Essays in American Diplomacy

Essays in American Diplomacy

Armin Rappaport / UNIVERSITY OF CALIFORNIA, BERKELEY

The Macmillan Company
NEW YORK

Collier-Macmillan Limited
LONDON

First Printing

Library of Congress catalog card number: 67–16713

The Macmillan Company, New York
Collier-Macmillan Canada, Ltd., Toronto, Ontario

Printed in the United States of America

TO PHILIP D. SPROUSE
DIPLOMATIST

Preface

In this volume I have collected twenty selections relating to the diplomatic history of the United States, each of which originally appeared as an article, a lecture, or a chapter in a book. Each is a self-contained piece, printed in its entirety. I have made no deletions or other changes and have retained all the footnotes, thereby permitting the author's argument or point to remain exactly as he conceived it with all his buttressing or qualifying explanations.

I was moved to edit such a collection because of the difficulty I have encountered over the years in assigning important articles or other scholarly writings to a large class of students. Copies of books and periodicals, even in large libraries, are in such short supply (rarely more than two of each number or copy) as to make it virtually impossible for students to do the reading from the original publication.

The criterion for each choice was the author's contribution to an understanding of the period or topic concerned—a new viewpoint, idea, or interpretation. The selections do not present the results of new research. They are all interpretive in nature, and my introductions serve only to present the setting, either historical or historiographical, for the interpretation and to point out the contribution. I have made no deliberate effort to provide coverage of all the principal topics or periods and never sacrificed quality for coverage; yet I have managed to select readings that touch many major aspects of our diplomatic history—the colonial period, the Federalists, the War of 1812, the Monroe Doctrine, Expansionism, the Mexican War, the Civil War, Latin America, the Far East, the Spanish War, both World Wars, the period between the two wars, and the period since the Second World War.

Berkeley   A. R.

Contents

1. Colonial Origins of American Diplomatic Principles
                              MAX SAVELLE   I

2. The Jay Treaty: The Origins of the American Party System
                              JOSEPH CHARLES   12

3. South Carolina—A Protagonist of the War of 1812
                              MARGARET K. LATIMER   47

4. The Age of Mercantilism: An Interpretation of the American
   Political Economy, 1763 to 1828
                              WILLIAM A. WILLIAMS   61

5. Manifest Destiny—An Emotion
                              EPHRAIM D. ADAMS   75

6. The Failure of Polk's Mexican War Intrigue of 1845
                              RICHARD R. STENBERG   87

7. Northern Diplomacy and European Neutrality
                              NORMAN A. GRAEBNER   106

8. A New Approach to the Origins of Blaine's Pan American Policy
                              RUSSELL H. BASTERT   121

9. Cuba, the Philippines, and Manifest Destiny
                              RICHARD HOFSTADTER   149

10. Progressivism and Imperialism: The Progressive Movement and American Foreign Policy, 1898–1916
WILLIAM E. LEUCHTENBURG   171

11. The Changing Concept of the Open Door, 1899–1910
RAYMOND A. ESTHUS   186

12. Wilson the Diplomatist
ARTHUR S. LINK   200

13. The Legend of Isolationism in the 1920's
WILLIAM A. WILLIAMS   215

14. The Stimson Doctrine and the Hoover Doctrine
RICHARD N. CURRENT   229

15. The President and the "Quarantine" Speech
DOROTHY BORG   252

16. History Through a Beard
SAMUEL E. MORISON   269

17. Reflections on the Yalta Papers
RAYMOND J. SONTAG   282

18. How the Cold War Began
STAUGHTON LYND   290

19. The Illusion of American Omnipotence
DENNIS BROGAN   302

20. On Dealing with the Communist World
GEORGE F. KENNAN   312

Essays in American Diplomacy

1

Colonial Origins of American Diplomatic Principles

MAX SAVELLE

A study of the diplomatic history of the United States does not properly begin in 1776 with the declaration of American independence but reaches back into the colonial period to the time of the earliest settlements. For about 250 years before the birth of the Republic the colonies that were later to compose the American nation had a diplomatic history that was shaped mainly by the struggle among the European powers for supremacy in the new world. To these nations—Portugal, Spain, Holland, France, England—the new world offered magnificent opportunities for increasing their wealth and their power. As one European diplomat noted, "It is possessions in America that will in the future form the balance of power in Europe. The nation which enjoys the monopoly of commerce of the new world will alone remain rich in Europe. Superiority in Europe will belong to the nation which has control of the greatest part of America."

For this reason the great powers rushed to discover, explore, colonize, and exploit the rich and virgin lands of the Americas, North and South. Portugal took the lead in the fifteenth century, followed closely by Spain. By the end of that century the two nations had, by means of several papal arbitrations and treaties, notably the papal bull Inter Caetera *(1493) and the Treaty of Tordesillas (1494), divided between themselves the new world their mariners had discovered. In the sixteenth and seventeenth centuries the entry of Holland, France, and England into the competition for colonies inevitably challenged the claims of Portugal and Spain and resulted in constant diplomatic sparring and finally war. From the sixteenth to the eighteenth centuries, the European nations were involved in almost continuous warfare, chiefly for dynastic reasons but increasingly involving their claims in the new world.*

By the end of the seventeenth century the dispute for possession of the mainland colonies of North America, the future United States, had narrowed to a two-power rivalry between France and England. For almost one hundred years, from 1688 to 1763, the two nations fought four great wars that ended with complete victory for England. In these wars the American colonies themselves were directly involved. They supplied troops, ships, money, and provisions to the British cause and participated in expeditions and campaigns. Their settle-

FROM *Pacific Historical Review*, III (1934), 334–356. By permission of the author and *Pacific Historical Review*.

ments were attacked, their houses raided, many of their people killed or taken prisoner, and their destinies were affected by the treaties of peace.

These experiences made a very great impression upon the colonists and profoundly shaped their outlook on international affairs. And when the colonies became a nation, the recollection of these experiences contributed to the development of certain basic principles of American diplomacy.

In the article that follows, Max Savelle of the University of Washington, a leading authority on the diplomatic and intellectual history of the American colonies, examines six such basic principles and finds their origins in the experiences of the colonial period. To him the ideas that underlay these principles "were already old, even traditional, long before the time of American independence. . . ." He sees their roots not only in the rivalry among the European powers but also in the relations between the colonies and the mother country and also among the French, Dutch, and English colonies, and in the geographic situation and economic development of the colonies.

In a survey of the "permanent bases" of American diplomacy, published a few years ago, Mr. John W. Davis lists six doctrines which, as he says, "seem to have run with reasonable persistence throughout the course of American diplomacy." [1] These are, according to Mr. Davis, the doctrine of isolation, the Monroe Doctrine, the doctrine of non-intervention, the freedom of the seas, the open door, and the pacific settlement of disputes. The first four Mr. Davis classifies as "negative" principles; the other two he calls "positive." For the purposes of this paper, Mr. Davis's classification will be used.

Now, in the words of Mr. James Brown Scott, "the foreign policy of a state or nation necessarily pre-supposes its existence as a political body." [2] Historians of American foreign policy have, therefore, generally begun their story with the appointment of a Committee of Secret Correspondence by the second Continental Congress and the sending of

Silas Deane abroad as the agent of the colonies on the eve of American independence. Deane and the American commissioners who followed him to Europe went with instructions which show that the basic principles of subsequent American diplomacy were already well developed in the minds of the American leaders in the Congress. Whence came the diplomatic principles embodied in the instructions of the American representatives abroad? Were they formulated, as it were, out of nothing, and without antecedents, to meet the need of the moment, or did they have some other, more remote origin? It is the purpose of this paper to suggest that the ideas underlying the permanent bases of American diplomacy were already old, even traditional, long before the time of American independence; that those ideas are as old as European settlement in America, because they arose out of needs which were inherent in the geographic situation of the colonies here; and that they developed simultaneously in America and in Europe, out of the intercolonial relations of English, Spanish, Dutch and French colonies, on the one hand, and out of the adaptation of European diplomacy to the new international situation presented by the appearance of

[1] John W. Davis, "The Permanent Bases of American Foreign Policy," in *Foreign Affairs*, x, 1–12.
[2] Samuel Flagg Bemis, ed., *The American Secretaries of State and Their Diplomacy* (New York, 1927–1929), Historical Introduction by James Brown Scott, i, 3.

colonial empires in the western hemisphere, on the other.

The doctrine of isolation, the first of these basic principles, probably dates from the beginning of Anglo-Saxon colonization in North America. The idea of escape from the entanglements of Europe, international, moral, religious and economic, appears in the thinking of the earliest permanent settlers, especially those who built their homes on the shores of Massachusetts Bay. "There never was a generation," wrote Increase Mather in 1677, "that did so perfectly shake off the dust of Babylon both as to ecclesiastical and civil constitution, as the first generation of Christians that came into this land for the gospel's sake." [3] William Bradford and Edward Winslow both express this feeling in explaining the move of the Pilgrims from Leyden to America,[4] and the same theme is repeated again and again in the history of Massachusetts Bay. The Massachusetts General Court, for example, in 1651 reminded Oliver Cromwell that it was to escape Europe that the founders of that colony came to America, and justified their feeling on the ground that "We know not any country more peaceable and free from Warre..." than this.[5] Francis Daniel Pastorius, speaking, perhaps, for thousands of the Germans who came to the middle colonies in the next century, expressed the same feeling when he said that "After I had sufficiently seen the European provinces and countries,

and the threatening movements of war, and had taken to heart the dire changes and disturbance of the Fatherland, I was impelled through a special guidance from the Almighty, to go to Pennsylvania." [6]

This deeply rooted feeling of escape from the turmoil of Europe, an escape guaranteed by three thousand miles of ocean, is the negative side of the colonial doctrine of isolation. The doctrine also had its positive side, which took the form of refusal, on occasion, to be drawn into European conflicts. Thus, for example, during the first Anglo-Dutch war, Governor Peter Stuyvesant of New Netherland proposed to the New England Confederation that the English and Dutch colonies maintain a policy of neutrality in the war between their "Nations in Europe." [7] At the same time, Massachusetts, who did not share Connecticut's prospect for territorial gain at the expense of the Dutch, was blocking the entrance of the New England Confederation into the war, because, as it seemed to the Massachusetts General Court, "it was most agreeable to the gospel of peace which we profess, and safest for these colonies at this season, to forbeare the use of the sword." [8]

The real reason for these actions by New Netherland and Massachusetts was probably less the gospel of peace than the fact that there was a very profitable intercolonial trade going on between them, which must inevitably have suffered in war. Their isolation was thus based largely upon self-interest; but the ideas inherent in the action are, none-the-less, the basic ideas of the doctrine

---

[3] Quoted in John Wingate Thornton, *The Pulpit of the American Revolution* (Boston, 1876), xviii; cf. Claude H. Van Tyne, *The Causes of the War of Independence* (Boston, 1922), 17.

[4] William Bradford, *History of Plymouth Plantation* (Massachusetts Historical Society edition. Boston, 1912), I, 52–60; Edward Winslow, *Hypocrisie Unmasked*, quoted, *idem*, I, p. 53, n.1 and p. 56, n.1.

[5] Thomas Hutchinson, *History of Massachusetts from the first settlement thereof in 1628 until the year 1750* (Boston, 1795–1828), I, appendix IX, 450–452.

[6] Quoted in J. Fred Rippy and Angie Debo, *The Historical Background of the American Policy of Isolation* (Smith College Studies in History, IX, Nos. 3 and 4, April–July, 1924), 71.

[7] N. B. Shurtleff and D. Pulsifer, eds., *Acts of the Commissioners of the United Colonies of New England* (Boston, 1859. Volumes IX and X of *Records of the Colony of New Plymouth*), II, 41, 64.

[8] Hutchinson, *op. cit.*, I, appendix X, 452–453.

of isolation, as subsequently developed. The geographic situation of the English and Dutch colonies not only took them outside the stream of European conflict, in this case, but had actually created interests for them which made for the maintenance of peace.

Nor was this an isolated case. Similar situations arose, from time to time, during the intercolonial wars of the eighteenth century; and the unwillingness of such colonies as New Jersey and Pennsylvania to contribute men or money for those wars, because their interests were not directly involved, is notorious.[9] Furthermore, as a part of the doctrine the two spheres, the principle of American isolation from European conflict was recognized and encouraged by the mother countries by treaty, as, for example, in the Anglo-French treaty of Whitehall, of 1686.[10]

John Adams expressed no new idea, therefore, when he formulated the American doctrine of isolation in 1776, to the effect that "we should make no treaties of alliance with any European power ... [but] that we should separate ourselves, as far as possible and as long as possible, from all European politics and wars."[11] Rather, he was expressing in terms of high policy a sentiment which was already a tradition in the American colonies, based upon a deep-seated feeling of escape from Europe and a strong tendency, encouraged by European diplomacy, to avoid becoming entangled in European conflict, whenever it was to their interest to do so.

Similarly, the ideological origins of the Monroe Doctrine, which is complemen-

tary to that of isolation, are to be traced far back into the beginnings of the colonial period. The basic theme in the Monroe Doctrine is the idea that "the political system of the allied powers [of Europe] is essentially different ... from that of America ... [and] we should consider any attempt on their part to extend their system to any portion of this hemisphere as dangerous to our peace and safety."[12] This is, in itself, a re-statement of the old international doctrine that America is a new world, separate and distinct from Europe, to which the European system of politics and diplomacy does not apply. In expressing his doctrine, Monroe thus falls back upon the older European principle of the two spheres, which had found both doctrinal expression and contractual implementation before the end of the sixteenth century.[13]

As early as 1532, Francisco de Vittoria proclaimed the inviolability of America.[14] It is true, of course, that Vittoria's argument is very different from that of Monroe. Vittoria based his principle upon the fact that the Indians had a civilization of their own, were the rightful owners of the new lands, and, therefore, could not legally be dispossessed, whereas Monroe based his doctrine upon the existence of an European-American civilization in America which had developed since the beginning of European settlement. They do have, however, a common premise, and that is that America is a new, different and independent

[9] Cf. Francis Parkman, A Half-Century of Conflict (Boston, 1910), I, 135–138 et passim.
[10] Frances G. Davenport, European Treaties bearing on the History of the United States and its Dependencies (Washington, 1917, 1929), II, 309–323.
[11] John Adams, The Works of John Adams, second President of the United States (Boston, 1851–1865), I, 201.

[12] James D. Richardson, ed., A Compilation of the Messages and Papers of the Presidents, 1789–1897 (Washington, 1899), II, 218.
[13] Camilio Barcia-Trelles, "La Doctrine de Monroë dans son Développement Historique, particulièrement en ce qui concerne les Relations Interaméricaines" (Hague Academy of International Law, Réceuil des Cours, XXXII, 1930), 391–605.
[14] Francisco de Vittoria, De Indis et de Jure Belli Reflectiones (James Brown Scott, ed., The Classics of International Law, Washington, 1917), 128 et passim.

world, over which Europe has no legal right to extend its control.[15]

Vittoria's philosophical pronouncement of the doctrine of the two spheres was not, however, the interpretation of that doctrine carried into the practice of European diplomacy. The early diplomatic application of this principle is to be seen, rather, in the practical dogma that "there is no peace beyond the Line." That is to say, to the diplomatists of the sixteenth and seventeenth centuries, Europe was one world and America, lying beyond the Line, was another; and piracy, territorial plundering, or intercolonial wars might take place in that new sphere without disturbing the peace and friendly relations of the mother countries in Europe. Likewise, under certain treaties, the reverse was true.

Such was the principle of the two spheres inherent in the oral agreement with regard to colonial affairs between French and Spanish diplomats at Cateau-Cambrésis, in 1559, and embodied in many subsequent treaties, notably the Anglo-Spanish treaty of 1604.[16] This was also the principle underlying the Anglo-French treaty of Whitehall, of 1686. In this latter case, however, the doctrine is a doctrine of peace, not war.[17] For Article XVII of this treaty provides that hostilities between the French and English colonies in America shall not be made a cause of war between the mother countries, and Article XVIII provides that war between England and France shall not be a cause of war in America; but that "true and firm peace and neutrality shall continue in America between the ... French and English nations, in the same manner as if no such rupture had occurred in Europe."[18]

The clearest example, perhaps, of the legal embodiment of the doctrine of the two spheres is the Hispano-Portuguese treaty of 1750. Not only is it provided in this treaty that the Spanish and Portuguese colonies shall remain neutral in case of war between the two nations in Europe, but, also, the treaty provides that, should either party to the treaty make an alliance with a third nation, the party making such an alliance, nevertheless, will not permit its ally to use its American ports or territories as bases of operations against the other party to the treaty or its colonies. In other words, even though enemies in Europe, they are to remain effectual allies for the maintenance of the *status quo* in America.[19] This treaty is significant, not only as showing the importance of the doctrine of the two spheres in European diplomacy, but, also, because it shows that the diplomats of Spain and Portugal, at least, were coming to think of the territorial *status quo* in America as fixed, and not subject to further change.

It thus seems clear that the principle of the two spheres was well established when John Adams and his colleagues embodied the idea in the form of treaties prepared for the American representatives abroad, in 1776. The interpretation now given to this principle, however, was new. Hitherto, the European treaties based upon the doctrine of the two spheres had legalized a system for America which was distinct from the system of Europe, in matters of commerce, territories, and war. But Adams went one step farther, and, while assuming the basic principle of the two spheres, claimed for the young United States a deciding voice in the disposition of ter-

[15] Barcia-Trelles, "La Doctrine de Monroë," *loc. cit.*, 398–400.

[16] Davenport, *op. cit.*, i, 219–222, 246–257.

[17] *Ibid.*, ii, 309–232.

[18] *Ibid.*, ii, 323.

[19] Pedro de Angelis, ed., *Collección de Obras y Documentos relativos á la Historia antigua y moderna de las provincias del Rio de la Plata* (Buenos Aires, 1910). "Tratado de limites, España y Portugal, 13 Enero, 1750," iii, 335–342.

ritories in North America still in the possession of Great Britain.[20]

At this point, a new factor enters into any consideration of the old doctrine of the two spheres. Basically, the doctrine remains the same; but henceforth affairs in the western sphere are not to be determined by the diplomats of Europe. On the contrary, there has now appeared in the western world a new and independent nation which may be expected to assume a decisive position in affairs pertaining to America. It was only a short step further that Monroe was to go, when, the Spanish colonies having, in the meantime, achieved their independence, he proclaimed the predominant interest of the United States, not only in any territorial change that might, in the future, take place, but in blocking, once and for all, the possibility of further change in the direction of extending European possessions in the entire western hemisphere.

It should be borne in mind, of course, that Monroe did not, necessarily, draw upon European precedents to justify his interpretation of the doctrine of the two spheres. The ingrained American sentiment of isolation produced, in its normal growth, the determination not only to stay out of European complications, but, also, to keep European complications out of America. The doctrine of isolation is the negative American aspect of the principle of the two spheres; the Monroe Doctrine is the positive American aspect of that same principle. It is sufficient for us to note that both the European doctrine of the two spheres and the American doctrine of isolation, culminating in the Monroe Doctrine, have a common origin and kinship in the elemental facts of the geography of the new world.

In a similar, if, perhaps, a more local and specific sense, the principle of nonintervention may be said to have grown out of the exigencies of colonial life in America. Perhaps the earliest opportunity for interference in the affairs of another nation or colony, and an occasion which demands the formulation of a policy, presented itself to the Commonwealth of Massachusetts Bay in the struggle of Charles de la Tour and the Sieur d'Aulnay Charnisé for the control of Acadia, in the fourth and fifth decades of the seventeenth century.

The merchants of the Bay were already trading for furs with La Tour when he made his first proposal for an alliance with Massachusetts in 1641.[21] His emissaries were unsuccessful, and La Tour himself came to Boston in June, 1643, to propose, for the third time, an alliance with Massachusetts in his fight against d'Aulnay. The legislature was not at the moment in session; so, probably at the prompting of the merchants in Boston,[22] Governor John Winthrop, on his own responsibility, allowed La Tour to hire such men and ships as were willing to go with him. This enabled La Tour to take out of Boston a filibustering expedition of four ships and a pinnace, with seventy land soldiers,[23] although there was no alliance.

This action by the governor aroused an immediate storm of disagreement in the Bay towns, and three of the magistrates, together with several other leading men of the colony, wrote Winthrop a strong letter of protest. The burden of the argument in this, the so-called "Ipswich letter," was that the governor's action was tantamount to intervention in an internal quarrel between two factions in the territory of the King of France, the merits of which the governor could

---

[20] *Journals of the Continental Congress, 1774–1789* (Library of Congress edition. Washington, 1904–1928), v, 668–697.

[21] John Winthrop, *Journal* (ed. by James K. Hosmer. New York, 1908), ii, 43, 88, 127–128.

[22] Justin Winsor, *Memorial History of Boston* (Boston, 1880–1881), i, 283. *Cf.* Winthrop, *Journal*, ii, 105ff.

[23] Winthrop, *Journal*, ii, 130.

not know. Not only was this a breach of intercolonial neighborliness, but it was positively dangerous. D'Aulnay was strong, he would certainly protest against the aid given to La Tour, and he was liable to be supported against the colony of Massachusetts Bay by the armed forces of France. And, they said, "He that loseth his life in an unnecessary quarrel dyes the Devill's martyr." [24]

Here is a clear, if homely expression of the doctrine of non-intervention, generated, as it were, not out of pure thought or precedent, but, rather, out of the actual circumstances of a particular situation. There can be no doubt, either, that it represents the feeling of the majority of the people of the colony and of New England. It was certainly effective, for it caused Governor Winthrop very carefully to repudiate, in a letter to d'Aulnay, all responsibility for the actions of La Tour's volunteers, while at the same time stoutly maintaining the right of the Massachusetts merchants to trade with whomsoever they would. As the governor disingenuously put it, "we thought not fit to give him [La Tour] aid, as being unwilling to intermeddle in the wars of any of our neighbors, yet considering his urgent distress, we could not in Christianity or humanity deny him liberty to hire for his money any ships in our harbor... And whereas some of our people were willing to go along with him... We had charged them to labor by all means to bring matters to a reconciliation... and ... that if they [should] do or attempt anything against the rules of justice and good neighborhood, they must be accountable therefor unto us at their return." [25] One might well have asked the governor for what purpose they were permitted to go, anyway.

Massachusetts was very careful, there-

after; and the Commissioners for the United Colonies, at the time of ratifying the commercial treaty later made between Massachusetts and d'Aulnay, wrote the doctrine of non-intervention into the records of the New England Confederation in unmistakable terms.[26]

In the case of the doctrine of non-intervention, then, we may say that its American origin lies in a practical situation in the experience of the colonies themselves. That is to say, after meddling rather gingerly in the civil strife in Acadia, and considering the possible consequences, the colony and the Confederation finally arrived at the conclusion that it was best not to intervene at all, except insofar as to claim the right of the "Bastonnais" to trade with both sides.

Out of this same episode with La Tour and d'Aulnay may be seen arising the beginnings of American diplomatic interest in the freedom of the seas. From the first, New England's major interests lay upon the sea; and when d'Aulnay protested against the Massachusetts trade with La Tour and threatened to seize the "Bastonnais" ships, the magistrates sent him a "sharp answer," asserting the right of the English colonists to travel the seas freely, trading with whomsoever they would. Winthrop had already voiced this principle in his reply to the "Ipswich letter": "it is lawful," he wrote, "for the owners and masters of shipps, and is in the way of their calling, to be hyred by laTour... But if our shipps shall be opposed in their lawful course, the justice of their cause will lye in that: as for example: a man travailing in a wagon in England, and carrying his goods with him, his creditor sets upon the wagon to take his debtors goods from him by force, the wagoner may defend him and his goods, [the traveller] being now in

[24] *The Hutchinson Papers* (Publications of the Prince Society. Albany, 1865), I, 131–132.
[25] Winthrop, *Journal*, II, 127, 128.
[26] Shurtleff and Pulsifer, eds., *op. cit.*, I, 56ff,

his charge without any respect to the former ingagement; for the justice of his cause ariseth upon another ground." [27]

Here Winthrop distinguishes between aid to La Tour and the mere carrying of La Tour and his goods. In the first case, he is arguing for the right of the citizens of Massachusetts to hire themselves and their ships to anyone who will pay them their price, which is essentially the argument of freedom of trade. In the other case, the emphasis is placed upon the right of the neutral carrier to carry his customer and the customer's goods without molestation by the customer's enemy. The justice of the neutral carrier's cause arises from the fact that he is not a party to the quarrel, and, therefore, may not be attacked by either party to it. This argument for the rights of neutral carriers, growing, as it did, out of the necessity for some expression of policy to meet the situation of the moment, voices a fundamental principle of later American diplomacy.

Now, while Winthrop's principle arose out of an immediate local need, the incident took place at a time when the question of the freedom of the seas was coming greatly to occupy the minds of European thinkers on international law. It is true that Francis I hurled his challenge to 'the Hispano-Portuguese monopoly of the seas of the new world in 1541,[28] and that, from that time forward, the international relations of Europe were full of the claims of the non-monopolizing nations, England, France and Holland, to the right to sail the seas beyond the Line without molestation. But it was not until 1609 that Grotius wrote his *Mare Liberum,* and it was 1635 when John Selden published his *Mare Clausum* in reply.[29] It is hardly probable that Governor Winthrop had

seen either of these books; if not, it seems apparent that the local need induced the principle, independently of the development of the principle in Europe. In any case, the question of the freedom of the seas is an important one in European diplomacy at least from the middle of the seventeenth century on.

Of particular interest to Americans, with regard to this principle, are the articles in the "Treaty of Navigation and Commerce" between England and France, signed at Utrecht, 11 April, 1713, that deal with the rights of neutrals on the high seas, the definition of contraband, and the doctrine that free ships make free goods.[30] These articles applied to the colonies as well as to the mother country, of course, and satisfied the needs of the colonies for such diplomatic protection. It is no wonder, therefore, that they were copied verbatim in the form of treaties prepared for the American commissioners to France in 1776,[31] and were embodied in the treaty of commerce with France signed 6 February, 1778.[32]

That is to say, the commercial interests of the colonies, which had appeared by the third decade of English settlement, coincided, to a degree, with the commercial interests of the mother country in 1713. In 1776, their commercial interests remaining the same, the United States, now independent, could appropriate bodily to their own use that part of the mother country's diplomatic policy which had served them so well as colonies. The history of this growing body

---

[27] *Hutchinson Papers,* I, 143.
[28] Charles de la Roncière, *Histoire de la Marine Francaise,* III, 300 (Paris, 1923).
[29] *Ibid.*

[30] Especially Articles XVII, XVIII, XIX, XXV, XXVI, XXVII, XXVIII. *A Collection of all the Treaties of Peace, Alliance and Commerce, between Great-Britain and other powers, from the Revolution in 1688, to the present time* (London, 1772), I, 142–167.
[31] *Journals of the Continental Congress,* V, 668–679.
[32] William M. Malloy, ed., *Treaties, Conventions, International Acts, Protocols and Agreements between the United States of America and Other Powers, 1776–1909* (Washington, 1910), I, 468–479.

of ideas with regard to the freedom of the seas furnishes an interesting case of a principle which originated simultaneously in Europe and America, but whose first legal expression as an American principle is not American at all, but British.

Turning now to the "positive" doctrines of American foreign policy, we find their evolution may be traced to similar beginnings. The principle of the freedom of trade, which now goes under the name of the "open door," goes back at least to that day in 1541 when Francis I espostulated against the Hispano-Portuguese monopoly of the land and commerce of the world: *"Le soleil luit pour moi comme pour les autres; je voudrais bien voir la clause du Testament d'Adam qui m'exclut du partage du monde."* [33]

But this principle, too, has an independent origin in the needs and the experiences of the British colonies in the new world. As early as 1627 we find the Pilgrim governors at Plymouth negotiating with an emissary from the Dutch colony of New Amsterdam for "mutual commerce and trading in such things as our countries afford." [34] And the chief provision in the treaty between the Commonwealth of Massachusetts and Governor d'Aulnay, of Acadia, in 1644, was that "it shalbe lawfull for all their people, aswell French as English, to trade each with other ... provided alwayes that the governor and Majestrates [of Massachusetts] aforesaid bee not bound to restrayne their Merchants from tradeing with the[ir] ships with what people soever, whether French or others, in what place soever inhabiting." [35] Here is a guarantee of the open door in Acadia; for one of the specific aims of this treaty,

so far as Massachusetts was concerned, was to prevent the closing of the lucrative trade between the Boston merchants and La Tour, d'Aulnay's rival.

A similar treaty was made at Jamestown, in the year 1660, between the English colony of Virginia and the Dutch colony of New Netherland, in flat defiance of the British Navigation Act of 1651.[36] And the freedom of trade provided by the treaty of Jamestown was further established, in Virginia, by legislation, in the Act of March, 1660, to the effect that "all strangers of what Xpian nation soever in amity with the people of England shall have free liberty to trade with us, for all allowable commodities ... and shall have equall right and justice with our own nation in all courts of judicature." [37] If England closed the door to Virginia, Virginia itself would open the door, to the Dutch and to all others, by treaty and by act of Assembly. Thus did the colony defy the mother country because the colony's economic interests ran counter to those of England; thus, also, did Virginia give expression to a principle, which Virginia was not able to maintain, it is true, in the face of the later Acts of Trade, but which has remained one of the permanent bases of American foreign policy.

Meanwhile, the "most favored nation" clause, itself a diplomatic lever for opening closed commercial doors, was making its appearance in European diplomacy, and was embodied in the Anglo-French commercial treaty of Utrecht.[38] This principle, too, was adopted for its own use by the United States, and embodied in the Franco-American commercial treaty of 1778; but it was inserted there only because it was found impossible to get from France that unrestricted free-

[33] Quoted in la Roncière, *op. cit.,* iii, 300.

[34] "Correspondence between New Netherland and New Plymouth," *Collections of the New York Historical Society,* Second series (1841–1857), i, 360–368.

[35] Davenport, *op. cit.,* i, 351–352.

[36] Davenport, *op. cit.,* ii, 55–56.

[37] William W. Hening, *The Statutes at Large; being a Collection of all the Laws of Virginia, from the first Session of the Legislature in the year 1619* (New York, 1823), i, 540.

[38] *Collection of all the Treaties,* i, 142–167.

dom of commerce with France and the French colonies which was the dearest wish of the young American nation, whose past growth and whose future prosperity were predicated upon an expanding commerce.[39]

Finally, the principle of peaceful settlement of disputes, as all these other permanent bases, has its origins both in the practices of European diplomacy with regard to the colonies and in the experiences of the colonies themselves. As early as 1655, Oliver Cromwell made a treaty with France which dealt, in part, with the issues raised in the informal war then going on between the two countries and with the seizure of Acadia by Major Sedgwick's expedition in 1654. This treaty provided for the establishment of a joint claims commission, composed of three appointees on each side, which was empowered, also, to settle the dispute with regard to the ownership of Acadia. In case the commissioners failed to agree, the disputes between the two countries were to be submitted to the city of Hamburg for arbitration.[40] The provisions for arbitration were not carried out; but the principle of the arbitration of colonial disputes was clearly recognized, and was embodied later, notably in the Anglo-French treaty of Whitehall, 1686.[41]

Meanwhile, in the colonies themselves, this principle had been established by the intercolonial treaty of Hartford, 1650.[42] For two decades the boundary line between the English and the Dutch in Connecticut and Long Island had been in dispute. Various suggestions had been made, on both sides, that the dis-

pute be settled by arbitration, but no action was taken until Peter Stuyvesant journeyed to Hartford in 1650 and negotiated with the Commissioners of the United Colonies a treaty which provided for the determination of the boundary by four commissioners, two to be appointed on each side.[43]

Thereafter, the principle of settlement of colonial disputes by arbitration or joint commission was given lip-service in the treaties of Whitehall (1686), Utrecht (1713), and Aix-la-Chapelle (1748); and an attempt was actually made to settle the dispute over the Acadian boundary by peaceful methods after 1749. This attempt collapsed, however, with the outbreak of the Seven-years War, and, apparently, there is no record of a successful application of this method of settling intercolonial disputes after the treaty of Hartford. The principle was, none-the-less, recognized; and it was embodied, as a principle by no means new, in the Jay Treaty of 1794, upon the basis of which certain disputes between the United States and Great Britain were actually settled.[44]

We have now considered certain suggestions with regard to the origins of the ideas underlying the six permanent bases of American diplomacy. In noting the existence and application of those ideas very early in the colonial period of American history, it has appeared that they were drawn from three sources. First, certain ideas were developed in the practical experiences of the colonies in America, in the course of their natural economic and political development and the relations of the French, Dutch and English colonies with each other. Second, we have seen that certain other ideas which later found a place in American diplomacy grew out of the relationships

[39] Malloy, op. cit., I, 469; cf. "Form of Treaties," Journals of the Continental Congress, v, 668–679; Emory R. Johnson, et al., History of Domestic and Foreign Commerce of the United States (Washington, 1915), I, 111–112, 122–123.

[40] Davenport, op. cit., II, 46, 47.

[41] Article XVII. Davenport, op. cit., II, 322.

[42] Davenport, op. cit., II, 1–6.

[43] Ibid.

[44] Malloy, op. cit., I, 590–606; Samuel Flagg Bemis, Jay's Treaty; A Study in Commerce and Diplomacy (New York, 1923), passim.

of the English colonies with the mother country; as, for example, those ideas and practices which underlie the doctrine of isolation. Third, we have seen that certain ideas later embodied in American diplomacy are drawn from European diplomacy, and, particularly, from the relations of England with other European nations, with regard to colonial commerce and related subjects. It is to be remembered, also, that the ideas underlying the six major doctrines we have discussed developed simultaneously in America and in Europe, sometimes with very little connection between the developments in Europe and those in America, and, sometimes, with a large amount of dependence by America upon Europe.

Looked at in this light, early United States diplomacy becomes a synthesis of American, English and European elements. This means, also, that the history of American diplomatic ideas does not really begin in 1776. On the contrary, it begins with the discovery of America and the appearance of the international doctrine of the two spheres. The permanent bases of American foreign policy are those concepts which grew out of the experiences of the European nations and the colonies in their efforts to direct the international destiny of the new world. They were laid down in the course of the first two centuries of exploration, annexation and settlement in North America.

So far as the colonies themselves were concerned, they contributed very little to the evolution of an American diplomatic system after the Stuart restoration of 1660. The reason for this fact is to be seen in the increasing importance of the colonies to the mother country, and the resultant increasingly important part the affairs of the colonies play in the determination of British foreign policy. From this time forward, British diplomacy is, largely, colonial diplomacy. On the other hand, however, the experiences of the colonies during the first five decades of their history, when they were most completely free from the political control of the mother country, were peculiarly like the experiences of the United States just after independence. They forecast, in unique fashion, the diplomatic needs of the United States, and the rudimentary policies then evolved similarly forecast the policies of the new republic. The mother country, after 1660, merely undertook to conduct the diplomacy of the colonies for them. It was not always conducted as the colonies would have liked; but, in so far as the British policies did satisfy the aspirations of the colonies, those policies were continued after independence without a break.

It is precisely in this first half-century of settlement, therefore, that the peculiarly American policies may be said most clearly to have had their origin. If the evolution of American diplomatic ideas paralleled the development of similar ideas in Europe, and if United States diplomacy adopted *in toto* certain doctrines of European diplomacy as its own, it is because the needs of America, arising out of its natural environment, were similar, in respect to the problems dealt with by such borrowed doctrines, to European needs.

Finally, we are to draw from this discussion one more suggestion. If it be true that the permanent bases of American diplomacy are rooted in the geography of North America, it becomes easy to understand why they remain consistent throughout the whole course of American history, and, therefore, come to be called traditional. Further, if this be a valid explanation of their traditional nature, it follows that they may be expected to remain the permanent bases of American foreign policy until, perhaps by mechanical agencies, the nature of the geographic relationship of North America to the rest of the world be changed or modified.

2

The Jay Treaty:
The Origins of the
American Party System

JOSEPH CHARLES

In February 1793 a war broke out between France and England that was to last for twenty-one years and end only with the defeat of Napoleon. In this war the United States eventually became involved, but not until 1812. For nineteen years it was able to maintain a neutral position, although with difficulty because the treatment of American commerce by the two warring nations brought the United States to the brink of war with both powers on a number of occasions.

With England relations were precarious from the outset of the war. As soon as hostilities erupted, the British government ordered the seizure of American vessels found trading with the French, and in the first months of the war several hundred American ships were taken by British men-of-war. At the same time, the British began visiting American vessels on the high seas and taking American seamen who were suspected of being British subjects and refugees from the British navy. Added to these maritime difficulties were other problems resulting principally from violations of the Treaty of 1783 which had ended the Revolutionary War. The British refused to evacuate five American posts in the Northwest and to return slaves carried away after the war. The United States, on its part, made little effort to fulfill its pledge regarding the restoration of property taken from the Loyalists and the payment of debts Americans owed Britons from before the war.

By the spring of 1794 war between the two nations appeared imminent unless a settlement of outstanding questions could be made. To effect such a settlement, President Washington sent John Jay, Chief Justice of the United States, to London in June of 1794. Five months later a treaty was signed and war averted. The treaty was not well received in the United States because the terms were not favorable for America. The Senate approved it by the barest margin of one vote; the House of Representatives appropriated the funds needed to carry out the terms of the treaty only after a prolonged and bitter debate.

To the whole problem of Jay's treaty, Joseph Charles brings a novel and interesting interpretation. While historians have generally viewed the treaty as purely a matter of foreign policy, Charles sees it in terms of domestic affairs,

FROM *William and Mary Quarterly*, 3rd ser., XII (1955), 581–630. By permission of Mrs. Joseph Charles.

as the decisive element in the formation of political parties in the first decade of the Republic. Hamilton's economic and financial measures generated opposition but did not, according to Charles, provide an adequate basis for the organization of political parties. What did provide the "suitable target" were the difficulties with England in 1793. James Madison made a bid for national support for his Republican party by a resolution in the House of Representatives to retaliate against British strictures on American commerce. Hamilton and the Federalists, fearful of defeat in the House on the measure, transferred the whole question of relations with England to the Senate and to the executive by sending Jay to London to negotiate a treaty. Thus, Charles sees the dispatch of Jay as a political maneuver to forestall a Republican victory. Similarly, he ascribes Washington's acceptance of the treaty and its approval by the Senate to the need of the Federalist party. The favorable vote in the House of Representatives on the appropriation of funds he views also as stemming from political considerations.

I. Early Phases of the Party Conflict [1]

In the preceding sections we have pointed out the dominant purpose of some of the outstanding political figures of the 1790's and the relation of each man to the more important issues of these years. We should bear in mind the stand of these men on the issues of the time, not only because they had a great deal to do with the way in which the issues were settled, but because both the men and the issues played a significant part in shaping public opinion. As important problems arose, the first question asked was how the leading figures stood upon them. Thus it would be easy to overemphasize the importance of the leaders and to picture our first political struggles merely as those of gigantic and shadowy figures. To assure balance, therefore, we must study the parties in action, where we see how they helped to shape and were in turn shaped by events. If we approach the parties from the functional point of view and can dis-

[1] This is the third of a three-part study on the origins of the American party system by Mr. Charles. The first and second, on "Hamilton and Washington" and "Adams and Jefferson" respectively, appeared in the April and July issues of the *Quarterly*.

cover what they were fighting for at various times during this period, we may be somewhat less dependent than heretofore upon definitions and formulas for our understanding of them.

The relation between the party conflict and the policies which the government followed during this period shifts and varies in many respects, but it remains constant in importance and interest. Division into parties cannot be studied apart from administration policy; for it was upon such issues as our commercial policy, Funding, Assumption, the establishment of the Bank, and the ratification of Jay's treaty that some of the ablest Republican leaders went into open opposition, and it was their stand against these and other government policies which brought them most of their followers.

Until the leading measures were formulated and debated upon, until sentiment upon them had taken shape, there was no way of telling what would be the contending forces in the new government. The political leaders of this time were slow to see the necessity for political parties, but they soon saw the necessity for having public support for their policies. Party growth came in response to this need. It both increased interest in public affairs and reflected the growth of that interest from other causes. The rise of national parties, the phenomenal increase in newspaper circulation, and the number of letters carried through the mails are all evidence that horizons were widening, that men were becoming citizens of the nation instead of the state, and that everywhere their minds were being increasingly occupied by the same problems. It was the growth of parties that gave the average voter his first chance to express himself on the new questions of the day, and parties became the medium through which this awakening of public opinion influenced government policy. The role of public opinion became greater as the decade progressed; and once the two parties took definite shape, government policy and party conflict began to resemble two unstable chemical compounds in a reversible reaction: whatever affected one affected the other. The fact that parties were only in the process of formation, that the allegiance of most of the voters was still to be won, that members kept passing from one party to the other, made the situation more rather than less complicated.

There had been parties of some permanence in almost all the states, but when and where did national parties first arise? One would naturally assume that they arose at the seat of government and that they first became evident in the House of Representatives, the branch of the government nearest the people. Orin G. Libby, an early investigator of this subject, has denied, however, that parties are to be found there at this time.[2] De-

spite his conclusions, there was during Washington's Presidency a progressive and rapid growth of parties which was reflected in the voting upon questions of importance in the House of Representatives. The increasing sharpness of the party division stands out most clearly if we measure it by showing the decline of no-party voting. The number of members who did not vote consistently with either party as measured by the percentage of the total in attendance fell sharply between 1790 and 1796. Selecting only those measures which were of national importance or those which members of the House felt to embody some important principle of government, we find that the no-party voting fell from 42 per cent in 1790 to 7 per cent for the Jay Treaty session, the lowest point it reached until 1798.[3] By this standard the years 1789 to 1797 would appear to be at least as important as the period from 1797 to 1801 for a study of party development.

The session table showing the number of representatives voting consistently in each party and the decreasing number of no-party voters is calculated by the voting on at least nine measures. The counting of the votes on the important measures of each session reflects a growing division in the House, but it does not show the causes for it. These causes

---

[2] Orin G. Libby, "Political Factions in Washington's Administrations," *Quarterly Journal of the University of North Dakota*, III (1912), 293–303. A close investigation of the measures which Libby selected as the basis for the tabulation of his votes and an analysis of the debates upon these measures show that Libby frequently counted anti-Administration votes as pro-, and pro-Administration votes as anti-. For example,

in the voting on the admission of Tennessee as a state, Libby counted the votes for the measure as pro-Administration and those against it as anti-, although the Federalists were making every effort to keep Tennessee out so that her vote would not be counted in the Presidential election of 1796. For a more detailed discussion of Libby's method of work and an explanation of the method followed here, see Joseph Charles, The Party Origins of Jeffersonian Democracy (Doctoral Dissertation, Harvard University, 1942), Appendix.

[3] These are the figures if we regard voting with one party 66⅔% of the time as the test of party regularity. If to be a regular party man a member must have voted 75% of the time with one party, the figures are 54% to 14% for the same sessions. See Joseph Charles, The Party Origins of Jefferson Democracy, 215.

were, of course, complex and went beyond the particular measures which were being debated in a given session. Any group of men voting on questions as they arise will discover communities and diversities of interest among themselves in the normal course of their business. When the individual no longer votes on the merits of questions as he sees them, when he thinks in terms of voting with those who have voted with him in the past or of winning support for some of his own measures which are to arise in the future, party division within the group is well on its way. If this division comes to the point where the decisions made on specific questions are secondary to the contest for power among the parties in the group, party division has reached an extreme and is furnishing motives of its own for action—which all concerned will deplore but will regard as forced upon them by their opponents.

If the nature of our problem is thus complex, it is, of course, useless to try to fix too precisely the moment at which two definite parties came into being in the House. Evidence other than that found in the party voting fixes the time when the Republicans first felt themselves in a position to offer a program of their own instead of remaining on the defensive. The program was expressed in Madison's resolutions on Jefferson's Commercial Report; and the date, January, 1794, immediately after Jefferson's retirement, may serve as the dividing point between the two earliest phases of the growth of the Republicans in the House of Representatives.

While Jefferson referred to the Republican party in letters as early as 1792, there is no reliable evidence that he was actively engaged that early in organizing a popular party, or indeed that what he spoke of as the Republican party existed. He probably used the term to prevent the Federalists from labeling all opposition to Hamilton's measures as anti-Federalism. The Republicans in the House of Representatives at this time had only two members from New England, one each from Vermont and Massachusetts; and their scattered Pennsylvania and New York members included no particularly active or able men. We might very well call Jefferson's "Republican" party at this time a group of Virginia representatives who picked up any support they could from the members of other delegations.[4]

What success this group had in the first sessions of Congress was limited largely to measures in which the issue was one of abstract republicanism.[5] They could usually get the support of the neutral members in limiting the executive powers and combating the threat of Cabinet government, but they failed to hold it on the vital questions of government finance.

Yet it was by their stand on finance that the Republicans hoped to win public support, and considerations of that issue dominated their own thinking on political subjects. They soon came to regard Hamilton's system as having been designed to strip them of the "power of the purse" and to prevent them from exercising control or restraint over the

[4] These conclusions were drawn from a careful study of the debates and the votes on the most important issues for the years indicated, *Annals of Congress* (Washington, 1834–56).

[5] Examples might include the following: a measure to have "all writs or processes, issuing out of the Supreme or Circuit courts" written in the name of the United States instead of "the President thereof" (carried 28 to 22); defeat of a Senate amendment giving the President the right to apply an appropriation for salaries of foreign service officers as he saw fit instead of specific salaries as the House had originally written the bill (defeated 38 to 18); refusal of the House to allow the Postmaster General the right to establish cross post roads; defeat of a Senate amendment to the coinage bill which would have put the President's head on our coins; and finally, defeat of a Senate amendment to an appropriation bill by which the army appropriation would not have been itemized. In that order: *ibid.,* Sept. 25, 1789; May 27, 1790; Jul. 22, 1790; Mar. 24, 1792; Feb. 22, 1793.

Tabulation of Party and No-Party Votes, by Sessions, House of Representatives, 1789–1802

	I 1 (Apr.–Sept. 1789)			I 2 & 3 (Jan.–Aug. 1790 / Dec. 1790–Mar. 1791)			II 1 (Oct. 1791–May 1792)			II 2 (Nov. 1792–Mar. 1793)			III 1 & 2 (Dec. 1793–Jun. 1794 / Nov. 1794–Mar. 1795)			IV 1 (Dec. 1795–Jun. 1796)			IV 2 (Dec. 1796–Mar. 1797)			V 1 (May–Jul. 1797)			V 2 (Nov. 1797–Jul. 1798)			V 3 (Dec. 1798–Mar. 1799)			VI 1 (Dec. 1799–May 1800)			VI 2 (Nov. 1800–Mar. 1801)			VII 1 (Dec. 1801–May 1802)		
	F	R	N	F	R	N	F	R	N	F	R	N	F	R	N	F	R	N	F	R	N	F	R	N	F	R	N	F	R	N	F	R	N	F	R	N	F	R	N
New Hampshire	1	1	1	1		2	1		2	2		1	2	1	2	3	1		2	1	1	4	3		4	2		4			4	2	2	4			4		
Massachusetts	3	2	3	4		4	7			8			12	1	1	11	3		8	5	1	10	1		10	2		11	2	1	10	2		11	3		7	6	
Connecticut	4		1	2		3	4			4		1	7			7			6		1	6		1	7			7			7			7			7		
Rhode Island	ab.			1			1			1			2	2		2			2			1			2			2			2		1	2			1	1	
Vermont														3		1	1		1	1		1			1	1		1	1		1			2		1	1	1	
New York	3	3		2		3	4	4	2	4	1		7	3	1	5	1	1	4	5	1	6	4		5	4		6	4		4	5		4	6		3	7	
New Jersey	3	3		3		1	2	2	2	2	2	1	4	4	4	2	1		2	1	1	4			5			4			2	3		2	3			5	
Pennsylvania	5	5		3		4	3	2	3	4	1	1	4	4		4	7	2	5	7	1	5	7	1	5	7		4	8	1	4	8	1	4	9		3	10	
Delaware	1	1		1			1			1		1	1			1			1			1			1			1			1			1			1		
Maryland	1	1	4	2	5	4	1	3	2	1	2	2	3	4	1	3	2	3	5	2	1	5	2	1	5	2	1	3	1	4	5	6	1	4	4		3	5	
Virginia	2	3	4	2		3		9	1		8	2	2	15	2		18	1	1	15	3	1	16	1	3	15	1	3	15	1	5	13		4	14	1	1	18	
N. Carolina	ab.				3	2	3	4	1	3	4	1		7	2		10		2	10		1	9	1	3	9	1	1	7	1	4	6		4	4	1	3	7	
S. Carolina	1	1	3	1	3	1	1	1	1	3	2	1	1		4	2	4		2	2		3	3		3	3		3	2		5	1		4	2		4	2	
Georgia	1	2	2		3			2			2			2	2	2	2		1	1		2			2			1	1		1	2		3			3		
Kentucky											2								1	1		2			1	2		2			2			2			2		
Tennessee																			1		1							1			1			1			1		
	25	11	21	22	15	27	28	23	14	29	25	11	45	38	20	40	57	7	36	55	12	49	50	4	51	48	6	50	44	8	55	46	5	51	52	2	38	64	0

F = Federalist   R = Republican   N = No-Party

The basis for the tabulation of the first three Congresses is to be found in Joseph Charles, The Party Origins of Jeffersonian Democracy (Doctoral Dissertation, Harvard University, 1942), Appendix. The balance of the table is based on computations from Manning J. Dauer, The Adams Federalists (Baltimore, 1953), Appendix III. Used by permission of the author.

Administration. One of the speeches of John F. Mercer of Maryland shows how the issue of the public debt was woven into Republican ideology.[6] Mercer maintained that the fact that we could not rightly bind another generation financially was "...as demonstrable as any proposition in Euclid." He stated that we should accumulate no debt which could not be paid off in twenty years. For to pass this line would destroy

> that great principle which alone was the cause of the war with Great Britain.... That taxation and representation should go hand in hand. We have no one quality of the Representatives of posterity—not elected by them, and not responsible to them.... It destroys one great check of free legislation—that the legislator should feel, in his own property, the burden of the tax he lays, and the contract he makes for society. It avoids that still greater check, that the constituents should feel the burdens their Representatives impose. The people never act but from feelings: so long, therefore, as their deputies contract for and at the expense of posterity, they act in perfect safety.

If we consider the long-run political effects of Hamilton's program and the public feeling which could have been stirred up against it at the time it was proposed, perhaps the most extraordinary thing about these measures is that they did not serve as the immediate basis for an effective opposition party. The reason is that the Republican party, like the Federalist, was made up of both former opponents and former supporters of the Constitution, and anti-Federalism was at no time their dominating principle. The leading Republicans were in favor of the Constitution, particularly after the amendments to it, and were willing to make almost any sacrifice to give the new government a fair start. Madison, for example, who had opposed both Funding and Assumption, voted for the Excise Bill. By the time this bill was offered, a large debt had been funded, and the cost of meeting it and

[6] *Ibid.*, Mar. 30, 1792, 504–05, *passim*.

other national expenses had to be paid if the new government was to succeed. During these years Madison showed a willingness to vote for almost any measure which would raise revenue.[7] Once Funding and Assumption were adopted, no opposition could be made to the steps necessary to pay the bill without threatening the existence of the new government. The basic measures of Hamilton's economic system were not, in 1790–91, a suitable target for a party which did not wish to weaken the new government or to endanger national unity.

Even after Jefferson had come to the conclusion that the success of Hamilton's plans was incompatible with the continued existence of a representative government, he for some years played little if any part in the creation of a popular national party. From the time when he and Hamilton became open antagonists in the spring of 1792 until he left the Cabinet, Jefferson's influence upon the opposition party seems to have been largely a negative one. He endeavored to persuade Washington that the opposition were not anti-Federalists, disorganizers, and Jacobins, as they were usually called;[8] and there are indications that he tried to get the party to avoid giving grounds for such charges. He wrote to Madison of the contested election between Clinton and Jay for the governorship of New York, at the time when the Republicans were considering supporting the former as Vice-President in 1792:

> It does not seem possible to defend Clinton as a just or disinterested man if he does not decline the Office, of which there is no symptom; and I really apprehend that the cause of republicanism will suffer and its votaries be thrown into schism by embarking it in support of this man, and for what?

[7] See his votes on revenue measures in *Annals of Congress.*

[8] Jefferson to Washington, Philadelphia, May 23, 1792, Paul Leicester Ford, ed., *The Works of Thomas Jefferson*, 12 vols. (New York and London, 1904–05), VI, 487 ff. Hereafter, Jefferson, *Works.*

to draw over the antifederalists who are not numerous enough to be worth drawing over.[9]

Until after Jefferson left the Cabinet at the end of 1793, the Republican members of Congress did little except try to prevent the passing of measures they regarded as harmful. It was in the following January that they took the offensive and attempted to win a large bloc of the Federalists' New England support away from them. The program with which Madison began the first strategic moves against the Federalists was not one which could be called anti-Federalist, particularist, or States' rights. It was based upon a strong and generally shared national sentiment, hatred of the British Navigation Acts and the commercial monopoly which had been erected upon them. Madison offered resolutions providing for higher duties upon the manufactured goods and the shipping of those nations with whom we had no commercial treaties. The resolutions were based upon Jefferson's "Report on the Privileges and Restrictions on the Commerce of the United States in Foreign Countries," [10] which he had submitted to the House before resigning from the Cabinet. The report showed that Great Britain was the only country with whom we had extensive trade who would not make a commercial treaty, and Madison's resolutions were designed to win commercial favors from her by putting a higher duty upon her goods and shipping than there was upon those of the countries who gave us commercial privileges. Madison stated that the purpose of his resolutions was to realize more fully that commercial independence which he had understood to be one of the main objects of the Constitution.

Against the background of general hostility to Britain because of her com-

[9] Jefferson to Madison, Jun. 21, 1792, *ibid.*, 123–24.
[10] *Ibid.*, 98 ff.

mercial policies since 1783,[11] the early debates of the new government are of particular interest. The question of our future commercial policy was the first serious matter to be taken up when Congress met in New York in 1789. To the great amazement of some of the staunchest supporters of the Constitution, it became apparent that there was a strong group opposed to any discrimination against the countries, including Great Britain, which were not in treaty with us. This group was successful when the question first arose in the summer of 1789, and their success has been laid to the influence of Washington and Hamilton,[12] though Washington has recorded that he went contrary to his own judgment on this point.[13] According to

[11] The commercial policy adopted by Great Britain toward the United States after the Revolution was apparently dictated by political circumstances in the House of Commons. See Helen Taft Manning, *British Colonial Government after the American Revolution, 1782–1820* (New Haven and London, 1933), 40. For protest of West Indies see *ibid.*, 42–43. Prices rose as high as 100% on the Islands when trade with the United States was stopped in 1783. See also *ibid.*, 10–12, for general importance of American trade to Great Britain, 1783–1800.
[12] After seeing the correspondence of Washington with Gouverneur Morris, who was then at the court of Great Britain, William Maclay wrote, "From the letters from the President it appears that the vote against discrimination which had involved us in difficulties with France was the work of the President, avowedly procured by his influence; and that he did it to facilitate a connection with Great Britain, thus offering direct offense to France and incurring the contempt of Great Britain, for she has spurned every overture made to her." Edgar Stanton Maclay, ed., *Journal of William Maclay* (New York, 1890), 392. See also 96–97.
[13] Washington gave the following explanation of his conduct with regard to the bill providing for commercial discrimination in his letter to David Stuart, New York, Jul. 26, 1789: "The opposition of the Senate to the discrimination in the Tonnage Bill, was so adverse to my ideas of justice and policy, that, I should have suffered it to pass into a Law without my signature, had I not been assured by some members of that body, that they were preparing another Bill which would answer the purpose more effectually without being liable to the objections, and to the consequences which they *feared* would have attended the

Madison's letter to Jefferson of June 30, 1789, the Federalists in opposing commercial discrimination were taking their first step away from the nationalism of their earlier views. It is not possible even now to say with certainty why they did so, but it would appear from earlier letters of John Adams, and from those of Madison and Washington written at the time, that Hamilton's policy of giving Britain the most-favored-nation status while she gave nothing in return marked a definite break with earlier Federalist views.[14]

According to Monroe,[15] Madison's presentation of his resolutions January 3, 1794, which revived the issue of discrimination, was an attempt to give the Republican party a national foundation. The Republicans regarded his resolutions as an effort to regulate commerce with an eye to the economic interests of every section. They were in particular a bid for New England support, and they

came at a time when that region, as well as the rest of the country, was in the first flush of its enthusiasm for the French Revolution. They came also when the shipping interests were feeling the first impact of large-scale confiscation of their ships by the British. By 1793 France very much needed supplies from the United States, and she presented such a market for our produce as never before. She also opened her West Indian islands to our shipping, and since we followed the policy of repaying our debt to her by letting her purchase supplies in this country with funds furnished by our government, British captures alone stood in the way of a great increase in our trade with her. Our business with Great Britain continued to increase also, as the French blockade was not so effective as the British one, and trade with Great Britain was still much greater than that with any other country. We sold her more than nine million dollars worth of goods and bought from her fifteen million.[16]

Great Britain's capture of our ships and her system of commercial monopoly were not our only grievances. She still held our western posts and was becoming increasingly threatening in that direction. On February 10, 1794, Lord Dorchester, Governor-General of Canada, made a highly inflammatory speech to the western Indians, one which was regarded by many Americans as a direct challenge to war.[17] Thus in the early

---

discrimination which was proposed in the Tonnage Law." J. C. Fitzpatrick, ed., *The Writings of George Washington from the Original Manuscript Sources, 1777–1805*, 39 vols. (Washington, 1931–44), XXX, 363. Hereafter, Fitzpatrick, *Washington's Writings*.

[14] *Letters and Other Writings of James Madison*, 4 vols. (Congress Edition, Philadelphia, 1865), I, 480–83. John Adams to Sam Adams, Jan. 26, 1786, New York Public Library (hereafter, NYPL) *Bulletin*, X (1906), 24; Jun. 2, 1786, *ibid.*, 242–43. Reference from Manning J. Dauer, *The Adams Federalists* (Baltimore, 1953), 78.

[15] Monroe to Jefferson, Philadelphia, Mar. 3, 1794, Jefferson Papers, Library of Congress (hereafter, LC). "You were aware of the motive in commencing the session by some act connected with the present state of our affairs, founded on the publick sentiment, and which should at the same time vindicate our rights & interests and likewise shun possible pretexts for war on the part of the power it was meant to affect, and the propositions introduced by Mr. Madison were tho't best calculated to accomplish this object. . . . An opposition to our carrying trade by their [the commercial states'] own members will affect them in such a manner, they will all know the fact & understand the motives. I therefore hope for the best from the discussion of these propositions and think symptoms to the Eastward authorize the expectation it will be verified."

[16] Jefferson's "Report on the Privileges and Restrictions on the Commerce of the United States in Foreign Countries," Jefferson, *Writings*, VI, 98 ff. The table from which the figures quoted are taken is on pp. 100–01.

[17] Evidence that feeling ran high against the British early in 1794 is found in at least two of Henry Van Schaack's letters to Theodore Sedgwick: Kinderhook, N.Y., Mar. 20, 1794, "Let me repeat that I believe Oswego and the little posts above and below the Falls of Niagra [sic] will be taken by our western citizens if in this session of Congress something effectually is not done. I rely much on the information that is now handed about." Sedgwick Papers, Massachusetts Historical Society (hereafter,

months of 1794 the Revolutionary generation looked out upon a familiar scene. No matter which way they turned, it seemed to them that the British stood in their path. Many Americans had been outraged by the behavior of Citizen Genêt, and the conduct of France was in some respects indefensible; but there was a difference between the provocations of France and those of Great Britain. The former were a blow, but the latter were a blow upon an old wound.[18]

Madison's resolutions, which had in the beginning been favored by the feeling against Great Britain, were put aside as that feeling became stronger and as people demanded more immediate and drastic steps than the resolutions provided. Between March and June of 1794 several measures were urged, and some of them passed, which went farther than any Madison had suggested. Congress empowered the President to lay a

complete embargo on our shipping for six months. Jonathan Dayton moved a sequestration of British debts, with at least a part of the money we owed to be used in compensating our citizens for their losses by British seizures. A Non-Intercourse Bill was passed. It should be observed, however, that all these were emergency measures, which went beyond anything Madison had contemplated but which would leave our commercial relations, once the measures should be removed, precisely as they had been before. The Non-Intercourse Bill passed, fifty-eight to thirty-eight, with the New Jersey and Pennsylvania delegations voting largely with the South,[19]—an alignment which, if it should persist, would be fatal to the Federalists. The measure sanctioned by this bill was defeated in the Senate, though only by the casting vote of John Adams, on the grounds that it would be harmful to the negotiations of the special envoy whom it had been decided to send to Great Britain.

Madison's resolutions were sidetracked, and it might appear that they had no particular political significance. Usually very little attention is given them in tracing the development of the two political parties. Yet because of their part in helping to set the stage for the Jay Treaty, they mark one of the milestones in the growth of parties. The debates on them brought the Republicans such a measure of support from the Middle states and New England as to convince the Federalists that the whole dangerous question of our commercial relations had to be taken out of the hands of the House of Representatives, where their party faced certain defeat, and put under the control of the Cabinet and Senate by being made the object of a special mission and a new treaty. Thus the first aggressive maneuver of the Republicans had great, if wholly unexpected, results.

MHS). Also Mar. 23, 1794, "Last Mondays paper confirms me more that there is a concerted plan to have hostilities committed independent of government." *Ibid.*

[18] The question of the relative damage inflicted upon our shipping by France and Britain during the 1790's is an extraordinarily difficult one, and appears to have been treated in a purely partisan manner at the time. Mr. Monaghan probably states the conventional view of present-day historians when he writes, "French depredations against American commerce were far greater than any ever committed by Great Britain." Frank Monaghan, *John Jay* (New York and Indianapolis, 1935), 412. No conclusive judgment on this point is given in Anna Cornelia Clauder, *American Commerce as Affected by the Wars of the French Revolution and Napoleon, 1793–1812* (Philadelphia, 1932). The only place where materials have been given which would permit the forming of even a tentative judgment on the relative damage inflicted on our shipping by France and Britain during the 1790's, appears to be in Samuel Flagg Bemis, *A Diplomatic History of the United States* (New York, 1936), 114–15, and 114 *n* (Court of Claims data). See also Timothy Pickering to Edward Stevens, Trenton, Sept. 5, 1800, Pickering Papers, XII, 10–12, MHS; Liston to Grenville, New York, Oct. 18, 1800, British State Papers (transcripts), LC; and Benjamin Goodhue to Fisher Ames, Dec. 20, 1800, and Mar. 20, 1801, Ames MSS., Dedham Historical Society.

[19] *Annals of Congress*, Apr. 21, 1794.

To the extent that the Federalists were moved by this consideration, the Jay Treaty, the most important measure in its political effects between the institution of Hamilton's financial program and the election of 1800, stemmed directly from the conditions of the party conflict in the early months of 1794.

Jefferson wrote of Jay's treaty in September, 1795:

A bolder party-stroke was never struck. For it certainly is an attempt of a party, which finds they have lost their majority in one branch of the legislature, to make a law by the aid of the other branch & of the executive, under color of a treaty, which shall bind up the hands of the adverse branch from ever restraining the commerce of their patron-nation.[20]

A study of the correspondence of the most eminent Federalists during the spring of 1794,[21] while they were planning to get a special envoy sent to England, would indicate that the judgment of Jefferson as to the origins of this treaty was a sound one, though the motive of most of these men was not pro-British, as he represented it. Above all, the sending of the mission was an effort to prevent the "mischievous measures" which Hamilton spoke of at the time,[22] a counterattack to defeat the Republican maneuver which had given that party a majority. As this majority was increased in the election of 1794,[23] giving the Republicans the only strongly Republican House they had between 1789 and 1800, the dependence of the Federalists upon the success of Jay's treaty grew greater. Their continued control of the government came to hang upon its adoption.

II. THE JAY TREATY

As we have seen, Jay was sent to Great Britain not only because of the strained relations between that country

---

[20] Jefferson to Madison, Sept. 21, 1795, Jefferson, *Writings,* VIII, 193. As to the actual inception of the treaty, Ralston Hayden says, "Probably the outstanding point in connection with the negotiation of the treaty, however, is the extent to which a small group of Federalist Senators, who were also among Washington's most trusted advisers, dominated the entire proceeding. These men suggested the mission; they secured its acceptance by the President, and practically directed the selection of the envoy; they secured his confirmation by the Senate; they sent him out fully cognizant with their views as to what sort of a treaty should be striven for and under very flexible instructions from the Department of State.

"It is also important to remember that this group prevailed upon the Senate to approve the general purpose of the mission by confirming the nomination of the envoy without demanding to be informed of and to pass judgment upon the particular instructions under which the negotiation was to be carried on." Joseph Ralston Hayden, *The Senate and Treaties, 1789–1817* (New York and London, 1920), 92.

[21] King kept a record of the events leading up to the sending of Jay, begining on Mar. 10, 1794 (Charles R. King, ed., *The Life and Correspondence of Rufus King,* 6 vols. [New York, 1894–1900; hereafter, King, *Correspondence*], I, 517 ff.), all of which should be read by anyone interested in the circumstances which gave rise to the mission. On Apr. 17, he recorded that Jay told the President that the resolutions (Madison's) were in the nature of a menace and that Great Britain would and ought to refuse to treat with us if they were

adopted. The comments of King, of Wolcott and his correspondents (George Gibbs, ed., *Memoirs of the Administrations of Washington and John Adams,* 2 vols. [New York, 1846; hereafter, Gibbs, *Memoirs*], I, 117 ff.), of Hamilton in particular (John Church Hamilton, ed., *The Works of Alexander Hamilton,* 7 vols. [New York, 1850–51; hereafter, Hamilton, *Works*], IV, 564), and of Sedgwick, (Sedgwick Papers, Jan.–May, 1794, MHS], would seem to support the view that the origin and main object of the Jay mission lay in the party conflict, though none of these men specifically affirmed it.

[22] Hamilton, *Works,* IV, 564.

[23] "Thus the entire Sea Coast area, which had been the Federal backbone in 1788, showed signs of Federal disintegration in 1794. This transition to Republicanism was permanent, although in certain places it met with a temporary check in the elections of 1796 and 1798." George Daniel Luetscher, *Early Political Machinery in the United States* (Philadelphia, 1903), 59 *n.* Luetscher's conclusion as to the long-run significance of Republican gains in the Congressional election of 1794 may not be sound, but there is no doubt that these gains were very disturbing to the Federalists at that time.

and the United States, which is the reason usually given for his mission, but also because of the party struggle and the condition of public opinion in this country. In order to understand the prolonged and bitter fight over the adoption of the Jay Treaty, it is necessary to keep in mind each of these factors in its immediate background: the one which grew out of the international situation and the one which sprang from domestic politics. Viewing only the relative situations of the two countries, the terms which Jay brought back may have been as good as we could have expected, as defenders of the Treaty have always maintained. The opposition, however, as well as many who had previously been strong Federalists, did not believe them to be, and the conditions of the Treaty put more powerful weapons into the hands of the Republicans for the struggle against it than any of them had expected beforehand. The party struggle had gone far enough that there would probably have been at least a perfunctory opposition to almost any treaty that could have been drawn up between the two countries in 1794, but only the conditions of the Jay Treaty itself could have brought about such widespread popular opposition as occurred. We must then, before plunging into the fight over the Treaty, examine its terms briefly.

Since Madison's proposal of the commercial resolutions directed against Great Britain had been of importance in bringing about the Treaty, it is interesting to note that all such regulation of British commerce and shipping to our shores as his resolutions proposed was barred under the Treaty. Although Jay obtained no commercial privileges except trade with the West Indies, and that on conditions so stringent that we refused to accept that part of the Treaty, we gave up for ten years the right to impose any tonnage or tariff discrimination upon British ships or goods.[24] Thus such questions as those raised by Madison's resolutions, which had afforded a strategic rallying point for Republicans, could no longer vex the Federalists once the Treaty was ratified. As far as trade with Great Britain was concerned, we were left in the same position that we had thought so intolerable under the Confederation. Other weaknesses of the Treaty, as evaluated by Samuel Flagg Bemis, include Jay's failure to maintain the honor of the Federal courts in the matter of debts owed to British citizens, which were now to be determined by a mixed commission; the lack of a provision to secure recognition of our adopted principles of international maritime law; the absence of an article protecting our seamen from impressment; and, finally, the failure to secure a mutual hands-off policy with regard to Indians in each other's territory.[25]

It would appear that this treaty could be defended, from the American point of view, only upon the assumptions which underlie "Admiral Mahan's statement that the signature by England of any treaty at all with the United States at that time was an event of 'epochal significance,' a recognition of the existence of American nationality of far greater import than the technical recognition of independence forced from George III in 1783."[26] This was not, however, the view which most Americans of that time took of the matter. They were not asking for recognition of the existence of American nationality. They were asking for a removal of grievances, some of which impaired our sovereignty, and for a basis of commercial and diplomatic relationship which would enable us to remain at peace with her without becoming a British satellite.

[24] Samuel Flagg Bemis, *Jay's Treaty* (New York, 1923), 257.
[25] *Ibid.*, 259–61.
[26] *Ibid.*, 269–70.

A deep and general aversion to the terms of the Jay Treaty is apparent throughout the whole effort to get it approved. As Gaillard Hunt says, "Washington did not pretend to like the treaty. After Jay had delivered it he kept it for four months before he could bring himself to submit it to the Senate."[27] When it was finally submitted, it was passed, after prolonged discussion, on June 24, 1795, by the minimum number of votes necessary. Senator Mason of Virginia, in violation of the resolution of complete secrecy passed by the Senate when consideration of the Treaty began, gave a copy of it to Benjamin Franklin Bache, editor of the *Aurora*,[28] who

printed it on June 29 and personally carried the news to Boston, scattering copies of the Treaty at all his stops along the way. Washington had expected to sign the Treaty if the Senate recommended it, but hesitated as the feeling against it began to mount. At the same time the Administration learned that the British had issued a new order for the seizure of our ships carrying provisions to France, an order mistakenly regarded at that time as a renewal of their provision order of June, 1793.[29] Britain continued to retain our posts, surrender of which was to be our one tangible benefit from the Treaty, until we should ratify, and the new order for the seizure of our ships was regarded as a further attempt at coercion on her part. According to Randolph, Washington told him on July 13 that he "might have informed Mr. Hammond that he [Washington] would never ratify if the provision-order was not removed out of the way."[30] Of Washington's Cabinet, Randolph alone opposed ratification before the order should be rescinded, though Wolcott wished us to ratify without communicating the fact that we had done so until the order was removed.[31]

While the question was in this state,

[27] Gaillard Hunt, Introduction to Bemis, *Jay's Treaty*, xiii.

[28] Mason has been accused of most unworthy motives in revealing the terms of the Treaty to the public. Howard Crosby Rice suggests that Mason got 500 guineas or $2,333 through James Swan from the French government for making the terms of the Treaty known. "James Swan: Agent of the French Republic, 1794–96," *New England Quarterly*, X (Sept., 1937), 481. Thomas Perkins Abernethy in his article on Mason in Allen Johnson and Dumas Malone, eds., *Dictionary of American Biography* (New York, 1928–44), says that his motives were undoubtedly honorable. Madison wrote to Monroe, Philadelphia, Dec. 20, 1795, "The Senate, after a few weeks consultation, ratified the Treaty as you have seen. The injunction of secrecy was then dissolved by a full House, and quickly after restored sub modo, in a thin one. Mr. Mason disregarding the latter vote sent the Treaty to the press...." Gaillard Hunt, ed., *The Writings of James Madison*, 9 vols. (New York, 1900–10), VI, 258. As a matter of fact, for some time various senators and other officials had been telling friends and relatives a part at least of what was in the Treaty. Gibbs, *Memoirs*, I, 199–202. Mason, in a letter which he gave Bache to print with the Treaty, claimed that he was giving it to the public to correct the impressions formed by garbled and incorrect versions that were floating about. Moncure Daniel Conway, *Omitted Chapters of History Disclosed in the Life and Papers of Edmund Randolph* (New York and London, 1888), 295. Hereafter, Conway, *Randolph*. According to Randolph, Washington gave him a copy of the Treaty to be published on the day it appeared. *Ibid.*, 261. Hammond wrote to Grenville, Jun. 5, 1795, "To be sure the proceedings of the Treaty have been secret, but your Lordship may be assured of the authenticity of the circumstances I have mentioned, as they

were last night communicated to me in confidence by Mr. Wolcott, the present Secretary of the Treasury." British State Papers (transcripts), NYPL.

[29] Josiah Turner Newcomb states that this was not a renewal of the provision order, seizures under which were contrary to Jay's treaty. "... there had been a complete shift in the legal basis for the seizures, for the British were now relying on the right to seize enemy property, in neutral bottoms, a course of action the legality of which in proved cases was sanctioned in the treaty and could not be denied under international law." "New Light on Jay's Treaty," *American Journal of International Law*, XXVIII (Oct., 1934), 687. Newcomb shows, however, that all Americans at the time believed that England was going contrary to the provisions of the newly concluded Treaty, and that it was ratified by us while under that impression.

[30] Conway, *Randolph*, 267.

[31] Wolcott to Hamilton, Aug. 10, Aug. 15, 1795, Hamilton Papers, LC.

Washington left for Mount Vernon to deliberate further on the matter. Fearful that if the Treaty were ratified, it would so divide the country as to give the French every opportunity to cause embarrassment to our government, he considered that there was more to be apprehended, whether the Treaty was signed or not, "than from any other crisis since the beginning of the government." [32] The inner circle of the Federalist party fairly held its breath, awaiting Washington's decision. Oliver Ellsworth wrote cryptically, "If the President decides wrong, or does not decide *soon, his good fortune will forsake him.*" [33] Noah Webster wrote to Oliver Wolcott, "The peace of our Country stands almost committed in either event. . . . A rejection sacrifices Mr. Jay & perhaps many of his friends, a ratification threatens the popularity of the President, whose personal influence is now more essential than ever to our Union." [34] Christopher Gore wrote to King that Washington's delay in signing the Treaty was doing the government incalculable harm in New England:

Of all the critical situations in which the government has been placed, this is the most extreme. . . . I know of but one step that can arrest this mania, that affords any hope of ‚ supporting the government. An address from the President to the people of the United States, stating that he had ratified the treaty. . . .[35]

When in 1791 Washington had hesitated and taken his full ten days before signing the Bank Bill, the Republicans claimed that the Federalists became very

impatient and even threatening.[36] In 1795 Federalist sources show that there would probably have been a split in the party had Washington failed them. Stephen Higginson wrote that if the Treaty were not ratified, "The President and Senate will be at open points, with Jay & Hamilton &c on the side of the latter." [37] We have no evidence that intimations of this sort reached Washington, and that they did seems highly improbable. Such threats would not have influenced him. What is significant is that during this period when the Republicans were most active in stirring up public opinion, the Federalists were comparatively quiet. Until they had obtained Washington's approval, they had little basis for an appeal to the public.

While the country was completely absorbed in the question of what Washington would do, Hammond, the British minister, showed Wolcott a dispatch written by Fauchet, the former French minister to the United States, which had been taken in March of that year when the corvette *Jean Bart* was captured by the British man-of-war *Cerberus*. The dispatch contained an account dated October 24, 1794, which stated that Randolph, the Secretary of State, had approached Fauchet at that time and had asked him for a sum of money with which he could insure the loyalty of three or four men whose conduct was believed to be of vital importance to the Republicans and hence to France.[38] Upon

---

[32] Washington to Randolph, Mt. Vernon, Jul. 29, 1795, Gratz Collection, Pennsylvania Historical Society (hereafter, PHS).

[33] William Garrett Brown, *The Life of Oliver Ellsworth* (New York and London, 1905), 220.

[34] Webster to Wolcott, Jul. 30, 1795, Emily Ellsworth Ford Skeel, ed., and Emily Ellsworth Fowler Ford, comp., *Notes on the Life of Noah Webster*, 2 vols. (New York, 1912), I, 393.

[35] Aug. 14, 1795, King, *Correspondence*, II, 23. Gore urged that King and Hamilton induce the President to act decisively in favor of the Treaty.

[36] See Henry Stephens Randall, *The Life of Thomas Jefferson*, 3 vols. (New York, 1858), I, 631, for account of Madison's remarks on Washington's aversion to the Bank Bill and the Jay Treaty.

[37] Higginson to Pickering, Boston, Aug. 16, 1795, Pickering Papers, XX, 32, MHS.

[38] The best of the Federalist sources for the account of Randolph's disgrace is Gibbs, *Memoirs*, I, 232 ff., though the preceding pages should also be read to form an estimate of Randolph's importance in the struggle over the Treaty. [*Editor's note:* See Irving Brant, "John Randolph Not Guilty," *William and Mary Quarterly*, 3d ser., VII (April, 1950), 179–98.]

news that a very urgent matter required his immediate presence, Washington left Mount Vernon and returned to Philadelphia on August 11. On the following day he saw the dispatch and said that he would ratify the Treaty. Randolph, from whom all news of this had been kept, was sent to tell Hammond, with whom he was not on good terms, that we would ratify the Treaty. When the dispatch was shown to Randolph in the presence of the Cabinet, he resigned and the Treaty was ratified. In the controversy which followed Randolph's attempt at self-vindication,[39] he and those Republicans who embraced his cause sought to prove that the accusations against him were merely part of a maneuver to get the Treaty accepted and that Randolph had been disgraced because he was the one Cabinet member who was not in favor of immediate and unqualified acceptance of the Treaty as passed by the Senate. In answer, Washington maintained that the charges against Randolph had had nothing to do with his decision to sign the Treaty.

It seems probable that the Republicans weakened their hold upon the public and their position with regard to the Treaty to the extent that they embraced Randolph's side of the dispute. Many Republicans thought that Washington had lost all his influence and popularity by signing the Treaty, but no matter how great his losses in this respect, few people were willing to hear him attacked in the terms which Randolph and his adherents used. In one letter Randolph said that Washington had shown toward him "treachery unexampled since Tiberius," and such charges as this only placed Randolph in a worse light than before. It seems clear that whatever motives lay behind his "exposure" and disgrace, the incident was highly effective

in diverting attention from questions relating directly to the Treaty, where the Republicans stood on comparatively firm ground with regard to the public opinion of the time, to a contest largely personal in nature.

While the events related above were taking place, the attention of the American people from Georgia to New Hampshire was engrossed as never before in a practical decision of government. Should we or should we not ratify the Treaty? The Republicans had taken the initiative with petitions, incendiary pamphlets, and a series of public meetings held in the larger cities, each of which addressed a memorial to the President. The Federalists denounced those who attended these meetings as the scum of society; but if it was the scum of society which showed this degree of interest—for some of the meetings were large—Jay's treaty is all the more noteworthy as a lesson in the political education of the public during this decade. John Beckley, who had taken a leading part in the planning of these meetings all over the country, wrote of the one in Philadelphia:

On Saturday, a memorial to the President will be presented, which if adopted will be carried through the different wards of the city and offered for the signature of the individual citizens, by which means we shall discover the names and numbers of the British adherents, old Tories and Aristocrats who modestly assume the title of Federalists, and stile themselves *the best* friends of our beloved President. At the same time it will effectually show the major and decided sense of the great commercial city of Philadelphia. Is it not a painful reflection, my friend, that the machinations and intrigues of a British faction in our country, should place our good old president in the distressing situation of singly opposing himself to the almost unanimous voice of his fellow citizens, and endangering the peace, happiness, and union of America, as well as destroying his own tranquillity, peace of mind, good name, and fame. But I trust in heaven to enlighten his mind and give

[39] Edmund Randolph, *A Vindication of Mr. Randolph's Resignation* (Philadelphia, 1795).

him wisdom and firmness to turn away the evil cup so insidiously prepared for him.[40]

Once the President had signed the Treaty, the real contest over it began, as the Republicans were determined to block the appropriation which the House of Representatives had to make in order to carry into effect certain provisions of the Treaty. After the President's signature, Beckley and his associates made a second attempt to whip up general public feeling, or at least to prevent its decline. To DeWitt Clinton, Beckley wrote:

We perfectly accord with you in sentiment, and are adopting measures on our part in furtherance of your ideas. A change in the public sentiment now so universally manifested against the treaty, is the great desideratum of our opponents, as they mean to influence a majority of the Representatives in its favor at the coming meeting of Congress;—to this object all their efforts will be pointed, and to frustrate them we have concluded an address to the people of the United States to be printed and dispersed in handbills in the same mode and subject to the same rules of secrecy that we observed in the case of the petition, respecting which not a suspicion is yet excited here—By this means, we hope to give the first effectual blow and to make it as impressive as possible, we shall incorporate in it ... a history of the late intrigues in the Cabinet, connected with the causes of Mr. Randolph's resignation, which produced the President's ratification of the treaty, and a revocation of his first determination officially made known to Hammonds [sic] not to ratify. ... Rely on every effort and cooperation here in pursuit of what we religiously think our country's political salvation rests on—the defeat of the treaty.[41]

Although public interest in the Treaty did not remain during the winter of 1795–96 at the level it had reached during the previous summer and fall, it soon revived. In March the question was brought before the House of Representatives of an appropriation to put the Treaty into effect. The parties fought now not only over the merits of the Treaty, but also over the question whether the House had the power under the Constitution to refuse to appropriate the money necessary for a treaty already ratified by the President and the Senate. Thus the passing of the Treaty had again come to depend largely upon extraneous factors. The Constitutional issue presented a true dilemma. Either the Senate did not have complete power as to treaties, or the House complete power to initiate financial measures, both of which powers had been generally assumed supreme.

The immediate effect of this apparent conflict of jurisdiction was to win some support for the Federalists from those who thought that the House was moved by jealousy of its powers or by mere political obstructionism, and who regarded its conduct as another example of the viciousness of party spirit. To many Republican representatives it must have appeared that the practical question for them to decide was whether it was best to defeat the Treaty and destroy the prestige of the House, or to pass the Treaty, vindicate their party and body as moderate and magnanimous, and hope thereby to prevent disaster to Republicanism later. Aaron Kitchell, a Republican representative from New Jersey who regarded the Jay Treaty as part of an effort to prepare the minds of the people for a rupture with France, nevertheless voted for it so that whatever evils followed could not then be laid on the House of Representatives. "Should this be the case it would exactly answer the wish of those who are wishing to destroy the check which the House of Representatives have in the government." [42]

---

[40] John Beckley to DeWitt Clinton, Philadelphia, Jul. 24, 1795, DeWitt Clinton Papers, Columbia University Library (hereafter, CUL). [Reprinted by permission of CUL.]

[41] Same to same, Philadelphia, Sept. 3, 1795, ibid.

[42] Aaron Kitchell to Ebenezer Elmer, Philadelphia, Mar. 31, 1796, PHS.

When the House voted to ask Washington for the papers which would explain the negotiations in the Treaty, his
negative reply, instructing the House to
limit its concern with treaties to appropriations,[43] must have been very gall-
ing to Madison and other Republicans
who knew at least as much as Washington of the view which the Federal Convention took on this and other matters.
On the other hand, it seems to have
strengthened the Federalist position in
the country at large.[44]

After the necessary funds were appropriated by the House, Washington
spoke of the public mind as having been
agitated at this time "in a higher degree than it has been at any period since
the Revolution."[45] The agitation was
stirred up by both parties and there are
letters extant from those who were in a
position to know, showing how the public excitement was induced. Beckley
wrote to DeWitt Clinton in April concerning three Republican congressmen
he considered unreliable on the coming
vote for appropriations to implement the
Treaty:

Elected by small majorities, and doubtful
from the present circumstance of your state
how the political scale will preponderate at
another Election, they perhaps wish to steer
that course which will best ensure their re-
election. So often and so fatally, my friend,
do personal supersede public considerations.
You can best judge of and will I am sure
pursue, *the most prudent* means to keep
our three friends in the true course—If *they*
go right, the British treaty will infallibly
be rejected. But remember whatever is done,
must be done quickly. You possibly know
their political connections, and from
whence they can be best encouraged and
supported.[46]

The development of party machinery
had gone a long way when party leaders
began to put pressure in this fashion on
representatives through their constituents. The Republicans were not the only
ones who employed these tactics, however. At about the same time, Rufus
King wrote to Hamilton of one of the
men Beckley mentions:

Van Cortlandt will leave this place on
Wednesday. Would it not be well to prepare a reception for him which may return
him in favor of the Treaty—His friends may
be induced to act upon his mind, which
balances, as to decide it.[47]

Hamilton was at the same time writing
to King, reporting on the situation in
New York and giving instructions for
the final effort so to arouse public opinion that the recalcitrant representatives
should be forced to grant the appropriation for the Treaty.[48] On April 16 he
wrote:

Our merchants here are not less alarmed
than those of Philadelphia & will do all
they can. All the insurance people meet today—The merchants and traders will meet
tomorrow or the next day. A petition will
be prepared and circulated among the other
citizens.

On April 18 he stated the steps which
must be taken in Philadelphia. First the
President must rebuke the House of
Representatives:

...then have the merchants meet in the...
cities & second by their resolutions the
measures of the President & Senate and
further address their fellow citizens to co-
operate with them, petitions afterward to be
handed throughout the United States. The
Senate to hold fast and consent to no ad-
journment till the expiration of the term
of service of the present house unless provision made. The President to cause a confidential communication to be made to the
British stating candidly what has happened,

[43] Mar. 30, 1796, Fitzpatrick, *Washington's
Writings*, XXXV, 2–5.
[44] Peter Van Schaack to Sedgwick, Kinderhook, N.Y., Apr. 15, 1796, tells of circulation
of this speech in handbills and of its great
effect. Sedgwick Papers, MHS.
[45] Washington to Pinckney, May 22, 1796,
Fitzpatrick, *Washington's Writings*, XXXV, 62.
[46] Beckley to DeWitt Clinton, Philadelphia,
Apr., 1796, DeWitt Clinton Papers, CUL.

[47] King to Hamilton, dated Apr. 17 with
1795 added in pencil (should be 1796), Hamilton Papers, XXIV, LC.
[48] Hamilton to King, Apr. 16, 18, and 20,
1796, King Papers, New-York Historical Society
(hereafter, NYHS).

his regrets, his adherence, nevertheless to the treaty, his resolution to persist in the execution as far as depends on the Executive & his hope that the faith of the country will be eventually preserved. But all this must begin with the President. P. S. If the Treaty is not executed the President will be called on in regard to his character & the public good to *keep the post* till another House of Representatives has pronounced.[49]

These are the concrete suggestions, in a time of crisis, of the man who professed to believe in majority rule.

The appropriations for the Treaty were passed because Republican members from New York, New Jersey, and Pennsylvania who had been opposed to the Treaty and who had not intended to vote the money to put it into effect were finally brought to do so. Washington thought that it was passed because of "the torrent of Petitions, and remonstrances which were pouring in from all the Eastern and middle States, and were beginning to come pretty strongly from that of Virginia . . ." [50] but it does not seem to have been the pressure of public opinion, stirred up as we have seen by both sides, which changed the views of these men. The vote of the doubtful members was changed by two means: by the threat that the Senate would not ratify Pinckney's treaty with Spain which gave us the use of the Mississippi, and by talk of breaking up the Union such as was used at the time the passing of Assumption was delayed. Chauncey Goodrich wrote to Oliver Wolcott, Sr., in April:

. . . 'tis well known that the Senate will, as soon as a vote shall be had on the resolution before us, if unfortunate, tack an amendment providing for the British treaty, to the Spanish treaty bill, and inflexibly adhere for all or none. I am not warranted to assert, but I trust they also will arrest the federal city loan bill, land office, perhaps appropriation for the army, refuse to rise; in short, arrest the whole government, and let the people decide.[51]

The way in which these threats affected Republicans may be seen in the letters of Aaron Kitchell, the center of resistance to the Treaty among the representatives from New Jersey, who wrote to Ebenezer Elmer late in March, ". . . my mind recoils from the issue. I must confess I have heard so many hints lately thrown out Seeming to espouse a wish for Separation of the union that I fear it is more than thought of." [52] A little earlier Kitchell had warned his friend Elmer against resolutions from the New Jersey legislature approving or disapproving the Treaty, lest their state offend some of the larger ones. He had heard, furthermore, that Judge Paterson of the Supreme Court had said that Jersey wished to break off from the Southern states and was ready to do so:

I fear a Separation may take place Sooner than wee would wish. In Such a case whether wee are joined to the Eastern or Southern states we are sure to be the Sufferers. I take it for Granted Mr. Patterson had no authority for what he said and he must have been drunk or a fool to make such a declaration.[53]

It was not Kitchell alone who heard rumors that there would be a separation of the Union if the appropriation were not granted. The British consul in Philadelphia, Phineas Bond, relied on the threat of dissolution ". . . for which the leaders of the democratic party, with all

---

[49] *Ibid.* [Reprinted by permission.] In the Jeremy Belknap Papers, the volume labeled 1620–1798, 83 ff., there is a number of letters and petitions which enable us to see how the Boston organization to push the Jay Treaty worked. The Church appears to have been the backbone of this organization, with the ministers urging their parishioners to sign petitions requesting the voting of appropriations for the Treaty. Pamphlets in its behalf appear to have been handed out at some of the rural churches. MHS.

[50] Washington to Pinckney, Philadelphia, May 22, 1796, *Washington's Writings*, XXXV, 62.

[51] Chauncey Goodrich to Oliver Wolcott, Sr., Philadelphia, Apr. 23, 1796, Gibbs, *Memoirs*, I, 331.

[52] Aaron Kitchell to Ebenezer Elmer, Philadelphia, Mar. 31, 1796, PHS.

[53] Same to same, Mar. 7, 1796, PHS.

that spirit of Disunion and Discontent, which marks their conduct are not yet ripe," [54] for the granting of the money. Early in March Sedgwick wrote "If Disorganization [meaning a refusal to vote the appropriation] prevails I see not but that it will then be demonstrated that We cannot live in the same family." [55] A month later he stated that the anxiety in the city of Philadelphia was the greatest he had ever seen. "The conversation of a separation is taking place in almost every company and even I am obliged to moderate the zeal and cool the passions of more cool and temperate men." [56]

There had long been a close connection between Sedgwick and Jonathan Dayton, a representative from New Jersey; and when the House met in December, 1795, Sedgwick had the bulk of the Federalist votes for Speaker, which had been cast unanimously for him in caucus, transferred to Dayton, "whom we carried in triumphantly." [57] During the last of March, Dayton, who had been expected by the Republicans to join them in the Treaty fight, told Sedgwick that he would no longer remain indifferent but would take a decided part for the Treaty. A few days later Sedgwick applied to him for aid on the bill, and Dayton then asked " 'what to do to be saved?' " Sedgwick told him to go to Findley, who was from Western Pennsylvania, and tell him that "he alone could save his country from anarchy & probably civil war." If he found Findley malleable, he was to suggest that the latter make the motion "that provision ought to be made for carrying into effect the several late treaties." Sedgwick then suggested to Dayton an outline of the speech Dayton should make at that time, and Dayton said he would "follow my directions explicitly." Sedgwick prided himself that he did not rely upon the patriotism of these men but the reverse:

Dayton is ambitious, bold, and vindictive. Because Jay has prevented the sequestration of debts he has incurred his mortal enmity. But New Jersey is alarmed and Dayton must regain her confidence or he is finished politically.... Findley knows that the Spanish treaty will meet the same fate as the British—the Senate will provide for the whole or none. The Spanish treaty is necessary to Findley's constituents and the opposition of the representative has already created prodigious sensibility. How disgusting it is, my friend, that on the weakness & wickedness of unprincipled men in a popular government the happiness of millions may frequently depend.[58]

Sedgwick's last letter on these maneuvers stated that the vote had been delayed until Monday because Dayton thought his influence would get the necessary votes by then. "New Jersey is perfectly electrified and Dayton is anxious to retrieve his character as are Kitchell, Samuel Smith and we hope even Findley and Gallatin ... it seems impossible to live long in the same family with these scoundrels." [59]

If Sedgwick did not exaggerate his part in getting the appropriation for the Jay Treaty passed and did not misrepresent the considerations which caused several Republicans to change their votes, the effect of the famous "tomahawk speech" of Fisher Ames, which is frequently credited with passing the bill, has been greatly overestimated. Ames's tone throughout the speech was one warning of the dire effects which would

---

[54] Bond to Grenville, Philadelphia, Mar. 31, 1796, British State Papers (transcripts), LC.
[55] Sedgwick to ———, Philadelphia, Mar. 2, 1796, Sedgwick Papers, MHS.
[56] Sedgwick to Ephraim Williams, Philadelphia, Apr. 1, 1796, ibid.
[57] Sedgwick to Loring Andrews, Philadelphia, Dec. 7, 1795, ibid.

[58] Same to same, Philadelphia, Apr. 5, 1796, ibid. [Reprinted by permission.]
[59] Ibid. Gallatin's constituents were so eager to get the treaty with Spain ratified that they put a great deal of pressure on him to vote for the Jay Treaty. Gallatin Papers, V, March through April, 1796, NYHS.

follow refusal to appropriate the money. Without the treaty, he stated, the Union would be endangered and Indian warfare would be brought to the frontiers. The concern of the frontiersmen for our commercial rights is well known; we see here the invalid recluse of Dedham pleading with frontier representatives for the lives of their wives and children.[60] Gallatin remarked in his answer to this famous speech:

I cannot help considering the cry of war, the threats of a dissolution of government, and the present alarm, as designed for the same purpose, that of making an impression on the fears of this house. It was through the fear of being involved in a war that the negotiation with Great Britain originated; under the impression of fear the treaty has been negotiated and signed; a fear of the same danger, that of war, promoted its ratification; and now every imaginary mischief which can alarm our fears is conjured up, in order to deprive us of that discretion which this House thinks it has a right to exercise, and in order to force us to carry the treaty into effect.[61]

The means by which support for the appropriation was won should be kept in mind when we read such statements as the following:

...he [Hamilton] cemented the Federalist group in Congress, and gave it such a pointed efficiency that even when the majority was in fact made up of Jeffersonians, he was able to dominate it and manoeuver it, as is proved by the long discussions and final votes on the Jay treaty.[62]

[60] Ames on Jay Treaty, *Annals of Congress,* Apr. 28, 1796.
[61] Henry Adams, *The Life of Albert Gallatin* (Philadelphia and London, 1880), 165.
[62] Bernard Faÿ, "Early Party Machinery in the United States," *Pennsylvania Magazine of History and Biography,* LX (Oct., 1936), 377. Faÿ refers to Edgar Eugene Robinson, *The Evolution of American Political Parties* (New York, 1924), 65. Henry Jones Ford writes, "Hamilton's success in carrying his measures through Congress, by sheer dexterity of management when numbers were against him, added bitterness to the natural chagrin felt by the defeated faction." *Washington and His Colleagues, A Chronicle of the Rise and Fall of Federalism* (New Haven, 1918), 165.

The above statement was made to prove the contention that Hamilton was a more able party leader than Jefferson; and if use of influence and coercion be the test of party leadership, he unquestionably was. An American counterpart of the scene so frequent in eighteenth-century London, the mob rioting outside a subservient House of Commons, apparently had no terrors for Hamilton. The question of Jefferson's party leadership at this time can hardly be discussed. As we have seen, it was the Jay Treaty more than anything else which made a party leader of him. In addition to this circumstance we must remember that Hamilton and Jefferson were party leaders of such different types that it is very difficult to compare them profitably, in spite of the common tendency to do so. Hamilton must be admitted to have had an undisputed supremacy in the use of the sort of management and pressure which we have seen exhibited in the struggle over the Treaty, but it ought always to be noted that the technique exhibited here is not, under a representative government, the whole story of party leadership. There is no indication that Hamilton ever realized how expensive this Federalist victory was to prove.

The immediate political results of the Jay Treaty may be seen in the changes of party affiliation which it brought about and in the way in which approval or disapproval of it became an issue in the elections of 1796. It altered party alignments and caused each group to close ranks. Because of the stand of the two parties on the Jay Treaty, such men as John Dickinson, Charles Pinckney, and John Langdon became active Republicans, although each was essentially conservative and each came from a state still dominated by the Federalists. Only one of these men, Pinckney, carried his own state for Jefferson in 1800, but each of them was a source of great strength to the Republicans through the country as a whole from 1796 to 1800.

Probably more important in the eventual Federalist defeat than the open defection of such leaders as these was the Federalist loss at this time of many less prominent men who had nevertheless been the backbone of the party. The disastrous effect of the Jay Treaty upon the Federalist party in the South may be estimated by the statement of Judge Iredell, who wrote, "...the sentiments *publicly* expressed by Mr. John Rutledge [who had attacked the Treaty], which procured his rejection by the Senate as Chief Justice, although nominated by General Washington, were shared by almost every other man south of the Potomac, even by those personally friendly to Mr. Jay and stanch Federalists.[63]

One of the immediate effects of the Treaty upon party organization was that it occasioned the first of the two Republican caucuses of the decade, thus taking the development of party machinery a step further.[64] In the Republican campaign to elect members of the House in 1796, attacks upon those who had voted for the Treaty were more prominent than any other form of appeal. In Pennsylvania, Republicans were rallied with the call to throw out "Gregg the Trimmer," and to substitute for Frederick Muhlenberg, Blair McClenachan, who had recommended "kicking the treaty to hell." The Republicans relied on this type of appeal almost as much in New York, where they were unsuccessful, as in Pennsylvania, which they carried.

It was not only the Republicans who

made an issue of the Treaty in the election of 1796. Hugh Williamson wrote in October, 1796, "Yesterday I returned from the Eastern States, having been about 200 miles beyond Boston. Nothing was talked of six weeks ago, but the measures of placing federal Members in the Place of those who voted against supporting the Treaty."[65] A little later William Vans Murray wrote from the Eastern Shore of Maryland that he "never knew an election so much of *principles,*" that although the Federalists had a candidate who was very unpopular personally, "...yet the language is, our choice is a party question, not a personal matter...."[66] William Bentley, the Unitarian minister of Salem, Massachusetts, noted that a new element appeared to have entered politics. "Electioneering goes on in our own state & in New Hampshire. It extends itself in Boston for the petty officers of the Town. This is the commencement of a new career."[67] Jefferson wrote later of the period following the struggle over the Jay Treaty:

One source of great change in social intercourse arose...tho' its effects were as yet scarcely sensible on society or government. I mean the British treaty, which produced a schism that went on widening and rankling till the years '98, '99, when a final dissolution of all bonds, civil & social, appeared imminent.[68]

If the Jay Treaty was of the importance in shaping the two parties which these quotations would indicate, we should inquire as to what was involved in the choice which this country had to make. What did acceptance or rejection

---

[63] Quoted in Mrs. St. Julien Ravenel, *The Life and Times of William Lowndes of South Carolina, 1782–1822* (Boston and New York, 1901), 33–34.

[64] Henry Adams, ed., *The Writings of Albert Gallatin,* 3 vols. (Philadelphia, 1879), III, 553. The other was held when news of the XYZ dispatches reached this country.

[65] Bernard Christian Steiner, *The Life and Correspondence of James McHenry* (Cleveland, 1907), 200.

[66] Nov. 2, 1796, *ibid.,* 200–01.

[67] William Bentley, *Diary,* Mar. 12, 1796, VI, 174, quoted in William Alexander Robinson, *Jeffersonian Democracy in New England* (New Haven, 1916), 12.

[68] Jefferson to Benjamin Hawkins, Washington, Feb. 18, 1803, Jefferson, *Writings,* IX, 445.

of the Jay Treaty mean? What were the aims of the Republican party in taking its stand on this very important issue? Was the opposition merely making political capital out of the necessities of the Administration? Were they simply making it more difficult to do something which had to be done?

The important question is, of course, whether or not war with Great Britain or a serious disruption of our trade with her were the sole alternatives to the Treaty. The only positive evidence on this point would be the statements of such men as Pitt or Lord Grenville as to what their course toward us would have been if we had not offered to open negotiations for a new treaty in 1794, or if we had refused to accept the treaty which resulted from these negotiations. There is no record that any reliable statement was ever made of what British policy would have been in this contingency; and under the circumstances, all that we can do is to look at the conditions in which that country found itself in 1793–94.

It would appear that Great Britain was more hard pressed abroad, more divided and straitened at home, and more isolated diplomatically in 1795 than she had been in 1775 or was to be in 1812. At the time when the Federalists were threatening that we would have war with Great Britain if we did not accept the Treaty, British leaders were wondering how long they would be able to maintain the war merely against France. In July, 1795, Lord Auckland wrote:

I will not be answerable that we can much longer find funds, however necessary, for the war on a large scale, without serious ill-humor, the tendency to which is much promoted by the very short produce in Europe and America of the last year's harvests, and by the harshness of the present summer.[69]

Under the circumstances, we may seriously question whether Great Britain would have wished to acquire another enemy. To bring about war with us in 1795 or 1796, she would have had to take the initiative in a way in which she did not have to either in 1775 or in 1812. This war would have been against her heaviest debtor and her best customer at a time when she was on the verge of bankruptcy, against the country which was her one certain source of food at a time when provisions were desperately scarce and very expensive. These were the years in which Great Britain was forced to adopt the Speenhamland system of outdoor relief to prevent general starvation. She had just been disastrously defeated in the French West Indies, one of the prizes for which she had gone to war and for which she had diverted men and supplies which would have been very useful to her on the Continent.[70] Would she have wished us to aid either France or the Negroes who were revolting in Santo Domingo?

According to Mahan in his *Influence of Sea Power upon the French Revolution and Empire*, Great Britain went to war with France in 1793 with less than one-fourth of the seamen she had had in active service during the last year of the American Revolution.[71] The conduct of her navy during the early years of this war, culminating in the mutiny at

Auckland, III, 309, quoted in Worthington Chauncey Ford, ed., *The Writings of John Quincy Adams*, 7 vols. (New York, 1913–17), I, 412, *n.*

[70] Sir John William Fortescue gives an estimate of the cost of the West Indian campaigns, "...which were the essence of Pitt's military policy," and shows how inadequate was the return for this effort. "For this England's soldiers had been sacrificed, her treasure squandered, her influence in Europe weakened, her arm for six hateful years fettered, numbed, and paralysed." *A History of the British Army*, 13 vols. (London and New York, 1899–1930), IV, Part I, 565.

[71] Alfred Thayer Mahan, *The Influence of Sea Power upon the French Revolution and Empire, 1793–1812* (Boston, 1895), 60.

[69] Lord Auckland to Hugh Elliott, Jul. 16, 1795, *Journal and Correspondence of Lord*

the Nore in 1797, was anything but reassuring. Would she have wished to spread these naval forces thinner, as she would have had to do to fight us? She would have had to make the decision before her victories of Camperdown, Cape St. Vincent, and the Battle of the Nile.

On the other hand, until Hamilton divulged to Hammond that we would not act with the League of Armed Neutrality, we stood in a stronger position with regard to Great Britain than we had done at any time between 1783 and 1812. The battle of Fallen Timbers had strengthened us along the entire Northwestern frontier. Englishmen later claimed that Lord Dorchester had spoken without official sanction when he attempted to incite the Indians against us in February, 1794, and that it would have cost him at least his command if hostilities had resulted from his speech. If we had been forced into war during those years, this country would not have been more divided than it was during the Revolution or the War of 1812. Revulsion against France had not yet become general, and a war against Britain would have been a crusade against the old order under slogans that had not yet become suspect in themselves or dishonored by those who bore them. Americans abroad wrote home that there was no fear of retaliation if we refused to sign a treaty which one of them called "the monster begot by Lord Grenville on Mr. Jay." [72] They seemed to be unanimously of the opinion that Great Britain needed our trade as she never had before,[73] though this evidence probably had little to do with the general Republican belief that war would not follow if we refused the Treaty.

The leading Republicans believed that in the condition in which Great Britain found herself, she would not fight us over the issues existing between the two countries at this time even if we rejected the Treaty. They thought, however, that we had already yielded as much as a self-respecting nation could and that if war came, it would be another fight for independence and would be generally regarded as such. No Republican leaders, as far as the writer can discover, ever offered any solution for the problems of government finance which would have arisen in case we had had to fight at that time. Their attitude on the whole question of finance and commercial relations appears to have been what it was during the Revolution, when our trade with the British was regarded mainly as a weapon which might be used against them. The belief in our national self-sufficiency underlay all American assumptions on this point. The spirit of ardent Republicans at this time can best be realized by recalling the attitude of men during the Revolution toward trade with the British. Early in that period a Philadelphia Committee of Correspondence wrote to a Committee in Boston:

By sea they will beat us; by land, they will not attempt us; we must try it out in a way of commerce. First, by suspending all trade with Great Britain.... Second, by suspending all trade with the West Indies. ... Third, by witholding flaxseed from Ireland.... These are the means we are coolly deliberating; we have other things in contemplation, as stopping our ports entirely and laying up all shipping.[74]

This had been the spirit of Americans at one time, and the belief of the Repub-

[72] Edward Fisher to Rush, Edinburgh, Aug. 30, 1795, Rush MSS., XLV, 29, Philadelphia Library Company, Ridgeway Branch.

[73] Ibid., and J. Speyer to Clinton, London, Feb. 20, 1795, "Should Congress refuse to confirm it, I think we might do anything with this country—for they dare not go to war with us —& wou'd rather give up any point, than hazard to ruin all their manufactures & the residue of their trade." DeWitt Clinton Papers, CUL.

[74] Quoted from Peter Force, American Archives, 4th ser., I, 441–42, by Edward Collins, "Committees of Correspondence of the American Revolution," American Historical Association (hereafter, AHA) Report for 1901, I, 271.

licans was that this spirit was as strong and as general as ever. The Republican leaders may have been guilty of a grave miscalculation here, but they were not playing politics with the Jay Treaty. They did not believe that we had given such hostages to fortune that we could not fight again if we had to.

When we attempt to learn what was involved in the choice which this country had to make at the time and what would have happened had we done other than we did, we run the risk of either writing "hypothetical history" or of being wise after the event. It is the former danger which is greater in the attempt to give the Republican view. One need not, however, try to say what would have happened if we had not made the overtures to Britain in the spring of 1794 which resulted in the sending of Jay, or if we had refused to accept the treaty which resulted from Jay's mission. It is enough to say that the Republican leaders believed that Great Britain would not make war, or that if she did, we should be in a much stronger position than we were in 1775, while hers would be weaker. To present these considerations as dominating the views of Republicans, however, is to represent their attitude as much more calculating than it was. In September, 1795, Jefferson wrote concerning the Jay Treaty that he hoped that the result of our policy toward Great Britain "will establish the eternal truth that acquiescence under insult is not the way to escape war." [75] When the terms of the Treaty became generally known in this country, a great many of our citizens felt that we had been merely enjoying the illusion of independence, that this period of illusion was now at an end, and that we were adopting a course which was certain to result in war with France simply because we would not stand up for our rights

[75] Jefferson to Henry Tazewell, Sept. 13, 1795, Jefferson, *Writings*, VIII, 191.

against England. Which party was right in its view of the Jay Treaty is not so much our concern as is the fact that the clash of their opposing views gave the most powerful stimulus to party division in this country that it had yet received.

III. THE AFTERMATH OF THE JAY TREATY

The basic conditions underlying both our foreign relations and our domestic politics were changed when we accepted the Jay Treaty. Until then, Great Britain was generally regarded as the enemy, actual or potential, and France as our friend and probable ally. Most Americans had thought up to that time that the future of our own experiment depended largely upon the success of the French struggle against monarchy and the old order, that a republican government in this country could not long survive if the coalition of kings should be supreme in Europe. After our acceptance of the Jay Treaty, however, each of these conditions changed in itself or appeared to us in a different light.

It may appear that in putting this emphasis upon our foreign relations after the Jay Treaty, we are wandering far from the development of parties, but the very reverse is true: events growing out of our foreign relations had a decisive influence in determining the course of the two parties in these years. The open split of the Federalist party was on the issue of the second mission to France in 1799. It was such war measures as the Federal land tax of 1799, the Alien and Sedition acts, and above all, the designs of suppression which were supposed to be behind them that finally roused the people of the country against the Federalist regime and swept it from power. It is impossible to separate foreign and domestic relations in this period, for in an epoch of war and revolution, all problems wear a double aspect.

For the period from May, 1796 to March, 1798, our relations with France are the most important phase of government policy. If the Jay Treaty was designed to bring us peace and to remove us from European entanglements, our conduct toward France at this time should have been conciliatory. She may not have deserved this consideration, but our national interest and the widespread desire in this country for peace, which had been so well utilized by Hamilton in the fight for the Treaty, did deserve it. We did not, however, follow a conciliating course. This was true, in part at least, because war with France was the keystone of High-Federalist policy during the latter years of the decade. This is demonstrated not only by what High-Federalists wrote, but also by their behavior after Adams dashed their hopes by sending the second mission to France. We are not, however, so much concerned with the more or less hypothetical uses to which they might have put this war as with the part these men had in bringing our foreign relations to the desperate situation of 1798 and 1799.

About six weeks after the House passed the appropriations for the Treaty, Hamilton wrote to Wolcott that he wanted three frigates completed at once, the money to be obtained by secret loans from the merchants. Ostensibly for Algerine service, these cruisers were really designed for use against French privateers which hovered around our coasts to prey on British shipping. Hamilton added, "The second object may circulate in whispers." [76] The capturing of an American ship off our coast a few days before by French privateers was apparently to serve as the excuse for our attack upon them. Wolcott answered Hamilton that the affair of the capture

was highly equivocal, that although the ship was registered in the name of an American, it had already been sold to an Englishman and after it had crossed the Atlantic was to be delivered to him. "Although the loading was in the name of Willing and Francis, it was in fact British property." He said further that these circumstances were known to or strongly suspected by the owner of the French privateer, that this capture need not alarm us, and that he could not learn that any other had been made.[77] Hamilton, however, continued to stir up feeling against France and wrote to Washington a few days later that Le Guen, a prominent New York merchant, had told him of French plans to seize supplies we were shipping to Great Britain.[78]

As was noted above, propaganda against the French Revolution became greater in volume and more bitter in tone during 1796 than it had been at any time before. It is very difficult to say to what extent this campaign was designed to stir up feeling against France herself and how much of it came naturally from the circumstances of the Presidential campaign of 1796, which was almost completely dominated by considerations of foreign policy. The Republicans claimed that the Treaty put us completely in the hands of Great Britain, that it was a betrayal of our Revolution; the Federalists claimed that opposition to the Treaty came only from those who were the tools of France. The French minister and his agents exerted themselves conspicuously for the election of Jefferson: apparently they had as little idea of the strength of nationalistic sentiment among Americans at this time as Britain showed so frequently between 1789 and 1812. Under the circumstances, Federalist attacks upon the

[76] Hamilton to Wolcott, Jun. 16, 1796, Hamilton Papers, LC.

[77] Wolcott to Hamilton, Philadelphia, Jun. 17, 1796, ibid.

[78] Hamilton to Washington, Jun. 23, 1796, ibid.

French Revolution were inevitable, but such attacks did not end with the election. They continued and were so plentiful and bitter that it seems probable that they marked some concerted effort, beyond that necessary to defeat Jefferson in 1796, to arouse feeling against France. Until a careful study is made of this propaganda campaign against France from 1796 on, however, it will be impossible to say how far there was a deliberate effort by some Americans to stir up trouble with her and how far Franco-American relations went from bad to worse merely in response to events that had already taken place.

France's refusal to accept C. C. Pinckney as minister in place of Monroe, who had been sacrificed by the Federalists for doing exactly as they wished—keeping France pacified while the Jay Treaty was pushed through—[79] took place early in 1797, and the first of John Adams's problems when he took office in March of that year was to decide what policy we should pursue toward France. Should we send a mission to attempt to reach a suitable basis for further relations, and risk a rebuff, or should we simply let matters drift, with all the risks that such a course would entail? Though Adams and Hamilton were bitter enemies, and the Cabinet subsequently worked with Hamilton against Adams, the question of whether or not to send an extraordinary mission to France presented at this time the spectacle of Adams and Hamilton in agreement and opposed by the Cabinet.[80]

Of the High-Federalist leaders only Fisher Ames appears to have supported the plan of Hamilton and Adams at this time. Wolcott showed one of his few signs of revolting against Hamilton's domination when he wrote to him at the end of March, 1797, after they had had considerable correspondence on the subject, that he was well enough aware of Hamilton's influence to be sure that his plan would be followed or that nothing would be done.[81] Hamilton tried to answer Wolcott's objections by writing "... a suspicion begins to dawn among the friends of the government that the actual administration [ministers] is not averse from war with France. How very important to obviate this." [82]

[79] Pickering, who had previously pried into Monroe's private correspondence to get evidence against him, was finally able to get him recalled in the summer of 1796. Monroe had written to George Logan from Paris, Jun. 24, 1795 giving instructions as to the way in which news that he planned to send from France should be made public. Benjamin Bache and John Beckley were to be associated with Logan in the dissemination of this news. Pickering Papers, XLI, 227, MHS. Since the only news which this country had from France came through Britain, and was usually highly colored to suit the purposes of that country, Monroe thought it necessary that there be some other means by which we could find out what was going on in France. The letter to Logan was opened by Pickering, who kept and used it against Monroe on more than one occasion thereafter. This letter was sent by Pickering to Edward Carrington to discredit Monroe in Virginia. Ibid., III, 530. He stipulated that the letter be returned and that Carrington not let it be known how it came into his possession. The use which Pickering made of it with Washington at the time Monroe was recalled in disgrace is a matter of more importance, though it is not possible to say how much it influenced Washington's decision. Pickering did not send the letter itself to Washington, or tell how it came into his hands, but he did use it as a basis for the most damaging accusations. See Pickering Papers, VI, 189, 191, 193, ibid., for use made of it in influencing Washington. The first of these letters has been printed in Worthington Chauncey Ford, ed., The Writing of

George Washington, 14 vols. (New York, 1889–93), XIII, 216 n. Monroe's conduct as minister cannot be defended in any absolute sense, but it appears to advantage when compared with the conduct of those who were maneuvering to get him dismissed.

[80] See Charles Francis Adams, ed., The Life and Works of John Adams, 10 vols. (Boston, 1850–56), IX, 286 (hereafter, Adams, Works); Wolcott to Hamilton, Philadelphia, Mar. 31, 1797, Gibbs, Memoirs, I, 487; Pickering to Hamilton, Philadelphia, Mar. 26, 1797, Hamilton Papers, LC; and Uriah Tracy to Hamilton, Philadelphia, Mar. 23, 1797, ibid.

[81] Wolcott to Hamilton, Philadelphia, Mar. 31, 1797, Gibbs, Memoirs, I, 487.

[82] Hamilton to Wolcott, New York, Mar. 30, 1797, ibid., I, 485.

We get a fuller specimen of Hamilton's arguments for the mission in a memorandum of sixteen closely written pages which he prepared and enclosed in a letter to William L. Smith of South Carolina. He concluded his arguments by saying, "The Plan of the government and the Federal party has been to avoid becoming a party in the present war." He feared that if we should become involved:

... the wisdom of the plan pursued will be questioned. The confidence in the government will be shaken. The adverse party will acquire the reputation & the influence of superior foresight. . . . The doubt entertained by many of the justifiableness of the treaty with Great Britain in respect to France may increase with suffering and danger & the management of affairs may be thrown into the hands of the opposite party by the voice of the people & government & the country sacrificed to France. Hence it is all important to avoid war if we can—if we cannot to strengthen as much as possible the opinion that it proceeds from the Unreasonableness of France. . . .[83]

If Hamilton hoped to avoid war with France, however, his response to Pickering's letters about the XYZ Affair does not indicate it: "I have this moment received your two favors of the 25th. I am delighted with their contents. . . .[84] Likewise, when Sedgwick first heard of the XYZ Affair, he wrote, "It will afford a glorious opportunity to destroy faction.

[83] Hamilton to William L. Smith, Apr. 10, 1797. Hamilton went on to say, "In addition to these [measures for defense which he is urging] it may be proper by some religious solemnity to impress seriously the minds of the people. . . . A politician will consider this as an important means of influencing opinion and will think it a valuable resource in a contest with France to set the Religious ideas of his countrymen in active competition with the atheistical tenets of their enemies. This is an advantage which we shall be very unskillful if we do not use to the utmost. And the impulse cannot be too early given. I am persuaded a day of humiliation and prayer, besides being very proper would be extremely useful." Enclosure, William L. Smith Papers, LC.
[84] Hamilton to Pickering, Mar. 27, 1798, Hamilton, *Works*, VI, 278. The "two favors" Hamilton mentions are *ibid.*, 272, 273.

Improve it."[85] The passing of a few days confirmed him in this view, and he whetted Henry Van Schaack's appetite for news with the report, "Orders will be given immediately to withdraw these envoys from France & there will be told a tale at which every ear will tingle; and unless I am mistaken will give a most fatal blow to the Jacobins."[86]

In June of 1798, Hamilton was sure that the XYZ Affair had destroyed the opposition. "Many of the leaders of faction will pursue and take ultimately a station in the public estimation like that of the Tories of our Revolution."[87] That he was still thinking of relations with France largely in terms of their effect upon the party struggle in this country is indicated by his comment in the margin of a letter King wrote to him in September, 1798, in which the latter stated "You will have no war." Hamilton wrote, "France will treat, not fight; grant us fair terms and not keep them. Meantime our election will occur & bring her friends into power."[88] The statement would seem to imply a belief that only war with France could insure continued Federalist control in this country.

Several circumstances connected with the sending of the mission suggest that Hamilton expected the venture would result in crisis. He had strongly urged that either Madison or Jefferson be included in the mission, accompanied by two staunch Federalists who could overrule the Republican member. Yet had such a group been successful, either of these two Republican leaders would in all probability have received the larger share of the credit for making peace

[85] Sedgwick to ————, Philadelphia, Mar. 7, 1798, Sedgwick Papers, MHS.
[86] Sedgwick to Henry Van Schaack, Philadelphia, Mar. 17, 1798, *ibid*.
[87] Hamilton to King, Jun. 6, 1798, King Papers, XLI, NYHS.
[88] King to Hamilton, London, Sept. 23, 1798, Hamilton Papers, LC.

with France. On the other hand, if a mission which included any eminent Republican leader had failed, the opposition party would have been silenced ahead of time. Is it likely that under these conditions Hamilton would have wanted Madison or Jefferson included if he thought that the mission had any strong probability of success?

Another fact which makes it appear that he was hoping for the failure rather than the success of the mission was his insistence that C. C. Pinckney be included. Pinckney had been embittered by the refusal of the French to accept him at the time Monroe was ordered home, and he had been loud in his complaints against the French. Sending him back at the head of the new mission was like sending Genêt back to us with additional marks of confidence after we had requested that he be withdrawn. Further, the mission was to ask additional concessions from a country which already felt itself to be the injured party. Our envoys were to ask France to let our ships go unmolested to Great Britain while the British seized our ships bound for the French ports. They were to offer nothing in return for these concessions except protestations of good will which were being constantly belied by the conduct of our government, particularly by that of Pickering, Secretary of State, who used diplomatic correspondence which should have been kept secret to stir up the people of the country further against France.[89] These circumstances do not justify Talleyrand's treatment of our envoys, but they do make it seem improbable that there was ever much hope of success for a mission constituted and instructed as was this one.

Hamilton's own temperament and his policies both before and after the mission to France make it appear probable that his sending of the mission was merely a maneuver in a complicated game which embraced both our foreign relations and our domestic politics. He appears to have valued highly a maxim which he copied into one of his notebooks from Demosthenes:

As a general marches at the head of his troups, so ought wise politicians, if I dare use the expression, to march at the head of affairs: insomuch that they ought not to wait the event to know what measures to take: but the measures which they have taken, ought to produce the event.[90]

The sending of a mission that had little chance of success would have been such a shaping of events as Demosthenes here recommends. It would have been in harmony with Hamilton's earlier policies, for he had tried from an early date to ally us with Britain against France.[91] His conduct in giving Beckwith and Hammond information which weakened our diplomatic position from 1792 to 1795 suggests that he thought that being a tail to the British kite was our natural role in foreign relations at this time.

1797, was doing nothing to support the Administration's foreign policy (see Fisher Ames to Hamilton, Philadelphia, Jan. 26, 1797, Hamilton Papers, LC; and Samuel Otis to William Smith, Philadelphia, Jun. 20, 1797, Smith-Carter Collection, MHS). Anything that would injure our relations with France or discredit the revolutionary regime would help to serve the purpose of the Federalists, and in fact, as Arthur P. Whitaker has pointed out, steps leading to hostilities with Spain, France's ally, in Florida were already being undertaken by members of the Cabinet. Arthur P. Whitaker, The Mississippi Question, 1795–1803 (New York, 1934), 125–27.

[90] An extract from Demosthenes copied in Hamilton's Memorandum Book, 250, LC.

[91] Dexter Perkins, Hands Off, A History of the Monroe Doctrine (Boston, 1941), 13–14.

[89] Murray to J. Q. Adams, Jun. 29, 1798, Worthington Chauncey Ford, ed., "Letters of William Vans Murray to John Quincy Adams, 1797–1803," AHA Report for 1912, 425–26. For Pickering's use of diplomatic correspondence as campaign documents, see Henry J. Ford's account of Pickering in Samuel Flagg Bemis, ed., The American Secretaries of State and Their Diplomacy, 10 vols. (New York, 1927–29), II, 230–31. Hereafter, Bemis, American Secretaries of State. The Federalists, lacking the appeal of Washington's name and facing a financial crisis, were in need of a popular issue to take to the people. The Congress, in

John Adams had also favored the sending of a mission to France, but there is no reason to believe that he conceived all the possibilities that Hamilton did in such a move, or that he urged it in any but complete good faith. He was enraged by the behavior of the French in the XYZ Affair, but he did not push hostilities against France after he saw the possibility of an honorable peace. He never used the war fever as an excuse for entrenching himself politically, and it was he and he alone who put an end to the schemes of Hamilton and his associates in 1799, though he terminated his own political career in doing so. Adams was among those who had accepted the Jay Treaty reluctantly, who regarded it as preferable to war with Britain but did not think of it as furnishing the occasion for war with France or for a complete reorientation of our policies which should put us under British domination. Unless further research into our foreign relations and our anti-French propaganda from 1796 to 1799 should disclose new evidence, we shall not be able to say what use Hamilton meant to make of the Jay Treaty. In the meantime, however, there seems to be ample ground to question whether he wished us to pursue the policy of neutrality and isolation which he had recommended in Washington's Farewell Address and whether he meant to further such a policy by his support of either the Jay Treaty or the first mission to France.

Our relations with England did not form a separate problem from our relations with France during those years. Our relations with each country were rather two aspects of a single fundamental problem, that of our neutrality or our participation in the European war; and this was in a sense the problem also of whether we were to be truly independent or were to be dominated by Great Britain. It was hard enough for us to stand on our own feet as a neutral, but once in the maelstrom of the European wars of this period, we should have been utterly unable to do so.

As our relations with France became more tense in 1797 and 1798, those with Britain became easier in their superficial aspect. They eased only superficially, however, for British offers and concessions, such as they were, were all made on the supposition that we were about to join them in a war upon France. For our rights as a neutral nation, as we conceived them, the British were to show the contempt which appears to have been their official attitude until after the War of 1812. Aside from finally giving us the western posts which we had been promised in 1783, the Jay Treaty did nothing to remove our basic difficulties with Great Britain. Some of the problems it was supposed to settle, such as our debts to Britain, were further complicated and confused by the commissions set up under the Treaty to handle them.

John Quincy Adams in London and Noah Webster in New York each wrote a description of British commercial policy as it touched our interest at this time. Adams warned that the concessions which England now had to make regarding our West Indian trade would be cut off the moment the British could obtain control of the French Islands:

One of the favorite objects of this government is an increase of their dominions in the East and West Indies. . . . There is no such thing as commercial liberality in the country. To engross the commerce of the world to themselves is the professed or secret wish of every heart among them.[92]

A few years later Noah Webster wrote to Rufus King, then ambassador to Great Britain, deploring the shortsighted policy behind British depredations and restrictions on our commerce. He said that

[92] J. Q. Adams to Pickering, London, Dec. 22, 1795, Pickering Papers, XX, 118–19, MHS. [Reprinted by permission.]

all we needed from Great Britain was that she give our vessels the freedom and privileges of "what is called the modern law of nations. . . . The jealousies and restrictions of Great Britain always appeared to me like the policy of a countertrader, who should attempt to limit the industry or destroy the Harvest of his customers." [93]

Republican denunciations of Great Britain's commercial policy are apt to be too heated and partisan, and the remarks of such moderate Federalists as Adams and Webster, who, though they were anti-French, were not blind to the dangers and difficulties of close Anglo-American relations, are perhaps as good contemporary evidence as can be found on this point.

In the face of these fundamental aspects of British policy, it may seem strange to us that the High-Federalists, many of them men with shipping and financial interests, should have been so pro-British in their views, though their attitude may have been due in part to their hope of greater concessions from Great Britain, which were at this time dangled before them. In April, 1797, Liston wrote to Grenville:

. . . the men of fortune, of weight and character now begin so generally to come forward to a close connection with Great Britain as the only wise system of American politicks, that I have considered it as necessary to the King's service, and consistent with the spirit of the instructions I have received from your lordship, that I should recommend it to the Commanders of His Majesty's ships upon this station to afford to the merchant vessels of the United States, especially to those bound for our West India Islands all the protection that is consistent with the general orders they may have received from home.[94]

Other concessions followed or were promised. A few days later Rufus King,

our ambassador in London, was entering in his journal the information that Lord Dorchester's taking the forts at Miami was contrary to orders he had seen at the Duke of Portland's office. He said that General Simcoe told him that if war with the United States had followed, Lord Dorchester would have forfeited his head,[95] a remark which at least indicates British policy in 1797. In June of that year King was notified by George Rose, a British official, that "Vessels coming from the States of America will not now be subject to a higher duty than those from Hamburgh or the nearest ports of Europe." This was presented as a great concession. He further stated "I cannot bring myself to think that the measures as at first proposed [against which King had protested vigorously] trenched in the slightest degrees either on the letter or spirit of the Treaty rightly understood." Rose went on to say that other duties originally contemplated in the bill had been given up, and that he would rejoice if these considerable sacrifices of Britain promoted friendly relations. "We may, and I hope we shall, be a Tower of strength to each other." [96]

In June, 1798, Grenville wrote to Liston suggesting that, since war seemed certain between the United States and France, British ships be used as convoys for American vessels and, in return, American seamen be used to man other British vessels. Grenville thought that France would not declare war on the United States, but that the United States would find it to her own interest to declare war on France. He said that Great Britain and France might make peace, but that if the United States should enter into any engagements with Great Britain, they would be scrupu-

[93] Webster to King, Jun. 1797, King Papers, XLI, 22, NYHS.
[94] Liston to Grenville, Philadelphia, Apr. 18, 1797, British State Papers (transcripts), LC.

[95] A long entry on unnumbered pages, Rufus King's Journal, May 3, 1797, King Papers, LXXIII, NYHS.
[96] George Rose to Rufus King, Jun. 22, 1797, Box VII, 83, *ibid.* [Reprinted by permission.]

lously observed by the latter. "You may with the fullest confidence assure the president that any proposals for concert and cooperation will be cordially received here."[97] A letter from Grenville in October stated that the British would loan the Americans cannon which they had at Halifax, but that these might be recalled at any time the King desired them.[98] Later another letter from Grenville urged Liston to disclaim any intention of Great Britain to bind the United States in any permanent system of alliance.[99]

Perhaps the most tempting bait Britain had to offer, although it was couched in the vaguest terms, was the hint that we might be admitted to a share in some of their more lucrative commercial monopolies. Pickering wrote to Washington, "It will give you additional pleasure to learn that such is the increased and increasing respectability of the United States among the European powers that from being viewed with indifference and even contempt, our friendship and commerce are courted." And later in the same letter he says:

Another striking proof of our national importance I must not omit; Mr. Pitt has made to Mr. King a proposition which implies an opinion that in certain articles (sugar & coffee in particular) Great Britain & the States may regulate the commerce of Europe. The subject has not been fully investigated—facts were sought for. But the idea presented by Mr. Pitt, whether it shall ever become a [illegible] or not demonstrates our commercial and even our political importance.[100]

To the High-Federalists it seemed that we were being admitted into partnership with Britain, albeit as a junior partner. The fact that our whole position and prosperity as they envisaged it would be entirely dependent upon Britain appears not to have bothered them in the slightest degree. Compared with John Adams, these men were colonials.

At the time that Great Britain was making or promising such concessions as these, the price that we were expected to pay for them and the consequences if we did not pay it were also being made clear to all who were inclined to see them. Britain was at this time relying heavily upon the prospect of our naval aid. Our forces had already joined with hers in operations against the French privateers in the West Indies; the two navies had drawn up a set of signals by which they would recognize each other,[101] and the British wished us to furnish the seamen to arm ten or twelve of their ships,[102] these to remain under the command of their officers. The solution for our two most crying grievances, captures and impressment, was thus clearly indicated. We had only to furnish first-class seamen for their shorthanded navy and to send our vessels in their convoys, by which our cargoes would of course be taken to British ports where they would be used or re-exported as the British wished.

If we followed those policies there would be no conflicts with the British. They did not, of course, put the alternative to us so directly. They merely made the offers and continued to capture and impress when we did not take advantage of them. British captures and impressments grew much worse after Adams showed his willingness to treat with France, but they had not ceased even before then. In November of that year, a British squadron took a part of the crew

[97] Grenville to Liston, Jun. 8, 1798, British State Papers (transcripts), LC.
[98] Same to same, Oct. 20, 1798, ibid.
[99] Same to same, Dec. 8, 1798, ibid.
[100] Pickering to Washington, Philadelphia, Feb. 8, 1799, Pickering Papers, X, 365–67, MHS. [Reprinted by permission.]

[101] Cited from Dudley Wright Knox, Naval Documents (Washington, 1935–38), I, 336 by Rayford Whittington Logan, The Diplomatic Relations of the United States with Haiti, 1776–1891 (Chapel Hill, 1941), 92.
[102] Grenville to Liston, Jun. 8, 1798, British State Papers (transcripts), LC.

from the American man-of-war *Baltimore.* "President Adams thereupon ordered all American commanders 'to resist every future attempt of the kind to the last extremity.' " [103]

Thus we were being offered a snug place within the imperial framework on the one hand, while being warned on the other, by British practices, of the difficulties and dangers of an independent policy.

In addition to offers of the protection of the British navy and vague hints of a future commercial partnership, Britain was inviting us to share in a vast and daring enterprise in Latin America. Miranda, the Spanish-American revolutionary leader, had been trying for some years to get British support for his scheme to overthrow Spanish rule in South America. In 1797, after France and Spain became allies, Pitt showed a renewed interest in this project. By the summer of 1798, Rufus King was writing frequent letters, particularly to Pickering and Hamilton, urging that we join in the venture against Spanish possessions. It is not surprising, in view of the interest of certain of our Cabinet members in Louisiana and Florida, that the plan of Miranda and Pitt was welcomed most enthusiastically by some Americans. King wrote of it late in 1798, "As *England is ready she will* furnish *a fleet and military stores and we should* furnish *the army.*" [104] And in January, 1799, he wrote to Hamilton:

For God's sake, attend to the very interesting subject treated of in my ciphered dispatches to the Secretary of State of the 10th, 18th, and 19th instant. Connect it, as it should be, with the main object, the time to accomplish which has arrived. Without superstition, Providence seems to have prepared the way, and to have pointed out the

instruments of its will. Our children will reproach us if we neglect our duty, and humanity will escape many scourges if we act with wisdom and decision. I am more confirmed than before, that an efficient force will be confederated to act against France. The combination is *not yet completed,* but, as I have reason to believe, will soon be.

That will be the moment for us to settle upon immutable foundations the extensive system of the American nation. Who can hinder us? One nation alone has the power; and she will coöperate in the accomplishment in South America of what has so well been done in North.[105]

Thus King, with Pickering, Ames, and many others, thought that our true destiny lay in close union with Great Britain. The destruction of France and the commercial exploitation with Great Britain of the French and Spanish colonies in this hemisphere seemed to him a dazzling opportunity.

There was at the same time still another plan afoot for Anglo-American collaboration, this time in support of Toussaint against the French in Santo Domingo.[106] It is impossible to say what

---

[103] Quoted from Liston Papers, Jan.–Jun., 1799, LC., by Arthur Burr Darling, *Our Rising Empire, 1763–1803* (New Haven and London, 1940), 304.

[104] King to Pickering, London, Oct. 20, 1798, King, *Correspondence,* II, 453–54.

[105] King to Hamilton, London, Jan. 21, 1799, *ibid.,* 519.

[106] General Maitland came to this country to arrange for our joint support of Toussaint. In June, 1798, Congress passed an act suspending commercial intercourse between the United States and France, and in the next session an act was passed continuing it but making it possible for the President to except from it any former French possession which became independent. (Pickering to Edward Stevens, Philadelphia, Mar. 7, 1799, Pickering Papers, X, 461–64, MHS.)

Most of the steps which we took in this affair appear to have been carried out behind Adams's back. It is very doubtful, for instance, that he ever knew that Hamilton had been asked by Pickering to draw up a scheme of government for Santo Domingo, or that he had intended, in opening trade with that island, to put Toussaint in the power of our merchants and politicians. (Pickering to Hamilton, Feb. 9, 1799, *ibid.,* 368.)

All our dealings regarding Santo Domingo were in the hands of Pickering, who apparently took his orders from Hamilton. Hamilton kept all the strings in his own hands in this delicate commercial and diplomatic venture by having Edward Stevens, a boyhood friend and, like himself, a native of the West Indies, appointed

actually went on there, or what the precise plans of the High-Federalists were regarding it; but our activities, whether rightly understood or not, had important consequences in our politics in this country. The South regarded any sort of encouragement to Toussaint as an invitation to their own slaves to revolt. Many of the Virginians thought that the New England Federalists would be glad to see slave insurrections in the South, and in their minds Adams bore the blame for much that went on in Santo Domingo of which he had no knowledge. Here as elsewhere, he bore the brunt of the responsibility both for what the High-Federalists were actually doing and for the plans attributed to them.

On the other hand, the designs which Adams himself attributed to the High-Federalists in connection with Santo Domingo appear to have had a prominent place among the considerations which caused him to send a mission to France in 1799. Something that he wrote years later would indicate that the plans in operation in Santo Domingo had influenced his decision upon crucial points in his conduct as President:

As I had been intimately connected with Mr. Jefferson in friendship and affection for five-and-twenty years, I well knew his crude and visionary notions of government as well as his learning, taste, and talent in other arts and sciences. I expected his reign would be very nearly what it has been. I regretted it, but could not help it. At the same time, I thought it would be better than following the fools who were intriguing to plunge us into an alliance with England, an endless war with all the rest of the world, and wild expeditions to South America and St. Domingo; and, what was worse than all the rest, a civil war, which I knew would be the consequence of the measures the heads of that party wished to pursue.[107]

Whatever the causes for Adams's decision, the sending of the second mission to France put an end to British efforts at collaboration with this country. Their captures of our ships and impressment of our seamen became again as numerous as at any time during the decade. The heavy captures of the British in 1800 were an important factor in bringing about the Republican victory in the election, particularly since one of these captures influenced the vote of New York City, upon which depended that of the state and less directly that of the whole country.

These seizures were by no means the only ground for contention between the two countries. Other causes of trouble and ill will against Great Britain arose out of the Jay Treaty. In regard to the question of the return to this country of Tories banished during the Revolution, as in some matters of commerce, the British were putting a construction on the Treaty which even such defenders of it as Jay and Hamilton did not think it could reasonably be made to bear. The sixth article, which provided for the collection of debts owed before the Revolution, was particularly troublesome, and negotiations on this point finally broke down completely.

Republicans, particularly the more partisan and unscrupulous ones, made the fullest use of the difference between the two countries which arose from different constructions of the various articles of the Jay Treaty. Several circumstances lent themselves to the charge that all the different ways in which the British injured or irritated us were a

a representative of the State Department in Santo Domingo. Our relations with Santo Domingo were to wear a somewhat different guise officially from what they were among the inner circle who were controlling them, for Hamilton instructed Pickering that the United States "must not be committed on the Independence of St. Domingo—no guarantee, no formal treaty—nothing that can rise up in judgment." (Hamilton to Pickering, Feb. 9, 1799, *ibid.*, XXIV, 65.)

[107] Adams to James Lloyd, Quincy, Mar. 31, 1815. Adams, *Works*, X, 154–55.

matter of design. *The Anti-Jacobin Review,* a British periodical which had some circulation here, contained much abuse and ridicule of this country and its prominent figures, and it did not confine itself to Republicans. As the journal was something of an official organ during the most reactionary phase of the Pitt administration, some Americans claimed that the British ministry at least approved of this abuse.[108] Some of the articles on America favored a close relationship with Britain.

The policy of the Pitt administration toward neutral countries added to the apprehension of the well-informed in this country, as the Prime Minister had declared it "a principle that the distance between friends and neutrals is immense; it is small, on the contrary, between enemies and neutrals; the slightest accident, a mere chance, the least mistrust, a false appearance, is enough to efface the distinction between them." [109] A High-Federalist of Philadelphia, Thomas Fitzsimmons, expressed the bewilderment at British policies which was felt by those in this country who had tried hardest to defend them.

To me it appears strange that the British ministry have never thought it their interest to try and conciliate this country; they cannot be uninformed of the state of parties here, or insensible to the advantages they derive from a good understanding with us. A very considerable portion of the commerce of this country is carried on with their manufacturers, and the payment for these insures them no small proportions of our exports. With all this their conduct is invariably cold and suspicious. They even never miss an opportunity of circumscribing our happiness, and though they may not directly sanction the depredations of their cruizers, they certainly take no pains to prevent them. I am not without my ap-

prehensions too, that their necessity as well as their monopolizing spirit will, when there is a peace, draw a circle round our commerce, that for a time at least, will narrow it down to a very small compass. ... If the British restrict our trade, let us meet them with restrictions on our part, and if we cannot find employment for our capital in commerce, let us employ it in either agriculture or manufactures.[110]

This conclusion was one which had been shared by many in the years preceding the Constitution and had been consistently urged by Jefferson and Madison from 1789 to 1800. Republicans would have said that we had passed by our best opportunities to win concessions from the British in the period from 1790 to 1795 and would have put the blame largely upon Hamilton. Most modern historians would deny such a statement, however, and would hold that, given Great Britain's commercial and naval power and the policies which naturally accompanied them, our relations with her were bound to have been about what they were from 1789 to 1800, regardless of the policies we sought to pursue.

Although our relations with France and England were not much different in 1800 from what they had been in 1795, the vicissitudes of those years had had a far-reaching effect in this country. The XYZ Affair had weaned all but the most deluded Republicans from an excessive attachment to France, and Britain's conduct had convinced even High-Federalists, at least for the moment, that we must stand on our own feet and not attempt to lean on Britain. At the first view it would appear that foreign relations had been the point upon which our domestic politics had turned between 1795 and 1800; for the Jay Treaty, the XYZ Affair, and the sending of the second mission to France had each in turn dominated and reshaped domestic

---

[108] King to Pickering, London, Oct. 11, 1799, King, *Correspondence,* III, 124.

[109] Quoted from *Godoy's Memoirs,* I, 468, by Andrew Jackson Montague in his article on John Marshall in Bemis, *American Secretaries of State,* II, 359.

[110] Thomas Fitzsimmons to Wolcott, Philadelphia, Jul. 24, 1800, Gibbs, *Memoirs,* II, 389.

politics for a time. Yet the first and last and perhaps the second of these three events was rooted as deeply in the domestic as in the international situation, and by 1800 the tendency toward nationalism and self-sufficiency was stronger than at any other time since 1789.

We achieve this view if we treat the period from 1789 to 1801 as a unit and if we attempt to trace the connection between our foreign relations and our domestic politics during that time. It is the development of parties and the growth of the party conflict which give continuity to the period and which provide the connection between the realms of foreign and domestic affairs. The party conflict is, of course, evident in the very circumstances of domestic affairs, but its relation to foreign policies has been somewhat obscured by the fact that they, being in the hands of the President and the Cabinet, did not exhibit the same open clash of views as could be seen in debates in the House of Representatives. Further, much of what happened in foreign affairs was kept from the public at the time, so that its influence in the forming of public opinion was not comparable to its intrinsic importance. Yet we should not forget that the High-Federalist leaders viewed their adversaries as enemies of society in league with fellow Jacobins in France, who must be discredited by any means. One of the most attractive features of a war with France to such men as Hamilton, Sedgwick, Ames, and Cabot was the opportunity it offered for "cleaning house" and putting it beyond the power of "demagogues and disorganizers" ever to seize control of the government. Many Federalists regarded their control of foreign affairs as their surest weapon against the Republicans. We cannot, however, go so far as to say that war with France was to be merely a blind, an excuse of the High-Federalists for proceeding against their opponents at home. Rather, they regarded the principles of liberty and equality as infections which must be stamped out wherever they were to be found.

This feeling was evident as early as the time of the Constitutional Convention, but it grew stronger during the decade. During that period the more obvious aspects of the party conflict shifted first from domestic questions to foreign relations and then back to domestic again. Until 1793 our foreign relations did not provide issues so pressing as those which grew out of Hamilton's domestic policy. From 1793 on, the questions of our neutrality, the Jay Treaty, and our relations with France engrossed the larger share of attention until we were faced with the question of war with France in 1798. Momentous as that issue was, public attention was gradually diverted from it by the emergency powers which the Federalists asked and by the means which they took to suppress opposition to their measures. The Federal land tax of 1798, the Alien and Sedition laws, the Ross election bill of 1800, all these and other measures gave the Republicans such an opportunity to arouse the ordinary voter of this country as they had never previously had. Even before news of the XYZ Affair had reached this country the Republicans had seen that they must shift their ground and leave the question of foreign relations, which was for the time taken completely out of the hands of the opposition party. Gallatin had written to his wife from Congress late in 1798, "... we mean, if possible, to avoid fighting on foreign ground. Their clamor about foreign influence is the only thing we have to fear, and on domestic affairs exclusively we must resist them." [111]

After the XYZ Affair it was more necessary than ever that the Republicans

[111] Dec. 14, 1798, Adams, *Life of Gallatin,* 224.

concentrate upon domestic issues. Feeling against France, whose conduct in the XYZ Affair could not be defended, rose high even among the Republicans themselves, and on the other hand, Federalist domestic policies became more and more open to attack. The reaction of the American people to the war measures of 1798–99, their evident distaste for militarism, their reluctance to pay the Land Tax, and their resentment of the Alien and Sedition laws do not fall, properly speaking, within the sphere of party origins. The public feeling these measures aroused is closely related to this topic, but its true significance is to be found rather in the fact that it constituted the background for the election of 1800, which was a part of the second rather than the first phase of party development.

If we observe the struggle of the two parties in the effort to shape our foreign policy, we see that the contest is not between abstract forces but between two groups of men. These men professed principles of constitutional interpretation, and they were moved in part by their economic interests, or their conception of them; but neither of these factors gives a full explanation of their conduct. If we regard this as a conflict of abstractions, we run into various pitfalls, not the least of which is that we are likely to interpret the struggle by what the actors in it said, both about themselves and their opponents, rather than by what they did.

We draw nearer the truth of the matter if, instead of viewing this as a contest of abstractions, we regard it as one between two shifting groups of men who, differing upon practical problems as they arose, came to suspect the views and purposes of those in the opposite camp and to regard their own pursuit of power and their determination to defeat their opponents as the supreme consideration. A party becomes an entity like a nation, and, as with a nation, the question of its own survival is likely to be paramount. This is not to say, however, that all the men of this time put the success of their party above every other consideration, but they tended to do so as the party struggle became more and more bitter. If we recognize this fact, we leave room for the play of motives, otherwise disregarded, which were frequently of the greatest importance.

If we put the emphasis upon a conflict of parties, a good deal which would otherwise furnish material for controversy, such as the inconsistencies of both Hamilton and Jefferson, is explained. If we ask what Hamilton was trying to accomplish at a given time—whether he was trying to get the Constitution ratified, or, that done, to "prop up the frail and worthless fabric," as he himself described his later policies—we shall understand his conflicting statements better than if we try to explain them solely in the light of his theories of government or by his concern for any economic interest. We shall also find an answer to the question why Jefferson was more concerned about strict construction while he was in the opposition than he was while he was President. If we place our emphasis upon party conflict, we shall understand how it was that Adams and Jefferson, both much closer in their economic interests and in their views on government than is generally recognized, were the rival candidates in one of the bitterest and most momentous elections which this country has ever seen. A comparison of their different views as they discussed them in letters to each other with those same differences as they were misrepresented and exaggerated by the partisans of 1800 is one of the best possible illustrations of how party feeling can put men into positions which they would never have taken from choice.

3

South Carolina—A Protagonist of the War of 1812

MARGARET K. LATIMER

The following article by Mrs. Latimer contributes significantly to an understanding of the complex problem of the causes of the War of 1812 by a close examination of the situation in South Carolina. So detailed a study of a single state enables the student to test broad generalizations and to see clearly the intricate wellsprings of action and the underlying motivation for conduct and policy. Although her investigations are confined to one state, Mrs. Latimer's conclusions may be applied to other agricultural states of the South and West.

Her researches weaken considerably the long-held and widely accepted thesis advanced by Julius Pratt. Pratt had argued that the war came because the states of the South and Southwest wished to conquer Florida from Spain, England's ally, for expansionist reasons and to deprive the Indians of the base from which they had been launching attacks on the frontier. Mrs. Latimer finds no evidence that South Carolina had any interest in winning Florida or any great concern about the Indian menace.

On the other hand, she finds ample evidence to support the generalizations made by George Taylor and A. L. Burt, who proposed the view that war was desired by the South and West for economic reasons connected with England's restrictions of American commerce on the high seas. South Carolina was feeling the pinch of the British blockade and the orders-in-council. Her farmers could not export their surplus, and, consequently, they suffered a serious depression. War was the only means to save American shipping. Similarly, she finds support for those historians who have emphasized "national honor" as a cause for war. South Carolinians felt aggrieved at Britain's presumptuous and arbitrary practice of impressment and demanded that Americans be protected.

Mrs. Latimer's analysis of the origin, character, and views of the three War Hawks of South Carolina—John Calhoun, William Lowndes, and Langdon Cheves—tells us a great deal that is new about all the War Hawks, those half-dozen young and aggressive newly elected congressmen who seized the leadership of the Twelfth Congress and were instrumental in marshaling the vote in support of war. The South Carolinians, although Republicans, had very little in common with the party of Jefferson and Madison; indeed, they opposed the Administration's policy of economic retaliation. They were conservatives and nationalists, and so in many ways closer to Federalism than Republicanism.

FROM *American Historical Review*, LXI (July 1956), 914–929. By permission of the author and American Historical Association.

They stood for election as Republicans but on a platform of changing the President's program of peaceful coercion of England to one of war.

Young Mr. Calhoun entered Congress prepared for a showdown. It was June 3, 1812, and the ambitious congressman from South Carolina would recommend war against England. The Foreign Relations Committee, of which he was chairman, had deliberated only two days on President Madison's message, but, after a forceful report in favor of war, John C. Calhoun presented a bill of declaration. A majority of the House followed his lead and on June 4 passed the act, the Senate concurring with some reluctance on June 18. Madison's signature, also of June 18, marked the official beginning of war.

The grievances against European powers for interfering with American ships and sailors on the high seas had gathered momentum in a continuous stream of events for more than a decade. The Jeffersonian policy of conciliation, restrictive measures, minimum armaments, and "peace at any price" had generally insured against violent ruptures.

Until the Twelfth Congress, legislation aimed at France or England had in reality been a jockeying of party strength in Congress. Although party voting was far from regular, the major portion of the Republicans and the Federalists debated hotly on the embargo and the succeeding restrictive measures. The erratic stands of the Quids accentuated the hodgepodge nature of congressional opinion as did certain courses taken by the New Englanders. Believing that the Republicans would never be forced into a war, Josiah Quincy of Massachusetts and many of his fellow New England Federalists voted steadily for armament and naval increases in order to antagonize the administration. Quincy wrote to Harrison Gray Otis on November 26, 1811, even

suggesting that New England stand for war.[1] However, when it became evident that the young Republicans in the Twelfth Congress had plunged their peace-loving party into just that war, the Federalists pitched their tents in the opposite camp.

Henry Adams estimated that only a third of Congress was in favor of war early in 1812, yet on June 4 the bill in the House was carried 79–49.[2] The crystallization of sentiment had been the work of an enthusiastic group of leaders in the Twelfth Congress who were responsible for a notable change in congressional foreign policy within the span of a few months. The story of the "War Hawks" is familiar, but still eminently impressive. It is important enough to warrant amplification and correction.

Of the five or six major "War Hawks" prominent in most accounts of the war, three were young South Carolina Republicans in Congress for the first time. John C. Calhoun, William Lowndes, and Langdon Cheves arrived in Washington with a motive in mind; they came if not pledged, at least committed, to oppose the prevailing Republican foreign policy. These three leaders in the war group frequently initiated actions so far from the old Jeffersonian line that even their fellow War Hawks sounded some misgivings.

Calhoun made his real debut in the Twelfth Congress on December 12, 1811, when he spoke in opposition to the mercurial John Randolph. The subject before the House was the recommendation for armament made by the Foreign Relations Committee, which in the opin-

[1] Samuel E. Morison, *Letters of Harrison Gray Otis* (Boston, 1913), II, 33–34.
[2] Henry Adams, *History of the United States of America* (New York, 1889–91), VI, 170.

ion of Mr. Randolph and many others had veered well off the Jeffersonian course. In an effective rebuttal, Calhoun presented ideas still further from the original tenets of the Republican party, which he nominally represented. "I know of but one principle to make a nation great," reasoned the South Carolinian, "...and that is to protect every citizen in the lawful pursuit of his business.... Protection and patriotism are reciprocal." [3] These sentences seemed almost to echo a phase of Hamiltonianism.

The second South Carolinian, Langdon Cheves, as chairman of the Naval Committee spoke at length in January maintaining the power of the President to use voluntary militia forces in time of war. Such nationalization, obviously anathema to old-line Jeffersonians, also appeared unduly risky to some of Cheves's belligerent cohorts. Later that month when Cheves requested an appropriation for twelve seventy-fours and twenty frigates at the cost of seven and a half million dollars, he was supported by a large number of the war group as well as the Federalists, but the bill failed by a close vote of 62–59. Clearly prompting Cheves's individual efforts were the underlying objectives of the South Carolinians—an effective navy and its complement, free-flowing international trade. William Lowndes of South Carolina, speaking on behalf of the frigates, well illustrated their policy:

The Constitution was not formed for the exclusive protection of commerce, but for the defense of all the interests of the United States.... But is it in this nation, and at this time that the profits of commerce are confined to the merchant? Your trade was, a few years ago unrestrained and flourishing —did it not enrich the most distant parts of your country? It has since been plundered and confined. Does the industry of the country languish? Is not the income of every man impaired?[4]

The concern of South Carolina with commerce became increasingly obvious. When the Committee on Foreign Relations in March, 1812, planned a ninety-day emergency embargo—information about which was supposedly to be withheld from public notice until passage— Calhoun opportunely informed Josiah Quincy, leader of the New England commercial interests. Eastern longshoremen were consequently set at work to load as many ships as possible and clear them from the ports, and undoubtedly the southern waterfronts were in the midst of similar activity.[5]

The joint efforts of Lowndes, Cheves, and Calhoun were directed in April toward a measure to authorize the importation of goods from Great Britain which had been contracted for before February, 1811. Having no success with this, on June 19 Cheves introduced a bill for the suspension of nonimportation, and Calhoun hastened to its support: "The restrictive system, as a mode of resistance ... has never been a favorite one with me.... I object to the restrictive system." [6] In essence, Calhoun was rejecting on the floor of Congress the major basis of the Jeffersonian foreign policy.

When Calhoun led his fellow congressmen in requesting a declaration of war, he was displaying not only the views of the three most aggressive South Carolina representatives but a real solidarity in the constituents whom he represented. True, not all eight South Carolinians in the House voted as a bloc on every measure. David R. Williams, chairman of Military Affairs, had been in Congress during most of the Jeffersonian decade and accepted in general such established

---

[3] *Annals of Congress,* 12 Cong., 1 sess., p. 479. All subsequent references to *Annals* except where specified denote the Twelfth Congress, First Session.

[4] *Ibid.,* p. 886.
[5] For Quincy's report of the incident, see *Niles' Weekly Register,* II, 110.
[6] *Annals,* pp. 1281–1312, 1511, 1539.

party measures as restriction, yet he had always acted independently and as early as the Tenth Congress had looked favorably toward war. He spoke forcefully for the cause of armaments and resistance to Great Britain: "It has been said our Constitution is not calculated to sustain a war. It surely is not calculated for submission."[7] The other representatives, Moore, Earle, Bulter, and Winn, had also been in earlier Jeffersonian Congresses, the latter two prominent Revolutionary soldiers. They belonged to a different generation from the young Calhoun, Cheves, and Lowndes, and their approaches to problems were similarly varied, but they shared fundamental principles based on the desires of their constituents at home. A majority of South Carolina representatives did support Cheves's bill for frigates, and all voted for the added military forces. When the crucial vote was taken, South Carolina cast a solid eight for war. The two senators, Gaillard and Taylor, likewise voted in its favor. Kentucky, Tennessee, and Georgia, casting in the House five, three, and three votes respectively, were the only other states which were unanimously in favor of war with England.[8]

The "War Hawks"—primarily from the four above-mentioned states—were given special emphasis by Julius W. Pratt in his *Expansionists of 1812*, which set forward in 1925 what has become one of the most popular and widespread

theories regarding the War of 1812. Basically, Pratt asserts that the Southwest and its war-minded leaders gave a major impetus to the war. Singling out the war group in Congress is highly significant in tracing the origins of the war sentiment, but the further direction taken by the Pratt school is more open to question: the "Southwest," including South Carolina as well as the inland states, is depicted as desirous of war largely because of an urge for frontier expansion and a concern with the Indian question. These basic ideas repeatedly occur in historical literature, most recently in a 1954 popularized account of the war, even though varying shades of doubt have from time to time been cast on the Pratt thesis. Not well enough known perhaps is the work of George Rogers Taylor in 1930 describing the dire economic conditions in the Mississippi Valley preceding the war and the resulting attitude of the western farmer toward international affairs.[9]

In A. L. Burt's study, *The United States, Great Britain and British North America* (1940), it is maintained that the War of 1812 was fought primarily for maritime rights; Burt discusses with thoroughness the diplomatic wrangles with Britain and France from the turn of the century onward, as an offshoot suggesting pertinent objections to Pratt. A historiographical article of 1941 by Warren H. Goodman gives a good progressive account of theories regarding the causes of the war, although it was unhappily prepared before the publication of Burt's work. Goodman does, however, make several elucidating observations about the Pratt thesis and

[7] *Ibid.*, p. 682. Williams was a Charleston planter. See James H. Wolfe, *Jeffersonian Democracy in South Carolina* (Chapel Hill, 1940), p. 218; *Dictionary of American Biography*, XX.
[8] *Annals*, pp. 287, 1637. There were no negative votes from these states. Senator Pope of Kentucky, however, did not favor war and refrained from voting on the issue. He did not thereby represent the feelings of his constituents, because his action resulted in disgrace at home and defeat in the next election. See John Bowman to Stephen F. Austin, Aug. 5, 1813, *Austin Papers*, ed. E. C. Barker, American Historical Association, *Annual Report*, 1919, II, 227–28.

[9] See currently, Glenn Tucker, *Poltroons and Patriots* (Indianapolis, 1954). The Taylor work appeared in two articles: "Agrarian Discontent in the Mississippi Valley Preceding the War of 1812," *Journal of Political Economy*, XXXIX (1931), 471–505; and "Prices in the Mississippi Valley Preceding the War of 1812," *Journal of Economic and Business History*, III (1930), 148–63.

takes successful issue with various of its aspects. Pointing to the need for much further investigation, Goodman concludes that the causes of the War of 1812 are still "singularly uncertain."[10]

Although South Carolina is included as an integral segment of the "South" and "Southwest" in the Burt and Pratt theses respectively, little has been said specifically about South Carolina's part in the drive for war. Nor in the many studies of John C. Calhoun has more than scant attention been given to his basic stands in the Twelfth Congress. During this era, South Carolina has been simply catalogued with the Jeffersonian states because of its nominal support of the Republican party in national elections from 1796 onward, and Calhoun and his fellow South Carolina "War Hawks" are neatly fitted into the same package. Many of the ambiguities associated with "Jeffersonian democracy" are regularly applied to South Carolina, which did of course share in the country-wide liberalizing trends. Sufficient attention has been given to the formal rise of the Republican party to control within the state;[11] yet too often overlooked in this period of history have been the other factors which explain South Carolina's important relation to the war and which at the same time elucidate the state-centered aims of the "young nationalist" Calhoun.

A unity had developed in the life of South Carolina which helped it achieve a share in the leadership of the nation at this critical period and which was to give impetus to its sectional prominence down to the Civil War. At the core of this unity was a fundamental political oneness which persisted despite the interplay of the two political parties. The spread of the electorate as settlement moved into the upcountry after 1800 indicated a liberalizing trend in South Carolina as did the election of an increasing number of young men to state offices; but the coming of age of the younger generation, who called themselves Republicans, had no effect on the ever-lingering conservatism in South Carolina which is normally associated with the Federalists. The upcountry farmer either young or old was severe and puritanical; he was also ambitious to gain the position in which he saw the planter slightly more prosperous than he. The planter as well as the farmer felt at all times that it was the purpose of government to maintain the orderly social and economic system, to protect the status quo. The representatives of the newer political alignment, led by the inherently conservative Charles Pinckney, were never enthusiastically "Republican" as a party group; they were indeed a distinct political faction increasingly dominant in South Carolina, but they upheld an all-pervading South Carolina political philosophy in much the same measure as their forerunners, the Federalists.[12]

[10] Warren H. Goodman, "The Origins of the War of 1812," *Mississippi Valley Historical Review*, XXVIII (1941), 171–86. Goodman's conclusion is based on the fact that nineteenth-century authors dealt primarily with military events and the twentieth century has netted only monographs on restricted phases of the question. No writer has attempted to "correlate and synthesize the various sets of causes," weighing the relative importance of the factors. Goodman makes an able suggestion of some eleven fields for investigation.

[11] J. H. Wolfe in his *Jeffersonian Democracy in South Carolina* gives a thorough factual discussion of this movement. Although the term "Jeffersonian democracy" has come into popular use, I question its preciseness of meaning for any area and especially with regard to South Carolina. Wolfe, however, is making in his title a correct distinction between the liberalism of this era and that of Jackson's, which South Carolina never accepted. See Wolfe, p. 286.

[12] Certain items in early South Carolina politics are interesting in this respect, in particular South Carolina's relation to the Virginia-Kentucky Resolutions, the vote on the Jefferson-Burr tie of 1800 in the Federal House of Representatives, and the nature of the Republican leader Charles Pinckney. On the latter, see Irving Brant, *James Madison, Father of the Constitution* (Indianapolis, 1950), pp. 79, 132.

Even though there were overwhelming numbers of Republicans in the state after 1800, many prominent conservatives of the purely Federalist variety were not without significant influence. The original solons of South Carolina politics had operated under the Federalist banner, and the presence of a Republican majority did not mean that the respect offered the older men came to an end. Thomas and Charles Cotesworth Pinckney, of course, were venerated elders. Abraham Blanding, William Crafts, William Drayton, Stephen Elliott, Daniel E. Huger, Keating Simons, and Henry W. DeSaussure, all notable Federalists, continued to wield a considerable power in state politics well after 1800.[13]

Of the thirty-four men recorded in the *Dictionary of American Biography* as outstanding in South Carolina political life from 1800 to 1812, one finds, surprisingly enough, that fifteen professed themselves Federalists. Contemporary accounts also indicate the political activity of these men: documents from Josiah Quincy were circulated by William Crafts among many "friends who still dare to call themselves Federalists, of whom there yet are many," and Henry W. DeSaussure wrote to Quincy that "many wise and good men view the course pursued by the Administration as you do.... They take a moderate share in the affairs of our own state, and are respected and permitted to have some share in the management."[14] DeSaussure, incidentally, had just been appointed to the Equity Bench by the Republican legislature. National crises during this period called forth widespread town meetings in which citizens joined together to pass resolutions. Participating on the local committees were as many nominal Federalists as Republicans—Keating Simons, William L. Smith, and Thomas Pinckney in company with Langdon Cheves, William Lowndes, and Peter Freneau.[15]

Major issues in state politics brought to the fore a rather uncanny agreement between the Federalist and the Republican members of the legislature. In fact, the part played by Federalist legislators in passing measures which are considered liberal and "Jeffersonian" is little short of amazing. The founding of South Carolina College in 1801 was a very special monument not only to the progress but to the unity of the state; it was located in Columbia, clearly a part of the upcountry, yet the impulse for the college was a patrician one solidly supported in the lowcountry Federalist circles.[16] The bill calling for a change in proportionment of representation was passed in 1807 with only two votes against it in each house. Some of the major pressure in its behalf had been exerted by Federalists, Robert Goodloe Harper having been especially active in this realm during the 1790's. The legislative act itself was introduced in 1807 by Abraham Blanding, a Federalist legislator from Kershaw, and had probably

[13] There is a discussion of the South Carolina Federalists from the Revolution to 1800 in Ulrich B. Phillips, "The South Carolina Federalists," *American Historical Review*, XLV (1909), 742.

[14] Edmund Quincy, *Life of Josiah Quincy of Massachusetts* (Boston, 1867), pp. 191, 192.

[15] Charleston *Courier*, Aug. 30, 1809, May 21, 1912, etc. In Georgia, similar public meetings also included representative Federalists. See John E. Talmadge, "Georgia's Federalist Press and the War of 1812," *Journal of Southern History*, XIX (November, 1953), 496–97.

[16] J. L. Petigru in later years claimed that the college was a work of the Federalists. Whether or not this was strictly true, Hollis describes it as an undertaking of lowcountry aristocrats. See Daniel W. Hollis, *South Carolina College* (Columbia, 1951), pp. 5–6. The patrician influence in the South Carolina legislature is interesting as contrasted with the rampant Republican Assembly of 1800 in North Carolina; the University of North Carolina was deprived of a portion of its income for fear the institution was drifting toward aristocracy. Delbert H. Gilpatrick, *Jeffersonian Democracy in North Carolina, 1789–1816* (New York, 1931), p. 142.

been prepared by Judge Daniel E. Huger, Federalist of Charleston.[17] Another notable gesture by a Federalist was the bill for free schools introduced into the legislature in 1811 by the botanist Stephen Elliott.[18] There seemed to be no particular clash of interests on basic issues between the majority Republican party and the minority Federalist party within the state. Their respective philosophies merged in concerted activities which were subsequently issued under the name of Republicanism.

The preponderance of Republicans in South Carolina politics within the state obviously was not the result of a distinct break with the older South Carolina Federalist school, nor did the South Carolina Republicans in national circles represent a close tie to national Republican policies. Actually the Republican party was so diverse that its national objectives defied accurate definition. Few would claim that Jefferson himself was consistent in political philosophy and actions. As an administrator, he initiated a duality which underlay the whole Republican era. His first inaugural spoke for restraint in government; the second showed the Jefferson who would negotiate the Louisiana Purchase and plan numbers of prospective states across the Mississippi, the Jefferson who found in the Constitution powers during the embargo which rivaled the hated Alien and Sedition Acts. The Jeffersonian tradition to which his followers have pointed sets up a noble set of social values, the secret of which is an appeal to America's better self, to her idealism and simplicity.

However, Jefferson made no headlong attack upon established institutions to make his principles work; Leonard White points out that "the Jeffersonian era in the field of administration was in many respects a projection of Federalist ideas and practice.... The ambivalence reflects the duality of the Republican party and of Jefferson himself." [19] The Jeffersonian party drew to it a tremendous variety of interests, and South Carolina had become a part of this group.

South Carolina's agrarian economy was one of the major factors which drew her originally into the Republican fold. But it was the growing preoccupation of South Carolina with the international commerce necessary to make agriculture profitable that took her somewhat off the path envisaged by Jefferson. Attacking the traditional Jeffersonian international policy, the Republican William Lowndes said to Congress, "The interests of agriculture and commerce are inseparable. What is commerce but the exchange of the surplus produce of ... one nation for those of another? ... it is this commerce which makes agriculture valuable." [20] Such a positive stand was not unusual, for South Carolina never demonstrated a very close adherence to the national party. The local Republican group so well represented the interests of the planting-business community of the state as a whole that its standard-bearers received almost no opposition from the Federalists in elections for national representatives, and the delegates in turn exercised a notable independence and lack of partisanship in Congress. Edward Hooker's description of Wade Hampton, one of the prosperous up-country Republicans, was almost generally applicable to South Carolinians: "In his politics he is, I hardly know what.

---

[17] William A. Schaper, "Sectionalism and Representation in South Carolina," A.H.A. *Annual Report*, 1900, I, 408, 428. This bill became a Constitutional amendment in 1808. See David D. Wallace, *History of South Carolina* (New York, 1934), II, 373, for information on Huger's preparation. Harriet Ravenel, *Life and Times of William Lowndes* (Boston, 1901), pp. 70–71, less convincingly ascribes the authorship to Lowndes.

[18] Wolfe, *Jeffersonian Democracy*, p. 175.

[19] Leonard D. White, *The Jeffersonians: A Study in Administrative History, 1801–1829* (New York, 1951), p. vii.

[20] *Annals*, pp. 805–806.

He is called a republican; yet he certainly has many notions and sentiments which are more characteristic of federalism. And he does not hesitate to condemn openly, and unequivocally some measures of the republican party."[21]

Calhoun, Cheves, and Lowndes had come to prominence in this era of independent Republicanism and conservative political unanimity. Calhoun was from Scotch-Irish upcountry stock, although the holdings of his father put him easily in the category of "planter."[22] After early training at the academy of Moses Waddell in Georgia, Calhoun went to Yale, where his seriousness and sternness must have made him well fitted for Timothy Dwight's domain. This Federalist president had a pervading influence over the students at Yale College, and it seems unlikely that Calhoun was untouched by his ideas. Experience in the Charleston law office of Henry W. DeSaussure and formal study at Litchfield Law School in Connecticut under Federalists James Gould and Tapping Reeve contributed further to Calhoun's background of conservatism. In 1811, his marriage to Floride Calhoun, a cousin who belonged to wealthy Charlestonian society, gave the Republican uplander a direct tie to the older, more staid South Carolina lowcountry.

Calhoun was a lawyer in the Piedmont region at the time that the Chesapeake-Leopard affair provoked indignant public meetings in many localities. His first chance at public oratory came when he was requested by the Abbeville committee to write and present its resolutions denouncing the incident; shortly thereafter he was elected to the state legislature, and in 1810 he became a representative to the United States Congress.

Langdon Cheves, also newly elected to Congress in 1810, had both upcountry and lowcountry connections as did Calhoun. He was born in Abbeville, a Piedmont district, and later became a lawyer in Charleston. The third new congressman, William Lowndes, was of lowcountry planting origin, and his attractive and intelligent wife was a confirmed Federalist, the daughter of Thomas Pinckney.[23]

Calhoun, Cheves, and Lowndes, Republicans with backgrounds strongly marked by conservative influences, expressed in the Twelfth Congress the conservatism which had become characteristic of South Carolina's "Federal"-Republicanism. All three were men of outstanding leadership abilities; and, when they made demands in the interest of their state, they also revealed a strong bent toward nationalization. Though nationalism can be the manifestation of both liberal and conservative movements, in 1811 nationalizing measures were definitely the latter. The conservatives during the Constitution-making era were the nationalists, and the South Carolinians were of this breed—conservatives in their desire to preserve the prevailing socio-economic system of

[21] J. Franklin Jameson, ed., "Diary of Edward Hooker, 1805–1808," A.H.A. Annual Report, 1896, I, 847. Among other South Carolinians in Congress who acted independently was Senator John Gaillard, who broke from his party in voting against the Chase impeachment. Thomas Sumter consistently voted against nonintercourse and the embargo; he and D. R. Williams have been singled out as particularly nonpartisan spirits among the Republicans. Senator John Taylor, concerned by the depressing effects of the embargo, worked for less extreme measures; he was the real author of Macon's Bill No. 2, which did grant some relief. See Albert J. Beveridge, The Life of John Marshall (Boston, 1919), III, 218; Anne King Gregorie, Thomas Sumter (Columbia, S.C., 1931), p. 260; Wolfe, Jeffersonian Democracy, pp. 203–206; letter to Joseph H. Nicholson from Nathaniel Macon, Apr. 10, 1810, in William E. Dodd, Nathaniel Macon (Raleigh, N.C., 1903), p. 259.

[22] Patrick Calhoun is credited with over 1000 acres of land and 31 slaves in 1790. Charles M. Wiltse, John C. Calhoun, II (Indianapolis, 1944), 17–23. See also Wallace, History of South Carolina, II, 386.

[23] See DAB, IV. XI, for biographies of Cheves and Lowndes; also Ravenel, Life and Times of William Lowndes.

their state. They sought federal power to protect this way of life.[24] Their nationalism was thus, in a sense, a sectionalism in disguise.

Calhoun, Cheves, and Lowndes were elected to Congress in 1810 with "reference to the critical condition of the country."[25] They were all in a belligerent mood, and they had spoken vigorously in pre-election campaigns. A clear statement of Calhoun's views on international affairs had been set forward as early as the Republican caucus in 1808: reviewing the struggle between the United States and European powers, he labeled the resort to the restrictive system an inefficient means of preserving American rights and pointed out that war with England was unavoidable. He later saw "in the low price of the produce, the hand of foreign injustice."[26] British minister Augustus J. Foster, who met the representatives in Washington, noted that the South Carolina members of Congress were "resolute," "particularly the younger Deputies... who seemed to have great influence and were very cool and decided on the propriety of going to war in order to protect the Commerce of the Country."[27] The South Carolina congressmen had a vital interest in the "Commerce of the Country," because on it depended the future of the prosperous economic developments which had taken place in South Carolina during the first decade of the nineteenth century.

By 1811 the entire state was in the middle of a tremendous cotton boom. The value and practicability of upland-grown short-staple cotton had become immediately apparent upon invention of the cotton gin and were demonstrated after the introduction of the gin into South Carolina in 1801; at the same time the demand for cotton went up as machine methods of manufacture became standard in England. When the slave trade was reopened in 1803, cotton production proceeded at full speed. South Carolina doubled its cotton output in the ten years following 1801, producing forty million pounds in 1811; the state had begun to export approximately forty per cent of the total cotton exports of the United States.[28] As David Ramsay wrote in 1808, cotton "has trebled the price of land suitable to its growth, and when the crop succeeds and the market is favorable, the annual income of those who plant it is double to what it was before the introduction of cotton."[29]

The increased use of the Negro slave was of course necessary for the phenomenal expansion of upland cotton, and during these years a constantly growing number of farmers and planters acquired property in slaves. It is important to note, however, that in twenty-three out of twenty-eight districts in 1810 whites still outnumbered blacks, the popular image depicting masses of Negroes working on all the farm lands being far from correct.[30] True, in coast districts such as

[24] Whether nationalization was a rightist or leftist move perhaps became questionable during the Jacksonian period. If one assumes Calhoun always to have been a conservative, his inconsistencies which appeared during the Jackson era have some basis for explanation.

[25] [John C. Calhoun], *Life of John C. Calhoun* (New York, 1843), p. 8.

[26] *Annals*, p. 482. For Calhoun's own description of the 1808 caucus at which he opposed the nomination of George Clinton for Vice President, see *Life of John C. Calhoun*, p. 7.

[27] MS Notes, Augustus J. Foster Papers, Library of Congress; see also MS Diary, Apr. 15, 1812, L.C.

[28] The amount of cotton produced in South Carolina is an approximation made by Frederick J. Turner, *Rise of the New West* (New York, 1906), p. 47, based on a group of figures. See Matthew B. Hammond, *The Cotton Industry* (New York, 1897), Appendix I, p. 358, for total yearly cotton production and exports of the United States in 1811. See *Niles' Weekly Register*, I, 399, for exports of each state in 1811.

[29] David Ramsay, *History of South Carolina* (Newberry, S.C., 1858), II, 121.

[30] Schaper, *Sectionalism and Representation*, p. 392, gives a map of the enlarging "Black belt" which shows a much greater preponderance of Negroes in South Carolina at this date. However, he lists no source. Census of 1810

Charleston and Colleton the black population was actually much greater than the white, but here cotton and rice production had probably been expanded to the limit before 1800 since the percentage of slave population even decreased slightly in the period 1800–1810. It was the upcountry legislators who insisted on the reopening of the slave trade in 1803, for it was their region in which cotton and slavery were spreading. A look at the United States Census figures for 1790, 1800, and 1810 shows as expected a steady increase in slaves for upcountry districts, the largest proportional gain coming after 1800. The following are sample Piedmont districts: [31]

same time that profits decreased. The southern agriculturalists incurred constant expenses whether or not their products sold, but the traditional planting system had to be kept. Manufacturing had no chance to develop because after 1803 the capital of the South had gone into buying slaves; the area was already in debt to New England.[32]

The Charleston *Courier* reported on January 20, 1808, that cotton was down to twenty-five cents per pound, and on February 10, 1810, that it had fallen to fourteen cents. A contemporary observer reported that in order to make ends meet, the South Carolinians had to get at least twenty cents for their cotton.[33]

	York Slaves	York Whites	Greenville Slaves	Greenville Whites	Edgefield Slaves	Edgefield Whites
1790	923	5,652	606	5,888	3,619	9,805
1800	1,804	8,417	1,439	10,029	5,006	13,063
1810	3,164	7,828	2,391	10,739	8,576	14,433

When the upland area like the coast became a significant producer of cotton, South Carolina could boast an amazing unity of economic interest. Corollary to this economic development was of course the spread of political power into the upcountry and the resulting era in which political and cultural oneness increased steadily. This unanimity of interest, political and economic, exhibited itself under the name of Republicanism.

The enactment of the embargo by the federal government in 1808 exactly coincided with the full realizations of South Carolinians that the primary economic interests of the state were much the same from coast to hill country, that a continuance of the cotton-planting system was essential to all areas. The discomforts brought on by the embargo gave the state an even greater unity as both sections were prey to the economic forces which made prices go up at the

One should note that the critical drop in price came between 1808 and 1810; this difference may partially account for South Carolina's growing concern with the world situation during that period, for attitudes which varied from passive endurance to active belligerence. The South Carolina legislature in June, 1808, had expressed its willingness to enforce the embargo, but in reporting the resolutions to Jefferson, Speaker Joseph Alston did tell the President that they represented a wholehearted patriotism, not necessarily a "perfect unanimity of political opinion." [34] As economic conditions became tighter, there was growing resistance to the embargo and to its successor, nonintercourse.

Calhoun's public speech against the embargo in 1808 has already been cited. Governor Charles Pinckney in December, 1807, blamed disputes with Great Britain for "an almost total stagnation of

bears out the above statement. See *Niles' Weekly Register*, I, 309.
[31] *Ibid.*, I, 309. See also Wiltse, *Calhoun*, II, 146.

[32] *Ibid.*, II, 45.
[33] MS Notes, Foster Papers.
[34] Note Wade Hampton's letter of April, 1808, and other comments in Wolfe, *Jeffersonian Democracy*, pp. 222–25.

commerce and stoppage of the sale of produce"; this caused "the great inconvenience of merchants and planters."[35] Fear that the international situation would bring the loss of markets gave impetus to such news stories as that which noted the phenomenal growth of South American cotton sales in Liverpool. By June, 1812, there were reports that cotton planters had been forced to turn to corn, that some upcountry men were turning to wheat.[36] The situation in Charleston is well mirrored in the letters of Margaret Izard Manigault to her mother: cotton prices of 1811 were down to eight cents; money in town was almost nonexistent; and worst of all, since early 1809 there had scarcely been a party.[37]

South Carolina depended on unrestricted trade—on "commerce" as British minister Foster called it—because this was a region where people cultivated the soil, sold most of what they produced, and purchased most of what they consumed. Although the nonimportation law which succeeded the embargo in 1809 was often unenforced, general economic conditions kept on the downgrade as long as there was a controversy with England, the chief purchaser and provider in the South.[38] By the time of the Twelfth Congress, the tone of the South Carolina legislature had changed notably from that of 1808. This group sent resolutions to President Madison demanding that definite action be taken to protect commerce and the honor of the nation. A firm stand from the beginning, it was explained, might have prevented much

loss to agriculture. D. R. Williams vigorously expressed the sentiments of his state before Congress:

But what is the condition of the commerce with Great Britain.... Truly miserable.... How is tobacco affected? ... Inquire into the state of the cotton market; where is the crop of 1810? A curse to him who meddled with it. Where is that of 1811? Rotting at home in the hands of the grower, waiting the repeal of the Orders in Council.[39]

South Carolina had developed a decided urge for war. Excited by considerations of her primary livelihood, the export trade in cotton, South Carolina became one of the main protagonists of the conflict. This was not the largest or wealthiest state in the union, but it had one special qualification for national leadership in 1812—the most at stake in the domestic export trade; South Carolina had more exports per individual white person than any other state in the union. With only 3.6 per cent of the total white population of the United States, South Carolina exported 10.3 per cent of the domestic goods.[40] Whether or not fighting a war with England was the logical step to take as a remedy to the commercial and thus agricultural distress is not the question—the South Carolinians of 1812 were convinced that a war would help.

To assess the total internal and external forces which produced the War of 1812

[35] Charleston *Courier,* Dec. 2, 1807.

[36] *Ibid.,* Sept. 26, 1809; June 2, July 3, 1812.

[37] Margaret I. Manigault to Alice Izard, February, 1809, Dec. 1, 1811, Ralph Izard Papers, II, III, Library of Congress.

[38] Wolfe, *Jeffersonian Democracy,* p. 236; *Niles' Weekly Register,* I, 133. Incidentally, Great Britain received 60 per cent of the American cotton exports in 1811. Hammond, *Cotton Industry,* p. 358.

[39] Speech of Jan. 6, 1812, *Annals,* p. 686. See also speech of Governor Henry Middleton giving a justification for war. *Niles' Weekly Register,* III, 275–76.

[40] *Ibid.,* I, 237, for figures from the Census of 1810; I, 399, for exports, domestic and foreign, for each state in 1811. South Carolina had 214,196 white population of the total 5,905,782 whites in the United States. (Counting the slave population full value, South Carolina had 5.8 per cent of the total.) South Carolina's domestic exports were valued at $4,650,-934, while the total was $45,294,043. Maryland came close to South Carolina in trade per individual; with 3.9 per cent of the white population, her domestic trade was 10 per cent. However, she also had over 14 per cent of the total shipping trade, a factor which would greatly complicate her attitude toward war.

will call for the investigation of a multitude of factors not yet understood. The effort in this paper has been primarily to set forth the position of South Carolina with regard to the war, thereby pointing out in particular the significant part played by the direct trade of the United States, by foreign markets for staple products, in determining the course of events.

In the realm of international diplomacy, A. L. Burt's study goes farther than any other in explaining how the United States, entangled with both Great Britain and France, finally chose war with Britain. Burt's suggestions regarding the attitudes of the various sections of the United States toward going to war are also well directed. Making note of the fact that the South was sorely pinched for markets (and South Carolina indeed received considerable support in her war effort from Georgia, Virginia, and North Carolina), Burt further points out that the Northeast was "betraying national honor . . . for selfish profit." All sources indicate in fact that New England experienced a great shipping and commercial boom because of continuing European hostilities; the United States government went to war to "champion maritime interests . . . in spite of their opposition." [41] Burt's observations, apparently sound, are directly supported by the conclusion of this paper that South Carolina, which played a significant role in the congressional campaign for war, had as its primary concern an alleviation of commercial distress.

The thesis of Julius W. Pratt, on the other hand, seems considerably weakened by the findings here reported. The coupling together of the South and South-west in interpreting the war sentiment is certainly justifiable, but this alliance was not altogether natural, and in many respects the relationships that have been singled out are not the significant ones. Indian troubles may have had some bearing on western sentiment, but these did not pose a serious problem in the South at this date; expansion into Florida was likewise an unimportant urge.[42]

[41] A. L. Burt, The United States, Great Britain, and British North America (New Haven, 1940), p. 306. Burt explains that Great Britain, in command of the sea, pressed harder on American neutrality than France, which had no foothold on the American continent and therefore was less vulnerable.

[42] Warren H. Goodman, taking issue with Pratt's thesis, grants that Pratt had sufficient evidence to justify listing the Indians as a definite problem, but not as an "overmastering" concern. In line with Goodman's statement on the Indian question, if sample data from middle Tennessee in this writer's files are of value, there seems to have been no particular concern with Indians or any other British-inspired difficulties in the Williamson County frontier settlement in the years before 1812; see Williamson County MS Records, 1800–1812, Court House, Franklin, Tennessee. It is also interesting to note from a slightly different angle that Ohio, which was closer to the British-Indian sphere of influence than Kentucky and Tennessee, cast one vote for war in the House yet one against war in the Senate, the negative vote being given by Senator Thomas Worthington, a future governor of the state. See DAB, XX. Pratt's contention that the southern desire for war was a part of its acquisitive impulse toward Florida is weak. No evidence can be found in congressional debates that Florida was a motive for war. Actually, part of Florida was taken without a thought of conflict with Britain, and in June, 1812, a move by the House of Representatives to permit the occupation of East and West Florida was blocked by the Senate (Annals, pp. 1684–92). The Florida thesis can certainly not be applied in any sizable measure to South Carolina; Thomas Sumter had opposed even the purchase of Florida in 1806 because too large a portion of seacoast would be left undefended. (Everett S. Brown, ed., William Plumer's Memorandum of Proceedings in the United States Senate, 1803–1807 [New York, 1923], p. 421.) In November, 1812, William Lowndes expressed the opinion that no law would be recommended for the occupation of Florida because Spain was likely to cede it anyway. (Lowndes to [Thomas Pinckney], Nov. 27, 1812, William Lowndes Papers, Library of Congress.) There was certain agitation in Georgia over the question of Florida because of the common boundary, but it seems unwise to visualize the entire South as an expansive-minded area. The contention that a sectional bargain was made between North and South regarding the acquisition of Canada and Florida has been left completely without basis by W. H. Goodman, who has pointed out that the conquest of Canada was openly advocated

The developing political philosophy of Kentucky and Tennessee could rarely be equated with that of conservative cotton-producing South Carolina, nor was the latter by 1812 in a position to share the frontier sentiments of the West. Indeed, the support of these states for similar measures in Congress lasted only a few years.

The significant basis of alliance between the South and the Southwest in 1812 was their common cry against foreign depredations on American shipping. As well-explained by G. R. Taylor, when depression replaced the early western prosperity of 1808 and 1809, discontent was rampant and settlers looked madly about them for the causes of their troubles. Economic analysts believe today that these were primarily difficulties within the frontier area itself—matters of transportation, communication, imperfect marketing, and insufficient financial organization. However, the westerners of 1808–1812 grasped for a time at the first likely cause; they began to be painfully aware of foreign restrictions on American commerce, and to these they directed more and more blame for their economic ills. Although western markets were actually far less directly connected to European trade than those of South Carolina, increased demands for western hemp, tobacco, cotton, and flour were hopefully anticipated as results of a war with Great Britain. In 1812, "the right of exporting the productions of our own soil and industry to foreign markets" seemed as real to the hemp and tobacco growers of Kentucky as to the large-scale cotton producers of South Carolina.[43]

The internal scene in South Carolina was ripe for a burst of political activity on behalf of commerce. Contrary to the impression left by authors who have elected to discuss in isolation the rise of the Republican majority in South Carolina, the state's over-all outlook was largely a conservative one based on an established political and economic philosophy. The South Carolina Republican party itself could only in a superficial sense be described as Jeffersonian; more specifically it was a state-centered group which kept well in line with the prevailing statewide views, these marked by ambition for gain yet an innate distrust of substantial change. Such conservatism, prompted by the immediate need to preserve the prosperous economic system of the state, was expressed by South Carolina in a nationalistic impulse for war.

In a sense the war marked the end of one era of Jeffersonianism and the beginning of a change in the nature of the Republican party. South Carolina, one of the foremost war-minded leaders, was a state whose Republicanism had never been more than an independent, local movement. The new generation in the Republican party, with an aim to protect and promote the direct commerce of the country that seemed more Federalist than Jeffersonian, was strongly spearheaded by men from the South and the Southwest who worked together successfully in a congressional drive for war. The effective leadership of Henry Clay in the Speaker's chair supplemented by other representatives of the frontier regions must never be minimized, but that provides matter for another paper. Working with Clay, the new delegation from South Carolina was the most aggressive force in Congress.

Paradoxical as it may seem, the desire of South Carolina to preserve and extend

---

in the South as early as 1807, no particular opposition to this move being voiced thereafter. Canada was often regarded in many parts of the country as possible remuneration for British damages to American commerce. See Goodman, "Origins of the War of 1812," pp. 177–82.

[43] The quotation is from a speech by Felix Grundy of Tennessee in which he singled out this right as the "true question in controversy." *Annals,* p. 424.

the status quo produced a determination not to be undone by the caprices of warring European powers. Going to Congress with the conviction that the older Republican measures would not solve the problems of 1812, South Carolina's young Congressmen Calhoun, Cheves, and Lowndes spoke for the protection of America's foreign commerce and not at all incidentally for the well-being of South Carolina's trade in cotton.

4

The Age of Mercantilism:
An Interpretation of the
American Political Economy,
1763 to 1828

WILLIAM A. WILLIAMS

The Monroe Doctrine has generally been interpreted by historians as a response to European events. Most scholars have pointed to the threat of the Holy Alliance to reconquer for Spain the colonies in South America that had declared their independence and to the advance of Russia southward from Alaska along the northwest coast of North America as the reasons for President Monroe's message of December 2, 1823. Almost immediately after the defeat of Napoleon, the European nations that had fought together to destroy the French Emperor joined in an alliance to preserve the settlement made at the Congress of Vienna. Their principal objective was to suppress any revolution in Europe that would threaten the status quo. After successfully quelling a revolt in Spain and restoring the deposed King Ferdinand VII, the allies quite naturally sought to restore his authority also in the Spanish colonies that had broken away from the Spanish crown during the Napoleonic Wars. In 1822 plans were under way for an expedition to the new world. At the same time, the Russian Czar issued a decree claiming the west coast of North America southward from Alaska to the present Canadian-American boundary and forbidding all foreign vessels to approach within one hundred miles of the coast. It was this dual threat, according to the most widely accepted historical theory, that generated the Monroe Doctrine.

There are some variations of this thesis. A number of writers have maintained that the Doctrine sprang primarily from a distrust of Britain's ambition to take Cuba and to extend her commercial hegemony to the new South American nations. Still another historian has seen the message as a challenge to French plans to send an expedition to South America. France was the only power capable of leading an invasion of the former Spanish colonies, and, indeed, Monroe himself stated that his chief concern was France. But all these interpretations are rooted in European factors. Whether directed against Russia, the Holy Allies, Great Britain, or France, Monroe's warning of "hands off" was a response to European factors.

William A. Williams, who teaches at the University of Wisconsin and who has written boldly and imaginatively on many aspects of the diplomatic history

FROM *William and Mary Quarterly*, 3rd ser., XV (1958), 419–437. Copyright © by *William and Mary Quarterly*. By permission of the author.

of the United States, suggests a new hypothesis for the genesis of the Monroe Doctrine. For him, the warning against further European colonization is "the negative side of the Monroe Doctrine [and] the least significant feature about it." The positive and important aspect of the Doctrine is that it propounded "the classic statement of mature American mercantilism." Williams sees the first half-century of American history in terms of the development of a mercantilist state. The new nation formed from thirteen colonies had learned its lesson from the British parent. It was determined to replace British mercantilism by American mercantilism. Hence, from the beginning it sought to achieve a balanced economy at home and to pursue a policy of commercial and territorial expansion, the two hallmarks of mercantilism. Presidents Washington, Adams, and Jefferson each contributed to the development of the mercantilist state, and Henry Clay embodied the concept in his "American system." Finally, when Spain lost control of South America, Monroe moved quickly to announce to Europe that the United States would replace Spain in that area. Thus, the Doctrine was "the manifesto of an American Empire" and the expression of the mercantilist philosophy.

Based upon the suggestion by Curtis P. Nettels that one of the consequences of British mercantilism was the creation "of a new mercantilist state on this side of the Atlantic," and upon recent re-evaluations of mercantilism by William D. Grampp, Gunnar Myrdal, Jacob Viner, Charles Wilson, and others, this essay advances the hypothesis that the central characteristic of American history from 1763 to 1828 was in fact the development and maturation of an American mercantilism.[1] Let it be emphasized that the interpretation is offered as a hypothesis and no more—as an idea to be examined and tested, then accepted, modified, or rejected on the basis of its relevance and validity. There is no intention, furthermore, even to imply that the approach as here stated offers final answers to all the vexing problems connected with understanding early American society. It is merely proposed that a re-examination of the era from this angle may lead to new insights, and hence contribute to a broader interpretation of the period.[2]

[1] Curtis P. Nettels, "British Mercantilism and the Economic Development of the Thirteen Colonies," *Journal of Economic History,* XII (Spring, 1952), 105–114; William D. Grampp, "A Re-examination of Jeffersonian Economics," *Southern Economic Journal,* XII (Jan. 1946), 263–282; "On the Politics of the Classical Economists," *Quarterly Journal of Economics,* LXII (Nov. 1948), 714–747; and "The Liberal Element in English Mercantilism," *ibid.,* LXVI (Nov. 1952), 465–501; Gunnar Myrdal, *The Political Element in the Development of Economic Theory* (London, 1953); Jacob Viner, "Power versus Plenty as Objectives of Foreign Policy in the Seventeenth and Eighteenth Centuries," *World Politics,* I (Oct. 1948), 1–29; Charles Wilson, " 'Mercantilism': Some Vicissitudes of an Idea," *Economic History Review,* 2d Ser., X (Dec. 1957), 181–188. This essay owes an equal debt to the extensive publications of Merrill Jensen and to his generous and helpful interest in this approach to the era. His

keen criticisms and perceptive suggestions were invaluable. It also benefited from the interest and intelligence of James Cooper, Lloyd Gardner, Kent Kreuter, Thomas J. McCormick, Walter La Feber, and Martin Sklar. This article is a foreshortened statement of the first section of a longer three-part essay dealing with the characterization and periodization of American history. Together with the other two portions, "The Age of Laissez Moi Faire, 1828–1896," and "The Age of Corporate Capitalism, 1896–1958," it will be published as The Contours of American History by the World Publishing Company.

[2] Some readers may feel that the vigor of the subsequent presentation contradicts these caveats. Perhaps they will be reassured by remembering that any tool has to be sharp, though later it may be laid aside out of preference for another.

At the outset, for example, the use of the concept of mercantilism restores to its properly central place the fact that Americans thought of themselves as an empire at the very beginning of their national existence—as part of their assertive self-consciousness which culminated in the American Revolution. Though it may seem surprising, especially when contrasted with the image of isolationism which has been accepted so long, in reality this early predominance of a pattern of empire thought is neither very strange nor very difficult to explain. Having matured in an age of empires as part of an empire, the colonists naturally saw themselves in the same light once they joined issue with the mother country.

Revolutionary leaders were confident of their ability "not only to take territory by the sword, but to hold and govern it under a colonial status." [3] Long before the break with England, for example, Benjamin Franklin was a leader of those who entertained a "burning interest in westward expansion." At the threshold of the revolution he visualized an American Empire including Canada, the Spanish Floridas, the West Indies, and perhaps even Ireland.[4] George Washington, John Adams, John Livingston, and Thomas Lee were among those who shared such conceptions of an American Empire.[5] By the

end of the war, such men as Silas Deane looked forward to the time when "Great Britain, America and Russia united will command not barely Europe, but the whole world united." [6] And in 1789, after remarking that "it is well known that empire has been travelling from east to west," Congregational minister and geographer Jedidiah Morse concluded that "probably her last and broadest seat will be America . . . the largest empire that ever existed." [7]

While the vigor, even cockiness, of such statements may be explained by the consciousness of having whipped the champion, the underlying emphasis on expansion and empire was an integral part of the general outlook of mercantilism, a conception of the world shared by most of the revolutionary generation. Though they revolted against British mercantilism, there is considerable evidence to suggest that early American leaders did not, as so often is assumed, rebel against the idea and practice of mercantilism itself. In stressing the role of natural-rights philosophy in the thinking of the leaders of the revolution, the traditional view of the American Revolution has slighted this key point.

An acceptance of natural law is not incompatible with mercantilism, as is indicated by John Locke's vigorous espousal of both systems. Much of the talk in America about natural rights, moreover, concerned what Thomas Paine called the "natural right" to one's own

[3] Albert Bushnell Hart, *The Foundations of American Foreign Policy* (New York, 1901), pp. 174–175. The best published study of the early empire outlook is Arthur B. Darling, *Our Rising Empire, 1763–1803* (New Haven, 1940).

[4] Gerald Stourzh, *Benjamin Franklin and American Foreign Policy* (Chicago, 1954), p. 54.

[5] On Washington see, among others, Charles H. Ambler, *George Washington and the West* (Chapel Hill, 1936), and Curtis P. Nettels, *George Washington and American Independence* (Boston, 1951). Also consult *Letters of Members of the Continental Congress*, ed. Edmund C. Burnett (Washington, 1921), III, 476; Malbone W. Graham, *American Diplomacy in the International Community* (Baltimore, 1948), pp. 9–24; and Max Savelle, "The Appearance

of An American Attitude Toward External Affairs, 1770–1775," *American Historical Review*, LII (July 1947), 655–666.

[6] *The Revolutionary Diplomatic Correspondence of the United States*, ed. Francis Wharton (Washington, 1889), II, 332.

[7] Jedidiah Morse, *The American Geography; or A View of the Present Situation of the United States of America* (Elizabeth Town, 1789), pp. 468–469, quoted in Richard W. Van Alstyne, "American Conceptions of Empire," a lecture delivered at the University of Chicago, May 5, 1953, copies available from the author.

empire.[8] And though they were willing to use Adam Smith's polemic in behalf of laissez faire as a weapon against British mercantilism (and against their domestic opponents), most Americans adhered firmly in their own practice to the principle that the state had to intervene in economic affairs. America's romance with Smith's laissez faire came later and was of relatively short duration. Hence it would appear that a better understanding of early American history depends in considerable measure upon a grasp of the nature and practice of American mercantilism as it developed between 1763 and 1825.

Traditionally thought of as little more than a narrow and selfish point of view held by the trading interest, mercantilism was in fact a broad definition and explanation of the world shared by most of Western Europe in the seventeenth and eighteenth centuries.[9] In this sense it was the basic outlook of those who labored to build a dynamic balanced economy of agriculture and business organized on a capitalistic basis within a nationalistic framework. Depending upon their specific function and power at any given stage in the process, mercantilists argued among themselves over the

best means to achieve and maintain such a system—and differed in their estimates of whether or not it had been established—but they agreed on the objective and upon the need to use the state as a tool.

Whether agrarian or urban, therefore, mercantilists were essentially nationalists who strove for self-sufficiency through increased domestic production and a favorable balance (and terms) of trade. Their emphasis on production and the control of export markets and sources of raw materials, rather than on consumption and economic interdependence, led them to fear surpluses as a sign of crisis and failure. Thus they dropped the old feudal restrictions on exports and replaced them with taxes on imports. Their greatest fear was a surplus of goods. In this respect, furthermore, mercantilism was reinforced—albeit in a backhanded and even unintentional way—by the broad ethical outlook of Puritanism (which frowned on luxury), even though mercantilism itself was a secular and almost amoral system. Likewise, the concept of a chosen people, so strong in Puritanism, also strengthened the secular and economic nationalism of mercantilism. Thus mercantilists constantly labored to build a tightly organized and protected national market and to increase their share of the world market. The key points in their program were integration at home and expansion abroad.

In the exuberant confidence of their victory over Britain, Americans tended to assume that each new state could survive and thrive as a mercantile empire unto itself. That attitude was not too surprising, for each of the new states appeared to enjoy the raw materials, labor supply, and trading facilities for a balanced economy. That estimate of the situation was supported and reinforced by the conviction, itself part of traditional theory, that a state could remain democratic in political and social life

[8] See Léon Dion, "Natural Law and Manifest Destiny in the Era of the American Revolution," *Canadian Journal of Economics and Political Science*, XXIII (May 1957), 227-247, as a supplement to Albert K. Weinberg, *Manifest Destiny* (Baltimore, 1935).

[9] Of the immense literature on mercantilism, the following items proved most stimulating: Max Beer, *Early British Economics from the Thirteenth Century to the Middle of the Eighteenth Century* (London, 1938); Philip W. Buck, *The Politics of Mercantilism* (New York, 1942); Edgar S. Furniss, *The Position of the Laborer in a System of Nationalism* (Boston, 1920); E. F. Heckscher, *Mercantilism*, rev. ed., ed. E. F. Soderlund (London, 1955), esp. Vol. II; E. A. J. Johnson, *American Economic Thought in the Seventeenth Century* (London, 1932), and *Predecessors of Adam Smith* (New York, 1937); Ephraim Lipson, *The Economic History of England* (London, 1948-49); Gustav F. von Schmoller, *The Mercantile System and Its Historical Significance* (New York, 1931); and the items cited in note 1.

only if it were small and integrated, and by the experiences of the colonies in dealing with Great Britain's imperial policy after 1763. Yet the political outlook and faith contradicted certain basic tenets of mercantilism, which Americans also entertained, or assumed.

The first attempt to reconcile the conflict produced the Articles of Confederation. That instrument of government stressed the independence of the states as self-contained units of mercantilism and democratic republicanism, yet also established a central government for the purposes of war and, as in the case of Canada, future expansion. But specific postwar developments, such as the serious recession, the expansionist conflicts between the states, and the difficulties in dealing with other countries in economic affairs combined to disillusion many Americans with their experiment in particularistic mercantilism.

Broadly speaking, the resulting movement toward a stronger central government grew out of internal and international economic difficulties analyzed and explained with the ideas of mercantilism. By 1785, for example, most of the states, including the agrarian ones, were switching from tariffs for revenue to tariffs for international retaliation and protection. Merchants demanded American navigation acts, artisans agitated for protection of their labor, and agricultural interests wanted help in balancing their political economy.[10] Various groups of Americans

who concerned themselves directly with the problem of strengthening the central government—and there were many who were preoccupied with local and immediate difficulties or opportunities—offered several proposals for handling the problem. Centered in New England, the smallest group favored establishing an aristocratic society at home and rejoining the British Empire as a contractual junior partner. Such men were not willing to return to colonial status, but they did favor economic and social reintegration. Most Americans opposed that solution, favoring instead either the delegation of more power to the central government under the Articles of Confederation or the substitution of an entirely new instrument of government.

A letter from James Madison to Thomas Jefferson in the spring of 1786 not only indicates that the agrarian as well as the urban interests favored one or the other of those last two approaches, but dramatizes the fundamental mercantilism of the entire movement. "A continuance of the present anarchy of our commerce," Madison explained, "will be a continuance of the unfavorable balance on it, which by draining us of our metals ... [will bring our ruin]. In fact, most of our political evils may be traced up to our commercial ones, and most of our moral may to our political." [11]

Against this background, the Constitution appears as an instrument of centralized national government framed in the classic manner by men thinking within the framework of mercantilism and blessed with the physical and human resources for a balanced economy. It provided the foundation for a national system of economics and politics and organized American strength for the

[10] Here see Oliver M. Dickerson, *The Navigation Acts and the American Revolution* (Philadelphia, 1951), on the attitude of the colonists toward the Navigation Acts per se. Then consult Oscar and Mary F. Handlin, *Commonwealth. A Study of the Role of Government in the American Economy: Massachusetts, 1774–1861* (New York, 1947); Louis Hartz, *Economy Policy and Democratic Thought: Pennsylvania, 1776–1860* (Cambridge, Mass., 1948); and Merrill Jensen, *The New Nation. A History of the United States During the Confederation, 1781–1789* (New York, 1950), on the development of an American mercantilism at the state level.

[11] Madison to Jefferson, Mar. 18, 1786, *Letters and Other Writings of James Madison. Published by order of Congress* (New York, 1884), I, 226–227.

struggle with other mercantile empires and for the conquest of less powerful peoples. The latter considerations were essential, for the Founding Fathers resolved the contradiction between the stress on expansion in mercantilism and the emphasis on a small state in existing democratic political theory by developing a theory of their own which held that democratic republicanism could be sustained by just such expansion. James Madison, often called the Father of the Constitution, provided the most striking formulation of this proposition, but Thomas Jefferson, John Adams, and other early leaders either shared or adopted it in one form or another within a reasonably short time.

Taking his cue from David Hume, the Englishman who attacked Montesquieu's argument that democracy was a system that could work only in small states, Madison asserted that a large state offered a much better foundation for republicanism.[12] Institutional checks and balances could help, and were therefore necessary, but they were not enough in and of themselves. "Extend the sphere," he argued, "and you take in a greater variety of parties and interests; you make it less probable that a majority of the whole will have a common motive to invade the rights of other citizens; or if such a common motive exists, it will be more difficult for all who feel it to discover their own strength, and to act in unison with each other...."[13]

While it is possible to conclude from Madison's remarks that he had in mind a static conception of such a large state,

three considerations would appear to weaken that reading of his thesis. First, Madison used the verb "extend" in its active, unlimited sense. Second, he was stating a general theory, not making an argument in behalf of a given territorial settlement. And third, he advocated and vigorously supported the continued expansion of the United States. It seems more probable, therefore, that Madison was proposing, *as a guide to policy and action in his own time,* the same kind of an argument that Frederick Jackson Turner formulated a century later, when he advanced his frontier thesis which explained America's democracy and prosperity as the result of such expansion.

Madison's theory became the key to an American mercantilism. Merchants and manufacturers who wanted their own empire found it convincing and convenient. And Jefferson's thesis that democracy and prosperity depended upon a society of landholding freemen was a drastically simplified version of the same idea. Edward Everett of Massachusetts captured the essence of the interpretation in his judgment that expansion was the *"principle* of our institutions."[14] Additional support for this interpretation is offered by Madison's later prophecy (in 1828–29) that a major crisis would occur in about a century, when the continent was filled up and an industrial system had deprived most people of any truly productive property. In the event, Madison's fears proved true sooner than he anticipated. For in the crisis of the 1890's, when Americans *thought* that the frontier was gone, they advanced and accepted the argument that new expansion was the best—if not the only—way to sustain their freedom and prosperity.[15]

[12] Robert L. Ketchum, "Notes on James Madison's Sources for the Tenth Federalist Paper," *Midwest Journal of Political Science,* I (May 1957), 20–25; Douglass Adair, " 'That Politics May Be Reduced to a Science': David Hume, James Madison, and the Tenth *Federalist,"* Huntington *Library Quarterly,* XX (Aug. 1957), 343–360.

[13] Madison, Federalist No. 10, *The Federalist,* ed. Henry Cabot Lodge (New York, 1900), pp. 58–60.

[14] Edward Everett, *Orations and Speeches on Various Occasions* (Boston, 1850–68), I, 210.

[15] Here see Charles S. Campbell, Jr., "American Business Interests and the Open Door in China," *Far Eastern Quarterly,* I (Nov. 1941), 43–58; Nancy L. O'Connor, "The Foreign Policy of the Farmers' Movements, 1890–1900,"

Madison's original statement of the expansionist thesis was important for two reasons. First, it provided the theoretical basis for an American mercantilism combining commercial and territorial expansion with political democracy. Second, by thus re-emphasizing the idea of empire, and proposing expansion as the key to national welfare, Madison opened the way for a discussion of the basic questions facing American mercantilism. Those issues concerned domestic economic affairs, the kind of expansion that was necessary and desirable, and the means to accomplish such gains while the nation was young and weak.

Washington's Farewell Address formulated a bipartisan answer to the problem of basic strategy. The solution was to build a commercial empire (which included markets for agricultural surpluses) by avoiding political involvement in the European system, meanwhile retaining complete freedom of action to secure and develop a continental empire in the Western Hemisphere. Washington's proposition was classically simple: play from the strength provided by America's basic economic wealth and geographic location in order to survive immediate weakness and emerge as *the* world power. "If we remain one people, under an efficient government," he promised, "the period is not far off when we may defy material injury from external annoyance ... when we may choose peace or war, as our interest, guided by justice, shall counsel." Sharing that objective, and quite in agreement with the strategy, Thomas Jefferson

unpubl. masters thesis, University of Oregon, 1957; William A. Williams, "The Frontier Thesis and American Foreign Policy," *Pacific Historical Review*, XXIV (Nov. 1955), 379–395, and "The Large Corporation and the Political Economy of American Foreign Policy: 1890–1958," paper read at the State University of Iowa Conference on Social Sciences, May 1958.

summed it all up a bit later in one famous axiom: "entangling alliances with none." And with the enunciation of the Monroe Doctrine, freedom of action became the avowed and central bipartisan theme of American foreign policy.

As a condition of that persuasive agreement, however, several serious conflicts had to be resolved. Perhaps they can be discussed most clearly by defining and considering them within the framework of the gradual defeat and amalgamation of the pro-British and pro-French minorities by a growing consensus in favor of an American mercantilism. Such an approach has the additional value of making it possible to organize the analysis around familiar personalities as symbols of certain ideas, functional groups, and special interests. Let it be posited, therefore, that the following men are key figures in the evolution of an American mercantilism: Timothy Pickering, John Adams, and John Quincy Adams of Massachusetts; Alexander Hamilton of New York; and James Madison, Thomas Jefferson, and John Taylor of Virginia.

In many respects, at any rate, Pickering and Taylor represented the nether fringes of American mercantilism. Pickering trod the trail from reluctant revolutionary to threatening secessionist in the name of a domestic merchant aristocracy functioning as a quasi-independent contractual member of the British Empire. His ideal was a central government charged with the responsibility (and armed with the power and authority) to establish and sustain a politically and socially stratified society and to provide the economic assistance (especially funded credit) that was necessary for the rationalized operations of overseas correspondents of British mercantilism and for domestic speculative ventures. Though Pickering and his supporters fit the traditional stereotype of mercantilists, they were in fact and function no more than the agents of British mercantilism. They were very successful agents, to be sure, but they did not view or define America in terms of its own mercantilism. Rather did they visualize it as a self-governing commonwealth of the British Empire. Hence it was only very late and with great reluctance, if at all, that they supported the measures necessary for a mercantilist state in America.

At the other extreme, John Taylor developed his program as a variation on a theme first stated by the French physiocrats. He emphasized the primacy of agriculture as narrowly as Pickering stressed the virtue and necessity of the merchant-trader-speculator. Taylor's tirades against funded debts and bank stock, and his soliloquies in praise of the noble farmer, seem alike in their total opposition to the principles of mercantilism. But in other respects his ideas were not so untainted by mercantilism as his rhetoric indicated. As with most other planters, for example, his theory of labor coincided at all essential points with the view held by British mercantilists.[16] So, too, did his conception of the role of western lands in the economy of the seaboard "mother country."

With respect to foreign trade, moreover, Taylor was trapped by the weakness of the physiocrats in that area of economics.[17] Ostensibly free traders, the physiocrats did not favor the navy essential to such a program. Taylor and other American imbibers of the physiocratic elixir awoke to discover that their vision did not correspond to reality. Taylor himself was not very adaptive, and ended his career in attacks on Jefferson and other agrarians who did develop

an American mercantilism. But Taylor's position does dramatize the dilemma faced by the agrarians.[18] The contradiction between theory and actuality confronted them with a rather apparent choice: either they could content themselves with slow economic stagnation or they could build an American maritime system, accept dependence upon a foreign naval power, or support an American industry. In that choice lies a key aspect of the rise of a mature American mercantilism; for it developed most consciously and was ultimately practiced most rigorously by the southern agrarians who are often assumed to have been most rabidly antimercantilist. If nothing else, the weakness of their ideal program drove them into mercantilism.

It is particularly important to keep that fact in mind when considering Hamilton, about whom the discussion of American mercantilism has billowed for so long. Joseph Charles was essentially correct in his view that "the standard works on Hamilton evade the main issues which his career raises," and his judgment remains relevant despite the plethora of centennial essays and biographies.[19] The entire question of Hamil-

---

[16] Though independently worked out, this analysis is supported by Charles R. Haygood, "Mercantilism and Colonial Slave Labor, 1700–1763," *Journal of Southern History*, XXIII (Nov. 1957), 454–464.

[17] Arthur I. Bloomfield, "The Foreign-Trade Doctrines of the Physiocrats," *American Economic Review*, XXVIII (Dec. 1938), 716–735.

[18] William D. Grampp, "John Taylor: Economist of Southern Agrarians," *Southern Economic Journal*, XI (Jan. 1945), 255–268, esp. pp. 258, 263, on Taylor's developing opposition to Jefferson.

[19] Joseph Charles, *The Origins of the American Party System* (Williamsburg, 1956), pp. 11–12. Also see John C. Livingston, "Alexander Hamilton and the American Tradition," *Midwest Journal of Political Science*, I (Nov. 1957), 209–224; Arnold A. Rogow, "Edmund Burke and the American Liberal Tradition," *Antioch Review*, XVII (June 1957), 255–265; James O. Wettereau, "Letters from Two Business Men to Alexander Hamilton on Federal Fiscal Policy, November, 1789," *Journal of Economic and Business History*, III (Aug. 1931), 667–686; Samuel Rezneck, "The Rise and Early Development of Industrial Consciousness in the United States, 1760–1830," *ibid.*, IV (Aug. 1932), 784–811. This approach to Hamilton had been worked out in all essentials prior to the publication of the most recent biographies, and for that reason it was deemed wise to present it in the form in which it was originally cast.

ton's mercantilism has to be decided with reference to three points: the meaning and significance of the *Report on Manufactures*, his role in the Jay Treaty episode, and his plans to join in the further expansion of the British Empire in the Western Hemisphere. However difficult it may be to pin him down with an alternate characterization, Hamilton simply cannot be considered the fountainhead of American mercantilism unless those aspects of his career can be interpreted within the framework of mercantilist thought and action.

Since the *Report on Manufactures* is often accepted as proof, as well as evidence, of Hamilton's mercantilism, it is convenient to give first consideration to that document. In doing so, it seems wise to recall the chronology of his three state papers on economic affairs. Hamilton was commissioned as Secretary of the Treasury on September 11, 1789; and there followed the manifesto on public credit in January 1790, the report on a central bank in December 1790, and the paper on manufacturing in December 1791. Even the most cursory review of those dates catches the two-year delay between the reports on credit and manufacturers. That interval becomes even more striking when viewed in the context of other events.

It was Madison rather than Hamilton, for example, who gave more attention to protective duties on manufactures during the Constitutional Convention. That is still more illuminating since associations for the promotion of American manufactures had appeared in New York, Boston, Providence, and Baltimore as early as 1785, and resolutions for domestic goods had followed the next year from such additional and widely separated localities as Hartford, Germantown, Richmond, and Halifax (South Carolina). By 1789, furthermore, not only had the anti-Federalists picked up political support from such groups in New England, New York, and Pennsylvania, but the special session of Congress received numerous requests and petitions from various manufacturing societies.[20]

Having passed an emergency revenue bill in the form of tariff legislation, the Congress then *ordered* Hamilton, on January 15, 1790, to prepare a specific report on manufactures. That makes his delay even more noticeable, whatever allowances may be granted for his other duties and the thoroughness of his research. As late as October 1791, moreover, the administration saw no need to increase the tariff of 1789. In matters of chronology, urgency, and emphasis, therefore, it seems clear that Hamilton gave priority to funding the debt and establishing the bank. Those operations represented precisely the needs and objectives of the merchants who were semi-autonomous correspondents of British mercantilism, and who were fundamentally opposed to a strong American industry. Their economic, political, and social position would be threatened by a vigorous program of industrialization; for at the very least they would have to make drastic changes in their outlook and actions. Since Hamilton's personal and political position was based on his rapport with that group, it seems relevant to consider whether Hamilton's mercantilism was as thoroughgoing as historians have assumed it was.

In Hamilton's behalf, it can be argued with considerable validity that domestic industry had to have a sound credit system as a cornerstone. But that approach only raises the question of why Hamilton did not present his funding and bank programs as the means to achieve an

[20] This section draws heavily on Charles, *Origins of the American Party System,* and on Vols. I and II of Irving Brant, *James Madison* (Indianapolis and New York, 1941—in progress). A more detailed account of these early episodes can be found in Vol. I of Edward Stanwood, *American Tariff Controversies in the Nineteenth Century* (Boston, 1903).

independent balanced economy. Since he did not, the most relevant explanation would seem to be that Hamilton was in fact a mercantilist who was hamstrung by his political dependence upon the Federalists around Pickering. His association with Tench Coxe would serve to strengthen that analysis.[21] The same argument could then be used to explain why Hamilton delayed his paper on manufactures for almost two years after the Congress had asked for it in January 1790.

The weakest point in that interpretation concerns Hamilton's response to Madison's resolution of January 3, 1794, that "the interests of the United States would be promoted by further restrictions and higher duties in certain cases on the manufactures and navigation of foreign nations employed in the commerce of the United States." Working through William Smith of South Carolina, Hamilton killed Madison's entire program which was designed to promote commercial and industrial independence. Instead, Hamilton's committee in the House reported in favor of more borrowing and further domestic taxes. For that matter, neither Hamilton nor the Federalist party acted to increase protection after 1792.[22]

The explanation of Hamilton's action which does the most to sustain his reputation as an American mercantilist is not as generous to his standing as a reformed monarchist. For given the broad and vigorous agitation from manufacturing societies for greater protection,

[21] Here see Rezneck, "The Rise and Early Development of Industrial Consciousness in the United States, 1760–1830"; and Joseph Dorfman, *The Economic Mind in American Civilization, 1606–1865* (New York, 1946), I, 253–256, 290–293.

[22] Stanwood, *American Tariff Controversies,* I, 108–110, 120–121; and for considerable insight into the role of Smith of South Carolina, consult Joseph Ernst, "Growth of the South Carolina Commons House of Assembly, 1761–1775," unpubl. masters thesis, University of Wisconsin, 1958.

Madison's resolutions offered Hamilton a striking opportunity to widen the base of the Federalist party. That would have strengthened his hand against the pro-British group within the party and have enabled him to give substance to the *Report on Manufactures.* If it be said that Hamilton favored domestic excise taxes in preference to domestic manufacturing, then his mercantilism appears even more questionable. A stronger argument could be made by reference to Hamilton's known reservations about democracy, which would account for his refusal to court the manufacturers as a counterweight to the merchants around Pickering.

It may be, however, that Hamilton's vigorous opposition to Madison's resolutions of 1794 derived in considerable part from the fact that Madison's program was aimed at Great Britain. Not only was that true in the immediate, particular sense, but it also was the case in that Madison's proposals pointed toward general economic independence. That approach to the question of Hamilton's mercantilism has the virtue of having considerable relevance to his role in Jay's Treaty. An American mercantilist could explain and defend Hamilton's basic attitude and maneuvers behind Jay's back by one or both of two arguments. First, England had to be courted while the United States built a navy. Second, Hamilton stressed the political side of mercantilism.

Neither of those explanations is very convincing: Hamilton always favored the Army over the Navy, and political mercantilism is such a contradiction in terms that it begs the entire issue. That interpretation becomes even less convincing when asked to account for the fact that at the end of his career Hamilton turned not toward manufacturing but in the direction of becoming a partner in Britain's imperial adventures in Latin America. Indeed, Hamilton's foreign policy does less to settle the question of his mercantilism than to recall the report in 1793 that "the English considered Hamilton, [Rufus] King, and [William] Smith, of South Carolina, as main supports of British interest in America. Hamilton, not Hammond, was their effective minister."[23] Perhaps the most to be said of Hamilton's mercantilism is that it was latent and limited, for his actions belied his rhetoric.

As in many other contexts, it is Madison who emerges as the central figure in the development of an American mercantilism. While there are many illustrations, perhaps his resolutions of January 1794 provide the most illuminating evidence. Once again Charles points the way: "The program with which Madison began the first strategic moves against the Federalists was not one which could be called anti-Federalist, particularist, or States' rights."[24] His plan was to combine landed expansion to the west with support for domestic manufacturing and an independent American commercial policy. Considered at the practical political level, it represented a bid to the growing numbers of dissident Federalists who opposed a one-way relationship with Britain. Some of those men eyed a bull market for domestic manufactures. Others thought of an expansionist foreign policy with the established states cast in the role of "mother country." Madison saw such groups as allies for the anti-Federalists, as well as the building blocks of an American mercantilism.

Madison's conception of an American mercantilism was possibly too comprehensive as well as too premature politically to be adopted by Congress in 1794, though it was extensively debated before being sidetracked by Hamilton and Smith. But it did serve as a keen analysis

[23] Eugene P. Link, *Democratic-Republican Societies, 1790–1800* (New York, 1942), n. 16, p. 49.
[24] Charles, *Origins of the American Party System,* p. 97.

and program for the growing consensus among anti-Federalists. That drive toward economic independence manifested itself in the Non-Intercourse Bill introduced in the summer of 1794, a move which was defeated only by the vote of Vice-President John Adams. Equally significant is the fact that it was backed by congressmen from Pennsylvania and Delaware as well as by those from southern states. Madison's mercantilism picked up new allies very rapidly, and two subsequent events served as catalysts in the process. Considered in the order of their importance, they were Jay's Treaty and the last stage in the defection of John Adams from High Federalism.

Following so closely upon the narrow defeat of the Non-Intercourse Bill, Jay's Treaty added injury to frustration. The great majority of Americans reacted bitterly and vigorously. Already weakened by deep fissures, the Federalist party cracked open under the ensuing attack. It cost them key leaders in such states as New Hampshire and Pennsylvania and alienated unknown numbers of voters south of the Potomac. As one who had cast the deciding vote against the Non-Intercourse Bill only with great reluctance, John Adams provided temporary leadership for such Federalist dissidents.

Adams strengthened his position even more by refusing to go quietly along to war with France at the bidding of the High Federalists. The differences between Hamilton and Adams were numerous, but perhaps none is so important to an appreciation of the maturing American mercantilism as the contrast between Hamilton's passion for a large army and Adams' emphasis on an American navy. Hamilton's military policy was that of the British nabob in North America, while that of Adams represented American mercantilism. Against that background, and in the context of his deciding vote on the Non-Intercourse Bill of 1794, it is possible to appreciate the full impact of Jay's Treaty on Adams. He made peace with France and forced Pickering out of the cabinet.

Little wonder, then, that Jefferson was willing to give way in favor of Adams. But thanks to Madison, who had been organizing a party as well as projecting a theory and a program, Jefferson became President. Once in power, Jefferson and his supporters were prodded by necessity and spurred by their own visions of empire toward the full development of an American mercantilism. There are several explanations for this phenomenon. Among the most important, one might list the following: the foreign-trade dilemma inherent in physiocratic theory (which was intensified by the wars stemming from the French Revolution); the creative leadership provided by such men as Madison and Albert Gallatin (who made his own *Report on Manufactures* in 1810); the political necessities and expediencies of unifying and sustaining a national party; and the maturing thought of Jefferson himself. But wherever one chooses to place the emphasis, the fact remains that the Jeffersonians in action were far more mercantilistic than the Federalists had been—even in theory and rhetoric.

As early as 1791, for that matter, Jefferson began to shift away from the physiocratic dogma of free trade. And by 1793 he concluded his *Report on Commercial Policy* with a series of retaliatory proposals that were as mercantilistic as any he criticized. Perhaps even more significant was his early ambivalence toward manufacturing, which he never condemned outright once and for all. Jefferson disliked cities and the factory system for what he judged their negative impact on politics and morals, and for the conditions and style of life they imposed upon human beings, but he never discounted the importance of home manufacturing and commerce. He could not afford to, either as the leader of agrarians beginning to produce surpluses for sale, or as one who sought and accepted support from the increasing number of urban groups of all classes who preferred an empire of their own to rejoining the British system. Even if Jefferson had not caught the intellectual flaw in physiocratic trade theory, its practical consequences were something he could not avoid. In substance, therefore, the Jeffersonians based their strength and their policies on the mercantilistic program of a balanced economy at home and a foreign policy of expansion.

Their strategy was to exploit the policy of neutrality initiated by Washington and continued by John Adams. To do so, Jefferson ultimately resorted to the intensely mercantilistic policies of the embargo and non-importation against Britain and France. It was with obvious pride that he remarked, in 1809, that those policies "hastened the day when an equilibrium between the occupations of agriculture, manufactures, and commerce, shall simplify our foreign concerns to the exchange only of that surplus which we cannot consume [in return] for those articles of reasonable comfort or convenience which we cannot produce."[25] Not even Madison ever provided a more classic statement of American mercantilism.

Quite in line with Jefferson's recommendations of the 1790's, and his actions between 1800 and 1809, his successors acted vigorously against such weaker opponents as the Barbary Pirates who threatened American trade. On a more general level, Jefferson's argument that American democracy depended upon a surplus of land was but another, even more overtly formulated, version of Mad-

[25] Quoted in Grampp, "A Re-examination of Jeffersonian Economics," p. 279.

ison's theory that extending the sphere
was the key to controlling factions.
Hence he and his followers initiated
and encouraged such expansion wherever
they could, as in Florida and to the
West; and it was precisely Jefferson's
general expansionist outlook which over-
rode his concern that the Louisiana Purchase was unconstitutional.

The Louisiana Purchase opened the
way to apply the tenets of American
mercantilism to the entire hemisphere.
It also encouraged an explicit American
formulation of the expansionist philosophy of history that was implicit in mercantilism. Americans began to call
openly and militantly for further expansion whenever and wherever they
encountered domestic or foreign difficulties. Indians and Spaniards had to
be pushed out of the way or destroyed.
Interference with exports had to be
stopped, by war if necessary. Canada
offered the solution to other domestic
economic problems, and should be taken
forthwith.

After 1807, when economic troubles
appeared at home, that expansionist outlook and program focused on Great
Britain as the chief offender against the
American Empire. Growing out of an
alliance of business and agrarian interests which favored war to relieve immediate difficulties and forestall future
crises, the War of 1812 was a classic
mercantilist conflict for trade and colonies.[26] The Jeffersonians' earlier economic and maritime warfare, which
almost secured the immediate objectives,
and which had appeared capable of
clearing the way for a general advance,
was just as mercantilistic in nature.
Though in many ways it failed to attain
its avowed objectives, the War of 1812

was in no sense a strategic defeat for
American mercantilism. If only in turning Americans to the west and the south,
it focused the general spirit of expansion
in a new and powerful manner. Perhaps
even more significant, the stalemate
strengthened the idea of an American
System as opposed to the rest of the
world. It was in the wake of the War
of 1812, after all, that the vapors of
Manifest Destiny gathered themselves
for an explosion westward to the Pacific.

John Quincy Adams formulated his
own concept of Manifest Destiny as
early as 1796, when he assured President Washington that the American
System would "infallibly triumph over
the European system...." [27] Fifteen years
later he defined America as "a nation,
coextensive with the North American
Continent, destined by God and nature
to be the most populous and most powerful people ever combined under one
social compact." [28] He pushed overseas
economic expansion just as vigorously.
Even his harshest critics, the High Federalists of New England who wanted to
re-enter the British Empire in some form
or another, recognized his mercantilism.
They called him one of the species of
"amphibious politicians, who live on
both land and water...." [29]

Both before and after he served as
Secretary of State under President James
Monroe, Adams devoted his energies to
building such an American Empire. His
rational program for a dynamic balanced
economy at home was too demanding for
his countrymen. They grew ever more
enamored of a philosophy that assured
them that expansion was the way to
ease their dilemmas and realize their
dreams. Hence they paid little heed to
his proposals for domestic development
or to his warning that America should

[26] On eastern urban votes for war see Warren H. Goodman, "The Origins of the War of 1812: A Survey of Changing Interpretations," reprinted in *The Shaping of American Diplomacy*, ed. William A. Williams (Chicago, 1956), p. 122.

[27] Quoted in Samuel F. Bemis, *John Quincy Adams and the Foundations of American Foreign Policy* (New York, 1949), p. 64.
[28] *Ibid.*, p. 180.
[29] *Ibid.*, p. 148.

go "not abroad in search of monsters to destroy." But to the extent that Adams wanted an empire big enough to sustain such a balanced economy, and to the degree thaat he partook of the expansionist elixir, he won support and influence. And, indeed, his very presence in the cabinet of Monroe was a symbol of the maturity of American mercantilism. Having broken with the old pro-British party to vote for the Louisiana Purchase and the measures of economic warfare against Europe, Adams became the leader of those business interests which supported territorial as well as commercial expansion.

In timing, authorship, and content, the Monroe Doctrine was the classic statement of mature American mercantilism. Seizing the opportunity presented by the decay of the Spanish Empire, Monroe and Adams moved quickly, decisively, and independently to give substance to Henry Clay's fervent exhortation to "become real and true Americans and place ourselves at the head of the American System." [30] Adams caught the tone and meaning of the doctrine in his famous remark that it was time for America to stop bobbing along as a cock-boat in the wake of the British Empire. Acting in that spirit, he spurned Secretary George Canning's not-so-subtle suggestion that America join England in a joint guarantee of Latin American independence and a pledge against their own expansion in the region. Canning claimed high honors for having brought in the New World to redress the balance of the Old, but one would like to think that Adams enjoyed a hearty chuckle over such ability to put a rhetorical gloss on a policy defeat. For what Canning had done was to block the old empires only to be confronted by the challenge of a mature American mercantilism.

In the negative sense, the Monroe Doctrine was designed to check further

European colonization in the Western Hemisphere. But Americans were quite aware of the positive implications of the strategy: it left the United States as the most powerful nation on the scene. America's ultimate territorial and commercial expansion in the New World would be limited only by its energies and its preferences—just as Washington had argued. [31] The negative side of the Monroe Doctrine is the least significant feature about it: the crucial point is that it was, in the minds of its authors, in its language, and in its reception by Americans, the manifesto of an American Empire.

The Monroe Doctrine was the capstone of a system destined to succumb to its own success. For in broad historical perspective, the classic function of mercantilism was to build a system strong enough to survive the application of the principles of Adam Smith. Without an American mercantilism there could have been no Age of Jacksonian Laissez Moi Faire. Perhaps, indeed, the greatest tribute to the leaders of American mercantilism lies in the fact that their handiwork withstood the trauma of a civil war and the sustained shock of unrestrained and irrational exploitation for some seventy years—until it became necessary in the Crisis of the 1890's to undertake the building of a new corporate system.

[30] *Ibid.*, p. 352; but cf. pp. 364, 127.

[31] The traditional neglect of commercial interests and pressures in connection with the formulation and enunciation of the Monroe Doctrine, an approach symbolized in Dexter Perkins, *Monroe Doctrine, 1823–1826* (Baltimore, 1929), is somewhat corrected by Charles L. Chandler, "United States Commerce with Latin America at the Promulgation of the Monroe Doctrine," *Quarterly Journal of Economics*, XXXVIII (May 1924), 466–486. Even more illuminating are Dorothy B. Goebel, "British-American Rivalry in the Chilean Trade, 1817–1820," *Journal of Economic History*, II (Nov. 1942), 190–202; Charles C. Griffin, *The United States and the· Disruption of the Spanish Empire, 1810–1822* (New York, 1937); and Arthur Preston Whitaker, *The United States and the Independence of Latin America, 1800–1830* (Baltimore, 1941).

5

Manifest Destiny—An Emotion

EPHRAIM D. ADAMS

One of the most compelling forces in American history has been expansionism. From the very beginning of the Republic men dreamed of extending the country's boundaries beyond the existing limits. George Washington talked of "our rising empire," and Thomas Jefferson said in 1786, "Our Confederacy must be viewed as the nest from which all America, north and south, is to be peopled." And in 1801 he further exclaimed, "However our present interests may restrain us within our limits, it is impossible not to look forward to distant times when our rapid multiplication will expand it beyond those limits to cover the whole northern, if not the southern, continent." His purchase of the vast territory of Louisiana may, indeed, be considered as a step toward the fulfillment of his prophecy. John Quincy Adams talked in the same vein after concluding the Transcontinental Treaty with Spain in 1819, when he noted, "It is a step to the absorption of all North America," and to a British minister he said two years later, "Keep what is yours but leave the rest to us."

The War of 1812 must also be viewed in expansionist terms, for however important were the maritime strictures by Britain as causes for the conflict, many Americans supported the war because they coveted Florida and Canada. Similarly, the Monroe Doctrine plays an important role in the development of the idea, in that President Monroe's warning to Europe to keep hands off the newly liberated colonies of Spain implied that they lay in the orbit of the United States.

It was in the three decades before the Civil War that the spirit of expansionism reached its height. That period saw the coining of the term Manifest Destiny, the annexation of Texas, the acquisition of Oregon by treaty, and a war against Mexico that brought vast new lands under the American flag.

What motives lay behind the urge to expand? There was, of course, a mixture of motives: economic and emotional, greed and glory, avarice and altruism. Many Southerners sought new land for cotton cultivation as the soil in older areas became exhausted. Undoubtedly, they also desired to form new slave states and thus add to the political power of the South. In the same way, Americans north of the Mason-Dixon line looked for new territory to replace their farms "back east"—extensive, not intensive, farming was the order of the day. And there were merchants and shipowners in the Northeast who saw in the acquisition of harbors on the Pacific stunning opportunities to increase their trade with the Orient. Thus commercial and agrarian imperialism figured heavily in the movement.

FROM *The Power of Ideals in American History* (New Haven: Yale University Press, 1913), pp. 65–94. By permission of the publishers.

But there was yet another impetus for expansion—the sense of a divine mission to spread democracy and extend the area where superior American institutions could operate. It is this drive which Ephraim D. Adams, long a professor at Stanford University and author of several important works on American diplomacy in the period 1830–1865, considers paramount. It is worth noting that the lecture in which he develops his view of the emotional quality in expansionism was delivered in the same year that Charles A. Beard published An Economic Interpretation of the Constitution.

Before attempting a narration of the origin and growth of the ideal of manifest destiny, in its territorial expansion aspect, I find it necessary, in order that its later phases may be understood, to state explicitly what I conceive to be the essence of the ideal of manifest destiny as a force in our history, actively recognized at the time it was exercised. The materialistic historians attribute the westward movement of population to a mere desire for the "gross comforts of material abundance." In answer to this, President Woodrow Wilson, the historian, has written:

The obvious fact is that for the creation of the nation the conquest of her proper territory from Nature was first necessary; and this task, which is hardly yet completed, has been idealized in the popular mind. A bold race has derived inspiration from the size, the difficulty, the danger of the task.

In my opinion both of these interpretations are in error. The purely materialistic historian loses sight of the fact that the people who took part in the westward movement up to 1830, carried with them the ideal of democracy. Mr. Wilson, regarding this wonderful movement from the point of view of later times, himself feeling the joy the pioneer must have had in the mere subjection of the soil, admiring his energy and courage, has depicted the movement in colors that serve to idealize it. But it is an error to assert that our understanding, our idealization, of events and conditions was also the conscious understand-ing and idealization of the men who were participants in those events and conditions. We of the present age rightly regard as heroic the American migration from East to West, and exalt the personal virtues of the men who led,—and of the women, those "Mothers of a Forest Land, whose bosoms pillowed *Men!*" But an ideal, unless it is consciously held by the actors, can not be considered as a living force on men's minds in their political activities. Now I very much doubt whether a man who "moved west," ever felt any "inspiration from the size, the difficulty, the danger of the task," and I certainly do not believe that before 1830, in thus moving west, he was at all consciously influenced by an ideal of expanding national territory. The inspiration which he did carry west with him was that of democracy, and when by 1830 there had been added the inspiration of nationality, the two operated to create a new element in manifest destiny, and that new element was territorial expansion,—a continent-wide national destiny. The westward movement did not create this new ideal, it was but the necessary preliminary condition in which certain inspirations, already held, took on a new form. It follows from this that I do not consider the mere shifting of population a result of the ideal of manifest destiny. That ideal included, up to about 1830, the sense of democracy and a belief in its superiority; afterwards, a desire to expand it, and to increase national power by territorial acquisition. The ideal of democracy and its manifestations, I reserve for a later lecture. The present lecture is primarily concerned, then, with the emotion of territorial expansion,— the emotion of manifest destiny. But it is to be understood that in each step forward in our territorial growth since 1800, there was a general. belief that democracy was expanding as well as national boundaries.

The sense of destiny is an attribute of all nations and all peoples. If we could penetrate beyond the veil of recorded history, and grasp the emotions of tribes and races, of whom it is known only that they existed, probably we should find that these tribes also felt themselves a people set apart for some high purpose. Possibly even the cannibal, as he sacrifices his victim, satisfies both his physical and his spiritual being,— though it is unlikely that the victim appreciates the service he is rendering. Among civilized peoples, national destiny has frequently been accompanied by cannibalistic rites,—also with an equal ignorance of a service performed by the absorbed. Certainly there is no great nation today that has not a belief in its destiny, both in respect to territory and of peculiar function. The larger nations seek "a place in the sun" for their peoples. The smaller are content to feel that their existence, as now established, is a manifestation of providence, and urge this against absorption threatened by powerful neighbors. But all nations that are worth anything, always have had, and always will have, some ideal of national destiny, and without it, would soon disappear, and would deserve their fate.

America has felt herself destined for various high purposes. In early colonial times, the New England communities felt more than all else that they were destined to occupy and preserve a small section of the earth, where those of like religious faith and practice could realize, without governmental interference, certain religious ideals. There were few who thought of a separate national existence from England, and it was not until shortly before the war of independence that there was any general conception of governmental ideals different from those of Great Britain. Even after independence was won, the eyes of America were still unconsciously turned toward the old world, the colonial instinct was still dominant, and it was only after the war of 1812 that America turned her gaze inward upon herself. At once she felt and expressed her "peculiar destiny,"—at first as the chosen servant of the spreading ideal of democracy, later in terms of territorial greatness. Militant patriotism came to reinforce this sense of a special national function in the cause of civilization, and that patriotism pictured Great Britain as the hereditary foe of America. This was inevitable, since stories of valor or of suffering were necessarily connected with the only nation with whom we had fought. The schoolboy, in selected orations and poetry, was trained in this hostility towards England,—a hostility which was, in fact, merely one expression of nationality. Captain Hall, an Englishman traveling in the United States, in 1827, was both amused and astonished on visiting the Boston public schools, that a boy called up to "speak" for the visitor's pleasure, should recite a "furious philippic" against Great Britain, while a second youth gave an oration beginning:

For eighteen hundred years the world had slumbered in ignorance of liberty, and of the true rights of freemen. At length America arose in all her glory, to give the world the long desired lesson!

The intolerance of America in thus training its youth in fixed hostility to old England, the arrogance of the young nation, in a new land, assuming to instruct the old world, were truly amusing, yet back of all bombast and back of all crudity of expression was the sincere conviction that America was destined to be the greater nation, that it would accomplish greater things, that it could offer exceptional enlightenment and bestow unusual favors.

The period from 1830 to 1860 is usually regarded as that in which the ideal of manifest destiny most affected our history. During these years the term "manifest destiny" vaguely expressed the sense of the American people that their government gave an example to the world of the success of the democratic principle, and that power went hand in hand with democracy. Previous to 1830 the westward shifting of population did not imply a belief in a continent-wide country. Year after year American citizens laboriously surmounted the Appalachian range, sought the sources of the streams flowing to the west, and followed these to the land of promise. Until the completion of the Erie Canal the bulk of this movement was from the middle and southern states, a poor white population finding in the rich soil of Kentucky, or Indiana, or Ohio, an improved industrial opportunity, and founding settlements marked by extreme simplicity and equality. Gradually the wide domain of the territory east of the Mississippi was dotted with villages and farms, and by 1830 the frontier had moved across the river into the lands of the Louisiana purchase. After 1825, there came an increased northern migration, swelled by a steady stream of British immigrants, though this last was never large and almost ceased temporarily in 1830. The German immigration of the early thirties added to this wave of humanity moving westward. But as yet there was room for all, and save for the uneasy frontiersman, restless if he had any neighbors, there could be no pressing need, for many years to come, of lands beyond the established boundaries of the country.

The controversy with Great Britain in the twenties over Oregon made clear that America, before 1830, had no thought of continental dominion and regarded as a dreamer the man who would still expand the national domain. Benton, senator from Missouri, was such a dreamer, but dared not give expression to his dream. In 1825, Russia, by treaties with England and the United States, had renounced her claims south of 54° 40', leaving the two remaining powers in joint possession. At once a bill was introduced in Congress for the military occupation of Oregon. A few supported it, more were opposed, but the great majority were wholly indifferent. Dickerson of New Jersey made the principal speech against the measure. "We have not," he said, "adopted a system of colonization, and it is to be hoped we never shall. Oregon can never be one of the United States. If we extend our laws to it, we must consider it as a colony.... Is this territory of Oregon ever to become a state, a member of this Union? Never. The Union is already too extensive." He then entered upon a calculation to prove the utter impossibility of a representative in Congress for Oregon, since mere distance would prove an effective barrier. Postulating that a representative must visit his constituents at least once a year, he stated the distance from the mouth of the Columbia to Washington as 4650 miles, or 9300 for the round trip. According to federal law granting mileage payment to congressmen, the average rate of travel was then twenty miles per day, but supposing the Oregonian to exceed this rate of speed, and to maintain the high average of thirty miles, "This," continued Dickerson, "would allow the member a fortnight to rest himself at Washington before he should commence his journey home.... It would be more expeditious, however, to come by water round Cape Horn, or to pass through Behrings Straits, round the North coast of this Continent to Baffin's Bay, thence through Davis Straits to the Atlantic, and so on to Washington. It is true, this passage is not yet discovered, except upon our maps,—but it will be as soon as Oregon shall be a State."

Benton himself was oppressed by the remoteness of the territory, and standing almost alone in the Senate, did not dare to profess a belief that Oregon could ever be admitted to the Union. He asserted, rather, that "the greatest of all advantages to be derived from the occupation of this country, is in the exclusion of foreign powers from it." He did assert, however, that Oregon would soon be settled, either by European or by American colonists, and declared that it lay with Congress to determine which. Seeking to persuade his hearers to action he pictured American settlement on lines of ultimate separation from the United States. The successive steps would be military occupation, settlements and a civil territorial government, then clamors against the hardship of dependence upon a government so remote as Washington, and finally independence willingly granted by the mother country. Continuing his plea for action, Benton even acknowledged that the Rocky Mountains formed the natural limit of the United States. To the west of that line, this offspring of our institutions would guard our interests, and America would have cause to rejoice in having aided "in the erection of a new Republic, composed of her children, speaking her language, inheriting her principles, devoted to liberty and equality, and ready to stand by her side against the combined powers of the old world."

The long journey to Oregon was indeed a barrier to settlement in the twenties. The next step of the American advance was to the southwest rather than to the northwest, and marks the faint beginnings of the expressed ideal of a territorial manifest destiny, later developed to great proportions. There were several elements merged in the American interest in, and desire for, Texas; the impulsion of the westward movement as lands further west and south became available to settlers; the natural and hopeful interest of Southerners who urged and anticipated annexation; and, in addition, the call of manifest destiny, —the yearning for power and territory. For a time, however, the more cautious and conservative opinion of the older states checked the cry for annexation and Texas was forced to rest under a separate sovereignty. Meanwhile, as evidence that the earlier movement on Texas was no mere slavery conspiracy, as Northern historians of the time declared, but was a manifestation of revived restlessness, and of a popular belief in the destined further expansion of America, we have but to note the conditions of the Canadian rebellion of 1837.

The causes of this miniature revolution do not call for narration, except to explain that in both Lower and Upper Canada the leaders proclaimed their admiration of American institutions and claimed that they were fighting for self-government. Easily defeated in Canada, they fled across the border, appealing to the "sympathy and generosity of a liberty-loving people," and there renewed their efforts to overthrow the Canadian governments. The revolution began in the last months of 1837. At that time the United States was in the throes of the most serious financial crisis in her history; everywhere there were great numbers of idle men, and as filibusters and meddlesome fighters are always recruited from the idle and lawless classes, there were many sympathizers, with empty pockets, ready to join the adventure to "redeem Canada." Yet there were higher motives, and higher-minded men concerned in the movement. Mac-Kenzie, the leader of the revolution in Upper Canada, was a man of unquestioned honor and high ideals, and won the sympathy of the American idealist who saw in his plans an effort to spread American political principles. In addition, there were those who thought that the revolution might be a first step toward the admission of Canada to the Union. The emotion of territorial greatness was beginning to be felt, and the riff-raff of the northern frontier, from Vermont to Michigan, were encouraged by the expression of ideals of democracy and expansion, in public meetings and in the press. The government at Washington condemned this border excitement, but at first was badly hampered in suppressing it, owing to antiquated and ineffective neutrality laws.

"The American," says Mr. Bryce, "likes excitement for its own sake and goes wherever he can find it." Americans of this spirit were the first to hasten to the call of the Canadian revolutionists, but their number was soon increased by the unemployed, and even by some who saw in the event a chance to attack privilege and property,—as the barber of Plattsburg, moulding musket balls, and rejoicing that "one ball would do the business of a man worth £2000 a year." The first rendezvous of these would-be American-Canadian "Patriots" was Navy Island, just above Niagara Falls on the Canadian side of the river. Here a camp of the "grand army of invasion" was established, and here a steamboat, the *Caroline,* carried supplies and men from the American side. In order to cut off this communication, a small Canadian force crossed the river in the night to the spot where the *Caroline* was anchored, cut her out, towed her into midstream, set her on fire, and left her to drift over the falls. The affair created a terrific excitement. American territory

had been invaded, her sacred soil polluted by the myrmidons of a despotic government. The Rochester *Democrat,* inspired to poetic frenzy, wrote:

As over the shelving rocks she broke,
  And plunged in her turbulent grave,
The slumbering genius of Freedom woke,
  Baptized in Niagara's wave,
And sounded her warning tocsin far,
From Atlantic's shore to the polar star.

For genius immersed in Niagara's wave, this was indeed a far cry. But the "Caroline Affair" was in truth a serious one, since it called for revenge, thus adding strength to the "patriot" cause.

On the Canadian side, the cry arose that Great Britain must gird herself to defend monarchical institutions and territory. Lieutenant-Governor Head, of Upper Canada, was as rabid and as melodramatic as the editor of the *Democrat.* He pictured this petty conflict as a contest between republican and monarchical institutions. In a public address he asserted:

The People of Upper Canada detest Democracy. . . . They are perfectly aware that there exist in the Lower Province one or two individuals who inculcate the Idea that *this* Province is about to be disturbed by the Interference of Foreigners [Americans], whose Power and whose Numbers will prove invincible.

In the name of every Regiment of militia in Upper Canada I publicly promulgate— Let them come if they dare.

"The enemy of the British Constitution," he said, "is its low-bred Antagonist, Democracy in America."

Later, in reporting a skirmish between a few Canadians and revolutionists, part of whom were American recruits, he wrote:

The Republicans stood their ground until the monarchical troops arrived within about twenty yards of them, when, abandoning their position, as also their Principle that all men are born equal, they decamped in the greatest confusion.

As apparently there were no shots exchanged in this fearful battle, the case does indeed seem one of those rare instances where principles were the sole contenders. Surely, if the American was fond of "twisting the Lion's tail," Head had revenge in "plucking the Eagle's feathers."

From a perspective of seventy-five years, the American relation to the Canadian rebellion seems ephemeral,—serio-comic. Yet the disturbances along the border gave evidence of a real intensity of feeling, and a genuine passion for expansion. The trouble lasted for two years, and was contemporary with a renewed dispute over the Maine boundary. There now came to the surface the feeling, later very powerful, that American destiny ran counter to that of England on this continent, and that one or the other must give way. Cushing, speaking in Congress in 1839, asserted that England was pursuing a definite policy of irritation, wherever she could press in upon the United States,—over the Maine boundary, in the Northwest, where the Indians were causing trouble, and in Oregon.

"Unless," he said, "this all grasping spirit of universal encroachment on the part of Great Britain be arrested, either by moderation in her councils, or by fear, the time must and will come, when her power and ours cannot co-exist on the continent of North America."

This meant that the United States would be forced to expand in defense of what she already possessed,—but back of this lay the desire of expansion for its own sake. In the late thirties this demand for territory and power was nation-wide, and though it was but one of the causes of the border troubles of that time, it first found expression in them. Failing to achieve results in Canada, interest easily turned to the southern border, where Texas waited.

When, in 1836, Texas declared her independence from Mexico, the Americans who had established that independ-ence, strongly desired annexation. The offer was declined, but the migration into this new country rapidly increased, and the newcomers reinforced annexation sentiment both in Texas and in the United States. By 1842, Texas had secured recognition from the stronger powers as an independent state, and to two of these powers, England and the United States, the future of Texas became a matter of great importance. Slavery existed, and cotton seemed destined to be the chief industrial product. England, hoping to free herself from dependence on American cotton, and at the same time establish a barrier to further American expansion, naturally encouraged Texan independence. The United States, while rejoicing over this new Anglo-Saxon nation, was yet in a doubtful position in regard to it. Mexico stubbornly refused to acknowledge Texan independence, and annexation might involve us in a war. Northern feeling was against a new slave state, so large that several slave states seemed then inevitable. In the South there rapidly developed enthusiasm for annexation on the score of Southern political influence, and the sentiment of manifest destiny was appealed to,—an effective appeal, since the hearts of all our Western people beat responsive to the cry. By 1842, the South was determined to have Texas, and the "Texan game," as Northern opponents termed it, was begun.

Manifest destiny was a strong factor in annexation sentiment, but a more specific argument was found in the national jealousy of England. Tyler and Calhoun raised the cry of British opposition, with more justice than the partisans of anti-slavery admitted. Great Britain did indeed hope that in Texas she would find a block to the increasing power of America, and even dreamed of inducing Texas to abolish slavery. Elliot, the British diplomat in Texas, confined his official efforts, however, to a preservation of the independence of Texas. He sought to check annexation sentiment, picturing the future greatness of an independent Texas. British colonists were introduced, but they were few in number compared with the steady stream from the United States, and, as Elliot himself sorrowfully confessed, they were wholly inferior in the art of pioneering. Like Peter Simple, the British colonist "preferred to walk, rather than to run, toward his goal, for fear he would arrive out of breath." Elliot, marveling at the difficulties and crudities of the American push westward, said "they jolt and jar terrifically in their progress, but *on they do get.*" With the coming of new American settlers, it became certain that Texas herself cared more for annexation than for independence. In the United States the sentiment of expansion grew steadily in strength, and though Calhoun, raising the cry of British interference, was at first defeated by the conservative and anti-slavery elements in the Senate, the campaign of Polk in 1844, when the rivalry with England for Oregon was also played upon, settled the destiny of Texas. In that campaign was heard, at last, no mere feeble and isolated assertion of a continent-wide destiny, but a positive and general profession of faith in the inevitable progress of democratic institutions and "Anglo-Saxon" ideals, destined to triumph over monarchical principles and inferior races. The clap-trap political oratory of this campaign is distressing to the patriotic historian, and I refrain from quotation, but it must be recognized that such oratory was used and was effective, simply because it reflected an American emotion. Manifest destiny, in terms of expansion, suddenly revealed itself as a powerful sentiment, against which the conservative minority struggled in vain. Nor was the expression of this sentiment confined to the political orator. Lyman Beecher, in a sermon enumerating the vices threatening American life, yet claimed for America a superior position among nations. "Our very beginning," he said, "was civilized, learned and pious." And even yet America is

still the richest inheritance which the mercy of God continues to the troubled earth. Nowhere beside, if you search the world over, will you find so much real liberty; so much equality; so much personal safety, and temporal prosperity; so general an extension of useful knowledge; so much religious instruction; so much moral restraint; and so much divine mercy, to make these blessings the power of God, and the wisdom of God unto salvation.

If these blessings were indeed peculiar to America, what reasonable opposition could exist to carrying them into new territory?

Polk's election determined the future of Texas, and Great Britain regretfully relinquished her hope of a barrier state, yet consoled herself with the thought that mere territorial weight would break the Union in fragments. But with Oregon it was a different matter. During the campaign, Democratic orators had declared for the extreme American claim,—"fifty-four forty or fight," and to this England would by no means agree. Southern leaders, gratified as to Texas, now sought to quiet the expansion sentiment they had used with so much success. Previously, in 1843, a bill for the organization of Oregon, offering lands to settlers, had been introduced in Congress. Senator McDuffie of South Carolina, who saw in slavery the "bulwark of republican institutions," was against it, saying:

I would not give a pinch of snuff for the whole territory. I wish to God we did not own it, I wish it was an impassable barrier to secure us against the intrusion of others. ...Do you think your honest farmers in Pennsylvania, New York, or even Ohio or Missouri, will abandon their farms to go upon any such enterprise as that? God forbid!

At the time McDuffie made this speech, other Southerners were more reserved, but no sooner had Tyler despatched the offer to receive Texas into the Union than the sentiments of Mc-Duffie were revived. But Polk, a determined expansionist, already planning to go far beyond Texas, and to carry American territory to the Pacific in the South as well as in the North, stood firmly for Oregon. Apparently he intended to exact the extreme American claim, and hostilities with England seemed near. At the same time, Mexico, still claiming Texas as her own, threatened war, while Texas unexpectedly delayed a formal acceptance of the annexation proposal. The situation seemed dangerous, and with a prospect of war on both northern and southern borders, wisdom urged caution. Horace Greeley, opposed to slavery expansion, argued in the *New York Tribune* against any expansion, citing Benton's speech of 1825 to prove that the Rocky Mountains formed a natural boundary. Winthrop, in Congress, answered the expansionist dogma, "The finger of God never points in a direction contrary to the extension of the glory of the Republic," by quoting:

Glory is like a circle in the water,
Which never ceaseth to enlarge itself,
Till by broad spreading it disperse to naught.

But Greeley and Winthrop were upheld by the anti-slavery faction alone. The *New York Sun* and the *New York Herald* strongly approved annexation and expansion, the latter asserting, "Our march is *onward* for centuries to come, *still onward*—and they who do not keep up with us, must fall behind and be forgotten,"—apparently a reference to Mexico. According to the *Evening Post,* Greeley stood alone in the North: "With the exception of the *Tribune* . . . there is not a press in the Union which does not say Oregon is ours and must be maintained." Polk had no intention of drifting into war with England, and, after a due amount of bluster, agreed to the forty-ninth parallel as the proper boundary of

Oregon; but before this was known, the *Herald,* with an eye on all North America, expressed the hope that war would ensue with both England and Mexico.

"The destiny of the Republic," it stated, "is apparent to every eye. Texas Annexation must be consummated, and the immediate results of that event may only precipitate the subjugation of the whole continent, despite of all the opposing efforts of the despotic dynasties of Europe."

Thus we were "destined" to have Mexico and Canada sometime;—why not now? The *Washington Union,* the administration paper, while relations with England and Mexico were still undetermined, expressed deep suspicion of Great Britain, and asserted that no nation could thwart American "destiny."

The march of the Anglo-Saxon race is onward. They must in the event, accomplish their destiny,—spreading far and wide the great principles of self-government, and who shall say how far they will prosecute the work?

Mingled with this emotion of destiny there was evident the appeal which the "West" made as a land of opportunity. A bit of verse appearing in a St. Louis paper was widely reprinted in the East:

COME OUT TO THE WEST
Come forth from your cities, come out to the West;
Ye have hearts, ye have hands—leave to Nature the rest.
The prairie, the forest, the stream at command—
"The world is too crowded!"—pshaw! come and *take* land.

Come travel the mountain, and paddle the stream;
The cabin shall smile, and the corn-patch shall gleam;
"A wife and six children?"—'tis wealth in your hand!
Your ox and your rifle—out West and take land!

Possibly it was by such means that Martin Chuzzlewit was induced to buy a corner lot in "Eden." The West had cast a glamor over the eyes of the nation, and the greater the distance, the more allur-ing the prospect. But with Oregon se-cured, and with Texas and California made definitely ours in the progress of the war with Mexico, Polk was satisfied and hastened the peace negotiations, that the fever of expansion should not rise too high. The Southern leaders were accus-tomed to bewail the fact that they would always be damned in history, since the historical writing was all done in New England. The South has indeed been thus damned for the annexation of Texas and the Mexican War, but in the former case alone can the slavery interest be re-garded as an important factor. Manifest destiny was the one great leading force in the war with Mexico.

At the end of the war, except for the extreme anti-slavery faction, there was united glorification in the power, and in the territorial greatness of America. The emotion of manifest destiny was at its height. Foreign observers were astounded by the national self-confidence, and ap-palled by the actual power of the United States. Warburton, an English traveler, arriving in America "in ignorance," as he himself says, went away astonished and fearful.

"We cannot," he writes, "conceal from ourselves that in many of the most im-portant points of national capabilities they beat us; they are more energetic, more en-terprising, less embarrassed with class in-terests, less burthened by the legacy of debt. This country, as a field for increase of power, is in every respect so infinitely be-yond ours that comparison would be ab-surd." ... All things "combine to promise them, a few years hence, a degree of strength which may endanger the existing state of things in the world. They only wait for matured power, to apply the incendiary torch of Republicanism to the nations of Europe."

Warburton overstates American desire to meddle in European affairs, yet he ex-presses American belief in the contagious qualities of the ideal of self-government. Witness our enthusiasm over the Euro-pean revolutions of 1848, when press, pulpit, and Congress gave credit to American ideals and institutions,—being woefully ignorant of the many sources of the most confused revolutionary move-ment in history. Yet there is a touch of truth in the theory that the prosperity and power of America, looked upon as a test of the success of her democratic insti-tutions, were an influence in expanding liberalism in Europe. Perhaps this was our most grandiloquent period. Here was this vast country,—its riches untold, sea-ports on two oceans, the one ideal form of government, and possibilities of power beyond telling. After the absorption of so much territory in so short a time, Amer-ica summed up her material blessings and was satisfied. But she hoped for domin-ion even beyond material things. A hand-ful of people as compared with the great powers of Europe, she arrogated to her-self leadership in the world of ideas, and proposed to make herself respected and feared in the family of Nations. Clay best expressed it in 1850, saying:

Our country has grown to a magnitude, to a power and greatness, such as to com-mand the respect, if it does not awe the apprehensions of the powers of the earth, with whom we come in contact.

The ebb of the tide of expansion craze began with the acquisition of the Pacific Coast. The discovery of gold in Califor-nia drew in a new direction the bulk of that adventurous population which had heretofore worried our neighbors. Before that discovery, Polk, in 1847, had advo-cated a waterway across the Isthmus of Panama, and Francis Lieber urged Amer-ica not to be afraid of her future, and to build the canal, writing:

Let the vastness not appal us;
Greatness is thy destiny.
Let the doubters not recall us:
Venture suits the free.

The gold rush at once forced into prom-inence the question of transit by the Isth-mus, and the Clayton-Bulwer treaty was signed with England, looking toward a canal. A ten-years' dispute as to the interpretation of that treaty followed, and Central America became the scene of a new "American movement," with William Walker, the "grey-eyed man of destiny," as the leading actor in filibustering expeditions, having for their object a tropical expansion, and finding favor in the South. Cuba also was an objective, but all this aftermath of the expansion craze was checked by the political exigencies of the dangerous situation within the United States, when the Kansas-Nebraska controversy arose.

Meanwhile Americans, generally, were proudly conscious of power, and of territorial greatness, and were not unduly modest in expressing this consciousness. Manifest destiny has indeed a characteristic of American humor,—exaggeration. The Englishman defined American humor as "merely a big lie,"—but he missed the fact that, to the American, the "big lie" was never quite an absolute impossibility. It was thus with the expression of the ideal of manifest destiny,—the bombast, however apparently absurd, was never wholly insincere, though it was tinctured with the love of humorous exaggeration for its own sake. This puzzled the English observer and he sometimes took American talk at its face value, as when the House of Lords solemnly recorded its indignation at an American proposal to repudiate all debts to foreign nations, on the ground that such creditors were fully recompensed in having aided in the spread of American civilization. The editorial in a Dubuque, Iowa, paper that inspired this British protest was a mere blatant absurdity and the editor must have been gratified, if he knew of it, to find his effort perpetuated in the pages of Hansard's Parliamentary Debates. Charles Dickens, in "Martin Chuzzlewit," revelled in the opportunity to caricature our assumption of superiority, and of the all-pervading influence of our institutions. Martin, under the guidance of Colonel Diver, editor of the *New York Rowdy Journal,* has made the acquaintance of several of "the most remarkable men of the country, sir," and has been astounded by their youth. At the dinner table in the boarding house, he is equally astounded to learn that the "little girl, like a doll," seated opposite, is the mother of two children. He expresses his wonder to Colonel Diver, who replies, "Yes, Sir, but some institutions develop human nature; others re-tard it." More serious English writers, accepting American estimate of the power and future expansion of the United States, struck the note of "hands across the sea," and declared a common destiny for the two nations, each in its own field. Charles Mackay, the "Ayrshire Poet," read at a banquet in Washington a poem called "John and Jonathan," disclaiming for John any wish to interfere with Jonathan's destiny:

Take you the West and I the East,
  We'll spread ourselves abroad,
With Trade and Spade, and wholesome laws,
  And faith in Man and God.

Take you the West and I the East,
  We speak the self-same tongue
That Milton wrote and Chatham spoke,
  And Burns and Shakespeare sung;
And from our tongue, our hand, our heart,
  Shall countless blessings flow
To light two darkened hemispheres
  That know not where they go.

The Civil War put a sudden end to the clamor for territorial expansion. The purchase of Alaska, in 1867, awoke no enthusiasm in American hearts. It was generally spoken of as "Seward's Folly," and regarded as a recompense to Russia for her friendly attitude during the war. For thirty years America was occupied with industrial development, satisfied to retain for herself the blessing of her institutions, with no inclination to confer them by force on other nations. Then came the Spanish-American war. Whatever its origin, the war awoke again, but only for the moment, the emotion of manifest destiny. President McKinley, in a message to Congress, following the cession of the Philippines by Spain, expressed the national sentiment:

"The war," he said, "has brought us new duties and responsibilities which we must meet and discharge as becomes a great nation on whose growth and career from the beginning the Ruler of Nations has plainly written the high command and pledge of civilization. Incidental to our tenure in the Philippines is the commercial opportunity to which American statesmanship cannot be indifferent."

A shrill voice from the East protested, but these words express briefly the true inwardness of manifest destiny at all times in our history. Even more briefly put they might be condensed to, "God directs us,—perhaps it will pay."

If, in this lecture, I have seemed to present to you an ideal simply as a target for caricature and ridicule, I shall be unfair to my own conception of manifest destiny and its influence. It is true that, as an ideal embracing territorial expansion, I have little respect for it, though I do not agree with Lowell:

Thet all this big talk of our destinies
Is half on it ign'ance and t'other half rum,

for it can not be denied that always there was present a spiritual exaltation, and not only the assertion, but the conviction of the superiority of American institutions. But the taint of sordid motives was there too. There was a golden ideal in the emotion, but there was also an alloy of baser metals. This criticism should not, however, lessen emphasis upon the force of the ideal of manifest destiny in American history, for whatever its origin, or however used, the ideal existed of and by itself. No economic basis whatever can be found for it after the annexation of Texas, and even in that instance, the emotion played as great a part as industrial interests. It was a fever in the blood that steadily rose, and was allayed only by the letting of blood.

In the introduction to this lecture I asserted that the westward movement, in and of itself, held no conscious ideal of a continent-wide destiny. Setting aside such a claim for that movement, there were, then, two phases of manifest destiny,—the earlier expressing merely the conviction of superiority in our form of government, and the greater happiness of our people; while the later phase carried with this belief the desire for new territory, and the responsibility of imposing upon other nations the benefits of our own. Present-day judgment repudiates the latter view, while holding firmly to the faith in our institutions, and to confidence in our future. In that ideal of manifest destiny,—a belief in our institutions, as the best in the world adapted to secure to *our* people "life, liberty, and the pursuit of happiness,"—we may still assert our faith. But in relation to those nations whose boundaries touch our own, or in whose peace and prosperity we have an interest, let us agree with Joseph Gilder's vision of the duty of America:

Be thou the guardian of the weak,
    Of the unfriended, thou the friend;
No guerdon for thy valor seek,
    No end beyond the avowèd end
Wouldst thou thy godlike power preserve,
Be godlike in the will to serve.[1]

[1] From *Harper's Weekly*. Copyright, 1900, by Harper & Bros.

6

The Failure of Polk's Mexican War Intrigue of 1845

RICHARD R. STENBERG

For an understanding of the reasons why the United States fought Mexico in 1846, a study of President James K. Polk is most important. Historians who have written on the causes of the war have stressed various factors, such as a conspiracy by Southern slaveowners to extend the "peculiar institution," a yearning by land-hungry Western farmers for virgin land to cultivate, a desire by New England commercial interests for the fine harbors of Mexican California, and a drive by proponents of Manifest Destiny to extend American democracy to the oppressed and American civilization to the benighted. But in the final analysis we must look to Polk, for it was he, as President, who made the decision for war. On May, 9, 1846, he announced to his cabinet his intention to ask Congress for a declaration of war. With the cabinet's unanimous consent, he sent the war message to Congress two days later.

The United States, said Polk, did not wish war and, indeed, had made every effort to "establish peace with Mexico on liberal and honorable terms." An envoy, John Slidell, had been dispatched in September 1845 to Mexico City to settle all differences—the two most serious being the Texas-Mexican boundary and unpaid claims by American citizens—but the Mexican government "refused to receive him or to listen to his propositions." And that was not all. On April 24, a party of Mexican soldiers had attacked an American force in the area between the Rio Grande and the Nueces River, which, he said, lay in the State of Texas, and had killed or wounded sixteen men. Mexico had "shed American blood on American soil," and thus war existed "by the act of Mexico herself."

A number of historians have claimed that Polk's reasons for war were not sound and that his message distorted the truth. Mexico's refusal to receive an envoy or to pay claims did not constitute sufficient grounds for war. Further, the statement that American blood had been shed on American soil was inaccurate. The territory between the two rivers was in dispute, and pending an adjudication of the controversy the President had no right to claim it as American or to send troops there in January 1846 "to provide for the defense of that portion of our country." And what of California? Polk made no mention of it in his message, yet it was well known that he coveted that Mexican province and had offered to buy it, but Mexico would not sell. Was that the real, if un-

FROM *Pacific Historical Review*, IV (1935), 39–68. By permission of *Pacific Historical Review*.

stated, reason for war? It was known, too, that Polk had decided for war on May 8 when Slidell arrived in Washington with the news of his rebuff—one day before the report of the attack on American troops reached the capital.

Other scholars have defended the President, claiming that he went to war only after all efforts to reconcile differences with Mexico had been exhausted. They agree with his statement in the war message that "our forebearance has gone to such an extreme as to be mistaken in its character." Polk indeed wanted California, but they find no evidence that he would have fought to get it. As for the presence of American troops in the disputed territory, these writers justify it on the grounds that Polk had the obligation to defend what he and the State of Texas considered American property.

To this controversy Richard R. Stenberg contributes an interesting and important item of evidence that supports the view that Polk sought war with Mexico to satisfy his expansionist ambitions. Stenberg, who in other articles has offered fresh and suggestive new interpretations of several aspects of the period between Jackson and Polk, finds that early in 1845, before the Slidell mission, Polk had intrigued with the Republic of Texas to provoke a war with Mexico by urging that Texan troops occupy the disputed territory. In such a war he promised to assist Texas and after Mexico was defeated, California and other parts of that Republic could be annexed to Texas (with the expectation that eventually Texas would become part of the United States). This plan for "covert aggression through Texas" failed, to be revived the following year with greater success.

History long accepted the contemporary view that Polk made war in 1846 very deliberately to seize the much-coveted Mexican borderlands from Texas to the Pacific, bringing up the private claims against Mexico merely as a justificatory pretext. Many still hold this opinion, dissenting from the recent presentation of "peaceful Polk" by G. L. Rives and J. H. Smith,[1] who, adding no salient facts to those already known, are essentially interpretative. Although the outstanding incidents—*e.g.*, Slidell's mission and Taylor's march to the Rio Grande—are of such uncertain meaning as to give

rise to conflicting interpretations, all recent writers have been at one in the manner of approach: in search for causal incidents, motives and maneuvers leading to the war, they have gone no further back than the Slidell mission in the latter half of 1845, neglecting Polk's diplomacy in the earlier half of the year. Perhaps they have been too confident in considering this earlier period (in which Texas was offered and accepted annexation) but one of "watchful waiting" and too hasty in assuming from the later "peaceable" Slidell mission that Polk consistently desired and worked from first to last for peace. This emphasis on the Slidell mission comes partly from the fact that historical sources are more abundant and available for the last part of 1845, Polk beginning his *Diary*, for example, about the first of September, showing the inception of this mission but leaving for the preceding period no comparable purported record of his mind ("pur-

[1] George Lockhart Rives, *The United States and Mexico, 1821–1848* (New York, 1913), 2 v.; Justin Harvey Smith, *The War With Mexico* (New York, 1919), 2 v. For dissent see, *e.g.*: Jesse Siddall Reeves, *American Diplomacy under Tyler and Polk* (Baltimore, 1907); Samuel Eliot Morison, *Oxford History of the United States* (London, 1927), II, 76–80; James Truslow Adams, *The Epic of America* (Boston, 1932), 229; James Wilford Garner, *American Foreign Policies* (New York, 1928), 71.

ported" is advisable, for the *Diary,* which on first sight and to those unconsciously biased in Polk's favor seems full and candid, appears on inspection of other sources to be incomplete and lacking in some very material respects). This neglect of the early half of 1845 seems an oversight of some moment, without which it would have been impossible to view Polk as scrupulous and peaceable.

According to President Anson Jones, of the Texas Republic, President Polk tried secretly, before the annexation of Texas was consummated, to instigate the "Lone Star Republic" to conquer the "disputed" territory between the Nueces River and the Rio Grande and so precipitate a Mexican war, which war he could then *annex* along with Texas—he, the American President, wishing to escape the invidious, well-nigh insoluble Texas boundary question and to have opened, apparently by some other hand than his own, the forbidden door through which he could lead "manifest destiny," stimulated to new eagerness by the anticipated triumph in Texas. As Jones says, too, such a movement was well calculated to precipitate Texas into the Union by frustrating the efforts then making towards a Texo-Mexican conciliation. But President Jones turned a cold shoulder and defeated the intrigue, leaving Polk the task and responsibility of provoking war. The truth of Jones's statement of this abortive intrigue (which curiously foreshadows the means by which Polk actually brought on the war) there seems no reason to question and every reason to believe, as the present paper will indicate. The few historians who have even so much as noticed Jones's version have rejected it summarily, upon the mere ground that it is "inconsistent" with the "peaceable" Slidell mission—whereas, of course, they might just as logically, on the contrary, have seen in this apparent inconsistency reason for doubting the "peaceableness" of the Slidell mission.

Mexico severed relations with the United States in March, 1845, when Congress passed the Texas annexation measure; and uttered threats to reconquer the "lost department." But all this proved mere "sound and fury," for she acquiesced in the annexation, desiring only to save appearances [2] and protect her right to her territory west of the Nueces, to which Texas had no right either legally or by conquest. It suited Polk to declare after war began that hostilities were commenced by Mexico because of annexation —a convenient fiction hardly plausible then and long since exploded. Yet in a certain way the annexation did lead to the war: Polk gave pledges to Texas, when trying to induce her to accept annexation, that he would maintain her claim to the Rio Grande, and in his fulfillment of this (by military occupation, or conquest, instead of by peaceable negotiation, as Congress had intended) he provoked the War with Mexico.[3] Such an outcome had been apprehended by many who had opposed Texas annexation; they saw in it only one link in a chain of forthcoming expansions towards Mexico. Certain senators, notably, had opposed the House resolutions for annexation largely from fear that the "re-annexation" of Texas with her unsettled western boundary would pave the way

[2] Brantz Mayer, *The War between Mexico and the United States* (New York, 1847), 69, note.

[3] Polk to Sam Houston, June 6, 1845, and Polk to A. J. Donelson, June 15, 1845, in Polk MSS. (in Library of Congress); Milo Milton Quaife, ed., *The Diary of James K. Polk* (Chicago, 1910), III, 196; Anson Jones, *Memoranda and Official Correspondence relating to the Republic of Texas* (New York, 1859), 53, 54; Smith, *War with Mexico,* I, 139. Despite the fact that Congress had plainly left the disputed boundary to be settled by negotiation with Mexico, Polk blandly affected in public pronouncement to be unaware of any boundary question. Observe how he announces the annexation of Texas in his message of December, 1845: "The jurisdiction of the United States . . . has passed the Capes of Florida, and been peacefully extended to the Del Norte," or Rio Grande.

to aggression upon Mexico and usher in war. President-elect Polk privately promised these senators, in late February, 1845, that he would proceed to annexation by new negotiations under Senator Benton's plan, which by amendment was then attached to the House resolutions as an alternative.[4] After his inauguration Polk similarly gave pledges to Texas to do many good things for her if she would accept annexation—pledges which likewise he made no effort afterwards to fulfill, save only that to uphold the Texan paper-claim to the Rio Grande. This last significant pledge placed him in an unpleasant dilemma. Texas claimed to the Rio Grande, though she had never extended west of the Nueces; and the advanced Democratic expansionists had seemingly endorsed the claim at the Baltimore Convention (May, 1844) by demanding the "re-annexation" of Texas, a most irrelevant expression historically.[5] But the Whigs and a strong section of the Democracy led by Benton and holding the balance of power in the Senate held that the Nueces, and not the Rio Grande, was the western boundary of Texas. If Polk should fail to uphold the Texan claim he would anger the Texans and many of his own countrymen; if he upheld it he would be forced to aggress

[4] The senators then voted for the measure; without their votes it would not have passed. Despite his pledge to negotiate, Polk offered the House resolutions to Texas. Later he denied having pledged himself in the matter; but his denial only serves to shed light on his character. For evidence as to Polk's pledges to senators and to Texas see Richard R. Stenberg, "President Polk and the Annexation of Texas," in *Southwestern Social Science Quarterly*, XIV, 333–356 (March, 1934); *Texas National Register* (Washington), June 19, 1845.

[5] The "re-annexationists" convenientlyy identified "Texas," a Spanish-Mexican state bounded on the west by the Nueces, with the old American claim (given up in 1819) to all the territory east of the Rio Grande as part of the Louisiana Purchase of 1803. This claim is discussed in Stenberg, "The Boundaries of the Louisiana Purchase," in *Hispanic American Historical Review*, XIV, 32–64 (February, 1934).

against Mexico—unless (which was very doubtful) she could be bought off or brought peacefully to acquiesce—and thereby would in all probability incur war and be attacked by a Whig-Benton coalition. In this dilemma it is not strange that Polk should have sought some remedy to relieve himself of an invidious task! The setting of circumstances was just that in which such an intrigue by Polk in Texas as Presedent Jones describes would have been logical, almost imperative—especially if Polk had ulterior aims against Mexico which only war could realize.

A word, therefore, as to Polk's aims: these were such as war only could fulfill (for it was impossible to suppose that Mexico would willingly dismember herself). Polk on taking office in March, 1845, told Secretary Bancroft that the acquisition of California was one of the chief measures he would endeavor to accomplish. In this he could expect the approval of his countrymen: expansive talk of "manifest destiny"—a term coined in 1845—was rife, and predictions assigned the whole continent to the ambitious Americans, who were now moving in ever-increasing numbers into California and Oregon, and perfecting a title (which diplomacy by itself had failed in) to the southern half of the Oregon territory. There were fearsome reports in 1844–45 that "grasping" England was about to gain California peaceably from Mexico. At the time the Slidell mission was conceived Polk records in his *Diary* his determination to take New Mexico and California by war if Mexico should refuse to yield a minimum of territory— that east of the Rio Grande—to satisfy private American claims against Mexico.[6]

[6] It is the writer's opinion that Polk neither intended the Slidell mission to be successful nor supposed that it would be—and that the mission was but a maneuver calculated to place Mexico in the light of wrong-doer to justify a declaration of war against her. This matter is beyond the purview of this paper, but will be

Such evidence is eloquent of Polk's imperialistic desires. The coercive Slidell mission, in which the private claims were newly and so much in evidence, gives Polk's conduct a peaceful and somewhat scrupulous appearance which it seems, when viewed closely and in the light of Polk's earlier and subsequent maneuvers, not even remotely to deserve. One may perhaps best judge whether the claims were the real cause, or were made the pretext, for war after observing the character of Polk's intrigue early in 1845, only after the failure of which the claims were brought on the scene by Polk and urged against bankrupt Mexico in so useful a way. And this was at a time when the American states had repudiated bonded debts, held largely by exasperated but helpless European creditors, to a sum beside which the claims against Mexico were as a crumb to a loaf.

Polk on entering the White House had an abundance of counselors for a policy of covert aggression through Texas, using her as a cat's-paw. Duff Green, who had been sent to Mexico by Tyler in September, 1844, "to aid in conducting the negotiation for the acquisition of Texas, New Mexico and California," reported that Mexico would never sell willingly and must be chastised. Returning to Texas he intrigued with the war party, which desired both annexation to the United States and the conquest of northern Mexico. His project, broached to high officials, was to employ "the Indians of the United States and Texas in the invasion of Mexico and revolutionizing the country from the Rio Grande to the Pacific under the flag of Texas." With the Texas officials it seems to have found little favor. Green wrote later of his scheme that

an arrangement was made for a movement in Texas which would enable the United States to interpose and thus obtain the concessions wanted. I came to Texas, explained to the President and to Congress the measure which had been agreed on, and which would have been approved and adopted but for the interference of Mr. Elliott, the British chargé to Texas, who induced the President, Mr. Jones, to believe that he could and would induce the Mexican Government to recognize the independence of Texas.

The "arrangement" and whom it was arranged with is now uncertain.[7] It is to be noted, however, that Green was back at Washington and was consulting with Polk in March, 1845. His advice was no doubt consonant with his late "project for the defense of the Western frontier and the invasion of Mexico."

The British consul at Galveston, Kennedy, reported on March 22, 1845, that a large force was preparing in the United States

with a view to invasion of the Mexican Provinces south of the Rio Grande. I have reason to believe that secret communications have for some time been carried on, between certain of the Federal leaders in those provinces, and parties resident in Texas, who, at present,—I am told—are in

[7] Donelson to Calhoun, November 18, 1844, and January 27, 1845, and Green to Calhoun, December 8, 1844, in J. Franklin Jameson, ed., *The Correspondence of John C. Calhoun*, 996–997, 1019–1022, 1006–1007, in American Historical Association *Report*, 1899, II; Duff Green, *Facts and Suggestions* (New York, 1866), 85. One wonders if Green's intrigue had any relation to the American government's instructions of September 17, 1844, to Donelson, American Minister to Texas, mentioning a report that Mexico or Mexican citizens were trying to incite the American border Indians to hostilities against the Texans, and advising him that if Texas should so desire the United States would intervene to restrain the Indians in Texas, under a treaty obligation. See Richard K. Crallé, ed., *The Works of Calhoun* (New York, 1883), V, 376–377; Ethan Allen Hitchcock, *Fifty Years in Camp and Field* (New York, 1909), 187; Raymond to Anson Jones, September 12, 19, 1844, in George Pierce Garrison, *Diplomatic Correspondence of the Republic of Texas*, II, 310–312, in American Historical Association *Report*, 1908, II; cf. *Report*, 1929, 287.

---

discussed, with other aspects of Polk's diplomacy not here touched on, in a study entitled "The Rise of American Imperialism, 1787–1850," which the writer has in preparation.

the United States, urging forward the military preparations reported to be in progress.[8]

Kennedy added: "The force to be raised and the object for which it was to be organized, were lately announced in Galveston by Doctor Branch T. Archer." Still later he learned that "Archer, and the partner of his counsels, General Thos. J. Green, who formed one of the Texian expedition beyond the Rio Grande in 1842, have spent the greater part of their time in Washington, ... where they appear to have been favourably noticed by the President, and the leading members of his cabinet." [9] The example and advice of these gentlemen was for expansion by conquest. But ever since 1841 the spirit of war against Mexico for revenge and conquest had been running high in Texas, so that Polk and his expansionist advisers would have needed no special counsel from Texas to have conceived the convenient scheme of inciting Texas to war against Mexico on the eve of annexation, a war which the United States could annex and so wage without suffering the odium of apparent responsibility or "war guilt."

President Jones, who was suspected (and probably rightly) of being opposed to the annexation of Texas to the United States, temporarily withheld the American offer from the people and sought hastily to procure through the mediation of the British chargé, Charles Elliot, a Mexican offer of recognition of Texan independence in return for a guaranty by Texas to preserve her independence. What was known of Jones's dealings with Elliot alarmed the American agents and the annexation party in Texas. The more militant of this party, which included the popular Texas commander-in-chief, Major-General Sidney Sherman (formerly of Kentucky), were in a ready mood for hostilities with Mexico, both to ensure annexation and for possible conquest.

Such was the situation when Polk sent a number of special agents to Texas with secret, confidential instructions,[10] to further his schemes and assist the regular Minister, Donelson. The first, Archibald Yell (ex-Governor of Arkansas), left for Texas on March 10, 1845; after him went Charles A. Wickliffe (Postmaster General under Tyler) at the end of March. Finally, thus preceded by Yell and Wickliffe, Commodore Robert F. Stockton of the Navy was sent to Texas, where he arrived off the coast May 12–15, anxious to extend the "protection" of his fleet. The Commodore—like Wickliffe, whom Polk had designated "confidential agent to Texas to counteract the contemplated interference of Great Britain and France to prevent the annexation of Texas to the United States" [11]—had secret unwritten instructions; and they were, as his secretary frankly told President Jones, to instigate Texas to seize the "disputed" territory west of the Nueces and start a war with Mexico, in which the United States would immediately join in "defense" of Texas.

Immediately, on reaching Texas, Stockton proceeded to interview General Sherman, who concurred enthusiastically with Stockton's proposal that Sherman gather and lead a force of Texans to occupy and

[8] Kennedy to Aberdeen, April 3, 1845, in *Southwestern Historical Quarterly*, XX, 154. [Reprinted by permission.]
[9] Kennedy to Aberdeen, December 8, 1845, in *Southwestern Historical Quarterly*, XX, 400. [Reprinted by permission.] Thomas Jefferson Green preached the Texan-American conquest of Northern Mexico to the Pacific on the ground of necessity and the "doctrine of usufruct." See Green's *Journal of the Texian Expedition against Mier; Subsequent Imprisonment of the Author ... with Reflections upon the Present Political and Probable Future Relations of Texas, Mexico, and the United States* (New York, 1845), 412 ff.

[10] See Polk to Donelson, March 28, 1845, in *Tennessee Historical Magazine*, III, 62, 63; *Southwestern Social Science Quarterly*, XIV, 353–355.
[11] Justin Harvey Smith, *The Annexation of Texas* (New York, 1911), 447, note; *Weekly Picayune* (New Orleans), May 26, 1845; cf. Charleston *Courier*, May 31, 1845; *National Intelligencer* (Washington), June 14, 1845.

eject the Mexican troops from the "disputed" territory. Stockton was to finance the scheme from his own wealth.[12] But let President Jones himself tell his story:

In May, 1845, Commodore Stockton, with a fleet of four or five vessels, arrived at Galveston, and with him Hon. C. A. Wickliffe. . . . These gentlemen had various interviews with Major Gen. Sherman, the chief officer of the militia of Texas, the result of which was active preparations at Galveston for organizing volunteer forces, the ostensible (and no doubt real) object of which was an invasion of Mexico. A party, it appears, was anxious that the expedition should be set on foot, under the auspices of the Major General and Com. Stockton; but these gentlemen, it appears, were unwilling to take so great a responsibility: it was therefore resolved that the plan should be submitted to me and my sanction obtained—(quere, forced?) indeed such, as afterwards became apparent, were the Commodore's instructions; and the organizing, &c., had been gone into for the purpose of forcing my consent to the proposed scheme. On the 28th of May, Gen. Sherman for himself and associates in the militia, and Dr. Wright, surgeon of the steamer Princeton, and secretary of the Commodore (as he informed me), took three days in unfolding to me the object of their visit. Dr. Wright stated that he was sent by Com. Stockton to propose that I should authorize Major Gen. Sherman to raise a force of two or three thousand men, or as many as might be necessary, and to make a descent upon the Mexican town of Matamoras, and capture and hold it; that Com. Stockton would give assistance with the fleet under his command, under the pretext of giving the protection promised by the United States to Gen. Murphy; that he

would undertake to supply the necessary provisions, arms and munitions of war for the expedition, would land them at convenient points on our coast, and would agree to pay the men and officers to be engaged; that he had consulted Gen. Sherman, who approved the plan, and was present to say so; and, besides, that the people generally from Galveston to Washington [Texas] had been spoken to about it, and that it met their unanimous approval; and that all that was now wanting was the sanction of the Government to the scheme. Gen. Sherman confirmed what Dr. Wright stated, said he had had various interviews with Com. Stockton, and hoped I would approve the mission. I asked Dr. Wright if he had written instructions from the Commodore, or any communication from him to me; that the matter was a grave one, and I did not well see how, without them, if disposed even, I could undertake such weighty responsibilities. As I expected, he replied in the negative, but that if I wished, Com. Stockton would visit me in person, and give me the same assurances in person. I asked him if the Minister of the United States [Donelson] was cognizant of the matter. He then stated to me that the scheme was rather a confidential and secret one, that it was undertaken under the sanction of the United States Government, but that the President did not wish to become known in the matter, but approved Com. Stockton's plan; —that as an evidence of that to me, Mr. Wickliffe was associated with the Commodore; that the President of the United States, satisfied that annexation was in effect consummated, wished Texas to place herself in an attitude of hostile activity towards Mexico, so that, when Texas was finally brought into the Union, *she might bring a war with her;* and this was the object of the expedition to Matamoras, as now proposed. He further stated that Com. Stockton was . . . very wealthy; that he had means of his own sufficient to support and carry on the expedition; and that it was desirable it should appear to the world as his individual enterprise, while at the same time I was given to understand that the Government of the United States was, in reality, at the bottom of it, and anxious for its accomplishment and for the reasons stated. I then said, smiling, "So, gentlemen, the Commodore, on the part of the United States, wishes me to *manufacture a war* for them"; to which they replied affirmatively. Subsequently I had an interview

[12] Anson Jones's *Memoranda* shows clearly that the proposed movement of Texans under Sherman was unheard of before the late part of May, before Stockton's arrival, and had no merely popular, or Texas, origin. Justin H. Smith believed that the scheme was a spontaneous move by the annexation party in Texas, not originating with Stockton and Polk; that the American agents merely fell in with and gave after-approval to Sherman's projected campaign. *The Annexation of Texas,* 446–448. Most writers on the Mexican War have nothing to say about the matter. *Cf.* Smith, *War with Mexico,* I, 130, 131, *passim;* Nathaniel Wright Stephenson, *Texas and the Mexican War* (New Haven, 1921), 178, 179.

with Gen. Sherman alone. He expressed to me his own anxiety that I should assent to Com. Stockton's proposals, represented that it was extremely popular among the people, and that he would have no difficulty in obtaining the requisite number of men, upon the assurances of Stockton that they should be provisioned and paid. I obtained all the information in my power from these parties as to their plans; and although indignant at the proposition ... I suppressed my feelings, and gave no expression of opinion, but suggested every objection and difficulty which presented themselves to my mind, and for three days kept them answering these objections or obviating difficulties, until they became preety thoroughly impressed with the belief that I was thinking very seriously on the matter; and so indeed I was, but not in the way they hoped. I ... found it necessary to temporize. There was much excitement in the public mind on account of my supposed opposition to annexation ... also a hatred of Mexico, and a burning disposition for revenge.[13]

Stockton's initiative in this scheme is seen again in a Galveston correspondent's letter of May 22:

The important event of the day is the arrival of Commodore Stockton, with his fleet. Two days after he anchored here, Col. Love received information from a reliable source from the West that the Mexican force on the Rio Grande would attempt to occupy and maintain the line of the Nueces, at the moment of the completion of annexation. This news he communicated to the Commodore, who advised an immediate occupation of that line by the Texan troops, offering his co-operation by sea. The Commodore, accompanied by Col. Love, Col. McKinney, Saml. Williams and C. A. Wickliffe, ... will sail tomorrow to obtain intelligence and will return in a week.— In the meantime, Maj. Gen. Sherman is to visit the Executive and ask his approval and co-operation. Should he refuse, Sherman contends that he is empowered by the general terms of an existing law to act independently of the President, *and he will do so.* He will call three thousand men into immediate service to rendezvous at Corpus Christi, *and the call will be promptly obeyed.* Things here are in great ferment.[14]

Thus on account of the popularity of the project and the danger of rebellion President Jones made no blunt refusal, but was dilatory. He was expecting Elliot to return from Mexico at any moment, and so told Wright and Sherman to go and confer further with Stockton while he took a "few days longer to reflect upon the matter," adding that Congress would soon convene and he would "in so grave a matter ... choose to have their advice." He adds in retrospect:

The *advocate for peace* for ten years, I naturally turned with disgust and abhorrence from a proposition of Mr. Polk's through Com. Stockton, "that I should manufacture a war for the United States." ... The anxiety of Mr. Polk for a pretext for a war with Mexico had been known to me for some time, through the agency of employees of the Texan Government at Washington city. That he was predetermined to have a war with that country so soon as a pretext was found I also well knew, and that such was the feeling of a large party in the ⏤United States. ... I thought, if she felt such cause existed, she should make the war *herself,* upon the right grounds.[15]

The fact—in which Professor Justin H. Smith found disproof of Polk's instigation or sanction of the Stockton intrigue —that Stockton's *written* instructions from Secretary Bancroft caution him to preserve American neutrality "unless Mexico herself should commence hostilities" is in no way inconsistent with Polk's *secret* sanction of an enterprise in which it was intended that *the United States should not appear as the instigator.* Indeed, we find rather a confirmation of Jones's account even in these written instructions, in which Polk consistently assumes the Rio Grande to be the boundary and arbitrarily tells his agents so to consider it and to view any attempt by Mexico to protect her occupation (for she was then actually occupying) the

---

[13] Jones, *Memoranda,* 46–52. See also 76–77, 95–97, 583.

[14] Quoted from New Orleans *Jeffersonian Republican* in *Democratic Statesman* (Nash-

ville), June 7, 1845, 136; and in *Niles' Register* (Baltimore), LXVIII, 213.

[15] Jones, *Memoranda, loc. cit.*

"disputed" territory as a "hostile invasion" of Texas. Observe further that, while Texas was not yet annexed, Stockton was advised: "In the interim should any foreign power invade Texas, the Texans themselves should be *encouraged* to repel the invasion." [16] Is this not precisely in accord with what Jones says of Polk's intrigue through Stockton? Similarly, Polk's organ, the Washington *Union,* declared on June 2 (on the basis of reports from Texas):

Intelligence had been received that the Mexicans were crossing the Rio del Norte under General Arista, and taking possession of an immense and valuable portion of the territory on the east side of that river. But is it possible that Mexico can be so infatuated as to believe that their mere occupancy of a territory, to which they have no legitimate pretension, can give them any shadow of claim to any portion of the country in which their troops may happen to be quartered at the moment of annexation? ... Our Government is prepared for any issue. Our squadron is off the coast. Three thousand troops will be on the borders of Texas to preserve our just rights and protect her from invasion.

This and abundant other evidence shows beyond doubt that Polk was quite aware that the Mexicans merely planned to maintain their claim to the "disputed" territory to which they had every right— that there was no intention to invade Texas proper. There is an evident hypocrisy in Polk's attitude towards the boundary question which Polk's apologists have tried in vain to ignore or read away, and which cannot easily be reconciled with his assumed peaceableness towards Mexico. That Polk favored the scheme to usurp the "disputed" territory—which rightly should have been left to diplomatic adjustment—is indicated again when the *Union* adds in the same piece

[16] Bancroft to Stockton, April 22, June 2, June 15, 1845, MSS. in Department of State, Washington, D.C.; also edited by C. T. Neu in *New Spain and the Anglo-American West: Historical Contributions Presented to Herbert Eugene Bolton* (Lancaster, 1932), II, 88–91.

of June 2: "But it is highly probable, if Gen. Arista does not retire ... the Texas volunteers will be sufficient to clear and protect their boundary." Indeed, the *Union* had stated as early as May 31 that if Mexico occupied the disputed territory the United States would be justified in driving her out (and it was well known, though naturally the fact was not spoken of, that the Mexicans were *already* in occupation of the territory in question—a fact that the administration found it convenient to try to ignore).

Wickliffe, who applied himself to the furtherance of Stockton's scheme, felt that it would be more efficacious if Polk would formally endorse it in a dispatch to Donelson, which could be used to bring the Texas authorities to accept it. He wrote a guarded letter to Secretary of State Buchanan on May 21 of his and Stockton's understanding with General Sherman as to the rumored Mexican "invasion":

The Texan Genl ... if he is satisfied that the information is correct will order out a sufficient force of Texas troops to expel the Mexican power east of the Rio Grande. Leading men here and elsewhere, say they are prepared at once to march ... I would have seen President Jones and conversed with him upon the subject but he might ask himself the question what right had I a private citizen of Kentucky to call his attention to this or any other matter, concerning the affairs of Texas ... It would be very easy to procure the passage of an act of [the Texas] Congress directing the President to strengthen the western posts and expel all foreign power west of the Rio Grande ... His [Polk's] opinions therefore may control the actions of Congress and if averse to such a movement I think it right Col. Donelson should be authorized to speak them. What will be the effect upon Annexation if Texas now renews the war with Mexico for the purpose of driving her Military and Governmental possessions beyond her claimed limits? What will be the right and duty of the American Government if Texas be admitted as a state and the entire country west of the Nueces so far as it is occupied at all, be occupied by the Mexican Power? If a war is in existence in fact between Texas and Mexico for this boundary at the time annexation is consummated, will not the United States have to interpose her power instantly in giving that aid and protection to the state which the constitution imposes? are questions worthy of the President and his Cabinet immediately if they have not already been considered and decided by them.[17]

Secretary Buchanan was by no means a confidant of the secretive, imperialistic President; and Polk's agents were sedulously representing the occupation scheme as being merely a plan to settle the boundary, keeping reticent as to its necessary result and ulterior object, of war. Perhaps Wickliffe was in some doubt as to whether Polk fully realized the inevitable and serious consequence of such a movement by Texas as he was seeking through Stockton's agency, and wished the President carefully to consider a course that could lead to only one destination. Wickliffe soon abandoned his doubts, if he really had any, and his private reports to Polk himself of June 3 and 4 show him favoring and working heartily for the success of the scheme, which, significantly, he assumes Polk to sanction. On June 3, just before hearing the outcome of Wright's and Sherman's visit to Jones, Wickliffe writes Polk from Galveston: "I shall leave here on Wednesfor Austin. My object is to see Capt Hays who commands the Rangers to see if I can get him to clear the country west of the Nueces of the Mexican military." He adds that he and Stockton after making a reconnaissance of the coast would return to Galveston

when and where we expect to hear through Genl. Sherman the views and wishes of President Jones. Col. Kinney has not yet arrived, neither have we heard from Genl. Sherman.

Fortunately Col. Donelson arrived on Saturday evening, and we will be governed

by his advice. It is my opinion, however, that Prest. Jones will discountenance the movement, under the impression that the United States will have the right and will be bound to remove the Mexican military from the east of the Rio Grande after annexation takes place. Would not this be an act of war upon Mexico by the United States?

Thus was Polk's apprehension reflected! The next day, June 4, Wickliffe further reported to Polk:

On last night Genl. Sherman returned from the seat of Government after having seen Prest. Jones and his cabinet. He explained to them the object of his visit, immediately on his arrival. They all, and at first President Jones, concurred on the propriety of removing the Mexicans west of the River Rio Grande. Genl. Sherman was directed to call next morning for a final decision. He did so and the President informed him that tho he saw the propriety and admitted the necessity of the movement which Genl. Sherman proposed yet he was so situated that he could not issue a proclamation without doing violence to any understanding which existed. When pressed harder upon this subject he at once said he expected to hear in a few days from Mexico as to her final determination and until he heard from her he could not without violating his pledge authorize any movement on the frontier... Genl. Sherman then remarked to him that he must be aware of the power vested in him Genl. Sherman by the act of Congress to call out the militia to defend the country without wating the orders of the President. He replied he was, but that he would esteem it as a personal favour if he would not act and that he might rest assured events in a few days would remove all obstacles against prompt action and co-operation on the part of the Executive... Genl. Sherman says that he does not believe that the cabinet concurred with the President at least one of them told him, as he did not.[18]

Donelson, at New Orleans when Stockton began his intrigue in Texas, heard a rumor that Stockton had actually "sailed to Santiago, to co-operate with

[17] Wickliffe to Buchanan, May 21, 1845, private, MS. in Department of State; published in New Spain and the Anglo-American West, II, 82–86.

[18] Wickliffe to Polk, June 3 and June 4, 1845, in Polk MSS. (in Library of Congress). Cf. Texas National Register (Washington), June 12, 1845; Telegraph and Texas Register (Houston), June 4, 1845.

General Sherman of the Texan militia in defending the occupation of the Rio Grande." On reaching Galveston, the Minister found the rumor inaccurate. On June 4, after interviewing the parties to the intrigue, he wrote to Secretary Buchanan, in a vein which shows that he had fallen in with the plan:

> From ... General Sherman, of the Texan militia, it appears that Mexico has already about seven thousand troops on the Rio Grande ... I will go tomorrow to see President Jones, who, I trust, will be prepared to take the steps which the safety of his country calls for in this critical emergency ... I look upon war with Mexico as inevitable—a war dictated by the British minister here for the purpose of defeating annexation, and ... to deprive both Texas and the United States of all claim to the country between the Nueces and the Rio Grande.[19]

Allen, the Texan Secretary of State, wrote to Jones, significantly, that the intriguers had also approached him and represented themselves as acting by authority from Polk. He says in his letter of June 5 that these

unaccredited and informal ... agents, acting in pretended behalf of the United States, are endeavoring to take advantage of the crisis to hurry us into hostilities with Mexico ... Until the terms from Mexico shall have been definitely rejected, I cannot apprehend danger of attack from that quarter. In the meantime could any possible harm, disadvantage, or danger accrue from a proclaimed armistice? ... Gen. Sherman, who returned from Galveston, is going up to-morrow to see Mr. D. [Donelson], who, as Gen. S. says, approves of a military occupation of the territory west of the Nueces by Texas, *but not as Minister of the United States*. I have only indirect news from Com. Stockton, who, in urging military operations on the part of Texas, seems to act through others, holding himself, in the meantime, wisely aloof. Under the circumstances I think that the policy of Texas should, for the present, be peaceful.[20]

Let Jones continue his narrative from the point where he put Wright and Sherman off, asking for a few days to reflect:

> In a few days ... Capt. Elliot ... returned from Mexico, and brought the preliminary treaty and an acknowledgement of our independence by that country. This enabled me to declare *my* independence of Com. Stockton, and Mr. Wright, Gov. Yell, Major Doneison, Mr. Polk ... I issued my proclamation, making known the Mexican arrangement early in June, and declaring a cessation of hostilities.

Jones's peace proclamation was issued on June 4. Jones heard that Wright and Sherman were on their way back to Washington-on-the-Brassos, hopefully and "in high feather," to learn the outcome of his reflection

> when my proclamation met them at Hamlin's, and dashed all their expectations. Gen. Sherman returned home from there; but Dr. Wright came on and saw me. *One word* settled Com. Stockton's business, and assured him I never had the least idea of *manufacturing a war for the United States*. Soon after which he left our waters and sailed for the Pacific in search of the same *un*pacific object which had brought him to Texas ... Many had been engaged and promised offices in the campaign to Matamoras, who were disappointed, and laid all the blame on me ... The public too were disappointed ... I could have been very popular if I had sanctioned the war scheme ... and probably there was no personal advantage which the United States Government had it in their power to bestow, or no emolument which I could not have stipulated for and received if I had so chosen, by acceding to involve the country afresh in war with Mexico ...
> It is true, the United States made the war *ostensibly* for the DEFENSE of Texas; but, in *reality*, to consummate views of conquest which had been entertained probably for many years, and to wage which, the

[19] Donelson to Buchanan, May 24, June 4, 1845, in *House Executive Documents,* 29 Cong., I sess., No. 2, 47, ·53–54.
[20] Allen to Jones, June 5, 1845, in Jones, *Memoranda,* 467, 468. Jones endorsed on Allen's

letter: "The suggestions in this letter are correct, in my opinion. I will not manufacture a war to please Mr. Polk. Commodore Stockton, through Dr. Wright, and Gen. Sherman, have received an emphatic No. The United States, I believe, have a good enough cause of war as against Mexico. Let their Congress determine. It is not my business to do so.—A.J." *Ibid.*

annexation of Texas afforded a pretext long sought and wished for. Texas never actually needed the protection of the United States; and the *protection* so much talked about... was all a trick...

Had the United States wished to consummate the measure of annexation in peace, that [Mexican] acknowledgment of our independence and that cessation of hostilities [by Jones's proclamation]... would have been *promotive* of such a result, at least... As these acts appeared opposed to Mr. Polk's belligerent policy, they were condemned, and violently censured by his friends; and the "Union" denounced them as "Treason!" in tones of thunder, which were reverberated far and wide over the country.[21]

Donelson, who eventually became convinced of the impolicy of Stockton's "occupation" project and gave Wickliffe and Stockton no support or encouragement in its furtherance after Jones's proclamation, wrote Buchanan on June 11: "Care will be taken to throw the responsibility of aggressive measures on the government of Mexico." [22] But in writing further on June 23 he could not conceal his chagrin because of Jones's defeat of the scheme:

It is the policy of those who are on the side of Mexico... to throw upon the United States the responsibility of a war for the country between the Nueces and the Rio Grande.[23]

Thus terminated the first phase, in Texas, of Polk's warlike policy. Stockton was later heard of in the conquest of California, while Wickliffe, says Jones, "remained as long as he had any hope, and left just in time to escape a legal investigation of his acts," he having "everywhere urged violence and rebellion against the Government of Texas." [24]

Jones's version of the affair—namely, that Stockton was acting by authority for

Polk, while wishing to shield Polk by assuming public responsibility—was no mere afterthought concocted by him years afterwards to assuage his disappointment at having been so violently denounced, and made a scapegoat of, by the annexationists and expansionists. His story finds confirmation in the contemporary report of the British chargé in Texas. Elliot writes to his government on June 11, 1845:

I learnt... from a source of information entirely to be depended upon that Commodore Stockton was using every effort to induce the President to issue a Proclamation calling out Volunteers for the purpose of occupying the Country *to the Rio Grande at once.*

The President frankly admitted to me that such was the case, and told me (I use his own words as nearly as I can remember them) that he said to those parties "I can see not one single motive for Annexation if it is not for security and protection, or if we are *to do our own fighting,* and I tell you plainly that I will not be made the scape goat in such an affair as you have proposed to me. The United States Government must take all the responsibility, and all the expense and labour of hostile movements upon Mexico. I will issue no Proclamation of the kind you wish, and authorize no movement *unless Mexico makes a movement upon us.* Somebody else must break up the state of peace. It shall not be me." You will see by the Proclamation that he has kept his word, and I remark already that it is a heavy blow to the violent partizans of the scheme here. Donelson... will probably enough disavow Stockton and at all events the Proclamation will be a sad disappointment to him... The American force here consists of "Princeton" (Steamer), "Saratoga" and St. Mary's Corvettes of 20 guns each, and Purpoise 10 gun brig. Their main business here is to spend money or as they have it in the U.S. to "log roll." [25]

[21] Jones, *Memoranda,* 51–54.
[22] Donelson to Buchanan, June 11, 1845, in *Senate Documents,* 29 Cong., I sess., No. 1, 68.
[23] Donelson to Buchanan, June 23, 1845, in *ibid.,* 83.
[24] Jones, *Memoranda,* 96–97.

[25] Elliot to Bankhead, Galveston, June 11, 1845, in *Southwestern Historical Quarterly,* xx, 181–184. [Reprinted by permission.] Regarding the occupation scheme Elliot wrote again on July 3: "Hence all the rumors of the Mexican Movement beyond that river in the prints of this Country [the United States] and Texas, and the extreme vexation which followed the President's proclamation of the

This seems sufficient corroboration of Jones's statement of his dealings with Wright, Stockton, and Sherman. Donelson, says Jones,

though originally engaged in the same cause, yet stood rather aloof himself, probably because, as he was the *authorized* minister of the United States, he was so instructed, lest he compromit the Government in a scheme which, although they desired its success, they dared not too openly avow; and finally, no doubt, because he became alarmed at the bold infamy of the plan... He has not, however, been quite able to conceal his chagrin and mortification at my defeat of all the schemes of this cabal; for this appears too plainly in his letters to Mr. Buchanan in 1845... While the President of the United States was acting the pious *"mawworm"* in reference to pretended "interference" on the part of France and England in the affairs of Texas, he was himself actively engaged in carrying on the most disgraceful system of intrigue.[26]

Sam Houston also gave Donelson credit for holding largely aloof from the intriguing of Stockton and Wickliffe, and later wrote the Minister that "Nothing but respect for President Polk has prevented the exposure of their conduct." [27] Ashbel Smith, Texan Secretary of State and ambassador, took the same view of the origin of the proposed campaign by Sherman:

Its purpose was by exasperating Mexico to destroy the prospects of peace... This project seems to have originated in the United States... for after the passage of the annexation resolutions by the American congress, the same policy of sending the Texas militia to the Rio Grande was vehemently urged on President Jones by the agents of the administration at Wash-

ington. Its purpose was to provoke Mexico to strike the first blow in the war which was deemed not improbable to grow out of annexation.[28]

Even if we had not evidence so positive of Polk's prime motivation behind the scene, it would be almost impossible to believe that his agents would without his sanction have assumed the grave responsibility of thus inciting Texas to precipitate a Mexican war. We find still further evidence: Wickliffe's suggestion to Polk in his dispatch to Secretary Buchanan of May 21, noted above, bore fruit in the following dispatch to Donelson, written by Buchanan for Polk on June 15 (before news of Jones's proclamation of June 4 blasting the intriguer's plans had reached Washington):

I shall proceed to present to you the views of the President upon the subject. There are many reasons why it is preferable that Texas herself should drive the intruders from her territory... The expenses of such an expedition must eventually be borne by the United States.[29]

It is strange that Polk's apologists should have overlooked this expression of Polk's wishes, which is so explicit! Stockton, who had perhaps originally suggested the intrigue to Polk, was faithful to the end in concealing the fact of Polk's having sanctioned and authorized its execution. His report of October 24, 1845, to Secretary Bancroft is quite circumspect:

Having performed, in the best way I could, the duty assigned to me in Texas, I returned to the United States, to bring the glad tidings of annexation, and to explain to you my views (the importance of which I no doubt overrated) in regard to our relations with Mexico. During those conversations I stated to you that I thought Mexico would probably, when ready commence hostilities... My great object in the first place was to be prepared, in the event

---

4th Utimo." *Ibid.,* xx, 277 278. See also Eliot to Aberdeen, June 15, 1845, in *ibid.,* xx, 185.

[26] Jones, *Memoranda,* 96–98.

[27] Houston to Donelson, December 9, 1845, in *Tennessee Historical Magazine,* iii, 160, 161. Houston assured Donelson that the intriguers wished him (Donelson) "at old Nick" for not joining in their plan to override Jones and to carry out their military project in spite of his opposition.

[28] Ashbel Smith, *Reminiscences of the Texas Republic* (Galveston, 1876), 66, 67.

[29] Buchanan to Donelson, June 15, 1845, in *House Executive Documents,* 29 Cong., i sess., No. 2, 135.

of a war with Mexico, to try to do something creditable to the navy.[30]

When news came to him that President Jones had opposed his belligerent design and declined to be his cat's-paw, Polk, it seems, was no little incensed, and could not refrain from expressing his chagrin. "Donelson has just received," Allen writes Jones on July 2, "a despatch from Mr. Buchanan... His despatch evinces a high state of excitement, not only among the people of the United States, but also in the Executive Cabinet, on the Texan Relations." [31] Why had Donelson not forced the scheme over the head of President Jones? That Donelson well understood Polk's desire and hand behind Stockton's project appears plainly in his references to the matter in his dispatches of July 2 and 11, 1845, to his government, complaining of Jones's not being "willing to fight" for the Rio Grande claim. Donelson wrote in that of July 2 (which, along with the subsequent one of July 11, Jones describes as "a labored apology for not *forcing* on the scheme of the United States Government through Stockton"):

It appeared wiser to me to look for some advantage from the assailing movement threatened by Mexico, than to risk the passage of such a law as Congress were disposed to pass, over the veto of the Presi-

[30] Stockton to Bancroft, Norfolk, October 24, 1845, in *Life of Com. Robert F. Stockton* (New York, 1856), 95, 96. This letter was in acknowledgment of orders to take the "Congress" to the Pacific. His "sealed" instructions, to be opened when he was "beyond the capes of Virginia," were that he should watch California and take that province whenever news of war between the United States and Mexico should reach him. How ardent an expansionist he was may be seen from his speech in Philadelphia in December, 1847, after his joint conquest, with Fremont, of California, which made him a lion of the hour. In *ibid.,* 169–178.
[31] Allen to Jones, July 2, 1845, in Jones, *Memoranda,* 476. Jones endorsed Allen's letter: "The United States Government have heard I have made peace with Mexico, which disappoints them in their hopes of my taking the initiative in bringing on a war. '*Inde hae lachrymae.*' Let them howl.—A. J." *Ibid.*

dent, putting the Texan force under the command of the major general, the effect of which would have been the immediate expulsion of all Mexican soldiers found on the east bank of the Rio Grande. If by such a law the whole of the Texan claim, in respect to limits, could have been taken out of dispute, its passage would have been insisted on [by Donelson]; but as there would have remained all the Santa Fe region, it occurred to me well enough that the subject is left as it is by this Congress.[32]

Donelson was further apologetic with regard to the boundary matter in his dispatch of July 11:

The joint resolutions of our Congress left the question an open one... [Jones's proclamation leaves] the question precisely as it stood when our joint resolutions passed— Mexico in possession of one portion of the territory, and Texas of another. If the President of Texas, instead of giving the proclamation the scope he did, had made it conditional upon the withdrawal of all Mexican authority to the west bank of the Rio Grande, or on failure thereof had notified Mexico that forcible measures would have been continued, to maintain the jurisdiction of Texas as far as that river, the case would have been different, and our rights and duties consequent upon an invasion of Texas, after her acceptance of our proposals, would have been accordingly changed... The proclamation... seemed to me inconsistent with the expectation that in defense of the claim of Texas our troops should march immediately to that river. What the Executive of Texas had determined not to fight for, but to settle by negotiation, to say the least of it, could as well be left to the United States on the same conditions...
There were many circumstances making it inexpedient in my judgment, after the issue of the proclamation referred to, for Texas to attempt a forcible possession of the Rio Grande, relying on the aid of the United States to maintain it. Leaving out of

[32] Donelson to Buchanan, July 2, 1845, in *House Executive Documents,* 29 Cong., I sess., No. 2, 79. Jones remarks indignantly on this that Donelson "saw in the precipitate flight of Mr. Wickliffe from the country, as well as from other indications too palpable not to be perceived by him, that he was greatly mistaken when he told Mr. Buchanan that he could *safely* interfere with my constitutional functions." *Memoranda,* 97.

view the difficulty of conducting such an enterprise against the consent of the Executive, ... Texas, by remaining passive, had an effectual shield in the aversion of the Mexican population [of northern Mexico] to war, and is gradually strengthening her ability to introduce, by peaceable means, her authority as far up the Rio Grande as she may please.

It is also apparent that no military expedition within the power of Texas to start, at this late period, could have placed the entire question of limits beyond the necessity of future negotiation ...

But whilst from such views I encouraged no aggressive movement on the part of Texas to take forcible possession of the Rio Grande, I have nevertheless omitted no opportunity of satisfying all parties here that the United States would, in good faith, maintain the claim.

Donelson sums up the matter baldly: "I have been far from admitting that the claim of Texas to the Rio Grande ought not to be maintained. This was not the question. It was whether, under the circumstances, we should take a position to make war for this claim, in face of an acknowledgement on the part of this [the Texas] government that it could be settled by negotiation." [33] As late as August 14 Donelson was still apologetic: "But for that [Mexican] treaty and the proclamation which grew out of it, our position on the question of boundary would have been less embarrassed. On

this subject, however, I wish to make explanations, as soon as I can visit Washington." [34]

In these dispatches of Donelson's after the abortion of the affair (which were published by Congress) Jones saw

a labored apology for not *forcing* on the scheme of the United States Government through Stockton, by procuring action on the subject by Congress or the Convention, and thus "manufacturing a war" *against the consent* of the Executive of Texas, and over his veto. In his efforts to throw blame upon me in opposing this scheme so anxiously prosecuted by Mr. Polk through his agents here, Major Donelson unwittingly has shown that the whole blame of the war with Mexico rests with the Government of the United States.

Jones says that Donelson, while at first favoring Polk's plan of making war by the instrumentality of Texas, became alarmed at Jones's opposition and the infamy of the plan, gave it up as impracticable, and after Jones's peace proclamation "has had the precaution to *seem* to denounce it from the beginning." Jones says:

I stated, on many occasions, to him my objections to the whole scheme attempted through Com. Stockton, not only of its impropriety, but its impolicy as far as Texas was concerned; and to get up a quarrel about a disputed territory and take forcible possession of Matamoras, under pretext of asserting our claim to the Rio Grande, by the "aid and comfort of the United States," just as we were on the eve of merging our separate nationality in theirs, could not in the least affect the justice of our claim, (favorably,) or aid in its ultimate adjustment in our favor ... His assertion ... that my "proclamation of a truce without stipulating that Mexico should withdraw her troops from Texas, was a virtual relinquishment of the claim of Texas to the boundary of the Rio Grande," is a very idle one, and savors more of spleen than knowledge of international law ... The *"status quo"* was not in the least affected by the proclamation at all. The "boundary and other

---

[33] Donelson to Buchanan, July 11, 1845, in *ibid.*, 89, 90; *Senate Documents*, 29 Cong., I sess., No. I, 102. Donelson, as Jones believed, probably had a revulsion from the infamy of the conquest plan. Of Polk's ordering General Taylor to the Rio Grande in 1846, which precipitated the War with Mexico, Donelson says: "I was one of those who regretted the movement ... in as much as the question of limits was one of negotiation unless Congress gave it a different character. Foreseeing that Mexico could give us no indemnity but land and dreading the application of the annexation principle ... I would have preferred almost any expedient to an aggressive measure." Donelson to Calhoun, January 8, 1848, in Boucher and Brooks, "Correspondence addressed to John C. Calhoun, 1837–1849," in American Historical Association *Report*, 1929, 421. In the disputed soil Texas held only Corpus Christi, on the west bank of the Nueces.

[34] Donelson to Buchanan, August 14, 1845, in *House Executive Documents*, 29 Cong., I sess., No. 2, 99.

questions were to be settled by negotiation," and not by occupation.[35]

The active British agent, Elliot, "the man with the white hat," also saw in Donelson's published dispatches confirming proof of what Jones had told him, that Polk had been behind the intrigue:

I had for some time been sensible that the disposal of this coveted Mexican territory was the single consideration left of any real moment in these affairs, and that it was highly desirable that colourable Texian occupation ... be suddenly intruded within it, before this Republic formally signified its willingness to join the North American Confederation... I was informed of plots in preparation ... for the seizure of the territory [of Mexico] which was not lost to her, nominally to [by] the Texian Militia, really by other Agency, and arms and funds... This correspondence confirms the impression I ... communicated to Mr. Bankhead at the time, namely, that the suspension of hostilities by proclamation of the Government had disturbed the fulfilment of dangerous purposes against Mexico.[36]

There is plentiful testimony of the disappointment of the schemers when Jones interposed his proclamation, which they

[35] Jones, Memoranda, 77, 78. Other contemporaries saw the same significance in Donelson's published dispatches. Edward D. Mansfield, The Mexican War (New York, 1852), 23.
[36] Elliot to Aberdeen, February 16, 1846, in Southwestern Historical Quarterly, XXI, 192. [Reprinted by permission.] On November 14, 1845, Elliot assured Aberdeen that it was now "generally understood by the people of Texas" that American desire to give them military "protection" and the desire of many of the Texans for the intrusion of American troops was "not attributable to any well founded apprehension of Mexican invasion, but chiefly to surrender the Country forthwith into Military possession of the Executive of the United States, for the purpose of overawing the friends of the independence of the Republic, and of silencing any inconvenient reconsideration of the subject in the Legislature of the United States. A state of actual war with Mexico would probably have that last effect; and a pretext for suddenly engaging the force in Texas and proceedings of still further aggression and invasion upon Mexico, rendering collision inevitable, could always be found at a short notice." Ibid., xx, 395; cf. Jones, Memoranda, 408.

feared to try to override. James Morgan wrote to Jones, from Galveston:

He [Sherman] was disappointed—greatly so, and thinks you humbugged him! For my part I was willing to see him go ahead ...Now if Sherman had once got 2,000 men together, the Rio Grande would not have been the stopping place (in my opinion). Some four or five of the Mexican States would most assuredly have fallen into the hands of the conquerors, and perhaps all Mexico...No one appeared to me more upset by your proclamation than Com. Stockton. I met him at Galveston.[37]

Polk expressed his mortification at the failure of his agents, and this not merely in a dispatch to Donelson, as seen above; Jones says that W. D. Lee, Texan envoy at Washington, wrote him in effect on September 13: "Mr. Polk, Mr. Walker, Mr. Marcy, and Mr. Ritchie [editor of the Union] are excessively angry that you did not agree to the proposals made by Com. Stockton, and authorize Gen. Sherman to invade Mexico. They wanted you to manufacture a war for the United States." [38] Jones adds, as to Buchanan:

[37] Morgan to Jones, July 12, 1845, in Jones, Memoranda, 478, 479. On the other hand, General Edwin Morehouse wrote Jones from near Gonzales, on July 17: "The people of the west feel gratified that the President put a stop on the Gen. Sherman & Co's. intention of sending Texas troops for their protection...It is all humbug as to Mexicans concentrating on the frontier." Ibid., 479. For Wickliffe's chagrin see his dispatch to Buchanan, June 13, 1845, in New Spain and the Anglo-American West, II, 89, 90. Wickliffe was one of the most rabid defenders of the Mexican War.
[38] Jones's endorsement on W. D. Lee to Jones, September 8, 1845, in Memoranda, 491, 492. In this endorsement Jones says that he has mislaid Lee's letter of September 13, but that it "was very explicit" and "clearly connects Mr. Polk and the Government with Com. Stockton, Mr. Wickliffe, Gov. Yell, and Mr. Donelson in the attempt to induce me to get up a war with Mexico." Jones adds the following later endorsement on Lee's letter of September 8: "Note.—Nov., 1850. I met Mr. Wm. D. Lee, formerly Chargé d'affaires of Texas near the Government of the United States, (acting,) in the city of New York, several times during this month, and had frequent conversations with him on the subject of his letter of the 13th September, 1845, now mislaid. He recollected the contents, and fully

"I do not think he had any thing to do with the cabal who were endeavoring to drive me into an adoption of hostile measures with Mexico. If he co-operated with them, it was from overexcited fears of English and French interference, and . . . in entire ignorance of the ulterior designs of those engaged in 'manufacturing a war.' " This seems a just estimate of Buchanan's part considering that on the outbreak of the Mexican War he suggested (but was the only cabinet member to favor) a public declaration that the United States intended no conquest of territory—a proposal that Polk, of course, would not listen to for a moment.

Those historians who have summarily rejected Jones's testimony would seem tacitly to consider his endorsements (which appear to be contemporary, to have been written in 1845 or as dated) mere later fabrications—and this for no reason except that Jones's version is "inconsistent" with Polk's "peaceable" Slidell mission. This assumption of gross dishonesty in Jones is utterly without proof and rests on very doubtful premise and assumptive reasoning. That Jones's statements are not mere fabrications conceived apologetically years later is shown by Charles Elliot's corroborative testimony in 1845. The British agent alluded significantly to what President Jones had told him when he wrote Jones, on June 12, 1845, of the disappointment of the intriguers at Galveston: "The proclamation seems to have been a blow to certain parties here. It was hugely wished that you should do the work of provoking hostilities, and that somebody else should

reap the advantage." [39] Jones also tells us: "Mr. J. C. Eldridge, formerly acting Secretary of State, who was sent to Washington in the summer of this year, informed me on his return, of the deep anxiety expressed by Polk for a war with Mexico." [40]

After the failure of the Stockton expansion scheme Polk turned to a new plan of coercion—the Slidell mission. Was he now really disposed to settle disputes with Mexico amicably, and renounce his designs on California if Mexico would yield merely the territory claimed by Texas, in satisfaction of the American claims? Or was the Slidell mission simply a hoax, its abortion foreseen and intended, its aim to make Mexico appear as an intransigent villain in order to justify a demand for a declaration of war by Congress? The writer believes (partly on the basis of evidence that has been overlooked) that the latter supposition is the more probable. The Slidell mission cannot be discussed here. Nor can we examine extensively its relation to American military movements in Texas after her acceptance of annexation (July, 1845). Immediately upon this Texan acceptance,

[39] Jones, Memoranda, 469. If Jones had fabricated his version of Stockton's intrigue in reference to Polk is it likely that he would have made the statement—so apparently weakening to his case—that he had "mislaid" Lee's letter of September 13, 1845? Would he not rather, for better verisimilitude, have simply forged such a Lee letter and inserted it among the other Lee letters of 1845 (which are given in full) in his Memoranda? It is the present writer's impression, from a study of Jones's career and his Memoranda generally, that Jones was a conscientious and honest man (albeit somewhat equivocal in denying that he had opposed annexation); and this is the impression of Texas historians generally.

[40] Endorsement on Lee to Jones, September 8, 1845, in ibid., 492. Colonel Eldridge returned to Texas late in September, 1845, serving the American government conveniently as "bearer of despatches from Washington to Gen. Taylor, at Corpus Christi." He reached Washington, Texas, on September 30. Texas National Register (Washington), October 2, 1845. On Polk's criticism of Jones, see Lee to Jones, October 20, 1845, in Jones, Memoranda, 499.

corroborates the fact as stated in the endorsement. . . The purpose of Mr. Polk and some of his Cabinet to induce me to 'manufacture a war with Mexico,' and their deep disappointment at my not complying with their views, was clearly and distinctly avowed by them to him, not once merely, but on repeated occasions." Ibid., 492. Unpublished MSS. Diary of Jones, 1850–51 (in the Texas State Library), records that he frequently dined with Lee in the winter of 1850.

Polk sent General Taylor with an army into the new state with instructions to occupy and protect its "frontier," which was confidently described to the General as the Rio Grande. All through the summer and autumn of 1845 Taylor was *subtly encouraged, but not explicitly ordered,* to march to the Rio Grande and occupy "the whole of Texas." The instructions sent him by Secretary of War Marcy were masterpieces of that cunning, deviousness and underhandedness which characterized Polk, whose policy it was never to assume responsibility for unscrupulous or invidious acts he wanted done if he could shift it to some cat's-paw. Consider Marcy's dispatch to Taylor of July 30, 1845:

> The Rio Grande is claimed to be the boundary ... and up to this you are to extend your position, only excepting any posts on the eastern side thereof, which are in the actual occupancy of Mexican forces, or Mexican settlements over which Texas did not exercise jurisdiction at the period of annexation, or shirtly before that event. It is expected that ... you will approach as near the boundary line—the Rio Grande— as prudence will dictate ... The President desires that your position ... should be near the river Nueces.[41]

Taylor *appears* to be ordered to move to the Rio Grande to occupy the "Texas" (now "American") territory west of the Nueces—while at the end of the dispatch are inconspicuously inserted a few saving words, wholly inconsistent with what preceded: "The President desires that your position ... should be near the river Nueces"! This last clause saves the President and will enable him later, if Taylor advances, to make the General the scape-goat of the aggression upon Mexico! Quite conscious of Polk's wish that he should go to the Rio Grande, Taylor noted that his orders were so equivocally worded as to place on his shoulders too great a share and burden of responsibility—so he remained at Corpus Christi, advising the administration that he would advance when explicitly ordered to do so.[42] Polk's apologists have been loath to perceive in Taylor's instructions this insidious character, which is nevertheless unmistakable. Only when Polk finally assumed full responsibility and expressly ordered Taylor to the Rio Grande on January 13, 1846, did the cautious General make the advance movement so long desired by his intriguing superiors. Was this order of Polk's peaceable in intent, as his apologists insist, or was it well calculated underhandedly to provoke the war which he now avowedly desired? (And he could scarcely have been so optimistic as to believe that, even after Slidell's failure in Mexico, he could produce war *constitutionally* by inducing Congress, on the mere basis of the claims, to declare it—a scheme that even President Jackson had tried in vain.) As to this, we will note only one fact which the late apologists of the war have failed to mention: namely, that some days before the issuance of his war message in May, 1846, Polk more than once remarks in his *Diary*, with evident anxiety and chagrin, that *he has not heard from* the "frontier," where he *anticipates*, using his own words, "a collision between the American and Mexican forces"—if he could only hear of which, he says, he would hesitate no longer, and send a war

[41] *House Executive Documents*, 29 Cong., 1 sess., No. 196, 70–71. Marcy's correspondence with Taylor is also found in *ibid.*, 30 Cong., 1 sess., No. 60. On the insidious character of Marcy's instructions, and Taylor's reactions, see also Oliver Otis Howard, *General Taylor* (New York, 1897), 91, 92; Hitchcock, *Fifty Years in Camp and Field, passim;* George Meade, *George Gordon Meade* (New York, 1913), I, *passim.*

[42] This southwestern border episode seems to the writer to find close parallel in that of 1836, in which President Jackson and General E. P. Gaines play the rôles played later by Polk and Taylor, but which was more complicated by the presence of other factors. Stenberg, "The Texas Schemes of Jackson and Houston, 1829–1836," in *Southwestern Social Science Quarterly*, xv, 229–250 (December, 1934).

message to Congress![43] Polk knew from the very beginning of his administration that Mexico was disposed to defend her occupancy and ownership of the "disputed" territory, a fact which has been obscured and even denied by Polk's apologists but which has been made sufficiently clear in this paper; thus his anticipation that the seizure of this (rightly Mexican) territory would result in hostilities was by no means new to his mind when he made the above confession, so inadvertently, in his *Diary*. A few days after the first querulous entry his anticipation was justified, news arriving of the engagements at Palo Alto and Resaca de la Palma on the Rio Grande, the "frontier"; he was then able to subordinate the claims against Mexico and to demand war of Congress on the ground that it existed in fact by the Mexicans' having "invaded" and shed American blood "on American soil." Without these hostilities —without his act which provoked them —it is extremely improbable that Polk could have induced Congress to make a war on Mexico, upon the grounds ostensibly of claims. Contemporary observers reject the idea that he could have succeeded in doing so. The private claims were, during the war, thrust more and more by Polk into the public eye by way of justification, to offset criticism of his usurpation of the boundary; but this could little conceal his aggression and real motive for war—his desire to seize northern Mexico from the Nueces to the Pacific—which the general public, infected strongly by the spirit of "manifest destiny," approved.

The strength of Polk's policy of expansion by covert aggression lay in the popular support he could count upon in bringing on war if Mexico should plausibly be presented as the aggressor. Confining his secret plans of conquest to the discreet circle of his immediate agents and advisers, and leaving the public to learn them only through events, Polk soon after the war began hypocritically assured the New York Democratic leaders —and doubtless others—that he "had no schemes of conquest in view in respect to Mexico, no intention to take possession of any portion of her territory with a view to hold it"![44] If he openly avowed his intention of taking a large territorial indemnity (which he had determined upon long before the actual coming of the war), the world would perhaps be even less credulous of his inconsistent assertions that he was waging a war "commenced by Mexico" to "redress American grievances." Even by magnifying the private claims—which could not be taken seriously as *cause* for a large and costly war—the apologists have not been able to make a very plausible case for "peaceable Polk," for vain is their endeavor to ignore or read away Polk's aggressive view and belligerent handling of the Texas boundary question, a matter in which contemporaries perceived the most significant key to the Mexican War and its instrumental cause. In conclusion, it may be noted that the foregoing view of an intriguing, war-desiring Polk invites one to accept fully, with regard to the much-mooted question of Frémont's activities in California, his own asseverations that he had been instructed secretly by Polk, through the messenger Gillespie and his father-in-law, Senator Benton, to seize or revolutionize California "if necessary to anticipate England."

[43] Quaife, ed., *The Diary of James K. Polk*, I, 379, 384–386 (May 5–9, 1846).

[44] John A. Dix to Silas Wright, July 10, 1846, in Morgan Dix, *Memoirs of John A. Dix* (New York, 1883), I, 202.

7

Northern Diplomacy
and European Neutrality

NORMAN A. GRAEBNER

The outbreak of the Civil War was the signal for the beginning of a diplomatic duel between North and South to capture the favor of the European nations, for everybody realized that the outcome of the war would be decisively affected by Europe's attitudes and policies. The Confederates did not expect direct military aid from the powers. They did, however, hope that England, France, and Russia would recognize their belligerent status (which would enable them to enjoy certain important rights under international law) and their independence, contest many of the Union's maritime practices (such as, the long-range blockade and the blockade of neutral ports, the application of the doctrine of continuous voyage to blockade and to contraband, and the extension of the contraband list), supply arms, ammunition, and ships, and, above all, mediate in the conflict to bring the fighting to an end on the basis of Southern independence. The federal government, on the other hand, aimed only to frustrate Southern diplomatic efforts.

Of the principal European powers, Russia, from the outset, favored the Union cause and never once contemplated acceding to Confederate diplomatic entreaties. The British and French governments, however, sympathized markedly with the South, yet they helped very little. All they did was recognize Confederate belligerency—in which action, as a matter of fact, the North preceeded them, for when Lincoln ordered the blockade of the South's ports, he tacitly recognized belligerency because only a belligerent can be blockaded—and provide a limited amount of military goods. They did not seriously challenge Northern maritime practices, nor did they mediate.

Historians have differed widely in ascribing reasons for the failure of Paris and London (principally London, because France would not have dared move without England's leadership) to take decisive action on behalf of the South. Some have pointed to the restraining influence of the British working classes, which viewed the North as champion of democracy and free labor; others have maintained that Union practices on the high seas were setting valuable precedents that would be extremely useful to England if, at some future time, the roles of England and America would be reversed; still others have emphasized British reluctance to cut off the lucrative Anglo-American trade.

Norman A. Graebner, who teaches American diplomatic history at the University of Illinois and who has written widely and perceptively on the subject,

FROM David Donald, ed., *Why the North Won the Civil War* (Baton Rouge: Louisiana State University Press, 1960), pp. 49–75. By permission of the publishers.

offers, in the essay that follows, yet another explanation of the failure by Britain and France to mediate. For him, the answer must be sought in the "realities of power." The European nations would not intervene "without the assurance of ultimate Southern success" and "until the South had demonstrated the power required to establish and maintain its independence." To have done otherwise would have been contrary to the European diplomatic tradition. And when, after the great Northern victories at Gettysburg and Vicksburg in 1863, it became clear that the South could not win the war, any possibility of mediation rapidly disappeared.

Major Robert Anderson's surrender of Fort Sumter in April, 1861, placed an unprecedented burden on American diplomacy. Not since the American Revolution had the foreign relations of the United States been reduced to a defense of the Republic's very existence. Diplomacy, to be sure, was only one element in the vast arsenal of resources upon which Northern leadership could draw to frustrate the South's determination to sever the Union, but from the outset of the struggle it assumed a primary importance. Even limited European power, thrown effectively into the scale against the North, could have rendered the Southern cause successful. The nation's future, therefore, rested on the efficiency of its diplomatic as much as its military corps.

Europe's involvement in the American Civil War comprised a persistent danger to the Union, for the Southern independence movement threatened all the fundamental power relationships between the Old World and the New. Despite its tradition of isolationism toward Europe, the American Republic had become by 1861 a significant force in world politics. Cassius Clay, President Lincoln's choice for the court at St. Petersburg, wrote in April, 1862, that it was "useless to deceive ourselves with the idea that we can isolate ourselves from European interventions. We became in spite of ourselves—the Monroe Doctrine—Washington's farewell—and all that—a part of the 'balance of power.'" To European

leaders the United States was a nation of consequence in world affairs, but the relationship of American strength and American traditions to the precise interests of Europe varied from country to country.

London promised to become the focal point of all wartime diplomatic maneuvering, for Britain was the dominant power of Europe and her control of Canada and the sea lanes of the north Atlantic created extensive commitments in the New World. France was equally concerned over events in America but lacked the power to escape the British lead. Keeping such interested and calculating nations neutral became the chief task of Northern diplomacy.

Fortunately for the North, Anglo-American relations had never been more cordial than they were in 1861. But this was no guarantee of British neutrality. Britain's powerful conservative classes, always cynical toward the democratic experiment of the United States, recognized the fundamental meaning of the American Civil War. Democratic institutions were on trial. The United States as a nation had passed beyond the normal control of Old World power, but if the American people were determined to destroy their national greatness and demonstrate the failure of their institutions, the least that reactionary Europe could do was to encourage them in their effort so that the work of destruction might succeed. British aristocrats had long regarded the American democratic example as a threat to their estate. For them the breakup of the American Union would impede the expansion of democracy everywhere. In July, 1861, *Blackwood's Magazine* declared: "It is precisely because we do *not* share the admiration of America for her own institutions and political tendencies that we do not now see in the impending change an event altogether to be deplored."

British conservatives resented American power and truculence as much as American institutions. What disturbed them especially was the growth of the United States into a formidable maritime rival. Edouard de Stoeckl, the Russian Minister in Washington, lamented in January, 1860, that in the approaching dissolution of the Union Great Britain would experience one of those "strokes of fortune" which occur but rarely in history. England, he predicted, would benefit more than any other nation from the disintegration of American power. "The Cabinet of London," he warned his government, "is watching attentively the internal dissensions of the Union and awaits the result with an impatience which it has difficulty in disguising." From St. Petersburg Cassius Clay warned Lincoln, "I saw at a glance where the feeling of England was. They hoped for our ruin! They are jealous of our power. They care neither for the South nor the North. They hate both."

Western Europe, moreover, had long been indignant at the American effort to keep the Western Hemisphere off limits for further European encroachment. For the ambitious Louis Napoleon of France, especially, events in America were encouraging, for they seemed to be rendering the Monroe Doctrine inoperative. No American fleet would block the contemplated movement of French troops to Vera Cruz or demolish his dreams of establishing a vassal empire in Mexico. A strong and friendly Confederate States of America would create a buffer between what remained of the United States and his new Mexican possessions. Secession appeared so consequential to Europe because it again exposed the western world to European partition. It was no wonder that Stoeckl advised his government in April, 1861, that "England will take advantage of the first opportunity to recognize the seceded States and that France will follow her."

In Washington, Henri Mercier, the French Minister, favored immediate action. He advised his government that in recognizing the Confederacy it would give the American conflict the character of a war and thereby extend to French seamen the benefit of neutral rights. The United States could not complain, he added, because it had recognized the revolutionary governments of Spanish America. Certainly this nation could not be offended merely because other nations accepted its democratic principles of self-determination. Yet Mercier was a realist. He admonished the French Minister in Paris to formulate his American policy only in agreement with the other powers of Europe.

Russia alone of the European states made the preservation of the Union a matter of conscious policy. For Stoeckl the destruction of the Union threatened the equilibrium of world politics. The United States, ran his argument, had become Europe's best guarantee against British aggression and arrogance. Traditional Russian-American friendship had been based on a mutual rivalry toward Great Britain. It had been the case of the enemies of a rival becoming friends. George Mifflin Dallas, when United States Minister at the Czar's court during the Van Buren administration, had recorded this significant phrase of Nicholas I, "Not only are our interests alike, our enemies are the same."

After the outbreak of the Civil War the *Journal of St. Petersburg,* official organ of the Czarist government, declared: "Russia entertains for the United States of America a lively sympathy founded on sentiments of mutual friendship and on common interests. She considers their prosperity necessary to the general equilibrium." Nothing, the Imperial Cabinet agreed, should be permitted to weaken this powerful counterpoise to England. Prince Gortchakov, the Russian Foreign Minister, instructed Stoeckl in July, 1861, to assure the American nation that it could assume "the most cordial sympathy on the part of our August Master, during the serious crisis which it is passing through at present." This *entente cordiale* between the world's greatest despotism and its leading democracy was *Realpolitik* at its diplomatic best, for despite the incompatibility of political principles, it served the best interests of both nations.

William H. Seward, Lincoln's Secretary of State, assumed the essential task of preventing the introduction of European power into the American Civil War. His diplomacy had but one objective—the preservation of the Union. Seward's devotion to this cause was so intense that in April, 1861, he recommended to Lincoln a foreign war, perhaps against Spain and France, to rally the seceded states around the American flag and thus reforge the Union. Lincoln tactfully ignored the proposal, but the Washington diplomatic corps was amazed. Lord Lyons, the British Minister, warned the Foreign Office in London that Seward would be "a dangerous foreign minister." Thereafter the British government regarded the American Secretary with suspicion. Charles Francis Adams, the American Minister in London, reported that Seward was viewed there as "an ogre fully resolved to eat all Englishmen raw." Lord John Russell, the British Foreign Secretary, addressed Lyons in February, 1861: "The success or failure of Mr. Seward's plans to pre-

vent the disruption of the North American Union is a matter of deep interest to Her Majesty's Government." From the opening guns of the war Seward's leadership was a matter of grave concern to the chancelleries of Europe.

To forestall European interference in American affairs after the fall of Sumter, Seward denied officially the existence of any war between North and South. "There is here, as there always has been," he informed the British and French governments, "one political power, namely, the United States of America, competent to make war and peace, and conduct commerce and alliances with all foreign nations." What existed, he explained, was an armed sedition seeking to overthrow the government. Its suppression did not constitute a war or in any manner modify the character, rights, and responsibilities of either the United States or foreign nations in their diplomatic relationships. Seward admitted that international law permitted the recognition of established *de facto* governments; he merely denied that one existed in the South.

What endangered Seward's rigid position toward Europe was the rapid expansion of the conflict between North and South onto the Atlantic. It was fundamental in Lincoln's strategy to weaken and destroy the Southern economy by cutting off Southern shipments of cotton to Europe through a blockade of the Southern ports. Shortly after the crisis of Fort Sumter the Confederate government issued a proclamation calling for privateers, and Lincoln announced his blockade. Seward warned Lyons that the North would tolerate no further European commerce with the South, but he denied that a formal blockade destroyed his own claims that war did not exist. Yet the United States could hardly proclaim a blockade without declaring itself a belligerent and claiming rights over foreign vessels admitted only in time of war. Lyons was disturbed, for the blockade imposed on Europe the choice of recognizing the Confederacy or submitting to the interruption of its commerce with the South.

Britain, fearful of being trapped in a maritime war, took immediate steps to protect her commerce. On May 13, 1861, without awaiting the arrival of Minister Adams, Queen Victoria issued a declaration of neutrality which called upon British subjects to avoid hostilities between the North and South. Soon France, Spain, the Netherlands, and Brazil followed the British lead. This recognition of Southern belligerency granted to Southern ships the privileges in neutral ports accorded the ships of the Federal government.

Washington was shocked at this British action, for it not only suggested collusion between Britain and France but also presaged the diplomatic recognition of the South. Charles Sumner, the Massachusetts Senator, termed the Queen's proclamation "the most hateful act of English history since the time of Charles 2nd." Seward's reaction was even more violent. "They have misunderstood things fearfully, in Europe," he wrote home in May. "Great Britain is in great danger of sympathizing so much with the South for the sake of peace and cotton as to drive us to make war against her, as the ally of the traitors. . . . It will be dreadful but the end will be sure and swift." Through Adams in London, Seward warned the British government, "If any European power provokes war, we shall not shrink from it."

Similarly Seward advised Mercier that French recognition of the Confederacy would result in war with the United States. This nation might be defeated, he admitted bluntly, but France would know that she had been in a war. To William L. Dayton, the American Minister in Paris, Seward wrote: "Foreign intervention would oblige us to treat those who should yield it as allies of the insurrectionary party and to carry on the war against them as enemies. . . . The President and the people of the United States deem the Union, which would then be at stake, worth all the cost and all the sacrifices of a contest with the world at arms, if such a contest should prove inevitable."

European interference meant war, but Seward offered the Old World powers the carrot as well as the stick. He reminded both Britain and France of their long tradition of friendship with the United States and assured them that this nation had cherished that peace. The American Republic, he instructed Adams, was "anxious to avoid all causes of misunderstanding with Great Britain; to draw closer, instead of breaking, the existing bonds of amity and friendship. There is nothing good or great," he added appealingly, "which both nations may not expect to attain or effect if they may remain friends. It would be a hazardous day for both branches of the British race when they should determine to test how much harm each could do the other." The Secretary extended similar assurances to the French: "We have no hostile or interested designs against any other state or nation whatever, and, on the contrary, we seek peace, harmony, and commerce with them all." Seward repeated ceaselessly his contention that the United States was one, and that the nations of Europe should not view themselves as neutrals between two imaginary belligerents in America, but as friends of the United States.

Seward's warnings were not without effect. When Lord Russell learned of the arrival in London of William L. Yancey, the Confederate Commissioner seeking recognition for his government, he wrote to Lyons in Washington: "If it can possibly be helped, Mr. Seward must not be allowed to get us into a quarrel. I shall see the southerners when they come, but unofficially and keep them at a proper distance." But even the unofficial reception of Yancey was too much for Seward. His next letter to Adams was so menacing that Lincoln revised certain passages and removed others. Nor would the President permit Adams to read the dispatch to Russell. Even in revised form the dispatch was little less than an ultimatum. It suggested that Adams break off his relations with the British government if Russell persisted in seeing the Confederate Commissioner. Not content with this warning, Seward invited William Russell, the noted Washington correspondent of the London *Times,* to his home and read to him deliberately the long dispatch with its insinuations that Britain would destroy the American Republic if she could. Russell, he hoped, would not keep his impressions to himself.

Adams regarded the Secretary's warning as little less than a declaration of war. "I scarcely know how to understand Mr. Seward," he admitted. "The rest of the Government may be demented for all I know, but he surely is calm and wise." Adams informed Lord Russell in London that further relations between the British government and the "pseudo-commissioners" of the Confederate States, whether unofficial or not, would be regarded as a manifestation of hostility by the United States. Lord Russell did not receive the Southern Commissioner again. In May the British Minister announced a hands-off policy: ". . . we have not been involved in any way in that contest . . . and for God's sake, let us if possible, keep out of it."

Through Dayton, Seward informed the French Minister that the United States would regard any further communications of his government with the Southern Commissioners as "exceptional and injurious" to American dignity and honor. Even an unofficial reception of the emissaries of disunion, he complained, would give them encouragement to prosecute their effort to destroy the American Republic. Perhaps a warning would be sufficient to relieve the United States of further action, for Seward declared that this nation could not tolerate, whatever the consequences of its resistance, the recognition of the Confederacy by the French government.

Mercier and Lyons in Washington, still determined to commit their nations to a settlement of the American conflict, suggested mediation, with their governments serving as umpires between North and South. Lord Russell judiciously declined and Seward caused the diplomatic corps abruptly to drop what remained of the scheme. In a statement to the governor of Maryland he made it clear that the Federal government would accept no foreign arbitrament in settling its differences with the Confederacy. The American Constitution, he reminded the Europeans, provided all the required means for surmounting internal disorders. Arbitration would endanger the nation's integrity by substituting non-Constitutional devices for the normal functioning of the American system.

United States relations with Britain were unnecessarily disturbed in December, 1861, when Captain Charles Wilkes of the Federal warship *San Jacinto* stopped the British mail steamer *Trent* off the coast of Cuba and removed two Confederate leaders, James M. Mason and John Slidell. These men, among the South's ablest, had been dispatched to London and Paris respectively to replace the earlier commissioners. To the zealous Wilkes their capture was an unprecedented coup, but unfortunately he had broken the cherished maritime principle for which this nation supposedly had fought the British in the War of 1812. In London Henry Adams, son of the American Minister, saw the issue clearly, writing to his brother: "Good God, what's got into you all? What do you mean by deserting now the great principles of our fathers, by returning to the vomit of that dog Great Britain? What do you mean by asserting now principles against which every Adams yet has protested and resisted?" Seward was embarrassed. He faced the necessity of satisfying the British who were wronged and at the same time of protecting American prestige abroad. "If I decide this case in favor of my own government," he admitted, "I must disavow its most cherished principles, and ...forever abandon its essential policy. The country cannot afford the sacrifice. If I maintain those principles, and adhere to that policy, I must surrender the case itself." Seward soon decided on the latter course and conceded to the British with remarkable grace, for nowhere did the *Trent* case challenge his Union policies. "In coming to my conclusion," he wrote to Adams, "I have not forgotten that if the safety of this Union required the detention of the captured persons it would be the right and duty of this government to detain them. But the effective check and waning proportions of the existing insurrection, as well as the comparative unimportance of the captured persons themselves, when dispassionately weighed happily forbid me from resorting to that defense." Federal officials released the two Confederates promptly and sent them on their way. Lord Russell was relieved. He wrote, "I do not believe that Seward has any animosity to this country. It is all buncom."

What gave the South the presumption of success in its effort to secure European recognition was the alleged economic power of cotton. Southern writers in 1861 assumed that Britain would break the Northern blockade to guarantee the flow of cotton into England. "Cotton," declared the Charleston *Mercury*, "would bring England to her knees." *De Bow's Review* in June predicted that a block-ade of the Southern ports would be "swept away by the English fleets of observation hovering on the Southern coasts, to protect English commerce, and especially the free flow of cotton to English and French factories." If cotton were king, the South had only to place an embargo on that commodity to force Britain to destroy the blockade. "Foreign nations will not recognize the independence of the Confederate States," admitted one Southern governor realistically, "until commerce with the Confederate States will become not only desirable, but necessary to their own prosperity." The Confederate Congress refused to establish an embargo, but Committees of Public Safety in the Southern seaport towns effectively halted the export of cotton to Europe.

By the spring of 1862 King Cotton had compelled neither Britain nor France to recognize Southern independence or break the blockade. Confederate efforts to force action in the British government by depriving Lancashire of raw cotton actually had the opposite effect. As one British leader observed, "I wonder the South do not see that our recognition *because* they keep cotton from us would be ignominious beyond measure, & that no English Parlt could do so base a thing." But the British resolve not to break the blockade resulted from a far more fundamental motive than a willingness to dispense with cotton, for the blockade defied America's own precedents and doctrines of neutral maritime rights. In undermining the principle of the Declaration of Paris that blockades to be binding must be effective, the United States was releasing England in a future conflict from this burdensome feature of the past. American action weakened the stand of the smaller maritime powers in their perennial effort to force Great Britain to recognize neutral rights in time of war.

Historians have agreed that cotton

failed as a diplomatic weapon because Britain enjoyed too much lucrative trade with the North, requiring especially huge quantities of Northern grain, and because the textile workers most affected by the cotton famine remained staunch friends of the Union. Professor Ephraim D. Adams has accounted for the allegiance of English workingmen to Lincoln's wartime leadership by citing the general threat to democratic progress imposed by Southern secession. Either the North would triumph or democracy everywhere would be in jeopardy. The eventual Northern success vindicated the democratic system so completely, says Adams, that it led directly to the British Reform Bill of 1867.

Lincoln's Emancipation Proclamation, although designed, at least partially, to influence European attitudes toward the Union cause, had little effect on European sentiment and none on European action. British conservatives thought it foolhardy and anticipated a servile insurrection. Even William E. Gladstone was unmoved by Lincoln's action, reiterating his conviction that "negro emancipation cannot be effected, in any sense favourable either to black or to white by the bloody hand of war, especially of Civil War." British liberals, abolitionists, and workingmen lauded the Proclamation, but these groups had always favored the Union because it represented the cause of democracy. None of these groups, moreover, wielded influence over British policy. Northern diplomatic success found its fundamental explanation less in specific interests and doubts than in a great diplomatic tradition.

Europe's diplomatic tradition cautioned against any recognition of the Confederacy until the South had demonstrated the power required to establish and maintain its independence. Without the assurance of ultimate Southern success, European involvement would assume the risk of either an eventual ig-nominious retreat from a declared diplomatic objective or an unlimited military commitment to guarantee the achievement of Southern independence. Confronted with Europe's traditional realism, the Southern diplomatic cause in London and Paris could be no more successful than the Southern military cause in Virginia and Pennsylvania. Diplomacy reflects the status of power, and Southern power never appeared greater than during the summer and autumn months of 1862.

News of General George B. McClellan's retirement from before Richmond in the early summer of 1862 merely confirmed a general European conviction that the American Union was doomed. To European military experts, diplomats, and statesmen, Northern power seemed incapable of overcoming the defensive nature of the Southern military commitment. The North, Europe understood, enjoyed an immense industrial superiority, but the advantages of strategy, terrain, and leadership appeared to lie with the South. Confederate armies had no obligation to conquer the North, but only to beat off the Union forces. This they appeared capable of doing. In June, 1862, the London *Times* broached the issue of European intervention, convinced that Southern independence was inevitable. "It is plain," said the *Times,* that the time is approaching when Europe will have to think seriously of its relations to the two belligerents in the American war. ... That North and South must now choose between separation and ruin, material and political, is the opinion of nearly every one who, looking impartially and from a distance on the conflict, sees what is hidden from the frenzied eyes of the Northern politicians." Recognition of a successful cause could be both legitimate and effective.

For many British editors and politicians, McClellan's retreat from the peninsula during the summer of 1862 was like redemption. So dominant was the pro-Southern trend in British opinion that Henry Adams wrote from London, "There is no doubt that the idea here is as strong as ever that we must ultimately fail, and unless a very few weeks show some great military result we shall have our hands full in this quarter." Only a decisive Northern victory, he observed, could prevent European intervention. Public hostility, Charles Francis Adams wrote on July 10 to his son in America, was "rising every hour and running harder against us than at any time since the Trent affair." There was nothing to do but retreat. "I shut myself up," he lamented, "went to no parties and avoided contact with everyone except friends." Reports in the British press of the capture of McClellan's entire army, Adams believed, had been fabricated "to carry the House of Commons off their feet" as it commenced its crucial debate on William Shaw Lindsay's resolution calling for a more vigorous pro-Confederate British policy.

In defense of his resolution, Lindsay pointed to the inevitability of final separation between North and South. He declared that the Southern cause was just and that the North would now accept mediation. Lancashire was in distress. Lindsay quoted from a letter written by a mill hand, "We think it high time to give the Southern States the recognition they so richly deserve." Friends of the North were assured that the British Ministry would not be influenced by the parliamentary debate and therefore chose the strategy of permitting the pro-Confederates to wear themselves out against a stone wall of silence. After two days of verbal effort Lindsay asked for a postponement of his motion to "wait for king cotton to turn the screws still further." Somehow the debate created a strong impression in England that public opinion favored intervention.

That critical summer found the Euro-pean diplomats confused and divided. Napoleon pondered the Southern victories, convinced that the moment for intervention had arrived. He informed the British Ministry that France would recognize Southern independence if the London government would follow. Edouard Antoine Thouvenel, the French Minister in Paris, did not share the Emperor's enthusiasm for intervention. He doubted that the French public had any interest in such involvement or that the Confederacy would win. He warned that French intervention, unless supported by both Britain and Russia, would result in an overcommitment of French power. Russia, he surmised, would reject every proposal for joint action. He was correct. Prince Gortchakov made it clear that his government would regard the dissolution of the Union as a catastrophe. In an interview with Bayard Taylor of the American Embassy in October, 1862, he said: "You know that the government of the United States has few friends among the Powers. England rejoices over what is happening to you; she longs and prays for your overthrow. France is less actively hostile; her interests would be less affected by the result; but she is not unwilling to see it. She is not your friend. ... Russia, alone, has stood by you from the first, and will continue to stand by you. We are very, *very* anxious that some means should be adopted—that *any* course should be pursued—which will prevent the division which now seems inevitable."

In Washington Mercier, still counseling mediation, stood alone. Lyons had no interest in confronting Seward with that issue again. To Stoeckl he observed, "We ought not to venture on mediation unless we are ready to go to war." Lyons did not share the European hostility toward the American Union. During his visit to England in the summer of 1862 he wrote to the British chargé d'affaires in Washington, with reference to McClellan's defeat, "I'm afraid no one but me is sorry for it." He believed that the debate on British policy in Parliament was ill-timed. "I do not think we know here sufficiently the extent of the disaster [to McClellan] to be able to come to any conclusion as to what the European Powers should do," ran his warning. Stoeckl concluded that the ravages of war would prompt the North eventually to beg for mediation, but not yet. He doubted, moreover, that British or French recognition of the South would achieve anything. "It will not end the war and what is more," he predicted, "it will not procure cotton for them, and the distress of the manufacturing districts will not be lessened. It can be accomplished only by forcing open the Southern ports, thus leading to a clear rupture with the North."

In London Mason, misled by the public evidence of British interventionism and unmindful of the disturbing doubts in the Foreign Office, moved to drive home his apparent advantage. He dispatched a brief note to Lord Russell requesting an interview. This Russell refused, assuring Mason that no advantage would result from it. In a second dispatch the Confederate Commissioner phrased his position in great detail, but again Russell replied that the moment for recognition had not arrived. For Mason the official British position had suddenly become clear. The Ministry would not alter its policies until the South revealed its ability to gain and maintain its independence, and reports from America indicated that the South was faltering at New Orleans, Memphis, and Shiloh. From Vienna John Lothrop Motley observed with accuracy that diplomacy would continue to reflect the course of war in America.

In Paris Slidell met with equal opposition. Thouvenel convinced him that it would be unwise even to ask for recognition. France, he said, was involved in Italy, but Slidell understood clearly the cause for French hesitancy. To the Confederate government he wrote on August 24: "You will find by my official correspondence that we are still hard and fast aground here. Nothing will float us off but a strong and continued current of important successes in the field." England, he warned, would avoid intervention until the North and South had become entirely exhausted. "Nothing," he lamented, "can exceed the selfishness of English statesmen except their wretched hypocrisy. They are continually casting about their disinterested magnanimity and objection of all other considerations than those dictated by a high-toned morality, while their entire policy is marked by egotism and duplicity."

Despite the lack of conviction in Europe's judgment of Confederate prospects, Southern victories were prompting the British Ministry to consider intervention. Russell admitted that nothing less than further Confederate successes would force mediation on the North. "I think," he wrote to the Embassy in Washington, "we must allow the President to spend his second batch of 600,000 men before we can hope that he and his democracy will listen to reason." Russell was convinced privately that October, 1862, will be the anticipated time for action. Stonewall Jackson's victories in Virginia prompted him to inform Lord Palmerston, the Prime Minister, that "it really looks as if he might end the war." Palmerston agreed, writing on September 14: "The Federals ... got a very complete smashing ... even Washington or Baltimore may fall into the hands of the Confederates. If this should happen, would it not be time for us to consider whether in such a state of things England and France might not address the contending parties and recommend an arrangement upon the basis of separation." The British Cabinet awaited word from France.

Before Napoleon could commit France to intervention, the British government passed the moment of decision. The wise and respected British politician, Earl Granville, warned Russell that involvement would mean war. "I doubt," he cautioned, "if the war continues long after our recognition of the South, whether it will be possible for us to avoid drifting into it." If Granville's words lacked conviction, Northern arms did not. Before the end of September news reached London of McClellan's success at Antietam and Lee's retreat down the Shenandoah Valley. Russell, who had been the ministry's most vigorous spokesman for involvement, now admitted, "This American question must be well sifted." Palmerston's support of Russell's position had been conditioned on the Southern invasion of Maryland. Now on October 2 in a letter to Russell he also acknowledged the wisdom of Granville's argument. Since mediation would favor the Southern position, its acceptance in the North hinged on Southern triumphs. Ten days earlier the necessary conditions seemed impending; now Palmerston counseled delay. He had no interest in exposing Canada and British commerce to a war against the United States. Nor would he venture into a qaurrel without the support of France and Russia. "The whole matter is full of difficulty," he concluded, "and can only be cleared up by some more decided events between the contending armies."

William E. Gladstone, Britain's liberal cabinet leader, continued to urge British involvement in the American conflict as a moral obligation. At Newcastle on October 7 he declared: "Jefferson Davis and the other leaders have made an army, they are making, it appears, a navy, and they have made what is more than either, they have made a nation." Gladstone denied that British mediation would be met by insult or war, for, he predicted in a memorandum to the Prime Minister, "America would feel the influence and weight of a general opinion on the part of civilized Europe that this horrible war ought to cease." Whatever the immediate Northern reaction, the British proposal would produce a powerful effect on opinion and alter affairs in America in favor of peace. But perhaps Gladstone was motivated by more than a moral revulsion to war. He had recently toured the North of England and was fearful that the unemployment in the cotton districts would produce a violent upheaval. By serving the cause of peace the great liberal might also serve the cause of the British cotton textile industry.

Palmerston, under pressure from the Cabinet, sought the advice of the Earl of Derby, leader of the opposition. Derby vigorously opposed both mediation and recognition. He reiterated the fundamental conviction of European conservatives that either action would merely irritate the North without advancing the cause of the South or procuring a single bale of cotton. Mediation, he added, would gain its apparent objective only if England were prepared to sweep away the blockade and invite a declaration of war from the Lincoln administration. Intervention was hopeless because there was no way in which England could influence events in America short of military involvement. Palmerston's decision reflected this fundamental reality. Britain, he informed Lord Russell, "could take no step nor make any communication of a distinct proposition with any advantage." The North, he pointed out, demanded no less than restoration of the Union and the South no less than independence. To offer mediation would merely pledge each party in the conflict more firmly to its uncompromising objective. Russell added his conviction that no British action would be effective unless it were supported by Russia, Prussia, Austria, and France. For nations of such diverse interests agreement on interventionist policy was impossible.

During the crucial months of October and November, 1862, Napoleon never disguised his sympathy for the Confederate cause. But sentiment and policy are not synonymous, and the French Emperor balked at involvement in the American conflict. He complained to Slidell of troubles in Italy and Greece and acknowledged his fear that if he acted alone England would desert him and would attempt to embroil him in a war with the United States. Slidell assured him that recognition would not be regarded by the North as a *casus belli* and that with his powerful navy he could defend French interests on the seas without difficulty. To Slidell joint mediation was worthless, for he had no faith in England or Russia. Napoleon answered with a proposal acceptable to the Southern Commissioner. France and Britain might seek a six-month armistice in the American Civil War in the interest of humanity. Napoleon's final program for joint action was dispatched to both London and St. Petersburg.

In London the tripartite proposal threw the Cabinet into confusion. Palmerston was displeased, for he no longer had any interest in European intervention. Lord Russell favored action provided European leaders could discover terms upon which the warring sections in America would agree. In lieu of this elusive formula he favored a Cabinet discussion of the French dispatch. At the Cabinet meetings of November 11 and 12 Russell conceded the issue to Palmerston. Reported Gladstone to his wife: "The United States affair has ended and not well. Lord Russell rather turned tail. He gave way without resolutely fighting out his battle." In its reply to the French government, the British Ministry declared that mediation in any form was useless since Lincoln would not accept it.

At issue in the final Cabinet decision was the attitude of Russia. As early as November 8, St. Petersburg had informed the Foreign Office that the Russian government had rejected Napoleon's proposal. Prince Gortchakov advised the French that it was "essential to avoid the appearance of any pressure of a nature to offend American public opinion, and to excite susceptibilities very easily roused at the bare idea of intervention." Russell yielded on this key question to Palmerston when he wrote, "We ought not to move at present without Russia." Russia's inflexibility created the basis for a harmonious decision within the British Cabinet, and even Gladstone could write, "As to the state of matters generally in the Cabinet, I have never seen it smoother."

Throughout the months of decision in Europe, Seward exerted relentless pressure on the British and French governments. When Mercier transmitted a French offer of mediation to him in July, 1862, the Secretary warned that "the Emperor can commit no graver error than to mix himself in our affairs. At the rumor alone of intervention all the factions will reunite themselves against you and even in the border states you will meet resistance unanimous and desperate." It was not in the French interest, he continued, to compromise the kindly feeling which the United States held for France. Mercier thereupon advised caution in Paris, adding that intervention could easily result in war. When Mercier apprised Seward of Europe's reaction to McClellan's withdrawal from Richmond, the Secretary again stormed back: "I have noticed it but as for us it would be a great misfortune if the powers should wish to intervene in our affairs. There is no possible compromise ... and at any price, we will not admit the division of the Union." Seward acknowledged the kindly sentiments of Europe but replied that the best testimony of those sentiments would be Old World abstention from American affairs. When Mercier suggested that restoration of the Union was impossible, Seward told him: "Do not believe for a moment that either the Federal Congress, myself or any person connected with this government will in any case entertain any proposition or suggestion of arrangement or accommodation or adjustment from within or without upon the basis of a surrender of the Federal Union."

Above all Seward sought to disabuse European leaders of their conviction that a Northern victory was impossible. Nothing had occurred, he once wrote to Dayton in Paris, to shake the confidence of the Federal government in the ultimate success of its purpose. To those Europeans who insisted that the United States was too large for one nation, Seward retorted that it was too small for two. When Europe gave evidence of interventionist tendencies in August, 1862, Seward wrote to Adams: "The nation has a right and it is its duty, to live. Those who favor and give aid to the insurrection, upon whatever pretext, assail the nation in an hour of danger, and therefore they cannot be held or regarded as its friends. In taking this ground, the United States claim only what they concede to all other nations. No state can be really independent in any other position."

In denying Europe the right to intervene, Seward insisted that he was defending the principle of civil government itself, for at stake was nothing less than the existence of the United States. "Any other principle than this," he said, "would be to resolve government everywhere into a thing of accident and caprice, and ultimately all human society into a state of perpetual war." American policy was dictated by the law of self-preservation, and no nation, he added, "animated by loyal sentiments and inspired by a generous ambition can ever suffer itself to debate with parties within or without a policy of self-preservation."

Seward, therefore, instructed Adams not to debate, hear, or receive any communication from the British government which sought to advise the United States in its relations with the Confederacy. This nation was fighting for empire, he admitted in October, 1862, but it was an empire lawfully acquired and lawfully held. "Studying to confine this unhappy struggle within our own borders," he wrote to Dayton, "we have not only invoked no foreign aid or sympathy, but we have warned foreign nations frankly and have besought them not to interfere. We have practised justice towards them in every way, and conciliation to an unusual degree. But we are none the less determined for all that to be sovereign and to be free."

Seward's reaction to the British Cabinet debate of November revealed both confidence and dismay. It was not pleasant for a loyal American, he admitted to Adams, to observe an English cabinet discuss the future of the American Republic. But the United States, he added, enjoyed the right and possessed the power to determine its own destiny; never before was it better prepared to meet danger from abroad. The wheel of political fortune continued to turn. England had once desired American friendship; she would do so aagin. "Neither politicians nor statesmen control events," the Secretary concluded. "They can moderate them and accommodate their ambitions to them, but they can do no more."

After November, 1862, all wartime diplomacy receded into insignificance. Whatever Southern hopes of European intervention still remained were shattered by the Confederate disasters at Gettysburg and Vicksburg in July, 1863. In September Mason informed Russell by note that his mission had been terminated. The British Secretary replied coldly: "I have on other occasions explained to you the reasons which have inclined her Majesty's Government to decline the overtures you allude to.... These reasons are still in force, and it is not necessary to repeat them." Europe's final refusal to involve itself in the American struggle was nothing less than a total vindication of Seward's diplomacy. Whatever the North's diplomatic advantages, he had understood them and exploited them with astonishing effectiveness. He made it clear that any European nation which committed itself to the destruction of the American Union would pay dearly if it sought to fulfill that commitment.

In one sense there was nothing unique in the diplomatic issues raised by the American Civil War. Many nations in the past had undergone internal revolution in which elements seeking power had sought either to overthrow the established government or to establish the independence of some portion of its territory. Such uprisings had succeeded and failed, but when major power was involved they had demonstrated invariably that other nations, whatever their moral and material interests, really could not intervene diplomatically without running the risk of military involvement.

Unfortunately Union diplomacy after 1861 placed this nation in the unprecedented and embarrassing position of appearing to defy its own democratic principle of self-determination. Americans in the past, Europe recalled, had not only made declarations in favor of the Greek and Hungarian revolutions and applauded such revolutionary leaders as Louis Kossuth, but they had furnished them money for the declared purpose of assuring new disorders. Now Americans were compelled to recognize what they had often denied Europe—that governments cannot exist without authority

and that to maintain their authority, they must resort to force. Cassius Clay, to explain American purpose, once declared that the United States was fighting for nationality and liberty. To this the London *Times* replied sarcastically that it was difficult to understand how "a people fighting ... to force their fellow citizens to remain in a confederacy which they repudiated, can be called the champions of liberty and nationalism." The Confederates were fighting for their independence, observed the *Times,* adding, "But with the Northerners all is different. They are not content with their own. They are fighting to coerce others."

Europe might have recalled that idealism had never established the official diplomatic tradition of the United States toward revolution and oppression. Whatever the concern of individual Americans toward events abroad, the nation's dictum since Washington's presidency had been one of abstention. John Quincy Adams had given it classical form in his Marcellus letters of 1794: "It is our duty to remain, the peaceful and silent, though sorrowful spectators of the European scene." Again in July, 1821, Adams declared that "America is the well-wisher to the freedom and independence of all. She is the vindicator only of her own." All national leaders prior to the Civil War, when holding positions of responsibility, agreed that any foreign intervention in behalf of liberal causes might well commit the United States beyond its national interest. President James Monroe recognized this when he refused to render aid to the revolting states of Latin America. They would receive recognition, he informed them, when they had demonstrated sufficient strength to establish their own independence. Palmerston was merely reflecting this diplomatic tradition when he admitted in October, 1862, that Britain "must continue merely to be lookers-on till the war shall have taken a more decided turn."

Tangible British and French interests were involved in the Southern struggle for independence, and to that extent neither nation could ignore events across the Atlantic. But until the South could demonstrate, as did the Latin American republics, that it could overcome the power and purpose of the North, European recognition would have defied one of the most significant and thoroughly established traditions of modern diplomacy. Except for one fleeting period in 1862, neither Britain nor France revealed any serious intention of breaking from their own past and assuming commitments which would endanger their territorial and commercial interests in the New World. Had Europe given expression to its moral sentiment by supporting the cause of the seemingly oppressed, it would merely have magnified the horror and confusion. Of this Seward left no doubt. He warned Europe in May, 1862, that its involvement in the affairs of the United States would not serve the interests of humanity. "If Europe will still sympathize with the revolution," he wrote, "it must now look forward to the end; an end in which the war ceases with anarchy substituted for the social system that existed when the war began. What will then have become of the interests which carried Europe to the side which was at once the wrong side and the losing one? Only a perfect withdrawal of all favor

from the insurrection can now save those interests in any degree. The insurrectionary states, left hopeless of foreign intervention, will be content to stop in their career of self-destruction, and to avail themselves of the moderating power of the Federal government. If the nations of Europe shall refuse to see this, and the war must therefore go on to the conclusion I have indicated, the responsibility for that conclusion will not rest with the government of the United States."

Seward here touched the central issue of Europe's relationship to the conflict in America. If after the summer of 1862 it was still within the power of the Old World to bring injury to the North, it was beyond its power to bring salvation to the South. There were no inexpensive means available to Europe to achieve the liberation of the South against the North's determination to hold it. Those Europeans who sought to cast from the South the yoke of alien rule might have been moved by the moral sentiment of Gladstone, but they had no influence on Palmerston. And since the realities of power are always the determining factors in international affairs, a Gladstone in office, whatever his sentimentalism and faith in moral pressure, could have influenced the internal affairs of the United States, wrapped in civil war, with no more success than the masters of *Realpolitik* who rejected such purpose as a matter of principle.

8

A New Approach to the Origins of Blaine's Pan American Policy

RUSSELL H. BASTERT

The policy of the United States toward Latin American has always had two aspects: one conciliatory, friendly, benevolent, rooted in the concept of equality and nonintervention; the other aggressive, belligerent, unilateral, based on the premise that the United States is the dominant power in the hemisphere and the protector of all the republics to the South.

During the first three quarters of the nineteenth century the second aspect predominated. It was demonstrated for the first time shortly after the enunciation of the Monroe Doctrine. At that time representatives of several South American countries, encouraged by the Doctrine's stated purpose to shield the newly liberated colonies from reconquest by Spain, sought to share with the United States the responsibility for protecting the hemisphere. The American reply to suggestions for bilateral alliances was brief and blunt. The United States, said the Secretary of State, needed no assistance in implementing the President's message. The same attitude soon appeared again in a speech by Henry Clay, an avowed friend of Latin America, who said, in commenting on an invitation from certain South American countries to attend a conference at Panama, "It is in our power to create a system of which we shall be the center and in which all South America will act with us." After that came Manifest Destiny, the war with Mexico, the seizure of two fifths of that nation's territory, and numerous private filibustering expeditions (condoned by the government in most instances) into Cuba and Central America. These last caused one Latin American to label the American government as "unprincipled [and] . . . scheming with its adventurous citizens to accomplish the spoliation of neighboring states." Even after the Civil War, when the foreign policy of the United States was not aggressive, a Secretary of State, and a notably nonbellicose one at that, could say that "the United States . . . occupy a prominent position on the continent which they neither can nor should abdicate and which entitles them to a leading voice and which imposes on them duties of right and honor regarding American questions."

In 1881 an abrupt change in the Latin American policy of the United States was proclaimed by the organization of a conference of American states by Secretary of State James G. Blaine. Blaine envisioned the replacement of the unilateral and aggressive course by one which emphasized harmony, unity, and friendship.

FROM *Hispanic American Historical Review*, XXXIX (1959), 375–412. By permission of the author and Duke University Press.

Why did the change come about? What impelled Blaine to pursue a new program?

Answers to these questions are suggested by Russell H. Bastert of Williams College, who is presently doing a book on Pan-Americanism. Bastert's article corrects many commonly held views on Blaine's motivation. It is his contention that Blaine "did not come into the State Department with a formula for dealing with Latin-America," nor was there anything in his career to 1881 that reveals that he had given the matter any serious thought. The evidence does indicate that Blaine took up the policy after assuming office and as a consequence of unsettled conditions in South America. It was because of the existence or menace of wars in Latin America that Blaine wished to call "a friendly conference of all the Nations of America to devise methods of permanent peace and consequently prosperity for all."

James G. Blaine unpredictably turned from politics to diplomacy late in 1880 by accepting the post of secretary of state in the cabinet of President-elect James A. Garfield. Blaine was a tallish, vigorous man, with a broad, expressive face, prominent nose, piercing brown eyes, and striking full beard, liberally streaked with gray; his appearance belied the fact that he worried about his health, and occasionally suffered from gout. A veteran of nearly twenty years in Congress, he was only fifty. His mind was quick, imaginative, shrewd; his manner genial, animated, and confident. Always lively and interesting, never at a loss for words, which flowed from him almost effortlessly, whatever he said or did commanded public attention.

For years he had been the most personally "magnetic" of Republican leaders. He had won the allegiance of countless Americans—they admired his brilliance; they envied his eloquence; they enjoyed his geniality; they laughed at his witty repartee; they respected him as a devoted family man; and they backed him with an enthusiasm and a loyalty which few of his rivals could command. The machinations of party politics—the personal maneuvers and intrigues which accompany the struggle for office—were food and drink to him. He fully expected to become President of the United

States. Even bitter political enemies, and he had many, among Republicans as well as Democrats, would not have wagered against his chances.

His becoming head of the State Department was essentially a by-product of the political process, a sign of his being Garfield's first adviser, not the result of interest in or qualifications for the art of diplomacy.[1] Ironically, however, in the world of foreign-policy making, so alien to his experience and nature, Blaine earned the gratitude and praise of posterity. As secretary of state, in November of 1881 he called for a conference of all the independent states of the New World, except Haiti.[2] After

[1] Significantly, Blaine's private letters between the election and inauguration in the James A. Garfield Papers (Division of Manuscripts, Library of Congress), deal with party and cabinet matters almost exclusively; there is no mention of diplomacy in them. Walker Blaine knew well his father's inclinations; he wrote from St. Paul, Minnesota, on January 3, 1881: "Did your going into the State Department simply mean that you were to be Secretary of State, I do not think any of your friends would greatly desire it. But your taking that position will mean—and the country will understand it—that you are the head of the administration under the President, and the chief counsellor of its policy." Gail Hamilton, *Biography of James G. Blaine* (Norwich, Conn., 1895), 530. Gail Hamilton was a pseudonym used by Mrs. Blaine's cousin, writer Mary Abigail Dodge.

[2] Rayford W. Logan, *The Diplomatic Relations of the United States with Haiti 1776–*

the death of Garfield by assassination, Blaine retired in December from the State Department, and suffered the embarrassment of seeing his invitations to a Pan American conference recalled, his diplomatic policy altered, his actions in South American affairs made the subject of a Congressional investigation.[3] Yet the idea of an international American conference grew in public favor in the United States. When a law of Congress finally brought about such a meeting in the fall of 1889, the honor of welcoming the delegates fell by a remarkable coincidence again to Blaine, once more secretary of state, now in the cabinet of Benjamin Harrison. The importance of Blaine's role in the first Pan American conference has given him a prominence among the advocates of Pan Americanism equalled only by Simón Bolívar and Henry Clay.

1

After more than half a century the genesis of Blaine's Pan Americanism is far from clear. Where did he get his idea for an inter-American conference? Eulogistic biographers and trained historians have ransacked Blaine's past in search of the answer. Some have hinted that he received his inspiration from the traditions of Simón Bolívar and the policies of Henry Clay, whom he greatly admired.[4] Others have pointed to the

interest in Latin America which Blaine exhibited in certain speeches made during his long career in Congress.[5] Still others have asserted that by the time he became secretary of state in 1881 he already had conceived the idea of fostering an American continental system in order to insure lasting peace and the growth of commerce among the independent republics of the New World.[6]

Little evidence exists to support these several contentions.

Bolívar's "grand idea," at best a shadowy rather than a substantial expression of latter-day Pan Americanism, seems to have influenced Blaine little if at all. By the 1880's the experiences with Latin America of Henry Clay and John Quincy Adams were over half a century old. The "traditional" Latin American policy of the United States was to admonish Europe to keep hands off the Western Hemisphere and to do very little else. Although Blaine recognized Clay's part in formulating a Latin American policy for the United States at the time of the Panama Congress,[7] never did he refer to Clay's, much less Bolívar's, Pan Americanism as providing the inspiration for his own. Blaine's silence on this score hardly justifies the eloquence of those historians who have spoken for him.

Co., 1893), 61; W. S. Robertson, *Hispanic American Relations with the United States* (New York, 1923), 390.

[5] David S. Muzzey, *James G. Blaine* (New York, 1934), 206; A. Curtis Wilgus, "James G. Blaine and the Pan-American Movement," HAHR, V (November, 1922), p. 669; Hamilton, *Biography of Blaine,* 439–440.

[6] Edward Stanwood, *James G. Blaine* (Boston, 1905), 241–244; Alice F. Tyler, *The Foreign Policy of James G. Blaine* (U. of Minnesota Press, 1927), 362–364; Joseph B. Lockey, "The Pan-Americanism of James G. Blaine," *Essays in Pan-Americanism* (U. of California Press, 1939), 52–53.

[7] James G. Blaine, "The Foreign Policy of the Garfield Administration," *Political Discussions* (Norwich, Conn., 1887), 413. It should be noted that this article first appeared in the Chicago *Weekly Magazine* on September 16, 1882, after Blaine had left the State Department.

1891 (U. of North Carolina Press, 1941), 366–367. After Haiti protested the exclusion, in 1882 Blaine's successor in the State Department, Frederick T. Frelinghuysen, gave official assurance that if the conference were held, Haiti would be included.

[3] Using previously unemphasized sources, I have analyzed the reasons behind Frelinghuysen's repudiation of Blaine's Pan American policy in my article, "Diplomatic Reversal: Frelinghuysen's Opposition to Blaine's Pan-American Policy in 1882," *Mississippi Valley Historical Review* (March, 1956), XLII, 653–671.

[4] T. C. Crawford, *James G. Blaine: A Study of his Life and Career* (Edgewood Publishing

If Blaine did not, then, receive his Pan Americanism from the past, did it emerge from his own concern for and study of Latin America? Curiously, his public record before 1881 revals little serious interest in any foreign policy matters.[8] When he did touch infrequently upon foreign relations, domestic concerns dominated his views. Thus he strongly favored Exclusion Acts against Chinese immigration. And he loved to indulge in the political sport of "twisting the lion's tail," openly emphasizing his marked suspicion and ill-will towards Great Britain.[9]

In several Congressional debates touching upon commercial relations in the Americas, Blaine clearly showed his animus against Great Britain more than he displayed any affection for Latin America. Early in June, 1878, he took a leading part in prolonged Senate discussions which focused on the use of federal subsidies to help support a private American steamship line to Brazil. Blaine supported such subsidies. He contended that our foreign commerce had declined primarily because it lacked shipping facilities, and that subsidies for American shipping lines would enable them to challenge the commercial supremacy of Great Britain. "Is this country willing calmly to resign the sceptre of the ocean to Great Britain" he thundered. "There is no rival left to her

in the commercial world, and if she can bluff us out, or buy us out, or bully us out of a tariff that shall protect American industries and any enterprise that shall stimulate lines of American steamships, she will have done all she desires to do for her factories and her commerce." [10] It is to read history in the light of later events, therefore, to assert that Blaine's public speeches in 1878 contained "the first actual development of the policy with which his name became afterwards inseparably associated, —the fraternization of the Americas." [11]

Did he promise more privately? One of Blaine's contemporay biographers, T. C. Crawford, asserts that he did, that he outlined to certain Southern senators, especially L. Q. C. Lamar, the details of his future Pan American policy, including a Peace Conference of the American republics, reciprocity, and a Pan American railroad—all of which were supported by those senators.[12] The assertion does not ring true. It does not rest on contemporary evidence, but instead follows in large part a description of Blaine's policy which he himself later gave. Certain ideas Crawford credits Blaine with having in 1881, such as supporting reciprocal trade agreements and an inter-American railway, were never expressed by him (and probably not held) until after his first term as secretary of state.

Further search for the origins of Blaine's Pan Americanism in his Con-

[8] Based upon a study of Blaine's speeches in the *Congressional Record* from 1863 to 1881; the few surviving James G. Blaine Papers (Division of Manuscripts, Library of Congress); Blaine's own selection of his writings and speeches printed in *Political Discussions;* and a search through issues in the 1870's of the New York *Tribune,* Blaine's chief spokesman among newspapers.

[9] See the frank comments on Blaine made by Edward Thornton, British minister to the United States, in "Private Letters from the British Embassy in Washington to the Foreign Secretary Lord Granville 1880–1885," edited by Paul Knaplund and Carolyn M. Clewes, *American Historical Association Annual Report,* 1941, I, 116 *passim.* Thornton distrusted Blaine and expected him "to get up a quarrel with a foreign power," very likely England.

[10] *Cong. Record,* 45 Cong., 2 Session, 4134.
[11] Hamilton, *Biography of Blaine,* 439. Historians have tended to follow earlier and often biased accounts in their search for the origins of Blaine's diplomatic ideas. Thus Hamilton asserts, but offers no proof, in connection with this speech: "He [Blaine] had made a study of the resources, needs, aspirations, possibilities of the southern hemisphere." Wilgus, "Blaine and the Pan-American Movement," HAHR, V, 669, merely paraphrases Hamilton.
[12] Crawford, *Blaine,* 490-91. Crawford was for many years Washington correspondent of the New York *World,* and, according to his own testimony, Blaine's close friend.

gressional outbursts has drawn attention to a Senate speech of late January, 1881. If, in Crawford's words, this speech was "generally regarded as an outline of the policy of the new administration," it must have seemed to those who heard it disappointingly narrow and unoriginal, far removed from the visions of a Pan American enthusiast. Blaine merely recorded his belief once again that an expansion of trade to South America (or elsewhere) was dependent upon government aid extended to private American shipbuilders.[13] He said nothing concerning the importance of improving either political or commercial relations with Latin America. Thus two months before he officially became secretary of state, but after he knew that the position was to be his, Blaine had not indicated publicly, and probably not privately, any preference or plans in favor of cooperation among the American Republics. He did not come into the State Department with a formula for dealing with Latin America.

In accordance with the political customs of the time, and in deference to the ability and initiative of his chief cabinet member, President Garfield left the control of foreign affairs almost entirely in the hands of his secretary of state. Garfield undoubtedly backed Blaine in the formative stages of his Pan American policy, but clearly the State Department originated it.[14] According to Blaine's apologia for his Latin American diplomacy, written after his retirement from the State Department, a Peace Congress of all the American nations was to be

the cornerstone of the foreign policy of the Garfield administration, which had two principal objects: "first, to bring about peace, and prevent future wars in North and South America; second, to cultivate such friendly, commercial relations with all American countries as would lead to a large increase in the export trade of the United States . . ." [15]

A public figure defending his record may have the right to reconstruct theory to harmonize with what has happened, but the historian must investigate the events themselves which shaped his actions *at the time.* Blaine developed his policy for dealing with Latin America after he became secretary of state and not before. It was the direct result of his own experience in the State Department; conditions in Latin America shaped his diplomacy from beginning to end. Blaine all but admitted this in a letter written by him to President Arthur in 1882:

. . . there are and have been serious troubles between the American nations. Peru, Chile and Bolivia have been for more than two years engaged in a desperate conflict. It was the fortunate intervention of the United States last spring that averted war between Chile and the Argentine Republic. Guatemala is at this moment asking the United States to interpose its good offices in Mexico to keep off war. . . . *It is the existence or the menace of these wars that influenced President Garfield and as I supposed influenced yourself to desire a friendly conference of all the Nations of America to divise methods of permanent peace and consequent prosperity for all.*[16]

A way to bring about peace in the Americas—the first and most important objective of Pan Americanism in 1881— interested Blaine because there was no

---

[13] *Cong. Record,* 46 Cong., 3 Sess., 961–64.
[14] Testimony of Blaine before the House Committee on Foreign Affairs, April 27, 1882, in "Chile-Peruvian Investigation," *House Reports,* No. 1780, 47 Cong., I Sess., 240. Muzzey, *Blaine,* 190–191, ably supplies the kind of analysis which refutes the conclusion of Theodore C. Smith, *The Life and Letters of James A. Garfield* (Yale U. Press, 1925), II, 1166, that Garfield was partly responsible for the idea of a Pan American conference.

[15] Blaine, *Political Discussions,* 411.
[16] Blaine to President Arthur, February 3, 1882, New York *Tribune,* February 4, 1882. The original letter is in the few remaining Chester A. Arthur Papers (Division of Manuscripts, Library of Congress). Blaine later included this letter in his *Political Discussions.* Italics inserted.

peace. The origins of Blaine's Pan American policy are to be found in the "existence or the menace of these wars."

2

In 1881 Latin America was in a time of troubles. The terrible War of the Pacific, pitting Chile against Peru and Bolivia, continued on the west coast of South America as it had since 1879. Territorial differences between Chile and Argentina seemed likely to drag in still another belligerent. Mexico and Guatemala were at odds in a diplomatic controversy threatening to involve them in a separate war of their own. Costa Rica and Colombia searched for a method of agreeing on their boundary. Thus from March until December, 1881, during the nine and one-half months Blaine served as secretary of state during the Garfield and Arthur administrations, his policy for Latin America developed while war and threats of war swept over that turbulent area. Unsettled conditions became the framework within which his diplomacy had to operate.

In 1881 the United States achieved only one success in helping to keep peace in Latin America. American diplomats ably assisted the Argentine Republic and Chile in agreeing, at least for the time, upon arbitration as a means of settling their long-standing boundary dispute in that land of the fabled giants, Patagonia, at the tip of the continent. Chile was eager for agreement because of its involvement in the War of the Pacific; the Argentine Republic was willing to press its case, but not to the point of war. Ministers Thomas A. Osborn in Santiago, and Thomas O. Osborn in Buenos Aires, unrelated to each other, kept diplomatic communications alive and made helpful suggestions to the two nations so discreetly and capably that

Blaine merely gave them his blessings.[17] He made it clear that the United States would not refuse to serve as arbitrator if asked, but Blaine wisely abstained from insisting upon such a solution.

The singularity of the Osborns' success was in itself significant. If the ordinary methods of diplomacy used to help settle the dispute between the Argentine Republic and Chile had succeeded equally well elsewhere in the New World, Blaine would not have needed to adopt a more comprehensive, Pan-American plan. Only after he embarked upon a more "spirited" policy did the extraordinary method of an inter-American conference to keep peace in the New World take on reason and necessity.

Such a need impressed Blaine as a result of his intervention in a dispute threatening war between Guatemala and Mexico.

For over a quarter of a century Mexico and Guatemala had engaged in serious diplomatic sparring over their boundary. When Central America separated from Mexico in 1823, the province of Chiapas had elected to remain Mexican. Guatemala had assumed the old Central American claims to Chiapas, but they were weak and tenuous by 1881. Having long been in possession of the province, Mexico considered its ownership as legal as it was actual. Within Chiapas, however,

[17] See the following group of selected dispatches: T. O. Osborn to Blaine, No. 324, July 1, 1881, Papers Relating to the Foreign Relations of the United States in 1881 (Washington, 1882), 6–8; T. A. Osborn to Blaine, No. 219, July 22, 1881, ibid., 134–135; Julio Carrié, minister of the Argentine Republic to the United States, to Blaine, July 28, 1881, ibid., 15–16; T. O. Osborn to Blaine, No. 334, October 8, 1881, Despatches Argentine Republic, XXIV (Department of State Records, National Archives); T. O. Osborn to Blaine, No. 338, October 27, 1881, Foreign Relations 1881, 10–13; Marcial Martínez, minister of Chile to the United States, to Blaine, October 27, 1881, ibid., 163. See also the brief sketch by Paul D. Dickens, "Argentine Arbitrations and Mediations with reference to United States participation therein," HAHR, XI (November, 1931), p. 470.

a district named Soconusco had denounced the annexation of Chiapas by Mexico and for seventeen years remained virtually an independent state. Mexico occupied Soconusco in 1842, and once again annexed it to Chiapas. At the time Guatemala had failed to protest, but it did so later. Both nations sent troops into the disputed area early in 1881. War seemed near.[18]

Reports making clear the gravity of this situation did not reach Blaine immediately. During his first three months as secretary of state the politican turned diplomatist sought primarily to facilitate American business opportunities in Mexico.[19] But his policy at that time did not associate the growth of commerce with the necessity for peace in the Americas, nor emphasize the need for an inter-American conference to promote either peace or commerce.

Blaine's involvement in Mexico's dispute with Guatemala shifted his policy away from economic considerations. Guatemala's minister to the United States, A. Ubico, wrote to Blaine on June 15, summed up the claims of his country to Chiapas and Soconusco, and asked the United States to intervene "as the natural protector of the integrity of the Central American territory." [20] Blaine responded to Guatemala's pleas eagerly, enthusiastically, and somewhat naïvely.

The United States did not look upon itself as "the arbiter of the destinies in whole or part of its sister republics," he magnanimously announced, but it did hold a distinctive place in the family of American nations. As founder and principal upholder of the true principles of liberty and a republican form of government the United States had the duty and right to give advice to its neighbors on matters which threatened their peace and prosperity. At Guatemala's request the State Department tendered its good offices and indicated that it expected Mexico to settle the dispute with Guatemala by peaceful means.[21] Although Blaine pleaded impartiality, actually he tended to favor Guatemala, and from the first reserved his suspicions and the provoking sting of his "spirited" diplomacy for the stronger power, Mexico.

An economic label has been pasted on Blaine's brand of peacemaking in Latin America, but it was a mixture of many motives, probably least of all economic.[22]

[18] Cornelius A. Logan, United States minister to Central America, to Blaine, No. 177, May 2, 1881, Despatches Central America, XVII (Department of State Records, National Archives); Logan to Blaine, No. 179, May 24, 1881, Foreign Relations 1881, 104–5. See also Dana G. Munro, The Five Republics of Central America (New York, 1918), 24–37; H. I. Priestley, The Mexican Nation (New York, 1935), 261; Chester L. Jones, Guatemala Past and Present (U. of Minnesota Press, 1940), 75–78.

[19] Blaine to Philip H. Morgan, United States minister to Mexico, No. 133, June 1, 1881, Foreign Relations 1881, 761–762; Blaine to Morgan, No. 137, June 16, 1881, Instructions Mexico (Department of State Records, National Archives), XX, 283–296.

[20] A. Ubico to Blaine, June 15, 1881, Senate Exec. Docs., No. 156, 47 Cong., I Sess., 5.

[21] Blaine to Ubico, June 16, 1881, ibid., 6. In a letter of reply written on June 19, Ubico termed Blaine's policy a "noble and generous course." Ibid., 7. Blaine to Morgan, No. 138, June 16, 1881, Foreign Relations 1881, 766–768.

[22] For interpretations which stress the primary importance of commercial considerations behind Blaine's peace-making efforts and proposal in 1881 for a Pan American conference, see Thomas A. Bailey, A Diplomatic History of the American People (New York, 1955), 435; Muzzey, Blaine, 207; Wilgus, "Blaine and Pan-American Movement," HAHR, V, 667. Tyler, Foreign Policy of Blaine, 165, and Joseph B. Lockey, "James G. Blaine," in Samuel F. Bemis (ed.), American Secretaries of State and Their Diplomacy (10 vols., New York, 1927–1929), VII, 275, are more judicious in balancing Blaine's interest in both peace and commerce.

I do not deny that in 1881 Blaine might have been thinking in terms of the increasing commercial opportunities for the United States which permanent peace in Latin America might bring. I do doubt that this was his first consideration. Those authors who have deemed it such are following Blaine's own analysis in his apologia, "The Foreign Policy of the Garfield Administration," written in 1882 after his retirement from the State Department. One would expect Blaine to point up in such a

If peace for the sake of Mexican commerce had been his primary aim, his vigorous intervention was such as to defeat its purpose, for it did nothing to smooth the way for the economic penetration of Mexico by American business men. Other considerations influenced him more in the Mexican-Guatemalan dispute. Blaine feared that the possibility of war anywhere in the Americas offered European powers their best chance to exert influence in the New World.[23] He wanted also to crush any desires Mexico might have harbored for an expansionist war against Guatemala. Such an outcome of the controversy would have destroyed future possibilities for an event opposed by Mexico but long desired by the United States—the reconfederation of the five Central American states.[24]

The day after Blaine first responded to Guatemala's pleas for intervention he received news which confirmed his worst suspicions. Cornelius A. Logan, United States minister to Central America, informed him that Mexico had sent 1,000 troops into Soconusco and was readying 2,000 more for action. "I believe," warned Logan, "that Mexico has every disposition to come to an open rupture with Guatemala on the boundary question, and that she may do so." [25] If no protection were forthcoming from the United States, Logan felt, Guatemala might appeal to one of the European powers for assistance, and offer Soconusco in return.

Blaine was aroused. He immediately informed United States minister to Mexico Philip H. Morgan that it appeared as if the country to which he was accredited planned deliberately to extend its borders by conquest. Blaine professed to believe that the Mexican government could not seriously entertain such plans, but he acted as if they already had been put into effect. The "Plumed Knight," veteran of many a political battle, sniffed the air of diplomatic combat and was eager for the fray. He now vigorously assumed a new and large responsibility, never given the attention it deserves in the history of the Latin American policy of the United States.

In relations with its sister republics in the New World, Blaine explained to Morgan, the United States would exert

document the material advantages which might accrue to the United States from his idea. Conditions in Latin America in 1881, however, were such that of the two motives Blaine admitted desiring—peace and commerce—the first was by far the more imperative and immediate objective. Neither Blaine's diplomatic instructions nor invitations to the conference mentioned commerce as an item to be placed on the agenda.

[23] Blaine was very much aware, since he had been in Congress at the time, of the advances which France had attempted to make in the Western Hemisphere while the United States fought its Civil War, and he did not intend that family quarrels should again offer such opportunities. See James G. Blaine, *Twenty Years of Congress* (Norwich, Conn., 1884), I, 597–598, 600–601; Blaine to Logan, No. 145, May 7, 1881, *Foreign Relations 1881*, 103.

[24] General J. Rufino Barrios, president of Guatemala in 1881, was a scheming and ambitious tyrant, but he did possess real military and political ability, and hoped to involve the United States in his boundary dispute with Mexico as a means of gaining assistance for a Central American union. No American secretary of state was willing to support Barrios, but the idea of a Central American confederation won favor both with Blaine and his immediate predecessor in the State Department, William M. Evarts. See Evarts to Logan, No. 53, March 4, 1880, Instructions Central America, XVIII, 73–78; Evarts to Logan, No. 85, August 3, 1880, *ibid.*, 113–115; Blaine to Logan, No. 145, May 7, 1881, *Foreign Relations 1881*, 102–103. For information on Barrios see J.

Fred Rippy, "Relations of the United States and Guatemala during the Epoch of Justo Rufino Barrios," HAHR, XXII (November, 1942), 595–605; J. Fred Rippy, "Justo Rufino Barrios," in A. Curtis Wilgus, ed., *Hispanic-American Essays* (U. of North Carolina Press, 1942), 280–298.

[25] Logan to Blaine, confidential, No. 179, May 24, 1881, *Foreign Relations 1881*, 105. The complete dispatch appears in *Despatches Central America*, XVII, and is even more alarming. Logan was convinced that Mexico had the idea of acquiring Guatemalan territory as compensation for that taken from it by the United States.

its influence "for the preservation of the national life and integrity of any one of them against aggression, *whether this may come from abroad or from another American republic*."[26] Blaine did not shrink from the implications of his bold stand. The United States stood for the territorial integrity of the independent republics of the New World, a diplomatic commitment of large order. Blaine enjoined Mexico to forswear aggression, use diplomatic methods or arbitration to settle its dispute with Guatemala, and support a "peaceful maintenance of the status quo of the American commonwealths."

Blaine's ministers in Guatemala and in Mexico sought to carry out his instructions, which went unchanged for months. A tragic disaster at home overshadowed the distresses of Latin America. President Garfield was shot on July 2, and through the long and wearisome weeks of the President's illness, until his death on September 19, Blaine waited and hoped for his recovery. Despite his grief the secretary had to assume many of his superior's political duties. Burdened with old responsibilities, troubled with new cares, and without Presidential concurrence for important diplomatic decisions, until late November Blaine made no effort to assist the negotiations underway to settle the dispute between Mexico and Guatemala.

They were carried on for the most part in Mexico. Philip H. Morgan, a lawyer of reputation and character in his private capacity, presented Blaine's views with persuasion and tact. He tendered the good offices of the United States to the Mexican minister for foreign affairs, Ignacio Mariscal, and urged him to settle matters with Guatemala by arbitration. Morgan's instructions obliged him to tell Mariscal frankly that the United States would look with extreme disfavor upon any Latin American nation which disturbed the territorial status quo of the Americas.[27]

Mariscal asserted that his country planned no aggression against any nation. He was equally vehement, however, in rejecting the proposal to submit Mexico's rights to arbitration. He hinted broadly that Guatemala's pleas for arbitration were a ruse, designed to delay the creation of a boundary commision and to obtain the backing of the United States for a Central American confederation. Mariscal's thinly veiled resentment against Blaine's diplomacy was more than matched by daily diatribes in the Mexican press. Morgan reported: "There is a prejudice here against all foreigners . . . this prejudice is more decided against Americans than against any others."[28]

Valiantly, but without success, Morgan tried to find a solution acceptable to both parties. But the tactics of both sides steadily pushed them into extreme and seemingly impossible positions to compromise. Late in September, therefore, Morgan wrote home a desperately frank dispatch, which gave a very bleak outlook for peace. He concluded: "unless the government is prepared to announce to the Mexican Government that it will actively, if necessary, preserve the peace, it would be the part of wisdom on our side to leave the matter where it is."[29]

While this demanding dispatch was on its way to Washington, Blaine was being besieged by Guatemala's special minister to the United States, Lorenzo

---

[26] Blaine to Morgan, No. 142, June 21, 1881, *Foreign Relations 1881*, 769. Italics inserted.

[27] Morgan to Blaine, No. 232, July 12, 1881, *Foreign Relations 1881*, 773–75; Morgan to Blaine, No. 240, July 19, 1881, *ibid.*, 775–778.

[28] Morgan to Blaine, confidential, No. 254, August 13, 1881, *Despatches Mexico*, LXXIII (Department of State Records, National Archives). This long (78 pages) and important report on Mexican commerce, industry, government, and classes, emphasized the hostility which many Mexicans felt for Americans, especially business men welcomed by the conservative Díaz regime.

[29] Morgan to Blaine, No. 273, September 22, 1881, *Foreign Relations 1881*, 809.

Montúfar. Montúfar was flattering: "The United States," he wrote, "... are the natural protectors of the integrity of the continent, and history shows how nobly and worthily they have fulfilled their high mission.... The Government of Guatemala lays its questions with Mexico in the hands of the United States Government."[30]

Blaine was ready for it. After his long period of inaction, he proved in new instructions late in November that he had lost none of his old fire. He reacted strongly to the pessimism of the latest dispatch from Morgan, who had confronted him with the alternative of actively intervening to preserve the peace or leaving the matter where it was. The use of force was out of the question, for Congress and the American people had no vital interests at stake in this particular territorial status quo of Latin America. Blaine did not expect to use or to need forcible means to gain his ends. Instead he instructed Morgan once again to urge arbitration on Mexico, limiting it to the question of the boundary and not the ownership of Chiapas, and urged him to exert to the full the "moral influence" of the United States in bringing about a settlement of the dispute.

But Blaine hinted also that a different approach probably held out more hope: "You will express the very deep and sincere regret which this government will feel if it shall find the powerful Republic of Mexico unwilling to join ... in maintaining and establishing the principle of friendly arbitration for international differences on the continent of America. Mexico and the United States, acting in cordial harmony, can induce all the other independent governments of North and South America to aid in fixing *this policy of peace for all the future disputes between the nations of the western hemisphere.... This country will continue its policy of peace even if it cannot have the great aid which the cooperation of Mexico would assure;* and it will hope, at no distant day, to see such concord and cooperation between all the nations of America as will render war impossible."[31]

Morgan must have wondered what Blaine meant. There can be little doubt of his meaning. On the very next day after sending instructions to Morgan, Blaine issued his circular inviting the independent nations of the Americas to a conference for the purpose of discussing ways to prevent war.

To place Blaine's conference invitations side by side with his specific policy regarding the Mexican-Guatemalan boundary dispute is to reveal the complexity of his purpose in issuing the circular. Obviously that dispute had impressed strongly upon Blaine the necessity for preventing such situations from developing in the future by providing for a general arbitration treaty to take care of them. Blaine deserves credit for his hopes, premature though they were, and highly inopportune though the time was, that the independent nations of the Western Hemisphere would be willing to approve such a treaty.

But calling an inter-American conference would serve a double purpose, would have meaning for the present as well as the future. No longer would the United States be the sole advocate of an arbitration scorned by Mexico and embraced by Guatemala. It would become a Pan American concern, shared by many. Thus even though Blaine ex-

[30] Montúfar to Blaine, November 7, 1881, *Senate Exec. Docs.,* No. 156, 47 Cong., 1 Sess., 20. Montúfar formerly had been minister for foreign affairs, and had been sent by General Barrios to convey Guatemala's regrets upon the death of President Garfield. The real purpose of Montúfar's visit undoubtedly was less humanitarian.

[31] Blaine to Morgan, No. 198, November 28, 1881, *Foreign Relations 1881,* 816–817. Italics inserted.

plicitly denied in his invitations that the conference would be concerned with present disputes, calling such a meeting would bring diplomatic pressure to bear on Mexico by publicly revealing its reaction to the idea of arbitration.[32] If Mexico continued to refuse Blaine's proposal that the dispute be arbitrated, he was powerless to do very much about it. But could Mexico refuse an invitation to such a seemingly idealistic proposal as a conference on arbitration? To put the question was to present Mexico with a puzzling dilemma.[33]

In summary, Blaine's involvement with the Mexican-Guatemalan dispute was an important reason, although not alone, in accounting for his Pan American policy. Essentially it was the expanded role which the new secretary of state defined for the United States in Latin American affairs—supporter of the territorial status quo in the Americas—which led him to adopt a policy that aroused the ire of the Mexican government.[34] In order to prevent such situations from arising in the future, as well as to rescue himself and his policy from an unfortunate mixup at the time, Blaine went ahead with his invitations for an inter-American conference.

A third Latin American boundary dispute, that between Colombia and Costa Rica, was for Blaine another convincing lesson that calling an inter-American conference fell "within the line of both duty and interest on the part of the United States." [35] There ‘was no danger by 1881 that this particular controversy would result in war, for Colombia and Costa Rica had agreed in treaty to settle their territorial differences by arbitration.[36] Ironically, however, the great

[32] Shortly after receiving word of the prospective conference, Logan, United States minister to Central America, wrote to Blaine: "As a means of restraining the aggressive tendency of Mexico in the direction of Central America, the Congress would be attended by the happiest results, should a full agreement be reached." Elsewhere in this same dispatch he referred to the "good" resulting from the conference by "tying the hands of Mexico . . ." but warned that "the latter may consider the Congress to be specifically levelled against her . . ." No. 227, December 16, 1881, *Despatches Central America,* XVIII. Officially, of course, Blaine could not reveal the full purpose of his proposal for a conference, but when the invitations were suspended by his successor Frelinghuysen early in 1882, on February 3 Blaine wrote an indignant letter to President Arthur and sent a copy for publication in the New York *Tribune,* defending the conference idea in these words: "Shall the United States now turn back, hold aloof, and refuse to exert its great moral power for the advantages of its weaker neighbors?" In such a way did Blaine himself suggest a purpose for the conference not stated in the invitations, but closely related to his own pressing and immediate Latin American problems.

[33] Mexico already had firmly declined one proposal for a conference on arbitration: that put forth by Colombia in October of 1880 for a meeting of the Latin American states a year later (postponed to December) for the purpose of approving a multi-lateral arbitration treaty. See Mariscal to Becerra, Colombian foreign minister, August 1, 1881, translation, enclosure 2 in Morgan to Blaine, No. 256, August 15, 1881, *Despatches Mexico,* LXXIII. It is interesting to speculate that possibly Blaine seized upon Colombia's lead. It was not until December 16 that Morgan transmitted Blaine's invitation to Mariscal. Mexico decided to deal with its dilemma by playing for time. Morgan informed Frelinghuysen on January 4, 1882, that Mariscal *thought* that someone from Mexico would be appointed, but "did not, however, inform me that his government had determined upon sending any commissioners." Late in

March Mariscal officially accepted the invitation. By that time, however, Frelinghuysen had made it clear that Blaine's strong policy in the Guatemalan dispute had been abandoned; Mariscal knew that Mexico had nothing more to fear from the United States, and also was aware that the conference probably would not be held. See Morgan to Frelinghuysen, No. 332, January 4, 1882, and No. 375, March 28, 1882, *Foreign Relations 1882,* 383–386.

[34] Matías Romero, Mexican minister to the United States in 1882, abundantly testified later to the scorn in which his government and his countrymen held Blaine in 1881. Romero was sorry for it, but he too felt that Blaine's policy had been wrong. See Matías Romero, "Mr. Blaine and the Boundary Question between Mexico and Guatemala," *American Geographical Society Journal* (New York, 1897), XXIX, 281–330.

[35] So he expressed himself later, in justification of his policy: "Foreign Policy of the Garfield Administration," *Political Discussions,* 414.

[36] For a translated copy of the treaty, signed December 25, 1880, see *Foreign Relations 1881,* 100–101.

champion of arbitration opposed such a settlement of this dispute.

Blaine's objection was based upon the kind and not the principle of arbitration employed. The treaty designated as possible arbitrators, in order of preference, the King of Belgium, the King of Spain, and the President of the Argentine Republic. Blaine deplored having foreign decisions become meaningful in the New World, but the additional fact that the United States was, under an 1846 treaty, the protector of Colombia's sovereignty over Panama, and the guarantor of the neutrality of the isthmus, caused him to conclude that such an arbitral proceeding affected the obligations of the United States and could not be binding without its consent.

He so informed his ministers to Colombia and to Costa Rica, and then quickly made his position clear to the responsible authorities in Belgium and Spain.[37] Although the price of his policy was resentment both official and unofficial in Colombia and Costa Rica, apparently his forceful messages did avert the danger that European influence might be exerted in a dispute of peculiar importance to the United States.

But Blaine held that the State Department must do more than make such isolated and individual interventions to prevent the increase of European influence in the New World. In situations threatening war in Latin America, he later urged, "Our own Government cannot take the ground that it will not offer friendly intervention to settle troubles between American countries, unless at the same time it freely concedes to European Governments the right of such intervention, and thus consents to a practical destruction of the Monroe doctrine and an unlimited increase of European influence on this continent."[38] However strained an interpretation of the Monroe doctrine this policy might rest upon, it required prompt and decisive action by the United States.

Such action could take place in an inter-American conference, whose purpose would be to draw up an inter-American arbitration treaty, and thus decrease the chances for Latin American nations to consult Europe. In such a way did Blaine hope to avoid for the future the kind of intervention which he felt necessary in the Colombian-Costa Rican controversy. His experience in that dispute thus led him by another path to see the value of and hence to propose an inter-American conference.

3

Territorial disputes in Latin America —the "menace" or threat of war dealt with above—played an important part in forming Blaine's Pan American policy. But, to use Blaine's words, the "exist-

---

[37] Blaine to Ernest Dichmann, United States minister to Colombia, No. 169, May 26, 1881, *ibid.*, 355–356; Blaine to Logan, No. 148, May 26, 1881, *ibid.*, 105–106; Blaine to James O. Putnam, United States minister to Belgium, No. 46, May 31, 1881, *ibid.*, 70–72; Blaine to Lucius Fairchild, United States minister to Spain, No. 148, June 25, 1881, *ibid.*, 1057–1058. Blaine tried but without success to get England's consent to a modification of the Clayton-Bulwer Treaty of 1850, which prevented a canal under exclusive United States control. See Mary W. Williams, *Anglo-American Isthmian Diplomacy, 1815–1915* (Washington, 1916), 276–286; Tyler, *Foreign Policy of Blaine*, 22–45.

[38] Again the historical example of the French intervention in Mexico is evident. Blaine, "Foreign Policy of the Garfield Administration," *Political Discussions*, 414. On June 13, 1882, before a House Foreign Affairs Committee, Blaine expressed similar views, with more heat and emotion: "I think it will be demonstrated in the very near future," he said, "that the United States will have to assume a much more decided tone in South America than the one which I took ... or else it will have to back out of it, and say that is a domain that does not belong to us, and we surrender it to Europe. Because the United States is almost big enough to do anything except to play dog-in-the-manger...." *House Reports*, No. 1790, 47 Cong., 1 Sess. (Washington, 1882), 352.

ence" of war—by which he meant the War of the Pacific [39]—proved to be far more significant than situations short of war in bringing about his invitations to a Pan American conference.

The War of the Pacific, pitting Chile against Bolivia and Peru, began two years before Blaine became secretary of state. Economic cupidity was a central cause. Explorations and scientific findings had revealed by the 1840's that Bolivia's Pacific littoral, which stretched between Chilean and Peruvian territory into the little known wastes of the Atacama desert, contained enormous guano deposits of great value as commercial fertilizer. Peru's province of Tarapacá did also. Atacama and Tarapacá contained besides large and valuable deposits of nitrate of soda.

Chile had an enterprising citizenry alive to commercial possibilities, and enjoyed a strong and stable government rare in Latin America. It sent an ex-

ploratory commission into the desert and proclaimed in 1842 that its territory included a part of Atacama. Weakened by a succession of insecure and incompetent governments, Bolivia ineffectively protested Chile's claims. They agreed upon a compromise boundary in 1866. To gain much needed revenue, however, Bolivia foolishly allowed its guano and nitrate deposits to be worked by Chilean companies, financed in many cases by British capital.[40] Disputes over complicated taxing arrangements created new tensions. In 1873 Bolivia sought and obtained an alliance of defense with supposedly powerful Peru, Chile's chief rival on the west coast. Over the years Peru had spent its rich nitrate revenues unwisely and without restraint. By the 1870's its guano deposits, though still great, were dwindling rapidly; Chilean competition had caused the market to slump somewhat; and Peru had hypothecated most of its income from nationalized nitrate mines in a series of complicated foreign loans and contracts.[41] The Peruvian foreign office tried, but without success, to widen the scope of its alliance with Bolivia so as to include the Argentine Republic.[42]

National rivalry and inept diplomacy now made their contributions. Chile in-

[39] There is a voluminous literature dealing with the origins of the War of the Pacific, but many of the significant accounts contain biased judgments. Important presentations of the Chilean point of view are Diego Barros Arana, *Histoire de la Guerre du Pacifique* (Paris, 1881), I; and Gonzalo Búlnes, *Historia de la guerra del Pacífico* (Valparaiso, 1912–1919), 3 vols., the first volume of which has appeared in English translation under the title *Chile and Peru The Causes of the War of 1879* (Santiago, 1920). Clearly favorable to Bolivia and Peru are C. R. Markham, *The War between Peru and Chile* (London, 1882), and V. M. Maúrtua, *The Question of the Pacific* (translated, revised, and enlarged by F. L. Pezot, New York, 1901). More recent and reliable accounts are W. J. Dennis, *Tacna and Arica* (Yale U. Press, 1931), and Jacinto López, *Historia de la guerra del guano y el salitre o Guerra del Pacfiico entre Chile, Bolivia y el Purú* (New York, 1930), I. The Tacna-Arica arbitration of 1928, which settled the longstanding "Alsace-Lorraine" territorial question between Chile and Peru growing out of the War of the Pacific, resulted in the translation into English and publication of important diplomatic correspondence in *The Appendix to the Counter-Case of Chile submitted to the President of the United States as Arbitrator* (Washington, D.C., n.d. 1923?), and *The Appendix to the Case of Peru in the matter of the controversy arising out of the Question of the Pacific* (Washington, 1923).

[40] V. G. Kiernan, "Foreign Interests in the War of the Pacific," HAHR (February, 1955), XXXV, 15; J. Fred Rippy, "British Investments in the Chilean Nitrate Industry," *Inter-American Economic Affairs* (Autumn, 1954), VIII, 3–11.

[41] The incredibly intricate history of Peru's nitrate finances has now been written, in definitive form, by William H. Wynne, *State Insolvency and Foreign Bondholders*, II (Yale University Press, 1951), 109–195. A good contemporary description of the state of Peru's guano resources in the 1870's is A. J. Duffield, *Peru in the Guano Age* (London, 1877).

[42] Agüero, Peruvian minister of foreign affairs, to Irigoyen, Peruvian minister to the Argentine Republic, May 20, 1873, *Appendix to Counter-Case of Chile*, 1–3. Robert N. Burr, "South America and the Balance of Power," HAHR (February, 1955), XXXV, 52–53, points out that a majority of South American nations had become involved in the balancing of power with this attempted integration of the power systems of the Plata and the Pacific.

creased its military and naval strength. A new boundary treaty with Bolivia went into effect in 1874, but provisions on taxes were still confusing. Bolivia's reaction to the spectacle of Chilean entrepreneurs forging ahead in their exploitation of Bolivian nitrates was perhaps inevitable. The immediate cause of the war was a change in the taxes levied by Bolivia upon the Chilean Antofogasta Company. Chile claimed that it was in violation of treaty obligations. Bolivia disagreed. When the company refused to pay, Bolivia ordered its appropriation. Chile met the order with force. Acting without a declaration of war, Chilean troops occupied Antofogasta and began a drive up the Atacama coast. Peru tried to mediate. Chile demanded an abrogation of the alliance between Bolivia and Peru. Peru refused. On April 5, 1879, Chile declared war on both Bolivia and Peru.

The war was a succession of Chilean military triumphs. In the winter of 1879, the allies failed to prevent Chile's conquest of Tarapacá. Early in 1880 Chile's armies began to advance farther north, into Peru's province of Tacna.[43] The prospect seemed clear: Chile probably would subjugate most of the western coast of South America. Such an outcome of the war would affect all of South America. In the United States it set off a sequence of events which culminated in Blaine's calling an inter-American conference.

That sequence began with the diplomacy of William M. Evarts,[44] Blaine's

predecessor in the State Department. Evarts hoped to see peace restored without provocative action by the United States. Strongly opposed to European interference in an American conflict, Evarts was equally against having the United States mediate unless called upon, and he disapproved of any coercion in disparagement of belligerent rights.[45]

One self-appointed bearer of the olive branch, Colonel Horace Fisher, an American citizen who was Chile's consul in Boston, traveled to South America after the war broke out and early in 1880 urged the United States to help solve Latin America's sufferings from boundary disputes by calling an inter-American conference. He and an earlier would-be mediator from Colombia, Dr. Pablo Arosemena, agreed that by such action the United States "would predominate in South America for the next century." And in December Bolivia's foreign minister, Juan C. Carrillo, suggested that a South American conference be called to keep the peace by guaranteeing the boundaries of 1810.[46] Such sug-

Exec. Docs., No. 79, 47 Cong., 1 Sess.; and upon the following secondary works: Chester L. Barrows, William M. Evarts (U. of North Carolina Press, 1941), Brainard Dyer, The Public Career of William M. Evarts (U. of California Press, 1933), and Claude Bowers and Helen Reid, "William M. Evarts," in Bemis (ed.), American Secretaries of State, VII, 217–259.

[45] For Evarts' reaction to German and British overtures in the summer of 1879 looking to a concerted mediation with the United States, see Evarts to Andrew D. White, United States minister to Germany, June 19, 1879 (telegram), Instructions Germany (Department of State Records, National Archives), XVI, 475; Evarts to White, No. 22, July 19, 1879, ibid., 486–487; and Evarts to Henry Howard (acting for Sir Edward Thornton, British minister to the United States), June 19, 1879, Notes to British Legation (Department of State Records, National Archives), XVIII, 76.

[46] Horace Fisher to Assistant Secretary of State William Hunter, February 27, 1880, Senate Exec. Docs., No. 79, 47 Cong., 1 Sess., 621–24. See also Fisher to Acting Secretary of State Frederick W. Seward, July 31, 1879, ibid., 604–607; Fisher to Hunter, December 26,

[43] See the report of Lt. Theodore Mason, military observer of the United States during the early stages of the war, in Senate Miscellaneous Documents, No. 30, 48 Cong., 1 Sess., 1–77. Dennis, Tacna and Arica, contains a good brief account of the military aspects of the war, 90–130.

[44] My impressions of Evarts' diplomacy are based upon a survey of the William M. Evarts Papers (Division of Manuscripts, Library of Congress); his diplomatic correspondence in connection with the War of the Pacific, almost all of which has been published in Senate

gestions are striking in view of Blaine's invitations a year later, but there is no evidence that Evarts gave the idea more than cursory attention.

The war's increasing tempo in 1880, accompanied by disturbing reports that European nations were contemplating interference, led Evarts to support a mediation initiated by the United States ministers to Bolivia, Peru, and Chile. Late in October, at a conference aboard the U.S.S. *Lackawanna,* anchored in Arica Bay, Chile produced harsh demands upon the allies for both territory and a financial indemnity. Peru and Bolivia refused a victor's peace, the views expressed by the three United States ministers present were conflicting and indecisive, and the conference ended in failure after three days. In the wake of the Arica talks the United States minister to Chile, Thomas A. Osborn, warned that if the State Department actively tried to bring peace to South America, it must expect bitter opposition from Chile.[47] Evarts was not so willing to involve the United States. He stood ready to promote peace properly. Beyond that he would not go.[48]

After the failure of the Arica conference Chile moved swiftly for an all-out drive on Lima. Peru stiffened its de-

fenses early in 1881, but could not prevent Chilean troops from conquering the Peruvian capital. The most important Chilean objective of the war had been won. Peru's remaining forces fled to the interior. Bolivian troops also retreated to inland defenses. The allies' military opposition was reduced to sporadic guerrilla operations. For purposes of peacemaking, Chile encouraged a new provisional government in Peru, that of García Calderón. To most Peruvians, Calderón appeared initially to be upheld primarily by Chilean bayonets, and though his government slowly gained support, his authority remained most pronounced within Chile's military lines. Nonetheless, when Blaine succeeded Evarts on March 4, 1881, he received Calderón's confidential agent in Washington, and issued instructions which resulted in the recognition of the Calderón government.[49]

Garfield and Blaine changed the personnel of the State Department as well as its policy. Two of their new ministers were diplomatists cut from military cloth, in the fashion of post-Civil War America. Stephen A. Hurlbut, sent to Peru, had been a war-time general and then served briefly as congressman from Illinois. As an army administrator on occupation duty in Louisiana, he had been

---

1879, *ibid.,* 617–621. Evarts appointed Fisher a special bearer of diplomatic dispatches; he delivered the mail without mishap, but unfortunately gave the impression in certain quarters that he was a special peace emissary from the United States. For the original printed circular of Carrillo, 9 pages, December 1, 1880, see the enclosure in Adams to Evarts, No. 52, December 16, 1880, *Despatches Bolivia,* VIII.

[47] Osborn to Evarts, No. 195, February 24, 1881, *Senate Exec. Docs.,* No. 79, 151–3.

[48] Herbert Millington, *American Diplomacy and the War of the Pacific* (Columbia U. Press, 1948), 78, interprets Evarts' mediation at Arica as putting the United States "on record as opposing any conquest by force in South America." There is no evidence for such a conclusion. Actually, Evarts never outlined the kind of peace preferred by the United States, and he never went on record as opposed, either in theory or practice, to Chile's demands for territory as the price of peace.

[49] Recognition was decided upon in a slipshod and careless manner. Isaac P. Christiancy, U.S. Minister to Peru, consistently had opposed it on the grounds that Calderón was not in actual control of Peru; Blaine instructed him to recognize the government if it "is supported by the character and intelligence of Peru and is really endeavoring to restore constitutional government with a view both to order within and negotiation with Chile for peace,..."; Christiancy concluded from this that his superior really favored recognition. See Blaine to Christiancy, No. 143, May 9, 1881, *Senate Exec. Docs.,* No. 79, 47 Cong., 1 Sess., 495; Christiancy to Blaine, No. 319, June 16, 1881, *ibid.,* 501–502, No. 320, June 21, 1881, *ibid.,* 503–505. Later Christiancy and Blaine quarreled publicly over the issue. Christiancy explained his misgivings about the recognition of the Calderón government in a press interview published in the New York *Herald,* December 14, 1881.

accused of corrupt financial practices. Apparently the charges had some validity. Nonetheless, in 1868 he was elected first commander-in-chief of the Grand Army of the Republic. From that exalted position he began what proved to be a disappointing career of opportunistic politicking.[50] Judson A. Kilpatrick, appointed to the post in Chile, had been a dashing cavalry commander with Sherman on his march to the sea, and also entered public life belatedly. His military record and political services to the Republican party had won him the post of minister to Chile once before, from 1865 to 1868. But by 1881 Kilpatrick was a sick man, his effectiveness severely limited by his physical infirmities.[51]

Blaine's first instructions to his new ministers were sympathetic to Peru. To Kilpatrick he pointed out that at the end of the war it might be necessary to have a readjustment of boundaries, but he strongly opposed having a territorial indemnity made the *sine qua non* of peace. "... nothing but a necessity proven before the world can justify it," Blaine maintained. "The United States Government ... believes that ... territorial changes ... should never be the result of mere force, but, *if necessary, should be decided and tempered by full and equal discussion between all the powers whose people and whose national interests are involved*."[52] To Hurlbut, Blaine made it clear that he hoped the Calderón government soon would become sufficiently independent of Chile so that peace negotiations could

begin. In regard to the peace itself he took the attitude that Peru had the right to substitute a financial for a territorial indemnity.[53]

In his diplomatic instructions Blaine maintained that his support of Peru's territorial integrity stemmed from his conviction that territorial changes brought about by force caused future international strife which might breed more wars, and kept alive in the New World an evil "European" right giving conquerors the privilege of taking what they wanted. A second explanation Blaine never expressed in his official diplomatic correspondence, but often ennough in emotional public statements he emphasized that he was also opposing England's commercial conquest of western South America: "Chile got ironclad ships from England," he asserted warmly in early 1882. "Chilean soldiers marched to Peru clad in uniforms of English cloth, with English muskets on their shoulders. English sympathy has stood behind [Chile] at every step in her conquest.... This Peru-Chilean war destroys American influence on the South Pacific coast and literally wipes out American commercial interests in that vast region.... Chile's victory throws the whole Peruvian business into English hands." [54]

[50] Theodore C. Pease, "Stephen A. Hurlbut," in Allen Johnson, Dumas Malone, and Harris M. Starr (eds.), *Dictionary of American Biography* (21 vols., New York, 1928–1944), IX, 425–426. Professor Pease wrote me that Hurlbut's family had destroyed his papers, probably because of a "skeleton in the closet."

[51] Charles Dudley Rhodes, "Hugh Judson Kilpatrick," *ibid.*, X, 374–75; New York *World*, December 7, 1881.

[52] Blaine to Kilpatrick, No. 2, June 15, 1881, *Senate Exec. Docs.*, No. 79, 47 Cong., 1 Sess., 157–159. Italics inserted.

[53] Blaine to Hurlbut, No. 2, June 15, 1881, *ibid.*, 500–501. Blaine was firmly convinced that Peru's territorial integrity should be preserved if possible, and said so on more than one occasion. In an interview given to the New York *Times*, January 30, 1882, he insisted that "Peru ought to have been allowed to pay a cash indemnity, and ought not to be subjected to a destruction of her nationality." Before the House Foreign Affairs Committee on April 27 of the same year he replied in the affirmative to the direct question: "Did you not urge on Chile through the diplomatic agents of the United States, that Chile should be satisfied to accept a pecuniary indemnity from Peru, and forego territorial acquision?" *House Reports*, No. 1790, 47 Cong., 1 Sess., 235.

[54] New York *Times*, January 30, 1882. See also Blaine's testimony before the House Foreign Affairs Committee, April 26, 1882, *House Reports*, No. 1790, 47 Cong., 1 Sess., 217.

Certain financial interests also endeavored to associate themselves with Blaine's diplomacy in the War of the Pacific. Most important of these was the Société Générale de Crédit Industriel et Commercial, a French corporation which acted as a giant holding company for many of Peru's European bondholders. The Crédit proposed to supervise the further exploitation of Peru's guano and nitrate deposits, and use the revenue to guarantee a financial indemnity to Chile, an annual income to Peru, payments to the bondholders, and a handsome profit to itself.[55] The Crédit was the chief financial group which tried to solicit aid from the State Department, but the lobbying activities of the Peruvian Company and its president, Jacob R. Shipherd, created a far greater sensation in the press. Early in 1881 Shipherd, a New York lawyer-promoter eager about get-rich-quick schemes in an age of easy money and easier virtue, worked out an audacious plan to exploit the long-standing and dubious Cochet claim against Peru—estimated by Shipherd at one billion dollars!—originated by Alexandre Cochet, a French explorer-scientist who claimed to have discovered and helped to increase the commercial value of certain Peruvian guano deposits. Shipherd's loosely organized Peruvian Company sought to gain control of Peru's nitrates

and guano, guarantee to Chile a financial indemnity, and pay off Peru's creditors and claimants, including the Peruvian Company itself.[56] Finally, there was the Landreau claim. Theophile Landreau, a French citizen, claimed that Peru illegally had cancelled a contract guaranteeing him a return on the value of guano deposits he had indentified. Landreau's brother, a naturalized American citizen, acquired an interest in the claim, appealed to the United States, and investigations had been undertaken before 1881 by both the State Department and the House of Representatives. The Landreau claimants hoped that diplomatic action by the United States would either cause Chile to desist from annexing Peruvian territory or recognize the claim as a lien upon any territory to be transferred.[57]

These three financial interests had in common the desire to prevent Chile from annexing Peru's guano lands. All tried to secure help from the State Department. And all got reactions. Blaine and Hurlbut probably looked upon the Crédit with favor, at least at first, hopeful that it would provide the means for Peru to pay Chile a financial indemnity. The rash and inexperienced Hurlbut, soon

Kiernan, "Foreign Interests in War of Pacific," HAHR, XXXV, 23, examined the British Foreign Office Records, and concluded that "So far as the British government was concerned, in this particular case, Blaine's suspicion was unfounded."

[55] Representatives of the Crédit submitted their plan and talked with Evarts before he left the State Department. He sent it on to Christiancy in Peru, but did not press the idea, as one of his advisers in the department, William Henry Trescot, urged him to do. See the documents enclosed in the communication from the Crédit's representatives in the United States, Count de Montferrand and M. Suárez, to Evarts, January 20, 1881, Senate Exec. Docs., No. 79, 47 Cong., 1 Sess., 686–696; Evarts to Christiancy, No. 129, confidential, February 17, 1881, ibid., 449–452; Trescot to Evarts (n.d., Jan. 1881?), Evarts Papers.

[56] The prospectus of the Peruvian Company, together with its outline of a proposed agreement with Peru, is printed in Senate Exec. Docs., No. 79, 47 Cong., 1 Sess., 634–678. See also Shipherd's testimony of March 22, 1882, before the House Foreign Affairs Committee, in House Reports, No. 1790, 47 Cong., 1 Sess., 36–46.

[57] For full documentation on the Landreau claim, see the sources prepared by the United States and Peru in the final settlement of this claim before an arbitral commission in 1922, which awarded $25,000 to the heirs of Landreau: Case of United States of America and Supporting Evidence on the Landreau Claim (Washington, 1922); Report of International Arbitral Commission on Landreau Claim: Answer of Peru and Supporting Evidence (Washington, 1922); Award of International Arbitral Commission on Landreau Claim (Washington, 1922); Numerical File, 1906–1910, vol. 168, Cases 1502/231 to 1504/96; vol. 1141, Cases 22909 to 22960 (Department of State Records, National Archives).

after his arrival in Lima on August 10, wrote that since Peru now had the means (no doubt he had the Crédit in mind) by which to pay an ample indemnity, Chile should not be allowed to insist upon territory.[58] Toward Shipherd and the Peruvian Company Blaine claimed to have been entirely hostile. An elaborate and unscrupulous campaign designed to give the impression that important public and financial figures were behind the Peruvian Company enabled Shipherd to obtain more than one interview with Blaine.[59] The promotor even attempted to bribe Hurlbut, who foolishly failed to report the offer.[60] Ship-

herd insisted that during the summer Blaine had been willing to support the Cochet claim and disowned it only on the eve of his retirement from the State Department.[61] Hurlbut, the promotor maintained, had been brought under the influence of the Crédit. No substantial evidence exists to support the charges of Shipherd, who mixed business, politics, and diplomacy by stirring with the crude spoons of guile and gain. Hurlbut may at first have contemplated the Cochet claim favorably, although he never pressed it upon Peru.[62] Blaine's mistake was in giving Shipherd more than one interview. To the Landreau claim Blaine was most partial. He insisted officially that if Chile annexed Peru's guano lands the claim must be considered a lien on the property annexed.[63] It is entirely speculative and probably misleading to suggest—as has been done[64]—that Blaine's and Hurl-

[58] Hurlbut to Blaine, No. 2, August 10, 1881, Senate Exec. Docs., No. 79, 47 Cong., 1 Sess., 510–512. Blaine's first instructions to Hurlbut did not mention the Crédit by name, but undoubtedly had it in mind when reference was made approvingly to ". . . a plan by which all the reasonable conditions of Chile can be met without sacrificing the integrity of Peruvian territory. . . ." See Blaine to Hurlbut, No. 2, June 14, 1881, 501; Blaine's testimony of April 27, 1882, House Reports, No. 1790, 47 Cong., 1 Sess., 226. Blaine's attitude toward the Crédit seems to have been that he wished it well in helping to allow Peru to meet Chile's demands for a financial indemnity, but would not interfere in its behalf. Robert Randall, the Crédit's New York lawyer, testified before the House committee that Blaine had led him to believe that he would go much further in his support: ibid., 304–313, 321–333.
[59] Shipherd wrote letters to President Garfield, to Blaine, to Hurlbut, and to Kilpatrick, peppering them with propaganda relating to the Cochet claim. His greatest coup, however, was in obtaining the services of United States Senator Henry W. Blair of New Hampshire as special counsel for the Peruvian Company. Blair was a close friend of Blaine's, and undoubtedly helped greatly in obtaining interviews for Shipherd. Testimony of Shipherd, March 21, 22, 1882, ibid., 24–176; testimony of Senator Blair, May 1, 1882, ibid., 242–304.
[60] Shipherd wrote Hurlbut that he was reserving for him, subject to approval, $250,000 worth of stock in the Peruvian Company. Shipherd to Hurlbut, June 2, 1881, enclosure in Hurlbut to Blaine, No. 2, November 2, 1881, Senate Exec. Docs., No. 79, 47 Cong., 1 Sess., 549. Hurlbut's brother, William Henry Hurlbut, editor of the New York World, claimed that the minister had been asked by President Garfield to look into the Cochet claim; Hurlbut advised his brother to make a complete investigation before informing his superiors of Shipherd's attempted bribe. Testimony of Hurlbut, April

20, 1882, House Reports, No. 1790, 47 Cong., 1 Sess., 184.
[61] Testimony of Shipherd, April 11, 1882, ibid., 115. See also his privately printed booklet, The Rejected Testimony of Jacob R. Shipherd (New York, 1882), 84 pages.
[62] Hurlbut's failure at once to report Shipherd's correspondence, which totaled twenty-two letters, leaves him open to suspicion of having contemplated the Cochet claim favorably until after he had investigated it in Peru. By the middle of September, in reply to a query from Blaine, Hurlbut was deprecatory of the Cochet claim and Shipherd: Hurlbut to Blaine, No. 12, September 14, 1881, Senate Exec. Docs., No. 79, 47 Cong., 1 Sess., 522.
[63] Blaine to Hurlbut, No. 7, August 4, 1881, ibid., 508–509.
[64] Frederic Bancroft (ed.), Speeches, Correspondence and Public Papers of Carl Schurz (New York, 1913), IV, 259; Thomas H. Talbot, The Proudest Chapter in His Life (New York, 1884); Edward H. Strobel, Mr. Blaine and His Foreign Policy (New York, 1884). Such charges were especially prominent during Blaine's campaign for the presidency in 1884. Perry Belmont, Democratic member of the House investigating committee in 1882, and an outspoken critic of Blaine's Latin American policy then and for more than sixty years thereafter, believed that Blaine switched his allegiance from the Crédit Industriel to the Landreau claim in order to gain public approval by supporting the claim of an American

but's sympathy toward the Crédit and support of the Landreau claim stemmed from backstairs intrigues for financial gain. Their interest in the Crédit seems to have originated in the hope that by utilizing its program Peru might avoid territorial dismemberment. The Landreau claim Blaine considered to be valid, although undoubtedly it appealed to him also as another obstacle in the path of Chile's aggrandizement, as well as a means of hitting at England.

Blaine later deprecated the importance of the claims to his diplomacy: "The fact of it is, the whole of this business about the Landreau claim and the Cochet claim [he did not mention the Crédit here] had no more to do with the administration's policy about South America than a barnacle on the bottom of the vessel that carried General Hurlbut into Lima had; not a bit; nothing whatever. It never interrupted the course of it for an hour, and never figured in it; never. ..." [65] But these three financial interests —all of foreign origin—did not have to interrupt the course of Blaine's policy in order to figure in it. Rumors grew that Blaine and his minister Hurlbut were practicing a "guano diplomacy" which placed private interests above the public welfare of either Peru or Chile.[66] Ship-

herd's wild charges came to be notorious on two continents. All three of the claims depended on saving Peru's territorial integrity, which came close enough to Blaine's own hopes for helping Peru that his policy disastrously became identified in many minds with theirs. Chile became more racalcitrant and Peru more hopeful because of the claims. The net effect was that Blaine's diplomacy, wittingly or not, became snarled in a tangle of charges and countercharges, rumors and rumors of rumors, and consequently, the inherent confusion in the diplomatic affairs of western South America became worse confounded.

In Chile and Peru, Kilpatrick and Hurlbut endeavored to translate Blaine's policy into practice. Hurlbut was the key figure of the two. He was Blaine's close and admired friend; he had conferred personally with him before leaving the United States; because Chilean authorities were present in Peru his post gave him a unique opportunity to conciliate the two antagonists. From the first he encouraged the Calderón government to resist demands by Chile for territory. In frequent and lengthy dispatches he vigorously expressed his conviction that Chile should not be allowed to annex Peruvian territory, but should give Peru a chance to pay a financial indemnity, which he was perfectly sure could be arranged.[67] In Hurlbut's eyes the United States had an obligation to end the war. Since his country looked with disfavor upon European intervention, it must assume such a responsibility itself. Blaine essentially agreed. When France in the

citizen. See Perry Belmont, *An American Democrat* (Columbia U. Press, 1940), 235–238.

[65] Testimony of Blaine, April 26, 1882, *House Reports*, No. 1790, 218.

[66] In the United States the press, depending on its attitude toward Blaine, speculated pro and con on the connection between the Peruvian Company and the State Department and Hurlbut. See New York *Times*, October 9, 17, November 26, 1881; New York *World*, October 9, 18, 1881; New York *Herald*, October 20, 1881; Washington *Post*, October 8, 22, November 28, 1881. For reactions in Peru and Chile see José Gaspar Rivadeneira, *Cochet y Landreau, breves observaciones sobre los derechos de Cochet y Landreau a propósito de la gran compañía americana destinado a explotar el Perú* (Valparaiso, 1882), 45 pages; Búlnes, *Guerra del Pacífico, III*, 96 *passim;* Federico J. Elmore, Calderón's representative in the United States, denied in an interview with the New York *Herald*, October 20, 1881, that agreements had

been made between his government and the Peruvian Company. Victor Drummond, British chargé d'affaires to the United States, speculated that Americans may have offered Calderón a secret loan on conditions favorable to their future commercial relations with Peru: see AHA *Annual Report, 1941*, I, 153.

[67] Hurlbut to Blaine, No. 2, August 10, 1881, *Senate Exec. Docs.*, No. 79, 47 Cong., 1 Sess., 510–512. See also his dispatches of August 17, 24, 27, in *ibid.*, 513–517.

summer of 1881 tried to come to an understanding with the United States on its policy toward the War of the Pacific, he was quick to disapprove any such negotiations.[68]

Late in August the uninhibited Hurlbut issued a flat warning to Admiral Lynch, commander-in-chief of Chile's occupation forces: ". . . the act of seizure of Peruvian territory . . . ," Hurlbut wrote, "would justly be regarded by other nations, as evidence that Chile had entered upon the path of aggression. . . ." [69] Lynch hurried a copy of the memorandum home, and Chile's able foreign minister, José Balmaceda, immediately got in touch with the tired and distraught Kilpatrick. Did Hurlbut, Balmaceda asked, accurately reflect American diplomacy? Eager to placate Balmaceda, and as unable as Hurlbut to restrain his prejudices in favor of the country to which he was accredited, Kilpatrick assured the Chilean that the United States intended no more than the tender of its good offices.[70] The two ministers were working at cross purposes, egregiously so.

Hurlbut continued to press the State Department. Late in October he summed up what in effect he had been saying since August: "It seems to me that the

opportunity for the United States will be to insist . . . and *forcibly*, that the principle of arbitration shall be accepted and acted on. . . . I hope to be promptly advised by telegraph or otherwise." [71] Instead the State Department sent no advice at all. Whether Blaine's silence through September and October resulted from Garfield's lingering illness and death, or whether it meant that he believed Hurlbut's bellicose tactics would cause Chile to modify its position, diplomacy by drift let things slide.

They rapidly slid into a new crisis. Early in November the Chilean authorities arrested Calderón. Hurlbut asserted that such action had been taken because Calderón would not make peace on Chile's terms, and suggested that it was possibly intended as a reply to the support of Calderón by the United States.[72] Blaine acted at last. Late in November he administered to Kilpatrick a reprimand for contradicting his colleague Hurlbut to Chilean authorities; Chile's complaints should have been made in Washington and answered there. At the same time Blaine gave Hurlbut a some-

---

[68] Levi P. Morton, United States minister to France, to Blaine, No. 6, August 11, 1881, *ibid.*, 596–597; Blaine to Morton, No. 30, September 5, 1881, *ibid.*, 597–598. Morton, who was to become Vice-President under Benjamin Harrison, was a member of the New York firm of Morton, Bliss and Company, which had signed a contract with a subsidiary of the Crédit Industriel for the sale of Peruvian nitrates in the United States. There was some question about Morton's propriety in this matter, but a House investigating committee in 1882 concluded that he had taken no part in the negotiations with the Crédit, and had acted properly.

[69] Hurlbut to Lynch, August 25, 1881, enclosure in Hurlbut to Blaine, No. 8, August 27, 1881, *Senate Exec. Docs.*, No. 79, 47 Cong., 1 Sess., 516–517.

[70] Kilpatrick to Balmaceda, enclosure in Kilpatrick to Blaine, No. 8, October 14, 1881, *ibid.*, 163–164.

[71] Hurlbut to Blaine, No. 23, October 26, 1881, *ibid.*, 539. Having gained the complete confidence and undying gratitude of Calderón and his government, Hurlbut proceeded in early October to draft a treaty with the provisional government of Peru granting the United States a coaling station in the Bay of Chimbote. Such a base, in what was one of the finest harbors in western South America, would perhaps not have been undesirable if negotiated in ordinary times, but Hurlbut coupled the cession with an extraordinary stipulation to the effect that American capitalists were to be given the right to purchase and develop a half-completed railway running from interior Peruvian coal mines to the coast at Chimbote; the minister even had the temerity to appoint himself as trustee of the railway line until an American company could be formed to take it over! See Hurlbut to Blaine, No. 19, October 5, 1881, *ibid.*, 530–31, with enclosures including the draft of a protocol.

[72] Hurlbut to Blaine, telegram, November 7, 1881, *Despatches Peru* (Department of State Records, National Archives), XXXVII; Hurlbut to Blaine, No. 26, November 9, 1881, *Senate Exec. Docs.*, No. 79, 47 Cong., 1 Sess., 560–561.

what milder rebuke by criticizing the emphasis and tactics of his diplomacy: getting Chile's agreement to a peace without territorial annexation should not have led him to insist that there could be no such annexation at all. Hurlbut complained privately to his brother in the United States that these instructions from Blaine backed down from the much stronger tone which he had taken previously.[73]

Troubled by the blunders of his ministers and the consequences of his own negligent policy, caught in the whirlwind of suspicion and mistrust stirred up by the financial interests, Blaine attempted a last minute move to save his Latin American policy. He sent news of the first importance to Hurlbut and to Kilpatrick: the President had decided to send a special envoy to South America, to deal with *"a condition now fast assuming proportions which make its settlement a matter of deep concern to all the republics of the continent."* [74] His choice for carrying a new policy into effect was William Henry Trescot. Blaine considered Trescot to be his department's "expert" on Latin America. A gifted writer and a dignified, if emotional South Carolinian, of impressive manners, brilliant speech, and wide public experience, as a special State Department assistant Trescot had helped Blaine greatly in his Latin American policy, "all of which he saw;" Blaine admitted, "a great part of which he was." [75] Trescot's

commission as envoy extraordinary and minister plenipotentiary to Chile, Peru, and Bolivia empowered him to take over the settlement of difficulties among the belligerents. Walker Blaine, son of the secretary and himself third assistant secretary, accompanied Trescot on the trip as an aide.

Secretary Blaine's instructions to Trescot, dated December 1, 1881, reviewed events from the fall of Lima early in the year. A decidedly strong stand was taken on Chile's arrest of Calderón; if it were a resentful reply to United States policy, Trescot was authorized to suspend diplomatic relations. But Blaine expected Chile instead to maintain that Hurlbut had so encouraged Calderón's resistance that a satisfactory treaty of peace became impossible; Trescot was to indicate to Chile that it had misconstrued Hurlbut's words and acts.

Trescot's next task would be to discuss the prospects for peace. Blaine repeated his strong belief that Peru should have the right to furnish a satisfactory financial indemnity rather than territory. But if Chile proved recalcitrant, the United States would not "regard with unconcern the destruction of Peruvian nationality." What action would it take? Blaine handed on to Trescot the trump he intended to play:

[73] Hurlbut to Hurlbut, dated December 29, 1881, in testimony submitted to the House Foreign Affairs Committee, April 20, 1882, *House Reports*, No. 1790, 47 Cong., 1 Sess., 181.

[74] Blaine to Kilpatrick, No. 13, November 22, 1881, *Senate Exec. Docs.*, No. 79, 169; Blaine to Hurlbut, No. 19, November 22, 1881, *ibid.*, 567. Italics inserted.

[75] Blaine to C. G. Williams, chairman of the House Foreign Affairs Committee, July 21, 1882, *House Reports*, No. 1790, 47 Cong., 1 Sess., 382. Trescot had become an assistant secretary of state by 1860, but his passionate Confederate loyalties during the war disbarred him from consideration later for a major diplomatic

position. Evarts had given him important duties to perform, perhaps the most striking of which was as head of a delegation to China in 1880 which arranged a successful modification of the Burlingame treaty. After his return to the United States, Evarts kept him on in the department, and he turned his attention more and more to Latin American affairs. Probably he made first drafts of certain of the instructions to Hurlbut, and undoubtedly was a great influence on Blaine's Latin American policies. The Trescot Papers, in the South Caroliniana Library at Columbia, South Carolina, constitute a valuable source of materials for a study of Trescot's career. Many important papers, unfortunately, including a special box containing letters, newspaper clippings, and notes on his South American mission, were burned in a fire which destroyed the family home in 1918, but enough remain to make them a significant collection.

If our good offices are rejected, and this policy of the absorption of an independent state be persisted in, this government... will hold itself free to appeal to the other republics of this continent to join it in an effort to avert consequences which cannot be confined to Chili and Peru, but which threaten with extremest danger the political institutions, the peaceful progress, and the liberal civilization of all America.[76]

To cause Chile to back down from its severe demands, Blaine had decided upon a Pan American appeal. Through consultations with the other American republics, not in a unilateral action, the United States could exert moral pressure in full panoply.

Two days before Blaine thus instructed Trescot, he had invited all the independent Latin American nations (except Haiti) to send representatives to a general conference on methods of preventing war in the Western Hemisphere, to be held in Washington a year later.[77] The invitations, dated November 29, stressed that "for years past" the United States had endeavored either to avert war or bring conflicts to an end by counsel or arbitration, and that "for some years past" a "growing disposition" in favor of arbitration had been manifested also by "certain states" in Latin America. It was also made clear that the conference would not deal with existing difficulties, but only with "the interests of all in the future"; the date for the meeting had been set "far in the future," to give good

reason for hope that "the present situation on the Pacific Coast will be happily terminated," so that those nations involved in it could take part in the discussions.

Blaine's hopes for a brave new American world without war were undoubtedly sincere. His own unfortunate experiences in dealing with the War of the Pacific and with Latin America's boundary disputes had made him deeply conscious that the distresses of Latin America meant diplomatic distresses for the United States as well. To prevent war in the Western Hemisphere would be insurance for all.

But in spite of Blaine's disclaimer that his "general congress" for 1882 was not to have anything to do with the war in the south Pacific, his proposal was linked to Trescot's mission in 1881. Significantly, Blaine instructed that the *neutral* republics of Latin America were to receive their invitations at once, but Trescot was to be in charge of those to Chile, Peru, and Bolivia.[78] If Chile insisted upon a harsh peace, it was to be threatened by the United States with an appeal to the other American republics. In such circumstances, Trescot wondered whether to invite Chile to the inter-American conference.[79] If invited, Chile probably would refuse. If not, it would consider the proposed conference a call for a hostile combination. In either case, however, Pan American pressure against Chile would have been applied. Blaine instructed Trescot, in case "such possi-

[76] Blaine to Trescot, No. 2, December 1, 1881, *Senate Exec. Docs., No. 79, 47 Cong., 1 Sess., 178.*

[77] Circular instructions of Blaine, dated November 29, 1881, to be found in full and original form, Blaine to Morgan, No. 199, *Instructions Mexico* (Department of State Records, National Archives), XX, 373–380, sent, under the same date, *mutatis mutandis,* to the legations of the United States in the Argentine Republic, Bolivia, Brazil, Central America (for each of the five governments of Costa Rica, Guatemala, Honduras, Nicaragua, and Salvador), Chile, Colombia, Mexico, Paraguay and Uruguay, Peru, and Venezuela. A copy was also sent, with an explanatory note, to the minister of foreign relations of Ecuador, in which country the United States had no diplomatic representation.

[78] Blaine delivered these instructions to Trescot verbally, and they do not appear in his written communications. Trescot referred to them, however, in various of his dispatches: Trescot to Blaine, No. 1, December 12, 1881, *Senate Exec. Docs., No. 181, 47 Cong., 1 Sess. (Washington, 1882), 8;* Trescot to Adams, United States minister to Bolivia, January 30, 1882, *ibid.,* 20; Trescot to Hurlbut, January 30, 1882, *ibid.,* 20–21.

[79] Confidential letter from Trescot to J. C. Bancroft Davis, January 27, 1882, J. C. Bancroft Davis Papers (Division of Manuscripts, Library of Congress). Why Trescot was writing to Davis will be made clear later in this essay.

ble contingency" made it worthwhile, to return home by way of Argentina and Brazil and impress upon those powerful nations the advantages to be derived from a conference.[80] Thus calling a Pan American meeting might help Trescot's mission to succeed, but even if it did not, if Chile refused to modify its demands, the future inter-American conference would overshadow Trescot's failure as well as the embarrassing rumors about claims and the bellicose bungling of Hurlbut.

Blaine put his most important Latin American policy decisions into effect *when he knew that he soon would be replaced as head of the State Department!* [81] Why revive during Arthur's presidency an idea which Blaine maintained he had given birth to before Garfield's assassination? Contentions have been made that Blaine sought either to complicate matters so much that President Arthur would have to keep him in office, or else to "sow the seeds" for his successor in the State Department, Frederick T. Frelinghuysen; but appealing though such charges were to Blaine's enemies,[82] they are impossible to prove.

The essential reason for Blaine's action lay in the critical situation of diplomacy which confronted him on the eve of leaving office. His country's prestige as well as his own future political career were at stake in the rapidly deteriorating diplomatic situation, which demanded drastic action. And so in a last and brilliant effort characteristically imaginative and ingenious Blaine placed in his brief record as secretary of state a new and striking proposal that would smooth over if not rub out his past mistakes.

Trescot and young Blaine took the regular route—a slow one—to the west coast of South America, sailing to the isthmus and then crossing by land to the Pacific. Upon their arrival at Panama, on December 12, they learned the distressing news that Kilpatrick had died suddenly at his post, thus silencing one of their most important sources of information. Hurlbut, however, was still very much alive in Peru. Having accepted an invitation of Peruvian notables to express his views at Calderón's house, Hurlbut told these influential gentlemen that the United States was firmly opposed to any territorial dismemberment of Peru.[83] When Trescot and young Blaine paid courtesy calls at Callao and Lima on their way to negotiate in Santiago, they were toasted as heroes of the hour. "I think if we had given a hint," wrote impressionable Walker Blaine to his parents, "they would have presented us with fortunes.

---

[80] Blaine to Trescot, No. 3, December 2, 1881, *Senate Exec. Docs.,* No. 79, 47 Cong., 1 Sess., 181.

[81] President Arthur asked Blaine to continue in the cabinet until after Congress met early in December, but already he was searching for Blaine's successor, and the latter knew that it would be impossible for him to continue in the Stalwart administration. See Frelinghuysen to Arthur, November 1, 1881, Arthur Papers; Frelinghuysen to Davis, December 8, 1881, Davis Papers. Frelinghuysen was ready to have his nomination presented to the Senate by December 6; Blaine suggested that he vacate on December 22; Frelinghuysen actually took over the State Department on December 20. See also Gail Hamilton, *Biography of Blaine,* 546–547.

[82] Hamilton Fish, former Republican secretary of state under Grant, who kept a close watch on the State Department's activities, wrote to his protégé J. C. Bancroft Davis, that he suspected Blaine of trying to "sow the seeds" for his successor. Fish to Davis, December 16, 1881, Davis Papers. See also William Henry Hurlbut, *Meddling and Muddling: Mr. Blaine's Foreign Policy* (New York, 1884).

[83] Hurlbut to the Notables of Lima, November 30, 1881, enclosure in Trescot to Blaine, No. 1, December 12, 1881, *Despatches Chile,* XXXI. (Department of State Records, National Archives.) By December 17 Hurlbut's speech had been reprinted and circulated in Chile: see Lucius M. Foote, United States consul at Valparaiso, to Blaine, No. 86, December 23, 1881, *Consular Despatches Valparaiso,* X. See also Hurlbut's pro-Peruvian version of the war and its antecedents, prepared as a memorandum to be submitted to Trescot and enclosed in Hurlbut to the Secretary of State, No. 41, January 10, 1882, *Despatches Peru,* XXXVII. An identical copy of this memo appears also in the Blaine Papers. How and when Blaine received it is impossible to determine.

... Trescott [sic] says it will be necessary to send a fleet to rescue us at the end of the mission, so little will the performance that we hope to succeed in correspond with Peruvian expectations." [84]

Before the two envoys had a chance to act at all, they received from the new secretary of state, Frelinghuysen, a vague wire, sent January 3, 1882, which read: "Exert pacific influence. Avoid any issue leading to your withdrawal from Chile." [85] The next day Frelinghuysen more seriously modified Blaine's demands on Chile. But these new instructions, mailed from Panama, did not reach Trescot until January 31! [86] He and young Blaine arrived in Santiago on January 7 aware only of Frelinghuysen's short and cryptic wire, not at all inconsistent with Blaine's original instructions, which Trescot continued to consider binding.

In Santiago public temper was at high pitch. Prevailing opinion was that the United States intended to dictate Chile's peace with Peru. Trescot was conciliatory, convinced that the more friendly his relations with Chile the better his chances of serving Peru. In confidential interviews the Chilean foreign minister, Balmaceda, assured Trescot that Calderón's arrest had not been intended as an affront to the United States. But Chile's peace proposals still went far beyond Blaine's hopes. Trescot believed that it was probably necessary for Peru to cede Tarapacá, and wired for such instructions. But he was also ready to invoke

Blaine's alternative order, warning that if Chile persisted in levying a harsh peace upon Peru the United States would take its case to the other American republics. [87]

Frelinghuysen was not willing to resort to such a Pan American appeal. Instead he changed the whole front of the Latin American policy of the United States, and by sending diplomatic correspondence to the House Foreign Affairs Committee, made his changes known publicly. [88]

Trescot, meanwhile, unaware that his instructions had become public property, was writing his inmost thoughts in confidential letters—hitherto unemphasized source material—to his good friend J. C. Bancroft Davis, the new assistant secretary of state. A letter of January 27 read in part:

The truth is the diplomatic situation is an awkward one.... Hurlbut has succeeded in making a muddle indeed.... The Chileans want peace ... [but] on their own terms. Now those terms are too harsh....

What are we to do? Recommend this to Peru? Why if we do instead of intervening to save Peru, we will practically have intervened to aid Chile....

... My idea is this.... we will advise Peru to cede Tarapacá but you [Chile] must stop there. If you won't do this we will withdraw. We will signify our grave disapprobation. We will hold ourselves free to do as circumstances seem to require without any further reference to our wishes, and *we believe the world will condemn the exactions of such terms.* I think

[84] Walker Blaine to Blaine, December 25, 1881, in Gail Hamilton, *Biography of Blaine*, 551–552.

[85] Frelinghuysen to Trescot, telegram, January 3, 1882, *Foreign Relations 1882*, 56. For the reasons behind Frelinghuysen's actions, see my article, "Diplomatic Reversal etc." *Miss Vall. Hist. Rev.*, XLII, 653–664.

[86] Frelinghuysen to Trescot, January 4, 1882, via United States Consulate at Panama, *Foreign Relations 1882*, 57. Even these instructions did not repudiate either the resort to a Pan American appeal or the invitations to a Pan American conference.

[87] Trescot to Frelinghuysen, January 23, 1882, telegram, *Senate Exec. Docs.,* No. 181, 47 Cong., 1 Sess., 12.

[88] In response to resolutions passed in the Senate on December 13 and in the House on January 24 Frelinghuysen submitted to Congress the outstanding correspondence, both miscellaneous and diplomatic, relating to attempts by the United States to bring about peace in the War of the Pacific, and even included his own instructions modifying the Trescot mission. This correspondence was printed as *Senate Executive Documents,* No. 79, 47 Congress, 1 Session, *Message from the President of the United States transmitting Papers relating to the War in South America and Attempts to bring about a Peace* (Washington, G.P.O., 1882), 742 pages.

a modification of such terms could be obtained—but not Tarapacá. That could be saved in my opinion but by force.

Trescot then reminded Davis that there was another card to be played:

Remember that you have invited a Congress of the American Republics in Washington....
If Chile will not modify her terms and you withdraw—will you ask her [to the peace conference] in face of such a refusal? And if you don't, will she keep a minister in Washington when she is the only state omitted?
Of course you can't invite her until you reach some solution of this imbroglio—and if you don't ask her will she not consider this a combination against her? ...
If [my] negotiations should terminate in failure, disturbing the amicable relations between us, the invitation would be either idle or offensive; *Chile might, if irritated by the position of the United States as defined in my instruction, construe it to mean an appeal to the public opinion of the American republics against her....*[89]

Trescot and Blaine realized that Chile would not consider the calling of the Pan American conference and the "threat to appeal to the other republics" as mere coincidence. But if in the face of such double persuasion Chile still refused to modify its peace terms, Trescot would be able to withdraw behind the prepared defenses of the proposed conference.

In any case he did not want to issue the invitations to the belligerent nations before the time was ripe. Upon reaching Panama he had discovered to his dismay that no word had arrived there explaining to Hurlbut and to Adams, United States minister in La Paz, that he was in charge of the conference invitations. Much concerned, Trescot both wired and wrote Blaine, asking whether such in-

structions had been "intentionally kept back" or accidentally omitted.[90] Upon Trescot's arrival in Santiago he wired both Adams and Hurlbut not to deliver the invitations without his approval.[91]

The warning came too late. Late in January Trescot received word that Hurlbut already had issued the invitation to Peru. For once Hurlbut, target of abuse from all except Peruvians, can be exonerated of blame. Blaine never did inform him that the invitation to Peru was to be in Trescot's keeping. Perhaps Blaine deliberately allowed Peru to receive its invitation before Chile, as a means of applying pressure Trescot preferred to postpone. More probably, however, Blaine simply neglected the matter during his last few hectic days in office, and assumed that the special envoy would handle it himself.

In any case, when Hurlbut prematurely issued the conference invitation to Peru, Trescot decided to deliver it at once to Chile, and to authorize Adams to do so in Bolivia. He saw Balmaceda on January 31, and took along with him Walker Blaine, who as temporary chargé d'affaires in Santiago was technically responsible for delivering the invitation. Trescot explained the presence of young Blaine.[92] Balmaceda interrupted

[89] Trescot to Davis, January 27, 1882, Davis Papers. Italics inserted. Apparently after Frelinghuysen replaced Blaine as secretary of state, Trescot felt that he could write less formally and more revealing to his old friend J. C. Bancroft Davis, who became assistant secretary under Frelinghuysen, and whose role was very important as policy maker.

[90] Trescot to Blaine, telegram, December 12, 1881, *Senate Exec. Docs.*, No. 181, 7; also his No. 1, December 12, 1881, *ibid.*, 8–9.
[91] Or so Trescot informed Frelinghuysen in his No. 8, February 3, 1882, with enclosures, *ibid.*, 17–21. Trescot's letters of warning to Adams and Hurlbut appear neither in the printed correspondence nor in the files of the State Department archives. A diligent search of the post records of Bolivia and Peru, did not reveal them: see Series 3 C, *Miscellaneous Letters Received*, United States Legation in Bolivia; C 8.7 *Legation and Consulate Correspondence*, United States Legation in Peru (Department of State Records, National Archives). This correspondence is quite incomplete, however: obviously these legations abroad did not take good care of their papers.
[92] Trescot to Frelinghuysen, No. 8, February 3, 1882, *Senate Exec. Docs.*, No. 181, 47 Cong., 1 Sess., 17–21. Trescot reproduced his conversations with Balmaceda in direct discourse.

brusquely to ask that the communication not be read: "It is useless," he said, "Your government has withdrawn the invitation." Trescot was astonished. Balmaceda added, with a touch of triumph in his voice: "Your instructions from Mr. Blaine have been published, and others are on their way to you modifying your original instructions in very important particulars. The whole question about Calderón is out of the way, and you are told to be entirely neutral." When Balmaceda hesitated to tell all he knew, Trescot said in disgust: "As you say that all this is confidential, don't make a half-confidence of it. If I am to receive my instructions through you let me know them in full." Instead the Chilean minister ventured the opinion that new instructions would be helpful in their negotiations. Then, according to Trescot, his manner became more heated and demonstrative. He objected at length to certain actions of Hurlbut and Adams, and said that he did not know how long Chile could continue to bear such interference. Trescot made no reply. He was nonplussed at the turn of events, and decided to remain silent until he had heard from Frelinghuysen.

Finally word arrived from Washington. Frelinghuysen proposed only to give counsel and aid to the negotiations: "whether Chile thinks it wise to listen to such counsel, Chile must determine." The new secretary considered Chile's terms exorbitant, especially the cession of Tarapacá and the levy of a high indemnity. Weakly he called for Chile "to be magnanimously just." [93] Late in February another wire from Frelinghuysen urged Chile to be moderate, but he was not willing to revive Blaine's tough policy toward Chile, with its final threat to appeal to the other republics. Having learned that other Latin American nations had received their invitations to

the conference, and fully aware that the proposal was no longer important in their mission, Trescot and Blaine decided not to omit Chile. Walker Blaine presented the invitation to Chile on Washington's birthday, in what Balmaceda might have looked upon as a mock ceremony. The Chilean minister need have no fears of a Pan American conference now, since he knew Frelinghuysen's own ungenerous attitude toward it. Therefore he accepted the invitation with good grace, approving the laudable purpose of such a meeting, and agreed to transmit personally the official reply of his government, when he knew its decision.[94] Actually, Chile never did accept the invitation. Thus passed into the limbo of diplomacy the proposal of a Pan American conference which Blaine had placed in Trescot's hands, its meaning crippled by the fate of his mission.

Although Trescot remained bitter, skeptical, and discouraged, when Frelinghuysen ordered him to stay and try to help the belligerents make peace, he dutifully stayed.[95] By the middle of March he was optimistic enough to believe that Chile might agree to forego further indemnity if it could obtain Tarapacá and purchase Tacna and Arica from Peru. He asked for and received permission to visit Peru and ascertain whether such terms would be acceptable there.

Pondering the State Department's new policy, in his private correspondence with Davis Trescot continued to complain of the method by which Blaine's course of action had been changed. Publication of his original instructions had been the worst offense. It had tipped off his every move, making it clear to Chile that the United States would not interfere; if Chile "had been allowed to feel

[93] Frelinghuysen to Trescot, telegram, February 4, 1882, ibid., 3.

[94] Walker Blaine to Frelinghuysen, No. 8, February 24, 1882, ibid., 57–8.
[95] Frelinghuysen to Trescot, telegram, March 1, 1882, Foreign Relations 1882, 79.

some doubt of what you might do," wrote Trescot, "you might have accomplished something." He pointed out further that Frelinghuysen's early wires and first dispatch had not recalled "the most dangerous paragraph of the original instructions ... to declare that the United States would appeal to the other American republics to take steps to stop this action. When Chile announced its terms and refused to modify them, that instruction was in full force and you could not have censured me if I had been the fool you seem to think and proceeded to exercise it." [96]

Trescot reached Lima on March 28, to discover that Hurlbut had died suddenly the day before. What a trail of tragedy followed Blaine's diplomacy in the War of the Pacific!—Kilpatrick dead, Hurlbut dead, the Trescot mission moribund, and the Pan American conference seriously ill. And now, from Peru, Trescot reported that public opinion was so excited and unstable that he thought it best not to report it in detail. Chile proposed modified but still severe peace terms for Peru. Trescot did not believe that the Peruvian government in the person of Calderón's vice-president, Lisardo Montero, could accept such terms, but that a counterproposal to cede Tarapacá might cause Chile to agree. So the indefatigable Trescot undertook an arduous one-hundred-mile trip into Peru's mountainous interior—most of it by pack-mule —to get to Montero's headquarters. Montero refused to accept Chile's terms, and instead asked Trescot to arrange an amistice during which Chile would recognize his government and give him an opportunity to ask the Peruvian National Congress to agree to a territorial cession. Trescot thought that Montero's requests were reasonable, and that "their refusal affords a fair ground for protest on the part of the independent powers

who desire to see peace restored." [97] To the very last Trescot could not refrain from harking back to Blaine's Pan American appeal.

In response to Trescot's repeated requests, Frelinghuysen finally wired him late in April that he and young Blaine could return home at their convenience. The two envoys were back in Lima by early May and left soon after for the United States on the U.S.S. *Lackawanna,* scene of the abortive discussions held a year and a half earlier, a fittingly symbolic ship for their departure. Only after his return did Trescot write his final report of the mission, an account of Chile's refusal even to recognize Montero's government unless and until he agreed to Chile's preliminary peace terms.[98] The peace talks had broken down completely.

Undoubtedly Trescot was glad to be relieved of what he confidentially called his "queer mission." [99] Nothing could disguise his failure. He had failed not only to bring the kind of peace to the War of the Pacific which Blaine had desired; he had failed to bring any peace at all. To speculate on what might have happened if Frelinghuysen had not blunted Blaine's principal diplomatic weapon—a Pan-American appeal—is to roam too freely in the realm of history-that-might-have-been. But if Trescot *had* threatened Chile with an appeal to the other republics of the New World, Blaine's proposed Pan-American conference would have been related properly—

[96] Trescot to Davis, March 16, 1882, Davis Papers.

[97] Trescot to Frelinghuysen, telegram, May 3, 1882, *Senate Exec. Docs.,* No. 181, 47 Cong., 1 Sess., 34; Trescot to Frelinghuysen, No. 24, May 8, 1882, *ibid.,* 36. Chile's terms were included in Trescot to Frelinghuysen, No. 19, April 5, 1882, *Despatches Chile,* XXXI (Department of State Records, National Archives). Trescot asked that these terms remain confidential, and they were not included in the printed documents.

[98] Trescot to Frelinghuysen, No. 26, June 5, 1882, *Senate Exec. Docs.,* No. 181, 47 Cong., 1 Sess., 48-50.

[99] Trescot to Davis, February 10, 1882, Davis Papers.

in 1881 and later—to his diplomatic difficulties relating to the War of the Pacific.

To conclude that the origins of Blaine's Pan American policy stemmed essentially from his own diplomatic experiences in dealing with Latin America's boundary disputes is to reveal the complexity of motives behind his proposal for an inter-American conference. The simple explanation he later gave of wanting merely to bring peace and commerce to Latin America will hardly suffice. No doubt he wanted these, especially the former. Such objectives were above reproach. By establishing a system of inter-American arbitration, such a conference might relieve Blaine's successors of unfortunate complications such as he had undergone. By ushering in a peaceful era it might also prepare the way for an increase in commerce among American nations, although such a consideration was certainly not uppermost in Blaine's mind in 1881.

But Blaine wanted and expected his proposal for a "peace congress of all the Americas" to be an extraordinary device for achieving other ends as well. He was much concerned about the possibility of European intervention and influence in the New World, and concluded that the role of the United States in Latin American affairs needed to be greatly expanded, as it would be by playing host to a Pan American conference. But something had to be done to rescue matters in the present as well as in the future. The extreme stand Blaine had taken in favor of the territorial status quo of Latin America led to a series of diplomatic predicaments

which plagued him on the eve of his retirement from the State Department. Invitations to an inter-American conference would strengthen his warnings to Mexico, and supplement the mission of Trescot, already instructed to threaten Chile finally with an appeal to the other American republics. Even if Trescot's mission failed, however, and Mexico continued to refuse arbitration, Blaine, still a rising political figure with itching presidential ambitions, would have in his diplomatic record a striking proposal that would turn public attention away from such regrettable concerns as claims, Hurlbut's blundering, Mexico's recalcitrance, Chile's bellicosity, and other difficulties. Put into execution on brief notice, and when he knew that he soon would leave the State Department, Blaine's invitations to a Pan American conference were a characteristically brilliant last-minute effort to save himself and his diplomacy. They came at a highly inopportune time, so far as the Latin American nations generally were concerned. Probably it was fortunate that the conference was never held in 1882, as Blaine proposed. Undoubtedly it would have been bypassed by Chile, probably by Mexico, perhaps by other Latin American states as well. Such an inauspicious result might have doomed the Pan American conference movement. At the very least it would have been a sad example standing in the way of future United States efforts to take the initiative in Pan Americanism. For in retrospect James G. Blaine's Pan American policy in 1881 appears to have been more politically astute than diplomatically wise.

9

Cuba, the Philippines, and Manifest Destiny

RICHARD HOFSTADTER

In 1898 the United States went to war against Spain and as a consequence took the Philippine Islands. Why did America find it necessary to fight Spain at that time, and why the willingness to accept a vast amount of territory in a distant ocean in such a sharp break with tradition? As for going to war, one reason may lie in the shock and revulsion felt by the American people over the harsh treatment of the Cuban revolutionaries by the Spanish. But Americans knew, before war was declared, that a new government that had come to power in Madrid had put a halt to some of the most objectionable features of Spanish policy and had dismissed the military commander who was responsible for the worst abuses. Another possible cause for the war may have been the indignation raised by the sinking of the battleship Maine *in Havana harbor. But such an incident, although outrageous, is not in itself a cause for war unless people crave war. The destruction of the* Lusitania *in 1915 and of the* Panay *in 1937 aroused great consternation in America, but there was no war because the people did not wish to fight.*

Some historians have suggested that the war came and the Philippines were taken because of the need by the business community for raw materials, market, and investment opportunities, and because of the demands by naval strategists and imperialists for colonies to serve as bases, coaling stations, and visible symbols of American power. But however significant these considerations may have been, they could not in themselves have propelled the nation to war unless the will to fight was present. Similarly, those who have attributed the war to the campaign by the "yellow press" fail to realize that the press "must operate roughly within the framework of public predisposition," which, at that time, was warlike.

It is, then, the will to war that must be investigated. It must be examined in light of the situation two decades earlier at the time of another and even bloodier Spanish-Cuban conflict, when each of President McKinley's reasons for war, as stated in his message of April 1898, was present, and yet, at that time, no war was fought. What conditions existed in the 1890s which were absent in the 1870s?

Richard Hofstadter, Pulitzer Prize-winning historian at Columbia University, offers a clue to an understanding of the change in the climate in the late 1890s and of the American will to war with an analysis of the "psychic crisis of the

FROM *The Paranoid Style in American Politics,* by Richard Hofstadter. Copyright 1952 by Richard Hofstadter. Reprinted by permission of Alfred A. Knopf, Inc.

1890's." In phenomena such as the depression of 1893, the closing of the frontier, the Populist movement, the agitation over free silver, the prevalence of corruption in public life, and the end of free competition in industry with the rise of great corporations and trusts, Hofstadter sees the sources of the "taste for battle." Frustration, fears, and discontent gave rise to jingoism, aggressiveness, and a need for self-assertion and "found a safe and satisfactory discharge in foreign conflict."

I

The taking of the Philippine Islands from Spain in 1899 marked a major historical departure for the American people, a breach in their traditions and a shock to their established values. To be sure, from their national beginnings they had constantly engaged in expansion, but almost entirely into contiguous territory. Now they were extending themselves to distant extra-hemispheric colonies. They were abandoning a strategy of defense hitherto limited to the continent and its appurtenances, in favor of a major strategic commitment in the Far East. Thus far their expansion had been confined to the spread of a relatively homogeneous population into territories planned from the beginning to develop self-government; now control was to be imposed by force on millions of ethnic aliens. The acquisition of the islands, therefore, was understood by contemporaries on both sides of the debate, as it is readily understood today, to be a turning point in our history.

To discuss the debate in isolation from other events, however, would be to deprive it of its full significance. America's entrance into the Philippine Islands was a by-product of the Spanish-American War. The Philippine crisis is inseparable from the war crisis, and the war crisis itself is inseparable from a larger constellation that might be called "the psychic crisis of the 1890's."

Central in the background of the psychic crisis was the great depression that broke in 1893 and was still very acute when the agitation over the war in Cuba began. Severe depression, by itself, does not always generate an emotional crisis as intense as that of the nineties. In the 1870's the country had been swept by a depression of comparable acuteness and duration which, however, did not give rise to all the phenomena that appeared in the 1890's or to very many of them with comparable intensity and impact. It is often said that the 1890's, unlike the 1870's, form a "watershed" in American history. The difference between the emotional and intellectual impact of these two depressions can be measured, I believe, not by the difference in severity, but rather by reference to a number of singular events that in the 1890's converged with the depression to heighten its impact upon the public mind.

First in importance was the Populist movement, the free-silver agitation, the heated campaign of 1896. For the first time in our history a depression had created a protest movement strong enough to capture a major party and raise the specter, however unreal, of drastic social convulsion. Second was the maturation and bureaucratization of American business, the completion of its essential industrial plant, and the development of trusts on a scale sufficient to stir the anxiety that the old order of competitive opportunities was approaching an eclipse. Third, and of immense symbolic importance, was the apparent filling up of the continent and the disappearance of the frontier line. We now know how much land had not yet been taken up and how great were the remaining possibilities for internal expansion both in business and on the land; but to the mind of the 1890's it seemed that the resource that had engaged the energies of the people for three centuries had been used up. The frightening possibility suggested itself that a serious juncture in the nation's history had come. As Frederick Jackson Turner expressed it in his famous paper of 1893: "Now, four centuries from the discovery of America, at the end of one hundred years of life under the Constitution, the frontier has gone, and with its going has closed the first period of American history."

To middle-class citizens who had been brought up to think in terms of the nineteenth-century order, the outlook seemed grim. Farmers in the staple-growing region had gone mad over silver and Bryan; workers were stirring in bloody struggles like the Homestead and Pullman strikes; the supply of new land seemed at an end; the trust threatened the spirit of business enterprise; civic corruption was at a high point in the large cities; great waves of seemingly unassimilable immigrants arrived yearly and settled in hideous slums. To many historically conscious writers, the nation appeared overripe, like an empire ready for collapse through a stroke from outside or through internal upheaval. Acute as the situation was for all those who lived by the symbols of national power —for the governing and thinking classes —it was especially poignant for young people, who would have to make their careers in the dark world that seemed to be emerging.

The symptomatology of the crisis would record several tendencies in popular thought and behavior that had previously existed only in pale and tenuous form. These symptoms were manifest in two quite different moods. The key to one of them was an intensification of protest and humanitarian reform. Populism, utopianism, the rise of the Chris-tian Social gospel, the growing intellectual interest in socialism, the social settlement movement that appealed so strongly to the college generation of the nineties, the quickening of protest and social criticism in the realistic novel—all these are expressions of this mood. The other mood was one of national self-assertion, aggression, expansion. The motif of the first was social sympathy; of the second, national power. During the 1890's far more patriotic groups were founded than in any other decade of our history; the naval theories of Captain Mahan were gaining in influence; naval construction was booming; there was an immense quickening of the American cult of Napoleon and a vogue of the virile and martial writings of Rudyard Kipling; young Theodore Roosevelt became the exemplar of the vigorous, masterful, out-of-doors man; the revival of European imperialism stirred speculation over what America's place would be in the world of renewed colonial rivalries, and in some stirred a demand to get into the imperial race to avoid the risk of being overwhelmed by other powers. But most significant was the rising tide of jingoism, a matter of constant comment among observers of American life during the decade.

Jingoism, of course, was not new in American history. But during the 1870's and 1880's the American public had been notably quiescent about foreign relations. There had been expansionist statesmen, but they had been blocked by popular apathy, and our statecraft had been restrained.[1] Grant had failed dismally in his attempt to acquire Santo Domingo; our policy toward troubled Hawaii had been cautious; in 1877 an offer of two Haitian naval harbors had been spurned. In responding to Haiti, Secretary of State Frelinghuysen had remarked that "the policy of this Government . . . has tended

[1] See Julius W. Pratt: *America's Colonial Experiment* (New York, 1950), pp. 4–13.

toward avoidance of possessions disconnected from the main continent." [2] Henry Cabot Lodge, in his life of George Washington published in 1889, observed that foreign relations then filled "but a slight place in American politics, and excite generally only a languid interest." [3] Within a few years this comment would have seemed absurd. In 1895, Russell A. Alger reported to Lodge, after reading one of Lodge's own articles to a Cincinnati audience, that he was convinced by the response that foreign policy, "more than anything else, touches the public pulse of today." [4] The history of the 1890's is the history of public agitation over expansionist issues and of quarrels with other nations.

II

Three primary incidents fired American jingoism between the spring of 1891 and the close of 1895. First came Secretary of State Blaine's tart and provocative reply to the Italian minister's protest over the lynching of eleven Italians in New Orleans. Then there was friction with Chile over a riot in Valparaíso in

[2] Albert K. Weinberg: *Manifest Destiny* (Baltimore, 1935), p. 252. There is a suggestive similarity to the conditions of the nineties in the circumstances attending the Cuban insurrection of 1868–78. The hostilities were even more bitter and exhausting than those of 1895–8; its latter phases also corresponded with an acute depression in the United States; the case of the *Virginius* offered a pretext for war almost as satisfactory as that of the *Maine*. The public and the press raised a clamor about it. But it did not rise even near to the pitch of overwhelming pressure for war. Several things were supplied in the nineties that were missing in the seventies: among them a psychic crisis that generated an expansionist mood; the techniques of yellow journalism; and an adequate navy that made a war with Spain possible to contemplate. Cf. Samuel Flagg Bemis: *A Diplomatic History of the United States* (New York, 1936), pp. 433–5. In the seventies the country was also too close to the completion of an exhausting internal war of its own.

[3] Samuel Flagg Bemis: op. cit., p. 432.

[4] Walter La Feber: *The New Empire* (Ithaca, 1963), p. 250.

which two American sailors were killed and several injured by a Chilean mob. In 1895 occurred the more famous Venezuela boundary dispute with Britain. Discussion of these incidents would take us too far afield, but note that they all had these characteristics in common: in none of them was national security or the natural interest vitally and immediately involved; in all three American diplomacy was extraordinarily and disproportionately aggressive; in all three the possibility of war was contemplated; and in each case the response of the American public and press was enthusiastically nationalist and almost unanimous.

It is hard to read the history of these events without concluding that politicians were persistently using jingoism to restore their prestige, mend their party fences, and divert the public mind from grave internal discontents. It hardly seems an accident that jingoism and populism rose together. Documentary evidence for the political exploitation of foreign crises is not overwhelmingly abundant, in part because such a motive is not necessarily conscious and where it is conscious it is not always confessed or recorded. [5] The persistence of jingoism in every administration from Harrison's to Theodore

[5] The most notable case in our earlier history was Seward's fantastic proposal during the crisis of 1861 that Lincoln attempt to reunite the North and South by precipitating a foreign war. A classic expression of the philosophy of this kind of statecraft was made by Fisher Ames in 1802, after the Federalists had been routed by the Jeffersonians. "We need as all nations do," he wrote to Rufus King, "the compression on the outside of our circle of a formidable neighbor, whose presence shall at all times excite stronger fears than demagogues can inspire the people with towards their government." Henry Jones Ford: *The Rise and Growth of American Politics* (New York, 1914), p. 69. One of the signal differences between the 1870's and the 1890's was that there was still a usable domestic enemy in the earlier period. "Our strong ground," wrote Rutherford B. Hayes in 1876, "is a dread of a solid South, rebel rule, etc., etc.... It leads people away from 'hard times' which is our deadliest foe." J. F. Rhodes: *History of the United States* (New York, 1906), VII, 220.

Roosevelt's, however, is too suggestive to be ignored. During the nineties the press of each party was fond of accusing the other of exploiting foreign conflict. Blaine was not above twisting the British lion's tail for political purposes; and it is hardly likely that he would have exempted Italy from the same treatment. Harrison, on the even of the Chile affair, for the acuteness of which he was primarily responsible, was being urged by prominent Republican politicians who had the coming presidential campaign in mind to pursue a more aggressive foreign policy because it would "have the . . . effect of diverting attention from stagnant political discussions." [6] And although some Democratic papers charged that he was planning to run for re-election during hostilities so that he could use the "don't swap horses in the middle of the stream" appeal, many Democrats felt that it was politically necessary for them to back him against Chile so that, as one of their congressmen remarked, the Republicans could not "run away with all the capital there is to be made in an attempt to assert national self-respect." [7]

Grover Cleveland was a man of exceptional integrity whose stand against pressure for the annexation of Hawaii during 1893–4 does him much credit. But precisely for this act of restraint he was accused by Republican jingoes like Lodge and by many in his own party of being indifferent to America's position in the world. And if Cleveland was too high-minded a man to exploit a needless for-

eign crisis, his Secretary of State, Richard Olney, was not. The Venezuela affair, which came at a low point in the prestige of Cleveland's administration, offered Olney a rich chance to prove to critics in both parties that the administration was, after all, capable of vigorous diplomacy. That the crisis might have partisan value was not unthinkable to members of Olney's party. He received a letter from a Texas congressman encouraging him to "go ahead," on the ground that the Venezuela issue was a "winner" in every section of the country. "When you come to diagnose the country's internal ills," his correspondent continued, "the possibilities of 'blood and iron' loom up immediately. Why, Mr. Secretary, just think of how angry the anarchistic, socialistic, and populistic boil appears on our political surface and who knows how deep its roots extend or ramify[1] One cannon shot across the bow of a British boat in defense of this principle will knock more *pus* out of it than would suffice to inoculate and corrupt our people for the next two centuries." [8]

This pattern had been well established when the Cuban crisis broke out anew in 1895. It was quite in keeping that Secretary Olney should get a letter during the 1896 campaign from Fitzhugh Lee, the American consul in Havana, advising that the conservative faction of Gold Democrats become identified with the strong policy of mediation or intervention in Cuba. Thus, he argued, "the 'Sound Democrats' would get, with the

[6] Donald M. Dozer: "Benjamin Harrison and the Presidential Campaign of 1892," *American Historical Review*, LIV (October 1948), p. 52; A. T. Volwiler: "Harrison, Blaine, and American Foreign Policy, 1889–1893," American Philosophical Society *Proceedings*, Vol. LXXIX (1938), argues plausibly that the imperial mood dawned during Harrison's administration.
[7] Earl W. Fornell: "Historical Antecedents of the Chilean-American Crisis of 1891–92," unpublished M.A. thesis, Columbia University (1950), p. 138; see especially Chs. 11 and 12, for Harrison's exploitation of the war crisis and the intense public reaction.

[8] Alfred Vagts: *Deutschland und die Vereinigten Staaten in der Weltpolitik* (New York, 1935), I, 511; for the domestic roots of administration policy, see Nelson M. Blake: "Background of Cleveland's Venezuela Policy," *American Historical Review*, XLVII (January 1942), 259–77. For a different view, see La Feber: op. cit., pp. 279–83. La Feber considers domestic pressures of minor consequence, and believes that Cleveland and Olney saw important long-rang American interests at stake in Venezuela.

Executive, the credit of stopping the wholesale atrocities daily practised here, the acquisition of Cuba by purchase, or by fighting a successful war, if war there be. In the latter case, the enthusiasm, the applications for service, the employment of many of the unemployed, might do much towards directing the minds of the people from imaginary ills, the relief of which is erroneously supposed to be reached by 'Free Silver.' " [9]

When President McKinley took office he was well aware that nationalist enthusiasm had reached a pitch that made war very likely. A few months earlier, he had told Senator Lodge that he might be "obliged" to go to war as soon as he entered the presidency, and had expressed a preference that the Cuban crisis by settled one way or another in the time between his election and inauguration. Although he had promised Carl Schurz that there would be "no jingo nonsense under my administration," he proved not to have quite enough strength to resist the current. He did not himself partake of the hysteria that was mounting throughout the country, and he was concerned that the country was unprepared to wage a war, uncertain even whether war could be confined to a contest with Spain. He soon found himself under incredible pressures for positive action, which he resisted as long as most Presidents would have been able to do. His failure was not in yielding too soon to the war fever but in not taking early initiative to rein it in. Sending the Maine to Havana proved to be one of his most vital mistakes, since it gave a hostage to the war party. The act was meant in part to curb the enthusiasm of the jingoes at home, but Cleveland had resisted just such a proposal on the grounds that an inflammatory incident was all too likely. No doubt the actual sinking of the Maine

on February 16 went even beyond anything that Cleveland or McKinley could have anticipated. From that time onward, the chances of avoiding war seemed slim.

Members of McKinley's own party put a great deal of pressure on him to give the people their war rather than endanger the Republican position. Some of them feared, as an infuriated senator put it to the Secretary of State, that Congress would declare war in spite of him. "He'll get run over and the party with him." [10] For McKinley himself the prospect that Congress might act without him was, by March, a very real fear.[11] It was widely argued that if war was inevitable, as presumably it was, it would be better for the President to lead rather than to be pushed; that resistance to war would be ruinous to the party; that going to war would prevent the Democrats from entering the next presidential campaign with "Free Cuba" and "Free Silver" as their battle cries.[12] After Senator Proctor's moving speech in the Senate on March 17 about conditions in Cuba, the Chicago Times-Herald, a McKinley paper, declared that intervention in Cuba, peaceful or forcible, was "immediately inevitable. Our own internal political conditions will not permit its postponement. ...Let President McKinley hesitate to rise to the just expectations of the American people, and who can doubt that 'war for Cuban liberty' will be the crown of thorns that Free Silver Democrats and Populists will adopt at the election this fall.... The President would be powerless to stay any legislation, however ruinous to every sober, honest in-

[9] Vagts: op. cit., II, 1266 n. Cf. Ernest R. May: Imperial Democracy (New York, 1961) pp. 75-76.

[10] H. Wayne Morgan: William McKinley and His America (Syracuse, 1963), p. 370.
[11] Ibid., pp. 369-70.
[12] Vagts: op. cit., II, 1308 n; Samuel Flagg Bemis: The Latin American Policy of the United States (New York, 1943), p. 407; Thomas A. Bailey: A Diplomatic History of the American People (New York, 1944), pp. 506-8; C. S. Olcott: The Life of William McKinley (Boston, 1916), II, 28.

terest of the country."[13] "The people want no disgraceful negotiations with Spain," cried the Chicago *Tribune*. "Should the president plunge his administration into that morass, he and his party would be swept out of power in 1900 by a fine burst of popular indignation. An administration which stains the national honor never will be forgiven."[14] Reporting to McKinley on sentiment in Massachusetts, Henry Cabot Lodge wrote in March: "If the war in Cuba drags on through the summer with nothing done, we shall go down in the greatest defeat ever known. ...I know that it is easily and properly said that to bring on or even to threaten war for political reasons is a crime & I quite agree. But to sacrifice a great party & bring free silver upon the country for a wrong policy is hardly less odious."[15]

In the facing of mounting pressure for war, McKinley was unable to sustain his negotiations with Spain long enough to exhaust the possibilities of a diplomatic solution. By the beginning of April some important demands had been conceded —an end to the *reconcentrado* policy and reparations for the *Maine*. But it is doubtful that a diplomatic solution could have been arrived at, since both the Cuban revolutionaries and the United States were insisting upon full Cuban independence, leaving no face-saving formula for the Spanish government. In the opening days of April, McKinley resolved upon war. On April 10, as he was about to send Congress his war message, word came from his ambassador in Spain, Stewart L. Woodford, that the Spaniards had yielded to the American demand for a prompt armistice, and Woodford also thought, rather optimistically, that even the demand for independence might still be met. This news McKinley incorporated anticlimactically at the end of the war message, thus passing up his chance for one final statesmanlike act, an appeal for further delay. That such a step could have avoided war, however, is doubtful. Americans seemed to want not merely the freedom of Cuba but a war for the freedom of Cuba. The Spanish government, insofar as it confronted the realities at all, seemed to think that it was preferable to lose the island "honorably," as the consequence of a war, than to back down. McKinley was caught between the aggressive irrationality of his own people and the decadent irrationality of the ancient Latin power.

Historians often say that the war was brought on by sensational newspapers. The press, spurred by the rivalry between Pulitzer and Hearst, aroused sympathy with the Cubans and hatred of Spain and catered to the bellicosity of the public. No one seems to have asked: *Why was the public so fatally receptive to war propaganda?* I believe the answer must be sought in the causes of the jingoism that had raged for seven years before the war actually broke out. The events of the nineties had brought frustration and anxiety to civically conscious Americans. On one hand, as Mark Sullivan has commented, the American during this period was disposed "to see himself as an underdog in economic situations and controversies in his own country";[16] but the civic frustrations of the era created also a restless aggressiveness, a desire to be assured that the power and vitality of the nation were not waning. The capacity for sympathy and the need for power existed side by side. That highly typical American, William Allen White, recalls in his *Autobiography* how during the nineties he was "bound to my idols—Whitman, the great democrat, and Kipling, the im-

[13] Walter Millis: *The Martial Spirit* (New York, 1931), p. 124.

[14] Morgan: op. cit., p. 368.

[15] May: op. cit., p. 146.

[16] Mark Sullivan: *Our Times* (New York, 1926), p. 137.

perialist."[17] In varying degrees the democrat and the imperialist existed in the hearts of White's countrymen—the democrat disposed to free Cuba; the imperialist, to vent his spleen on Spain.

I suspect that the readiness of the public to overreact to the Cuban situation can be understood in part through the displacement of feelings of sympathy or social protest generated in domestic affairs; these impulses found a safe and satisfactory discharge in foreign conflict. Spain was portrayed in the press as waging a heartless and inhuman war; the Cubans were portrayed as noble victims of Spanish tyranny, their situation as analogous to that of Americans in 1776.[18] When one examines the sectional and political elements that were most enthusiastic about policies that led to war, one finds them not primarily among the wealthy eastern big-business Republicans who gave McKinley his strongest support and read the dignified conservative newspapers, but in the Bryan sections of the country, in the Democratic party, among western Republicans, and among the readers of the yellow journals.[19] A great many business-

men were known to fear the effects of a war on the prosperity that was just returning, and some thought that a war might strengthen the free-silver movement. During the controversy significant charges were hurled back and forth: conservative peace advocates claimed that many jingoists were hoping for a costly war over Cuba that could be made the occasion of a return to free silver; in reply, the inflammatory press often fell into the pattern of Populist rhetoric, declaiming, for example, about "the eminently respectable porcine citizens who—for dollars in the money-grubbing sty, support 'conservative' newspapers and consider the starvation of . . . inoffensive men, women and children, and the murder of 250 American sailors . . . of less importance than a fall of two points in a price of stocks."[20] As Margaret Leech has remarked, peace "had become a symbol of obedience to avarice."[21] In the case of some of the war enthusiasts it is not clear whether they favored action more because they bled for the sufferings of the Cubans or because they hated the materialism and the flaccid pacifism of the *haute bourgeoisie*. Theodore Roosevelt, who was not in the habit of brooding over the wrongs done to the underdog in the United

[17] William Allen White: *Autobiography* (New York, 1946), p. 195.

[18] On the role of the press, see J. E. Wisan: *The Cuban Crisis as Reflected in the New York Press* (New York, 1934); and M. M. Wilkerson: *Public Opinion and the Spanish-American War* (Baton Rouge, 1932). On the evolution of human-interest journalism, see Helen M. Hughes: *News and the Human Interest Story* (Chicago, 1940); and the same author's "Human Interest Stories and Democracy," *Public Opinion Quarterly*, I (April 1937), 73–83.

[19] Wisan (op. cit., p. 445) notes: "It was no mere accident that most of the leading proponents of intervention in Congress represented southern and western states where populism and silver were strongest." Cf. pp. 125–6, 283, 301. A resolution of May 20, 1897, in favor of granting belligerent rights to the Cubans was passed by the Senate, 41–14, with 33 senators not voting. The yeas came from 19 Democrats, 2 Populists, 3 maverick Republicans, and 17 regular Republicans. The nays came from 12 Republicans and 2 Democrats. The 17 Republican votes for recognition broke down as follows: 10 west of the Mississippi, 2 South, 3 Midwest, 2 New

England. A New York *Journal* poll of the House in December 1897, on the question of recognizing Cuban belligerency, showed: for, 40 Republicans, 117 Democrats, and 27 Populists, total 184; against, 165 Republicans, 5 Democrats, and 2 Populists, total 172 (Wisan: p. 359); cf. Julius W. Pratt: *Expansionists of 1898* (Baltimore, 1936), pp. 224, 234–6, 242–3. It is noteworthy that dominant sentiment in the labor movement favored recognition of Cuban belligerency from an early date, and that Cleveland's conservative policy was considered to be another instance of the "coldness" toward the underdog that was held to characterize his labor policies. Cf. John C. Appel: "The Relationship of American Labor to United States Imperialism, 1895–1905," unpublished Ph.D. thesis, University of Wisconsin (1950), Ch. 2. Cf. Ernest May: op. cit., pp. 81–2.

[20] Wisan: op. cit., p. 394.

[21] Margaret Leech: *In the Days of McKinley* (New York, 1959), p. 179.

States, expressed some of this when he cried at Mark Hanna: "We will have this war for the freedom of Cuba in spite of the timidity of the commercial interests." [22]

Although imputations of base motives were made by both sides, it is also significant that the current of sympathy and agitation ran strong where a discontented consistency, chagrined at Bryan's defeat, was most numerous. An opportunity to discharge hatred of "Wall Street interests" that were coolly indifferent to the fate of both Cuban *insurrectos* and staple farmers may have been more important than the more rationalized and abstract linkage between war and free silver.[23] The primary significance of this war in the psychic economy of the 1890's was that it served as an outlet for expressing aggressive impulses while presenting itself, quite truthfully, as an idealistic and humanitarian crusade. It had the advantage of expressing in one issue both the hostilities and the generous moral passions of the public. The American public on the whole showed little interest in such material gains as might accrue from an intervention in Cuba. It never dreamed that the war would lead to the taking of the Philippines, of whose existence it was hardly aware. Starting a war for a high-minded and altruistic purpose and then transmuting it into a war for annexation was unimaginable. That would be, as McKinley put it in a phrase that later came back to haunt him, "criminal aggression."

[22] H. F. Pringle: *Theodore Roosevelt* (New York, 1931), p. 179.

[23] To say this is not to say that the war "originated" among southern and western farmers, a point on which I have been misunderstood. (Cf. May: op. cit., pp. 75, 145.) The clamor for intervention and war was clearly nation-wide, urban as well as rural. My proposition is that it was much stronger among those who were otherwise discontented than among those who were well off. The agrarians, being particularly discontented, are merely a test case for one side of this proposition, just as the reluctant big-business interests are for the other.

William James, who deplored the war fever from the beginning, correctly diagnosed the popular mood when he wrote to a friend in France: "The basis of it all is, or rather was, perfectly honest humanitarianism, and an absolutely disinterested desire on the part of our people to set the Cubans free.... Congress was entirely mad, supposing that the people was in the same condition, as it probably was, in less degree.... War... was the only possible discharge. We were winning the most extraordinary diplomatic victories, but they were of no use. We were ready (as we supposed) for war and nothing but war must come." Although he reiterated that the American disclaimer of desire for conquest was "*absolutely* sincere" he also shrewdly predicted that once the excitement of military action was aroused, "the ambition and sense of mastery which our nation has will set up new demands," and he accurately forecast that although we would never annex Cuba we might take Puerto Rico and the Philippines.[24]

One might add that inhibitions against going to war were not so strong as they would have been if a major power had been involved. Spain, hardly a formidable foe in a war whose main strategic object was in the Caribbean, had been described by the press as weak, bankrupt, degenerate, and friendless, and her military incompetence was demonstrated by the events in Cuba itself. As T.R. put it to Lodge: "I do not think a war with Spain would be serious enough to cause much strain on this country." Lodge himself had a shrewder estimation than many timid financiers of the bearing of war on the currency question. "If we should have a war," he wrote in March 1898, "we will not hear much

[24] Ralph Barton Perry: *The Thought and Character of William James* (Boston, 1935), II, 307; William James: *Letters* (Boston, 1935), II, 73–4.

of the currency question in the elections."[25]

III

There is one odd paradox in the evolution of sentiment from a war over freeing Cuba to a peace treaty ratifying the acquisition of the Philippines by conquest. The big-business-conservative-Republican-McKinley element, which was overwhelmingly hostile to this romantic and sentimental war, quickly became interested in the imperialism that grew out of it.[26] The popular Populist-Democratic-Bryanite element, which had been so keen for the war, became the stronghold—although by no means resolute or unbroken—of opposition to the fruits of war. This much, however, must be said of both the populace and the business community: if the matter had been left either to public clamor or to business interests, there would have been no American entrance into the Philippines in 1898.

The dynamic element in the movement for imperialism was a small group of politicians, intellectuals, and publicists, including Senator Henry Cabot Lodge, Theodore Roosevelt, John Hay, Senator Albert J. Beveridge, Whitelaw Reid, editor of the New York *Tribune,* Albert Shaw, editor of the *American Review of Reviews,* Walter Hines Page, editor of the *Atlantic Monthly,* and Henry and Brooks Adams.

Most of these men came from what are known as good families. They were well educated, cultivated, patrician in outlook, of Anglo-Saxon stock, and conservative reformers in politics whose personal goals and standards were non-commercial. Although living in a commercial world, they could not accept business standards for their own careers or become absorbed into the business community. Although they lived in a vulgar democracy, they were not democratic by instinct. They could not and did not care to succeed in politics of the corrupt sort that had become so common in America. They had tried their hands at civic reform, had found it futile, and had become bored with it. When they did not, like Henry Adams, turn away from American life in despair, they became interested in some large and statesmanlike theater of action, broader than American domestic policy. Although there were men of this sort in the Democratic ranks, like Walter Hines Page, they were most influential within the Republican party, which had become committed to a policy of aggressive commercial diplomacy.[27]

In general, this group of imperialists was inspired by the navalist theories of Mahan and by the practical example of what they on occasion called Mother England. They saw that a new phase of imperialism had opened in the Western world at large, and they were fearful that if the United States did not adopt a policy of expansion and preparation for military and naval struggle, it would be left behind in what they referred to as the struggle for life or the march of the nations. They were much concerned that the United States expand its army and particularly its navy; that it dig an isthmian canal; that it acquire the naval bases and colonies in the Caribbean and the Pacific necessary to protect such a canal; that it annex Hawaii and Samoa. At their most aggressive they also called for the annexation of Canada and the

[25] H. C. Lodge (ed.): *Selections from the Correspondence of Theodore Roosevelt and Henry Cabot Lodge* (New York, 1925), I, 243; Morgan: op. cit., p. 369.
[26] Pratt: *Expansionists of 1898,* Ch. 7, has a classic treatment of the business attitude.
[27] The best account of the little imperialist elite is in Matthew Josephson: *The President Makers* (New York, 1940), Chs. 1–3; See also Pratt: *Expansionists of 1898,* and Vagts: op. cit., Vol. II, passim.

expulsion of European powers from the Western Hemisphere. They were much interested in the Far East as a new theater of political conflict and of possibilities for investment. They were, indeed, more interested than business itself in the Pacific area, particularly in China, as a potential market. As Julius W. Pratt has observed: "The need of American business for colonial markets and fields for investment was discovered not by business men but by historians and other intellectuals, by journalists and politicans." [28]

The central figure in this group was Theodore Roosevelt, who more than any other single man was responsible for our entry into the Philippines. Throughout the 1890's Roosevelt had been eager for a war, whether it be with Chile, Spain, or England. A war with Spain, he thought, would get us "a proper navy and a good system of coast defenses," would free Cuba from Spain, would help to free America from European domination, would give "our people ... something to think of that isn't material gain," and would try "both the army and navy in actual practice." Roosevelt feared that the United States would grow heedless of its defense, take insufficient care to develop its power, and become "an easy prey for any people which still retained those most valuable of all qualities, the soldierly virtues." "All the great masterful races have been fighting races," he argued. There were higher virtues than those of peace and material comfort. "No triumph of peace is quite so great as the supreme triumphs of war." [29] Such was the philosophy of the man who obtained for Commodore Dewey his ap-

pointment to the Far Eastern Squadron and alerted him before the actual outbreak of hostilities to be prepared to proceed from Hong Kong to engage the Spanish fleet at Manila. These orders were confirmed by McKinley two months later, shortly after war was actually declared.

Our first step into the Philippines presented itself to us as a "defensive" measure. Dewey's attack on the Spanish fleet in Manila Bay was made on the assumption that the Spanish fleet, if unmolested, might cross the Pacific and bombard the west coast cities of the United States. I do not know whether American officialdom was aware that this fleet was so decrepit that it could hardly have gasped its way across the ocean. Next, Dewey's fleet in Manila Bay seemed in danger unless its security were underwritten by the dispatch of American troops to Manila. To be sure, having accomplished his mission, Dewey could have removed this "danger" simply by leaving Manila Bay—and McKinley once remarked to H. H. Kohlsaat that "If Old Dewey had just sailed away when he smashed that Spanish fleet, what a lot of trouble he would have saved us!" However, in war one is always disposed to hold whatever gains have been made, and to Dewey's request American troops were dispatched very promptly after the victory and arrived at Manila in July 1898.

Thus our second step into the Philippines was again a "defensive" measure. The third step was the so-called "capture" of Manila, which was actually carried out in co-operation with the Spaniards, who were allowed to make a token resistance, and in exclusion of the Filipino patriots under Aguinaldo. The fourth step was an agreement, incorporated in the protocol suspending hostilities between the United States and Spain, that the United States would occupy the city, bay, and harbor of Manila pending

[28] Pratt: *Expansionists of 1898*, p. 22; for a succinct statement of the outlook of Republican expansionists, see Henry Cabot Lodge: "Our Blundering Foreign Policy," *The Forum*, XIX (March 1895), 8–17; for Mahan's position, see A. T. Mahan: *The Interest of America in Sea Power* (New York, 1898).
[29] See Roosevelt: *Works* (New York, 1925), XIV, 182–99; Pringle: op. cit., Ch. 13.

a final settlement in the peace treaty. The fifth step came much later, on December 21, 1898, when McKinley instructed the War Department to extend the military government already in force at Manila to the entire archipelago. This set off a fierce revolt by the Filipino patriots, who felt that they had been led to expect a much different policy from the American government. Two days before the vote was taken in the Senate on the ratification of the peace treaty, the patriots and the American forces fought their first battle and American soldiers were killed, a fact that seems to have had an important influence on public discussion. Once again, administrative action had given a sharp bias to the whole process of political decision. Tyler Dennett goes so far as to say that by authorizing a campaign of conquest while the Senate was still discussing the issue, McKinley "created a situation . . . which had the effect of coercing the Senate." [30] This is a doubtful conclusion,[31] but there is some reason to believe that the hand of the expansionists was strengthened by the feeling that opposition to the administration's policy would be unpatriotic.

By the time our policy toward the Philippines could be affected by public discussion a great deal had already been accomplished by the annexationists. The argument was already weighted toward staying in simply because we were there. As McKinley put it: "It is not a question of keeping the islands of the East, but of leaving them." [32] It is not an easy

thing to persuade a people or a government, at a high pitch of war enthusiasm, to abandon a supposed gain already in hand. Moreover, a great social interest hitherto indifferent to the Philippines, the business community, quickly swung around to an expansionist position. Business began to talk about the Philippines as a possible gateway to the markets of eastern Asia, the potentialities of which were thought to be very large.[33] The Protestant clergy, seeing a possible enlargement of missionary opportunities, also threw in its weight. For the first time the group of imperialists and navalists had powerful allies. Its members took heart and, with the help of navy officers, put increasing pressure upon a rather hesitant administration to follow through.

There seemed four possible ways of disposing of the Philippine problem. The first, returning the islands to Spain, found favor nowhere. The second, selling or otherwise alienating the Philippines to some other power, seemed to invite a general European war; and it would hardly be more justified morally than remaining in possession ourselves. Moreover, we were being encouraged by England to remain in the Philippines, for American possession of those islands was much more palatable to England than possession by any other power. The third possibility, leaving the Philippines to themselves and giving them the independence Aguinaldo's men had been fighting for, was equivalent in the minds of most Americans to leaving them to anarchy or to conquest. It also seemed to be another way of encouraging a scramble among other powers interested in the Far East—flinging, as McKinley put it, "a golden apple of discord among the rival powers." [34] The final possibility was American possession, in the form

[30] Tyler Dennett: *Americans in Eastern Asia* (New York, 1922), p. 631.
[31] W. Stull Holt: *Treaties Defeated by the Senate* (Baltimore, 1933), pp. 170–1, concludes that the struggle in the Philippines had no important effects on the debate; see, however, José S. Reyes: *Legislative History of America's Economic Policy toward the Philippines* (New York, 1923), pp. 33–4; cf. Lodge: op. cit., p. 391; and Morgan: op. cit., pp. 421–2.
[32] *Speeches and Addresses of William McKinley from March 1, 1897, to May 30, 1900* (New York, 1900), p. 174.

[33] Pratt: *Expansionists of 1898*, pp. 233, 261–78.
[34] Morgan: op. cit., p. 403.

of a protectorate or otherwise. In the beginning there was much sentiment for merely retaining a naval base and coaling station on the island of Luzon, or perhaps the island of Luzon itself. Second thoughts suggested, however, that such a base would be endangered if the rest of the islands were left open to possible occupation by other nations. The dynamics of the situation suggested an all-or-none policy, and the administration drifted rapidly toward annexation of the entire archipelago. "I didn't want the Philippine Islands," McKinley said in retrospect, "and in the protocol to the treaty I left myself free not to take them; but—in the end there was no alternative." [35] The sincerity of his own doubts about annexation may be measured by the fact that it took him all of five months to decide that we should take not merely a part but the entire archipelago.

IV

Previously the American public had not been either informed about or interested in the Philippines. In the entire eighty-year period from 1818 through May 1898, only thirty-five articles about the islands had appeared in American magazines.[36] At the moment of Dewey's victory, the press, although given over to encouraging the public jubilation, did not show an immediate interest in taking the islands. However, such sentiment grew with remarkable rapidity. As early as July 1898, the *Literary Digest* noted that the leading Republican papers were pro-expansion. A sample of 65 newspapers taken by the magazine *Public Opinion* in August showed that 43 per cent were for permanent retention of the Philippines, 24.6 per cent were opposed, and 32.4 per cent were wavering. In this case, "wavering" usually meant formerly opposed to expansion but apparently changing views. By December 1898, when the vital debate in the Senate was beginning, the New York *Herald* polled 498 newspapers on the subject of expansion and found that 305, or 61.3 per cent, were favorable. New England and the Middle States showed clear margins in favor of expansion, the West an overwhelming margin. The South alone, by a thin margin, was opposed. The state of press opinion does not *measure* public feeling, but probably does indicate the direction in which public opinion was moving.[37]

To President McKinley, a benign and far from aggressive man, public sentiment was of great importance, and he studied press opinion assiduously. He was not a man to lead the American people in a direction in which their sympathies were not already clearly bent. There was a current joke: "Why is McKinley's mind like a bed? Because it has to be made up for him every time he wants to use it." However unjust to the President, this does characterize his response to public opinion. He was not by temperament an expansionist, but if his immediate advisers and the public at large were preponderantly for annexation, he was willing to go along, and was thoroughly capable of finding good reasons for doing so. During the fall of 1898 he left Washington for a tour of

[35] Jacob Gould Schurman: *Philippine Affairs* (New York, 1902), pp. 1–2.
[36] A. A. Greenberg: "Public Opinion and the Acquisition of the Philippine Islands," unpublished M.A. thesis, Yale University (1937), pp. 2, 18. What is most impressive is the absence of any conscious commitment of the public to the imperial idea before the outbreak of war. Referring to the failure of proposals of Hawaiian annexation, T.R. wrote as late as January 13, 1898, that he was "a good deal disheartened at the queer lack of imperial instinct that our people show." W. A. Russ, Jr.: *The Hawaiian Republic* (Selinsgrove, Pa., 1961), p. 219.

[37] For the development of press opinion, see surveys cited in *Literary Digest,* XVII (July 1898), 32 ff., (September 10, 1898), 307–8; and *Public Opinion,* XXV (August 4, 1898), 132–5, (December 29, 1898), 810.

the West, and made a great many brief speeches sounding out public opinion on annexation of the Philippines, on which he seems to have tentatively been determined in his own mind. He was warmly received and his references to expansion met with an enthusiastic response. Evidently his intent was confirmed by this exposure to public opinion and also by advices concerning the state of the public mind from correspondents and advisers. When he returned to Washington those who were opposed to expansion found him unmovable.[38] The Peace Commission negotiating the treaty in Paris was instructed to ask for all the Philippine Islands, and this provision was included in the peace treaty signed on December 10, 1898.

The debate over the retention of the Philippines then went through two phases. During the first, which lasted from December 1898 to the second week in February 1899, the question was argued both in the Senate and in the forums of public opinion.[39] This phase neared its end when, on February 6, the Senate narrowly voted to ratify the peace treaty; it was definitively closed on February 14, when a resolution sponsored by Senator Bacon of Georgia, calling for early Philippine independence, was rejected by the preciously narrow margin of one vote—the vote of the Vice-President, which resolved a 29–29 tie. The second phase of the debate extended throughout 1899 and 1900, when American policy toward the Philippines was a matter of general public discussion and a partisan issue in the presidential campaign of 1900.

Who was for and who against annexation? In large measure it was a party issue. The New York *Herald* poll showed that of 241 Republican papers 84.2 per cent were for expansion, and of 174 Democratic papers 71.3 per cent were against expansion. In some degree it was also a young man's movement. Geographically it extended throughout all sections of the country, and seems to have been predominant everywhere but in the South, although even there it was strong. We do not have a clear index of public opinion for the period, but the practical politicians, whose business it was to gauge public sentiment in the best way they knew, concluded that the preponderant feeling was overwhelmingly for annexation.[40]

The debate over the acquisition of the Philippines was perhaps no more than a ceremonial assertion of the values of both sides. The real decisions were made in the office of Theodore Roosevelt, in the Senate cloakroom, in the sanctums of those naval officers from whom the McKinley administration got its primary information about the Philippines during its period of doubt over annexation, and, by McKinley's own testimony, in the privacy of his chambers late at night. The public was, by and large, faced with a *fait accompli* that, although theoretically reversible, had the initial impetus of its very existence to carry it along. The intensity of the public discussion, at any rate, showed that the conscience of at least some Americans had really been shocked. No type of argument was neglected on either side. Those who wanted to take the Philippines pointed to the potential markets of the East, the White Man's Burden, the struggle for existence, "racial" destiny, American traditions of expansion, the dangers of a general war if the Philippines were left open to a

[38] Greenberg: op. cit., pp. 84–6. "None of us," said Secretary of the Interior Cornelius Bliss, "have been able to move him since he returned from the west"; Morgan: op. cit., p. 408.

[39] For the debate in the Senate, see *Congressional Record*, 55th Cong., 3rd sess., passim; Reyes: op. cit., Ch. 2; Holt: op. cit., Ch. 8; Marion Mills Miller: *Great Debates in American History* (New York, 1913), III, 245–324; Pratt: *Expansionists of 1898*, pp. 345–60.

[40] For impressive evidence on this point, see Greenberg: op. cit., pp. 35, 42–3, 46–7, 49–50, 60, 67–9, 71, 86.

European scramble, the almost parental duty of assuming responsibility for the allegedly childlike Filipinos, the incapacity of the Filipinos for self-government. The anti-imperialists based their essential appeal on political principle. They pointed out that the United States had come into existence pledged to the idea that man should not be governed without his consent. They suggested that the violation of these political traditions (under which the nation had prospered) was not only a gross injustice to others, of which we should feel deeply ashamed, but also a way of tempting Providence and risking degeneration and disintegration as a sort of punishment for the atrophy of one's own principles. They pointed also to the expense of overseas dominions, standing armies, and navalism, and the danger of being embroiled in imperialist wars, and argued that it would be unwise to try to absorb peoples who were racially incapable of self-government.

Many leading anti-imperialists were men of great distinction; their ranks included by far the greater part of the eminent figures of the literary and intellectual world. Most of them were, however, in the unfortunate position of opposing the fruits of a war that they had either favored or failed to oppose. Unlike the expansionists, they did not have complete control of a major party (there were more expansionists among the Democrats than there were anti-expansionists among the Republicans). They were hopelessly heterogeneous: Gold Democrats, Bryan Democrats, New England-conscience Republicans, and a scattering of reformers and intellectuals.[41]

They organized late—the Anti-Imperialist League grew up in the months after November 1898—and their political leadership, however ardent in sentiment, pursued a hesitant and uncertain course. Their most eminent political leaders were chiefly old men, and the anti-imperialist movement seems to have had its strongest appeal among the old, high-principled elements in the country, while the imagination of the young was fired far more by the rhetoric of expansionism.[42] It seems clear that the main chance of this minority was to use its position in the Senate to deny the necessary two-thirds approval to the peace treaty by which the islands would be acquired from Spain. Here the opponents of annexation might have delayed it long enough to give themselves a chance to reach the public. But William Jennings Bryan, for reasons that are not altogether clear, persuaded enough members of his party to vote for the treaty to lose the case. Bryan hoped to continue the fight, of course, and grant independence later, but over his conduct and his explanations there hangs a heavy sense of inevitable defeat, stemming from his recognition that the voice of the majority

[41] On the anti-imperialist movement, see Fred H. Harrington: "The Anti-Imperialist Movement in the United States, 1898–1900," *Mississippi Valley Historical Review*, XXII (September 1935), 211–30. On the intellectual class and anti-imperialism, see the same author's "Literary Aspects of American Anti-Imperialism,

1898–1902," *New England Quarterly*, X (December 1937), 650–67; William Gibson: "Mark Twain and Howells: Anti-Imperialists," *New England Quarterly*, XX (December 1947), 435–70. Christopher Lasch has pointed out that the anti-imperialist argument, North and South, was almost universally based on racist premises; "The Anti-Imperialists, The Philippines, and the Inequality of Man," *Journal of Southern History*, XXIV (August 1958), 319–31.

[42] Harrington points out that the average age of the prominent Republican members of the Anti-Imperialist League was 71.1 years; that of the forty-one vice-presidents of the League, 58.3. By contrast, the average age of fourteen leaders of expansionism in 1898 was 51.2. The American consul in London, William M. Osborne, wrote to McKinley: "If what I hear and what I read is true there is a tremendous party growing up for expansion of territory, *especially by the younger and more active elements in the country.*" (Italics added.) Quoted by Greenberg: op. cit., pp. 46–7.

demanded the bold and aggressive policy.[43]

V

In the arguments for annexation two essential moral and psychological themes appeared over and over again. These themes were expressed in the words Duty and Destiny. According to the first, to reject annexation of the Philippines would be to fail of fulfilling a solemn obligation. According to the second, annexation of the Philippines in particular and expansion generally were inevitable and irresistible.

The people had entered the war for what they felt to be purely altruistic and humanitarian reasons—the relief and liberation of the Cubans. The idea that territorial gains should arise out of this pure-hearted war of liberation, and the fact that before long the Americans stood in the same relation to the Filipinos as the Spaniards had stood to the Cubans, was most uncomfortable. This situation raised moral questions that the anti-imperialists did not neglect to express and exploit. The imperialists were accused of breaking our national word, of violating the pledge made by McKinley himself that by our moral code

forcible annexation would be "criminal aggression." They were also accused of violating the solemn injunctions of the Founding Fathers, particularly the principles of the Declaration of Independence. The rhetoric of Duty was a reassuring answer to this attempt to stir feelings of guilt.

The quick victories won by American arms strengthened the psychological position of the imperialists. The feeling that one may be guilty of wrongdoing can be heightened when the questionable act is followed by adversity.[44] Conversely, it may be minimized by the successful execution of a venture. Misfortune is construed as Providential punishment; but success, as in the Calvinist scheme, is taken as an outward sign of an inward state of grace. One of the most conspicuous things about the war was the remarkable successes achieved by American arms, of which the most astonishing was Dewey's destruction, without losing a single American life, of the entire Spanish Eastern Fleet in Manila Bay. Victories of this sort could readily be interpreted as Providential signs, tokens of divine approval. It was widely reported in the United States that this was Dewey's own interpretation. "If I were a religious man, and I hope I am," he said, "I should say that the hand of God was in it." [45] This was precisely the sort of reassurance that was needed. "The magnificent fleets of Spain," declared a writer in a Baptist periodical, referring to Spain's senile and decrepit navy, "have gone down as marvelously, I had almost said, as miraculously, as the walls of Jericho went down." The victory, said an editor of the *Christian and Missionary Alliance*, "read almost like the stories of the

[43] Bryan argued that the treaty should be ratified because "a victory won against the treaty would prove only temporary if the people really favor a colonial policy," and because the opponents of the treaty, if they won, "would be compelled to assume responsibility for the continuance of war conditions and for the risks which always attend negotiations with a hostile nation." A minority, he argued, could not permanently thwart annexation. His policy was to appeal to the voters in the election of 1900; but it is impossible to make a presidential election a clear referendum on foreign policy. Bryan found, during the campaign of 1900, that anti-imperialism was not a strong talking point. Cf. Bryan: *The Second Battle* (Chicago, 1900), pp. 126–8; *Bryan on Imperialism* (Chicago, 1900), p. 16. On the election, see Thomas A. Bailey: "Was the Presidential Election of 1900 a Mandate on Imperialism?" *Mississippi Valley Historical Review*, XXIV (June 1937), 43 ff.

[44] Cf. Sigmund Freud: *Civilization and Its Discontents* (London, 1930), pp. 110–11.
[45] Louis A. Coolidge: *An Old-Fashioned Senator: Orville H. Platt* (New York, 1910), p. 302.

ancient battles of the Lord in the times of Joshua, David, and Jehosophat."

Furthermore, what might have seemed a sin became transformed into a positive obligation, a duty. The feeling was: *Providence has been so indulgent to us, by giving us so richly of success, that we would be sinful if we did not accept the responsibility it has asked us to assume.* The Protestant clergy, as guardians of the national conscience, did not hesitate to make lavish use of such arguments. "To give to the world the life more abundant both for here and hereafter," reasoned a writer in the *Baptist Missionary Review*, "is the duty of the American people by virtue of the call of God. This call is very plain. The hand of God in history has ever been plain." "If God has brought us to the parting of the ways," insisted a writer in the *Churchman*, "we cannot hold back without rejecting divine leadership." [46] The rhetoric of secular leaders was hardly less inspired. "We will not renounce our part in the mission of our race, trustees under God, of the civilization of the world," said Senator Albert J. Beveridge. "God has not been preparing the English-speaking and Teutonic peoples for a thousand years for nothing but vain and idle self-contemplation and self-admiration. No! He has made us the master organizers of the world to establish system where chaos reigns. He has made us adepts in government that we may administer government among savages and senile peoples." [47]

The theme of Destiny was a corollary of the theme of Duty. Repeatedly it was declared that expansion was the result of a "cosmic tendency," that "destiny always arrives," that it was in the "inexorable logic of events," and so on. The doctrine that expansion was inevitable had of course long been familiar to Americans; we all know how often Manifest Destiny was invoked throughout the nineteenth century. Albert Weinberg has pointed out, however, that this expression took on a new meaning in the nineties. Previously destiny had meant primarily that American expansion, *when we willed it,* could not be resisted *by others* who might wish to stand in our way. During the nineties it came to mean that expansion "could not be resisted by Americans themselves, caught, willing or unwilling," in the coils of fate.[48] A certain reluctance on our part was implied. This was not quite so much what we *wanted* to do; it was what we *had* to do. Our aggression was implicitly defined as compulsory—the product not of our own wills but of objective necessity (or the will of God).

"Duty," said President McKinley, "determines destiny." While Duty meant that we had a moral obligation, Destiny meant that we would certainly fulfill it, that the capacity to fulfill it was inherent in us. Ours had been a continuous history of expansion; it had always succeeded before, therefore it was certain to succeed in the future. Expansion was a national and "racial" inheritance, a deep and irresistible inner necessity. Here was a plausible traditionalist answer to the accusation of a grave breach of tradition.

It is not surprising that the public should have found some truth in this concept of inevitable destiny, for the acts that first involved their country with the fate of the Philippines were willed and carried out by others and were made objects of public discussion and decision only *after* the most important commitments had been made. The

---

[46] The quotations are from Pratt: *Expansionists of 1898*, pp. 289–90, 294, 305.

[47] Claude G. Bowers: *Beveridge and the Progressive Era* (New York, 1932), p. 121.

[48] Weinberg: *Manifest Destiny*, p. 254. Appropriately enough, as Weinberg shows (p. 279), when independence was at last granted to the Philippines, it was portrayed not as an act of "destiny" but as an act of "our own free will."

public will was not freely exercised upon the question, and for the citizens at large, who were in the presence of forces they could not understand or control, the rhetoric of Destiny may have been a way of softening and ennobling the *fait accompli* with which they were presented. But what of the men whose wills were really effective in the matter? If we examine their case, we find that the manufacturers of inevitability believed deeply in their own product. Indeed, while the extent to which the idea of Destiny was generally accepted is unknown, its wide prevalence among influential politicians, editors, and publicists is beyond argument. When Senator Lodge wrote to Theodore Roosevelt in 1898 that "the whole policy of annexation is growing rapidly under the irresistible pressure of events," when President McKinley remarked in private to his secretary, concerning the taking of Hawaii, "It is manifest destiny," when he declared in his private instructions to the peace commissioners that "the march of events rules and overrules human action"—what was involved was not an attempt to sell an idea to the public but a mode of communication in which the insiders felt thoroughly at home; perhaps a magical mode of thought by which they quieted their own uncertainties. It is easy to say, from the perspective of the twentieth century, that where contemporaries heard the voice of God we think we can discern the carnal larynx of Theodore Roosevelt. But if the insiders themselves imagined that they heard the voice of God, we must be careful of imputing hypocrisy. It is significant that the idea of Destiny was effective even among people who had very grave doubts about the desirability of remaining in the Philippines. Secretary of the Navy John D. Long, who was affectionately regarded by Theodore Roosevelt as an old fuddy-duddy on this score, confided to a friend

in 1898 that he would really have preferred the United States to remain what it had been during the first half of the nineteenth century—"provincial," as he expressed it, and "dominated by the New England idea. But," he added, "I cannot shut my eyes to the march of events—a march which seems to be beyond human control." [49]

It would be false to give the impression that only high moral and metaphysical concepts were employed in the imperialist argument. Talk about entry into the markets of Asia was heard often after Dewey's victory; but even those who talked about material gains showed a conspicuous and symptomatic inability to distinguish between interests, right, and duties. Charles Denby, former minister to China and a member of McKinley's commission to study the Philippines, contributed to *The Forum* two interesting articles full of this confusion. The central business of diplomacy, confessed Denby, was to advance commerce. Our right to hold the Philippines was the right of conquerors. So far, Mr. Denby was all *Realpolitik*. But, he continued, he favored keeping the islands because he could not conceive any alternative to doing so except seizing territory in China, and he did not want to oppress further "the helpless Government and people of China"! Thus a rather odd scruple crept it; but Mr. Denby quickly explained that this was simply because China's strength and prosperity were in America's interest. "We are after markets," he went on, sliding back into *Realpolitik,* and along with these markets"—sliding back into morality—"will go our beneficent institutions; and humanity will bless us." In a second article Mr. Denby shuttled back to "the cold, hard practical question. ...Will the possession of these islands benefit us as a nation? If it will not,

[49] Greenberg: op. cit., p. 89.

set them free tomorrow, and let their people, if they please, cut each other's throats." And yet, Mr. Denby made it clear, we did come as benefactors, bringing to our cut-throat friends "the choicest gifts—liberty and hope and happiness." [50] There was, besides the oscillatory rhetoric of Mr. Denby, a "let's be candid" school, whose views were expressed by the Washington *Post:* "All this talk about benevolent assimilation; all this hypocritical pretense of anxiety for the moral, social, and intellectual exaltation of the natives ... deceives nobody, avails nothing.... We all know, down in our hearts, that these islands ... are important to us only in the ratio of their practical possibilities, and by no other.... Why not be honest?" [51]

There were others who found the primary benefit of our new imperial status in the social cohesion and military spirit that would result when the energies of the country were deflected from internal to external conflict. "Marse" Henry Watterson, the well-known editor of the Louisville *Courier-Journal,* told a New York reporter: "From a nation of shopkeepers we become a nation of warriors. We escape the menace and peril of socialism and agrarianism, as England has escaped them, by a policy of colonization and conquest. From a provincial huddle of petty sovereignties held together by a rope of sand we rise to the dignity and prowess of an imperial republic incomparably greater than Rome. It is true that we exchange domestic dangers for foreign dangers; but in every direction we multiply the opportunities of the people. We risk Caesarism, certainly; but even Caesarism is preferable to anarchism. We risk wars; but a man has but one time to die,

and either in peace or war, he is not likely to die until his time comes.... In short, *anything is beter than the pace we were going before these present forces were started into life.* Already the young manhood of the country is a goodly brand snatched from the burning, and given a perspective replete with noble deeds and elevating ideas." [52]

Probably the most remarkable statement of the meaning of the war and the whole imperial adventure for American thinking was written by Walter Hines Page in the *Atlantic Monthly* not long after the battle of Manila. Page thought the American people would face graver problems after the war than they had experienced in the preceding years. "A change in our national policy may change our very character," he said, "and we are now playing with the great forces that may shape the future of the world—almost before we know it." Up to then, the nation had been going about the prosaic business of peace, a commercial nation absorbed in problems of finance and administration. Now it had come face to face with the sort of problems connected with the management of world empires, and its isolation was at an end. "Shall we be content with peaceful industry, or does there yet lurk in us the adventurous spirit of our Anglo-Saxon forefathers? And have we come to a time when, no more great enterprises awaiting us at home, we shall be tempted to seek them abroad?"

His own conviction was clear. The Americans had sprung from "a race that for a thousand years has done the adventurous and outdoor tasks of the world." Stemming from the English, themselves explorers, conquerors, and founders of states, the Americans had always been engaged with great practical enterprises—fighting Indians, clearing forests, building a new government,

[50] Charles Denby: "Shall We Keep the Philippines?" *Forum,* XXVI (October 1898), 279–80; "Why the Treaty Should Be Ratified," ibid., XXVI (February 1899), 644, 647.
[51] Quoted in Grayson L. Kirk: *Philippine Independence* (New York, 1936), p. 25.

[52] *Literary Digest,* XVII (July 2, 1898), 214; italics added.

extending territory, developing wealth, settling the great issues connected with slavery and the Civil War. These had been "as great enterprises and as exciting, coming in rapid succession, as any race of men has ever had to engage it." The old outdoor spirit of the Anglo-Saxon had thus had wide scope in recent experience.

"But now a generation has come to manhood that has had no part in any great adventure." The chief tasks of domestic politics, like civil service and the reform of the currency and of municipal government, had not been exciting to the imagination, and our politics had been attractive only to petty brigands and second-rate men. In literature too we had fallen into decline. In fact, the three books which had found the most readers and most affected the masses were books of utopian social programs and fantastic philosophy—*Progress and Poverty, Looking Backward,* and *Coin's Financial School.* The proliferation of movements for petty social reforms, "societies for the prevention of minor vices and for the encouragement of minor virtues," denoted a lack of adventurous opportunities. It was quite possible that a life of quiet had grown irksome, that it was not "natural" to us. "Is it true that with a thousand years of adventure behind us we are unable to endure a life of occupations that do not feed the imagination?" Perhaps we were still the same old colonizing and fighting race of Anglo-Saxons at heart. "Before we knew the meaning of foreign possessions in a world ever growing more jealous, we have found ourselves the captors of islands in both great oceans; and from our home-staying policy of yesterday we are brought face to face with world-wide forces in Asia as well as in Europe, which seem to be working, by the opening of the Orient, for one of the greatest changes in human history.... And to nobody has

the change come more unexpectedly than to ourselves. Has it come without our knowing the meaning of it?"[53]

VI

Since Julius W. Pratt published his *Expansionists of 1898* in 1936, it has been obvious that any interpretation of America's entry upon the paths of imperialism in the nineties in terms of rational economic motives would not fit the facts, and that a historian who approached the event with preconceptions no more supple than those, say, of Lenin's *Imperialism* would be helpless. This is not to say that markets and investments have no bearing; they do, but there are features of the situation that they do not explain at all. Insofar as the economic factor was important, it can be better studied by looking at the relation between the depression, the public mood, and the political system.

The alternative explanation has been the equally simple idea that the war was a newspapers' war. This notion, once again, has some point, but it certainly does not explain the war itself, much less its expansionist result. The New Deal period, when the political successes of F.D.R. were won in the face of overwhelming newspaper opposition, showed that the press is not powerful enough to impose upon the public mind a totally uncongenial view of public events. It must operate roughly within the framework of public predispositions. Moreover, not all the papers of the nineties were yellow journals. We must inquire into the structure of journalistic power and also into the views of the owners and editors to find out what differentiated the sensational editors and publishers from those of the conservative press.

[53] Walter Hines Page: "The War with Spain, and After," *Atlantic Monthly,* LXXXI (June, 1898), pp. 721–7, esp. pp. 725–7.

There is still another qualification that must be placed upon the role of the press: the press itself, whatever it can do with opinion, does not have the power to precipitate opinion into action. That is something that takes place within the *political* process, and we cannot tell that part of the story without examining the state of party rivalries, the origin and goals of the political elites, and indeed the entire political context. We must, then, supplement our story about the role of the newspapers with at least two other factors: the state of the public temper upon which the newspapers worked, and the manner in which party rivalries deflected domestic clashes into foreign aggression. Here a perennial problem of politics under the competitive two-party system became manifest again in the 1890's. When there is, for whatever reason, a strong current of jingoism running in the channels of public sentiment, party competition tends to speed it along. If the party in power is behaving circumspectly, the opposition tends to beat the drums. For example, in 1896, with Cleveland still in office, the Republican platform was much more exigent on the Cuba issue. When McKinley came into office and began to show reluctance to push toward intervention, the Democratic party became a center of interventionist pressure; this pressure was promptly supplemented by a large number of Republicans who, quite aside from their agreement on the issue, were concerned about its effect on the fate of their party.

When we examine the public temper, we find that the depression, together with such other events as the approaching completion of the settlement of the continent, the growth of trusts, and the intensification of internal social conflict, had brought to large numbers of people intense frustrations in their economic lives and their careers. To others they had brought anxiety that a period of stagnation in national wealth and power had set in. The restlessness of the discontented classes had been heightened by the defeat of Bryan in 1896. The anxieties about the nation's position had been increased among statesmen and publicists by the revival of world imperialism, in particular by the feeling that America was threatened by Germany, Russia, and Japan. The expansionist statesmen themselves were drawn largely from a restless upper-middle-class elite that had been fighting an unrewarding battle for conservative reform in domestic politics and looked with some eagerness toward a more spacious field of action.

Men often respond to frustration with acts of aggression, and allay their anxieties by threatening acts against others. It is revealing that the underdog forces in American society showed a considerably higher responsiveness to the idea of war with Spain than the groups that were satisfied with their economic or political positions. Our entry into the Philippines then aroused the interest of conservative groups that had been indifferent to the quixotism of freeing Cuba but were alert to the possibility of capturing new markets. Imperialism appealed to members of both the business and the political elites as an enlargement of the sphere of American power and profits; many of the underdogs also responded to this new note of national self-assertion. Others, however, looked upon our conduct in the Philippines as a betrayal of national principles. Anti-expansionists attempted to stir a sense of guilt and foreboding in the nation at large. But the circumstances of the period 1898–1900—the return of prosperity and the quick spectacular victories in war—made it difficult for them to impress this feeling upon the majority. The rhetoric of Duty and Destiny carried the day. The anti-expansionists had neither the numbers nor the morale of their opponents. The most conspicuous result of their lack of drive and confidence can be seen in the lamentable strategy of Bryan over the ratification of the treaty.

Clearly this attempt to see the war and expansion in the light of social history has led us onto the high and dangerous ground of social psychology and into the arena of conjecture. But simple rationalistic explanations of national behavior will also leave us dissatisfied. What I have attempted here is merely a preliminary sketch of a possible explanatory model. Further inquiry might make it seem more plausible at some points, more questionable at others.

This study has been narrowly focused on a single incident. Other expansionist crises in our own history would show important differences. I have not tried to compare American imperialism with that of other countries, or to decide how far our behavior is unique to our own country or similar to that which has been found elsewhere. In the history of other nations we can find many parallels to the role of the press and political parties in whipping up foreign crises, and to the role of the administration in committing the nation to a foreign policy before it could be made a matter of public discussion. The rhetoric and ideology of expansion also were not singular to us; duty, destiny, racism, and other shibboleths were widespread.

I cannot refrain from adding to these notes on the methods of historical understanding another note on the tragicomic procedure of history itself. It may be of some value to us to be reminded how some of the more grandiose expectations of the nineties were realized. Cuba, to be sure, which might have been freed in peace, was freed in the war—insofar as the little country of Batista, Machado, and Castro can be considered free. The sensational newspapers that had boomed the war lost money on expensive extras, costly war-news coverage, and declining advertising.[54] I do not know whether those silverites who wanted the war really expected that it would remonetize silver, but if they did they were rewarded with McKinley's renewed triumph and the Gold Standard Act of 1900. As for business, the gigantic markets of the East never materialized, and the precise value of the Philippines in getting at them is arguable. The islands themselves proved to be a mildly profitable colony that came to absorb a little over 1 per cent of all United States investments abroad. Yet within a generation the United States had committed itself to restoring independence to the Philippines. When this promise was enacted in 1934 many descendants of Aguinaldo's rebels were unenthusiastic about their new economic and strategic position.[55] Finally, the exact estimation that is to be put on our strategic commitment in the Far East, which began with the Philippines, is still a matter of debate. We should, however, make note of the earlier opinion of one of our most brilliant and farsighted statesmen, who declared in 1907 that the Philippines were the Achilles' heel of our strategic position and should be given "nearly complete independence" at the "earliest possible moment."[56] The author of these remarks was Theodore Roosevelt.

[54] Frank Luther Mott: *American Journalism* (New York, 1947), pp. 537–8.

[55] Pratt: *America's Colonial Experiment*, pp. 243–4, 291–310.

[56] Pringle: *Theodore Roosevelt*, pp. 408–9.

10

Progressivism and Imperialism: The Progressive Movement and American Foreign Policy, 1898–1916

WILLIAM E. LEUCHTENBURG

In the period in American history from the end of the war with Spain to American intervention in World War I, two themes predominated: the Progressive movement and the vigorous pursuit of an imperialist policy in the western hemisphere.

The Progressive movement sprang from a desire to reform the evils that had resulted from the growth of cities, rapid industrialization, and the influx of large numbers of immigrants. It sought to put an end to the slums, the vice, and the crime of the urban centers; to help the poor, the sick, and the oppressed; to curb the power of the large corporations and the trusts; to destroy the corrupt political machines; to restore true democracy to the political process; to effect a more equitable distribution of the country's wealth. It was a liberal and humanitarian movement. The Progressives dreamed of a better America in which there would be no "pyramids of money in a desert of want." And they hoped to achieve their aims by legislation for an eight-hour day, the direct primary, civil service reform, regulation of child labor, prosecution of trusts, fair wages, workers' insurance, income and inheritance taxes, and similar social, political, and economic measures.

The imperialist policy of the United States grew out of the necessity to make secure the approaches to the Panama Canal. Its aim was to convert the Caribbean into an American lake and to achieve United States hegemony in Central America. Between 1898 and 1916 this policy, pursued with equal vigor by the Republicans Roosevelt and Taft and by the Democrat Wilson, resulted in the acquisition of two colonies (Puerto Rico and the Virgin Islands), five protectorates (Dominican Republic, Haiti, Cuba, Nicaragua, Panama), and several naval bases. These gains were effected by armed intervention, when marines were sent to restore order after local revolutions and then frequently remained in occupation for a number of years, and by American money in the form of loans floated by American bankers.

Did these two movements have anything in common? Were they compatible?

FROM *Mississippi Valley Historical Review*, XXXIX (Dec. 1952), 483–504. By permission of the Organization of American Historians.

To these questions the answer generally has been a negative one, and superficially, at least, it would appear unlikely that Progressive reformers would have condoned a harsh and aggressive foreign policy. But William E. Leuchtenburg marshals an imposing body of evidence to demonstrate that an affirmative answer is warranted. Leuchtenburg, a professor of history at Columbia who has written extensively on Progressivism, points out that the Progressives, with but few exceptions, gave unqualified support to the imperialist policies. Indeed, they frequently urged a program more militant than any administration was willing to take. In 1914 they were demanding that Wilson take strong preventive action against Mexico and refuse to indemnify Columbia for the alleged complicity by the United States in the success of the Panama revolution of 1903.

For Leuchtenburg, the link between Progressivism and imperialism is not strange. Firm proponents of democracy at home, the Progressives saw in imperialism the opportunity to export democracy to less fortunate people in foreign lands. Committed to social reform for their own people, they supported every effort to make it available to their neighbors.

No distinction is more revered by the American historian than that between domestic and foreign affairs and in few periods of our history has that distinction been more religiously observed than in the Progressive era. The Theodore Roosevelt who fought the trusts, defied the special interests, and stood at Armageddon to battle for the Lord, and the Theodore Roosevelt who preached jingoism and "took" Panama have been divorced on grounds of incompatibility.[1] The leaders of the Progressive movement, we are given to understand, welcomed Roosevelt's aid in fighting the railway kings and the coal barons, but dissented vigorously from his imperialism and chauvinism. The Progressives were deeply disturbed by Roosevelt's racism, and even more by such episodes as the acquisition of the Canal Zone, but accepted his leadership because of his avowed hostility to corporation control of American life. George Norris' biographer represents the prevailing attitude in asserting that "Western progressives

...had never adhered to the big-stick doctrines of Roosevelt." [2]

The thesis of this article is that the Progressives, contrary to the orthodox accounts, did not oppose imperialism but, with few exceptions, ardently supported the imperialist surge or, at the very least, proved agreeably acquiescent. The majority of the Progressive members of Congress voted for increased naval expenditures and for Caribbean adventures in imperialism. At no time did the Republican insurgents in the Taft administration take issue with Dollar Diplomacy, even when the Progressives were searching for campaign issues in 1912. Not until after the 1912 elections did they concern themselves actively with foreign affairs and then it was not to combat imperialism but to urge the use of American force in Mexico and an increase in armaments. By 1916 the Progressive party had forsaken its program of domestic reform to condemn the foreign policy of the Wilson administration, and a fondness for a "strong" foreign policy was an important cause of the death of the party. Moreover, the ideological content and the motiva-

[1] Insofar as any link has been made between the domestic and foreign aspects of the Progressive period, it has been to present a tableau of Theodore Roosevelt, the warrior, brandishing a big stick at American corporations on the one hand and foreign potentates on the other.

[2] Alfred Lief, *Democracy's Norris* (New York, 1939), 155.

tion of imperialism and progressivism had much in common, a relationship made explicit in the writings of Herbert Croly.

Senator Albert J. Beveridge of Indiana epitomized the two interlocking forces, although his imperialistic views were unquestionably more fervently held than those of the average Progressive. One of the most eloquent orators of the period, he made the keynote speech at the Progressive convention of 1812 in Chicago. Beveridge's fame as an orator started with his declamatory avowal of American imperialism in the Spanish-American War, and he maintained this enthusiasm for imperialism throughout the Progressive era. " 'The opposition tells us we ought not to rule a people without their consent. I answer, the rule of liberty, that all just governments derive their authority from the consent of the governed, applies only to those who are capable of self-government'," he told an enthusiastic Indianapolis meeting in 1898.

The proposition of the opposition makes the Declaration of Independence preposterous, like the reading of Job's lamentations would be at a wedding, or an Altgeld speech on the Fourth of July....Cuba not contiguous? Porto Rico not contiguous? The Philippines not contiguous? Our navy will make them contiguous!...Dewey and Sampson and Schley have made them contiguous, and American speed, American guns, American heart and brain and nerve will keep them contiguous forever.[3]

No member of the Senate in the first decade of this century contributed more to the Progressive movement than Senator Beveridge. He sponsored the bill for federal meat inspection and carried the fight against the bitter opposition of the slaughterhouses. He fought a long, courageous, abortive campaign to end child labor in America. In the 1910 cam-

paign in Indiana he urged federal control of railways, the eight-hour day, and the regulation of trust capitalization. It was Beveridge who managed the insurgent revolt against the Payne-Aldrich tariff. He walked out of the Republican party with the Progressives in 1912, and he fought against the drift toward reconciliation after the election, even accepting the hopeless assignment of Progressive candidate for the Senate in 1914.

Yet his faith in America's imperialist mission continued to be just as strong as his belief in economic reform, and Beveridge's imperialism ultimately proved his undoing as a Progressive. Many of the reforms dearest to Beveridge, which the Republican party had opposed and Roosevelt had shunned, were pushed through Congress by Woodrow Wilson, and Beveridge could have little quarrel with the President's domestic program, but by 1914 he was bitterly opposed to him. Wilson should have recognized Huerta, for Mexico needed a strong man, and the repeal of the Panama tolls was a "fatal blunder." "The Progressive Party in Congress will be solid against the repeal." [4] In 1916 he lashed into Wilson for refusing to use arms to support American investments in China, for his proposal to withdraw from the Philippines, and, strangely, for not increasing the tariff to meet new European competition. Beveridge, faced with the necessity to choose between progressivism and imperialism for the first time, chose the latter. By 1920 he was crying out against " 'Organized labor's assault on American institutions!' " interspersing speeches against the League of Nations with demands for the repeal of the excess profits tax. Inflation was caused by the draining of money to Europe through foreign propaganda and unreasonable demands of labor unions for higher wages.[5] Once more Beveridge's views on

[3] Claude G. Bowers, *Beveridge and the Progressive Era* (Boston, 1932), 73–76.

[4] *Ibid.*, 448.
[5] *Ibid.*, 511–12.

domestic and foreign policy had merged, and this new outlook persisted until his death.

At the outbreak of the Spanish-American War few men saw any conflict between social reform and democratic striving at home and the new imperialist mission; indeed, the war seemed nothing so much as an extension of democracy to new parts of the world, and few political figures exceeded the enthusiasm of William Jennings Bryan for the Spanish war.[6] As the war continued and its consequences were realized, as the dream of *Cuba libre* gave way to the realities of Aguinaldo's insurrection, a few of the Progressives, like Hazen Pingree and Jane Addams, joined the anti-imperialist forces, but, first and last, it was the conservatives who bore the burden of the anti-imperialist campaign.

In late March, 1899, William Allen White explained the Emporia *Gazette's* support of the war. " 'Only Anglo-Saxons can govern themselves.... It is the Anglo-Saxon's manifest destiny to go forth as a world conqueror'," [7] he observed. Years later he wrote of this time:

And we in Emporia, and "Our Charley" in Washington, thought we were free to spout and jower and jangle about the atrocities of the "brute Weyler" without in the slightest affecting the reality of our lives. We were as little boys making snoots across the fence, throwing rocks into the next yard, but innocent of the fact that we were starting wars that would last far into the next century, threaten all that we loved and wreck much that we cherished.[8]

"Though I hate war *per se*," wrote Elizabeth Cady Stanton, "I am glad that it has come in this instance. I would

[6] Merle Curti, *Bryan and World Peace,* Smith College *Studies in History* (Northampton), XVI, Nos. 3–4 (1931), 117 ff.
[7] Walter Johnson, *William Allen White's America* (New York, 1947), 111.
[8] *The Autobiography of William Allen White* (New York, 1946), 305–306.

like to see Spain ... swept from the face of the earth." [9]

A few of the Progressives, and many of the older generation of radicals like Henry Demarest Lloyd, joined forces with the anti-imperialists, but it was conservative Republicans like Thomas B. Reed, Democrats like Grover Cleveland and Bryan, frequently for partisan ends, businessmen like Andrew Carnegie, and Mugwumps like Carl Schurz who provided the bulk of the leadership. "The Republicans who joined the anti-imperialist movement were, almost without exception, Republicans of the older generation.... The anti-imperialists made great efforts to attract labor support, but, on the whole, were unsuccessful." [10] The important political figure who persistently linked the fight for progressivism with the struggle against imperialism was the ineffective Silver Republican, Senator Richard Pettigrew of South Dakota, and he was retired from office in 1900, partly because of his anti-imperialist views.[11]

Theodore Roosevelt's accession to the presidency brought the new imperialist

[9] Merle Curti, *Peace or War: The American Struggle, 1636–1936* (New York, 1936), 171.
[10] Fred H. Harrington, "The Anti-Imperialist Movement in the United States, 1898–1900," *Mississippi Valley Historical Review* (Cedar Rapids), XXII (September, 1935), 218–19. See also Fred H. Harrington, "Literary Aspects of American Anti-Imperialism, 1898–1902," *New England Quarterly* (Baltimore, Portland), X (December, 1937), 650–67. The support given by organized labor to various imperialist ventures may be traced in John C. Appel, "The Relationship of American Labor to United States Imperialism, 1895–1905" (Ph.D. dissertation, University of Wisconsin, 1950).
[11] Cf. Richard Pettigrew, *Imperial Washington* (Chicago, 1922); William G. Carleton, "Isolationism and the Middle West," *Mississippi Valley Historical Review*, XXXIII (December, 1946), 379. Even Senator Pettigrew favored war with Spain, "because I believe it will put us on a silver basis." Arthur W. Dunn, *From Harrison to Harding...1888–1921,* 2 vols. (New York, 1922), I, 232. There was a close tie, in fact, between the jingoes and the silverites. Julius W. Pratt, *Expansionists of 1898* (Baltimore, 1936), 242 ff.

movement to full flower, and, in all of his foreign ventures, in Santo Domingo, Panama, the Far East, in building a greater American fleet, Roosevelt had the support of a majority of the Progressives. "I confess that the half-hearted criticism I hear of the way of the administration with Panama provokes in me a desire to laugh," Jacob Riis noted. "I am not a jingo; but when some things happen I just have to get up and cheer. The way our modern American diplomacy goes about things is one of them." [12] Gifford Pinchot warmly admired Roosevelt's policy in Panama,[13] while Oscar Straus, the Progressive candidate for governor of New York in 1912, helped prepare the dubious legal defense of Roosevelt's course with Panama, with his concept of a " 'covenant running with the land'." As John Bassett Moore observed cynically to Straus, it was "indifferently, a question of the 'covenant running with the land' or a question of the 'covenant running (*away!*) with the land'!!" [14] When Bryan negotiated a treaty of indemnity and apology with Colombia, the Progressives were outraged. The Colombians, said Senator Joseph L. Bristow heatedly, were "a lot of blackmailers." As for the contention that Roosevelt had acted immorally in Panama, "there could be no greater slander pronounced against the Government and nothing more unjust, and in my opinion it borders on treason." [15] The final word on the Progressive position on Panama was had by George Norris over forty years later, when he ruefully observed:

Often those years I followed him [Roosevelt] when I had some doubts as to the

righteousness of his course.... Yet he built the Panama Canal after other governments and a great corporation had spent a vast amount of money and had failed in their efforts. He threw his heart into the construction of this waterway, whose long useful service has caused the struggle for it to be forgotten; but during its progress the means by which the Panama Canal was accomplished in some respects seem doubtful to me. *I followed him step by step in that fight.* Doubts assailed me at the time, and I have since reached the conclusion that our government's decision to establish the new republic of Panama, which in reality prevented Colombia from defending her own territory with her army, was open to argument.[16]

The Progressives were scarcely less cooperative in promoting American hegemony in the Caribbean and defending Roosevelt's big stick diplomacy there. On the Platt amendment Senators Beveridge and Jonathan P. Dolliver voted with the majority, and the Silver Republicans, Pettigrew and Henry M. Teller, cast the only dissenting Republican votes.[17] Roosevelt's action in taking over the customhouse of the Dominican Republic received the approval of Senators Beveridge, Moses E. Clapp, Dolliver, and Robert M. La Follette, with not a single Progressive senator voting against the treaty.[18] By March, 1907, Charles Joseph Bonaparte, who prosecuted the trusts under Roosevelt and was to be a bitter foe of George W. Perkins in 1916, could sound a popular note in praising the President's skill in "promoting the peace of Central America, in staying civil strife in Cuba, in discouraging rebellion in Santo Domingo." [19] Bonaparte also shared with a great many Progressives Roosevelt's enthusiasm for a big navy, a viewpoint of in-

[12] Jacob A. Riis, *Theodore Roosevelt, The Citizen* (New York, 1903), 384, 385.
[13] Cf. Gifford Pinchot, *Breaking New Ground* (New York, 1947).
[14] Oscar S. Straus, *Under Four Administrations; From Cleveland to Taft* (Boston, 1922), 175, 176.
[15] New York *Times*, October 14, 1914, p. 10; Claudius O. Johnson, *Borah of Idaho* (New York, 1936), 191 ff.

[16] *Fighting Liberal; The Autobiography of George W. Norris* (New York, 1945), 145–47 (italics supplied).
[17] *Cong. Record,* 56 Cong., 2 Sess., 3151–52.
[18] *Ibid.,* 59 Cong., 2 Sess., 3917.
[19] Charles J. Bonaparte, "Two Years of a Government That Does Things," *Outlook* (New York), LXXXV (March 16, 1907), 600.

estimable advantage for a secretary of the navy. When Roosevelt appointed him to this post in 1905, Bonaparte assured him: "It is perhaps proper to say, in this connection, that I am in hearty sympathy with your frequently expressed views as to the importance and, indeed, necessity of a very strong and very efficient Navy to the United States." [20] The antinavy bloc in Congress was led not by the Progressives but by the conservative Eugene Hale in the Senate and the conservative Theodore Burton in the House, and their main supporters were likewise conservatives.[21]

The first uprising of the insurgents against Nelson W. Aldrich occurred not over the Payne-Aldrich tariff, but on behalf of Roosevelt's request for four new battleships in 1908 against the outspoken opposition of the Old Guard. Led by Senator Beveridge, two fifths of the Republicans deserted Aldrich in a debate featuring repeated attacks on the leadership of the Old Guard. The debate, which ended in a compromise on two battleships, badly shook Aldrich's domination of the Senate. "The Senate oligarchy is in a bad way," reported the *Saturday Evening Post*. "It is tottery and wobbly at the knees. Its members do not know just what it was that hit them, but they do know that they have been hit hard." [22] On the final vote on the Piles amendment for four battleships, which was defeated 50 to 23, Beveridge, William E. Borah, and Jonathan Bourne voted with the big navy minority against Aldrich, W. Murray Crane, Thomas C. Platt, and other Old Guard leaders. Senator Weldon B. Heyburn expressed the general sentiment of the debate in observing: "I care nothing for the poetic idea of turning swords into plowshares and spears into

pruning hooks. This is a business proposition." On this occasion two of the Progressives, Clapp and Joseph M. Dixon, voted against navalism, and Clapp launched a brilliant, bitter attack on Beveridge for raising false issues "that the public might be prejudiced." [23]

The degree to which the majority of the Progressives were bound to Roosevelt's foreign policy is indicated in a letter of Brand Whitlock's:

I have your note asking me if I could help you with a letter against wasting $32,000,000 on two more useless battleships. I am not sure that anything I can say on that subject will be of any use in stopping the construction of battleships; if it would I would say a great deal, for; of course, it is all but a part of the vast and amazing superstition of war.... I suppose that as long as there are some nations in the world who want to go to war, and so long as there are commercial interests that will keep up revolutions in Mexico and Central and South America, we shall need a navy and army to do police duty and keep the peace in this hemisphere, for which, under the Monroe Doctrine, I suppose we are responsible; but I know of no reason for going beyond this need.[24]

Whitlock was an intelligent, eloquent critic of Roosevelt's foreign policy who once observed that "Thayer can see the megalomania which afflicted Garibaldi but cannot see it when the same symptoms are repeated in Roosevelt." [25] Yet even the hostile Whitlock accepted reluctantly the obligations of "police duty" and the Monroe Doctrine, and from these premises much could follow.

In March, 1909, Theodore Roosevelt gave way to his heir apparent, William Howard Taft, and for the next four years the Progressives were confronted

[20] Joseph B. Bishop, *Charles Joseph Bonaparte* (New York, 1922), 100.

[21] Curti, *Peace or War*, 220.

[22] *Saturday Evening Post* (Philadelphia), CLXXX (May 23, 1908), 18–19.

[23] *Cong. Record,* 60 Cong., 1 Sess., 5291, 5284, 5274.

[24] Brand Whitlock to General Isaac R. Sherwood, February 26, 1913, Allan Nevins (ed.), *The Letters and Journal of Brand Whitlock*, 2 vols. (New York, 1936), I, 158–59.

[25] Whitlock to Albert J. Nock, June 14, 1916, *ibid.*, 195.

by the phenomenon of Dollar Diplomacy. Philander C. Knox, who had prosecuted the Northern Securities case, directed the new Caribbean policy, while Willard D. Straight, who in 1914 was to found the *New Republic* "to explore and develop and apply the ideas which had been advertised by Theodore Roosevelt when he was the leader of the Progressive party," [26] fostered Dollar Diplomacy in the Orient. The liberal character of Straight's Oriental diplomacy, which attempted to force American capital to go into China where it did not care to enter, rests on the nice distinction between territorial integrity and economic hegemony, and the dubious assumption that the investments of Edward H. Harriman, who allegedly asserted he could buy Congress and, if need be, the judiciary, would be more beneficial to the Chinese people than French and Russian capital. Ultimately Straight ended up attempting to raise a foreign loan to crush the Chinese revolution, on the assumption that what China needed was a dictator. The British and Germans were unsympathetic, and Straight was forced to allow the Chinese people to determine their own political destiny.[27]

From the days of the Payne-Aldrich tariff dispute, the rift between the insurgents and Taft grew wider, and Taft was beleaguered by a Progressive bloc which at times opposed him on purely ideological grounds, on occasion out of personal spite, but at no time because of disagreement with Taft's Dollar Diplomacy. While the Progressives were meeting in Chicago in 1912 to establish their third party, Taft was landing American marines in Nicaragua, but no word of condemnation for Taft's foreign policy appears in the Progres-

sive platform of 1912. Instead, the platform stated:

It is imperative to the welfare of our people that we enlarge and extend our foreign commerce. In every way possible our federal government should co-operate in this important matter. Germany's policy of co-operation between government and business has in comparatively few years made that nation a leading competitor for the commerce of the world.... The Panama Canal, built and paid for by the American people, must be used primarily for their benefit. ... American ships engaged in coastwise trade shall pay no tolls.

Roosevelt's speech to the Progressive convention called for building a larger navy,[28] and Frank Munsey assured his readers that "The new Progressive party believes in a navy that will insure peace, that will give us a rightful position among the powers of the world, and that will make the Monroe Doctrine an actuality." [29]

The two issues of foreign policy which did affect the Progressive bolt of 1912 were the arbitration treaties and Taft's Mexican policy, both of which earned the ire of Theodore Roosevelt, and with Taft's prosecution of United States Steel, brought about the final break between Roosevelt and Taft. "Describing the treaties as an outrage, born of some very 'sloppy thinking,' Roosevelt furiously set about to destroy them. He wrote innumerable letters to [Henry Cabot] Lodge, chairman of the Senate Foreign Relations Committee, corresponded with [Elihu] Root, and indirectly reached [Albert B.] Cummins and Borah." [30] In a series of articles in the *Outlook*, starting on May 20, 1911, Roosevelt lashed out at the arbitration

[26] Walter Lippmann, "Notes for a Biography," *New Republic* (New York), LXIII (July 16, 1930), 250.

[27] Herbert Croly, *Willard Straight* (New York, 1924), 422 ff.

[28] Chicago *Record-Herald*, August 7, 1912, p. 5.

[29] Frank A. Munsey, "The New Progressive Party—What It Is and Why It Is," *Munsey's Magazine* (New York), XLVII (August, 1912), 678.

[30] George E. Mowry, *Theodore Roosevelt and the Progressive Movement* (Madison, 1946), 187 ff.

treaties with thinly veiled references to Taft. We should not indulge in "amiable sentimentality"; it is "our duty not to indulge in shams, not to make believe we are getting peace by some patent contrivance which sensible men ought to know cannot work"; "to speak of it as silly comes far short of saying what should be said." [31] When the treaties reached the Senate floor, the Progressive forces were divided, Borah, Bourne, Bristow, and Cummins voting for the crippling amendment to exclude from arbitration questions affecting the admission of aliens to the United States or any question involving the Monroe Doctrine, while Clapp and John D. Works voted against it, a courageous act on the part of Senator Works, who came from the alien-conscious state of California.[32] Roosevelt denounced as "flabby" Taft's firm action in refusing to intervene on behalf of American oil interests in Mexico.[33] "Of all the misconduct of the Administration," Roosevelt concluded, "no misconduct had been greater than that relating to foreign affairs." [34]

The campaign of 1912 offered the Progressives another excellent opportunity to attack Taft's Dollar Diplomacy, but they were strangely silent. Scarcely had the election returns of November, 1912, been counted, however, than they began their attack on Woodrow Wilson and a movement started within the Progressive party to return to the Republican fold at almost any price. The Progressives were embarrassed by Wilson's commendable record in domestic affairs, and as Wilson drove through one reform after another in 1913 it became clear that their only choice was between joining forces with

Wilson or maintaining their party organization intact with a more radical approach to domestic problems; there were no grounds for choosing the Republicans over the Wilson administration. Instead, they chose to fight it out with the administration on foreign policy. For the first time in the history of the Progressive movement foreign affairs determined the line of direction, and by 1916 the Progressives were completely absorbed with foreign policy issues and their movement was moribund.

On July 11, 1914, Roosevelt announced the new direction of the party when he resigned as contributing editor to the Outlook to devote his time to opposing the Wilson administration for its foreign policy which had "meant the abandonment of the interest and honor of America." [35] In later years Roosevelt indicated that his violent turn against the administration was over Wilson's indifference to the plight of Belgium, but in September, 1914, Roosevelt was urging American neutrality with respect to Belgium. "Of course it would be folly to jump into the gulf ourselves to no good purpose; and very probably nothing that we could have done would have helped Belgium." [36] The main grievances of Roosevelt and the Progressives with Wilson were originally not over the European war at all, but over the treaty of apology and indemnity with Colombia, Bryan's cooling off treaties, and the "mushy amiability" of Wilson in withdrawing from Mexico and agreeing to arbitration by the ABC powers.[37]

Borah announced a "last ditch" fight against Wilson's bill to repeal the Panama Canal tolls, and on the vote for final passage, Borah, Bristow, Clapp, Cummins, La Follette, Miles Poindexter, and Works all voted in opposition, with only

[31] See particularly Theodore Roosevelt, "The Peace of Righteousness," Outlook, XCIX (September 9, 1911), 66 ff.
[32] Cong. Record, 62 Cong., 2 Sess., 2954–55.
[33] Mowry, Theodore Roosevelt and the Progressive Movement, 307.
[34] Ibid., 187 ff.

[35] Outlook, CVII (July 11, 1914), 569.
[36] Theodore Roosevelt, "The World War: Its Tragedies and Its Lessons," ibid., CVIII (September 23, 1914), 169–78.
[37] New York Times, June 25, 1914, p. 2.

Asle J. Gronna and Norris voting with the Wilson administration.[38] Mexico was an even hotter issue. In March, 1915, Walter A. Johnson, New York state chairman of the Progressive party, asserted in an interview in the New York *Sun* that Wilson, instead of following the policy of "watchful waiting" in Mexico, should follow the sterling example of Theodore Roosevelt in the Perdicaris case in Morocco by sending warships and issuing an ultimatum.[39] A few months later Dr. H. Nelson Jackson, chairman of the Progressive party of Vermont, issued a statement to the Burlington *Free Press:*

While hundreds of Americans were being murdered, their wives and daughters outraged, their property destroyed, and have received no protection from our spineless, psalm-singing administration, thousands of our citizens thought that President Wilson was locked in his study praying and planning for peace and good will to this beloved country of ours, but in the past few weeks they suddenly realized that his time had been taken up otherwise, with courting. ...Oh! God give us a leader that will keep our country in the exalted position made possible by such leaders as Washington and Abraham Lincoln and that will make Americans feel no matter where they go, no matter where they invest their capital, that they, their families, and their properties will be respected and protected, and above all that our dear flag will be honored among all nations.[40]

In December, 1914, the Progressives issued a statement completely omitting the progressive planks of the 1912 platform and concentrating on demands for a higher protective tariff, a far cry from

the insurgency of 1909 and a clear bid for amalgamation with the Republican party. By the fall of 1915 domestic issues had almost completely disappeared from the Progressive program, and the one issue that was hammered home in Progressive publications and meetings was the need for military preparedness. On September 25, 1915, Victor Murdock, the Kansas radical who was chairman of the National Committee of the Progressive party, wrote Walter Johnson:

I was greatly gratified to find this view [the necessity for maintaining the Progressive party] confirmed at a dinner given by Mr. Perkins to me at the Manhattan Hotel here on Wednesday evening.... There was straight-out, complete candor in the addresses made by all of them, and an absence of boast and fustian. They were in favor of holding the line, facing forward and throwing themselves into the campaign of 1916 with uncompromising aggression, behind a ticket and platform which will challenge the sense and patriotism of the nation.

The strong notes sounded were for military and economic preparedness. The men present favored insuring peace for the nation by placing us in a position to command respect and for an adjustment of the tariff under the Progressive plan of a tariff commission to meet the abnormal selling campaign by Europe which will follow inevitably the cessation of hostilities abroad.[41]

Not only had foreign policy become a key issue, but it had been linked by now with the need for high tariff walls, a prophecy of the economic policy of Warren G. Harding and Herbert Hoover.

In December Chairman Murdock issued a statement emphasizing the main points of the Progressive party program:

The Progressive Party proposes to bring, first of all, a constructive program for business ills, the proposal of a sane protective tariff policy and a demand for social justice and for straight-out preparedness both on the military side and the industrial and economic sides. The Progressive Party's policy of 1912 for a tariff commission with

[38] *Cong. Record,* 63 Cong., 2 Sess., 10247–48. This is not to say that the Wilson administration was free from imperialist manifestations. Indeed, the degree to which Woodrow Wilson was involved with American imperialist aspirations makes the attitude of the Progressives all the more remarkable. The relation of the New Freedom to American foreign policy merits further study, but it necessarily lies outside the scope of this short paper.

[39] *Progressive Opinion* (New York), I (March 27, 1915), 7.

[40] *Ibid.,* II (January, 1916), 3.

[41] *Ibid.,* II (October 2, 1915), 2.

broad powers has already the endorsement of the whole country and must be enacted into law if the industrial invasion from Europe after the war is to be forestalled.[42]

On January 11, 1916, the Progressive National Committee, meeting in Chicago, issued a statement, adopted unanimously, condemning the Wilson administration for its failure "to deal adequately with National honor and industrial welfare."

The Wilson administration has repudiated the faith of our forefathers which made the American flag the sufficient protection of an American citizen around the world. It has suffered American men, women and children to be slaughtered in Mexico and on the high seas, American property to be destroyed and American liberty to travel and trade to be subject to the arbitrary and lawless coercion of foreign belligerents.... We need a reawakening of our elder Americanism, of our belief in those things that our country and our flag stands for.

At their national convention in 1916 the Progressive party, which had had only a few sentences on foreign policy in its 1912 platform, devoted almost its entire platform to preparedness, Americanism, and the excoriation of the Wilson program on Mexico and the European war. The Progressives demanded a regular army of 250,000 men, compulsory universal military training, and "a navy restored to at least second rank in battle efficiency." When Roosevelt refused the nomination, the party turned to Charles E. Hughes, who Roosevelt told them stood for "clean-cut, straightout Americanism," and the party decided to support him, because only he could "serve the two vital causes of Americanism and Preparedness."[43]

For many it was a hard choice. The Republican platform of 1916, as the *New Republic* observed, was a "stupidly, defiantly and cynically reactionary docu-

ment." "The Republican party of 1916 does not differ in any essential respect from that portion of the party which nominated Mr. Taft.... They have revised none of their professed principles; they have dismissed none of their objectionable leaders; they have not by a single act or declaration betrayed a leaning towards liberalism, such as would make an honest Progressive welcome reunion."[44]

When Raymond Robins of Illinois, chairman of the national convention, heard Roosevelt tell him that "Mr. Hughes would answer the preparedness, Americanism and progressive demands of our party," Robins dissented. On June 26, at a meeting of the Progressive National Committee, Robins announced: "At this hour, if I had to vote or declare my sentiments, I should declare for Woodrow Wilson and vote for him."

Robins sounded out the other Progressive leaders. Hiram W. Johnson, Gifford Pinchot, and James R. Garfield all told him that the only hope was to go back to the Republican party and support Hughes, Pinchot explaining it was necessary because of "this national crisis." Soon Robins was announcing his support of Hughes, in part because "we must develop a national mind that will comprehend our social, industrial and military unpreparedness. It must appreciate the domestic injury and national danger that lies in our lack of a definite foreign policy." He further asserted his warm support of compulsory military training, the Oriental Exclusion acts, and "our obligations under the Monroe Doctrine."[45]

In the campaign of 1916 the Progressive party frankly announced its abandonment of its earlier political ideals. On June 26, 1916, the National Committee, after listing recent important gains in

---

[42] *Ibid.*, II (December 4, 1915), 3.
[43] Progressive Party, National Committee, *The Progressive Party; Its Record From January to July, 1916* (New York, n. d.), 6 ff.

[44] *New Republic*, VII (June 17, 1916), 160.
[45] Progressive Party, National Committee, *Progressive Party; Its Record From January to July, 1916*, pp. 102 ff.

progressive legislation, which it termed "national advance," observed that the war had brought

an issue deeper than national advance, the issue of national unity and the nation's existence, of Americanism and of Preparedness. The Progressive Platform of 1916, therefore, placed foremost as our immediate need preparedness in arms, industry and spirit.... The Progressive National Committee recognizes that such are now the issues that immediately confront the country and *looks only to the duty that arises therefrom*.[46]

The Republican and Progressive platforms of 1916 were almost identical, except that Lodge could not get the Republicans to accept the provision for universal service.[47] Partly out of political desperation, partly out of loyalty to Roosevelt, in large part because of their views on foreign affairs, the mass of the Progressives supported Hughes, although the Republicans made no pretense of progressivism and Wilson had enacted much of the Progressive platform. The 1916 campaign was the last presidential election the Progressive party entered; imperialism and militarism had replaced the old liberal formulas of protest, and within a year the party was dead.

How does one account for the wide divergence between Progressive principle and practice, between a concern for democratic processes at home and a disregard of them abroad, for antagonism to financial empires in America and encouragement of them overseas, for the destruction of American progressivism in the interest of imperialism, militarism, and Americanism?

In the first place, many Progressives were able to convince themselves that there was no conflict at all, that their domestic and foreign policies were two sides of the same coin. The Spanish-American War was not merely a struggle

to bring freedom to Cuba and end Spanish tyranny but a crusade for principle against the greed of Wall Street interests opposed to the war. "Cuba is free and she thanks President Roosevelt for her freedom," wrote Jacob Riis. "But for his insistence that the nation's honor was bound up in the completion of the work his Rough-Riders began at Las Guasimas and on San Juan Hill, a cold conspiracy of business greed would have left her in the lurch, to fall by and by reluctantly into our arms, bankrupt and helpless, while the sneer of the cynics that we were plucking that plum for ourselves would have been justified." [48] "We will have this war for the freedom of Cuba in spite of the timidity of the commercial interests," Roosevelt told a Gridiron dinner.[49] We must save the "wretched Cubans" from Spain, Roosevelt averred, and then noted, "It would be a splendid thing for the Navy, too." [50]

Compulsory military training was likewise a phase of progressivism. "The proposed continental army is utterly undemocratic; it denies to the patriotic man of small means the chance to train which it gives to his well-to-do brother," Roosevelt asserted.[51] Compulsory universal military training, agreed Raymond Robins, "will do more in one generation to break down class and section prejudice, develop disciplined, vigorous and efficient citizenship, and to unify the diverse groups of our national life in a vital Americanism than all other forces combined." As opposed to this Progressive program, Robins added, the Democrats, in opposing universal training, offer only

[46] *Ibid.*, 112 ff.
[47] Mowry, *Theodore Roosevelt and the Progressive Movement*, 348.

[48] Riis, *Theodore Roosevelt, The Citizen*, 383.
[49] Arthur W. Dunn, *Gridiron Nights* (New York, 1915), 70 ff.
[50] Theodore Roosevelt to Henry C. Lodge, August 3, 1897, Henry C. Lodge (ed.), *Selections from the Correspondence of Theodore Roosevelt and Henry Cabot Lodge, 1884–1918*, 2 vols. (New York, 1925), I, 268.
[51] *Progressive Opinion*, II (December 4, 1915), 6.

"a state-dominated militia with its menace of shiftless incompetence, spoils politics and organized snobbery as a national defense force, at a time of world peril." [52]

Secondly, it is impossible to understand the acquiescence of many Progressives in the imperialist movement without realizing the remarkable hold that Theodore Roosevelt had on his followers. Norris' testimony that "often those years I followed him when I had some doubts as to the righteousness of his course" is not an isolated instance. To many American liberals "Roosevelt was ... [by 1912] something more than a revered political leader. He was gradually becoming a minor deity." [53] Years later, William Allen White described his first meeting with Roosevelt:

I met Theodore Roosevelt. He sounded in my heart the first trumpet call of the new time that was to be. ... I had never known such a man as he, and never shall again. He overcame me. And in the hour or two we spent that day at lunch, and in a walk down F Street, he poured into my heart such visions, such ideals, such hopes, such a new attitude toward life and patriotism and the meaning of things, as I had never dreamed men had.[54]

Even after Roosevelt had deserted the Progressives and helped disrupt the movement, even after he had had the obtuseness to suggest Lodge as the standardbearer, Harold Ickes could see only George Perkins as the Iago of the movement and had no harsh words for Roosevelt.[55]

Thirdly, the attitude of the Progressives toward the American Negro made them more receptive to American imperialism. They readily accepted the no-

tion that the little brown brother was a ward of the United States, not fit for self-government, because they regarded the southern Negro as a ward when they did not think of him as a corrupt politician attempting to sell his vote to the highest bidder at Republican conventions. The Progressive party plan with respect to the Negro, wrote Roosevelt, was "to try for the gradual re-enfranchisement of the worthy colored man of the South by frankly giving the leadership of our movement to the wisest and justest white men of the South." [56] Despite the fact that the Negro vote in Maryland was credited with giving Roosevelt his margin of victory over Taft in the 1912 primaries, he persisted in his aim to make the Progressive party a lily white party in the South, with Senator Dixon, his national campaign manager, publicly disavowing a Progressive organization in South Carolina because of its Negro membership and the convention refusing to seat any southern Negro delegates, despite the dissent of Jane Addams.[57] W. A. D. Venerable, head of the Colored Men's National Progressive Association, denounced the Progressive party for holding the Negro unfit for suffrage in the South, and, immediately after the convention, his organization announced for Wilson in the 1912 elections.[58]

Nor was this policy limited to the Progressive party. At the American Socialist Congress in 1910, over a third of the dele-

[52] Progressive Party, National Committee, *Progressive Party; Its Record From January to July, 1916*, pp. 121 ff.
[53] Mowry, *Theodore Roosevelt and the Progressive Movement*, 243.
[54] *Autobiography of William Allen White*, 297.
[55] Harold L. Ickes, "Who Killed the Progressive Party?" *American Historical Review* (New York), XLVI (January, 1941), 306–37.

[56] Theodore Roosevelt, "The Progressives and the Colored Man," *Outlook*, CI (August 24, 1912), 911.
[57] "Official Minutes of the (Provisional) Progressive National Committee," Theodore Roosevelt Collection (Widener Library, Harvard University, Cambridge); George E. Mowry, "The South and the Progressive Lily White Party of 1912," *Journal of Southern History* (Baton Rouge, Lexington), VI (May, 1940), 237–47.
[58] Chicago *Record-Herald*, August 6, 1912, p. 1; August 9, 1912, p. 2. See also the attack on the action of the convention in "No Square Deal," *Independent* (New York), LXXIII (August 15, 1912), 391–93.

gates, led by Victor Berger, favored legislation against Asiatic immigration. Ernest Untermann, the Socialist candidate for governor of Idaho, asserted: "The question as to what race shall dominate the globe must be met as surely as the question of what class shall own the world. We should neglect our duty to the coming generation of Aryan peoples if we did not do everything in our power, even today, to insure the final race victory of our own people." Both Robert Hunter of the National Executive Committee of the Socialist party and Adolph Germer of the Miners' Union attacked foreign and Negro labor as hostile to unionism, and Untermann stated, " '*we should be false to our Socialist agitation if we insisted first on doing away with the race prejudice'.*" [59]

Hostility toward and contempt for Oriental labor, in particular, was an avowed part of the Progressive campaign of 1912, a legacy of its trade union support and the sectional attitudes of the west coast which made an unsympathetic attitude toward Oriental nations a concomitant part of the outlook of many Progressives. The *Progressive Bulletin,* the official organ of the party, attacked Wilson in 1912 because he "prefers Chinese immigrants to white," and inquired whether "the Chinese are more desirable immigrants than the white people who dig our ground?" The first two points listed on Roosevelt's "labor record" in the 1912 campaign were "renewing the Chinese Exclusion Act and extending its provisions to the island territory of the United States," and "prohibiting the employment of Mongolian labor on irrigation works." [60] Nor did the Progressives always view southern European labor with favor. "These hearty

'hunkies' and 'dagoes' feel that they are working to make America rich and that their services should be appreciated, but are they?" asked the leading Progressive magazine on the west coast. "Are they not rather displacing the American of forty-five to fifty, when otherwise, he would work on until sixty without showing the white feather?" [61]

Most important, imperialism and progressivism flourished together because they were both expressions of the same philosophy of government, a tendency to judge any action not by the means employed but by the results achieved, a worship of definitive action for action's sake, as John Dewey has pointed out,[62] and an almost religious faith in the democratic mission of America. The results of the Spanish-American War were heartily approved not merely because the war freed subject peoples from tyranny, but because, since the United States was the land of free institutions, any extension of its domain was *per se* an extension of freedom and democracy. It was an age that admired results, that was not too concerned with fine distinctions and nice theories. The Progressives, quite apart from sharing in the general excitement of middle-class America in the rise of the United States as a world power and the sense of identity with the nation which imperialism afforded in a time of national stress, admired anyone who could clean up the slaughterhouses or link two great oceans, who could get a job done without months of tedious debate and deference to legal precedents. The Progressives believed in the Hamiltonian concept of positive government,

[59] William E. Walling, *Progressivism—And After* (New York, 1914), 377–81.
[60] *Progressive Bulletin* (New York), I (September 16, 1912), 5. At the same time, however, the *Bulletin* attacked the nativism of the Republican party.

[61] *California Outlook* (Los Angeles and San Francisco), XII (February 10, 1912), 5. William Allen White recalled that "of course, I read the popular pseudo-sciences of the day, such as 'Anglo-Saxon Superiority,' by Edmond Demolins." *Autobiography of William Allen White,* 326.
[62] John Dewey, *Characters and Events,* 2 vols. (New York, 1929), I, 91.

of a national government directing the destinies of the nation at home and abroad. They had little but contempt for the strict construction of the Constitution by conservative judges, who would restrict the power of the national government to act against social evils and to extend the blessings of democracy to less favored lands. The real enemy was particularism, state rights, limited government, which would mean the reign of plutocracy at home and a narrow, isolationist concept of national destiny abroad, which would deny the democratic mission of America and leave the brown peoples pawns of dynastic wars and colonial exploitation.

No writer better demonstrates the close link between progressivism and imperialism, with the concept of the Hamiltonian state and the democratic mission, than Herbert Croly, whose *The Promise of American Life* (1909) influenced the Progressive movement more profoundly than any other work. Roosevelt was more deeply moved by Croly's book than by anything he had read since the early Alfred T. Mahan. A few months after his return from Africa, Roosevelt was preaching the "New Nationalism" of Croly in his Osawatomie address and the war against the Old Guard was on in earnest.

"The American nation, just in so far as it believes in its nationality and is ready to become more of a nation, must assume a more definite and a more responsible place in the international system," wrote Croly. "... In spite of 'old-fashioned democratic' scruples and prejudices, the will to play that part for all it was worth would constitute a beneficial and a necessary stimulus to the better realization of the Promise of our domestic life." [63] We should shun the Jefferson administration's policy of basing "its international policy not upon the firm

[63] Herbert Croly, *The Promise of American Life* (New York, 1909), 289.

ground of national interest, but on the treacherous sands of international democratic propagandism." [64]

The first task of a truly national foreign policy was to develop hemispheric solidarity, and Croly left no doubt of what he meant by "a stable American international system."

In all probability no American international system will ever be established without the forcible pacification of one or more centers of disorder.... In short, any international American political system might have to undertake a task in states like Venezuela, similar to that which the United States is now performing in Cuba.... The United States has already made an effective beginning in this great work, both by the pacification of Cuba and by the attempt to introduce a little order into the affairs of the turbulent Central American republics.[65]

Our work was greatly simplified by the fact that the political condition of Mexico, under the dictatorship of Diaz, had "become more stable and more wholesome," and "any recrudescence of revolutionary upheavals in Mexico would enormously increase the difficulties and perils of the attempt." [66]

The Spanish-American War was a great boon to the American people for it ushered in the Progressive era.

Not until the end of the Spanish War was a condition of public feeling created, which made it possible to revive Hamiltonianism. That war and its resulting policy of extra-territorial expansion, so far from hindering the process of domestic amelioration, availed, from the sheer force of the national aspirations it aroused, to give a tremendous impulse to the work of national reform ... and it indirectly helped to place in the Presidential chair the man who, as I have said, represented both the national idea and the spirit of reform. The sincere and intelligent combination of those two ideas is bound to issue in the Hamiltonian practice of constructive national legislation.[67]

[64] *Ibid.*, 290.
[65] *Ibid.*, 302–303.
[66] *Ibid.*, 301, 303.
[67] *Ibid.*, 169.

Bryan's campaign of 1900, on the other hand, Croly continued, was composed of two disastrous mistakes. "In seeking to prevent his countrymen from asserting their national interest beyond their own continent, he was also opposing in effect the resolute assertion of the national interest in domestic affairs. He stamped himself, that is, as an anti-nationalist, and his anti-nationalism has disqualified him for effective leadership of the party of reform." [68]

Far from being isolated movements, our international mission and our domestic reform program were interlocking forces, and frequently one and the same thing, Croly concluded, for "it is entirely possible that hereafter the United States will be forced into the adoption of a really national domestic policy because of the dangers and duties incurred through her relations with foreign countries." [69]

As Felix Frankfurter observed, "Unlike almost all American prewar writers on politics (with the notable exception of Captain Mahan, because of his special interest in navalism) Croly saw the American situation with its international implications." [70] He did more than that. He provided an intelligible rationale for the union of progressivism and imperialism, ordering the apparently unrelated events of the Roosevelt administration into a coherent political system and contending that imperial ventures were an important phase of the new religion of national reform, steps toward the fulfillment of the promise of American life.

The attitude of the Progressives toward imperialism explains much about the basic character of the Progressive movement. Despite the evangelical aura about the 1912 convention, the movement was not an attempt to remold the world anew, to discard the old system for a new society. The Progressives were completely a part of American life, accepting the traditional values and ideals, cherishing the aspirations of middle-class America, including the new sense of delight in the rise of the United States as a world power. Although a few leaders like Jane Addams saw the movement as an aspect of a broad humanitarian philosophy, the most influential spokesmen thought not in terms of universals but of providing remedies for certain specific political abuses and economic ills. Insofar as they thought in more general terms, they were concerned less with the rights of *all* men, with universal brotherhood, than with the promise of *American* life. They were interested not only in a more equitable division of the pie but in a larger pie to divide, and consequently saw nothing incongruous in supporting American investments abroad in the interest of expanded markets while condemning the same businesses at home for excessive profits and substandard wages. The same group of men who could tear the Republican party asunder because of a discriminatory tariff in 1909 could outdo the Old Guard in arguing for protectionism in 1916 when they feared foreign goods would undercut the home market.

In the final analysis the Progressive movement suffered from a contradiction between humanistic values and nationalist aspirations, which, if not inherent, had certainly beset other democracies from the time of the wars of the French Revolution. In arguing for a positive national government, the followers of Croly ultimately lost sight of the distinction between the state as an instrument and the state as an end. The consequences were not only the endorsement of an imperialistic foreign policy but the death of the Progressive party in the interest of their nationalist zeal.

[68] *Ibid.*, 157.
[69] *Ibid.*, 310.
[70] Felix Frankfurter, "Herbert Croly and American Political Opinion," *New Republic,* LXIII (July 16, 1930), 248.

11

The Changing Concept of
the Open Door, 1899–1910

RAYMOND A. ESTHUS

The "open door" policy of the United States was enunciated by Secretary of State John Hay in the form of two notes, sent on September 6, 1899, and July 3, 1900, to all the great powers that had interests in China. The first urged the powers to support the principle of equal commercial opportunity for the citizens of all nations trading in China. The second announced the American intention to preserve Chinese territorial integrity and indirectly suggested that the powers join in taking the same pledge.

The immediate occasion for the first note was the seizure by the great powers of parts of China in the form of leaseholds and spheres of influence for the purpose of granting to their own nationals in those areas preferential treatment in respect to trade and investment opportunities. This action presented a serious threat to American businessmen who faced discrimination in many sections of China. The second note was prompted by the Boxer rebellion, a revolt led by a Chinese secret society to put an end to all foreign influences in China. To suppress the uprising, an international army consisting of Japanese, European, and American soldiers was formed and sent to Peking, then under siege by the Boxers. During the operation there was considerable speculation that the relief of the Chinese capital and the punishing of the Boxers might lead to the permanent occupation of parts of China by foreign troops. Such a partition of China would, obviously, affect American interests adversely.

The great powers replied to Hay's suggestions evasively and equivocally. They had no intention of permitting foreigners to share equal commercial rights with their own citizens in areas under their control, nor did they abandon their ambitions to exert political control over parts of China. Indeed, within a few years after the notes were sent, the powers were strengthening their entrenched positions and were "closing the door" to all but their own people. But Hay made no effort to enforce the policy of the two notes. He was content merely with reiterating the position and repeating the suggestions.

Not so his successors in office. Under Elihu Root and Philander C. Knox, the "open door policy underwent progressive and finally radical modification." Raymond A. Esthus, who has contributed several interesting new interpretations of American Far Eastern policy in the first decade of the twentieth century, describes the great changes that took place in the application of the open door policy, especially during Knox's administration. It took on a vigorous and

FROM *Mississippi Valley Historical Review*, XLVI (Dec. 1959), 435–454. By permission of the Organization of American Historians.

positive cast and became a challenge to the pretensions of any power that threatened to exclude the citizens of any nation from the enjoyment of equal commercial opportunity in any part of China. Soon it developed into a weapon aimed principally at Japan, which was emerging as the most aggressive exploiter of Manchuria, the area of China in which American interests were greatest. Esthus makes a particularly noteworthy contribution in his reassessment of the Root-Takahira agreement, which, in his view, cannot be construed as giving Japan a "free hand" in Manchuria.

For over four decades after Secretary of State John Hay dispatched his famous notes of September 6, 1899, and circular of July 3, 1900, American Far Eastern policy was based upon the twin principles of the open door and the integrity of China. Moreover, Hay's fame as one of America's foremost secretaries of state rests in large measure upon his enunciation of these principles, which have taken their place beside the Monroe Doctrine and the policy of non-entanglement as fundamentals of American foreign policy. It is one of the ironies of history, however, that the policy pursued by the Department of State over the years under the name of John Hay's open door policy bore little resemblance to the policy which Hay himself had advocated and applied. Indeed, his contribution to later American diplomacy lies more in the words he used than in the manner in which he defined them. Many of his successors were to repeat his phrases while pursuing a fundamentally different policy.

The history of the open door policy, at least in its earlier period, is therefore the story of a changing interpretation of the original concept. If in the 1920's and 1930's the phrases "open door" and "integrity of China" seemed to determine policy and impart to it a measure of rigidity, as George F. Kennan has suggested, it is also true that in the earlier period a variety of policies evolved within the framework of Hay's phraseology. Under Hay's successors, Elihu Root and Philander C. Knox, the open door policy underwent progressive and finally radical modification. The chief architects of that modification were not the secretaries of state themselves, but rather two subordinates, Willard Straight and Francis M. Huntington Wilson. These two young diplomats, both possessing strong antipathy toward Japan, were to leave an imprint upon future American policy which was perhaps more decisive than that of Hay.

The story of the open door policy during Hay's secretaryship has been so ably told that it needs only brief summary here.[1] At a time when the major world powers were marking out spheres of influence in China—areas where they would have superior investment rights and presumably concomitant political influence—Hay had sought to preserve equal commercial opportunity within the spheres. His objectives were limited, for he had no illusions about the inability of the United States to prevent the erection of spheres of influence. Equality of opportunity for capitalistic investment in such enterprises as railway construction and mining was gone and could not be retrieved. Hay did hope, however, to preserve the right of Americans to trade freely in commercial goods, that is, to sell such products as textiles, kerosene, and tobacco. In his open door notes of

[1] See especially A. Whitney Griswold, *The Far Eastern Policy of the United States* (New York, 1938), Chap. II; Tyler Dennett, *John Hay: From Poetry to Politics* (New York, 1933), Chap. XXIV; and George F. Kennan, *American Diplomacy, 1900–1950* (Chicago, 1951), Chap. II.

September 6, 1899, he asked, therefore, only for the minimum guarantees necessary for commercial equality: no interference with the treaty ports, equitable administration of the Chinese customs tariff, and no discriminatory railroad rates or harbor dues.[2] Despite Hay's assertion that the replies to his notes were "final and definitive," the record shows that the replies amounted to a rejection.[3] When in the following year, in a circular to the major governments, Hay enunciated the second principle of his now famous policy, he met with little more success. In this circular of July 3, 1900, he declared that the United States desired a solution of the Boxer troubles which would preserve the Chinese "territorial and administrative entity." But within three years the Secretary, along with President Roosevelt, was in full retreat from this second principle. The Russians had used the Boxer troubles as an excuse to send fifty thousand troops into Manchuria, and in the face of this Russian penetration both Hay and Roosevelt were willing to scrap the second principle if only commercial equality could be saved. "In this Manchurian matter," Roosevelt wrote in 1903, "we are not striving for any political control or to help any nation acquire any political control *or to prevent Russia from acquiring any political control of the territory in question.*"[4]

The open door policy as applied by Hay over a period of some six years was based upon a realistic appreciation of the limitations of American policy. He did not undertake to attack the spheres of influence; he felt that it was hopeless to try to bring those structures tumbling

down through note-writing and that the American public would not support a policy based upon the use of force, even if the military power were available. He therefore fought a limited campaign, hoping to save commercial equality within the framework of special rights and interests. His support of China's integrity was an exceedingly qualified one. He supported it to the extent of opposing complete partition, but he never supported it to the point of attacking the spheres of influence, though the spheres themselves were undoubtedly an infringement of China's integrity.

By the time of Hay's death in 1905 his open door principles had achieved so little success that it might have been expected that they would not long survive him. Yet the principles not only survived, but within five years after his death had been expanded to include a demand for equal investment, as well as equal commercial opportunities, and the phrases open door and integrity of China had become bywords in a crusade against Japan in defense of China. Indeed, by the time of Secretary of State Knox's neutralization proposal of 1909–1910 (the attempt to "smoke Japan out" of Manchuria) Hay's policy had been so transformed that he would scarcely have recognized it. It seems even less likely that he would have claimed it as his own. The words were the same—"the open door and integrity of China"—but the substance was not. The five years following his death, therefore, constitute a crucial period in the evolution of the open door policy.

It was left to Hay's successor, Elihu Root, to wrestle with the problems of the open door policy during the remaining four years of Roosevelt's administration. When Root took over his duties at the Department in the summer of 1905 the power relations in the Far East were undergoing drastic realignment as a result of the Russo-Japanese War. By the middle of 1905 the Japanese had driven

[2] Department of State, *Papers Relating to the Foreign Relations of the United States, 1899* (Washington, 1901), 131–33.
[3] *Ibid.*, 133–43.
[4] Roosevelt to Lyman Abbott, June 22, 1903, Elting E. Morison (ed.), *The Letters of Theodore Roosevelt* (8 vols., Cambridge, 1951–1954), III, 500–501. Italics mine.

the Russians from South Manchuria, and at the Portsmouth Conference in September, 1905, had proceeded to take over Russian rights and interests there, including the leasehold at Port Arthur and that part of the Russian-controlled Chinese Eastern Railway stretching from Changchun in central Manchuria to Port Arthur. Root had to contend, therefore, with two powers in that critical area of international rivalries, the Russians in North Manchuria and the Japanese in South Manchuria, both possessing far-reaching rights and interests in their respective spheres. As in the time of Hay, so in Root's time, the issues relating to the open door and the integrity of China were to revolve around this particular portion of the Chinese Empire.

Root's first statements on the open door policy evidenced some initial confusion as to the nature of Hay's principles. The months following the Portsmouth settlement had witnessed the emergence of serious questions resulting from Japan's temporary military occupation of South Manchuria. Complaints coming to the State Department from American commercial interests there led Root to make vigorous representations to the Japanese government over Japan's delay in opening the interior to foreign commercial agents. Root told Tokyo bluntly that while military exigencies might explain temporary restrictions, such an explanation did not meet "the rapidly developing situation of the absorption of a great part of the commercial and mining opportunities of Manchuria by the freely admitted Japanese." Furthermore, said Root, "If this condition continues, China will find itself after the Japanese occupancy has ceased, the merely nominal sovereign of a territory the material advantages of which have been appropriated by the temporary occupants." [5]

Though this note was to be Root's most vigorous statement on the open door policy, the phraseology used indicates that there was some misunderstanding within the Department of State regarding the meaning of Hay's principles. The reference to "mining opportunities" gives a hint that Root was contesting the right of Japan to have superior investment rights in South Manchuria. Only a few months before, however, Japan had gained at Portsmouth such substantial rights that the State Department should have been under no illusions regarding the Japanese intention to have superior investment rights in South Manchuria. These rights had been transferred to Japan with the full blessing of President Roosevelt.[6] It is true that Roosevelt, before arranging the peace conference, had exacted a pledge from Japan to observe the open door, but Japan naturally interpreted this obligation in terms of Hay's open door for commercial equality, not investment rights. Nevertheless, Root's notes did achieve the immediate objective of getting the Japanese to open the interior to trade, and in the subsequent months there appeared to be little need for further representations to Japan. Reports came from Ambassador Luke E. Wright at Tokyo, Minister William W. Rockhill at Peking, and Consul General Thomas Sammons at Newchwang in South Manchuria, and they all agreed that Japan was not using her military occupation to discriminate against other foreign interests and that Japan would observe the open door.[7]

Japan, V, State Department Records (National Archives).

[6] Roosevelt to William W. Rockhill, September 10, 1905, Morison (ed.), *Letters of Theodore Roosevelt*, V, 18.

[7] Luke E. Wright to Roosevelt, June 7, 1906, Theodore Roosevelt Papers (Manuscript Division, Library of Congress); Rockhill to Root, October 11, 1906, State Department Records, File 551; Thomas Sammons to Assistant Secretary of State Robert Bacon, March 10, 1906, Consular Letters, Niuchwang, VII, State Department Records.

[5] Root to Chargé d'Affaires Francis M. Huntington Wilson, March 30, 1906, Instructions,

The fact that Root made no further energetic assertion of the open door principles was due primarily to the improvement of conditions in South Manchuria. Even if the situation there had not improved, however, Root would doubtless have spoken softly about the open door policy, because of the emergence of serious crises in Japanese-American relations. Beginning with the school segregation trouble in California in the fall of 1906, one crisis followed another, culminating in a serious war scare in the summer of 1907. Root and Roosevelt both believed that the war scare was a product of sensational journalism and that Japan had no intention of going to war.[8] They nevertheless realized that it was not an auspicious time for any vigorous assertion of the doctrine of the open door and the integrity of China if it must be invoked against Japan.

In spite of Washington's desire to restore friendly relations with Japan, it was during these very years (1907–1908) that there began to develop an expanded concept of the open door, directed specifically against Japan. The determination of Root and Roosevelt to tread warily in questions relating to Japan's position in South Manchuria was not shared by some of the younger members of the Department and the Foreign Service. This was particularly true of the twenty-eight-year-old consul general at Mukden in South Manchuria, Willard Straight. By the summer of 1907 the Japanese military occupation of South Manchuria had come to an end, and it was apparent that Japan was going to abide by her pledge (given to Roosevelt in 1905) to observe the open door so far as commerce was concerned. Observance of Hay's limited open door was not, how-

ever, sufficient for Straight. As vice consul at Seoul in 1905 he had witnessed the demise of Korea, and he felt that Manchuria could be saved from Japan only by an extensive program of capitalistic investment carried out by the United States and other Western powers. At his Mukden post, Straight embarked upon an anti-Japanese crusade which, resting on an enlarged concept of the open door doctrine, claimed equal opportunity in investment as well as commercial enterprise and was intended, also, to give forcible support to China's integrity.

The nature of Straight's anti-Japanese program may be seen by examining just one of his many projects, that for a new railway line in Manchuria. With J. O. P. Bland, of the British and Chinese Corporation, and Lord ffrench, of Pauling and Company, he promoted the building of a railroad from Hsinmintun to Fakumen as the first leg of a line running to Tsitsihar in North Manchuria, paralleling the Japanese-owned South Manchuria Railway. In November, 1907, Lord ffrench signed a contract at Mukden with Tang Shao-yi, governor of Fengtien Province, providing for the construction of the line as far as Fakumen. At the same time, a secret agreement was signed for the construction of the rest of the line to Tsitsihar.[9] Straight was quite frank in describing the anti-Japanese nature of this project to Huntington Wilson, the third assistant secretary of state:

The Hsinmintun-Fakumen line will surely be extended to Tsitsihar, will very seriously compete with the South Manchurian Railway, will not only tap a rich and rapidly developing country, part of the produce of which is now carried over the Japanese road, but will almost certainly attract all the through European traffic as well as secure all the mails. More than that even, it will threaten the Japanese strategic posi-

[8] Roosevelt to Root, July 26, 1907, Morison (ed.), *Letters of Theodore Roosevelt*, V, 729–30; Root to Roosevelt, August 8, 1907, Roosevelt Papers; Root to Whitelaw Reid, September 3, 1908, Elihu Root Papers (Manuscript Division, Library of Congress).

[9] Straight diary, November 5, 1907, Willard Straight Papers (Albert R. Mann Library, Cornell University); George Marvin diary, November 6, 1907, Straight Papers.

tion and place a splendid line of communication along the Japanese flank and within easy reach of the Russians whose activities in Mongolia have already aroused the apprehensions of their late, and possible future enemies.[10]

This project was clearly a direct attack upon the Japanese sphere of influence, and Japan countered promptly. She revealed the provisions of the so-called secret protocols, the signed minutes attached to the Sino-Japanese Treaty of 1905 whereby China had agreed that no parallel lines would be constructed in the neighborhood of the South Manchuria Railway. The instigators of the new railway project were left high and dry. An ironic note was added by the fact that it was none other than Governor Tang Shao-yi himself who had signed the understanding with Japan in 1905. Confronted with the Japanese disclosure, the wily governor at first asserted that China had never agreed to supplementary conditions to the treaty of 1905, but, as Bland reported from Peking, "this is denied even by the Chinese who are familiar with all the facts." [11] An Associated Press representative at Peking likewise reported to Straight that nobody in the Chinese Foreign Office "denied the binding force nor the actuality of those minutes forbidding China to build a competitive line." [12] Governor Tang himself admitted to Straight that he and the Japanese negotiator in 1905 had agreed to something vague about parallel lines, but, he now explained, this was not an issue, for the proposed line would not be parallel or compete with the South Manchuria Railway.[13] Straight knew the implications of the project too well to

accept such specious reasoning: "if the Chinese can only excuse themselves by saying that the new road would not compete," he confided to Bland, "they had better chuck it as a rotten bad case." [14]

Any hope for success of the railway project was soon killed by the refusal of the British government to countenance this attack upon the position of its ally, Japan. The London government announced in March, 1908, that it would not give diplomatic support to the British interests involved in the project. The failure of the enterprise might have discouraged a less adventurous crusader than Willard Straight. He had already turned, however, to new schemes. At this time the United States was negotiating for the return to China of approximately half of the Boxer indemnity funds, and Straight saw an opportunity to secure the funds for his Manchurian projects. The State Department's reaction to his efforts indicates that Root was not in sympathy with the anti-Japanese crusade. Straight was bluntly informed that the indemnity remission issue was "a delicate matter of diplomacy with which the Consulate General at Mukden has no direct concern." [15] Root was determined to have this matter handled at Peking by Minister Rockhill, who wished to have the funds devoted to the education of Chinese students in the United States.

While Straight was out in the Three Eastern Provinces attempting to breathe new life and meaning into the open door, Third Assistant Secretary Huntington Wilson was working along parallel lines at the Department of State. In the spring of 1908 he was commissioned to draw up a comprehensive information series circular on the open door policy, to be sent to all major American embas-

[10] Straight to Huntington Wilson, January 31, 1908, ibid. [Reprinted by permission.]
[11] J. O. P. Bland to Straight, January 23, 1908, ibid.
[12] Frederick McCormick to Straight, February 21, 1908, ibid.
[13] Straight to Bacon, January 4 and February 12, 1908, State Department Records, File 6625.

[14] Straight to Bland, February 6, 1908, Straight Papers.
[15] Wilbur J. Carr (Chief Clerk) to Straight, February 10, 1908, State Department Records, File 2413.

sies and legations. The manner in which this project was carried out indicates both the confusion of thought and the division of opinion which existed in the Department regarding the policy. Huntington Wilson compiled a large collection of documents, adding what he considered to be appropriate interpretations. According to his optimistic estimate, all the major nations had pledged their adherence to the American doctrine. Every treaty repeating the phrases was brought to the support of the record. He even included the Anglo-German agreement of October 6, 1900, apparently unaware that German Chancellor von Bülow, in a speech before the Reichstag, had specifically excepted Manchuria from the open door in his interpretation of this agreement.[16]

When the circular was completed it was apparent that Huntington Wilson was not constructing an objective analysis of the open door policy. Rather, he was drawing up a propaganda statement directed against the Japanese in Manchuria. He had spent many years at Tokyo as secretary of the American legation, and he had brought back to Washington a distinct dislike of the Japanese, a fact that was quite apparent in the content and emphasis of his statement. The key part of the circular, an appended commentary on the situation in Manchuria, was a severe indictment of Japan. It accused the Japanese of violating the open door and the integrity of China by opposition to the Hsinmintun-Fakumen railway project, by the granting of preferential treatment to Japanese goods on the South Manchuria Railway, by the designation of Japanese consuls in Manchuria as secretaries to the Governor General of the Kwantung leased territory, and by the operation of telegraph and postal stations outside the railway

area. With the exception of the last charge, all these allegations were either without foundation or were not related to the open door policy as enunciated by Hay.[17] When the galley proof of the publication was submitted to Root for his approval, he recognized Huntington Wilson's handiwork for what it was— and here was have a clear insight into Root's position. He took his blue pencil and struck out the long indictment of Japan.[18] When Information Series Publication Number 3, Section A, was sent out on April 10, 1908, it consisted only of a long compilation of documents accompanied by a bit of innocuous interpretation.

Huntington Wilson and Straight were engaged in what was essentially the same program. They proposed to invigorate and reinterpret the policy of

[16] William L. Langer, *The Diplomacy of Imperialism, 1890–1902* (2 vols. in 1, New York, 1951), 722.

[17] The blocking of the Hsinmintun-Fakumen project was no more a violation of the open door than many other railway agreements signed by China. The agreement between China and the American-China Development Company signed on July 13, 1900, for the construction of the Hankow-Canton line, and the agreement between China and the British and Chinese Corporation signed on July 9, 1903, for the construction of the Shanghai-Nanking line, both contained clauses protecting the lines from parallel or competing lines. Texts of these agreements are in Percy H. Kent, *Railway Enterprise in China: An Account of Its Origin and Development* (London, 1907), Appendix. The designation of Japanese consuls as secretaries to the Governor General related only to police matters and was intended to resolve a conflict in authority between the Foreign Office and the Governor General regarding consuls in the railway zone. When the State Department asked Ambassador Thomas James O'Brien at Tokyo for a full report, he saw in it no violation of China's integrity. O'Brien to Root, May 26, 1908, State Department Records, File 560. The charge that the South Manchuria Railway granted preferential rates was never substantiated. Consul Roger S. Greene at Dairen stated emphatically that no specific cases had been brought to his attention. Greene to Bacon, January 29, 1908, *ibid.*, File 551. The telegraph and postal offices issue was shortly settled by an agreement between China and Japan, October 12, 1908, whereby China purchased those lines and offices which were outside the leased territory and the railway zone.

[18] Galley proof is in State Department Records, File 551.

the open door and the integrity of China. The effect of their reinterpretation would be to slough off the inherent limitations of that doctrine, which had been only too apparent to Hay, and to expand it into an all-encompassing concept directed toward the vigorous support of China's integrity and against every infraction of equal opportunity, investment as well as commercial.

Secretary of State Root, however, had shown no sympathy for the anti-Japanese crusade of the two young diplomats. Beyond this his views are difficult to assess, for he left only scant evidence in his personal correspondence. Some historians have suggested that he not only resisted the crusade against Japan, but actually gave the Japanese free rein in Manchuria by the oft-quoted Root-Takahira exchange of notes of November 30, 1908. The fact that Root was able to secure through that exchange a guarantee of the Philippines without apparent *quid pro quo* has led to the allegation that there was a hidden meaning in the exchange of notes, namely, that Japan would be accorded a free hand in Manchuria.[19] Since this accusation affects the understanding of Root's and Roosevelt's Far Eastern policy, it requires careful examination.

The "free hand in Manchuria" interpretation of the exchange of notes in 1908 has been supported largely from Roosevelt's letters to President William Howard Taft in 1910, at the time of the ill-fated Knox neutralization scheme. In these letters the former President evidenced much respect for Japan's strategic interests in Manchuria, as well as her commercial and investment interests there.

Our vital interest [he said] is to keep the Japanese out of our country, and at the same time to preserve the good will of Japan. The vital interest of the Japanese, on the other hand, is in Manchuria and Korea. It is therefore peculiarly our interest not to take any steps as regards Manchuria which will give the Japanese cause to feel, with or without reason, that we are hostile to them, or a menace—in however slight a degree—to their interests.... The "open-door" policy in China was an excellent thing, and will I hope be a good thing in the future, so far as it can be maintained by general diplomatic agreement; but as has been proved by the whole history of Manchuria, alike under Russia, and under Japan, the "open-door" policy, as a matter of fact, completely disappears as soon as a powerful nation determines to disregard it, and is willing to run the risk of war rather than forego its intention.[20]

These letters, however, written more than two years after the exchange of notes, were designed to counter an aggressive policy against the Japanese in Manchuria which was then being pushed by Knox, Huntington Wilson, and Straight. The letters accurately expressed Roosevelt's realistic views, but they did not necessarily state the policy toward Japan that actually had been followed during his administration, nor did they necessarily express the policy underlying the Root-Takahira exchange of notes. Though Roosevelt doubtless held such views while he was President, and though his views influenced over-all policy toward Japan, it was Root rather than Roosevelt who dealt with Manchurian affairs during the years 1906–1908. One looks in vain in the Roosevelt correspondence of those years for any reference to Manchuria. There are letters about Japanese immigration, the sending of the fleet around the world, and other matters relating to Japan, but nothing on Manchuria. The State De-

[19] Griswold, *Far Eastern Policy of the United States*, 129; Harley F. MacNair and Donald F. Lach, *Modern Far Eastern International Relations* (New York, 1950), 161–63; Claude A. Buss, *The Far East: A History of Recent and Contemporary International Relations in East Asia* (New York, 1955), 378–79.

[20] Roosevelt to Taft, December 22, 1910, Morison (ed.), *Letters of Theodore Roosevelt*, VII, 189–90. See also his letter of December 8, *ibid.*, 180–81.

partment records reveal, however, that Root himself wrestled daily with the exceedingly complex issues relating to Manchuria.

Root's policy toward Japan was generally that of following the middle road between the aggressive policy of Straight and Huntington Wilson and the concession policy later advocated by Roosevelt. This is clearly seen from his action in the controversial Harbin issue which arose early in 1908, and Root's policy during the Root-Takahira exchange of notes must be interpreted against the background of this important issue relating to Manchuria. When in 1908 Russia began actively to put regulations into effect at Harbin in North Manchuria enforcing her claim to an exclusive right of administration, Root began a long and determined struggle in defense of China's sovereignty in Manchuria.[21] The question was first presented to Root when the Russian ambassador called to protest the support given to China by the American consul at Harbin. The Secretary was not long in discerning that the issue was of unusual significance for both the Russian and the Japanese spheres in Manchuria. On the occasion of the ambassador's call he took a piece of paper and drawing two lines across it said: "If there is to be a broad belt of sovereignty drawn through the center of Manchuria, Russian at the one end and Japanese at the other, like our Canal Zone across the Isthmus of Panama, it may be very serious." [22] His private comment was even more explicit: "We cannot recog-

nize this attempt to exclude Chinese sovereignty." [23]

Root was well aware that there was more at stake in the Harbin question than the status of the municipal administration at that city, a place where American commercial interests were practically non-existent. The larger question was the effect it might have in encouraging similar action by Japan in South Manchuria where the United States had sizable commercial interests. Chargé d'Affaires Henry P. Fletcher at Peking had already reminded Root that if the right of municipal administration were conceded to the Russians in Harbin, the Japanese, having succeeded to the rights of the Chinese Eastern Railway Company in Southern Manchuria, would claim the same privilege there.[24] William Phillips, who was head of the newly created Far Eastern Division in the State Department, also warned Root of this same threat:

Japan is undoubtedly waiting for the moment to attempt to enforce a similar proposition in Southern Manchuria. The result of a recognition now by the United States Government of an absolute Russian administration of Harbin would be our formal acquiescence in the principle of the erection by Russia and Japan of large foreign and commercial cities within Manchuria wholly independent of China, and maintained on the supposition that they are appurtenances to railway property. The integrity of China would be at an end.[25]

In the succeeding months Root made determined efforts to prevent Russia from perfecting her claim at Harbin. He put pressure upon Sir Edward Grey in order to get him to restrain the Japanese from making a similar demand. "We do not wish to have any controversy on the subject," Root wrote to Ambassador Whitelaw Reid at London, "but all

[21] Under Article VI of the agreement of 1896 for the construction of the Chinese Eastern Railway, Russia claimed the absolute and exclusive right of administration in the railway zone and was attempting to erect a municipal government at Harbin which would be under the complete control of the railway company. Straight to Bacon, February 22, 1908, State Department Records, File 221.

[22] Memorandum by Root, March 26, 1908, ibid., File 4002.

[23] Note by Root, March 10, 1908, ibid.

[24] Henry P. Fletcher to Root, February 14, 1908, ibid.

[25] Memorandum by William Phillips, March 6, 1908, ibid.

the treaty powers would seem to be equally interested in having the municipal government to be established at Harbin and at other points along the line of the railroad, both in Russian and Japanese control, based upon an extraterritorial right under the treaties rather than upon an erroneous construction of the railroad grant." [26] In June Reid cabled that Sir Edward had seen the Japanese ambassador and had told him that he hoped that Japan would be very cautious about committing herself to a claim of such consequence to the open door and to the territorial integrity of China.[27] Root also sought and obtained the support of the German government on the matter.[28] At Washington he had several conferences with Minister Kogoro Takahira during the spring and summer of 1908 at which he sought to dissuade the Japanese from supporting the Russian contention or from asserting similar rights in their railway zone in Manchuria.[29]

Throughout the summer and fall of 1908 Root continued to oppose the threat to China's sovereignty in Manchuria, reluctant though he was to become involved in a vexatious controversy over the Harbin issue. "We do not want to get into the position of being a protagonist in a controversy in China with Russia and Japan or with either of them," he wrote to Ambassador Reid in July. "At the same time we feel that the position taken by the Russian Railroad Company is quite without just foundation." [30] In September, 1908, just

two months before the Root-Takahira exchange of notes, William Phillips, in a letter to Rockhill, accurately summed up Root's attitude. "I do not think," he said, "that the Department intends to have trouble in Manchuria, either with Russia or Japan. The Secretary is especially anxious not to become embroiled in little incidents with either of those two powers; but when Russia makes a demand that we relinquish our extraterritorial rights in Harbin and on all railway property, in favor of Russia, we can not very well agree to her proposal without hitting China pretty hard." [31] The conclusion of the Root-Takahira exchange of notes in November brought no change in Root's policy on the Harbin issue. In December, 1908, he was still making it clear to the Russian ambassador that the United States would oppose such a serious infringement of the open door and China's integrity.[32] The issue outlasted Root's service as secretary of state, but his policy was to meet with some measure of success. In May, 1909, a Russian-Chinese preliminary agreement was signed which recognized the sovereignty of China in the railway zone as a fundamental principle.[33]

[26] Root to Reid, April 11, 1908, Whitelaw Reid Papers (Manuscript Division, Library of Congress). Root continued to urge the matter in instructions and personal letters to Reid: Root to Reid, May 20, 1908, State Department Records, File 4002; Root to Reid, May 22, 1908, Reid Papers.

[27] Reid to Root, June 18, 1908, State Department Records, File 4002.

[28] Ambassador David J. Hill to Root, July 1, 1908, ibid.

[29] Root to Reid, May 22, 1908, Reid Papers.

[30] Root to Reid, July 31, 1908, Root Papers.

[31] Phillips to Rockhill, September 19, 1908, William W. Rockhill Papers (Houghton Library, Harvard University).

[32] Root to Baron Rosen, December 29, 1908, Department of State, Papers Relating to the Foreign Relations of the United States, 1910 (Washington, 1915), 207–208.

[33] Rockhill to Secretary of State Philander C. Knox, May 14, 1909, State Department Records, File 4002. If Root made any departure at all from his middle-of-the-road policy during the Harbin question, it was not in the direction of giving the Japanese a free hand in Manchuria, but rather in the direction of Straight's program of investment in Manchuria. In July, 1908, Straight was called home at Root's instance, and William Phillips believed it was for the purpose of furnishing information to "Wall Street" regarding Manchuria. At this time Edward H. Harriman and his bankers, Kuhn, Loeb and Company, had some hope of purchasing, or helping China to purchase, the Chinese Eastern Railway and the South Manchuria Railway. It is possible that Straight was called home to lend his knowledge to the support of this project.

What then was the meaning of the Root-Takahira exchange of notes? It is impossible to reconcile Root's policy on the Harbin issue with the allegation that he gave the Japanese a free hand in Manchuria. Both before and after the Root-Takahira exchange he pursued a consistent policy of resisting any extension of Japanese and Russian rights which would further infringe China's integrity. Moreover, there is no evidence in either the American or the Japanese records of the Root-Takahira negotiations which supports the "free hand in Manchuria" thesis.[34] Indeed, only once—and then in the Japanese records—was mention made of Manchuria. When Root suggested to Ambasador Takahira that a statement be included in the joint declaration of policy supporting the "territorial and administrative entity of China," the Japanese Foreign Minister, Jutaro Komura, raised objection to the inclusion of such a statement. His objection, as he confided in a cablegram to Takahira, was based upon the fact that it might lead to misunderstandings in the future about the rights which Japan had by treaty to exercise some administrative powers in the leased territory and the railway zone in Manchuria.[35] Just what those rights in the railway zone included had not been determined at this time, for the Harbin issue was still pending. The Japanese, however, did not press their objection. Takahira merely told Root that the Japanese government preferred to omit any reference to China's integrity, giving as the reason the fact that such a declaration was no longer necessary and that it might offend the Chinese to have other nations making decisions between themselves about China. In the very same note Takahira agreed to the inclusion of a modified statement, requesting only that it express support for the "independence and territorial integrity of China," rather than the "territorial and administrative entity of China."[36] Root readily accepted this phraseology. There is no evidence in the Japanese or American records that Takahira told Root the real objection to the use of the phrase "administrative entity." If Root discerned the reason for the change in wording, he did not press the Japanese on the matter. To have done so would have compelled them to commit them-

---

Inherent in the negotiations which were being carried on by the bankers with the Russian representative, however, was the understanding that the project would be carried out only with the co-operation of Japan. Indeed, Jacob Schiff of Kuhn, Loeb and Company was willing to go into the project only on the condition that "Russia and Japan will act concurrently." As for other possible investment projects, Root was apparently willing that American capital venture into Manchuria on its own initiative, but he scrupulously avoided giving any official encouragement to such undertakings. His great reluctance to become involved in a controversy with Japan and Russia in Manchuria, which was evident throughout the Harbin issue, indicates that he would not countenance an aggressive investment project, such as the Hsinmintun-Fakumen scheme, which was directed against Japan's established interests there. Phillips to Rockhill, July 16, 1908, Rockhill Papers; Phillips to Straight, October 9, 1908, Straight Papers; Edward H. Zabriskie, *American-Russian Rivalry in the Far East: A Study in Diplomacy and Power Politics, 1895–1914* (Philadelphia, 1946), 149–50; Herbert Croly, *Willard Straight* (New York, 1924), 270–71.

[34] The American records are in State Department Records, File 16533; the Japanese records are in *Reference Materials on the Anglo-Japanese Alliance, the Takahira-Root Agreement, and the Ishii-Lansing Agreement* (Nichi-Ei kyōyaki, Takahira-Rūto kyōtei, oyobi Ishii-Ranshingu kyōtei ni kansuru sankō shiryo), microfilm collection of the Japanese Ministry of Foreign Affairs Archives, PVM 12–43, Reel P30 (Library of Congress).

[35] Jutaro Komura to Takahira, November 12, 1908, *Reference Materials ...*, PVM 12–43, Reel P30.

[36] Takahira to Root, November 14, 1908, State Department Records, File 16533. In Root's later counterdraft the word "territorial" was dropped, making the phrase read "independence and integrity of China." Root to Takahira, November 20, 1908, *ibid*. There is no evidence in either the Japanese or the American records to suggest that this was done at the request of the Japanese, or that it was omitted for the purpose of weakening the phrase, as some scholars have conjectured.

selves categorically on the Harbin issue, and Root was not ready to force a showdown on that matter. He was depending principally upon British pressure upon Russia and Japan to win that issue, and in the final result this strategy was successful.

It seems reasonably clear that the Root-Takahira exchange of notes was not a bargain in *Realpolitik* giving the Japanese a free hand in Manchuria, as has often been asserted. The available records give no support to such a thesis and Root's consistent defense of China's integrity in Manchuria in the Harbin issue indicates that the exchange of notes had no such hidden meaning. The exchange, rather, was just an air-clearing joint declaration of policy designed to smooth over the ill will which had been generated during the school segregation and immigration crisis of 1906 and the war scare of 1907. The clauses of the exchange, declaring it the common policy of both powers to support the status quo, to respect one another's possessions in the Pacific area, and to support the open door and integrity of China, were well chosen to achieve the desired effect.[37]

The rapprochement between Japan and the United States did, of course, run counter to the crusade of Huntington Wilson and Straight against the Japanese position in Manchuria. Huntington Wilson later noted in his memoirs, with obvious displeasure, that he was not consulted during the negotiations.[38] Straight, who was also then at the Department and had been consulted, raised sharp objections to the exchange of notes.[39] At this very time his old associate of the Manchurian crusade, Tang Shao-yi,

was on his way to the United States, ostensibly to express China's appreciation for the remission of the Boxer indemnity funds. Actually, Tang hoped to negotiate a loan agreement for the Manchurian enterprises and perhaps promote a Chinese-American-German alliance. Straight felt that the Root-Takahira exchange would give the deathblow to these projects. But, regardless of the exchange, Tang's schemes had not the remotest chance of realization. Though Root gave Tang some encouragement concerning use of the indemnity funds as security for a general loan designed to facilitate currency reform and the removal of the *likin* (internal transit tax),[40] Roosevelt and Root were far too realistic to consider a projected alliance with a strengthless China and an isolated Germany.[41]

The refusal of the Roosevelt administration to enter the alliance scheme or to follow the policies advocated by Straight was not, however, tantamount to giving the Japanese a free hand in Manchuria. It meant only that the administration was not going to join in any anti-Japanese crusade. Root's whole policy was based upon the proposition that American policy was not confined

[37] Department of State, *Papers Relating to the Foreign Relations of the United States, 1908* (Washington, 1912), 510–12.
[38] Francis M. Huntington Wilson, *Memoirs of an Ex-Diplomat* (Boston, 1945), 169–70.
[39] Straight to Root, November 11, 1908, State Department Records, File 16533.

[40] Memorandum by Root of his conversation with Tang Shao-yi, December 9, 1908, Roosevelt Papers.
[41] Roosevelt made this clear in a conversation with German Ambassador Count Johann von Bernstorff on December 31, 1908. The Ambassador reported to Berlin: "My predecessor had often discussed with him the idea of a joint guarantee of China's integrity by Germany and America in conjunction with China. He had been unable to go into it, because it might have driven China into a policy hostile to Japan. A Chino-Japanese conflict would have found China totally unarmed, in which case neither Germany nor America were prepared to defend her against Japan.... He had explained this idea quite frankly to the Chinese Ambassador, Tang Shao Yi as far as it concerned America, for complete frankness was the right policy." Von Bernstorff to the Foreign Office, January 2, 1909, *Die Grosse Politik der Europäischen Kabinette, 1871-1914* (40 vols., Berlin, 1922–1927), XXV, 97.

to the choice between giving the Japanese a free hand and aggressively attacking their sphere of influence. He believed that another alternative existed, and he seems to have followed it rather consistently. It was a policy which on the one hand recognized Japan's sphere in South Manchuria as an established fact and avoided an attack upon it. On the other hand, it sought to keep the Japanese claim of rights within the bounds of reasonable treaty interpretation and resisted especially any interpretation of those rights which would further infringe upon China's integrity. Within the framework of that policy Root attempted to preserve equal commercial opportunity.

When the Taft administration came to office in 1909 Root's middle-of-the-road policy was quickly abandoned in favor of Straight's expanded concept of the open door. Huntington Wilson, who had been designated minister to Argentina, became instead first assistant secretary of state and Secretary Knox's chief adviser on Far Eastern matters. Straight himself was soon made the agent of the newly formed American banking group which was seeking investment opportunities in China. He skillfully turned the interest of the bankers to the Manchurian field, and, together with his old associates Lord ffrench and J. O. P. Bland, concocted still another plan to thwart the Japanese in Manchuria. This time it took the form of a Chinchow-Aigun railway project. Though this line was not as close to the South Manchuria Railway as the ill-fated Hsinmintun-Fakumen line, its objective was the same.[42] Taft and Knox were willing supporters of the enterprise, and the Secretary of State, late in 1909, even came forward with a proposal for putting all the railways of Manchuria under inter-

national control. Moreover, he formally proposed to England that, in the event the Japanese refused to go along with such a neutralization proposal, the United States and England jointly support the Chinchow-Aigun project.[43] The Knox neutralization proposal and the Chinchow-Aigun project were destined to founder upon the rock of the Anglo-Japanese alliance, just as the Hsinmintun-Fakumen project had done. The only concrete result of the abortive proposal was that Japan and Russia were driven closer together and in 1910 signed an agreement pledging mutual support for their respective spheres of influence.[44] The expanded open door policy thereby came to fruition—and utter failure.

During the years 1899 to 1910 the policy of the open door and integrity of China thus went through three phases of development. In each of the phases the words used remained the same: "open door" and "integrity of China." But the policies tacked to those words had a very different meaning. In the Hay period the open door policy meant the preservation of equal commercial opportunity in an area where equal investment opportunity was hopelessly gone. Though the accompanying "integrity of China" concept was asserted, Hay was eventually driven to abandon that tenet in the face of Russian power in Manchuria. When, shortly before his death, Hay restored the concept of Chinese sovereignty in Manchuria to American diplomacy, he was able to do so only because Japanese power, not American note-writing, had driven the Russians from Manchuria.

Under Hay's successor, Elihu Root, the open door policy entered a second phase. Root accepted the basic assumption that the spheres of influence were

[42] Charles Vevier, *The United States and China, 1906–1913: A Study of Finance and Diplomacy* (New Brunswick, 1955), 125.

[43] Griswold, *Far Eastern Policy of the United States,* 153–56.

[44] Ernest B. Price, *The Russo-Japanese Treaties of 1907–1916 Concerning Manchuria and Mongolia* (Baltimore, 1933), 113–16.

established facts and that probably more harm than good would result from a direct attack upon them. He was less willing than Hay, however, to abandon or water down the "integrity of China" concept, and he struggled doggedly to prevent a further infringement of China's integrity. In the third phase, that of dollar diplomacy, American policy demanded equal investment as well as commercial opportunity—that is, an end to the spheres of influence—and was intended to give vigorous support to China's integrity. In this phase the policy of the open door and integrity of China had no more connection with the policies of Hay and Root than semantics could provide. If this substitution of new policies for old words is confusing to the historian, how confusing it must have been to the Japanese. Having pledged their adherence to the open door policy of Hay in 1905, they found themselves bitterly criticized in subsequent years for not abiding by the entirely different open door policy of dollar diplomacy.

Unfortunately for the Japanese, and perhaps for American policy as well, the new and expanded policy of the open door did not die, despite its ignominious failure in 1909–1910. Straight himself, in a few years, was becoming disillusioned with the new policy. In 1914 he wrote to Bland belaboring him for "trying to set our Russian and Japanese friends by the ears by stirring up the Chinchow-Aigun once more." [45] Straight now knew that no such project could succeed. A later letter to Bland revealed his complete disillusionment.

All our information here [he wrote in 1916] leads us to believe that your government has practically recognized Japanese domination in China.... Take it all in all, I am not sure that it is a bad thing. We love our China, but our Chinese friends seem to be so persistently inapt and so incorrigibly foolish, that I don't believe they can ever work out their own salvation, nor do I believe they will ever let their friends do it for them. [46]

Yet the imprint of Straight and his associates upon the open door policy was to be a lasting one. The expanded concept of the open door became the basis for future policy. The gap between objectives and capabilities (in terms of both military power and diplomatic support) had been widened tremendously. In the subsequent years American policy seemed to vacillate dizzily between a recognition of harsh realities (which had been so apparent to Hay) and an attempt to implement the expanded open door policy. The enlarged concept seemed to have much to recommend it. It plàced American policy in a high moral position, setting it in sharp contrast to the power diplomacy of the Old World powers and Japan. It even had a genuine element of altruism. In short, it seemed to possess all the elements of good policy—all except the one indispensable component: a reasonable chance of succeeding.

[45] Straight to Bland, March 24, 1914, Straight Papers.

[46] Straight to Bland, November 13, 1916, ibid. [Reprinted by permission.]

12

Wilson the Diplomatist

ARTHUR S. LINK

The problems in the field of foreign affairs that faced Woodrow Wilson as President were vast and complex. During his eight years in office crisis conditions in every continent save Africa affected the interests of the United States and demanded that the President develop policies and make decisions. In Asia the Japanese, already in control of Korea and southern Manchuria, were in the process of extending their influence into China. It was no secret that the Island Empire planned to reduce China to the status of a Japanese protectorate. The Twenty-One Demands, presented by Tokyo to Peking in the spring of 1915, was the legal instrument for such a takeover. Obviously, the Japanese course of action presented a serious challenge to the American position in eastern Asia— to the security of the Philippines and to the pledge made in the open door notes of 1899 and 1900 concerning the maintenance of the territorial integrity of China and of equality of commercial opportunity for the citizens of all nations. And in addition to the problems created by Japanese ambition, there were others that grew out of the transformation of China from a monarchy to a republic as a result of the revolution of 1911.

No less serious were conditions in the western hemisphere. There the republics of the Caribbean and of Central America were kept in constant turmoil by the rivalries of aspiring dictators. These frequent and bloody revolutions posed a serious threat to the security of the Panama Canal, in that they offered European nations the occasions for sending ships and troops to protect their nationals caught in the conflicts. The European powers also saw the opportunities to intervene when Latin American rulers failed to pay interest or principal on money they had borrowed from European nationals. Then there was Mexico, whose contiguity to the United States as well as proximity to the Canal made it a very special problem. During Wilson's Administrations that unhappy country was involved in continuous strife, rendering it weak and unstable and thereby dangerous to its northern neighbor.

Finally, there was Europe, which proved to be the most serious problem that the President had to meet. In the second year of his Administration erupted the great contest pitting Germany against the Allied powers, and Wilson was caught in the difficult position of a neutral attempting to "do business as usual" and reap the profit of nonbelligerency without getting involved in the war.

What training, experience, and background did Wilson bring with him to the White House? How well was he equipped to handle such serious matters? Of

FROM *Wilson the Diplomatist* (Baltimore: The Johns Hopkins Press, 1957), Chap. I. By permission of the author and the publishers. With notes by the author, 1966.

what significance were his qualities of mind and character, his personality and temperament?

Few historians are better qualified than Arthur S. Link to suggest answers to these questions. Author of a multivolume life of Wilson and editor of his letters and papers, Link has examined minutely every aspect of the President's life. In the essay that follows, Link analyzes the President's strengths and weaknesses in his approach to foreign affairs. He sees a consistency in Wilson's policies because his reactions to all events were grounded in a "body of principles and assumptions that supplied motive power and shaped and governed policy in the field of action."

The asterisk footnotes in the selection have been added by Arthur Link, 1966.

A gaunt man of serious mien walked to the stands outside the east front of the Capitol on Tuesday, March 4, 1913, to take the oath as twenty-eighth president of the United States. He was Woodrow Wilson, born in Staunton, Virginia, on December 28, 1856, educated at Davidson College and Princeton University, trained in law at the University of Virginia, and prepared for a career in teaching and scholarship in history and political science at The Johns Hopkins University. From 1885 to 1902 he had taught in succession at Bryn Mawr College, Wesleyan University in Connecticut. The Johns Hopkins University, and Princeton University. Elevated to the presidency of Princeton in 1902, he had helped to transform that venerable college into a university of distinction. Embroiled in a personal controversy with the Dean of the Graduate School, he had escaped the troubled Princeton scene by accepting nomination for the governorship of New Jersey in the summer of 1910. Elected governor, he had gone on with irresistible momentum to capture the Democratic presidential nomination and the presidency itself in 1912.

The man who was inaugurated on that March morning in 1913 was privileged to guide the destinies of the United States during eight of the most critical years of the modern epoch. For the American people, the period 1913 to 1921

was a time at home of far-reaching attempts to confront and resolve the dilemma posed by the existence of private economic autocracy in a political and social democracy. Abroad, it was a time of revolutionary upheaval in countries near and far, of cataclysmic world war, and of portentous shifts in the balance of power that threatened to crumble the foundations of the international community.

As a domestic leader, articulating American democratic ideals and utilizing the resources of party and presidential leadership to devise and achieve solutions for the problems raised by twentieth-century economic developments, Wilson succeeded so well that he earned an undisputed place among the first rank of presidents. As a leader in foreign affairs, guiding the American people from provincialism toward world leadership and responsibilities, Wilson's contribution was even more significant for the long future than were his immediate achievements in domestic affairs. The sources of his strength and weakness as a maker of foreign policy will perhaps become evident, both implicitly and explicitly, as we proceed in these lectures.

There is considerable revelation in the nature of Wilson's training as a diplomatist, which was, insofar as it went, exclusively theoretical. Few men have come to the White House better equipped in the philosophy or more adequately trained in the techniques of domestic leadership than Woodrow Wilson. He is saved from the reverse generalization—that few men have ever begun the presidency with less experience and training in the field of foreign affairs than he had had—only because of the naïveté of most beginners in the White House in this field. "It would be the irony of fate if my administration had to deal chiefly with foreign affairs," Wilson remarked to a Princeton friend a few days before he went to Washington in 1913. It was a frank acknowledgement of the fact that, as a scholar and analyst, he had been almost exclusively concerned with domestic politics in the Anglo-American tradition and interested only casually in the mechanisms and history of foreign relations.

To be sure, in the late nineteenth century, when Wilson did most of his scholarly writing, the average American was caught up in great political and economic movements at home and knew next to nothing about affairs abroad. But Wilson was not an average American; he was a distinguished writer and teacher in the fields of government, history, and international law. Yet at least before the turn of the century he wrote and spoke almost as if foreign policy were a minor concern of great powers.

In his first book, *Congressional Government*, an inquiry into the practical functioning of the federal government published in 1885, Wilson made only a passing reference to foreign affairs, and that in connection with the Senate's treaty-making power.[1] Four years later Wilson published *The State*, an excellent pioneer text in comparative government. Out of a total of more than one hundred pages devoted to the develop-

ment of law and legal institutions, he gave a page and a half to international law. In his analysis of the administrative structures of modern governments, he described the machinery of the foreign relations of the British Empire in five words, but devoted twenty-six pages to local government in England; and he gave thirteen times as much space to the work of the Interior Department as to the Department of State in the American government. Finally, in his summary chapters on the functions and objects of government, he put foreign relations at the bottom of his list of what he called the "constituent functions" and then went on to elaborate the functions and objects of government without even mentioning the conduct of external affairs![2]

Wilson began to evince more than a casual interest in foreign affairs for the first time in the late 1890's and early 1900's. In part he was reacting to disturbing new shifts in international power and in American thinking about the future role of the United States in the world as a consequence of the Venezuelan controversy, the war with Spain, the extension of American interests to the Far East, and the acquisition of an overseas empire. Thus Wilson approved President Cleveland's assertion, made during the Venezuelan boundary dispute with Great Britain, of the right of the United States to compel a European state to arbitrate a territorial controversy anywhere in the Western Hemisphere.[3] After some earlier doubts about the wisdom of the war with Spain and of acquiring overseas possessions, he concluded that the war was the natural outgrowth of American industrial might and that it was America's duty to retain the Philippines and teach the Filipinos

---

[1] *Congressional Government, A Study in American Politics* (Boston and New York, 1885), pp. 232–34.

[2] *The State, Elements of Historical and Practical Politics* (Boston, 1889), *passim*.

[3] "Mr. Cleveland as President," *Atlantic Monthly*, LXXIX (March, 1897), 298.

order and self-government, even if the effort required the use of force.[4] To cite a final example, he echoed the propaganda of imperialists like Alfred T. Mahan and Albert J. Beveridge in declaring that the flag must follow trade and that the United States must acquire colonies and markets abroad.[5]

Wilson, however, did more than merely react to the epochal developments at home and abroad around the turn of the century; he also thought seriously about their future impact upon American policies and institutions. The war with Spain, he asserted with growing conviction, had been only one sign of a more important underlying development —the end of American isolation and the inevitable beginning of a new era in which the United States would have to play an ever-widening role in world politics. "Of a sudden, as it seemed, and without premeditation," he wrote in the concluding pages of his *History of the American People,*

the United States had turned away from their long-time, deliberate absorption in their own domestic development, from the policy professed by every generation of their statesmen from the first, of separation from the embarrassing entanglements of foreign affairs; had given themselves a colonial empire, and taken their place of power in the field of international politics. No one who justly studied the courses of their life could reasonably wonder at the thing that had happened. . . . A quick instinct apprised American statesmen that they had come to a turning point in the progress of the nation, which would have disclosed itself in some other way if not in this, had the war for Cuba not made it plain. It had turned from developing its own resources to make conquest of the markets of the world.[6]

It followed inexorably, Wilson added in a revealing essay in 1901, that Amer-

icans were living in a new and more perilous age, in which changed circumstances had rendered meaningless and dangerous the time-honored traditions of self-sufficiency and of security through isolation. "There is no masking or concealing the new order of the world," he warned. "It is not the world of the eighteenth century, nor yet of the nineteenth." There were radically new forces at work which would determine the future of mankind; there were shifts in the balance of power that portended new rivalries and threatened the peace. The American people, he concluded, were now neighbors to the world, whether they liked it or not; they could not escape the coming challenges by ignoring them; they had, perforce, to devise new foreign policies and to become efficient in executing them.[7]

Wilson also saw clearly that the sudden emergence of the United States to world power would have a profound and enduring impact upon the location of authority and the system of leadership in the federal government. "Much the most important change to be noticed," he wrote in the preface to the fifteenth edition of *Congressional Government* in 1900,

is the result of the war with Spain upon the lodgment and exercise of power within our federal system: the greatly increased power and opportunity for constructive statesmanship given the President, by the plunge into international politics and into the administration of distant dependencies, which has been that war's most striking and momentous consequence.[8]

"The war with Spain again changed the balance or parts," Wilson asserted in 1907.

Foreign questions became leading questions again, as they had been in the first days of the government, and in them the Presi-

---

[4] "The Ideals of America," *ibid.,* xc (December, 1902), 727–30.
[5] *History of the American People* (5 vols.; New York, 1902), v, 296.
[6] *Ibid.,* pp. 294–96.

[7] "Democracy and Efficiency," *Atlantic Monthly,* LXXXVII (March, 1901), 292.
[8] *Congressional Government* (15th ed.; Boston and New York, 1900 [?]), p. xi.

dent was of necessity leader. Our new place in the affairs of the world has since that year of transformation kept him at the front of our government, where our own thoughts and the attention of men everywhere is centred upon him. . . . The President can never again be the mere domestic figure he has been throughout so large a part of our history. The nation has risen to the first rank in power and resources. . . . Our President must always, henceforth, be one of the great powers of the world, whether he act greatly and wisely or not. . . . We have but begun to see the presidential office in this light; but it is the light which will more and more beat upon it, and more and more determine its character and its effect upon the politics of the nation.[9]

There is the temptation to conclude from this analysis of Wilson's observations during the decade 1898–1907 that, as one authority has said, he had demonstrated an understanding of the foreign relations of his country and considerable preparation for their conduct by the time he entered the White House.[10] Much, of course, depends upon the criteria that one applies. Compared to a Grant or a Harding, Wilson does indeed seem an eminent authority. On the other hand, to compare Wilson with a Jefferson or a John Quincy Adams is to point up some of the deficiencies in the latter-day President's intellectual and practical training for the difficult business of managing the foreign affairs of a great power.

The strengths and weaknesses in Wilson's unconscious preparation as a diplomatist will, I trust, become more fully evident as we proceed in this analysis, but it might be well to summarize them at this point. There was to his advantage the fact that he had done much serious thinking about general principles of politics and national ideals that transcended geographical boundaries. That is to say, Wilson came to the presidency equipped

with a coherent and deeply rooted philosophy about the nature and ends of government, a philosophy that could be readily translated into the basis of a foreign policy. Also to his advantage was the fact of his awareness of the larger dimensions of the diplomatic revolution of the period and the impact of that revolution upon American political institutions.

Balanced on the debit side were certain obvious deficiencies in Wilson's thought and training in foreign affairs. The most serious of these was his failure before 1913 to do any systematic thinking about the nature, complexity, and difficulties of foreign policy and his assumption that the main task of diplomacy was the simple one of translating national ideals into a larger program of action.

Secondly, there was Wilson's apparent ignorance of or unconcern with the elementary facts about the main thrusts of American diplomacy from 1901 to 1913 and about the tensions that were impelling Europe toward a general war during the same period. Even about those events on the international scene in which he evidenced a keen interest, the war with Spain and its immediate aftermath, much of Wilson's thinking was superficial and reflected more the faddish thought of the time than an astute understanding of what was taking place. Indeed, after the thrill of the war and of empire had quickly passed, Wilson apparently lost virtually all interest in affairs abroad. There were tremendous new developments in American foreign policy and furious partisan debates at home between 1901 and 1913. There were recurrent crises in Europe during the prolonged prelude to the war that would break out in 1914. Yet throughout this period, during which Wilson emerged as a pre-eminent political leader, he spoke and acted as if foreign problems did not exist. For example, during a brilliant campaign for

[9] *Constitutional Government in the United States* (New York, 1908), pp. 59, 78.
[10] Harley Notter, *The Origins of the Foreign Policy of Woodrow Wilson* (Baltimore, 1937), p. 145.

the Democratic presidential nomination and for the presidency from 1911 to 1912, he never once mentioned a foreign issue that was not primarily a domestic concern.

A good argument can be made to the effect that Wilson was so absorbed in plans for Princeton from 1902 to 1910 and so engrossed in his political apprenticeship from 1910 to 1913 that he had neither time nor energy for a serious study of foreign policy. The argument has some merit, but we must also conclude that Wilson did not concern himself seriously with affairs abroad during the period 1901 to 1913 both because he was not interested and because he did not think that they were important enough to warrant any diversion from the mainstream of his thought. Therefore, Wilson was not being unduly self-deprecatory when he remarked before he went to Washington how ironical it would be if his administration had to deal chiefly with foreign affairs. He was simply recognizing the obvious fact of his primary concern with domestic issues and his superior training for leadership in solving them.

Regardless of the adequacy or inadequacy of his preparation, Wilson after 1913 faced foreign problems of greater magnitude than any president had confronted since the early years of the nineteenth century. Whether he responded wisely or unwisely to the mounting international challenges of the years from 1913 to 1920, he executed policies that were on the whole firmly grounded upon a consistent body of principles and assumptions that supplied motive power and shaped and governed policy in the fields of action. These principles and assumptions were deeply rooted in Wilson's general thinking before 1913 about cosmology, ethics, the nature and ends of government, and the role of his own country in the creative development of mankind; they were in turn enlarged and refined as Wilson sought to apply them in practical affairs after his inauguration. Determining and controlling, they gave both strength and weakness to the diplomatist in action.

The foundations of all of Wilson's political thinking were the religious and ethical beliefs and values that he inherited from the Christian tradition and from his own Presbyterian theology. In matters of basic Christian faith, Wilson was like a little child, never doubting, always believing, and drawing spiritual sustenance from Bible reading, church attendance, and prayer. Having derived his beliefs from the Shorter Catechism, his father's sermons, and the Presbyterian scholastics, Wilson was Calvinistic in theology. He believed in a sovereign God, just and stern as well as loving; in a moral universe, the laws of which ruled nations as well as men; in the supreme revelation and redemption of Jesus Christ; and in the Bible as the incomparable word of God and the rule of life. He was a predestinarian, not so much in his apparent belief in election as in his conviction that God controlled history and used men and nations in the unfolding of His plan according to His purpose. Few ministers of the gospel gave more eloquent voice to these beliefs than did Wilson in his day; to point out that there was nothing unique about them is not to detract from their underlying and pervasive importance.[11]

From such spiritual roots grew a sturdy tree of character, integrity, and concern for first principles in political action—in brief, all the components of the idealism that was the unifying force

[11] For examples of Wilson's religious addresses and writings, see "The Ministry and the Individual" and "The Bible and Progress," printed in Ray S. Baker and William E. Dodd (eds.), *The Public Papers of Woodrow Wilson, College and State* (2 vols.; New York, 1925), II, 178–87, 291–302; for a description and analysis, see Arthur S. Link, *Wilson: The New Freedom* (Princeton, N. J., 1956), pp. 64–65.

in Wilson's life. In the conduct of foreign affairs this idealism meant for him the subordination of immediate goals and material interests to superior ethical standards and the exaltation of moral and spiritual purposes. This is not to say that he ignored the existence and powerful operation of economic forces in international life. Indeed, for a brief period following the Spanish-American War he seemed almost to verge upon an economic determinism in his analysis of developments, both past and present, upon the international scene. As president, moreover, he was not unmindful of the necessities of a viable international economic life, of the material interests of Americans abroad, or of the economic rivalries that helped to produce conflict among nations. Even so, idealism was the main drive of Wilson's thinking about international relations. As he put it, foreign policy must not be defined in "terms of material interest," but should be "more concerned about human rights than about property rights." [12]

A second main theme in Wilson's political thinking with large consequences for his foreign policy was his belief in democracy as the most humane and Christian form of government. From the beginning to the end of his adult career he studied, wrote about, and put into practice the essential aspects of democratic government, and it would be superfluous here to review his splendid synthesis of the Anglo-American democratic theories and traditions. More important for our purposes is an understanding of the way in which these assumptions helped to form his objectives and to determine his actions in the field of foreign affairs.

Much, of course, depended upon Wilson's view of the nature and capacities

of man. There is in his thinking an implicit if never an outright repudiation of the classical Presbyterian emphasis upon original sin, and a strong strain of nineteenth-century Christian optimism and social Darwinism. To be sure, he never completely lost sight of man's capacity for evil, but he seems often to have forgotten it, so strong was his faith in man's inherent goodness and in the possibility of progress.

These were the controlling assumptions. It followed in Wilson's mind that all people were capable of self-government because all were endowed with inherent character and a capacity for growth. He was no visionary in these beliefs; following his master Burke, he repudiated and condemned utopianism and taught that people learned democracy only by long years of disciplined experience. The fact remained, none the less, that he thought that all people, whether they be Mexican peons or Russian peasants, whites or Orientals, were capable of being trained in the habits of democracy. "When properly directed," he once declared, "there is no people not fitted for self-government." [13]

These assumptions inevitably had profound implications for Wilson's thought about the development and relationships of nations. His belief in the inherent goodness of man, in progress as the law of organic life and the working out of the divine plan in history, and in democracy as the highest form of government led him straight to the conclusion that democracy must some day be the universal rule of political life. It ultimately led him even further, to the belief that a peaceful world community, governed by a universal public opinion and united for mutual advancement, could exist only when democracy was itself triumphant everywhere. This conviction

[12] For a rewarding amplification of the foregoing generalizations, see William Diamond, *The Economic Thought of Woodrow Wilson* (Baltimore, 1943), pp. 131–61.

[13] Samuel G. Blythe, "Mexico: The Record of a Conversation with President Wilson," *Saturday Evening Post*, CLXXXVI (May 23, 1914), 4.

was more than an assumption underlying Wilson's foreign policy; it was also an imperative force that propelled him into bold plans for Mexico, the Caribbean region, and, afterward, the entire world.

The final main assumptions of Wilson's thought about international relations grew out of his attempt to define America's role in world affairs within the context of his general principles and in light of the contribution that the United States could make. The American people, he believed, had a peculiar role to play, indeed a mission to execute in history precisely because they were in so many ways unique among the peoples of the world. They were unique politically, not because they alone possessed democratic institutions, but because they had succeeded in organizing diverse sections and a hundred million people into a federal system such as one day (he at last conceived) must provide a structure for a world organization. The American people were unique socially, first, because of their radical affirmation of equality and their historic repudiation of everything for which the caste- and class-ridden societies of Europe and Asia stood, and, second, because they were in fact a new people, the product of the mixing of all the nationalities of Europe. Finally and most importantly, they were unique morally and spiritually. America, Wilson believed, had been born that men might be free; Americans had done more than any other people to advance the cause of human welfare; Americans, above all other peoples, were "custodians of the spirit of righteousness, of the spirit of equal-handed justice, of the spirit of hope which believes in the perfectibility of the law with the perfectibility of human life itself."

Thus America's mission in the world was not to attain wealth and power, but to fulfill the divine plan by service to mankind, by leadership in moral purposes, and above all by advancing peace and world brotherhood. As one scholar has written in summary of Wilson's view:

[America's] mission was to realize an ideal of liberty, provide a model of democracy, vindicate moral principles, give examples of action and ideals of government and righteousness to an interdependent world, uphold the rights of man, work for humanity and the happiness of men everywhere, lead the thinking of the world, promote peace,—in sum, to serve mankind and progress.[14]

These assumptions and ideals bore so heavily upon the formation of Wilson's foreign policies that we cannot be content with a mere desecription of them. We must also attempt to see the way in which they equipped or unfitted the President for the needs of practical statesmanship during a critical period.

Only a confirmed cynic would fail to recognize that a large measure of Wilson's strength as a diplomatist and much of his contribution in the field of international relations derived in the first instance from his spiritual resources. To begin with, there were certain practical advantages in idealism. By rejecting narrow nationalism and materialism as bases for foreign policy, and by articulating the noblest traditions of Western culture, Wilson could and did speak as with universal authority, whether in pleading with the Imperial German government to respect human life in using the submarine, in proclaiming a people's war for justice as much to the vanquished as to the victors, or in appealing for a world organization based upon the ideals of peace and co-operation. That is to say, ideals are a dynamic force in cultures that acknowledge their validity, and Wilson was a more effective war leader, a more fearful antagonist of the German military dictators on the ideological battlefield, and a more indomitable fighter for a just peace settlement because he

[14] Harley Notter, *Origins of the Foreign Policy of Woodrow Wilson,* p. 653.

stood for what most men in the Western world (including his opponents) were willing to acknowledge were their own best ideals. Besides, on several occasions, particularly in his relations with Mexico, he was able to escape the consequences of a blundering policy only because he had made his real, that is, his ideal, purposes clear.

We should not measure the significance of Wilson's idealism in practical terms alone. Men violate or more often simply ignore the ideals by which they profess to live; but without ideals to recall lost visions and to give guidance for the present and future, societies degenerate into tyrannies of individuals, classes, or ideologies. It was Wilson's great contribution that while hatreds and passions threatened to wreck Western civilization, he held high the traditions of humanity and the ideal of justice, and by so doing he helped to salvage them for a future generation.

It does not detract from the significance of the foregoing to point out that Wilson's assumptions and principles also impaired to some degree his leadership in the mundane affairs of state. This was true in the first place because his philosophy and thought, even more about foreign than about domestic matters, failed to take sufficient account of what theologians call original sin or what diplomatic specialists call "realities." The qualifying adjective *sufficient* has a key importance here. Wilson was never a fool or a visionary incapable of facing reality; he was keenly intelligent and often shrewd. And yet his faith in the goodness and rationality of men, in the miraculous potentialities of democracy, and in the inevitable triumph of righteousness sometimes caused him to make illusory appraisals of the situations at hand and to devise quixotic or unworkable solutions.

In executing foreign policy generally, Wilson assumed that foreign relations among the great powers consisted of intercourse between civilized gentlemen controlled by an enlightened public opinion and common moral standards, and that decency, good will, and free discussion sufficed to settle all international disputes. This assumption in turn led him to rely mainly upon enlightened instruments of diplomacy—conciliation treaties, the invocation of universal principles in diplomatic correspodence, and displays of friendship—and, conversely, almost to refuse to think in terms of threat or violence. His dependence upon moral suasion in the protracted controversy with Germany over the submarine is one example of his nearly inveterate reliance upon the spirit rather than the sword in foreign relations.

In the second place, Wilson's uncommon concern with the fundamental principles of national and international life sometimes led him to oversimplify the vast complexities of international politics. This deficiency stemmed also from his methods of thinking and arriving at conclusions—methods that were as much intuitive as rational and deductive rather than inductive; it stemmed also from his tendency to invoke analogies between domestic and international politics without taking sufficient account of the enormous differences between the two.

There is a good example of the danger of an almost exclusive reliance upon general principles in the formation of foreign policy in the manner in which Wilson dealt with an important Far Eastern question in 1913, the issue of American participation in the Six-Power Consortium, which had been formed in 1911 to supply capital to the Chinese government. The full records of his discussions about this matter reveal clearly how Wilson's mind worked in making policy. First he set up the general propositions that the European and Japanese governments involved in the

Consortium were scheming in the usual imperialistic manner to impair Chinese sovereignty and to gain control over the internal affairs of a democracy struggling to be born. Reasoning deductively, Wilson quickly concluded what the American government should do in these circumstances. Since imperialism and such an attempt to subvert a democracy in its birth were morally wrong, the United States should withdraw from the Consortium and should help the Chinese people in other and more honorable ways.

It was a "moral" decision, based upon reasoning not altogether unsound as far as it went. The trouble was that the Chinese situation in 1913, domestic and external, could not be encompassed by a few moralizations that ignored the unpleasant realities—the fact that Chinese sovereignty was well nigh a fiction, that there was no Chinese "democracy," and that China desperately needed capital to survive. The consequences of Wilson's "moral" decision were soon obvious: The American withdrawal caused the virtual collapse of the Consortium, and the failure of the Western powers to extend financial assistance weakened the Chinese government precisely at the time when the Japanese were beginning their first great drive to control their continental neighbor.[15]

An even more important example of the consequences of oversimplification through too much reliance upon obvious moral principles was Wilson's response to the situation created in Mexico in 1913 when a military usurper, General Victoriano Huerta, overthrew a constitutional government headed by Francisco Madero. To Wilson the issues were as plain as daylight, and he refused on moral grounds to recognize the Huerta government even though it controlled

most of Mexico and was constitutional in form. More than this, Wilson went on to devise a new test of recognition for Mexico, which he later applied to the Bolshevik regime in Russia. It was a test of constitutional legitimacy, which involved going behind the exterior to determine whether a government was legitimate, or politically moral, as well as constitutional in form or de facto in authority.[16] It was "moral" diplomacy, but it soon involved Wilson and the American government in far-reaching meddling in the internal affairs of Mexico, and this in turn led to consequences nearly disastrous for both countries.[17]

But let us return to my analysis of the way in which Wilson's assumptions and principles impaired his statesmanship in the field of foreign relations. I have already mentioned his tendency to take insufficient account of hard realities and to oversimplify the complexities of international life. A third point was the unreal quality of some of his thought and policy that resulted from his almost romantic faith in the sufficiency of democratic solutions. This was revealed in his attempts to apply constitutional and democratic criteria to Central America and the Caribbean states,[18] to the revolutionary upheaval in Mexico led by Madero's successors, the Constitutionalists, and finally to the revolutionary situation in Russia between the fall of the czarist government and the triumph of the Bolsheviks.[19] In all these

[15] For an extended discussion, see the excellent study by Tien-yi Li, *Woodrow Wilson's China Policy, 1913-1917* (New York, 1952).

[16] Howard F. Cline, *The United States and Mexico* (Cambridge, Mass., 1953), p. 142, has an illuminating discussion of this point.

[17] I have told this story at length elsewhere, in *Wilson: The New Freedom*, pp. 347-416, and in *Woodrow Wilson and the Progressive Era* (New York, 1954), pp. 107-44.

[18] As Samuel Flagg Bemis has pointed out in a telling way in "Woodrow Wilson and Latin America," MS in possession of the present writer.

[19] George F. Kennan, *Soviet-American Relations, 1917-1920, Russia Leaves the War* (Princeton, N. J., 1956), particularly pp. 140-48.

situations ordinary democratic concepts simply did not apply, yet Wilson insisted upon believing that solutions lay in the establishment of enlightened and responsible governments through free elections.*

The fourth and final peril of an excessive concern for ideals and principles in foreign policy was in Wilson's case particularly acute. It was the danger of Pharisaism, which often results from too much introspective concern about the standards of right conduct. It was revealed, among other things, in Wilson's assumption that his motives and purposes were purer than those of the men with whom he happened to be contending. Even though they were actually often well grounded, such convictions left little room for a saving humility and gave Wilson the appearance of the Pharisee who thanked God that he was better than other men.

In the final reckoning, Wilson will be judged not so much by what he thought about foreign policy as by what he did, and I conclude this introductory lecture with a word about his techniques and methods as a diplomatist. They stemmed in an all-pervasive way from his temperament, and we can ease some of the problems that puzzle the biographer if we begin by frankly confronting those aspects of his personality that bore directly upon his practice of leadership. Endowed with an intense nervous and emotional constitution, Wilson was in temperament an extreme activist, never satisfied with mere speculation or willing to apply slow-working remedies, but

* [The author, if he were writing this paragraph again, would make it clear that this generalization applies to Wilson only during the early stages of his policies toward Mexico and the Bolshevik Revolution. In both cases he came to realize that constitutional solutions were impossible and accepted the triumph of the revolutions, even though, to be sure, he never approved of the Bolshevik regime. —A. S. L., 1966.]

driven as if by demons to almost frenzied efforts to achieve immediate and ideal solutions.

Was the challenge one of transforming Princeton into a leading institution of higher learning in the United States? Then the task had to be done thoroughly and at once, and no vested social interest or obstreperous individuals could be permitted to stand in the way. As Wilson put it, all had to be "digested in the processes of the university." Did the job at hand encompass the reform of federal economic policies? Then Congress must be driven and public opinion must be maintained at a high pitch of excitement in order that all might be finished during a single congressional session. Were the tasks those of reconstructing the world order and of propelling the American people into an international leadership? Then nothing less than total reconstruction and a total commitment would suffice. This driving force, relentless energy, and striving for the whole achievement characterized all of Wilson's major efforts in the field of foreign affairs; they were at once sources of power and of danger.

Two other aspects of personality or temperament had an equal impact. One was Wilson's egotism, manifested in his remarkable conviction that he was an instrument of divine purpose, or his sense of destiny, in his awareness of his own intellectual superiority over most of his associates and, above all, in his urge to dominate. The other was a driving ambition, fired as much by a longing for personal distinction as by a desire to serve God and mankind. Egotism and ambition combined with a compelling activism to produce in Woodrow Wilson a leader of extraordinary strength and daring, one who would play not merely an active but the dominant role in foreign affairs while he was president.

Mature conviction from scholarly study concerning the role that the president should play also helped to determine Wilson's methods as a diplomatist. Even during that period in his scholarly writing when he emphasized congressional government, Wilson recognized the president's wide latitude in the conduct of affairs abroad. That recognition had grown into a sweeping affirmation of presidential sovereignty by the time that Wilson had reached maturity in his thought about the American constitutional system.

"One of the greatest of the President's powers," he said in 1907,

I have not yet spoken of at all: his control, which is very absolute, of the foreign relations of the nation. The initiative in foreign affairs, which the President possesses without any restriction whatever, is virtually the power to control them absolutely. The President cannot conclude a treaty with a foreign power without the consent of the Senate, but he may guide every step of diplomacy, and to guide diplomacy is to determine what treaties must be made, if the faith and prestige of the government are to be maintained. He need disclose no step of negotiation until it is complete, and when in any critical matter it is completed the government is virtually committed. Whatever its disinclination, the Senate may feel itself committed also.[20]

It was a striking characterization of Wilson's own management of foreign affairs a few years after these words were spoken. In the areas that he considered vitally important—Mexico, relations with the European belligerents, wartime relations with the Allied powers, and the writing of a peace settlement—Wilson took absolute personal control. He wrote most of the important notes on his own typewriter, bypassed the State Department by using his own private agents, ignored his secretaries of state by conducting important negotiations behind their backs, and acted like a divine-right monarch in the general conduct of affairs.

[20] Constitutional Government in the United States, pp. 77–78.

Perhaps as good an example of Wilson's personal diplomacy as any I could choose was his handling of the Mexican problem during the period of Huerta's tenure in Mexico City from March, 1913, to August, 1914. Ignoring the men in the State Department who knew anything about the subject, the American Ambassador and the Chargé in the Mexican capital, and the consuls in field, Wilson proceeded to make a Mexican policy in his own way, as follows: He first sent a journalist whom he trusted, but who knew nothing about Mexican affairs, to Mexico City to investigate. Accepting this reporter's recommendations, Wilson next sent a former Governor of Minnesota, who had neither experience in diplomacy nor any knowledge about Mexico, to present certain proposals for a solution to Huerta. Then, after the Dictator had repudiated the President's right to interfere, Wilson pursued a relentless personal campaign to depose Huerta, one that culminated in armed intervention and Huerta's downfall. Time and again Wilson used the same methods and almost always with the same results: the formation of faulty policy through sheer ignorance, men working at cross-purposes, confusion in the State Department and in the embassies and legations, and the like.*

To be sure, there were some extenuating circumstances. Wilson often ignored the professionals in the State Department and the Foreign Service because he genuinely distrusted them, because he thought that they, or many of them, were either aristocrats, the products of exclusive schools and a snobbish society,

* [In retrospect, the author wonders whether this judgment is just to Wilson. Wilson, knowing that Ambassador Henry Lane Wilson had been implicated in Huerta's overthrow of a constitutional regime, had good reason to distrust the United States mission in Mexico City. The American President, in spite of his mistakes, did, after all, play a vital role in the success of the Constitutionalist Revolution. —A. S. L., 1966]

or else sycophantic imitators of the wealthy classes. "We find," he explained in 1913,

that those who have been occupying the legations and embassies have been habituated to a point of view which is very different, indeed, from the point of view of the present administration. They have had the material interests of individuals in the United States very much more in mind than the moral and public considerations which it seems to us ought to control. They have been so bred in a different school that we have found, in several instances, that it was difficult for them to comprehend our point of view and purpose.[21]

There was also the fact that many of the men through whom Wilson would normally have worked in the conduct of foreign relations *were,* to a varying degree, incompetent, and this because of the necessities of politics and the paucity of Democrats with any experience. Simply and solely because he had to have William J. Bryan's support for domestic policies, Wilson appointed the Great Commoner secretary of state. Because he did not trust Bryan in delicate matters, Wilson turned more and more away from regular channels and leaned increasingly upon unofficial advisers like Colonel Edward M. House.

In the selection of ambassadors for important stations, moreover, Wilson tried desperately to find the best men and to break the custom of using ambassadorships as rewards for party service. Except in a few cases the "best" men would not accept appointment, and Wilson had to yield to pressure and name party hacks to places like Berlin, St. Petersburg, Rome, and Madrid. The classic example was James W. Gerard, a generous contributor to the Democratic treasury and an active Tammany politician, whom Wilson named as ambassador to Germany after vowing that he would never stoop so low. Thus it

[21] Wilson to C. W. Eliot, September 17, 1913, Wilson Papers, Library of Congress.

happened that during a period of extreme tension in German-American relations Wilson had as his spokesman in Berlin a man for whom he had no respect and not a little contempt. The President's opinion of Gerard is rather pungently revealed in the following examples of the comments that he penciled on copies of dispatches from the Ambassador:

10 Sept. [1915]
Ordinarily our Ambassador ought to be backed up as of course, but—this ass? It is hard to take it seriously. W.
11 Sept. [1915]
Who can fathom this? I wish they would hand this idiot his passports! W.

As he had not much more confidence in most of his other ambassadors, it was little wonder that Wilson used them only as messenger boys.

Thus circumstances that he could not control were in part responsible for Wilson's extreme individualism in conducting foreign affairs. Yet they were not entirely responsible, and the conviction remains that the chief causes of his exercise of an exclusive personal control were his urge to dominate, his egotism, and his reasoned jealousy of the presidential power, that is, his belief that it would be constitutionally dangerous to delegate essential power for national good or ill to men, even able men, not directly responsible to the people.

The essential validity of this conclusion is to some degree revealed in the nature of Wilson's relations with two men of considerable talents, Robert Lansing and Walter H. Page. Lansing, who served as counselor of the State Department from 1914 to 1915 and as secretary of state from 1915 to 1920, was thoroughly trained in international law and practice, keenly intelligent, and completely loyal to the President. Yet Wilson never really trusted Lansing's mental processes (once he remarked that Lansing "was so stupid that he was constantly afraid he would commit some serious blunder"), never thought of him as much more than a dignified clerk, and consequently never took full advantage of the resources that Lansing had to offer.*

The reasons for this lack of confidence shed an important light upon the Wilsonian character. To begin with, the two men were fundamentally different in their thought processes: Where Wilson was intuitive and idealistic, Lansing was inductive in reasoning, coldly analytical, and realistic. But the chief cause of Wilson's distrust was Lansing's refusal to give the kind of loyalty that his chief demanded, which was intellectual submission and agreement as well as understanding. Lansing was a little too strong in mind and character thus to subordinate himself, or even to pretend that he did. He survived in office as long as he did only because he became fairly adept in handling the President and only because it was usually inexpedient for Wilson to dismiss him.

Unlike Lansing, Page had no special preparation for his tasks as ambassador to Great Britain, but he had an abundance of natural ability and was soon the master of his functions. So long as he reported what the President wanted to hear, Page was Wilson's intimate friend and best source of opinion abroad, but he soon lost all standing at the White House once he began to offer unwanted advice, to criticize, and to report opinions that disturbed his superior.†

* [The author would write this paragraph very differently were he writing it today. The evidence in the author's third, fourth, and fifth volumes of his biography of Woodrow Wilson shows that Wilson's estimate of Lansing was not far from the mark. It is particularly inaccurate to speak of Lansing as "completely loyal." He was guilty of several gross betrayals, for example, his torpedoing of the President's peace move of 1916–17. —A. S. L., 1966.]

† [Perhaps it is expecting too much to ask a President to take seriously an Ambassador who totally disagreed with his superior's policies! —A. S. L., 1966.]

Wilson maintained his personal control over foreign policy, finally, by applying the same techniques of leadership of public opinion and of Congress that he used with such spectacular success in domestic struggles. His instruments of public leadership were public papers, statements to the press, and speeches, by means of which he established direct communication with the people and spoke for them in articulating American ideals in foreign policy. Wilson was a spellbinder of immense power during an era when Americans admired oratory above all other political skills, and he was irresistible in leadership so long as he voiced the dominant national sentiments.

In the business of controlling Congress, Wilson's methods were influenced by his conception of the president as the unifying force in the federal government. Believing as he did that the president alone was responsible for the conduct of foreign relations, he had no thought of a genuine collaboration with the legislative branch in the formulation of policies abroad. Believing as he did in party government and responsibility, Wilson never seriously considered a bipartisan approach to foreign policy. To be sure, he took careful pains to render periodic accountings to the members of the House and Senate foreign affairs committees. On several occasions he even asked Congress to approve policies that he had already decided to pursue. Yet one has the suspicion that on all these occasions he was simply observing certain forms in order to buy congressional support cheaply.

The most revealing examples of Wilson's methods of dealing with Congress on matters of foreign policy arose, after all, not during periods of quietude and agreement, but during times of sharp controversy with the legislative branch. Wilson's leadership was challenged by a threatened or an actual revolt in Congress on three occasions—in 1914, during the debate over the repeal of a provision in the Panama Canal Act of 1912 exempting American coastwise shipping from the payment of tolls; in 1916, over the issue of the right of Americans to travel in safety on belligerent armed merchant vessels; and in 1919 and 1920, over ratification of the Treaty of Versailles. To all these challenges Wilson replied with incredible vigor and boldness. In these important tests Wilson revealed his conviction that in foreign affairs the President should lead and the Congress should follow.

This ends my account of Wilson's preparation, thought, and methods as a diplomatist. There are many pitfalls in such an attempt as I have just made. There are dangers of overemphasis, of distortion, and of exploring certain aspects of thought and character to such a degree that they seem unique instead of normal. There is the danger of permitting weaknesses in method to assume a larger importance than they deserve in the total estimate. Worse still, there is the danger that inevitably arises when one paints a composite portrait, that of viewing the subject in static form and of forgetting his capacity for growth and his ability to learn by his mistakes. The ordinary risks involved are multiplied when one deals with a person as complex and contradictory as Wilson assuredly was. I only hope that the whole man as diplomatist will reveal himself in all his strength and weakness more fully in the lectures that follow.*

* [The author would emphasize that this portrait is one of Wilson as an apprentice in foreign policy, and that subsequent chapters in *Wilson the Diplomatist* show his remarkable growth both in skill as a diplomatist and leadership of humane and liberal opinion in the world. —A. S. L., 1966.]

13

The Legend of Isolationism
in the 1920's

WILLIAM A. WILLIAMS

In his book The Trail of a Tradition, written in 1926, Arthur Vandenberg, the editor of the Grand Rapids Herald, urged his countrymen to continue in the isolationist tradition of the Founding Fathers. By isolation he did not mean that the American people should sever all contacts with the world, but only that the government should steer clear of alliances and entanglements. He was warning against making any diplomatic or military commitments and pleading that complete freedom of action be retained.

If Vandenberg's concept of isolation is used, then indeed the United States in the period between the two world wars may be said to have been isolationist. The people did not cut themselves off from the world. Quite the reverse—America was very much a part of the world. Hundreds of thousands of Americans traveled abroad; American money in the form of loans and investments reached every corner of the globe to build railroads in Poland, dig for oil in the Middle East, plant sugar in Cuba, and develop public utilities in South America; American sewing machines, typewriters, refrigerators, bicycles, and other products were sold in every continent. At the same time, representatives of the United States government attended hundreds of international meetings of all types, ranging from high-level disarmament conferences, such as those held at Washington in 1921–22, Geneva in 1927, and London in 1930, to nonpolitical meetings on the control of anthrax, the regulation of opium traffic, the standardization of customs formalities, and other social, economic, and administrative matters. But not once was the United States willing to enter into diplomatic commitments. Not once did it entertain the requests by France and other powers for a guarantee of their security should they disarm. No heed was paid Belgium's plea, "Give us an assurance of safety and we Belgians will gladly dismiss our soldiers." And when the Council of the League of Nations met in 1931 and 1932 to consider the Manchurian crisis, the United States did not participate in the deliberations, except at one brief session, lest its hands be tied by some League action.

Unfortunately, almost all historians writing about the 1920s have missed Vandenberg's fine distinction concerning isolation. They have, instead, used the term to describe American foreign policy in general and thus have conveyed the erroneous impression that the government and people were insular and withdrawn. Recently an eminent historian described the majority of the American people in 1920 as "ready to adopt an attitude of comfortable and

From *Science & Society*, XVIII (Winter 1954), 1–20. By permission of *Science & Society*.

prosperous isolationism." It is no wonder that most students of United States history, if asked to describe American foreign policy in the 1920s, would reply almost instinctively with the word isolationism.

It is to combat this view that Professor William A. Williams of the University of Wisconsin has written the following article. He considers that the "assumption that the United States was isolationist from 1920 through 1932 is no more than a legend" and seeks to demonstrate that during those twelve years the policies pursued "were marked by express and extended involvement with—and intervention in the affairs of—other nations of the world."

The widely accepted assumption that the United States was isolationist from 1920 through 1932 is no more than a legend. Sir Francis Bacon might have classed this myth of isolation as one of his Idols of the Market-Place. An "ill and unfit choice of words," he cautioned, "leads men away into innumerable and inane controversies and fancies."[1] And certainly the application of the terms *isolation* and *isolationism* to a period and a policy that were characterized by vigorous involvement in the affairs of the world with consciousness of purpose qualifies as an "ill and unfit choice of words." Thus the purpose of this essay: on the basis of an investigation of the record to suggest that, far from isolation, the foreign relations of the United States from 1920 through 1932 were marked by express and extended involvement with—and intervention in the affairs of—other nations of the world.

It is both more accurate and more helpful to consider the twenties as contiguous with the present instead of viewing those years as a quixotic interlude of low-down jazz and lower-grade gin, fluttering flappers and Faulkner's fiction, and bootlegging millionaires and millionaire bootleggers. For in foreign policy there is far less of a sharp break between 1923 and 1953 than generally is acknowledged. A closer examination of the so-

called isolationists of the twenties reveals that many of them were in fact busily engaged in extending American power. Those individuals and groups have not dramatically changed their outlook on foreign affairs. Their policies and objectives may differ with those of others (including professors), but they have never sought to isolate the United States.

This interpretation runs counter to the folklore of American foreign relations. Harvard places isolationism "in the saddle." Columbia sees "Americans retiring within their own shell." Yale judges that policy "degenerated" into isolation— among other things.[2] Others, less picturesque but equally positive, refer to a "marked increase of isolationist sentiment" and to "those years of isolationism." Another group diagnoses the populace as having "ingrained isolationism," analyzes it as "sullen and selfish" in consequence, and characterizes it as doing "its best to forget international subjects." Related verdicts describe the Republican party as "predominantly isolationist" and as an organization that

[1] F. Bacon, *Novum Organum,* Headlam's translation as received by C. P. Curtis and F. Greenslet, *The Practical Cogitator* (Boston, Houghton Mifflin Co., 1945), pp. 14–16.

[2] A. M. Schlesinger, *Paths to the Present* (New York, The Macmillan Co., 1949), 69, 201; L. M. Hacker, "American International Relations," in *The United States and Its Place in World Affairs, 1918–1943,* ed. by A. Nevins and L. M. Hacker, (Boston, D. C. Heath and Co., 1943), p. 166; S. F. Bemis, "The Shifting Strategy of American Defense and Diplomacy," in *Essays in History and International Relations in Honor of George Hubbard Blakeslee,* ed. by D. E. Lee and G. E. McReynolds (Worcester, Clark University, 1949), p. 9.

"fostered a policy of deliberate isolation."[3]

Most pointed of these specifications is a terse two-word summary of the diplomacy of the period: "Isolation Perfected."[4] Popularizers have transcribed this theme into a burlesque. Their articles and books convey the impression that the Secretaries of State were in semiretirement and that the citizenry wished to do away with the Department itself.[5] Columnists and commentators have made the concept an eerie example of George Orwell's double-think. They label as isolationists the most vigorous interventionists.

The case would seem to be closed and judgment given if it were not for the ambivalence of some observers and the brief dissents filed by a few others. The scholar who used the phrase "those years

of isolationism," for example, remarks elsewhere in the same book that "expansionism ... really was long a major expression of isolationism." Another writes of the "return to an earlier policy of isolation," and on the next page notes a "shift in policy during the twenties amounting almost to a 'diplomatic revolution'." A recent biographer states that Henry Cabot Lodge "did not propose ... an isolationist attitude," but then proceeds to characterize the Monroe Doctrine—upon which Lodge stood in his fight against the League of Nations treaty—as a philosophy of "isolation." And in the last volume of his trilogy, the late Professor Frederick L. Paxson summed up a long review of the many diplomatic activities of the years 1919–1923 with the remark that this was a foreign policy of "avoidance rather than of action."[6]

But a few scholars, toying with the Idol of the Market-Place, have made bold to rock the image. Yet Professor Richard Van Alstyne was doing more than playing the iconoclast when he observed that the "militant manifest destiny men were the isolationists of the nine-

[3] In sequence, these quotations come from S. Adler, "The War-Guilt Question and American Disillusionment, 1919–1928," *The Journal of Modern History*, XXIII, No. 1 (March, 1951), p. 27; A. K. Weinberg, *Manifest Destiny. A study of Nationalist Expansion in American History* (Baltimore, Johns Hopkins Press, 1935), p. 473; L. M. Hacker and H. S. Zahler, *The United States in the 20th Century* (New York, Appleton-Century-Crofts, Inc., 1952), pp. 278, 302; W. Wilson, quoted in Weinberg, *Manifest Destiny*, p. 473; F. D. Roosevelt, *Foreign Affairs*, VI, No. 4 (July, 1928), p. 577; W. Johnson, *The Battle Against Isolation* (Chicago, Chicago University Press, 1944), p. 132. For similar expressions see S. F. Bemis, *A Diplomatic History of the United States* (3rd ed., New York, Henry Holt and Co., 1950), p. 705; J. D. Hicks, *The American Nation* (Boston, Houghton Mifflin Co., 1949), p. 565; D. Perkins, *The Evolution of American Foreign Policy* (New York, Oxford University Press, 1949), p. 110; and A. Nevins, *America in World Affairs* (London, Oxford University Press, 1941), p. 80.

[4] D. F. Fleming, *The United States and World Organization, 1920–1933* (New York, Columbia University Press, 1938), title of Chapter VI.

[5] This literature is far too vast to cite, but even a perusal of *The Reader's Guide to Periodical Literature* will indicate the great volume of such material. It is vital to note, however, that the so-called disillusionment writers did not make this mistake—whatever their other errors. They criticized the policies of the time, but documented, in such journals as *The Nation*, the active character of the diplomacy.

[6] Quotations, in order, from Weinberg, *Manifest Destiny*, pp. 473, 454; H. U. Faulkner, *American Political and Social History* (6th ed., New York, Appleton-Century-Crofts, Inc., 1952), pp. 700, 701; J. A. Garraty, *Henry Cabot Lodge. A Biography* (New York, Alfred A. Knopf, 1953), pp. 348, 364–65; F. L. Paxson, *American Democracy and the World War. Postwar Years. Normalcy, 1918–1923* (Berkeley, University of California Press, 1948), p. 367. For other examples of this ambiguity see D. Perkins, *American Approach to Foreign Policy* (Cambridge, Harvard University Press, 1952), p. 26; T. A. Bailey, *A Diplomatic History of the American People* (4th ed., New York, Appleton-Century-Crofts, Inc., 1950), p. 682—where he says that the Harding Administration "retreated into what ex-President Wilson described as 'sullen and selfish isolation' "; H. J. Carman and H. C. Syrett, *A History of the American People* (New York, Alfred A. Knopf, 1952), pp. 264–65, and title of Chapter XII; S. E. Morrison and H. S. Commager, *The Growth of the American Republic* (4th ed., New York, Oxford University Press, 1950), Volume II, p. 497; and H. B. Parkes, *The United States of America* (New York, Alfred A. Knopf, 1953).

teenth century." For with this insight we can translate those who maintain that Lodge "led the movement to perpetuate the traditional policy of isolation." Perhaps William G. Carleton was even more forthright. In 1946 he pointed out that the fight over the League treaty was not between isolationists and internationalists, and added that many of the mislabeled isolationists were actually "nationalists and imperialists." Equally discerning was Charles Beard's comment in 1933 that the twenties were marked by a "return to the more aggressive ways ...[used] to protect and advance the claims of American business enterprise." All these interpretations were based on facts that prompted another scholar to change his earlier conclusion and declare in 1953 that "the thought was all of keeping American freedom of action." [7]

[7] R. W. Van Alstyne, "The Significance of the Mississippi Valley in American Diplomatic History, 1686–1890," *Mississippi Valley Historical Review*, XXXVI, No. 2 (September, 1949), p. 238; L. L. Leonard, *Elements of American Foreign Policy* (New York, McGraw-Hill Book Co., Inc., 1953), p. 220; among the many others who characterize Lodge in this manner is S. Adler in his recent article on isolation, "Isolationism Since 1914," *The American Scholar*, XXI, No. 3 (Summer, 1952), p. 340; W. G. Carleton, "Isolationism and the Middle West," *Mississippi Valley Historical Review*, XXXIII, No. 3 (December, 1946), pp. 381–82; C. A. and M. R. Beard, *The Rise of American Civilization* (New Edition. Two Volumes in One. Revised and Enlarged. New York, The Macmillan Co., 1933), pp. 681–83; and compare D. Perkins, *The American Approach to Foreign Policy*, 26, with D. Perkins, "The Department of State and Public Opinion," Chapter IX in *The Diplomats 1919-1939*, ed. by G. A. Graig and F. Gilbert (Princeton, Princeton University Press, 1953), p. 308. Interestingly enough, both Carleton and Van Alstyne addressed their remarks to meetings of the Mississippi Valley Historical Association, and their articles later appeared as lead articles in the *Review*. On the same program with Van Alstyne, furthermore, was Professor Richard Leopold, whose comments were of a similar nature and whose paper was also printed. The professional audience seems to have ignored their keen suggestions. Professor Weinberg's article, "The Historical Meaning of the American Doctrine of Isolation," *The American Political Science Review*, XXXIV (1940), pp. 539–47, offers certain concepts that would

These are perceptive comments. Additional help has recently been supplied by two other students of the period. One of these is Robert E. Osgood, who approached the problem in terms of *Ideals and Self-Interest in American Foreign Relations*.[8] Though primarily concerned with the argument that Americans should cease being naive, Osgood suggests that certain stereotypes are misleading. One might differ with his analysis of the struggle over the Treaty of Versailles, but not with his insistence that there were fundamental differences between Senators Lodge and William E. Borah—as well as between those two and President Woodrow Wilson. Osgood likewise raises questions about the reputed withdrawal of the American public. Over a thousand organizations for the study of international relations existed in 1926, to say nothing of the groups that sought constantly to make or modify foreign policy.

Osgood gives little attention to this latter aspect of foreign relations, a surprising omission on the part of a realist.[9]

go far to resolve the contradictions in his earlier *Manifest Destiny*, but he did not apply the ideas to any later period. H. Feis writes of America's active foreign economic policy in *The Diplomacy of the Dollar, First Era, 1919–1932* (Baltimore, Johns Hopkins Press, 1950), but fails to note that these facts contradict the idea of isolation. The same approach is taken by G. Soule, *Prosperity Decade. From War to Depression: 1917–1929* (New York, Rinehart and Co., Inc., 1947), pp. 252–74. Far more stimulating than either Feis or Soule is S. Kuznets, "Foreign Economic Relations of the United States and Their Impact Upon the Domestic Economy," Chapter 11 in his *Economic Change* (New York, W. W. Norton and Co., 1953), pp. 296–333. See also the neglected work of A. D. Gayer and C. T. Schmidt, *American Economic Foreign Policy. Postwar History, Analysis, and Interpretation* (New York, no publisher given, 1939), especially pp. 11–17.

[8] R. E. Osgood, *Ideals and Self-Interest in America's Foreign Relations. The Great Transformation of the Twentieth Century* (Chicago, University of Chicago Press, 1953).

[9] This is strange for a realist trained in the school of Professor Hans J. Morgenthau's *Realpolitik*. For the realists emphasize the fact that the relationship between power and ideals is re-

But the underlying assumption of his inquiry cannot be challenged. The foreign policy issue of the twenties was never isolationism. The controversy and competition were waged between those who entertained different concepts of the national interest and disagreed over the means to be employed to secure that objective. Secretary of State Charles Evans Hughes was merely more eloquent, not less explicit. "Foreign policies," he explained in 1923, "are not built upon abstractions. They are the result of practical conceptions of national interest arising from some immediate exigency or standing out vividly in historical perspective." [10]

Historian George L. Grassmuck used this old-fashioned premise of the politician as a tool with which to probe the *Sectional Biases in Congress on Foreign Policy*. Disciplining himself more rigorously in the search for primary facts than did Osgood, Grassmuck's findings prompted him to conclude that "the 'sheep and goats' technique" of historical research is eminently unproductive. From 1921 to 1933, for example, the Republicans in both houses of Congress were "more favorable to both Army and Navy measures than ... Democrats." Eighty-five percent of the same Republicans supported international economic measures and agreements. As for the Middle West, that much condemned section did not reveal any "extraordinary indication of a ... tendency to withdraw." Nor was there "an intense 'isolationism' on the part of [its] legislators

with regard to membership in a world organization." [11] And what opposition there was seems to have been as much the consequence of dust bowls and depression as the product of disillusioned scholars in ivory towers.

These investigations and correlations have two implications. First, the United States was neither isolated nor did it pursue a policy of isolationism from 1920 to 1933. Second, if the policy of that era, so generally accepted as the product of traditional isolationist sentiment, proves non-isolationist, then the validity and usefulness of the concept when applied to earlier or later periods may seriously be challenged.

Indeed, it would seem more probable that the central theme of American foreign relations has been the expansion of the United States. Alexander Hamilton made astute use of the phrase "no entangling alliances" during the negotiation of Jay's Treaty in 1794, but his object was a *de facto* affiliation with the British Fleet—not isolation. [12] Nor was Thomas Jefferson seeking to withdraw when he made of Monticello a conselling center for those seeking to emulate the success of the American Revolution. A century later Senator Lodge sought to revise the Treaty of Versailles and the Covenant of the League of Nations with reservations that seemed no more than a restatement of Hamilton's remarks. Yet the maneuvers of Lodge were no more isolationist in character and purpose than Hamilton's earlier action. And while surely no latter-day Jefferson, Senator Borah was anything but an isolationist in his concept of the power of economics and ideas. Borah not only favored the recognition of the Soviet

ciprocal. Not only do ideas fail to have consequences without power, but the sources and the nature of the power have some correlation with the character of the ideals. Thus it would seem doubly unrealistic to slight the sources of power and at the same time discuss the ideas without reference to the private as well as the public record of the groups and individuals in question.
[10] C. E. Hughes, "The Centenary of the Monroe Doctrine," *The Annals of the American Academy of Political and Social Science,* Supplement to Volume CXI (January, 1923), p. 7.

[11] G. L. Grassmuck, *Sectional Biases in Congress on Foreign Policy* (Baltimore, Johns Hopkins Press, 1951), pp. 32, 93, 162, 49.
[12] Hamilton to the British Minister, as quoted by S. F. Bemis, *Jay's Treaty. A Study in Commerce and Diplomacy* (New York, Macmillan and Co., 1924), p. 246.

Union in order to influence the development of the Bolshevik Revolution and as a check against Japanese expansion in Asia, but also argued that American economic policies were intimately connected with foreign political crises. All those men were concerned with the extension of one or more aspects of American influence, power, and authority.

Approached in this manner, the record of American foreign policy in the twenties verifies the judgments of two remarkably dissimilar students: historian Richard W. Leopold and Senator Lodge. The professor warns that the era was "more complex than most glib generalizations . . . would suggest"; and the scholastic politician concludes that, excepting war, there "never [was] a period when the United States [was] more active and its influence more felt internationally than between 1921 and 1924." [13] The admonition about perplexity was offered as helpful advice, not as an invitation to anti-intellectualism. For, as the remarks of the Senator implied, recognition that a problem is involved does not mean that it cannot be resolved.

Paradox and complexity can often be clarified by rearranging the data around a new focal point that is common to all aspects of the apparent contradiction. The confusion of certainty and ambiguity that characterizes most accounts of American foreign policy in the twenties stems from the fact that they are centered on the issue of membership in the League of Nations. Those Americans who wanted to join are called internationalists. Opponents of that move became isolationist. But the subsequent action of most of those who fought

participation in the League belies this simple classification. And the later policies of many who favored adherence to the League cast serious doubts upon the assumption that they were willing to negotiate or arbitrate questions that they defined as involving the national interest. More pertinent is an examination of why certain groups and individuals favored or disapproved of the League, coupled with a review of the programs they supported after that question was decided.

Yet such a re-study of the League fight is in itself insufficient. Equally important is a close analysis of the American reaction to the Bolshevik Revolution. Both the League Covenant and the Treaty of Versailles were written on a table shaken by that upheaval. The argument over the ratification of the combined documents was waged in a context determined as much by Nikolai Lenin's *Appeal to the Toiling, Oppressed, and Exhausted Peoples of Europe* and the Soviet *Declaration to the Chinese People* as by George Washington's Farewell Address.[14]

Considered within the setting of the Bolshevik Revolution, the basic question was far greater than whether or not to enter the League. At issue was what response was to be made to the domestic and international division of labor that

[14] None of the authors cited above makes this association of events central to his discussion of the League issue. Few of them even connect the two. The integration has, of course, been made: most notably by E. H. Carr, *The Soviet Impact on the Western World* (New York, The Macmillan Co., 1947); M. Dobb, *Political Economy and Capitalism. Some Essays in Economic Tradition* (New York, International Publishers, 1945), Chapter VII, and *Studies in the Development of Capitalism* (New York, International Publishers, 1947), Chapter VIII; H. J. Laski, *Reflections on the Revolution of Our Time* (New York, 1947); Sir L. Namier, *Conflicts. Studies in Contemporary History* (London, The Macmillan Co., 1942), Chapter I; and, of especial significance, H. Hoover, *American Individualism* (Garden City, Doubleday, Page and Co., 1923).

[13] R. W. Leopold, "The Mississippi Valley and American Foreign Policy, 1890–1941: an Assessment and an Appeal," *Mississippi Valley Historical Review*, XXXVII, No. 4 (March, 1951), p. 635; H. C. Lodge, "Foreign Relations of the United States, 1921–1924," *Foreign Affairs*, II, No. 4 (June, 1924), p. 526.

had accompanied the Industrial Revolution. Challenges from organized urban labor, dissatisfied farmers, frightened men of property, searching intellectual critics, and colonial peoples rudely interrupted almost every meeting of the Big Four in Paris and were echoed in many Senate debates over the treaty. And those who determined American policy through the decade of the twenties were consciously concerned wih the same problem.

An inquiry into this controversy over the broad question of how to end the war reveals certain divisions within American society. These groupings were composed of individuals and organizations whose position on the League of Nations was coincident with and part of their response to the Bolsheviks; or, in a wider sense, with their answer to that general unrest, described by Woodrow Wilson as a "feeling of revolt against the large vested interests which influenced the world both in the economic and the political sphere." [15] Once this breakdown has been made it is then possible to follow the ideas and actions of these various associations of influence and power through the years 1920 to 1933.

At the core of the American reaction to the League and the Bolshevik Revolution was the quandary between fidelity to ideals and the urge to power. Jefferson faced a less acute version of the same predicament in terms of whether to force citizenship on settlers west of the Mississippi who were reluctant to be absorbed in the Louisiana Purchase. A century later the anti-imperialists posed the same issue in the more sharply defined circumstances of the Spanish-American War. The League and the Bolsheviks raised the question in its

most dramatic context and in unavoidable terms.

There were four broad responses to this reopening of the age-old dilemma. At one pole stood the pure idealists and pacifists, led by William Jennings Bryan. A tiny minority in themselves, they were joined in terms of general consequences if not in action, by those Americans who were preoccupied with their own solutions to the problem. Many American business men, for example, were concerned primarily with the expansion of trade and were apathetic toward or impatient with the hullabaloo over the League.[16] Diametrically opposed to the idealists were the vigorous expansionists. All these exponents of the main chance did not insist upon an overt crusade to run the world, but they were united on Senator Lodge's proposition that the United States should dominate world politics. Association with other nations they accepted, but not equality of membership or mutuality of decision.

Caught in the middle were those Americans who declined to support either extreme. A large number of these people clustered around Woodrow Wilson, and can be called the Wilsonites. Though aware of the dangers and temptations involved, Wilson declared his intention to extend American power for the purpose of strengthening the ideals. However noble that effort, it failed for two reasons. Wilson delegated power and initiative to men and organizations that did not share his objectives,

[15] W. Wilson, remarks to the Council of Ten, January 16, 1919, *Papers Relating to the Foreign Relations of the United States, Paris Peace Conference* (13 vols., Washington, D. C.), III, p. 583.

[16] See the excellent essay by J. H. Foote, "American Industrialists and Foreign Policy, 1919–1922. A Study in Attitudes," Master's Thesis, University of Wisconsin, Madison, 1947; for a typical expression see the remarks of Senator Walter E. Edge—"we wasted, practically wasted, two years of the opportunity presented to us at that time, unequaled, as I say, in the history of the world"—in National Foreign Trade Council, *Official Report of the Eighth National Foreign Trade Convention, 1921* (New York, 1921), p. 553.

and on his own part the president ultimately "cast his lot" with the defenders of the status quo.[17]

Led by the Sons of the Wild Jackass, the remaining group usually followed Senator Borah in foreign relations. These men had few illusions about the importance of power in human affairs or concerning the authority of the United States in international politics. Prior to the world war they supported—either positively or passively—such vigorous expansionists as Theodore Roosevelt, who led their Progressive Party. But the war and the Bolshevik Revolution jarred some of these Progressives into a closer examination of their assumptions. These reflections and new conclusions widened the breach with those of their old comrades who had moved toward a conservative position on domestic issues. Some of those earlier allies, like Senator Albert J. Beveridge, continued to agitate for an American century. Others, such as Bainbridge Colby, sided with Wilson in 1916 and went along with the president on foreign policy.

But a handful had become firm antiexpansionists by 1919.[18] No attempt was

made by these men to deny the power of the United States. Nor did they think that the nation could become self-sufficient and impregnable in its strength. Borah, for example, insisted that America must stand with Russia if Japan and Germany were to be checked. And Johnson constantly pointed out that the question was not whether to withdraw, but at what time and under what circumstances to use the country's influence. What these men did maintain was that any effort to run the world by establishing an American system comparable to the British Empire was both futile and un-American.

In this they agreed with Henry Adams, who debated the same issue with his brother Brooks Adams, Theodore Roosevelt, and Henry Cabot Lodge in the years after 1898. "I incline now to antiimperialism, and very strongly to antimilitarism," Henry warned. "If we try to rule politically, we take the chances against us." By the end of the first world war another generation of expansionists tended to agree with Henry Adams about ruling politically, but planned to build and maintain a similar pattern of control through the use of America's economic might. Replying to these later expansionists, Borah and other antiexpansionists of the nineteen-twenties argued that if Washington's influence was to be effective it would have to be used to support the movements of reform and colonial nationalism rather than deployed in an effort to dam up and dominate those forces.

For these reasons they opposed Wilson's reorganization of the international banking consortium, fearing that the financiers would either influence strongly or veto—as they did—American foreign policies. With Senator Albert B. Cummins of Iowa they voted against the Wilson-approved Webb-Pomerene Act, which repealed the anti-trust laws for export associations. In the same vein they

[17] W. Wilson, remarks to the Big Five, February 14, 1919, *Foreign Relations, Russia, 1919* (Washington, D. C., 1937), p. 59.

[18] C. Vevier reviewed these early expansionist sympathies of the Progressives in "The Progressives and Dollar Diplomacy," Master's Thesis, University of Wisconsin, Madison, 1949. W. E. Leuchtenburg later published a summary of his own study of the same question as "Progressivism and Imperialism: The Progressive Movement and American Foreign Policy, 1898–1916," *Mississippi Valley Historical Review*, XXXIX, No. 3 (December, 1952), pp. 483–504. It would seem, however, that Leuchtenburg missed the split within the Progressives over Wilson's foreign policy. For in note 38, page 493, he considers it "remarkable" that the Progressives fought Wilson in view of the degree to which the president "was involved with American imperialist aspirations." This writer's information on the division comes from the manuscript papers of Calvin Coolidge, William E. Borah, William Judson, Samuel N. Harper, Theodore Roosevelt, Alexander Gumberg, Raymond Robins, and Woodrow Wilson; from the materials in the National Archives; and the *Congressional Record*.

tried to prevent passage of the Edge
Act, an amendment to the Federal Reserve Act that authorized foreign banking corporations.[19] Led by Borah, they
bitterly attacked the Versailles Treaty
because, in their view, it committed the
United States to oppose colonial movements for self-government and to support
an unjust and indefensible status quo.
From the same perspective they criticized and fought to end intervention in
Russia and the suppression of civil liberties at home.[20]

Contrary to the standard criticism of
their actions, however, these anti-expansionists were not just negative die-hards.
Senator Cummins maintained from the
first that American loans to the allies
should be considered gifts. Borah spoke
out on the same issue, hammered away
against armed intervention in Latin
America, played a key role in securing
the appointment of Dwight Morrow
as Ambassador to Mexico, and sought
to align the United States with, instead
of against, the Chinese Revolution. On
these and other issues the anti-expansionists were not always of one mind, but

as in the case of the Washington Conference Treaties the majority of them
were far more positive in their actions
than has been acknowledged.[21]

Within this framework the key to the
defeat of the League treaty was the defection from the Wilsonites of a group
who declined to accept the restrictions
that Article X of the League Covenant
threatened to impose upon the United
States. A morally binding guarantee of
the "territorial integrity and existing
political integrity of all members of the
League" was too much for these men.
First they tried to modify that limitation.
Failing there, they followed Elihu Root
and William Howard Taft, both old
time expansionists, to a new position
behind Senator Lodge. Among those
who abandoned Wilson on this issue
were Herbert Hoover, Calvin Coolidge,
Charles Evans Hughes, and Henry L.
Stimson.

Not all these men were at ease with the
vigorous expansionists. Stimson, for one,
thought the Lodge reservations "harsh
and unpleasant," and later adjusted other
of his views.[22] Hoover and Hughes
tried to revive their version of the
League after the Republicans returned
to power in 1920. But at the time all of
them were more uneasy about what one
writer has termed Wilson's moral imperialism."[23] They were not eager to
identify themselves with the memories
of that blatant imperialism of the years
1895 to 1905, but neither did they like
Article X. That proviso caught them

[19] See, for example, the debates on the Webb-Pomerene Act in *Congressional Record*, Volume 56, Part 1, pp. 69–71; and the votes on the same legislation, pp. 168, 186.

[20] Especially pertinent are the remarks of Borah, *Congressional Record*, V54:1:636; V57:1:190; V58:3:3143–44; and his letter to F. Lynch, August 1, 1919, *Papers of William E. Borah*, Library of Congress, Manuscript Divi-sion, Washington, D.C. Also important are the comments of Senator Hiram Johnson, *Congres-sional Record*, V53:1:503, 505. Eric Goldman's penetrating study of the Progressives, *Rendez-vous With Destiny. A History of Modern Ameri-can Reform* (New York, Alfred A. Knopf, 1952), completely misses this development. In pp. 273–74, Goldman remarks that the "most striking deviation of American progressivism in foreign affairs from its attitudes in domestic af-fairs was the enthusiasm for international order in the form of the League of Nations." He pro-ceeds, then, to argue that if the progressives had applied the same criticism to the League as they had to its laissez faire counterpart in domestic affairs "they could hardly have emerged with a favorable attitude." But the key point is that the hard core of the Progressives did exactly this and came out in opposition to the League.

[21] This paragraph is based on much the same material cited in note 18. But see, as repre-sentative, Cummins' remarks on the loans, *Con-gressional Record*, V5511:757, 762; Borah on economic factors, V64:1:930–31; and the par-liamentary maneuvers over the Liberian Loan, V63:1:287–88.

[22] Stimson, Diary entry of December 3, 1919, quoted in H. L. Stimson and McGeorge Bundy, *On Active Service in Peace and War* (New York, Harper and Brothers, 1948), p. 104.

[23] H. F. Cline, *The United States and Mexico* (Cambridge, Harvard University Press, 1953), p. 141.

from both sides, it illegalized changes initiated by the United States, and obligated America to restore a status quo to some aspects of which they were either indifferent or antagonistic. But least of all were they anxious to run the risk that the Wilsonian rhetoric of freedom and liberty might be taken seriously in an age of revolution. Either by choice or default they supported the idea of a community of interest among the industrialized powers of the world led by an American-British entente as against the colonial areas and the Soviet Union.

This postwar concept of the community of interest was the first generation intellectual off-spring of Herbert Croly's *Promise of American Life* and Herbert Hoover's *American Individualism*. Croly's opportunistic nationalism provided direction for Hoover's "greater mutuality of interest." The latter was to be expressed in an alliance between the government and the "great trade associations and the powerful corporations."[24] Pushed by the Croly-Hoover wing of the Old Progressive Party, the idea enjoyed great prestige during the twenties. Among its most ardent exponents were Samuel Gompers and Matthew Woll of the labor movement, Owen D. Young of management, and Bernard Baruch of finance.

What emerged was an American corporatism. The avowed goals were order,

stability, and social peace. The means to those objectives were labor-management co-operation, arbitration, and the elimination of waste and inefficiency by closing out unrestrained competition. State intervention was to be firm, but moderated through the cultivation and legalization of trade associations which would, in turn, advise the national government and supply leaders for the federal bureaucracy. The ideal was union in place of diversity and conflict.[25]

Other than Hoover, the chief spokes-

[24] H. Croly, *The Promise of American Life* (New York, The Macmillan Co., 1909); H. Hoover, *American Individualism*, p. 43; and Hoover, quoted in Goldman, *Rendezvous With Destiny*, p. 309. Goldman makes this identification between Croly and Hoover, but does not develop it, either as corporatism or in foreign affairs. Other Americans had spoken the language of the community of interest. J. P. Morgan used it to describe his ideal in the economic realm. Brooks Adams warned ·Theodore Roosevelt that such coordination at the national level was necessary to insure American supremacy in the world. The Adams argument emphasized the need for an intellectual and political elite chosen from the upper classes to supervise the community of interest through control of the national government.

[25] American corporatism is a neglected field. This writer is greatly indebted to Professor Paul Farmer, University of Wisconsin, for many long discussions of the question. Farmer brought to these conversations his intimate and extended knowledge of French corporative theory and practice as it developed to and culminated in the Vichy Government. His insights into the American scene were equally penetrating. At a later date M. H. Elbow, *French Corporative Theory, 1789–1948. A Chapter in the History of Ideas* (New York, Columbia University Press, 1953), was helpful in review. Of other published material, the following were most helpful: S. D. Alinsky, *Reveille For Radicals* (Chicago, University of Chicago Press, 1946); G. A. Almond, "The Political Attitudes of Wealth," *Journal of Politics*, VII, No. 3 (August, 1945); R. A. Brady, *Business as a System of Power* (New York, Columbia University Press, 1938); R. Bendix, "Bureaucracy and the Problem of Power," *Public Administration Review*, V, No. 3 (Summer, 1945); J. A. C. Grant, "The Guild Returns to America," *Journal of Politics*, IV, Nos. 3 and 4 (August, November, 1942); W. E. Henry, "The Business Executive: the Psycho-Dynamics of a Social Role," *American Journal of Sociology*, LIV, No. 1 (January, 1949); E. J. Howenstine, "Public Works Policy in the Twenties," *Social Research*, XII (December, 1946); F. Hunter, *Community Power Structure. A Study of Decision Makers* (Chapel Hill, University of North Carolina Press, 1953); R. S. Lynd, "Power Politics and the Post War World," in *The Postwar World. The Merrick Lectures for 1944* (New York, Abingdon-Cokesbury Press, 1945); and M. Weber, *The Theory of Social and Economic Organization*, trans. by A. M. Henderson and T. Parsons, ed. by T. Parsons (New York, Oxford University Press, 1947). For a revealing glimpse of the later bi-partisan movement toward corporatism, and the consequences thereof, see *The Welfare State and the National Welfare. A Symposium on Some of the Threatening Tendencies of Our Times*, ed. by S. Glueck (Cambridge, Addison-Wesley Press, Inc., 1952); and the last chapter in Goldman, *Rendezvous With Destiny*.

men of this new community of interest as applied to foreign affairs were Secretaries of State Hughes and Stimson. In the late months of 1931 Stimson was to shift his ground, but until that time he supported the principle. All three men agreed that American economic power should be used to build, strengthen, and maintain the co-operation they sought. As a condition for his entry into the cabinet, Hoover demanded—and received—a major voice in "all important economic policies of the administration." [26] With the energetic assistance of Julius Klein, lauded by the National Foreign Trade Council as the "international business go-getter of Uncle Sam," Hoover changed the Department of Commerce from an agency primarily concerned with interstate commerce to one that concentrated on foreign markets and loans, and control of import sources.[27] Hughes and Stimson handled the political aspects of establishing a "community of ideals, interests and purposes." [28]

These men were not imperialists in the traditional sense of that much abused term. All agreed with Klein that the object was to eliminate "the old imperialistic trappings of politico-economic exploitation." They sought instead the "internationalization of business." [29] Through the use of economic power they wanted to establish a common bond, forged of similar assumptions and purposes, with both the industrialized nations and the native business community in the colonial areas of the world. Their deployment of America's material strength is unquestioned. President Cal-

vin Coolidge reviewed their success, and indicated the political implications thereof, on Memorial Day, 1928. "Our investments and trade relations are such," he summarized, "that it is almost impossible to conceive of any conflict anywhere on earth which would not affect us injuriously." [30]

Internationalization through the avoidance of conflict was the key objective. This did not mean a negative foreign policy. Positive action was the basic theme. The transposition of corporatist principles to the area of foreign relations produced a parallel policy. American leadership and intervention would build a world community regulated by agreement among the industrialized nations. The prevention of revolution and the preservation of the sanctity of private property were vital objectives. Hughes was very clear when he formulated the idea for Latin America. "We are seeking to establish a *Pax Americana* maintained not by arms but by mutual respect and good will and the tranquillizing processes of reason." There would be, he admitted, "interpositions of a temporary character"—the Secretary did not like the connotations of the word intervention—but only to facilitate the establishment of the United States as the "exemplar of justice." [31]

Extension to the world of this pattern developed in Latin America was more involved. There were five main difficulties, four in the realm of foreign relations and one in domestic affairs. The internal problem was to establish and integrate a concert of decision between the government and private economic groups. Abroad the objectives were more sharply defined: circumscribe the impact of the Soviet Union, forestall and control potential resistance of

[26] *The Memoirs of Herbert Hoover. The Cabinet and the Presidency, 1920–1933* (New York, The Macmillan Co., 1952), p. 36.
[27] *Official Report of the 18th Foreign Trade Convention, 1931* (New York, 1931), p. 287.
[28] C. E. Hughes, remarks concerning a substitute for Article X of the League Covenant, Union League Club Speech, New York, March 26, 1919.
[29] J. Klein, *Frontiers of Trade* (New York, The Century Co., 1929), p. 40, 46.

[30] C. Coolidge, Address of May 30, 1928, *Congressional Record*, V69:10:10729.
[31] C. E. Hughes, "Centenary of the Monroe Doctrine," *Annals*, p. 17; and Hughes, remarks to the Havana Conference, 1928.

colonial areas, pamper and cajole Germany and Japan into acceptance of the basic proposition, and secure from Great Britain practical recognition of the fact that Washington had become the center of Anglo-Saxon collaboration. Several examples will serve to illustrate the general outline of this diplomacy, and to indicate the friction between the office holders and the offce dwellers.

Wilson's Administration left the incoming Republicans a plurality of tools designed for the purpose of extending American power. The Webb-Pomerene Law, the Edge Act, and the banking consortium were but three of the more obvious and important of these. Certain polishing and sharpening remained to be done, as exemplified by Hoover's generous interpretation of the Webb-Pomerene legislation, but this was a minor problem. Hoover and Hughes added to these implements with such laws as the one designed to give American customs officials diplomatic immunity so that they could do cost accounting surveys of foreign firms. This procedure was part of the plan to provide equal opportunity abroad, under which circumstances Secretary Hughes was confident that "American business men would take care of themselves." [32]

It was harder to deal with the British, who persisted in annoying indications that they considered themselves equal partners in the enterprise. Bainbridge Colby, Wilson's last Secretary of State, ran into the same trouble. Unless England came "to our way of thinking," Colby feared that "agreement [would] be impossible." A bit later Hughes told the British Ambassador that the time had come for London's expressions of cordial sentiment to be "translated into

something definite." After many harangues about oil, access to mandated areas, and trade with Russia, it was with great relief that Stimson spoke of the United States and Great Britain "working together like two old shoes." [33]

Deep concern over revolutionary ferment produced great anxiety. Hughes quite agreed with Colby that the problem was to prevent revolutions without making martyrs of the leaders of colonial or other dissident movements. The despatches of the period are filled with such expressions as "very grave concern," "further depressed," and "deeply regret," in connection with revolutionary activity in China, Latin America, and Europe.[34] American foreign service personnel abroad were constantly reminded to report all indications of such unrest. This sensitivity reached a high point when one representative telegraphed as "an example of the failure to assure public safety...the throwing of a rock yesterday into the state hospital here." Quite in keeping with this pattern was Washington's conclusion that it would support "any provisional government which gave satisfactory evidence of an intention to re-establish constitutional order." [35]

Central to American diplomacy of the twenties was the issue of Germany and Japan. And it was in this area that the government ran into trouble with its partners, the large associations of capital.

[32] The story of the fight over diplomatic immunity for consular officers can be followed in Foreign Relations, 1925, pp. 211–54; the quote from Hughes is by J. Butler Wright, in Official Report of the 12th National Foreign Trade Convention, 1925 (New York, 1925), p. 165.

[33] Colby to Wright, November 5, 1920, National Archives of the United States (hereafter cited as NA), 574.D1/240b; Hughes, Memorandum of conversation with Geddes, September 20, 1921, NA, 500.A 4/190.5; Stimson, Memorandum of July 20, 1931, NA, 462.00 R 296/4594.5.

[34] Colby to Russell, August 13, 1920, NA, 333.3921 L 96/3; Hughes to Cottrell, April 9, 1923, NA, 824.51/174; Hughes to Morales, June 30, 1923, NA, 815.00/2609; same to same, May 15, 1923, NA, 815.00/2574.

[35] Kodding to Hughes, October 10, 1924, NA, 375.1123 Coleman and Delong/89; Hughes to Welles, April 10, 1924, NA, 815.00/3077a supplement.

The snag was to convince the bankers of the validity of the long range view. Hoover, Hughes and Stimson all agreed that it was vital to integrate Germany and Japan into the American community. Thus Hughes opposed the French diplomacy of force on the Rhine, and for his own part initiated the Dawes Plan. But the delegation of so much authority to the financiers backfired in 1931. The depression scared the House of Morgan and it refused to extend further credits to Germany. Stimson "blew up." He angrily told the Morgan representative in Paris that this strengthened France and thereby undercut the American program. Interrupted in the midst of this argument by a trans-Atlantic call from Hoover, Stimson explained to the president that "if you want to help the cause you are speaking of you will not do it by calling me up, but by calling Tom Lamont." Stimson then turned back to Lamont's agent in Europe and, using "unregulated language," told the man to abandon his "narrow banking axioms." [36]

Similar difficulties faced the government in dealing with Japan and China. The main problem was to convince Japan, by persuasion, concession, and the delicate use of diplomatic force, to join the United States in an application of its Latin American policy to China. Washington argued that the era of the crude exploitation of, and the exercise of direct political sovereignty over, backward peoples was past. Instead, the interested powers should agree to develop and exercise a system of absentee authority, while increasing the productive capacity and administrative efficiency of China. Japan seemed amenable to the proposal, and at the Washington Conference, Secretary Hughes went a great distance to convince Tokyo of Amer-

ican sincerity. Some writers, such as George Frost Kennan and Adolf A. Berle, claim that the United States did not go far enough. [37] This is something of a mystery. For in his efforts to establish "cooperaton in the Far East," as Hughes termed it, the Secretary consciously gave Japan "an extraordinarily favorable position." [38]

Perhaps what Kennan and Berle have in mind is the attitude of Thomas Lamont. In contrast to their perspective on Europe, the bankers took an extremely long range view of Asia. Accepting the implications of the Four and Nine Power Treaties, Lamont began to finance Japan's penetration of the mainland. Hughes and Stimson were trapped. They continued to think in terms of American business men taking care of themselves if given an opportunity, and thus strengthening Washington's position in the world community. Hughes wrote Morgan that he hoped the consortium would become an "important instrumentality of our 'open door' policy." [39] But the American members of the banking group refused to antagonize their Japanese and British colleagues, and so vetoed Washington's hope to finance the Chinese Eastern Railway and its efforts to support the Federal Telegraph Company in China.

In this context it is easy to sympathize with Stimson's discomfort when the Japanese Army roared across Manchuria. As he constantly reiterated to the Japanese Ambassador in Washington,

[37] G. F. Kennan, *American Diplomacy, 1900–1950* (Chicago, University of Chicago Press, 1951), p. 82; A. A. Berle, Jr., review of H. Feis, *The China Tangle,* in the *New York Times,* Book Review Section, October 4, 1953.
[38] Hughes to Judge Hiscock, April 24, 1924, quoted in M. J. Pusey, *Charles Evans Hughes* (2 vols., New York, The Macmillan Co., 1951), II, p. 516; Hughes to Bell, October 22, 1924, *NA,* 893.51/4699; Hughes, Memorandum of conversations with Kato and Balfour, December 2, 1921, *NA,* 500.A4b/547.5.
[39] Hughes to Morgan, August 8, 1921, *NA,* 861.77/2184.

[36] Stimson, Memorandum of talks with representatives of J. P. Morgan and Co., Paris, July 17, 1931, *NA,* 462.00 R 296/4587.5.

Tokyo had come far along the road "of bringing itself into alignment with the methods and opinion of the Western World." [40] Stimson not only wanted to, but did in fact give Japan every chance to continue along that path. So too did President Hoover, whose concern with revolution was so great that he was inclined to view Japanese sovereignty in Manchuria as the best solution. Key men in the State Department shared the president's conclusion.[41]

[40] Stimson, Memorandum of November 21, 1931, NA, 793.94/2865; and see Stimson, Memorandum of February 27, 1933, NA, 793.94/5953, for a clear review of his changing attitudes.
[41] This writer is greatly indebted to Professor Richard N. Current, University of Illinois, for sharing his extended knowledge of the Manchurian Crisis. Professor Current's study will be published in the spring of 1954 by Rutgers University Press.

Stimson's insight was not so limited. He realized that his predecessor, Secretary of State Frank B. Kellogg, had been right: the community of interest that America should seek was with the Chinese. The Secretary acknowledged his error to Senator Borah, who had argued just such a thesis since 1917. Stimson's letter to Borah of February 23, 1932, did not say that America should abandon her isolationism, but rather that she had gone too far with the wrong friends. The long and painful process of America's great awakening had begun. But in the meantime President Hoover's insistence that no move should be made toward the Soviet Union, and that the non-recognition of Manchuko should be considered as a formula looking toward conciliation, had opened the door to appeasement.

14

The Stimson Doctrine and
the Hoover Doctrine

RICHARD N. CURRENT

One of the principal foreign policy objectives of the Republican Administration that came to power in 1921 was to stabilize the diplomatic situation in the Far East by international agreement. This was achieved at the Washington Conference for the Limitation of Armament in 1921–22 in two treaties, the Four-Power Treaty and the Nine-Power Treaty. By the former the United States, Japan, France, and Great Britain pledged to respect each other's "rights in relation to their insular possessions...in the Pacific Ocean." In the latter the United States, Japan, France, Great Britain, Belgium, the Netherlands, China, Portugal, and Italy agreed to adhere to the principle of the open door in China and to respect that country's sovereignty, independence, and territorial and administrative integrity.

With these treaties signed and ratified, the United States hoped that the great powers, having renounced every aggressive design and having tied their hands by self-denying pledges implicit in the treaties, would pursue a peaceful policy in Asia. It was expected that even Japan, whose ambition to dominate in Asia was greatest and whose favorable geographic position made conquest most feasible, would abide by the settlement. After all, her government had in good faith signed the treaties and her Parliament had ratified them. Further, the party in power in Tokyo was liberal and pacific and more concerned with social reform than military adventure. Her leaders favored cooperation with the West and looked to the League of Nations as the instrument for solving the world's problems. It appeared reasonable to believe that the aggressive program of the Twenty-One Demands of 1915 would not reoccur.

The American hope, however, was not fulfilled, for the militarists in Japan had not given up their plan to dominate China and other parts of Asia and to achieve that domination by force of arms. Indeed, during the decade of the 1920s they sought several times to gain the permission of the Emperor and of the Cabinet Council for an attack on China. Failing to obtain imperial sanction, the army moved without it. On the night of September 18, 1931, following a minor explosion on the South Manchurian Railway, Japanese soldiers, stationed in Manchuria by virtue of treaties with China, quickly took possession of most of the southern part of that province and moved to exercise political control of the area.

Both government and people in the United States were shocked by the Japa-

FROM *The American Historical Review*, LIX (1954), 513–542. By permission of the author and the American Historical Association.

nese assault on Chinese territory. Not only the Nine-Power Treaty but also the Kellogg-Briand Pact had been violated. And it was further feared that Tokyo's action in Manchuria was only the prelude to a large-scale operation in other parts of China. After much discussion and debate in the fall of 1931, in Washington by President Hoover and Secretary of State Stimson and others in the State Department, and in Geneva with members of the League of Nations, the United States finally made its response to the Japanese move in the form of a note to both China and Japan on January 7, 1932. It stated that Washington would not recognize any treaty or agreement entered into by these two governments that might curtail the rights of American citizens in China. This nonrecognition policy has come to be known as the Stimson Doctrine, the Hoover Doctrine, or the Hoover-Stimson Doctrine.

Professor Richard N. Current of the University of Wisconsin, in the course of writing an evaluation of Stimson's statecraft, came to the view that using the names of Stimson and Hoover interchangeably to designate the policy conveys the erroneous impression that the two agreed on the intent and implication of the note on nonrecognition. In the article that follows, Current attempts to demonstrate that each had something very different in mind. For Hoover, nonrecognition was the end; it "remained a final and sufficient measure," an alternative for "economic pressure or military force." For Stimson it was "a preliminary to economic and military sanctions,...a means of laying down the ideological grounds for war if, as he expected, war eventually should come."

In response to Japanese activities in the Far East, 1931–1933, the Hoover administration adopted a policy of refusing to recognize political or territorial changes made in violation of American treaty rights. This was not entirely new. At the time of Japan's Twenty-One Demands upon China, in 1915, Secretary of State William Jennings Bryan had announced a similar nonrecognition policy. But the Hoover administration elaborated the formula by associating it with the Kellogg-Briand or Paris Pact of 1928, whose signatories (including Japan) renounced war as an instrument of national policy, and with the Nine-Power Treaty of 1922, which bound the nine powers (including Japan) to respect the Open Door in China and Chinese territorial and administrative integrity. Nonrecognition—as a corollary of these treaties—came to be known variously as the Stimson, the Hoover-Stimson, or the Hoover doctrine. The interchangeable use of these terms gave

the impression that President Hoover and his Secretary of State, Henry L. Stimson, had one and the same policy in mind. In his book *The Far Eastern Crisis* (1936) Stimson did not disabuse his readers of that impression, but afterward some of the published papers of Hoover suggested and the memoirs of both men revealed serious disagreements between them about the authorship and implications of the doctrine.[1] Now, with access to the unpublished diaries of Stimson and of William R. Castle, Hoover's Undersecretary of State, a more circumstantial account of policy making with

[1] Henry L. Stimson, *The Far Eastern Crisis: Recollections and Observations* (New York, 1936), pp. 6–7 and *passim;* Ray L. Wilbur and Arthur M. Hyde, *The Hoover Policies* (New York, 1937), pp. 600–601; William S. Myers, *The Foreign Policies of Herbert Hoover, 1929–1933* (New York, 1940), pp. 157–73, 229n.; Henry L. Stimson and McGeorge Bundy, *On Active Service in Peace and War* (New York, 1948), pp. 220–81; *The Memoirs of Herbert Hoover*, II: *The Cabinet and the Presidency, 1920–1933* (New York, 1952), pp. 362–79.

respect to nonrecognition can be presented.[2]

During the first two or three weeks of the Manchurian crisis, which began with a Japanese attack upon Mukden, September 18, 1931, the policy makers in Washington saw eye to eye. Neither President Hoover nor Secretary Stimson then believed that American treaty rights would be involved. Both men felt a kind of godfatherly concern for the Kellogg Pact, they having sponsored the Washington ceremony at which it was finally proclaimed, and in 1929 Stimson had invoked the pact when Russian and Chinese troops clashed in Manchuria. In 1931, however, the Japanese army appeared at first to be proceeding without authorization from Tokyo, and so it seemed that the Japanese government could hardly be accused of violating its antiwar pledge. Day after day Stimson kept looking for signs that the Japanese were retreating to their own railroad zone, were "crawling back into their dens," and he listened eagerly to the assurances and reassurances of Ambassador Katsuji Debuchi.[3]

Meanwhile the Chinese government and the League of Nations were making futile attempts to enlist the United States in some kind of joint action. China appealed to this country as sponsor of the Kellogg Pact and to the League under Article XI of the Covenant, and the League in turn queried the State Department about the applicability of the pact. After authorizing an appeal to China and Japan to preserve peace, the League Council forwarded copies of its proceedings to Washington and

then began to discuss a proposal for creating a neutral commission, including an American representative, to deal with the Manchurian affair.[4] None of these overtures elicited a favorable response from the American Secretary of State. He suspected that the League was "trying to pass the buck to us," and he resented the way the League kept "nagging" him.

Stimson's own thinking at this stage centered upon two points. For one thing, he wished to avoid antagonizing Japan against the United States. For another, he feared that positive action by any outside agency might strengthen the military element in Japan, weaken the relatively moderate Wakatsuki-Shidehara ministry, and make it impossible for the latter to recover and maintain control over the rampageous army. Accordingly he thus formulated his basic aim: "My problem is to let the Japanese know we are watching them and' at the same time to do it in a way that will help Shidehara, who is on the right side, and not play into the hands of any Nationalist agitators on the other." In keeping with this object he cautioned Ambassador Debuchi that, although he was "making every effort to save Japan's face and give them time to settle this by themselves with China," the Japanese must realize that he "thought the situation was very grave" and "they must settle it mighty quick." [5] To the American minister in Geneva, Hugh Wilson, he laid down three successive lines of action for the United States in relation to the League: First, while opposing the plan for a neutral commission, we should support the League in urging "that Japan and China themselves effect a settlement through direct negotiation." Second, if "outside action" should be-

[2] The author is indebted to Mr. McGeorge Bundy for permission to use the Stimson diary, which is available (to 1933) on microfilm in the Yale University Library, and to Mr. William R. Castle for permission to use his diary, which is in his possession in Washington, D.C. [Reprinted by permission.]
[3] Stimson diary, Sept. 19, 21, 22, 23, 28, 1931.

[4] Sara R. Smith, *The Manchurian Crisis, 1931–1932: A Tragedy in International Relations* (New York, 1948), pp. 28–50.
[5] Stimson diary, Sept. 22, 23, 24, 1931.

come necessary, we should "favor China and Japan's submitting to machinery set up in the League of Nations Covenant." Third, "should it develop for any reason that this line is impracticable," we should "consider the machinery of" the 1922 Nine-Power Treaty "or action such as may be practicable under the 1928 Kellogg-Briand Pact." [6]

This program Stimson himself authored, but he did so with the approval of his advisers in the State Department on the one hand, and the President on the other. At the outset Hoover endorsed Stimson's analysis of the problem, and, as the days passed, Stimson was reassured to find that Hoover "throughly agreed" with him in his "caution." [7] Undersecretary Castle rejoiced to see that Stimson was "looking at the whole thing very sanely" and not contemplating any such "precipitate action" as in 1929. Castle told Stanley K. Hornbeck, chief of the division of Far Eastern affairs, that Japanese control of Manchuria might prove to be the least of possible evils, and Hornbeck "ruefully agreed." [8]

Even the isolationist leaders of the Senate could find little fault with the State Department during these weeks of watchful inactivity. True, the irrepressible Hiram Johnson sarcastically inquired: "Where now is the bugle call Mr. Stimson trumpeted so loudly and prematurely but a short time ago, when Russia and China were making faces at each other? Where is the League of Nations? Where is the sacrosanct Kellogg Pact?" [9] But William E. Borah, chairman of the Senate committee on foreign relations, agreed with Stimson "throughout" when Stimson took him aside to

explain how he was co-operating with the League while preventing it from "leaving any baby" on his "doorstep." Stimson learned with satisfaction that Lord Reading, the British Foreign Secretary, was "taking very much the same policy ...and not getting excited the way they did down in Geneva." [10] The *Times* of London, spokesman for the Foreign Office, complimented Stimson on his "tactful" diplomacy. Tokyo as well as London applauded American policy, and so did most of the rest of the world except Geneva—and Nanking.[11]

From Nanking came demands for a stronger stand by the United States, pleas for action by all the signatories of the Kellogg Pact, threats of a raprochement with Russia as China's only alternative. All this did not swerve Stimson in the slightest from his adopted course. The League having adopted a resolution asking "both parties" in Manchuria to restore "normal relations," he merely advised the Nanking government that time must be allowed for Japan and China to carry out the League's request. And at length he reaffirmed his official attitude in a conversation with the Chinese *chargé d'affaires* in Washington: "We have not attempted to go into the question of right and wrong.... we are not taking sides.... we are 'playing no favorites.' " [12]

That was on October 8. On the very same day Stimson's thinking and American policy reached a turning point. The change was precipitated by the news that Japanese planes were bombing the city of Chinchow in southern Manchuria, far from the railroad zone. From the "dis-

---

[6] Stimson to Hugh Wilson (telegram), Sept. 23, 1931, in *Papers Relating to the Foreign Relations of the United States, 1931* (Washington, 1946), III, 49.

[7] Stimson diary, Sept. 24, 1931.

[8] Castle diary, Sept. 29, 1931.

[9] Quoted in Drew Pearson and Constantine Brown, *The American Diplomatic Game* (New York, 1935), p. 308.

[10] Stimson diary, Sept. 25, Oct. 6, 1931.

[11] London *Times*, Sept. 26, 1931, and Tokyo *Jiji*, Oct. 1, 1931, both quoted in Smith, *Manchurian Crisis*, pp. 44–45, 66–67.

[12] Memorandum of conversation between T. V. Soong and the American consul-general in Nanking, Oct. 2, 1931; Stimson to the American minister in China, Oct. 7, 1931; memorandum by Hornbeck, Oct. 8, 1931, in *Foreign Relations, 1931*, III, 104–106, 136, 137–39.

quieting telegrams" he read, Stimson had to conclude that, for all Debuchi's promises, the Japanese army was expanding rather than contracting its operations. He told himself, "I am afraid we have got to take a firm ground and aggressive stand toward Japan." So far as he was concerned, the policy of "playing no favorites" was no sooner stated than, by the force of events, it had to be abandoned.[13] Here his views and those of the President began to diverge a bit. When (October 9) he reported to the cabinet the new and ominous turn in Manchurian events, he felt that Hoover was not sufficiently impressed. The President, as Stimson noted, did not seem to realize quite what it meant "to have Japan run amok and play havoc with its peace treaties." Instead, the President insisted that we must be careful "not to get ourselves into a humiliating position, in case Japan refused to do anything about what he called our scraps of paper or paper treaties."

As Stimson saw it, the time had come to take the third and ultimate step among the alternatives he earlier had outlined— that is, to consider action under the Nine-Power Treaty or the Kellogg Pact. The latter he now put first, thinking that he would "probably push forward the Kellogg Pact" and hold the Nine-Power Treaty "in reserve" to facilitate an eventual peace conference between China and Japan. He decided, however, "not to initiate action" but to wait for the League.[14] When he discussed his plan with his advisers, Castle and Hornbeck, he got their concurrence.[15] And when

he talked again with the President (October 10) he found him more than willing to go along. Hoover "even went so far as to say that we should authorize our man in Switzerland to sit with the Council." This suggestion had come originally from Norman Davis, head of the American delegation to the preparatory disarmament commission in Geneva, and Stimson had dismissed it as one of Davis' "rather wild propositions." He now welcomed the idea.[16]

The United States must be represented officially on the Council of the League! Having arrived independently at the same bold conclusion, Hoover and Stimson together determined to carry it out in the most cautious way possible so as not to offend public opinion whether American or Japanese. Hence the invitation must appear to come unprompted from the League, and the business of the extraordinary session must be confined strictly to the Kellogg Pact. When the Council began to discuss the invitation Stimson became alarmed at the Japanese opposition. "It lines us up vis-a-vis Japan," he thought, "just the position that I have been trying to avoid." In cabinet he raised the question (October 16) whether at the last minute the United States should not decline the Council's invitation. But he discovered that "the President was very strong that we should keep right on. He has been first-rate throughout . . . taking a clear and unequivocal stand." [17]

And so, despite Japan's dissenting vote, the American consul in Geneva, Prentiss Gilbert, sat at the Council table in an open meeting and then in a secret session to discuss the invocation of the Kellogg Pact. The conferees decided, on October 17, that the Council should call

---

[13] Stimson diary, Oct. 8, 1931. See Paul H. Clyde, "The Diplomacy of 'Playing No Favorites'; Secretary Stimson and Manchuria, 1931," *Mississippi Valley Historical Review,* XXXV (1948), 187–202.

[14] Stimson diary, Oct. 9, 10, 1931. See also Stimson and Bundy, *On Active Service,* pp. 232–33.

[15] "Stimson's ideas as to what should be done seem to me excellent," Castle wrote, but Hornbeck apparently was less enthusiastic. "I must

ask Hornbeck to try his darndest to work in the Secretary's manner and not stir him up as he did yesterday." Castle diary, Oct. 10, 1931.

[16] Stimson diary, Sept. 23, Oct. 10, 1931. See also Stimson, *Far Eastern Crisis,* p. 60.

[17] Stimson diary, Oct. 10, 13, 15, 16, 1931.

upon all the signatories to remind China and Japan of their obligations under the pact of peace. This decision, with a representative of the United States participating, climaxed the first phase of American policy making with respect to the Manchurian crisis.

The rest was anticlimax. As soon as the decision had been made, Stimson "thought it advisable to terminate the outward appearance at least of Gilbert's connection with the Council." Castle and Hornbeck concurred. But the British and the French protested against the withdrawal of Gilbert: it might look like a gesture disapproving the League's action. Reluctantly Stimson concluded to "let him go on sitting at the damned table" on the condition that he "keep his mouth shut" to show that he was no longer a participant, only an observer. Then, to re-emphasize the League's initiative, Stimson delayed sending his note on the Kellogg Pact to China and Japan until three days after Great Britain, France, and other League members had sent theirs. And when the Council passed a resolution calling upon Japan to evacuate Chinese territory by November 16, he hesitated to endorse it. Some of its points he thought were "unwise" and might "lead to a deadlock"; his "problem" was to compose for Japan a statement which would "back up the things which we believe in and back their [the League's] position up in general" without committing this country to the "unwise things." He accepted as the basis of his note on the League resolution a draft prepared by Castle, who "had rather cleverly met the difficulties which faced us of putting our statements in an inoffensive form." This note omitted any reference to the November 16 deadline, the nub of the League's resolution, and was not communicated to Japan until two weeks after the League had acted.[18]

So the United States followed the League—at a distance and with qualifications—in making a verbal application of the Kellogg Pact to the Manchurian affair. This was Stimson's policy, and it was also Hoover's. The two men had agreed upon each careful step, but the one was willing to consider going farther, and the other was beginning to fear that they had gone too far already. As Castle observed on November 4, after lunching with the President, "he wants to get completely out of the League connection and thinks it might have been wise, politically, to make Stimson keep out."[19]

The assumption underlying American policy at the start of the Manchurian crisis did not remain tenable for long—the assumption that forbearance by the United States would enable the Japanese moderates to retain power and check the militarists. As early as November 7, 1931, Stimson observed, "It looks now as if the military element in Japan might get control." On November 19, after hearing that Japanese troops had taken Tsitsihar, in far northern Manchuria, he inferred that "the Japanese government which we have been dealing with is no longer in control; the situation is in the hands of virtually mad dogs." On December 11 he imparted to the cabinet the news that the Wakatsuki-Shidehara ministry had actually fallen, and he pointed out the "imminent danger of a new movement by the Japanese army." On January 2, 1932, he learned that the army had occupied Chinchow and so had brought "the Manchurian matter up to a final climax": the conquest of Manchuria was an accomplished fact. Meanwhile, as soon as they foresaw this as the probable outcome, he and Hoover had begun to con-

[18] The quotations are from *ibid.*, Oct. 19, 20, 29, Nov. 3, 1931. See also Stimson, *Far Eastern Crisis*, p. 60; Pearson and Brown, pp. 312–16; Smith, *Manchurian Crisis*, pp. 92–127; Clyde, pp. 196–98.
[19] Castle diary, Nov. 4, 1931.

sider "eventualities" and ways to deal with them.[20] The upshot was the announcement of the famous nonrecognition doctrine. That was the work of both the President and the Secretary, the one proposing the general principle and the other developing and applying it, but before concurring in it they debated another possible line of action—co-operation with the League in the exertion of economic pressure upon Japan.

Stimson first broached this subject to Hoover, rather tentatively, on October 17, while the American representative was sitting with the League Council. At that time some of the delegates in Geneva were thinking, unofficially, of the possibility of the League's resorting to economic sanctions. The question arose whether the United States would co-operate, at least passively, by refraining from the use of its navy to maintain the freedom of the seas against a League blockade. Even before the Manchurian crisis this question had come up repeatedly in a theoretical form, and Hoover always had refused to yield on American neutral rights, while Stimson had inclined to the belief that in an actual test the United States would not employ its navy to frustrate concerted action against an aggressor.[21] Now that the issue apparently was becoming a prac-

tical one, Stimson faced the problem of making his position acceptable to the President, as well as to the American people, and he thought he had hit upon a brilliantly simple solution when someone suggested to him the relevancy of the Kellogg Pact. Let the pact be the touchstone: the United States could judge other nations by it and refuse to interfere with sanctions against a violator.

When Stimson recommended this to the President, it provoked a long argument, but Hoover "promised finally that he would think it over with an open mind." [22] After thinking it over, he addressed the entire cabinet with a statement in which he limited American action to "moral pressures" alone and ruled out economic and military sanctions as "roads to war." [23] Though not a specific reply to Stimson's proposal, the President's blast seemed to impress the Secretary of State. "I concur with him as to the danger of a blockade leading to war," he told his diary (November 7) after Hoover once more had spoken against the use of economic pressure. Again, in answer to Secretary of War Patrick J. Hurley, who insisted in cabinet that "the Japanese were going to seize Manchuria anyhow," unless stopped by force, Stimson averred that "the policy of imposing sanctions of force" had been "rejected by America in its rejection of the League of Nations." Hoover backed him up "very fully." [24]

Then the sudden extension of warfare in Manchuria, culminating in the capture of Tsitsihar on November 17, induced some change of heart in both the President and the Secretary of State. The move of the Japanese army looked like a defiant reply to the League resolution calling for withdrawal from Chinese territory by November 16. The

[20] Stimson diary, Nov. 7, 19, Dec. 11, 1931; Jan. 2, 1932.
[21] In the discussions of naval limitations in 1929 and 1930 Hoover opposed food blockades as violating the freedom of the seas, and he refused to consider a consultative pact which might bind the United States to co-operate, at least passively, in a British blockade against an aggressor designated by the League. Stimson favored such a consultative pact. He also told Prime Minister Ramsay MacDonald, August 7, 1931: "...I could not believe that any American Government would seek to use our Navy to enforce an extreme doctrine of neutrality under which American merchants were seeking to trade with an aggressor nation so declared by the League and against whom Britain and British public opinion were sanctioning the use of the British Navy." Hoover Memoirs, II, 345–48; Stimson diary, Aug. 7, 1931. See also New York Times, Mar. 27, 1930.

[22] Stimson diary, Oct. 17, 1931.
[23] Wilbur and Hyde, pp. 600–601; Myers, Foreign Policies of Herbert Hoover, pp. 156–59; Hoover Memoirs, II, 368–70.
[24] Stimson diary, Nov. 9, 13, 1931.

Council now reconvened in Paris, and Stimson prevailed upon Hoover to send Ambassador Charles G. Dawes there from London to be accessible to its members, though not to join their sittings. Dawes reported to Stimson that the League now would probably consider sanctions and that even Sir John Simon, the new British Foreign Secretary, was "inclined to think" that "the League should go to the limit of its powers." Stimson informed Dawes that an embargo meant war and therefore the United States could not aid in enforcing one, but he assured Dawes that the American fleet would not interfere with it. Hoover, who struck Stimson as "quiet but determined," approved the message to Dawes. "The President added," according to Stimson, "that he thought I could tell him [Dawes] again that the sympathy of our people undoubtedly would be with the embargo, and that there might be a private embargo put on here by voluntary action in refusing to trade with Japan." [25]

For the President, this was going pretty far, and yet Stimson soon began to wonder whether it was far enough. On November 27 he proposed to Hoover that they reconsider the question of American participation in an embargo. He argued, first, that sanctions against Japan would be brief if all the powers, including the United States, joined in ("She would have to surrender very quickly"); second, "that the militaristic elements in Japan could learn only through suffering and not by the sanctions of public opinion"; third, that it would be a tremendous blow to world peace "if Japan really gets away with this." The President, however, refused to reverse himself. He still thought of sanctions as the road to war; his Secre-

tary was beginning to think of sanctions as a way to peace, though he admitted to his diary, "I have not yet made up my own mind on the subject." [26]

Stimson, thus undecided, fluctuated during December between the President's position and that of the "many people" who, he said, were "getting impatient and urging drastic steps or words" upon him. Among these people were his closest personal advisers in the State Department: his special assistant, Allen T. Klots, and the Assistant Secretary of State, James Grafton Rogers. Hornbeck inclined at times toward these extremists, but Castle remained the advocate of circumspection. The four of them, with Stimson presiding, took part in a "vigorous meeting" at Woodley, his Washington residence, on December 6, while in Geneva the League Council was considering not sanctions but an investigation (ultimately to be carried out by the Lytton Commission). The question at Woodley was what "the next step" for the United States should be if the League plans for a neutral commission fell through. Three of the experts, Castle alone dissenting, favored "economic measures," but, as Stimson noted, "We all agreed that if possible action should come from the other nations first." On the whole the Secretary himself was noncommittal at the meeting, though he confided to his diary that Hornbeck went "too far against Japan" for him. Castle assumed that the Secretary leaned in Castle's own direction. After this conference Stimson saw Hoover at the White House and was surprised to find "he was not absolutely and to the last against a boycott." The President felt, however, that we would have to base the action on the Nine-Power Treaty and "not go into it behind the League." Accordingly Stimson began hopefully to think of planning a nine-power confer-

[25] Dawes to Stimson, Nov. 18, 1931; memorandum of transatlantic telephone conversation between Stimson and Dawes, Nov. 19, 1931, in *Foreign Relations, 1931*, III, 484, 488–98; Stimson diary, Nov. 19, 1931.

[26] Stimson diary, Nov. 27, 1931.

ence, then became discouraged when the President in his special message to Congress on foreign affairs, December 10, omitted a "warning sentence" which Stimson wanted him to include. Senator Borah decried the current "talk of the use of force or intervention," while the Scripps-Howard newspapers ,were "pounding the government for not being more aggressive towards Japan." Stimson finally invited Roy Howard and his chief editorial writer to lunch and tried to make them "see the folly of taking an aggressive step" at that time.[27]

Casting about for an alternative to economic pressure, the President weeks earlier had begun to make suggestions, one of which was to lead eventually to the nonrecognition announcement. On November 7 he proposed to Stimson that the American government recall its ambassador from Japan but, at the same time, to make the protest a strictly peaceful one, issue a public statement disclaiming all thought of war. Then he got what he considered a better idea. "He is beginning to swing against the idea of withdrawing the Ambassador," Stimson recorded as of November 9, "and thinks his main weapon is to give an announcement that if the treaty [presumably to be made between Japan and China] is made under military pressure we will not recognize it or avow it." At once Stimson discussed this proposal with his advisers. Castle favored it, especially if the announcement were made "together with the rest of the world," though he cautioned the Secretary that "even then we must be careful" because, "if the resultant treaties should be eminently fair," it might prove embarrassing to refuse to recognize them. Hornbeck opposed the plan, arguing that Secretary Bryan had tried it in 1915 without re-

sults. But Stimson himself thought that, even as used in 1915, by the United States alone, nonrecognition had become "one of the potent forces" that finally brought about a Far Eastern settlement at the Washington conference of 1921–22. Now, if the "disavowal" were "made by all of the countries, it ought to have a very potent effect" in bringing about an "ultimate solution," which would "of course involve elements of compromise." [28]

Stimson delayed acting on the nonrecognition plan, partly because almost to the last he had lingering hopes that the Japanese might yet reverse themselves in Manchuria; [29] partly because he was waiting to see what the League would do, especially with regard to sanctions; and partly because some American experts on the Far East, even more cautious than the President, considered the plan too drastic. One of those counseling caution was Stimson's old friend, former law partner, and highly respected mentor in international affairs—Elihu Root. "Allen Klots brought me back interesting news from Mr. Root," Stimson noted on November 14. "Rather to my surprise Mr. Root is more sympathetic with Japan then with China; and he is very fearful lest we do not recognize her real claims to Manchuria." [30] Nevertheless the Secretary continued to ponder and to elaborate the nonrecognition idea, associating with it the Nine-Power Treaty and the Kellogg Pact, and planning to reveal, simultaneously with its announcement, some of the documents bearing on the Manchurian affair. As he informed Dawes in Paris, Novem-

---

[27] *Ibid.*, Dec. 6, 8, 9, 1931; Castle diary, Dec. 7, 1931; New York *Times*, Nov. 22, 1931, quoted in Smith, *Manchurian Crisis*, pp. 179–81.

[28] Stimson diary, Nov. 7, 9, 1931; Castle diary, Nov. 9, 1931.

[29] As late as November 30, 1931, Stimson said in his diary: "... the Japanese Ambassador came in with some more news from Manchuria, which was pretty good this time. I think now the Japanese don't intend to let their army do any more solo work, and I think they will go ahead and make a settlement."

[30] Stimson diary, Nov. 14, 1931.

ber 19, ". . . the only act we see we could do would be to publish the papers and the correspondence, announce our disapproval of the action of Japan, possibly calling it a violation of these treaties and then announce as we did in 1915 that we would not recognize any treaties that were created under military force." [31] By December 2 he was almost ready to cable Dawes a "final statement" warning Japan about the refusal to recognize. But his assistant Klots, after consulting three State Department experts, reported back to him that they all advised holding up the message for fear "it would make Japan so recalcitrant in any future negotiations over Manchuria that it would simply invite trouble." He "put aside the cable for the present." [32]

A month later, January 2, 1932, when he got news of the Japanese occupation of Chinchow, which brought "the Manchurian matter up to a final climax," Stimson suddenly decided to act. The next morning, a Sunday, he arose at six "with my mind rather clarified on what I wanted to do. I went down to my library and there wrote out in long hand a short note to the Chinese Government and to the Japanese Government, based largely upon the note of 1915. Previously we had been thinking of a longer note. . . ." In the evening he showed his draft to Klots and the foreign policy specialists Hunter Miller, Ransford Miller, and George· H. Blakeslee. "They were staggered by it at first because it was so different from what we had been thinking [of], but they gradually came around to it. . . ." On the following day, January 4, after conferring with Rogers, Klots, and Hornbeck, he took a revised draft of the new and relatively pointed note, together with a copy of the old and more diffuse one, to the White House, where he showed Hoover the short version first. Hoover

approved it. Stimson "pointed out the dangers . . . if the Japanese called our position . . . and tried to annex Manchuria," but Hoover was "willing to take that risk." [33]

The President approved, but the Secretary still faced some opposition within the State Department. In a "brief final session on the draft of the note," on January 6, Castle was in general enthusiastic and especially liked "bringing the Kellogg Pact in," but he objected to a sentence which made the United States as a signatory of the Nine-Power Treaty appear, incorrectly, to "guarantee" (rather than merely "respect") the integrity of China, and the wording was changed.[34] Hornbeck not only objected to the wording—he thought "does not intend" to recognize was better than "will not"—but, according to Stimson, he also "fought rather tenaciously against a definite statement" at all. "I thought his words were a little too weak," Stimson said in his diary, "although I consented to making the note a little bit softer than it had been originally." [35]

Next day, January 7, 1932, copies of the note went off to China and Japan. The essence of it was as follows:

. . . the American Government deems it to be its duty to notify both the Government of the Chinese Republic and the Imperial Japanese Government that it can not admit the legality of any situation de facto nor does it intend to recognize any treaty or agreement entered into between those governments, or agents thereof, which may impair the treaty rights of the United States or its citizens in China, including those which relate to the sovereignty, the independence, or the territorial and administrative integrity of the Republic of China, commonly known as the open-door policy; and that it does not intend to recognize any situation, treaty, or agreement which may be brought about by means contrary to the covenants and obligations of the pact of Paris of August 27, 1928, to which treaty

[31] Foreign Relations, 1931, III, 496–97.
[32] Stimson diary, Dec. 2, 3, 1931.
[33] Ibid., Jan. 2, 3, 4, 1932.
[34] Castle diary, Jan. 7, 1932.
[35] Stimson diary, Jan. 6, 1932.

both China and Japan, as well as the United States, are parties.[36]

This was a unilateral *démarche* by the United States and not a joint announcement with other powers such as Stimson at first had envisaged. After the sending of the notes, however, and almost as an afterthought, he did carry out Castle's last-minute suggestion of inviting the other signatories of the Nine-Power Treaty (but not those of the Kellogg Pact) to dispatch similar notes.[37]

The *Times* of London published the Foreign Office reply of January 9 and endorsed it in a sarcastic editorial. The Foreign Office referred to Japanese statements describing Japan as "the champion in Manchuria of the principle of equal opportunity and the open door," then declared that "in view of these statements" his majesty's government had "not considered it necessary to address any formal note to the Japanese Government on the lines of the American Government's note." Of this rebuff, Stimson observed that "it was not at all unexpected so far as I was concerned." True, he had told the British ambassador two days in advance what he was going to do, and had "hoped that his government would take a similar stand." On the night of January 7, however, he learned from the French ambassador that Great Britain was refusing to join in a French protest against Japan's taking Chinchow. "So, therefore, No. 1 is backing out," he inferred, but he did not blame "poor old England," beset as she was by "troubles with India" and "financial troubles at home."

The American reaction to the notes was most encouraging to him. He tactfully explained to Senator Borah that he "had not consulted him beforehand" because he "did not want to dump the

responsibility on him," and Borah responded by praising the *démarche* in general and in detail. Then the two men made arrangements for the delivery to the Senate of the State Department's correspondence on Manchuria.[38]

Though the publication of the correspondence was intended to "educate" American public opinion, Stimson, for the time being, looked upon the nonrecognition warning itself as a step toward "the eventual settlement of Manchuria by negotiation" and not as a step toward forceful measures. So he could not agree when Senator Claude A. Swanson of the naval affairs committee commented on the unusually "strong language" of the notes, then "suggested that we move the fleet to Hawaii, merely as a demonstration." Stimson remarked to the Senator that *that* would be unusually "strong." And to Representative Cordell Hull, who was promoting a bill "to give the President discretionary power to put an embargo on exports on [*sic*] nations which violate the Pact of Paris," the Secretary said "it would be very dangerous to have it brought up just now, because everybody would discuss Japan." [39] Within a few days his attitude was to change rather abruptly with the march of events in the Far East.

A new phase of the policy debate within the American government began during the last week of January, 1932, when Japanese troops moved against the Chinese in and around Shanghai.

As soon as it appeared that thet Japanese were going to attack in China proper, to break the Chinese boycott against Japan, Stimson took the lead in demanding vigorous action by the United States and Great Britain. He was urged on by his law partner, Bronston Winthrop, who was "quite het up about the

[36] *Foreign Relations of the United States: Diplomatic Papers, 1932* (Washington, 1948), III, 8.
[37] Stimson diary, Jan. 6, 7, 1932.

[38] London *Times,* Jan. 11, 1932; Stimson diary, Jan. 7, 9, 1932.
[39] *Ibid.,* Jan. 14, 21, 1932.

Japanese threat against Shanghai" and wanted "to see the British and American fleets lined up there against any attempt to overawe the Chinese or to prevent a real honest boycott." When, however, the Secretary called in Hornbeck, Klots, Castle, and a couple of other State Department advisers (January 25) he found them all so hesitant that he "had to put on the pressure."[40] Castle, who noted that the Secretary was "in a high state of excitement," agreed with him that Japan had less excuse in Shanghai than in Manchuria but thought that Japan did have a real grievance in the boycott, enforced by arson and murder, and in the general disorder and lack of a stable government in China.[41] Even Navy Secretary Charles F. Adams and Admiral William V. Pratt were slow to see things as Stimson did. "They were not alive to the situation," he observed after a conversation with them, "but became so after the talk got on." The President himself, by contrast, was "thoroughly alive" from the start and quickly endorsed Stimson's "proposition" embracing a joint Anglo-American protest to Japan and the movement of British and American naval forces to Shanghai. Stimson then presented his case to the British ambassador, Sir Ronald Lindsay.[42]

After the Japanese had launched their threatened move against Shanghai, Hoover did as Stimson had proposed: he quickly sent men and ships to join the British at the scene of fighting, and he later reinforced the American bases in Hawaii and the Philippines. He was willing enough to use the navy, but his purpose was considerably narrower than Stimson's. His own object was "to protect the lives of Americans"; "strict orders were issued that our forces should

confine themselves to the task of protecting Americans."[43] And Castle believed, "This is, of course, for the protection of American life and property, seriously endangered, in all probability more from the Chinese than from the Japanese."[44] Stimson, however, had other ends in view. When he first spoke to Sir Ronald Lindsay on the subject, he did say that "our Consuls up the River were calling for additional war vessels because they anticipated the possibility that we would have to rescue and remove our nationals." He also said he "did not intend any threat against Japan; our Asiatic squadron was not large enough to constitute a threat." But he added that the presence of American and British warships would have a "beneficial effect" on Japan, would "strengthen the hands of Chiang Kai-Shek," and would help to salvage the Anglo-American policy of the Open Door.[45]

In the cabinet discussions preceding and accompanying the dispatch of naval forces, Stimson made it perfectly clear that, unlike Hoover, he wished to bluff and threaten Japan. He said (January 26) he "realized the importance of having Japan fear this country" and was glad it happened that "the fleet was going to have its battle practice this time off Hawaii." War Secretary Hurley, opposing further notes and protests and deprecating nonrecognition, argued that we should put up or shut up, should either use our fleet (along with the British) to restrain Japan or else say and do nothing. The President stood in between the two secretaries. For Hurley's benefit he warned of the "folly of getting into a war with Japan on this subject" and "said he would fight for Continental United States as far as anybody, but would not fight for Asia." Turning to

---

[40] *Ibid.*, Jan. 23, 25, 1932.
[41] Castle diary, Jan. 25, 1932.
[42] Stimson diary, Jan. 25, 1932. See also Stimson and Bundy, *On Active Service*, pp. 241–42.

[43] *Hoover Memoirs*, II, 374; Myers, *Foreign Policies of Herbert Hoover*, p. 162.
[44] Castle diary, Feb. 2, 1932.
[45] Stimson diary, Jan. 25, 1932.

Stimson, he complimented him on his mobilization of public opinion behind the Kellogg Pact in 1929 and his non-recognition notes of January 7, 1932, but refused to approve a policy of threat. Stimson reflected afterward upon "the great difference and difficulty" which he was having with the President. "He has not got the slightest element of even the fairest kind of bluff." At the next cabinet meeting (January 29) Stimson requested "that there should be no talk or action by anyone which should indicate that we were not going to use any weapon that we might have, whether it be the fleet or the boycott." [46]

Instead of heeding this request, Hoover turned to conciliatory methods of ending the fighting in Shanghai. At the end of January he suggested that he and King George appeal publicly to the emperor of Japan, but Prime Minister Ramsay MacDonald replied that this would be contrary to royal etiquette. Next morning, February 1, according to Castle's record, "the President had a new idea which was to make joint representations to the Chinese and Japanese to stop fighting and to open direct negotiations with neutral observers." [47] After Great Britain, France, and Italy had joined the United States in this mediation offer, the President spoke out to show that it was not intended as a means of bluffing or coercing Japan. "He came out with one of his statements that we weren't going to fight," Stimson later complained, and he thereby "spoiled the impression" which Stimson had desired to make.[48]

At the moment Stimson was thinking much in terms of naval power, little in terms of economic pressure. When China appealed to the League under Article XV of the Covenant, talk of sanctions was revived in Geneva, and discussions of an arms embargo began "making a good deal of a rumpus," as Stimson put it, in the House committee on foreign affairs. Again, as with Congressman Hull a few weeks earlier, he tried (February 13) to discourage consideration of such a law. He instructed Rogers to tell Representative Linthicum, "...we have a treaty with Japan which really prevents an embargo, and to denounce that treaty ...involves a very serious question because it would terminate all our port arrangements and everything else with Japan." And when an emissary came to him with a petition sponsored by A. Lawrence Lowell and endorsed by Newton D. Baker, "asking us not to block the way for the sanctions of the League by refusing to refrain from trade with Japan in case the League leads the way," he replied that the League members obviously were *not* leading the way; "none of them were willing to apply sanctions, whatever we did." He reflected to himself, "It is very curious now to have a peace man trying to urge action which normally leads to war." For the moment, he could see no point in trying to cooperate with the League. He was returning to his "old view" that the United States could not "dispense with police force; and the only police force I have got to depend upon today is the American Navy." [49]

Comparing the Japanese attack on Shanghai with the German invasion of Belgium, he remembered "how outraged we were when President Wilson did nothing to show the shame that we felt," and he was "anxious that Mr. Hoover should not be put in the same position." So he wished to do something to "sum up the situation officially" and "put the situation morally in its right place." To his "relief" he found that Hoover was "very sympathetic" with this particular

[46] *Ibid.*, Jan. 26, 29, 1932. See also Stimson and Bundy, *On Active Service*, pp. 243–45.
[47] Castle diary, Jan. 30, Feb. 1, 1932.
[48] Stimson diary, Mar. 29, 1932.

[49] *Ibid.*, Feb. 13, 18, 1932.

proposal. When he went farther, however, and spoke his mind to the President about the need for "leadership" and for avoiding Wilson's timid example, the two men "had a set-to back and forth." And Stimson later learned to his dismay that Hoover lacked "appreciation of the real nobility of the traditional and standard American doctrine towards China of the 'Open Door.'" He himself appreciated it so much that he even regretted to see the "prospect of the cessation of hostilities" in Shanghai. "I am unhappy," he confessed to his diary, "because if they cease they will cease without America having said her word on the morality of this great situation." [50]

What he had specifically in mind, on and after February 8, was a restatement of the nonrecognition doctrine. This time he intended to emphasize the Nine-Power Treaty rather than the Kellogg Pact, and he hoped to persuade Great Britain to join with the United States. "He has been working on a new note, based on the Nine Power Treaty," Castle observed on February 12, "which really only re-iterated the point in our note of January 7th that we will not recognize treaties resulting from the present military operations." After this note had "occupied him exclusively for a week," however, he gave it up because the British government, as he learned in mid-February, preferred to act with the League.[51]

Looking to the future, he began to consider what the United States could or would do in case the League should ever proceed against Japan with either an economic or a diplomatic boycott. Having changed his own mind again about an embargo, he tried to change the President's mind, without success. But he did persuade Hoover at least "to intimate in some way to the League," as Castle had it from Stimson, "that if that

august body finds Japan guilty of creating a state of war we will go along with the other powers in withdrawing our Ambassador." Stimson was encouraged. "This," he thought, "is a long step towards combativeness for the President."

Meanwhile he still longed to have his say on the "morality of the situation," to express his "sentiments on the Open Door without making a speech. The British have pocketed me on the note method of doing it. I do not dare to send a note on the Nine-Power Treaty for fear of the yellow-bellied responses that I will get from some of the countries." On February 21 Rogers suggested that the Secretary "might write a letter to somebody." And after a conference at Woodley that day Castle noted that "it was finally decided that the Secretary should write a letter to Borah, if possible, setting forth the ideas of this Government as to the Open Door, etc. in a fashion which would get public sentiment behind us in this country and at the same time show the League how far we were willing to go." [52]

Stimson's Borah letter, drafted with the aid of Hornbeck, gave a long exposition of the Open Door policy, denied the Japanese contention that the Nine-Power Treaty needed to be revised, reaffirmed the nonrecognition principle, and recommended that "the other governments of the world" adopt it, so as to express a "caveat" which would "effectively bar the legality hereafter of any right or title sought to be obtained by pressure or treaty violations." The letter also added a new and distinctive element to the American case against Japan. This was the contention that the three Washington conference treaties of 1922—the Nine-Power, Five-Power, and Four-Power pacts—were "interdependent and interrelated." The United States, Stimson argued, had agreed to limit its

[50] Ibid., Feb. 8, 18, 20, 1932.
[51] Castle diary, Feb. 12, 15, 16, 19, 1932.

[52] Ibid., Feb. 21, 1932; Stimson diary, Feb. 21, 1932.

battleship construction and to leave its bases at Guam and the Philippines without further fortification in return for Japan's agreeing to respect the Open Door and the integrity of China. He indicated that, if Japan was to persist in violating Chinese integrity, the United States would consider itself released from the limitations on its navy and its Pacific fortifications.[53]

Castle, "after a hasty reading of the letter," gave it his "wholehearted approval" and said to himself, "That is the kind of thing which the Secretary, a lawyer, can do admirably." But Hoover, when Stimson showed the draft to him, "suggested putting in a sentence which would relate to the public opinion of the world as the sanction behind our note of January 7th and behind the action which the Borah letter proposes." Stimson "persuaded him to cut it out" with the argument that the sentence would "be used to indicate that under no possibility would we use any sanction of a boycott." Stimson "preferred to leave the Japanese guessing on that point still." [54]

The letter was dated February 23 and published on February 24. Next day Stimson went to show the President a batch of congratulatory cables he had received. "It was lucky I did," he thought. Hoover "was proposing to tell the people of the United States that under no circumstances would we go to war. He has been rather frightened by the reaction of the big Navy people to my letter . . . without stopping to remember that the reaction of the peace people had been equally favorable." Stimson told Hoover that a no-war announcement "would make people think he did not endorse my letter instead of endorsing it most thoroughly as he had and it

would remove the last little lingering doubt in the minds of Japan as to the possibility of our doing something which would be serious against them." And again on the following day Stimson talked Hoover out of making a public statement to the effect that the United States would use absolutely nothing but *moral* sanctions.[55]

The Borah letter, Stimson said in retrospect, was intended for "at least five unnamed addressees" and was designed to "encourage China, enlighten the American public, exhort the League, stir up the British, and warn Japan." [56] It achieved at least a partial success, though at first, on March 3, Stimson felt "slapped in the face" when he saw London press reports indicating that the British were "not going to follow our action in regard to recognition." He thought, "This is a singular and rather startling eventuality in view of the attitude which Sir John Simon has been taking to me over the telephone from Geneva." Then, within a few days, Sir John himself began to champion nonrecognition before the League, and on March 11 the Assembly adopted a resolution incorporating the principle.[57]

But Stimson had much more in mind than merely nonrecognition when he thought of encouraging China, enlightening the American public, exhorting the League, stirring up the British, and warning Japan. He was now looking toward the eventual use of economic sanctions. "If a situation should ultimately arise when the American government felt it necessary to recommend the imposition, in cooperation with the rest of the world, of an embargo upon Japanese goods," he wrote in 1936, "I believed that such a measure would have more chance of

[53] Stimson, *Far Eastern Crisis*, pp. 166–75; Stimson and Bundy, *On Active Service*, pp. 246–56.
[54] Castle diary, Feb. 23, 1932; Stimson diary, Feb. 24, 1932.

[55] *Ibid.*, Feb. 25, 26, 1932.
[56] Stimson, *Far Eastern Crisis*, p. 175; Stimson and Bundy, *On Active Service*, p. 249.
[57] Stimson diary, Mar. 3, 1932; Stimson and Bundy, *On Active Service*, p. 257.

being adopted by Congress if it were recommended following the invocation of the Nine Power Treaty than if it had been recommended solely by the League of Nations." [58] And he was also looking, more immediately, toward the use or at least the threat of American naval power. Though he protested that he "had been very careful not to make any threats" in the Borah letter,[59] his reference to the interdependence of the Washington conference treaties clearly implied the threat of a new naval race, if not actually a war, in the Pacific. To him, though not to Hoover, the publication of the letter as well as the naval display at Shanghai was a far-seeing move in a game of diplomatic bluff and power politics.

Peace came to Shanghai early in May, the Japanese withdrawing in frustration, which Stimson attributed largely to his own policy of bluff.[60] In Manchuria, however, they proceeded with the creation of a puppet state. Throughout that spring and summer of 1932, as they consolidated their newly won position in Asia, the policy of the United States became increasingly ambivalent.

While the Shanghai incident was still dragging on, Stimson began to think in terms of an eventual Japanese-American war. There was "shaping up an issue between the two great theories of civilization," he believed, and it was "almost impossible that there should not be an armed clash between two such different civilizations." [61] Hornbeck, too, predicted that the conquest of Manchuria would lead to the conquest of China and "eventually to war" between Japan and the United States. "And if this might lead to war in the future," queried Castle, "is that any less bad than to take

steps with regard to Manchuria which would lead to war now?" [62] In the cabinet (April 5) Stimson talked at length on "the challenge which Japan had made to the civilization of the West," and ended with "a warning that the President had better keep his powder dry." The Secretaries of War and the Navy seconded him, but the President was not impressed. He only said something about "phantasmagorias." [63]

War sometime—maybe soon. Stimson thought there was a "ticklish situation in Shanghai and Tokyo," and "at any moment an accident might occur which would set the whole world on fire." And so he became concerned about instant as well as ultimate readiness. He consulted Admiral Pratt about the relative states of preparedness of the Japanese and American navies, Chief of Staff Douglas MacArthur about the maintenance of American troops in China, and banker Thomas W. Lamont about the "financial susceptibility" of Japan in case of war. He was "much alarmed about the present situation of the Navy," which appeared to be "more unequal" than he had thought "to meeting Japan," and he told Hoover so. "The President said that was all the more reason for not having an offensive Navy," Stimson noted. "I said I wasn't talking about an offensive but a defensive Navy." [64]

Hoover's attitude depressed Stimson, especially after Norman Davis returned from Geneva and called at the State Department (March 29). Davis told Stimson that Hoover's disclaimer of any intention to fight, at the time of the joint representations to Japan early in February, had left a very unfortunate impression at the League capital. He advised the Secretary to go in person to Geneva, presumably to correct that bad impression. According to Stimson's diary,

[58] Stimson, Far Eastern Crisis, pp. 161–62.
[59] Stimson diary, Feb. 25, 1932.
[60] Stimson, Far Eastern Crisis, pp. 137–38; Stimson and Bundy, On Active Service, p. 242.
[61] Stimson diary, Mar. 9, 1932. See also Stimson and Bundy, On Active Service, p. 255.
[62] Castle diary, Apr. 4, 1932.
[63] Stimson diary, Apr. 5, 1932.
[64] Ibid., Mar. 2, 8, 10, 16, 1932.

Hoover readily consented to his making the trip with the object of discussing both disarmament and the Far Eastern crisis.[65] According to Hoover's press statement (April 5) announcing Stimson's departure, the object of the mission was to assist the work of the disarmament conference and nothing else: "This is the sole purpose of the Secretary's visit." [66] According to Stimson's memoirs, "Stimson set himself at Geneva ... to the purpose of obtaining ... a world judgment against Japan," so that, if worse should come to worst, "it would lay a firm foundation of principle upon which the Western nations and China could stand in a later reckoning." [67]

For several weeks in April and May, while Secretary Stimson was abroad pursuing one line of policy, Undersecretary Castle took his place in the cabinet and, together with the President, laid down a quite different line. Hoover long had wanted to claim the nonrecognition doctrine as his own and define it in his terms. As early as February 18 Castle had written:

The President said a couple of days ago that for the coming election he must have all the support he can get. He wants Stimson—if we get across the Nine Power note making more or less universal the idea that the world will not recognize treaties, etc. which result from the use of force—to make a speech somewhere and proclaim this as the Hoover doctrine. As the President says, it is a tremendous step, a longer step toward eliminating force from international affairs than anything which has been done. He said that he had to wrestle with Stimson for days to get it across, that the Secretary wanted always to go in for withdrawal of diplomats or an economic embargo, either or both of which measures would almost inevitably lead to war. I knew that the Secretary had always played with those ideas, but gathered from him that he had, with great difficulty, put across the idea embodied in his note of January 7. It would hurt his feelings terribly to have this called the Hoover doctrine because he thinks of it as one very important star which history will put to his credit.

Stimson declined to speak out as the President desired him to, on the grounds that it was improper for members of the State Department to make political speeches.[68] And he still held back when, as he himself put it, "Secretary Hurley came in to talk to me about the 'Stimson Doctrine' of the Borah letter" and said he was "anxious to have me say something to indicate that the President had actively shared in this matter, so that it could be used in the campaign in his favor. I pointed out that I had already done this in my letter to Borah, where I pointed out that my note of January seventh had been sent at the President's instructions." [69] Stimson having repeatedly refused to champion the "Hoover doctrine," the President turned to Castle, who wrote (April 1), "He wants me to talk about the new doctrine ... of not recognizing ... which he rightly feels is his own." [70] After Stimson had left for Europe—where he was to reach an "understanding" with Sir John Simon about "working hand in hand with regard to the Far East" [71]—Castle made two addresses in which he assured the American people that their government's policy excluded sanctions of economic pressure or military force. The people did not realize that at the

---

[65] Ibid., Mar. 29, 1932.

[66] William S. Myers, ed., The State Papers and Other Public Writings of Herbert Hoover (New York, 1934), II, 157–58.

[67] Stimson and Bundy, On Active Service, p. 258.

[68] Castle diary, Feb. 18, Apr. 8, 1932.

[69] Stimson also took occasion, when talking with a couple of newspapermen, to "emphasize again the President's part in this matter." Stimson diary, Mar. 12, 1932. In his book of 1936, however, he did not emphasize the President's part but wrote of the origin of the nonrecognition idea, without mentioning Hoover: "I find from my diary that as early as November 9th I discussed it with my assistants as an ultimate possible weapon to be used, and thereafter it was constantly cropping up in our discussions." Far Eastern Crisis, p. 93.

[70] Castle diary, Apr. 1, 1932.

[71] Stimson diary, May 17, 1932.

moment the United States was engaging in a kind of dual diplomacy almost comparable to that of Japan herself!

Hoover dreaded Stimson's return, and the Secretary on his arrival home was indeed incensed on account of Castle's speeches. He waited for an explanation. After a few days, taking full responsibility, Hoover offered one. He said, according to Stimson, that "he had gotten very nervous about the excited feeling in Japan" while Stimson was away. He had been "afraid it might lead to some attack on us and thought the best way to prevent it was to come out and say that we were not going to boycott them." Meanwhile Stimson was already planning a continuation of his policy of naval display and an extension of the nonrecognition doctrine. He now thought the fleet, after the completion of its war games, should remain at Hawaii as a restraining influence upon Japan. In addition, he thought the United States should announce its refusal to recognize not only territorial changes made by aggression but also belligerent rights claimed by an aggressor. We should "implement the Kellogg Pact with a declaration as to what we would do in not recognizing a nation which was declared an aggressor by the League of Nations, and who had also broken the Kellogg Pact." So Stimson told Hoover, but he inferred that the President, while "in favor of the proposition," was "afraid to do it during the presidential campaign." With the aid of Admiral Pratt he did persuade the President to keep the fleet at Pearl Harbor.[72]

Hoover looked upon disarmament, rather than sanctions, as a proper corollary of the Kellogg Pact. The pact, he reasoned, meant that the nations of the world should use their arms only for defense. They should increase the power

of defense by "decreases in the power of attack," by drastic cuts in their land, air, and naval forces.[73] Such was Hoover's idea, but Stimson thought it "just a proposition from Alice in Wonderland," and he objected vehemently to it.[74] "He feels," wrote Castle, "that our fleet, intact, is essential in the Pacific to keep Japan in order."[75] In spite of his opposition the President finally went ahead and, on June 22, announced his comprehensive disarmament plan: "I propose that the arms of the world should be reduced by nearly one-third."[76]

Stimson now set to work on a speech "in defense of the nonrecognition policy" according to his own interpretation of it, as distinct from the Hoover-Castle view. "My speech is intended to support the Kellogg Pact as the fulcrum upon which we will have our issue with Japan," he said to himself. "The speech is intended to rally the European countries around the Pact, so that when the issue with Japan comes up, they will support us intelligently on this central point." When he showed his draft to Hoover, he ran into trouble and, though he explained that he was defending the pact against the assaults of "the intelligentsia," he had to cancel part of what he had written and revise some of the rest.[77]

After arranging for an invitation,[78] he

[72] Castle diary, May 2, 15, 1932; Stimson diary, May 16, 18, 19, 20, 1932. See also Stimson, *Far Eastern Crisis*, pp. 137–38.

[73] Hoover's press statement of June 22, 1932, in Myers, *State Papers*, II, 211–13. Castle commented in his diary, June 23, 1932: "The President's arms statement has been well received in this country and on the whole well received by Governments abroad. . . . What is unfortunate, I think, is that such a move was not made long ago, and in fact the President is being criticized just for this. . . . It is very hard to understand why he allowed himself to be overpersuaded by the Secretary because . . . he told me he had pled with Stimson at least to send it to Geneva for the Delegation to discuss."
[74] Stimson diary, May 22, 24, 1932.
[75] Castle diary, May 30, 1932.
[76] Myers, *State Papers*, II, 212.
[77] Stimson diary, July 20, 25, 26, 27, 1932.
[78] Stimson had telephoned Walter Lippmann to ask if the Council on Foreign Relations would like to hear a speech from him. *Ibid.*, July 23, 1932.

delivered his censored address on August 8, 1932, before the Council on Foreign Relations in New York. In it he proclaimed a "revolution in human thought" as expressed in the League Covenant and the Kellogg Pact. War, except for the "right of self-defense," was now "an illegal thing," and neutrality was out of place. The nonrecognition policy of the United States reflected "this new viewpoint and these new covenants." True, the Kellogg Pact had no "sanctions of force," only those of "public opinion," but the American notes of January 7, 1932, would lead eventually to a worldwide "moral disapproval" of aggression and to "consultation between signatories of the Pact." [79]

So Stimson declared, and if he was a bit cryptic, if he did not make clear what the objects of "consultation" might be, the fault was not entirely his own. Years afterward, in his memoirs, he admitted that at the time he "did not himself accept" the position that moral sanctions alone were adequate, but "he was bound to ... acknowledge that the Kellogg Pact would not have had general support if it had included stronger sanctions than that of public opinion." [80] He might have added that the Kellogg Pact, with such a gloss upon it, would not have had Hoover's support, either. As Castle wrote during a visit at Hoover's summer camp on the Rapidan: "The President told me ... he was always afraid Stimson would get us into real trouble through his earnest and entirely laudable desire to support the various peace treaties. He said that he was thankful that he had forced Stimson to omit the last three pages of his speech on the Kellogg Pact because in those pages he

went the whole limit, expressed our willingness to join in sanctions, etc." [81]

Even in its truncated form the speech provoked a violently anti-American reaction in Japan.[82] When Senator Swanson expressed concern over a possible impasse, Stimson assured him "that we would not go to war unless Japan attacked us, but in that case we would fight like the devil." And Stimson half expected this to happen, as he discussed with a couple of admirals "the absolute necessity of keeping the Navy in such a condition in which it would be airtight against any sudden attack by the Japanese." [83] President Hoover feared that his Secretary's attitude invited war. Soon after his defeat for re-election he spoke to Castle about the latter's writing a book on the foreign policy of the administration. He said Stimson would feel that *he* ought to write it. "But," observed Castle, "the President does not want Stimson to make himself the center of the book because, as he said, 'he would have had us in a war with Japan before this if he had had his way.' ..." [84]

On September 15, 1932, while the Lytton Commission, after months of investigation in the Far East, was preparing its report to the League, the Japanese government announced its recognition of the state of Manchukuo, newly erected in conquered Manchuria. With this *fait accompli* the Japanese presented a challenge both to the American policy of nonrecognition and to the forthcoming Lytton Report. Grimly accepting the

[79] The speech, entitled "The Pact of Paris: Three Years of Development," was published as a special supplement to *Foreign Affairs*, XI (October, 1932).

[80] Stimson and Bundy, *On Active Service*, pp. 259–60.

[81] Castle diary, Aug. 20, 1932.

[82] In a letter from Tokyo, Aug. 13, 1932, Ambassador Joseph C. Grew informed Stimson of the "outburst in Japan against your speech before the Council on Foreign Relations," and explained that the "violent Japanese press reaction was based ... on the Foreign Office's inflammatory interpretation of Debuchi's cabled account." *Papers Relating to the Foreign Relations of the United States: Japan, 1931–1941* (Washington, 1943), I, 99.

[83] Stimson diary, Aug. 10, Sept. 16, 1932.

[84] Castle diary, Nov. 18, 1932.

challenge, Stimson throughout the fall and the winter of 1932–33 strove to bring about a final statement of the nonrecognition doctrine by the League and the United States, acting together.

He was not deterred by warnings of Japan's increasing hostility toward the United States nor by rumored threats of a rapprochement between Japan and the Soviet Union. From Tokyo, Ambassador Joseph C. Grew cautioned him on September 3: "The Japanese regard the United States as their greatest stumbling block, although they expect the report of the Lytton Commission to be unfavorable. At present talk of friction with Soviet Russia is comparatively quiescent."[85] And by way of the diplomatic grapevine, information came to the State Department that, as Castle phrased it, "Russia would have no difficulty in recognizing Manchukuo when Japan did," and "this would probably be followed by a non-aggression pact between Japan and the Soviet." According to Castle, "It makes the Secretary itch to recognize Russia just to prevent this—and why should recognition prevent it?"[86] But the Secretary decided, as he announced in a letter of September 8 to Senator Borah, that if "we recognized Russia in disregard of her very bad reputation respecting international obligations," the rest of the world would look upon our action as "a maneuver to bring forceful pressure upon Japan," and we would "lose the moral standing we had theretofore had in the controversy" with her.[87] Though Stimson did not shrink from the possibility of an ultimate application of force, he wanted first to make the "moral" issue absolutely clear.

He therefore welcomed the Lytton Re-

port as condemning Japan and justifying his own position. Castle, however, viewed the report as anything but an indictment —"so judicial in temper, so fair to both countries"—and the President and his cabinet, to the disgust of Stimson, "did not take any great interest" in what he considered "probably the greatest event that has happened in foreign relations for a long time." What was worse, the columnist Walter Lippmann argued that the Lytton Report and the nonrecognition doctrine were incompatible, since the report recommended for Manchuria a regime different from either the old one under China or the new one under Japan, while the nonrecognition notes of January 7, 1932, if taken literally, would estop the United States from agreeing to anything except a restoration of the status quo! Indignantly denying this, Stimson went ahead "stiffening up the League on Manchuria" and urging its members to act upon the Lytton Report and nonrecognition together. Some of them, "pretty wishy-washy," hoped to make the report a basis for conciliation between China and Japan, but he insisted that the League must "do its duty as to principles before they start conciliation."[88]

His self-appointed task of "stiffening up the League" was complicated and yet facilitated by the results of the presidential election of 1932. Soon after election day he heard a newspaperman describe Roosevelt as "not knowing anything about foreign affairs" and not having any interest in Manchuria.[89] So, when he got an invitation to a personal conference with Roosevelt, he thought he ought to accept it, but Hoover at first refused his permission. "I told Hoover," he noted, "that I was sufficiently interested in his [Hoover's] policy to want to do anything I could to perpetuate

[85] Foreign Relations: Japan, 1931–1941, I, 102.
[86] Castle diary, Sept. 7, 1932.
[87] Foreign Relations of the United States: Diplomatic Papers, 1933 (Washington, 1949–52), II, 778–79.

[88] Stimson diary, Sept. 20, 27, Oct. 5, Dec. 12, 15, 1932; Castle diary, Oct. 5, 1932.
[89] Stimson diary, Nov. 11, 1932.

it."[90] Actually he advanced his own rather than Hoover's policy when, on January 9, 1933, with Hoover's grudging consent, he called upon Roosevelt at Hyde Park. During the five-hour talk Roosevelt "expressed most warmly his approval" of Hoover's disarmament proposal, and Stimson "cautioned him not to be too hasty, pointing out that Japan was not likely to agree to the naval portions of the Hoover plan." Stimson discussed with Roosevelt, more sympathetically than he could do with Hoover, the possible imminence of war with Japan, problems of naval strategy, and the question of Philippine independence. Roosevelt "fully approved of our policy in the Far East" as Stimson described it to him, his "only possible criticism" being that "we did not begin it earlier." He asked whether the American ambassador should not be removed from Tokyo as a gesture, and Stimson replied that it would be fatal for the United States to act alone. The gist of the conversation, as Stimson reproduced it, was this:

I told him of the present ticklish situation at Geneva and the likelihood that it might be advisable for me to make another statement as to this Government's position. I said to him, "I do not wish to ask any commitment from you but I certainly do not wish to make any such statement and then have you immediately afterward come out with a contrary position or statement." He replied, "You need have no fear of that."[91]

Thus reassured by the President-elect, Stimson found himself in a stronger position than before for dealing, on the one hand, with the reluctant President and, on the other, with the hesitant League. On January 11, after resisting Stimson's entreaties for weeks, Hoover recommended to Congress the passage of

an arms embargo bill which would have empowered the United States to reinforce League sanctions against Japan. His own message was brief and perfunctory, but he accompanied it with an elaborate memorandum provided (at his request) by Stimson, and Roosevelt came out with an enthusiastic endorsement.[92] Congress, however, soon stalled the arms embargo bill. Meanwhile, on January 13, Hoover again yielded to Stimson by vetoing a bill for Philippine independence. Hoover favored independence in principle, but Stimson did not, and he contended that the prospect of American withdrawal from the Philippines had invited and brought on Japanese expansion in the Far East.[93] On the day of the veto, when Stimson called up Roosevelt to say he was going to inform the British that he did "not expect the American policy towards the Japanese to be changed," Roosevelt "at once responded that that was all right" and that he would back him up. So Stimson went ahead "with much greater confidence" and telephoned a message for Sir John Simon in which he said that, "as a lawyer," he "did not see how they could get away without approving the Lytton Report, which amounted to findings of fact, and then making a decision of the League on these findings, which should include an application of the non-recognition policy directly to Manchoukuo." Roosevelt backed him up with a statement to the press.[94]

Roosevelt's support made Stimson

[90] Jan. 3, 1932. Stimson and Bundy, On Active Service, p. 292.

[91] "Memorandum of Conversation with Franklin D. Roosevelt, Monday, January 9, at Hyde Park," Stimson diary.

[92] Stimson diary, Dec. 14, 1932; Jan. 12, 1933; Myers, State Papers, II, 565–66; Raymond Moley, After Seven Years (New York, 1939), pp. 93–95.

[93] Myers, State Papers, II, 569–76; Hoover Memoirs, II, 359–61; Stimson diary, Jan. 12, 1933. Earlier Stimson had said that "the whole trouble with Japan and her intransigence is based upon her belief that we are going to give up the Philippines and do not wish to remain a Far Eastern power," and Hoover had concluded that "it was no time to give up the Philippines." Stimson diary, Feb. 3, 1932.

[94] Ibid., Jan. 12, 13, 1932.

"feel better" than he had felt "for a long time," and when the two men met again, they laughingly agreed that they did "pretty good teamwork." Stimson was troubled, however, by the delicacy of his position as between the incoming and the outgoing President.[95] After incautiously remarking at a press conference, "I am Roosevelt's acting Secretary of State," [96] he confessed to Hoover "that the only thing that upset me was the thought that he felt that he was being humiliated by what I had done with regard to Roosevelt." [97] To Castle it seemed that the President was placed "in a very embarrassing position since his own defense of American rights is ignored in the press accounts and Roosevelt and Stimson are played up as the heroes." [98]

Already Hoover was resuming his effort to establish, for history, his own defense of American rights. He got statements from Secretary of War Hurley and Secretary of the Interior Ray Lyman Wilbur testifying that he had proposed nonrecognition, insisted upon it as against sanctions or other "aggressive action," and started the "discussions and decisions" out of which "came the Hoover doctrine." [99] While, behind the scenes, he was trying to name and define the policy of nonrecognition, those on the outside assumed, with unconscious irony, that they knew the significance of the policy, whatever its name. The New York *Herald Tribune,* in one issue, reported that Roosevelt was "putting himself behind what is alternatively called

the Hoover doctrine or the Stimson doctrine" and, in the next issue, editorialized that in consequence of the "Stimson doctrine" this country was "drifting into a quarrel with Japan to no clear end." [100] And Roosevelt's brain-truster Raymond Moley later supposed that the President-elect had declared his "wholehearted acquiescence in the Hoover-Stimson rejection of the traditional concept of neutrality" and had "endorsed a policy that invited a major war in the Far East." [101]

During February, as events in Geneva approached their fateful climax, the struggle between President and Secretary over the control of American policy came to its inconclusive denouement. Sir John Simon wanted assurances of close American co-operation with the League, but Stimson had difficulty in satisfying him because of the restraining hand of Hoover, who on February 14 returned with corrections and additions a review of the administration's foreign policies which Stimson had prepared. "I feel the memorandum gives the impression of too strong an alliance with the League," the President said. "I have insisted upon the aloofness of the United States from the League of Nations in that the sanctions of the League are those of force either economic or military, whereas the United States could not and would not enter into force sanctions...." [102]

Stimson scored a partial victory when, on February 24, the League Assembly adopted the Lytton Report with essentially the kind of recommendations he had desired, recommendations which did "not provide for a mere return to the status quo" but did "exclude the maintenance and recognition of the existing

[95] Stimson and Bundy, *On Active Service,* p. 293.
[96] This remark was "off the record." Castle diary, Jan. 24, 1933.
[97] Stimson diary, Jan. 24, 1933.
[98] Castle diary, Jan. 24, 1933.
[99] Myers, *Foreign Policies of Herbert Hoover,* pp. 163–68. In his *Memoirs* (II, 373) Hoover, crediting Bryan as the prime author of the nonrecognition doctrine, said: "... Secretaries Hurley and Wilbur wrote me letters of protest, both having been present at Cabinet meetings when I first proposed this idea (originally Bryan's)."

[100] New York *Herald Tribune,* Jan. 17, 18, 1933.
[101] Moley, p. 94. See also Myers, *Foreign Policies of Herbert Hoover,* p. 229n.
[102] Memorandum by Stimson, Feb. 18, 1933, in *Foreign Relations, 1933,* III, 186–87; Myers, *Foreign Policies of Herbert Hoover,* pp. 251–54.

regime in Manchuria."[103] The British ambassador, congratulating him, said that at last the nations of the world had done a good job. "And he added," according to Stimson, "that he thought I had hothoused them a little into 'more prompt action than they would have taken.'"[104]

Stimson's triumph was, however, to be qualified. On the very day the Assembly acted, he and the President had a final showdown about the meaning of nonrecognition. He had passed on to Hoover a cable from Ambassador Grew in Tokyo about Japan's probable reaction to the League resolution. "There is no bluff in her attitude," Grew warned. "The military themselves, and the public through military propaganda are fully prepared to fight rather than to surrender to moral or other pressure from the West." This ominous message raised in Hoover's mind "a most serious question," and he at once sent word to Stimson that "some occasion should be taken to make it clear" that nonrecognition presupposed absolutely no sanctions other than those of public opinion. Furthermore, "The whole doctrine of nonrecognition is not alone a method of invoking world opinion but it is equally important in the phase that it avoids precipitant action and allows time to work out proper solutions." Stimson promptly talked Hoover out of making any such public declaration.[105] But the next day Stimson's official response to the Assembly's resolution fell somewhat short of the reply he had promised Sir Eric Drummond, the secretary-general of the League. "As I read your reply to Drummond," Minister Wilson in Geneva cabled to Stimson, "we have neither 'as-sociated the Government of the United States' with the views expressed in the Assembly's report although we declare ourselves to be in substantial accord therewith nor have we stated that we would 'concert our action and attitude if necessary.'" And Stimson had to keep on explaining, in answer to Chinese, British, and other inquiries, that the United States did not and could not contemplate an arms embargo for the time being.[106]

The American policy of nonrecognition of territorial changes made in violation of treaties, though originated by Bryan in 1915, may properly be called the Hoover-Stimson doctrine in the form in which it developed from 1931 to 1933, since it was then suggested by Hoover and formulated by Stimson. In the mind of the President, however, nonrecognition remained a final and sufficient measure, a substitute for economic pressure or military force, a formula looking toward conciliation and peace and relying on the moral force of public opinion for its effect. That was the Hoover doctrine. In the thinking of the Secretary of State, nonrecognition became not an alternative but a preliminary to economic and military sanctions, a way of drawing sharp the issue between the United States (along with the League of Nations) and Japan, a means of laying down the ideological grounds for war if, as he expected, war eventually should come. That was the Stimson doctrine—or, perhaps, the Stimson-Roosevelt doctrine. That was the view which ultimately prevailed, and so it is quite fitting that the policy of nonrecognition should, as it generally does today, bear Stimson's name.[107]

[103] League of Nations, *Official Journal,* Special Supplement no. 112 (Geneva, 1933), p. 75.
[104] Memorandum by Stimson, Feb. 23, 1933, in *Foreign Relations, 1933,* III, 197.
[105] Grew to Stimson, Feb. 23, 1933; Hoover to Stimson, Feb. 24, 1933, and penciled notation by Stimson, in *Foreign Relations, 1933,* III, 195, 209–10.

[106] *Ibid.,* III, 197–98, 204–205, 210–11, 214; *Foreign Relations: Japan, 1931–1941,* I, 114–16.
[107] For an account of the widespread acceptance and application of the Stimson doctrine after 1933, see Robert Langer, *Seizure of Territory: The Stimson Doctrine and Related Principles in Legal Theory and Diplomatic Practice* (Princeton, 1947), pp. 123–290.

15

The President and the "Quarantine" Speech

DOROTHY BORG

Franklin D. Roosevelt came to the White House in 1933 fully expecting to concentrate all his efforts and his energies on domestic problems and on pushing his New Deal through Congress. He had no great interest in foreign affairs, nor did he have any desire to play an active role in curing the ills of the world. But as the situation in Europe and in Asia grew ominous in the mid-thirties, the President nevertheless found his attention turning to overseas affairs. He became concerned over the possible effect on American security of the policies of Germany, Italy, and Japan. There were strong indications that those nations were determined to pursue an aggressive course that would unquestionably lead to another great war in which the United States might well become involved.

To the President, it was becoming clear that the United States could not stand aloof from the events in Europe and Asia and that the economic and military resources of the country might have to be used to aid the Western European democracies resist the aggressions of the dictators. But he feared that the American people would not recognize the dangers confronting them and the need to take sides in the coming struggle. What better evidence was there than the rejection by Congress, when considering neutrality legislation in 1935, of the President's recommendation that in the event of a war he be empowered to withhold arms and munitions from the side he deemed the aggressor and to supply matériel to the nation that was attacked. The law as passed required the President to embargo war matériel to all the belligerents without distinction.

In the hope of helping the American people to appreciate and understand the responsibilities they faced, and to make them aware of the realities of international life, Roosevelt made several speeches in various parts of the country. He always assured his audience that it was the intention of the Administration to stay out of any future war, but at the same time he cautioned that such a course, however desirable, might not always be possible. Thus at Chautauqua, New York, on August 14, 1936, he said, "I hate war. We shun political commitments which might entangle us in foreign wars.... Yet we must remember that so long as war exists on earth there will be some danger that even a nation which most ardently desires peace may be drawn into war."

On October 5, 1937, he spoke in Chicago in the same vein. It was his celebrated "quarantine" speech, in which he reassured the American people of his

Reprinted by permission of the publishers from Dorothy Borg, *The United States and the Far Eastern Crisis of 1933–1938.* Cambridge, Mass.: Harvard University Press, Copyright, 1964, by the President and Fellows of Harvard College.

"determination to pursue a policy of peace" but said also that if war should occur in some part of the world, "let no one imagine that America will escape, that America may expect mercy, that the Western Hemisphere will not be attacked. . . ." In that speech, however, he went beyond these ideas. Noting "that the epidemic of world lawlessness is spreading," he said, "when an epidemic of physical disease starts to spread, the community approves and joins in a quarantine of the patients in order to protect the health of the community against the spread of the disease."

The speech was widely interpreted at the time as heralding a major departure in the Administration's foreign policy in the direction of firm and positive action to "quarantine" the aggressor nations by means of economic sanctions. Historians have, for the most part, agreed with the contemporary interpretation and have, additionally, viewed the address as a "trial balloon" to test the public reaction to so radical an alteration in policy.

Dorothy Borg, who has made an intensive study of the diplomacy of the period between 1933 and 1938, dissents from the usually accepted interpretations of the speech. Her researches have led her to conclude that the President was not announcing a change in the Administration's foreign policy, nor was he proposing economic sanctions. The purpose of the address was to counteract the rising isolationism in the country. The "quarantine" figure did not appear in the State Department's draft and was only inserted by the President on the train to Chicago. It was not related to sanctions but rather to explorations that Roosevelt was making at the time as part of a search for a new formula to bring peace to the world.

○

ROOSEVELT'S SEARCH FOR A PEACE PROGRAM

By the middle 1930's, Roosevelt had inevitably become greatly concerned over the international situation and the possibility of future conflicts in Europe and Asia. Therefore, as already related, he began to think in terms of finding some new method of solving the world's problems which would be sufficiently bold and imaginative to dispel the threat of war and establish a durable peace. This led him in the summer of 1936 to entertain the notion that he might invite the heads of all the large European nations to meet with him on board a battleship where, seated around a conference table isolated from all other influences, they would try to work out a blueprint for a "lasting peace."[1] As he discussed the

feasibility of such a project with a number of people, word of his idea spread and on August 26 Arthur Krock published an article, together with the pictures of the leaders of five European governments, on the front page of the *New York Times* under a startlingly large headline which declared that ROOSEVELT IF ELECTED MAY CALL KINGS DICTATORS AND PRESIDENTS TO GREAT POWER CONFERENCE. The President, Krock said, felt that he had made a "new discovery in world leadership" in what he regarded as the greatest cause of mankind: the cause of peace. He had invented a plan which involved calling a conference of the heads of the most important states in order to devise a means of assuring the peace of the world. While none of the details had yet been considered, he was contemplating the presentation of a program which would in

[1] *The Memoirs of Cordell Hull*, I, 646.

general be patterned after the Pan-American agreements. The President had no intention of taking any action, however, until after the forthcoming election campaign, as he was afraid that the Hearst papers and the *Chicago Tribune* would attack him for launching a foreign policy that was even worse than Wilson's effort to drag the United States into the League of Nations.

Roosevelt subsequently by implication took the position that Krock's story was a figment of the writer's imagination and the project for a high-level meeting at sea was dropped.[2] But the President did proceed to carry out another scheme which, as described earlier, was to be his first concrete attempt to develop some sort of a peace plan. While he had actually set the wheels in motion for the convening of an extraordinary conference at Buenos Aires as early as January 1936, he waited until after his election in November to announce that he himself expected to attend the opening session. His trip to Argentina in December proved to be a triumphal tour which fulfilled his purpose of attracting widespread attention to the proceedings at the conference so that it became possible to impress upon the peoples of other continents that the program for the maintenance of peace which was to evolve from the deliberations at Buenos Aires was not intended to have only regional implications but rather to serve as a model for the whole world to follow.[3]

[2] See note concerning the Krock article in Elliott Roosevelt (ed.), *F.D.R. His Personal Letters 1928–1945* (1950), I, 649. On January 9, 1937, in a letter to Ambassador Dodd in Berlin, the President wrote with characteristic humor: "That story by Arthur Krock was not wholly crazy. If five or six heads of the important governments could meet together for a week with complete inaccessibility to press or cables or radios, a definite, useful agreement might result or else one or two of them would be murdered by the others! In any case, it would be worthwhile from the point of view of civilization!" (*Ibid.*, 648.)

[3] Contemporary publications are full of the

Of all the proposals advanced at Buenos Aires, the draft of a neutrality treaty submitted by the United States delegation probably created most agitation. The draft was introduced by Hull when, in his Eight Pillars of Peace speech, he posed the question: "Can we in the Conference work out for ourselves a common line of policy that might be pursued during a period of neutrality?"[4] The Secretary declared that an agreement embodying such a policy would be a "tremendous safeguard" to each of the American nations and "might be a powerful means of ending war." The draft itself provided that, in case of war on the continent of the Americas, the states not parties to the conflict would enforce measures similar to those incorporated in the existing United States neutrality law; in the event of war outside the Americas, the signatories would consult with a view (it was implied) to concerting their policies as neutrals *vis-à-vis* the belligerents.[5]

The United States proposal was an outgrowth of the general controversy of the times over neutrality and collective security.[6] At one extreme were the advocates of a collective security system of

worldwide impact of the President's trip to Buenos Aires. Thus the *New York Times* said on December 2 that Roosevelt's "instincts led him right." His presence at Buenos Aires made the conference a world event rather than a regional gathering. And while nothing the President said at the conference was directly addressed to Europe, no European government could "fail to take note of every word spoken by such a man at such a place in such a time." (Editorial entitled "The President's Speech.") There are interesting comments on the European reaction in *The United States in World Affairs*, 1936, p. 207, and *Survey of International Affairs*, 1936, p. 823.

[4] *Peace and War: United States Foreign Policy 1931–1941*, p. 342.

[5] Text of the draft is in *Documents on International Affairs*, 1936, p. 77.

[6] Frederick J. Knauer, "American Neutrality Reconsidered," in the *Columbia Law Review*, January 1936, p. 505, surveys many of the ideas current at the time. A very colorful demonstration of different views held by different people is to be found in the proceedings of the Com-

the Geneva variety who maintained that the outbreak of war anywhere was the responsibility of every nation and that countries that were not belligerents should, if necessary, resort to sanctions against an aggressor even though as a result they might be drawn into the hostilities. At the other extreme were the isolationists who favored the kind of neutrality that was embodied in the United States neutrality legislation of the 1930's, which was essentially based upon the principle that a government should concern itself with keeping its own people out of war and not with attempting to influence the conflict. In between these two schools of thought there existed a great variety of people holding many different opinions. Among them were those who believed that it must be possible to find a middle-of-the-road solution that would enable the nonbelligerents to have an impact upon the course of a war while at the same time protecting themselves from becoming involved in it. Within this group it was often argued that in order to reduce the risk of involvement the nonbelligerents would have to assume the status of neutrals and enforce whatever measures they adopted against both sides in a conflict equally. While neutral nations might find it difficult—or maybe even impossible—to discover a way of playing a decisive part in defeating an aggressor, they might at least be able to curtail the scope and duration of the hostilities if they operated collectively and followed a policy such as refusing to trade in war materials and perhaps other essential supplies with any of the belligerents. Moreover if an international agreement were concluded so that it were known in advance that all neutrals would auto-

matically apply certain embargoes, it might prevent a potential aggressor from resorting to force. Also, to reduce the danger of their own involvement even further, it was thought that neutrals should disavow any intention of using military pressures and should in general adopt as unprovocative methods as possible. Many different kinds of methods were, however, regarded as unprovocative, even including at times a ban upon all commercial intercourse between neutrals and belligerents. Professor Philip C. Jessup, for example, in one of the most detailed studies of "techniques of neutral cooperation" to be published at the time, contended that a plan—which he himself favored—for neutrals engaging in "only interneutral trade," in contrast to the sanctions system of the League Covenant, would not tend to invite retaliation on the part of the belligerents because the renunciation of trade did not constitute an act of intervention in a war but rather of aloofness from it.[7]

The draft treaty which the United States presented at the Buenos Aires Conference was part of the effort to discover a middle-of-the-road course. In effect, it was an attempt to apply in practice the famous provision of the Saavedra Lamas Anti-War Pact accepted by the American Republics in 1933 which stated that, if war broke out between two or more of the American nations, the signatories that were not involved in the hostilities would "in their character as neutrals" adopt a "common and solidary attitude." In the end the United States draft was rejected by the delegates at Buenos Aires because

mittee on Neutrality at the Buenos Aires Conference recorded in the stenographic reports of the Conference published under the title of *Inter-American Conference for the Maintenance of Peace, Proceedings.*

[7] Philip C. Jessup, *Neutrality, Its History, Economics, and Law, IV: Today and Tomorrow* (1936), p. 187. Jessup thought that total nonintercourse, while theoretically possible, was not practical for the present and suggested that a beginning might be made by neutrals agreeing to the adoption of common measures for withholding shipments of arms, ammunition, and implements of war from the belligerents.

some of the Latin American governments felt that it would conflict with their responsibilities as members of the League of Nations. Nevertheless, as a consequence of the United States proposal the general idea that the neutral countries of the Americas might, under certain circumstances, adopt a common neutrality policy was inserted in other agreements which were approved by the conference. Moreover, in the following years the Roosevelt administration, far from departing from the concept of collective neutrality, continued to try to implement it. The result was in part that the General Declaration of Continental Neutrality was adopted at the inter-American Conference at Panama in 1939. But, as in the meantime the threat of war in Europe had progressively increased and finally materialized, the administration in Washington went one step further and sought to get the American nations to manipulate their "continental neutrality" so that it would work to the advantage of the democracies against the Axis powers. This aim was actually achieved through the development of a policy which, though imposed upon all belligerents alike, by its very nature favored the war effort of the British and French.

Aside from considering the United States draft, the Buenos Aires Conference discussed a wide variety of other plans which aimed at enabling the non-belligerents to deal with the problem of war short of reliance upon any of the more drastic forms of collective security or neutrality.[8] One consequence of these

discussions was the passage by the conference, with extraordinary acclaim, of the Declaration of Principles of Inter-American Solidarity and Cooperation, which emphasized in particular the possibility of collective action by the American states in the face of a conflict outside of this hemisphere. The action was to be pacific but might or might not be neutral. The whole history of the declaration suggests, however, that, if unneutral, the pressures applied against the aggressor were to be relatively moderate. For the declaration was patterned after a well-known decree issued by Uruguay during the first World War for the purpose of organizing a united front of the American nations, that were not involved in the conflict, so that they would give moral support to the United States and the other American Republics that were fighting for the cause of democracy.[9] The kind of measures that were under consideration were the severance of diplomatic relations with Germany. Although the declaration was therefore not likely to involve the non-belligerents in hostilities, in addition, in accordance with the whole Pan-American peace structure, it had a moral character which might also serve to prevent reprisals. For it declared in substance that the American nations formed a "moral union" which, if confronted with a war outside of this hemisphere, would act on behalf of the common interests of its members, prominent among which was their faith in the ideal of democracy. The collective action of the nonbelligerents was therefore invested with the high purpose of protecting and

[8] For pertinent material on the Buenos Aires Conference, in addition to the proceedings cited in note 6, see *The Report of Delegation of the United States to the Inter-American Conference for the Maintenance of Peace*, which among other matters contains the official texts of the treaties, resolutions, etc., passed at the conference; Professor Charles G. Fenwick's article on "The Inter-American Conference for the Maintenance of Peace," in the *American Journal of International Law*, April 1937, p. 210 (Professor Fenwick was a member of the United States Delegation to the Conference); *The Memoirs of Cordell Hull*, I, Chap. 35; Sumner Welles, *The Time for Decision* (1944), pp. 205ff. and *Seven Decisions That Shaped History* (1950), pp. 103ff.; Samuel Flagg Bemis, *The Latin American Policy of the United States* (1943), Chap. XIV, Sec. 3.

[9] Percy Alvin Martin, *Latin America and the War* (1925), p. 361.

furthering the welfare of the "international American community" as a whole. As far as the United States government was concerned, the most important part of the Buenos Aires Conference was, however, not any single agreement adopted by the delegates but the entire program for peace which resulted from the discussions. In the opinion of many United States officials, the main value of the program lay in what they termed its "constructive" and "comprehensive" approach, by which they meant that it sought to improve the political, social, and other conditions leading to war and treated them as interrelated problems. Even before the Marco Polo Bridge incident, Hull stated repeatedly that the application on a world-wide scale of a program similar to that which had been worked out at Buenos Aires was the best —if not the only—means of averting another World War; and after the incident he appears to have felt even more convinced than earlier that the key to the solution of the international crisis lay within the framework of the Buenos Aires Conference.[10]

The President attached as much significance as Hull to the Buenos Aires agreements. Nevertheless, he continued to explore other ways of stabilizing the world situation. When the Canadian Prime Minister, Mackenzie King, who was a close friend of Roosevelt's, visited Washington in early 1937, they had a long talk in which they discussed the possibility of creating a new world organization which might be called "Permanent Conference on Economic and Social Problems."[11] The main purpose of this body would be to demonstrate to the world that "collective security should not be identified with reliance upon force," whether in the form of military or economic sanctions, but rather with "reliance upon reason—public opinion." It was therefore not to concern itself with political problems but to investigate "fundamental" causes of war—that is, "economic and social injustices"—and expose them so that they could be cured by the pressure of an aroused public opinion. The President and Prime Minister agreed that, as this new method of dealing with international tensions proved its effectiveness, the League of Nations would inevitably change in the direction of seeking to preserve peace by peaceful means only and, as a result, would probably merge with the Permanent Conference to form one large international organization with a universal membership such as President Wilson had originally envisaged.

Roosevelt carried the scheme which he discussed with King a step further some two weeks later. It was at this point that Norman Davis was preparing to go to London for the International Sugar Conference and that the President instructed him to obtain the views of European statesmen on the trend of world events while he was abroad. In speaking to Davis before his departure, the President said that he might discreetly try to ascertain the reaction of European statesmen to the idea of possibly reorganizing the League of Nations so as to divest it of its political functions and transform it into a sort of Economic Council in which case "the United States ought to be able to go along."[12] But this was not the only kind of peace plan Roosevelt proposed. It will be recalled that he also told Davis to sound out European statesmen on the subject of a general agreement to "neutralize" the Pacific area

[10] For an expression of Hull's views before the Marco Polo Bridge incident, see for example the extraordinarily comprehensive statement of his opinions which appears in a memorandum of a talk that he had with Prime Minister Mackenzie King of Canada, printed in *FR* 1937, I, 641.

[11] Roosevelt, *F.D.R. His Personal Letters,* I, 664.

[12] Memorandum of telephone conversation between the President and Norman Davis, March 19, 1937. (Davis papers.)

which he regarded as a possible Far Eastern counterpart to the Buenos Aires agreements. In addition, Roosevelt wanted Davis to see if he could find a means of bringing the European governments together in a cooperative attempt to arrest the rapid deterioration of the international situation.

That Roosevelt was making increased efforts in the spring of 1937 to search for a plan by which peace might be maintained, was in no way remarkable. The President was widely regarded as having led his country out of the shadow of a fearful depression into a new economic era through courageous experimentation with the political and economic techniques of the New Deal. Consequently, as the international crisis deepened, many people believed that Roosevelt alone had the capacity to avert another World War. The early part of 1937 saw an upsurge of wishful thinking which gave rise to new rumors that the President intended to convene an international conference to settle the differences of the European powers before it was too late. By May the rumors had reached such proportions that Mussolini regarded it as expedient to declare, in a widely publicized interview, that he would greatly welcome Roosevelt's initiation of such a conference.[13] There can be no doubt that the President himself felt increasingly that the world was thrusting upon him the responsibility of solving its problems. When, for example, he was asked at a press conference whether he intended to respond to Mussolini's apparent desire for an international meeting, the President said that "almost everybody in Europe" felt that they were at the end of their tether so they naturally looked to him to pull a rabbit out of a hat; but, he added, not without

poignancy, "I haven't got a hat and I haven't got a rabbit in it."[14] Somewhat later he wrote across the top of a memorandum which contained a proposal for a solution of the international situation that "so many leaders of nations in every part of the world" were appealing to him "to *do* something."[15]

Davis in his conversations with European statesmen concentrated largely upon an effort to get a movement under way whereby the leaders of various nations of the world would come together in an attempt to settle the problems which divided their countries.[16] Davis spoke first to the French Minister of National Economy, Charles Spinasse, who declared that animosity among the peoples of Europe was running so high that no European government would dare to take the initiative in making a move toward political or economic "appeasement"; nevertheless, if Roosevelt, with his enormous prestige, would set the wheels going there might be some prospect of success.[17] Spinasse and Davis agreed that in any move which was undertaken the political, economic, and disarmament problems would have to be tackled comprehensively. Davis next saw Anthony Eden who, while he favored the idea of a comprehensive approach, said that Great Britain could not propose any scheme for a general international agreement, as her doing so would be regarded as a sign of weakness and would thereby detract from the beneficial effect that her rearmament program was having upon Japan, Germany, and Italy. Like Spinasse, he thought that the initiative would have to

[13] *FR* 1937, I, 655. The same volume contains papers on the German reaction to Roosevelt's calling a world conference to stabilize the European situation (29, 638, 640, 649).

[14] Press conference of July 13, 1937, Roosevelt papers.

[15] Roosevelt papers, PSF State Department 1933–1938, marked: "F.D.R.'s first draft."

[16] The following accounts of Davis' conversations with European statesmen are all based on memoranda in his files.

[17] It must be recognized that the word "appeasement" was consistently used at this time and did not have the unpleasant connotations it acquired after the Munich settlement.

come from President Roosevelt but he did not believe that the time was as yet quite ripe for action. Davis, on his part, declared repeatedly that he was absolutely certain that the President would not allow himself to become involved in the political controversies of the European powers but that he would be willing to participate wholeheartedly in a concerted effort to find a solution to economic questions and to the problems posed by the competitive construction of more and more armaments. In the end, it was decided that the United States and Great Britain would continue to exchange views about the possibility of reaching an international agreement—by convening a conference or by some other means—in the hope that the situation would have shaped itself so that some undertaking could be started in September. Subsequently Davis talked with Joachim Von Ribbentrop, then German Ambassador to Great Britain, who insisted that Germany desired a peaceful settlement of the international crisis and who also said that President Roosevelt as a "world figure with greater prestige than any living person" must take the initative.

The most important interviews which Davis had during his stay in London were, however, his meetings with Neville Chamberlain who, while he expressed great sympathy with the general idea of trying to bring the European dictatorships and democracies closer together, strongly implied that he wished to pursue this objective in his own fashion. He explained that in his judgment "political appeasement" would have to precede "economic collaboration" and any further attempt to obtain a limitation of armaments. Moreover he told Davis that the British government had just instructed its ambassador in Berlin to impress upon Hitler that the British wanted to establish "more friendly relations and a sound basis for peace" as soon as they were convinced that Germany genuinely

desired the same thing. Davis replied in effect that he did not question the British desire to reach an understanding with Germany; nevertheless he wondered whether in view of the critical state of the world it was practicable to postpone for much longer an effort to adjust the differences of the European powers on a wider scale than would be attained by discussions of purely political issues. Chamberlain, however, showed no disposition to change his mind on this point and instead reverted to the problem of the Far East which he said was still giving him great concern. This part of the Davis-Chamberlain talks has already been noted in an earlier chapter but, despite some repetition it seems worth reviewing its main features here. The Prime Minister reiterated the view he had expressed in his letter to Morgenthau, namely, that he feared if England should get into trouble with Germany, Japan would take advantage of the situation to attack British interests in the Pacific area. And he again suggested that this could be avoided by a firm Anglo-American stand in the Far East which, in his opinion, would cause the Japanese to abandon their hostile attitude in favor of cooperating with England and America to "promote peace and economic recovery in China and the Pacific." Davis' response was that if the Japanese were genuinely ready to cooperate on a "proper basis"—one which did not violate the integrity of China—"this might be a very constructive thing to do." Davis then brought up the President's proposal for "neutralizing" the Pacific area although he made no mention of Roosevelt's own connection with it. Chamberlain expressed considerable doubt about the wisdom of this suggestion, saying that he questioned "the practicability of trying to do anything so important before there should be an improvement in the political situation in Japan."

In addition to discussing means of

solving the situation in Europe and Asia with Chamberlain, Davis raised the question of the possibility of the Prime Minister's coming to the United States so that he could talk with Roosevelt directly and received the impression that Chamberlain would be glad to do so if the matter could be conveniently arranged. There is no record of a conversation between the President and Davis on this subject after the latter's return home, but Roosevelt must have approved the idea of such a trip as on June 10 Davis wrote to the Prime Minister, on the President's behalf, to ask him to come to Washington around late September.[18] The President, Davis said, was ready to make arrangements immediately to have an agenda drawn up for their meeting. Davis stated further that he believed it might "become possible and advisable within a few months to make a concerted and comprehensive effort to achieve economic rehabilitation, financial stability, a limitation of armaments and peace" so that it would "seem most desirable for Great Britain and the United States to do what they can to ... prepare the way for a broader move to establish more healthy ... conditions in the world." But the Prime Minister replied that he did not believe that the time had yet arrived for meetings with the Germans and, if these materialized, they might provide "a valuable indication of the direction in which the lines of advance might run and in this way would be a useful preliminary to any conversation between the President and myself." [19]

By this time Roosevelt was apparently firmly convinced of the importance of a meeting with Chamberlain. For at the end of July he wrote personally to the Prime Minister to say that he appreciated his desire to make progress along other lines which would have a bearing upon the timing of his trip to the United States but that he would nevertheless like some suggestions as to any preparatory steps that might be taken to expedite his visit.[20] Chamberlain did not answer Roosevelt's letter until two months later, when he stated that, given the existing international situation, he was afraid that he could not suggest any way in which his meeting with the President could be expedited.[21] While conditions in Europe were less menacing than they had been a few months earlier, things were still "a long way from the resumption of cordial relations between the Totalitarian States and the democracies." Moreover, developments in the Far East had justified all the worst fears and there appeared little prospect of effecting any improvement through action by the Western powers.

The President was awaiting Chamberlain's reply at the time that he delivered his "quarantine" speech at Chicago so that he still had in mind getting under way some plan for securing peace by bringing the various powers together in a cooperative movement to achieve that end.[22] Indeed, only one day after the "quarantine" speech a new such plan— which was destined to attain considerable fame—was drafted by Sumner Welles.[23] Welles' thought was that it would be easier to get the democracies and the totalitarian states together to work out a broad program for the solution of political, economic, and armaments problems if they first succeeded in reaching an accord on less explosive issues. He therefore proposed trying to conclude an

[18] Davis papers. A draft appears also in the Roosevelt papers, PSF Great Britain 1933–38, Box 7.
[19] Davis papers.

[20] FR 1937, I, 113.
[21] Ibid., 131.
[22] Chamberlain's letter was not delivered to the President until October 14 (see FR 1937, III, 608, footnote 24).
[23] FR 1937, I, 665. Welles' own account of his plan appears in The Time for Decision, p. 64, and Seven Decisions that Shaped History, Chap. I. See also the discussion of the Welles plan in Langer and Gleason, The Challenge to Isolation, p. 22.

agreement concerning the fundamental rules which ought to govern international behavior such as certain rules of international law. Although Welles recognized that this project was exceedingly modest, he believed that, apart from all other considerations, it marked the limits to which the administration could go without awakening isolationist opposition at home, especially in Congress.

Welles discussed his plan with the President in the first week of October. Roosevelt seems to have reacted with enthusiasm but characteristically sought a means of imbuing the whole idea with a dramatic and human appeal. He therefore suggested holding a meeting of diplomatic representatives, accredited to Washington, at the White House on Armistice Day at which he would read a message outlining the proposal and appealing to the world for support in the interests of peace. Welles subsequently incorporated the President's suggestion in a detailed memorandum preparatory to action. But the entire undertaking was dropped before Armistice Day because Hull felt that it was too "pyrotechnical." It was nevertheless revived in early January 1938 in a manner which will be discussed later.[24]

All in all, the President's search for a plan that would reduce the danger of war in the immediate and distant future covered a period of time which started considerably before and continued after the "quarantine" speech. The most important feature of his plans was that they aimed at bringing the various powers together to settle their differences, an objective which Roosevelt for the most part assumed could best be achieved through the negotiation of an international argeement dealing with some of the basic causes of war.

At some point, however, Roosevelt also began to make groping efforts to find a technique of international organization which would provide a better solution than any as yet suggested to the question of how, if the outbreak of war proved unavoidable, nonbelligerents could have an influence upon the hostilities without becoming embroiled in them. The President developed a vague idea of his own to which he referred in talks with various people—talks that form part of the rest of this story—and in the "quarantine" passage of his Chicago speech. One of his reasons for returning to this idea on a number of occasions may well have been that he tended to follow a practice of giving expression to some half-formulated concept in the hope that others would be stimulated to improve upon it until it reached the point of furnishing a possible basis for action. At any rate, not only was Roosevelt's concept of a new technique for collaboration between nonbelligerents or neutrals vague, but, equally significantly, his plan for the use of it was also very nebulous.

Shortly after the Marco Polo Bridge incident, Eichelberger of the League of Nations Association sent the President a letter which indicates the substance of a conversation they had had about a week earlier.[25] Eichelberger wrote that he felt certain that some time before leaving the presidency, Roosevelt would find the occasion to fulfill the desire he had expressed during their talk of making a "dramatic statement" which would "not have the effect of 'simply another speech' " but would "lead the world on the upward path." Eichelberger suggested that such a statement should emphasize certain principles which the President had stressed as, for example, the need to establish economic and social justice throughout the world. "Once the world had accepted your principles," Eichelberger declared, "the denial of trade to the aggressor would be accepted by the American

[25] Roosevelt papers, OF State Department, Box 6.

people. Instead of sanctions being voted piecemeal they would take the form of a denial of the economic benefits of the more nearly just international society to the nation that would make war."

On September 14, about a week before he was to leave on the trip that ended in the "quarantine" speech, Roosevelt had a talk with Ickes which the latter recorded in his diary.[26] The President, Ickes wrote, said that he was thinking of addressing a letter to all the nations of the world, except possibly the "three bandit nations" (Germany, Italy, and Japan) in which he would "suggest that in the future if any nation should invade the rights and threaten the liberties of any of the other nations, the peace-loving nations would isolate it." What the President had in mind was to "cut off all trade with any such nation and thus deny it raw materials." However, he did not intend to apply his plan to the situation in China and Spain as what had been done could not be undone; what he wanted was to evolve a "new policy for the future" in which case "it would be a warning to the nations that are today running amuck." Ickes on his part expressed approval of the President's scheme, as it offered a "method of keeping out of war ourselves" and preventing wars from occurring. The conversation ended with a discussion of whether Roosevelt's letter should be sent before or after his tour out west and with Ickes advising the President to wait until his return.

But only two days after speaking with Ickes, the President mentioned a plan to Morgenthau which did not include any reference to possible collective action against any aggressor and, in fact, had little in common with any of Roosevelt's other proposals. The President told Morgenthau that he continued to have a hunch about the international situation and thought he might publicly declare

his readiness to act as a clearing house for peace between the governments of the world. Almost imediately thereafter he reiterated this statement to Hull. Both expressed their opposition to the President's embarking upon any such undertaking and, whether for this or some other reason, Roosevelt informed Morgenthau before he left for his western tour that he had changed his mind and had decided not to make any move that would call for any response or action from any other quarter, preservation of peace being a matter of long-term education.

The idea that Roosevelt should give a major foreign policy address during his trip across the country had first been suggested by Hull, who thought that something should be done to counteract the isolationism which he felt was rapidly increasing throughout the United States, especially in the middle west.[27] Roosevelt had readily accepted the Secretary's proposal and it was decided that the President would deliver the speech on the last day of his journey, at Chicago. Both men clearly had in mind that the address should also serve as a medium to convey to the world the revulsion felt by the American people to the outrages being committed by the "bandit nations." The original draft of the speech consisted of four memoranda, two of which were written (as far as can be learned) by Hull and Norman Davis while the remaining two were definitely written by Davis alone.[28] The memoranda as a whole were characterized by a strong tone of moral condemnation of Japan, Germany, and Italy (though these countries were not

[26] The Secret Diary of Harold L. Ickes, II, 213.

[27] The Memoirs of Cordell Hull, I, 544.

[28] For a detailed discussion of these memoranda and the manner in which Roosevelt used them, see my "Notes on Roosevelt's 'Quarantine Speech,'" in the Political Science Quarterly, September 1957. The four memoranda are in both the Roosevelt and Davis papers, although there are some differences in the texts and also in the accompanying letters and notations (see note 30).

named) and described with great forcefulness the chaos being created by their brutal actions over wide areas of the globe. In addition, two points were made repetitively: that disorder in any part of the world could not fail to affect every nation and that peace-loving nations must make a concerted effort to uphold the "laws and principles" without which peace could not exist.

Roosevelt related subsequently that while traveling in his railroad car through the great western prairies he took out the memoranda which had been furnished him by the State Department and dictated his Chicago address; the dictation flowed with a readiness he rarely attained and he made few changes after re-reading the speech.[29] A comparison of the texts makes clear that Roosevelt used the four memoranda almost *in toto* and for the most part limited himself to editing them by rearranging and shortening sentences, so that they would conform to his own brilliantly vivid and terse style of writing, and by adding a few paragraphs largely for the sake of color. The President did, however, make two important changes in the section of the draft composed by Davis without Secretary Hull's collaboration. Davis, who was known for a tendency to express his feelings about the international situation with a lack of restraint unusual in statesmen, had written a characteristic passage which said that the United States was dedicated to certain principles "without which life would not be worth living" and that, if the time ever came when the American people were not willing to defend these principles to the utmost of their ability, they would cease to have the vitality and stamina to keep this nation alive.[30] Any such assertion could clearly be interpreted as meaning that, if pushed too far, the United States would fight. Roosevelt discarded this passage and in its place put his famous "quarantine" statement.[31] Under the circumstances, in doing so he may partially have been trying to tone down the original text while striking a note which, though vague, still sounded sufficiently strong to give pause to the totalitarian states. In any case he wrote:

It would seem to be unfortunately true that the epidemic of world lawlessness is spreading.

When an epidemic of physical disease starts to spread the community approves and joins in a quarantine of the patients in

we are unable or unwilling to defend our rights and interests we will lose the respect of other nations and we will also lose our own self-respect.

This nation was dedicated to certain principles which our forebears considered to be of greater value than life itself and without which life would not be worth living. If the time ever comes when we are no longer willing or able to defend to the utmost of our ability the principles which are the foundation of freedom and progress we will sacrifice our great national heritage and will cease to have the vitality and stamina to keep this nation alive.

The original memorandum, which exists in the Davis files and which the President may or may not have seen, contains an even stronger version of this passage: "We recognize, however, that a policy of peace at any price will not ensure peace... This nation was born fighting for certain principles which our forebears considered to be of greater value than life itself."

It should be added that the only part of the first two memoranda which the President did not use was a paragraph that laid itself open to the same interpretation.

[31] The "quarantine" simile may have been suggested to the President by the fact that one of Davis' drafts prominently featured the sentence: "War is a contagion." Secretary Ickes, however, thought that Roosevelt took the simile from a talk in which he (the Secretary) said that neighbors had a right to "quarantine" themselves against the spread of an infection such as existed in the international situation. Welles has still a different version. In any case, it is a simile quite often found in political speeches and writings of the time dealing with the issue of collective security. (*The Secret Diary of Harold L. Ickes*, II, 221; Welles' version is in Samuel I. Rosenman, *Working with Roosevelt* (1952), p. 164.)

[29] William Phillips, *Venture in Diplomacy* (1952), p. 207.
[30] The passage which the President omitted read in full:
It is my determination to pursue a policy of peace... We recognize, however, that if

order to protect the health of the community against the spread of the disease.

The second change that Roosevelt made was in the ending of the speech. At the conclusion of his final memorandum, Davis had declared that "there must be positive endeavors to preserve peace" and had written an unusually moving statement to the effect that there was a tendency, in the welter of conflicting ideologies that were battling for control of the modern world, to overlook one basic truth: that "man, the human being ... is the supreme end of society." One might have expected these lines to have a special appeal for the President in view of his own constant emphasis in political matters upon the overriding importance of the individual. But he set them aside and wrote his own ending instead:

There must be positive endeavors to preserve peace.
America hates war. America hopes for peace ... Therefore America actively engages in the search for peace.

The President delivered the final text of the speech in Chicago on the morning of October 5. Immediately thereafter he went to lunch at the house of Cardinal Mundelein where he entered into a conversation in which he tried to define his "quarantine" idea further. Again, the record of his remarks is an indirect one, consisting of a letter written on the following day by Cardinal Mundelein to the Apostolic Delegate to the United States which said in part:

Yesterday the President of the United States delivered here in Chicago a strong and important address which may affect the future peace and tranquility of the world. Afterwards, in my own house, he continued discussion of the subject to which he had given considerable thought. He asked me whether he might invite participation of the Holy See in the movement and, as it is for the purpose of establishing permanent peace in a war-torn world, I answered that I thought he should. His intention in this

case would be to send a special envoy to the Vatican ... a man of ambassadorial rank ...

His plan does not contemplate either military or naval action against the unjust aggressor nation, nor does it involve "sanctions" as generally understood, but rather a policy of isolation, severance of ordinary communications in a united manner by all the governments in the pact. It does seem that if an end is to be put to the present wave of lawlessness both in Europe and Asia, it must come from a united action of the civilized peoples of the .world.[32]

Looking back over the events that began with the President's talk with Eichelberger, it is evident that the idea to which Roosevelt kept returning was, stated in its simplest form, that in case of war nonbelligerents might "quarantine" or isolate an aggressor thereby depriving him of the benefits of "ordinary communications" in the interests of the entire society of law abiding nations. This idea, as Roosevelt's subsequent remarks showed, was closely associated in the President's thinking with suggestions for possible collective action by neutrals or nonbelligerents such as had been made at the Buenos Aires Conference and elsewhere. In short, the President was trying to find a formula which would enable nonbelligerents to exercise an influence upon a war to the extent of actually defeating an aggressor while still limiting themselves to the use of methods which would not provoke reprisals that would involve them in hostilities. The President's "quarantine" idea was nonprovocative in that it contained features such as the moral overtones of the Pan-American agreements; but, on the other hand, it called for exceedingly drastic action on the part of the nonbelligerents without providing them with the protection that might be afforded by the much more positive safeguard of retaining the status of neutrals. Roosevelt never consistently faced up to the fact that his "quarantine" device departed from the principle of neutrality

[32] Roosevelt papers, special file on foreign policy statements.

and at moments seems even to have persuaded himself that the common isolation of an aggressor by nonbelligerents was a form of neutral cooperation. This, however, required quite a *tour de force* so that the whole quarantining concept never reached the stage of providing a usable medium for action and although Roosevelt referred to it even after his Chicago speech none of the available evidence suggests that he ever really intended to push it. Indeed, he continued, as he himself emphasized, to grope for a genuinely satisfactory formula.

The theory that the President's "quarantine" idea was and remained a confused and unsuccessful attempt to solve the dilemma of how to restrict aggression without resorting to threatening measures such as sanctions is supported by two incidents that followed Roosevelt's Chicago speech. The day after his return from Chicago, the President held an off-the-record press conference which has since become famous.[33] The reporters, convinced that the President's references to a "quarantine" in his Chicago address

[33] Samuel I. Rosenman, ed., *The Public Papers and Addresses of Franklin D. Roosevelt, 1937* (1941), p. 414. On the same day the President also saw William Phillips, who was in the United States on a short leave of absence from his post as ambassador in Rome. In his *Ventures in Diplomacy* (p. 206), written many years later, Phillips states that during the course of their conversation he asked Roosevelt what he meant by a "quarantine" and the President said that, in dictating the text of his speech he had "searched for a word which was not 'sanctions' and had settled upon a 'quarantine' as a 'drawing away from someone.'" Phillips felt that the President, in developing his thought further, showed a "willingness to go very far in drawing away." But Roosevelt's comments do not seem to have added up to anything very concrete for Phillips merely says that the President seemed to him to be taking a "new position" which showed a "disposition to favor the so-called peace-loving countries as against Japan, Italy, and Germany, the three bad boys." Moreover, as the ambassador apparently devoted much of the time to telling the President about the benefits that Mussolini was bringing to Italy, it is hard to evaluate how much Roosevelt's remarks reflected his reaction to the ambassador's statements.

had been carefully chosen to convey to the American people and the world that Roosevelt had decided to use sanctions— economic and perhaps military—against Japan, subjected him to many questions. His answers seemed to them meaningless, from which they concluded that, fearful of the almost hysterical attacks launched against his speech from certain quarters, the President was intentionally being evasive, having determined to beat a hasty retreat; but in retrospect Roosevelt's replies sound like a genuine attempt to explain what he had in mind. The main point which the President tried to make was that he was searching for a method of furthering the cause of world peace, that his "quarantine" concept was one of a variety of ideas related to this search, but that he was still in the process of seeking the right solution. The reporters were especially persistent in asking whether a "quarantine" concept was a sanction, to which the President responded by stating with considerable vehemence that "sanction" was a "terrible word" which should be thrown "out of the window" and by admonishing the correspondents not to "get off on the sanctions route" as he had "never suggested" sanctions. A reporter explained that by "sanctions" he meant "going further than moral denunciation" but the President declared: "That is not a definition of sanctions." When the same reporter said: "Are you excluding any coercive action? Sanctions are coercive," Roosevelt replied, "That is exactly the difference." When the reporter asked: "Better then to keep it in a moral sphere?" the President retorted "No, it can be a very practical sphere."

The correspondents also repeatedly questioned the President as to whether a "quarantine" was "neutral" and felt that on this point in particular his answers were so confused they must reflect a deliberate attempt to be misleading. But the key to Roosevelt's answers seems to lie in the fact that he had in mind techniques for neutral collaboration of the kind which the United States itself had suggested at the Buenos Aires Conference and in his tendency to regard his "quarantine" idea as similarly based upon the concept of neutrality. In general, the President said that it was "by no means" necessary that the method of international action he wanted to find would be "contrary to the exercise of neutrality." When asked whether he would not at least admit that a "quarantine" would essentially amount to a repudiation of the United States neutrality law, Roosevelt asserted, "Not for a minute. It may be an expansion." At another point when a correspondent, who from the outset had shown marked skepticism, said that in his opinion a "quarantine" was no longer neutrality, Roosevelt replied that "On the contrary, it might be a stronger neutrality." The President further declared: "There are a lot of methods in the world that have never been tried yet."

About two weeks after the President's press conference, Norman Davis, who was about to depart for Brussels, where he was to represent the United States at the Nine Power Conference which had been called as a result of the League's action, went to Hyde Park to receive his final instructions from Roosevelt.[34] In notes, written the day after their meeting, Davis recorded that the President "particularly objected to the word *sanctions* being used and said that this was a word that ought not to be used any more, some other word must be found." Roosevelt then asserted that every effort must be made at the Nine Power Conference to settle the Sino-Japanese conflict by mediation but that if none of these efforts succeeded, all of the countries that wished to stop the war and protect themselves from its consequences "or in other words the *so-called neutral nations,* should band to-gether for their own protection against this contagion." One thing that might be considered was having the other powers agree to give to China every facility for acquiring arms, et cetera, although in that case the United States could do nothing because its laws would not permit. "Another alternative would be for *neutrals* to ostracize Japan, break off relations." [35]

Attached to these notes in Davis's files is a paper marked "Handed me by the President as of possible use." The paper contains what must be an excerpt from an article or book which states that "the principle of neutral cooperation, short of obligation to use force," as embodied in the Saavedra Lamas Anti-War Pact and reaffirmed at the Buenos Aires Conference, might "offer a useful formula for the United States at the present time" as it "suggests the possibility of a constructive program in which a group of neutrals, acting together, but without threat of force, might make their influence felt. If stressed by the President it could be made the instrument for a positive . . . policy."

If the President's remarks to the press and to Norman Davis showed among other things the extent to which his "quarantine" concept was loosely conceived, it cannot be emphasized too strongly that Roosevelt's idea of the use to which he wanted to put his "quarantine" device was equally ill defined. The furthest the President went in discussing a plan was in his talk with Cardinal Mundelein when he indicated that he had two purposes in mind: one of initiating a movement for the establishment of a "permanent peace" and the other of arresting the "present wave of lawlessness both in Europe and Asia." While he suggested that the first aim might be achieved by the conclusion of a universal pact involving some method of collective

---

[34] Davis papers.

[35] Italics inserted in both these quotations.

action designed to isolate an aggressor, Roosevelt apparently said nothing about any means of attaining the second objective. In speaking to Secretary Ickes, he had referred to the possibility of reaching an international agreement from which the "three bandit nations" would be excluded. But he evidently abandoned this proposal nor was he likely to appeal to the Pope to assume the leadership of a political venture overtly directed against the governments of Germany, Italy, and Japan.[36] Moreover, in so far as he had a plan, the President was not very intent upon pursuing it for Cardinal Mundelein stated specifically in his letter to the Apostolic Delegate that Roosevelt had not indicated what he intended to do next. It is in fact quite possible that in his conversation with Cardinal Mundelein, the President was not so much interested in advancing any specific scheme as in reaffirming his desire to establish closer relations with the Vatican through the appointment of an envoy, a matter with which he had been concerned for some time, as he believed that religious and lay leaders by pooling their influence could create a better spiritual climate in which peace was more likely to thrive.[37]

The detailed story of the "quarantine" speech seems therefore to indicate clearly that Roosevelt was not trying through his statements at Chicago to prepare the world for the enforcement of a policy of sanctions against Japan which he had already decided to adopt. Indeed, besides

expressing the vigor of the reaction of his countrymen to the acts of aggression being committed in Europe and Asia and sounding a very general note of warning to the totalitarian states, the President probably wanted his Chicago speech to convey one message: that, in response to the outcry of the many people who were appealing to him to forestall the tragedy of another major war he was trying "to *do* something" in terms of uniting the world and opening the door to the possibility of unlimited peace. Roosevelt's own explanation of his speech was in essence that its significance lay in this message and in view of his long effort to find a peace plan which would involve a concerted attempt on the part of all the powers to reach an agreement —especially a "constructive" agreement— there is little reason to doubt that he meant what he said. Thus when questioned at the press conference held after his return from Chicago about the meaning of his Chicago address as a whole, the President replied: "I don't know that I can give you spot news because the lead is in the last line, 'America actively engages in the search for peace' ... We are looking for some way to peace." When one of the correspondents then said that "foreign papers put it as an attitude without a program," the President answered: "It is an attitude and it does not outline a program but it says we are looking for a program." In addition, in a Fireside Chat on October 12, which was devoted to a discussion of his tour out west, Roosevelt, in referring to his remarks at Chicago, said that it was the duty of a president to think in terms of peace not only for one but for many generations and that peace must therefore be "sound and permanent," built on a "cooperative search" for peace by all nations desiring that end.[38] In conclusion he declared:

---

[36] For a discussion of the Pope's policy at this time and how far he was likely to go in interfering in the temporal conflicts of other governments, see Camille M. Cianfarra, *The Vatican and the War* (1944). Also for the kind of relationship the President did ultimately establish with the Vatican in regard to the international situation, see *Franklin D. Roosevelt and Pius XII: Wartime Correspondence* (the introduction by Myron C. Taylor describes this relationship very well).

[37] Langer and Gleason, *The Challenge to Isolation*, section on "A Special Mission to the Vatican," beginning on page 347.

[38] Rosenman, comp. and coll., *The Public Papers and Addresses of Franklin D. Roosevelt, 1937*, p. 429.

The common sense, the intelligence of America agree with my statement that "America hates war . . . America hopes for peace, therefore America actively engages in the search for peace."

. . . It may be said therefore that Roosevelt had not abandoned the hope to which he was so intensely committed, of securing peace by peaceful means. And that he definitely had not settled upon any policy of drastic action, let alone sanctions, either in order to support the general principle of restraining lawlessness by collective measures or to stop the advance of the totalitarian nations as a whole or of Japan individually.[39]

[39] One further point should be mentioned. Sumner Welles, writing in the 1950's, said that in the summer of 1937 the President was far more preoccupied with the Far East than with Europe and that Roosevelt had, on several occasions, talked to him about the possibility of stationing units of the American and British navies at certain points in the Pacific to enforce an embargo against Japan. Welles stated further

that as he was in Europe during most of September 1937 he knew little about the writing of the "quarantine" speech but believed the President had in mind the embargo and quasi blockade he had mentioned earlier.

However, Welles' recollection closer to the event does not bear out the thesis that the Chicago address reflected Roosevelt's determination to use sanctions against Japan but instead supports the interpretation that the President was thinking of some program to stabilize the world situation. For in 1944 Welles wrote:

Partly because of the issues involved in the Spanish war, and partly because the real nature of Hitlerism was becoming increasingly apparent, the President determined to make a vigorous effort to persuade public opinion that in its own interest the United States should propose some constructive plan for international action to check the forces of aggression before they succeeded in engulfing the world. For this effort he selected the very heart of isolationism—the city of Chicago.

Welles then went on to quote the "quarantine" speech. (See Welles' *Seven Decisions That Shaped History*, pp. 8, 13–14, 70–75, 91–93; *The Time for Decision*, p. 61. There is a letter from Welles on the "quarantine" speech in Rosenman's *Working with Roosevelt*, p. 164.)

16

History Through a Beard

SAMUEL E. MORISON

Each of the five foreign wars the United States has fought has engendered a spirited historiographical controversy. Historians using generally the same sources have come to very different conclusions on the causes of America's participation in the wars. But the writing on the two great conflicts of the twentieth century differs in two important ways from that on the three wars of the nineteenth. In the first place, all the historians who have written on the First or Second World Wars, regardless of their specific emphasis, may be classified in one of two groups—as defenders or attackers (more commonly labeled revisionists) of the administration that took the nation into war. Secondly, the writing is more passionate, and the positions taken are more rigid. This second difference may be accounted for by the fact that most of the authors who wrote on the two wars of the twentieth century lived through the events they described; whereas the scholars who in this century studied nineteenth century wars (and the significant works on those wars were done in this century), obviously, had no personal experiences.

Regarding intervention in 1917, there are those who strongly defend President Wilson's decision for war whether they believe he fought to protect the rights of Americans to travel unmolested on the high seas and to trade with the belligerents, or to prevent a German victory which would endanger American security. The revisionists accuse the President of having taken the country into the conflict because he succumbed to pressure by bankers, munitions makers, and others involved in supplying the Allies or by the British who duped him and his advisors, or because of his own excessive Anglophilism, which caused him to adopt an unneutral course in favor of the Allies from the very beginning.

The historiographical dispute on the Second World War is different from that of the First again in two significant ways. The passions are more intense, the arguments more heated, and the positions more rigid and dogmatic. For not only did most of the writers live through the events they narrated, but many were personally and deeply involved before the war in the public debate on the wisdom of aiding the Allies. Secondly, the revisionists who consider entry into the war a colossal blunder not only place the blame squarely on President Roosevelt but accuse him of duplicity, deception, and mendacity. Their personal hatred of the President and their hostility to his domestic program colored their analysis of his foreign policy. No historian of World War I, however severe his indictment of Wilson's course of action, ever questioned the President's honesty or integrity.

FROM *By Land and by Sea*, by S. E. Morison. Copyright 1951, 1953 by Priscilla B. Morison. Reprinted by permission of Alfred A. Knopf, Inc.

Of all the revisionists, none criticize President Roosevelt more harshly or castigated him more relentlessly than Charles A. Beard in his President Roosevelt and the Coming of War, 1941: A Study in Appearances and Realities, *published in 1948, nor has any account had a greater influence in shaping the public attitude toward the coming of the war. Beard contends that Roosevelt foisted a diabolical plot upon the American people. After deceiving the people into re-electing him in 1940 on a pledge to keep them out of the war, he then pursued such policies against Japan as to make inevitable that country's attack on the United States fleet at Pearl Harbor, thus precipitating the war.*

So damning an indictment of the President inevitably elicited a large number of rebuttals. The best of them is in the form of a book review by Samuel E. Morison, one of America's most distinguished historians, biographer of Columbus, author of numerous works on United States history, and official historian of the operations of the United States Navy in World War II. Morison not only exposes Beard's "every error, innuendo, or misconception" but also attacks his historical method and attempts an explanation of why so eminent a scholar should have so distorted history.

HISTORY BY INNUENDO

About twenty years ago Oliver Wendell Holmes in a letter to his friend Sir Frederick Pollock had something to say about Charles A. Beard's *Economic Interpretation of the Constitution*. Beard, said Holmes, argued "that the Constitution primarily represents the triumph of the money power over democratic agrarianism and individualism. Beard ... went into rather ignoble thought most painstaking investigation of the investments of the leaders, with an innuendo even if disclaimed. I shall believe until compelled to think otherwise that they wanted to make a nation and invested (bet) on the belief that they would make one, not that they wanted a powerful government because they had invested. Belittling arguments always have a force of their own, but you and I believe that high-mindedness is not impossible to man."

That famous book came out in 1913. The "innuendo" that Holmes alluded to has been disclaimed by the author more than once, and his penultimate work, *The Enduring Federalist* (1948), might have pleased Alexander Hamilton. But his latest, *President Roosevelt and the Com-*

ing of the War (1948), may also be characterized as a "rather ignoble though most painstaking investigation." It is a coldly passionate argument, posing as objective history, to prove that Franklin D. Roosevelt planned to pull his country into World War II shortly after it commenced, deceived the American people into re-electing him a second time by swearing to keep them out, plotted with Winston Churchill to provoke some incident which he could call an "attack" by Germany; and, when Hitler refused to fall into the trap, "maneuvered" Japan into hitting the Pacific Fleet at Pearl Harbor. All this, it seems, for personal power. Beard could see no menace to the United States if Hitler conquered all Europe, and Japan took the other half of the world, suppressing liberty as they proceeded. He had taken care of that in an earlier book, *A Foreign Policy for America* (1940).

Nobody can laugh Beard off. He is, by any standards, an important historian and a fine man. Born in Indiana seventy-three years ago, he went through the regular mill for professional historians, rose to be full professor at Columbia, and taught students effectively for several years. His *Rise of American Civilization,* which appeared twenty-odd years ago, is still, in my opinion, the most brilliant historical survey of the American scene ever written; a delight to read; stimulating, witty, and revealing. He has been president of the American Historical Association. His *American Government and Politics* has been a standard text for almost forty years.

As a man, Beard is and should be an object of admiration. His resignation from Columbia University in 1917, as a protest against the dismissal of Professors Cattell and Dana, was a noble and a courageous gesture. No American since John Fiske had been able to earn a living by writing history, apart from an academic milch cow. But Charles and Mary Beard, the forthright lady whom he had married in 1900, preferred four-legged cows to the academic variety. They established themselves on a hilltop farm in New Milford, Connecticut, created a successful dairy farm, and continued to write books which have been no less profitable. Farmer Beard has been a good neighbor and a power in his community, while Dr. Beard has performed countless acts of kindness and encouragement to younger students, including myself. I won't pretend that I hate to write what follows, for I enjoy controversy quite as much as does the Sage of New Milford; but my esteem for Beard the man far outweighs my indignation with Beard the historian.

No more rugged individualist exists than Charles Austin Beard. Since his salad days he has belonged to no party and joined no sect. He takes a puckish delight in shocking the smug and the complacent; but he also enjoys letting down with a thump any group of liberals who claim him as their own. At the present moment he is the darling of the McCormick-Patterson Axis, but I doubt whether he enjoys their patronage. Beard is no joiner, his name never appears on those long letterheads that spill down the margins, and he is always one jump ahead of the professional patrioteers. On rare occasions when a Legionnaire goes after Charles, or a D.A.R. after Mary, the assailant retires howling from the scene, like a jackal that attacks a lion; for Beard keeps a blunderbuss loaded with facts and figures at his barn door.

One of the amusing if unamiable devices of Beard's historical method is an effective use of innuendo, as Holmes observed. A typical one, in *The Rise of American Civilization* (II, 83), describes how "on one occasion" during the American Civil War, "Gladstone, whose family fortune contained profits from the slave trade... virtually acknowledged southern Independence." Admiral Mahan, anathema to Beard, makes his bow in *A Foreign Policy for America* (p. 39) as "the son of a professor and swivel-chair tactician at West Point," who "served respectably, but without distinction, for a time in the navy," and "found an easy berth at the Naval War College." In the Roosevelt book (p. 254), referring to a constitutional opinion that he dislikes, written by the Assistant Solicitor General, Beard remarks: "Mr. Cox, with a B.A. acquired at Christ Church, Oxford, England, whose knowledge of the American Constitution may have been slighter than his knowledge of the English Constitution...." Mr. Cox spent three years at Oxford as a Rhodes Scholar, after graduating from the University of Nebraska, and, for several years before his government appoinment, practiced law in New York. With equal unfairness I might write: "Mr. Beard, whose favorable reception in Japan many years ago predisposed him to favor that country rather than his own in 1941."

BEARD'S NEW JERUSALEM

Another trait that runs through Beard's writings is a disbelief in the

Great Man. One looks in vain for any appreciation of Washington, Hamilton, Jefferson, Jackson, Clay, Webster, Lee, or Cleveland as men. Their intellectual qualities may be praised, not their moral stature. Some are treated with subtle disparagement; others appear as wan products of economic forces. In all his work I can remember but three clear, well-rounded pictures of eminent personalities: Lincoln in the *Basic History,* Theodore Roosevelt and Jonathan Edwards in the *Rise;* and even T.R. is described as a natural product of a bourgeois background. Jonathan Edwards appears to be one of Beard's few objects of admiration, and an instructive parallel might be drawn between his theology and Beard's historiography. If Charles could only have moved to Connecticut two centuries earlier, how he and Jonathan would have lambasted each other from rival pulpits!

A third constant in Beard's work is his attitude toward war and those who fight and direct wars. Since his youth, when he tried to get into the summer frolic of 1898, Beard has detested war. Consistently in his works he has ignored war, minimized its results, and derided military men. He would probably say, in defense of ignoring war, that his writings are largely on political subjects or on cultural history, in which war has a slight part; but Albert J. Beveridge could find place for the impact of the War of Independence on the federal debates of 1787–8, and could point out that some of the differences between the doctrines of Marshall and those of Jefferson were due to the fact that Marshall had been a soldier.

Now, one may share Beard's detestation of war as a barbarous survival; but one must admit that American liberty, union, and civilization would never have been unless men had been willing to fight for them. Whether well directed or not, an immense amount of American

effort has gone into preparation for war, making war, and paying for war; and to leave war out of any general history of the United States, whether it be called Basic, Political, Constitutional, or Cultural, is an evasion of essential truth. Beard, aloof on his Connecticut hilltop, was unofficial high priest for the thousands of churchmen, teachers, and publicists who promoted disarmament in a world where aggressive nations were arming, and who prepared the younger generation for everything but the war that they had to fight.

The clue to Beard's inconsistencies and tergiversations is furnished by the historical method he has consciously adopted and consistently preached. This method, spread at large in several articles and books, is well known to the profession but hardly to the public, who have no reason to suspect that his standards of truth and objectivity differ from those of any other professional historian. He starts with a negative, the denial of Ranke's classic dictum to write history "as it actually happened" (*wie es eigentlich gewesen ist*). Nobody, says Beard, can do that, since history, conceived as the sum total of human activity, is so multifarious and multitudinous that nobody could possibly put it all down in writing; and if he did, nobody would read it. (Of course that is not what Ranke meant, but never mind.) The historian therefore tries to make sense out of the totality of history by selecting facts that to him are significant. Consciously or not, he selects and arranges these facts according to some "frame of reference" as to what is socially desirable for the time, place, and circumstances in which he writes. "The historian who writes history ... performs an act of faith, as to order and movement. ... He is thus in the position of a statesman dealing with public affairs; in writing he acts and in acting he makes choices, large or small, timid or bold, with respect to some conception of the nature of things, and the degree of his influence and immortality will depend upon the length and correctness of his forecast." [1]

G. M. Trevelyan reminds us that "the object of history is to know and understand the past on all its sides"; but Beard will not have it so. The object of history, according to him, is to influence the present and future, in a direction that the historian considers socially desirable. The ordinary, dumb, as-it-really-happened historian admits he has some frame of reference; but he does not consciously go about polishing one up before he starts writing, nor does he reject facts that do not fit the frame. He believes that he has an obligation to keep himself on the alert for facts that will alter any tentative conclusions with which he starts. Moreover, an historian conceives it to be his main business to illuminate the past in the light of his acquired knowledge and skill; not to use the past to project the future. He may wish to influence the future, but that should not be his main preoccupation. I naturally hope, through my naval history, to help persuade the American people not to scrap their navy; but that is incidental. My real task is to tell what the navy did in World War II, mistakes and all.

History fitted to a consciously set frame, with the historian's sights set for the future, not the past, is really a kind of preaching. However noble or generous the objective set by such a writer may be, his end product could only by exception be history in any modern or reputable meaning of that word. It would ordinarily be in a class with the violent sectarian histories of past centuries, or with those in which Communist historians throw the "party line." When Beard set himself up as preacher

and prophet, he was lost as an historian. One may quote against him the lines that James Russell Lowell wrote on himself:

There is Lowell, who's striving Parnassus to climb
With a whole bale of isms tied together with rhyme;

. . . .

His lyre has some chords that would ring pretty well,
But he'd rather by half make a drum of the shell,
And rattle away till he's old as Methusalem,
At the head of a march to the last new Jerusalem.

Beard's last new Jerusalem is a socialized, collectivist state in isolation. "Does the world move, and if so, in what direction?" he asked in 1933, after both Hitler and Roosevelt were in power. "Does it move forward to some other arrangement which can be only dimly divined—a capitalist dictatorship, a proletarian dictatorship, or a collectivist democracy? The last of these is my own guess...." And in an article, "The World as I Want It," which he wrote for the *Forum* in June 1934, he showed clearly that by "collectivist democracy" he meant a "workers' republic" without poverty or luxury; "a beautiful country ... labor requited and carried on in conditions conducive to virtue." A fair vision indeed, such as his Fabian friends had dreamed of at the turn of the century.

Within two years, however, there appeared a disturbing shadow, the threat of war. While Beard was not a pacifist in the strict meaning of the term, he felt he had been sold by Woodrow Wilson and the Treaty of Versailles. Although he had time and again urged students to get behind the documents and discover the reality behind the phrase, warning them to be skeptical of "the next grand committee on public mystification," [2] he swallowed the famous Nye Committee

---

[1] "Written History as an Act of Faith," *American Historical Review*, XXXIX (1934), 226; *The Nature of the Social Sciences* (1934); *The Discussion of Human Affairs* (1936).

[2] Review in the *New Republic*, XLIV (1925), 311.

report complete. During the interval between world wars he actively supported disarmament and cast ridicule on the generals and admirals who opposed stripping the national defense.

"CONTINENTAL AMERICANISM"

Beard realized, however, that negative criticism was not enough. Hating war, yet faced with a world where Japan and Germany were arming feverishly, he conscientiously sought a way out. And in a series of publications he presented a positive program which he believed would let America live in peace and prosperity even if the rest of the world went to hell.[3] The United States should evacuate the Philippines, renounce all "engines of war and diplomacy," and .apply its entire political thought and energy to a super New Deal directed by a super TVA, the "Standard of Life Authority." Foreign trade would be controlled by a National Trade Authority with an eventual purpose of attaining complete economic isolation. Immigration must cease, except for students and tourists; the merchant marine must be allowed to sink, and the navy be reduced to a submarine or coast-defense force.

"Continental Americanism," as Beard called this blueprint for the future, made no headway. It looked too much like that which the Chinese Empire had followed for some five hundred years, the end product of which was not alluring. It also had a disquieting resemblance to the economic autarchy practiced by Hitler. His friends wondered how a scholar of Beard's knowledge and experience could propose anything so extravagant. Perhaps the answer is that

[3] Especially *The Open Door at Home, a Trial Philosophy of National Interest* (1934). My quotations are from Samuel F. Bemis's review in *American Historical Review*, XL, 541–3; *Giddy Minds and Foreign Quarrels* (1939); *A Foreign Policy for America* (1940).

isolation breeds isolationism. In a university there is an intellectual rough-and-tumble that one lacks on a hilltop. You get more back talk even from freshmen than from milch cows.

This pacifistic super-isolationism has apparents become Beard's frame of reference for recent history. In a thoughtful letter to the *Saturday Review of Literature* (August 17, 1935), answering an article by Julian Huxley, he declared that there was an objective test for every system of economics or sociology; namely, "its continuing appropriateness for life and thought amid the remorseless changes of human affairs in time—which is the subject of historical inquiry." In other words, did the prophet make good? One would suppose that if Hitler and Tojo had not convinced Beard that a Chinese policy was inappropriate for America, the atomic bomb would. On the contrary, the whole Roosevelt book falls within that same frame. Beard is trying to show that Roosevelt dragged the nation into an unnecessary war. He is trying to revive the same masochistic state of public opinion into which he and most of the American people fell at the end of World War I. Wilson then, Roosevelt again, sold us down the river; watch out that Truman does not pick a quarrel with Russia.

Indeed, Beard is so firmly and emotionally enmeshed in this new frame of reference that he has smashed his earlier ones. Time was when history through a Beard moved with the sweep of relentless, dynamic forces. The American Revolution and the Civil War were foreordained by economics; the concept of the former as a quarrel caused by George III and his ministers "shrinks into a trifling joke";[4] the latter "was merely the culmination of the deep-running transformation that shifted the center of gravity in American Society. . . ."[5] In a

[4] *Rise of American Civilization*, I, 201.
[5] Ibid., pp. 632–3.

little book of 1936, entitled *The Devil Theory of War,* he again stressed dynamic economic-social forces, and reserved his most devastating sarcasm for the "childish" theory that "wicked politicians, perhaps shoved along by wicked bankers," marshaled innocent people into war; that the politician "is a kind of *deus ex machina* ... making the people do things they would never think of doing otherwise."

Yet, note how the *deus* (or rather *diabolus*) *ex machina* emerges ten years later. Franklin D. Roosevelt, personally, without dynamic forces or economic interests behind him, is accused of changing the orientation of his country in *American Foreign Policy in the Making, 1932–1940* (1946); and now appears in full diabolic array, with Stimson, Hull, Knox, Stark, and Marshall as attendant imps, in *President Roosevelt and the Coming of the War* (1948).

The premise of both books is stated in the opening sentence of the second: "President Roosevelt entered the year 1941 carrying moral responsibility for his covenants with the American people to keep this nation out of war—so to conduct foreign affairs as to avoid war. Those covenants, made in the election campaign of 1940, were of two kinds. The first were the pledges of the Democratic Party.... The second were his personal promises....

"The anti-war covenants of the Democratic Party ... were clearcut: 'We will not participate in foreign wars, and we will not send our Army, naval or air forces to fight in foreign lands outside the Americas, except in case of attack. ... The direction and aim of our foreign policy has been, and will continue to be, the security and defense of our own land and the maintenance of its peace.' "

This is the first time, to the writer's knowledge, that any historian has honored a party platform with the old Puritan name of "covenant." As Beard is a great stickler for semantics, the use of so solemn a word for flimsies like party platforms and campaign promises is astonishing. Yet, even if we concede that a party platform is a promise binding the candidate, all promises have implied predicates. If Farmer Beard promises to sell twenty heifers on a certain date for a certain price, it is understood that if in the meantime the heifers die or the other party goes bankrupt, or if he dies and his widow needs the heifers for her support, the promise no longer binds. So, political promises imply no important change of conditions that will make their implementation contrary to the public interest. A party platform is a party platform, not the supreme law of the land. The presidential oath of office —that the President will, to the best of his ability, "preserve, protect and defend the Constitution of the United States"— must override any campaign promise. Moreover, that platform had the saving clause: "except in case of attack." Not that that daunts Beard! Off he goes, like Don Quixote, to prove that the Japanese did not attack us at Pearl Harbor; F.D.R. attacked them.

ROOSEVELT'S FOREIGN POLICY

The main object of foreign policy is not peace at any price, but the defense of the freedom and security of the nation. It is clear that Beard still firmly believes that nothing that the European Axis or Japan did or could do endangered the freedom or security of the United States, which he holds no less dear than does any other citizen. His argument for the faithlessness of President Roosevelt to his "covenant" is carried out in a sort of dialectic isolationism, as if the issue of peace or war, the most momentous the nation had to face since 1861, was merely a matter of debate and negotiation between the two ends of Pennsylvania

Avenue, Washington, D.C., with Charles A. Beard of New Milford, Connecticut, in the role of God Almighty delivering the last judgment. If all books on the war before 1942 but Beard's should perish from the earth, the curious reader in the far future would have to infer that a dim figure named Hitler was engaged in a limited sort of war to redress the lost balance of Versailles; that Japan was a virtuous nation pursuing its legitimate interests in Asia; and that neither threatened or even wished to interfere with any legitimate American interest.

Beard would answer, maybe the Nazis and Japs were devils too, but what the hell? Adopt my Chinese foreign policy and America is safe. Those responsible for American foreign policy naturally did not see it that way. Unlike the Sage of New Milford they lacked the imagination to suppose that American freedom could be defended if Japan was allowed to bring half the world's population under her hegemony, and Hitler controlled most of the other half.

Even his stoutest supporters will not deny that President Roosevelt failed to take the American people into his complete confidence or that he attempted to build up national defense without clearly indicating what the dangers were. Secretary Stimson was evidently troubled by this and still believes that Theodore Roosevelt by sounding the trumpet earlier and more frequently would better have prepared the people psychologically for war. Robert E. Sherwood in his book based on the Harry Hopkins papers regrets that the President had to utter soothing phrases in 1940 in order to be re-elected. No one can be certain whether they are right or not. Let the reader, however, cast his mind back to 1940, or read a few newspapers or magazines of that year, and he will recall or ascertain a climate of opinion which compelled the President to do good by stealth. The American people were still

bogged down in the most pacifistic or anti-war phase of their history since 1806. Disillusion with the results of World War I, the Nye Report, the appeasement of Hitler by Neville Chamberlain, the Communist propaganda against an "imperialist war," and the speeches and writings of hundreds of able men, of whom Beard was one of the best, had brought about a state of opinion that regarded American entry into World War II as unthinkable. During the first half of 1940 men of good will, leaders in business and the professions, journalists and crossroads philosophers, were virtually united in the belief that the European war was "no concern of ours," that to stop Hitler was not worth the life of one American, that the oceans were a sure defense of the United States, and that if Hitler tried any monkey business in South America, the American nations could stop him without aid from anyone. The fall of France and of the Low Countries and the expected attack on Britain shook this complacency but failed to break it.

Thus, the essential problem of the administration was to support Great Britain (and after June 1941, Russia) as much and as far as Congress and public opinion would permit, to build up American armed strength, and to keep Japan quiet by diplomacy; hoping by measures "short of war" to prevent an Axis victory or, if that did not suffice, to come into the war prepared to win it. There is no distinction of kind, in a world at war, between measures that a neutral takes to prevent being involved, and measures taken to win if finally involved; only a difference of degree. James Madison, Beard's great hero among the founding fathers, once wrote: "The means of security can only be regulated by the means and the danger of attack. They will, in fact, be ever determined by these rules and by no others."

Exactly when President Roosevelt and his advisers decided that "short of war" would not suffice may never be known. It is improbable that they knew, themselves. As the fortunes of war fluctuated in Europe, it seemed one day that with Lend-Lease and indirect aid Britain and Russia would win; then would come a sudden blitz in North Africa or Crete or elsewhere that dashed Allied hopes. Under those circumstances, inconsistency appeared between the administration's words and its deeds. It is an easy matter to draw a brief of Rooseveltian "hypocrisy." Other great men under similar circumstances, puzzled and baffled under myriad pressures, have been subject to the same accusation. James Monroe published in 1797 a furious diatribe against Washington's inconsistent conduct of foreign affairs; Lincoln was accused of vacillating over the issue of secession; Sir Edward Grey lay under the same charge in 1914; even Winston Churchill was not so firm and consistent as he makes out in *The Second World War*.

APPEARANCES AND REALITIES

Now for a few sordid details on *President Roosevelt and the Coming of the War*, a book so full of *suppressio veri* and *suggestio falsi* that it would take one of almost equal length to expose every error, innuendo, or misconception. The book is divided into three parts, "Appearances," "Unveiling Realities," and "Realities as Described by the Pearl Harbor Documents"; but there is a rather confusing interplay of the three, as Beard's principles of division are subjective or polemical. "Appearances" includes a good many genuine realities, and "Realities" includes the conjectures of Washington gossip columnists, articles by *Chicago Tribune* writers, and odd scraps from any sources that support Beard's thesis.

Thus, Beard taunts Roosevelt with doing nothing to help Britain until he was re-eelected; but the destroyer-naval bases deal, the first "short of war" aid, was consummated on September 2, 1940. An entire chapter, "Patrols as Appearances," is vitiated by Beard's confusion of the Neutrality Patrol, set up as early as September 5, 1939, and approved by the Act of Panama on October 2, with escort-convoy operations; nor does he distinguish between escorting ships to occupied Iceland and escorting ships to belligerent Britain. The first Lend-Lease Act was passed by Congress March 11, 1941; Iceland was occupied by United States forces on July 7; and the navy was ordered to escort convoys to Iceland only a few days later. The first transatlantic convoy to be assisted by the U.S. Navy sailed from Halifax September 16; and until war was formally declared by Germany on the United States, the American escort dropped such convoys at a mid-ocean meeting point. The President's denials in April that the navy was escorting British ships to Britain were true and not false, as Beard contends; and the reference Beard gives on page 98, note 16, to prove the contrary proves only that the Atlantic Patrol was being augmented at the expense of the Pacific Fleet. For a neutral nation to provide armed escorts to protect ships against submarine attack was illegal according to pre-1914 conceptions of neutrality. But the elaborate structure of neutral rights and duties erected at the Hague Conventions had completely broken down by 1940. Hitler's Germany flouted the Kellogg-Briand Pact, broke the treaty against unrestricted submarine warfare on the very first day of the European war, and showed no respect for the most scrupulous neutrality observed by Denmark, Norway, and the Netherlands. Consequently the legal advisers of the Roosevelt administration very properly regarded the United States as no longer bound by pre-1914 conceptions of neutral duties.

Part II, "Unveiling Realities," affords Beard a marvelous opportunity, by quoting all manner of guesses, editorials, speeches and the like, to build up in the reader's mind an impression of frightful iniquity on the part of the administration. For instance, David Lawrence is quoted on pages 289–90 as asking a number of rhetorical questions, such as: "Why were all our battleships in harbor in Hawaii on December 7, 1941, instead of out at sea, and who in Washington gave the orders to keep them there?" But Beard never gives the answer: that they were there by Admiral Kimmel's order, in accordance with normal peacetime routine, after he had received the "war warning" meassage of November 27.

Again, Lawrence is quoted to the effect that Admiral Richardson protested in 1940 against concentration of ships in Pearl Harbor on the ground that it "was dangerous and offered the Japanese a chance to destroy much of the Navy at a single blow." But Beard, after combing through the Richardson testimony before the Joint Congressional Committee, is not candid enough to state that the Admiral expressly disclaimed danger as motive for his protest, which was based entirely on logistic grounds—the difficulty of supply and the deprivation of leave and liberty to naval personnel.

The "Realities as Described by the Pearl Harbor Documents" are "realities" only in the Beardian sense; namely, such selections from the multitude of available facts as fit his conscious frame of reference, to the effect that President Roosevelt was a villian and the war was unnecessary.

An important insinuation against "the management of the Congressional Committee" (probably meaning its counsel, Seth Richardson) appears in a note on page 420. The "management" is accused

of leaving out of the printed record, "for reasons of its own," a letter of Admiral Stark, dated April 3, 1941, to the commanders in chief of the three United States fleets, in which Stark says: "The question of our entry into the war now seems to be *when* and not *whether*." "Students of history" are pompously warned by Beard to be "on guard" against such omissions. The Committee, however, did print this letter, but in another place in its voluminous report: Part 33, Exhibit No. 73, p. 1357. And it also printed Stark's private letter to Kimmel on April 4, in which he says: "Something may be forced on us at any moment which would precipitate action, though I don't look for it as I can see no advantage to Mr. Hitler in forcing us into the war.... On the surface, at least, the Japanese situation looks a trifle easier, but just what the Oriental *really* plans, none of us can be sure." This does not, of course, fit the Beard frame of reference.

Beard concludes his handling of Stark with another unjustified sneer. "Perhaps it was for this 'indiscretion,'" he says— said indiscretion being the generous submission of his private correspondence file to the Congressional Committee—"that Admiral Stark, after services in the war for which he was awarded high honors, was cashiered by Secretary Forrestal..." (p. 585). Admiral Stark was never "cashiered"; the reproof by Admiral King and Secretary Forrestal, to which Beard refers, was dated almost two years prior to the Joint Congressional Committee's Report; and after that report was submitted, Admiral King withdrew his reproof. In other words, the real story is the exact converse of Beard's "reality."

As part of the case for Japanese innocence and Rooseveltian guilt, Beard adduces the American-Dutch-British staff conversations at Singapore in March 1941. It is suggested (pp. 450–1) though not directly stated, that a military agreement of the three nations to go to each other's defense if any one were attacked was an "encirclement" that justified aggression on the part of Japan. One is reminded of Buffon's *cet animal est méchant*— "this animal is wicked, he defends himself when attacked." However, the ADB Plan of the Singapore Conference was rejected by Admiral Stark and General Marshall on July 3, 1941. Whatever cooperation existed between the three powers in the disastrous Southwest Pacific campaign was improvised.

By harping on a rather unfortunate use of the word "maneuver" in the diary of Secretary Stimson (who, unlike Beard, is no expert in semantics), the author tries to prove that Japan was prodded and pushed into the attack on Pearl Harbor. Stimson, recording the Cabinet meeting of November 25, 1941, noted (p. 516) that the President predicted "we were likely to be attacked perhaps next Monday.... The question was how we should maneuver them into the position of firing the first shot without allowing too much danger to ourselves." Why should this caution be regarded as iniquitous? Throughout modern history Western nations in danger of war have chosen to await the first blow rather than give it. If Beard is right, American history will have to be rewritten; Captain Parker, who at Lexington Green said: "Stand your ground. Don't fire unless fired upon, but if they mean to have a war let it begin here," must be called a warmonger.

Although Beard gives the chronology of the approach of war well enough, and makes accurate summaries of the voluminous notes that were exchanged, he relates so little of what the Japanese were doing as to make a distorted picture. And it is strange that an historian so identified with economic influences should almost wholly ignore the significance of oil. The assets-freezing order of July 26, 1941, which included complete stoppage of oil exports to Japan, is

mentioned as a provocation without observing that it was an answer to the Japanese occupation of French Indo-China.

Again (p. 496), Roosevelt is attacked for his secrecy as to Prince Konoye's proposed personal conference in September; but Beard fails to inform his readers that the secrecy was urgently requested by the Prince Premier, because he knew that if the proposal leaked, the Tojo crowd would throw him out—which is exactly what happened. We now know from Japanese sources, published by the Joint Committee, that Konoye promised us one thing and Tojo another. That is just what Hull suspected, and that is why he urged the President not to meet Konoye, as he had originally intended to do.

Beard gives the Japanese a break by describing their proposals of November 20 as a *modus vivendi* (pp. 506 ff.). They were not that, but (as the Japanese Foreign Minister said) an ultimatum: Japan's last alternative to making war on us and the British and the Dutch. They required the United States to cease reinforcing the Philippines and to stop sending naval vessels into the South Pacific; but Japan was to be free to pour more troops into French Indo-China. The United States must unfreeze Japanese assets, restore the flow of oil and other strategic materials, and stop all aid to Chiang Kai-shek. The only thing Japan offered to do in return for these concessions, appropriate for a nation already defeated in war, was to move troops from southern Indo-China into northern Indo-China (whence she was planning to cut the Burma Road) and to evacuate that French colony after forcing China to conclude peace. Such is the proposed Japanese settlement which Beard considers fair and equitable, and the rejection of which by Hull and Roosevelt "proves" that they were bent on war at any price.

There then came the episode of the

proposed *modus vivendi* which the administration decided not to present because it smelt too strongly of Munich; and the "Outline of Proposed Basis of Agreement" of November 26, 1941. This, again, is misrepresented as a deliberate stepping-up of demands to provoke Japan. Actually, as Tojo admitted at his trial, the "Outline" contained nothing more than was in the Nine-Power Treaty on China, to which Japan was a party. It was not an ultimatum, but a penultimate attempt—the final one being the President's personal appeal to the Emperor—to make a peaceful settlement. An ultimatum means a last alternative to war; but war was neither threatened nor suggested by Secretary Hull if Japan should reject this "Outline." In order to avoid war with the United States, Japan merely had to keep what she already had taken, and conquer nothing more. That is what Prince Konoye wished the Tojo government to do; but the Konoye memoirs prove that Tojo was bent on war unless the United States gave in completely.

PEARL HARBOR

As for Pearl Harbor, Beard carries over from the minority report of the Joint Congressional Committee the insinuation that Washington knew all along that Japan was going to strike, and where. What Washington knew, as early as November 25, was that Japanese forces were moving southward and that something unpleasant was going to happen soon. But everyone made two grave errors in evaluating the information at hand. They believed the Japanese to be incapable of more than one major operation at a time; and they assumed Tojo's government had more sense than to arouse America by a sneak attack. Nobody in authority at Washington, civil or military, anticipated the assault on Pearl Harbor.

Perhaps the most indecent of Beard's numerous innuendos in this book are those respecting the Roberts Commission. Secretary Stimson suggested Justice Roberts to head the Pearl Harbor Commission, not only because of his personal integrity, but because he was an experienced lawyer who had investigated the Teapot Dome scandal, and had been appointed by President Hoover. Nevertheless, Beard insinuates (p. 380) that Justice Roberts's appointment was part of a triple play to put Kimmel and Short "out," and conceal the iniquities of F.D.R. and Stimson in a cloud of dust. He creates suspicion by declaring (p. 378) that the appointment of a Justice of the Supreme Court to head an investigating commission was improper, unprecedented, and unconstitutional. That is pure nonsense. In *Hayburn's Case,* to which Beard refers, the Supreme Court under Chief Justice Jay refused as a Court to accept the additional duty of passing on pension claims, but at the same time declared that individual justices might do it. Chief Justice Hughes served as chairman of President Taft's committee to determine postal rates to be paid by newspapers; Justice Reed and others have recently served on civil service commissions. Even if Justice Roberts were the man to accept the dishonorable role imputed to him, how could he have played it, with two generals and two admirals, one a former commander in chief of the fleet, as colleagues?

Since the discrediting of the Roberts Report is necessary for Beard's case, the Justice's testimony in the congressional investigation is also attacked. Beard's three charges against him on page 362— that he had been uninformed on vital matters, that Senator Brewster forced him to concede error on a "crucial point," and that he showed "unbecoming levity"—are not supported by the record.

The point was trivial and not crucial, and the "vital matter" was not relevant to the scope of his inquiry. Justice Roberts did keep his balance and sense of humor under the badgering to which he was subjected by Senators Ferguson and Brewster, frustrating those who hoped to trap him; that seems to be what Beard regards as "unbecoming."

After all, the Roberts Commission was only concerned with the question whether the military authorities in Hawaii had shown "derelictions of duty or errors of judgment" on the basis of the information they then had; it had no competence or means to investigate the political aspects.

Beard's statement (page 604) that Admiral Kimmel was "exonerated by the Navy Board" is incorrect. Admiral King's endorsement on the report of that board, dated November 6, 1944, and without which the report is incomplete, brackets Stark with Kimmel as committing "derelictions" which were "faults of omission rather than faults of commission," indicating a "lack of superior judgment." The Roberts Commission said no more as to Kimmel, and the conduct of Stark did not come under its jurisdiction. The final report of the Joint Congressional Committee, after consuming months of time, examining hundreds of witnesses and tens of thousands of documents, found few significant facts relating to the conduct of the armed forces at Oahu that were not disclosed by the brief investigation of Justice Roberts and his four military colleagues; nor did it reach any different conclusion as to the responsibility of Kimmel and Short. The "official thesis," as Beard calls the Roberts Report, never has been "undermined," except by partisan Congressmen or so-called historians who are unwilling to face the facts fairly.

So one might continue through the book, demonstrating page after page how cleverly facts and opinions have been selected to fit the Beard "frame of reference." For it is by selection and rejection that Beard makes his effect. He never misquotes or garbles a document or quotation, he never invents (though he often insinuates) something false; he merely jumbles the multitudinous facts, opinions, surmises, and events of a very crowded and recent era into the pattern that he believes to be socially desirable. He is desperately trying to prove to the American people that they were "sold down the river" by Roosevelt, and anxious to prevent them from being tricked by Truman into a war with Russia.

In concluding, I wish long life and much happiness to Charles the Prophet and to Mary his wife, who have done so much in the past to illuminate American history. May they rise above the bitterness that has come from brooding over their lost horizon of a happy, peaceful, collectivist democracy insulated from a bad world. May Dr. Beard recast his frame of reference once again, raise his sights a little higher than the Connecticut hills, and apply his erudition, wit, and craftsmanship to writing history without innuendo, history tolerant of mistakes that men make under great stress; may he try to understand rather than to blame and to sneer, and even discover before he dies "that highmindedness is not impossible to man."

17

Reflections on the
Yalta Papers

RAYMOND J. SONTAG

During World War II the Allied powers met from time to time to coordinate their military effort and to make plans for the postwar world. In October, 1942, the foreign ministers of the United States, Great Britain, and the Soviet Union convened in Moscow and agreed to fight until the unconditional surrender of the Axis, to work together "for the organization and maintenance of peace and security," to destroy Fascism in Italy and restore democracy in that country, and to reconstitute Austria as a free nation.

In November of the same year, at Teheran, the heads of state of the three great powers met for the first time. In a spirit of cordiality and intimacy Roosevelt, Churchill, and Stalin resolved to "work together in war and in the peace that will follow." They agreed on the scope and timing of the campaign to defeat Germany, on the launching of a second front in Europe and in Asia, and on matters regarding Iran, Turkey, and Yugoslavia.

The next meeting, which took place at Yalta in the Crimea in February, 1945, was the most important of all the wartime conferences and the one that has generated controversy. At Yalta the three leaders considered a wide range of important questions, including the entrance of the Russians into the Japanese war, the boundaries and government of Poland, the military occupation and the borders of Germany, and the formation of the United Nations. Complete agreement was reached on all these vital problems, and when the conference ended, the American delegates left in "high exultation." They believed that "this was the dawn of a new day, . . . that the first great victory of the peace" had been won.

But within a few weeks after the conference ended, it became clear that the agreements were chimerical and the friendship an illusion, for Joseph Stalin, far from cooperating with the Allies, was beginning to follow a unilateral course in Eastern Europe, extending Soviet influence in that area by establishing Communist-dominated governments in newly liberated countries. Critics of the Roosevelt Administration ascribe this state of affairs to inept American diplomacy at the conference. They claim that the President gave Stalin too many concessions in Eastern Europe that amounted to a free hand for the Soviet dictator and paved the way for the takeover. They maintain that the Russians had been handed large amounts of territory in Asia, making the Soviet Union a formidable Pacific power and a potential foe of great strength. Furthermore, it is said

Reprinted by special permission from *Foreign Affairs*, July 1955. Copyright by the Council on Foreign Relations, Inc., New York.

that those concessions, which were granted to assure Stalin's entry into the war against Japan and his continued cooperation in the struggle against Germany, were unnecessary, because Japan and Germany were on the verge of defeat and Soviet help was not needed.

There are, of course, defenders of the Administration. One of the most thoughtful is Raymond J. Sontag, a professor of history and an authority on the diplomatic history of modern Europe. On the occasion of the publication by the Department of State in 1955 of the documents on the Yalta conference, Sontag wrote the following essay, in which he assesses American diplomacy as revealed in the record. For him, the key to an understanding of our diplomacy at the conference lies in an appreciation of the "circumstances of the time." That is to say that given existing conditions, no other course was possible. In the light of the situation in 1945, Soviet cooperation was essential and had to be bought by concessions.

The Yalta papers could not have appeared under worse auspices. The decision to publish them was colored by partisan political motives. The leakage during the process of selection and editing of sensational passages throws a strange light on the supposedly tightened security regulations of the Department of State. The circumstances under which the documents as a whole were released to the press in the form of uncorrected galley proof were, to put it mildly, peculiar. Finally, it is doubtful whether all the important papers in the Pentagon files have been included.

The most unfortunate effect of the release of the documents to the press in proof form, months before publication of the finished volume, is that attention has been focused on the minutes of the conference itself. This is inevitable, because the minutes have by far the greatest interest as "revelations." Of the pre-conference documents, which fill almost half the volume, only a few have attracted attention. Yet it is only from these papers that a clear view of the world as seen by the American negotiators, and of the objectives of American policy, can be obtained.[1]

[1] The pre-conference documents make untenable Mr. Byrnes' belief that Mr. Roosevelt "had made little preparation for the Yalta Con-

The foreign policy objectives of the United States in 1944–45, as set forth in the pre-conference papers, can still be studied with pride by Americans; and they should be placed by the rest of the world in contrast to Soviet policy as it has unfolded over the last decade. To see that contrast it is necessary to cite only a few examples. On Italy: "United States policy toward Italy is, briefly, to encourage the development of Italy into a democratic and constructive force in the future Europe and to assist Italy to become politically independent and economically self-supporting as quickly as possible." On Iran: "Our policy in this case is based on the American Government's recognition of the sovereign right of an inde-

ference," as well as the less directly stated suggestion that Mr. Roosevelt had no knowledge of the contents of the Briefing Book prepared for him by the Department of State (James F. Byrnes, "Speaking Frankly." New York: Harper, 1947, p. 23). The Briefing Book consisted of papers summarizing the status of the problems likely to be discussed at Yalta, and stating American policy, or making policy recommendations, on each problem. It is almost certainly true that Mr. Roosevelt did not read most of the papers. However, there is clear evidence that the main points of many of the papers were known to him, and that he was familiar with the policy statements or recommendations in most of the important papers. I have used the statements of policy as given in the Briefing Book only when it seems clear that the statement was, in fact, American official policy.

pendent nation such as Iran, acting in a nondiscriminatory manner, to grant or withhold commercial concessions within its territory." On liberated countries: "In so far as the United States is concerned, the following two criteria could be applied to any proposed interim government: (1) that it should be dedicated to the preservation of civil liberties; (2) that it should favor social and economic reforms." [2]

These are not isolated instances. Through every statement of policy in the period preparatory to the conference there is evident the conviction that American interests would be best served by the independence and the economic revival of other nations, by the liberation of subject peoples, by the spread of social reform, and by the free coöperation of all countries in the United Nations. And throughout it is evident that the one central problem was believed to be to obtain Soviet support for the attainment of these objectives. That support obtained, the conviction was general that the world would enjoy peace.

Yalta was the supreme effort of the Uninted States Government to obtain Soviet support for these objectives, an effort which ended in disastrous failure. The Yalta papers, for the first time, give the American people an opportunity to understand clearly why the effort was made and why it failed, and it is vitally important that we should achieve this clear understanding. The present writer

had no part in the formation of policy during World War II, and at the time he viewed what was known of our policy toward the Soviet Union with foreboding. Examining the record a decade later, however, he is driven to the conclusion that in the circumstances of the time, and given the accepted military view of the probable duration of the war and of the distribution of power in the world after the war, no other policy was possible. One can go farther and say that if the policy of the American Government in 1944–45 had not been attempted, wholeheartedly and to the point where its failure was clear without a shadow of doubt, the firmness of will and the serenity of conscience with which the American people today face a world full of ominous portent would have been impossible to attain.

In the winter of 1944–45 the duration of the war was uncertain. For planning purposes, it was assumed that the European war would be over, at the earliest, by July 1, 1945.[3] At the time of the Yalta Conference, the Russian armies seemed to have a clear road ahead of them across the great European plain; the Western armies hd not yet crossed the Rhine. In this situation, it was possible that the end of the war would find the Russians in possession of most of Germany, as they were already in possession of nearly all of what we now call the satellites.

Beyond the ending of the European war, there stretched the unknown duration of the Pacific war. For planning purposes, the end of the war against Japan was set at 18 months after the defeat of Germany.[4] While this date was tentative and set merely for logistical purposes, there is clear evidence that the Joint Chiefs saw a hard fight ahead, as indeed there was. The probability that

[2] As only the galley proofs of the Yalta papers are available at this writing, and the precise title of the volume is uncertain, location of a paper within the volume can be given only by chapter and section within the chapter. The first quotation above is from a Briefing Book Paper on "United States Policy Toward Italy," printed in Chapter 2, section entitled "The Italian Cabinet Crisis;" the second is from a dispatch from Stettinius to Harriman, October 30, 1944, printed in Chapter 2, section entitled "Iran;" the third is from a Briefing Book Paper on "Liberated Countries," printed in Chapter 2, section entitled "Liberated Europe and Spheres of Influence."

[3] February 9, 1945, Report of the Combined Chiefs of Staff to President Roosevelt and Prime Minister Churchill, paragraph 18, printed in Chapter 8.
[4] *Ibid.*

one atomic bomb would be ready by July 1, 1945, and more by the end of the year, was known.[5] But there is no evidence that the military had yet assessed the probable effect of atomic weapons on the length of the war, either in Europe or Asia.

If the war developed in this way, the whole strength of the United States would be concentrated in Asia for some time after the ending of the war in Europe, and if, during this time, the Russians were in undisturbed occupation of most of Europe north of the Alps and east of the Rhine, how would they use this time? Ambassador Harriman reported that, "the overriding consideration in Soviet foreign policy is the preoccupation with 'security'. . . . The Soviet Union seeks a period of freedom from danger during which it can recover from the wounds of war and complete its industrial revolution. The Soviet conception of 'security' does not appear cognizant of the similar needs or rights of other countries and of Russia's obligation to accept the restraints as well as the benefits of an international security system." [6] This was ominous.

The situation in Asia was even more ominous. Within China, according to the Briefing Book Papers of the Department of State, "there is now Kuomintang China, Communist China, and puppet [i.e. Japanese dominated] China. Kuomintang China is being weakened by dissident elements and widespread popular discontent. Communist China is growing in material and popular strength. Puppet China is filled with pockets of Communist guerrilla resistance." A continuance of this situation would be "detrimental to our objective of a united, progressive China capable of contributing to security and prosperity in the Far East." There

was an even more dangerous possibility. If the U.S.S.R. entered the Far Eastern war, one line of attack might be from Outer Mongolia; Soviet troops could strike east and take over all of north China and Manchuria. The Department believed that as yet there was little to substantiate the fear that Russia intended "to establish an independent or autonomous area in north China and Manchuria," but an open break between the Kuomintang and the Chinese Communists would tempt Russia to abandon her declared policy of nonintervention in the internal affairs of China. "It is our task to bring about British and Russian support of our objective of a united China which will coöperate with them as well as with us." [7]

Reading these documents, one sees clearly that the American policy-makers, civil or military, had no confidence in their ability, while the war continued, to *compel* the U.S.S.R. to accept the American plans for the organization of the Asiatic mainland. Moreover, our Government was eager to secure early Soviet military intervention in the war against Japan, and recognized the necessity to pay for it. The problem as seen in Washington was both to ensure early Soviet intervention and to bring the U.S.S.R. to recognize that "a strong and friendly China" was the best guarantee of Soviet security in Asia.[8]

Even after victory over Japan, in the view of American policy-makers, the power of the United States directly to

[5] December 30, 1944, Groves to Marshall. Printed in Chapter 2, section entitled "Entry of the Soviet Union Into the War Against Japan."

[6] January 10, 1943, Harriman to Stettinius, printed in Chapter 4.

[7] Briefing Book Papers on "Political and Military Situation in China in the Event the U.S.S.R. Enters the War in the Far East," and "Unity of Anglo-American-Soviet Policy Toward China," printed in Chapter 2, section entitled "China."

[8] *Ibid*. It should be emphasized that the American objective was not simply to bring the U.S.S.R. into the war against Japan: "Russia's entry at as early a date as possible . . . is necessary to provide maximum assistance to our Pacific operations" (January 23, 1945, The Joint Chiefs of Staff to the President, printed in Chapter 2, section entitled "Entry of the Soviet Union Into the War Against Japan").

shape the future would be very limited. The strategic situation expected after the war is most clearly outlined in a letter which Admiral Leahy wrote to Secretary Hull on May 16, 1944, giving the view of the Joint Chiefs of Staff on a British proposal for the disposition of the Italian colonies.[9] While this letter was written many months before Yalta, it was accepted as the basis for policy by the Department of State in the Briefing Book for the conference, and, so far as can be determined from the available evidence, the views of the Joint Chiefs had not altered during the intervening months The central theme of the letter was the "revolutionary changes in relative national military strengths" resulting from the war, and particularly the "phenomenal development" of Soviet strength, absolutely, and relative to the impaired strength of Britain. The situation which was expected to result from this shift now seems so remote that it is almost forgotten, but it must be recalled if American policy in 1945 is to be understood. Admiral Leahy wrote:

It would seem clear that there cannot be a world war, or even a great war, which does not find one or more of the great military powers on each side. At the conclusion of the present war, there will be, for the foreseeable future, only three such powers—the United States, Britain and Russia. Since it would seem in the highest degree unlikely that Britain and Russia, or Russia alone, would be aligned against the United States, it is apparent that any future world conflict in the foreseeable future will find Britain and Russia in opposite camps....

In a conflict between these two powers the disparity in the military strengths that they could dispose upon that continent [i.e. Europe] would, under present conditions, be far too great to be overcome by our intervention on the side of Britain. Having due regard to the military factors involved—resources, manpower, geography and particularly our ability to project our strength

across the ocean and exert it decisively upon the continent—we might be able to successfully defend Britain, but we could not, under existing conditions, defeat Russia. In other words, we would find ourselves engaged in a war which we could not win even though the United States would be in no danger of defeat and occupation.

It is apparent that the United States should, now and in the future, exert its utmost efforts and utilize all its influence to prevent such a situation arising and to promote a spirit of mutual coöperation between Britain, Russia and ourselves. So long as Britain and Russia coöperate and collaborate in the interests of peace, there can be no great war in the foreseeable future.

The greatest likelihood of eventual conflict between Britain and Russia would seem to grow out of either nation initiating attempts to build up its strength, by seeking to attach to herself parts of Europe to the disadvantage and possible danger of her potential adversary. Having regard to the inherent suspicions of the Russians, to present Russia with any agreement on such matters as between the British and ourselves, prior to consultation with Russia, might well result in starting a train of events that would lead eventually to [to] the situation we most wish to avoid.

Seen in the light of Admiral Leahy's letter, much that is puzzling in the Yalta period becomes understandable: Mr. Roosevelt's elaborate efforts to avoid the appearance of intimacy with Britain, even to create the impression of friction between Britain and the United States; American opposition to the delimitation of Ango-Soviet spheres of influence in Southeastern Europe; what seems now the shortsighted preoccupation of the Department of State with the possibility that the British and Soviet Zones in Germany might be administered along divergent lines. These and other aspects of American policy should be seen in relation to the conviction that, in the future, war between the U.S. and U.S.S.R. was "in the highest degree unlikely," that Anglo-Russian enmity was the one likely cause of war, and that the United States must avoid appearing to line up with Britain on questions of direct interest to

[9] May 16, 1944, Leahy to Hull, printed in Chapter 2, section entitled "Liberated Europe and Spheres of Influence."

Russia "lest postwar disunity of the three great powers be thereby fostered with all the possibility of ultimate impact upon the military position of the United States which such a disaster would entail." [10]

It is probable that one can go farther. On many questions Mr. Roosevelt's position at Yalta seems to waver, even to involve contradiction. When Mr. Churchill insisted that France must participate not only in the occupation of Germany but also in the Control Commission, Mr. Roosevelt at the outset joined Marshal Stalin in opposing the British proposal, and made disparaging remarks about the French which, read now, cause justified resentment. At the end of the conference, however, Mr. Roosevelt moved to the British position. Surely, in such cases the position of a statesman should be judged, not by isolated remarks on a single occasion, but by his long-term policy, and the policy of his responsible advisers. Mr. Roosevelt had shown himself a friend of France, and historians of the future are likely to describe American policy toward France, before and after Yalta, in the words the Secretary of State addressed to the President:

It is in the interests of the United States to assist France to regain her former position in world affairs in order that she may increase her contribution in the war effort and play an appropriate part in the maintenance of peace.... In the long run this Government will undoubtedly gain more by making concessions to French prestige and by treating France on the basis of her potential power and influence, than we will by treating her on the basis of her actual strength at this time.[11]

Similarly, the real state of Anglo-American relations in 1945 cannot be determined on the basis of a few quips made by Mr. Roosevelt to Marshal Stalin; much more can be learned from the few words

with which General Marshall justified his refusal to insist on precise formulation of American right of access to Bremen: "The broad policy had been decided and the good will was there." [12]

What requires explanation is the fact that, at the end of the Yalta Conference, the American delegation was convinced (so far as can be determined from evidence set down at the time, and not from undocumented afterthought) that Soviet support had in fact been won. In the last days a note of relief, even of rejoicing, breaks through the cold summaries of the proceedings.

To understand this rejoicing it is necessary to stress, not the concessions made by the Americans and the British, but the attitude and the promises of the Russians. On Poland, the Americans and the British stood firm until Stalin said that free elections could be held in about one month; then agreement was quickly achieved. On Germany, what seemed important at the time was that the Soviet Union agreed to a single administration for all the zones, thus apparently eliminating the possibility of disastrous friction between the occupying Powers. On the Far East, the concessions to Russia in Manchuria, Sakhalin and the Kuriles seemed justified not only because they insured Soviet military intervention in the war against Japan; these concessions also set limits to Soviet expansion in an area where there was no effective force to oppose Soviet expansion; finally, these concessions brought a Soviet promise to support the government of Chiang Kai-shek. When Molotov agreed to accept the American proposal that in the United Nations the veto should not be used in questions involving the peaceful adjustment of disputes, Mr. Roosevelt "felt that this was a great step forward" and Mr. Churchill echoed the President's words, adding that the decision "would bring

[10] Ibid.
[11] January 4, 1954, Stettinius to Roosevelt, printed in Chapter 2, section entitled "The Rôle of France."

[12] February 6, 1945, Meeting of the Combined Chiefs of Staff, printed in Chapter 8.

joy and relief to the peoples of the world."[13]

Over and above concrete concessions, there were Marshal Stalin's repeated protestations of his determination to "create for the future generation such an organization as would secure peace for at least fifty years,"[14] and, in contrast to earlier exchanges between the Allied Governments, his disarming friendliness and apparent eagerness to continue the wartime coöperation into the years of peace which lay ahead. Even Mr. Churchill, whose detestation of Communism went back to 1917, was persuaded to hope that "we were all standing on the crest of a hill with the glories of future possibilities stretching before us," while Mr. Roosevelt felt that the atmosphere "was as that of a family, and it was in those words that he liked to characterize the relations that existed between our three countries."[15]

Seldom in history has deception been so successful and so decisive as that perpetrated at Yalta by the Soviet leaders at the expense of Britain and the United States. Immediately after the conference closed, evidence began to accumulate that the Soviet promises were worthless. If the Americans alone had been deceived, one would be driven to conclude that they were deceived only because they were blind to the nature of their antagonists. Blind they certainly were. Nowhere in this volume is there anything which suggests that American statesmen were conscious that they were dealing, not with Russian national leaders, but with Communist revolutionaries determined to outwit and eventually destroy their allies, allies not from choice but because of the mad decision of Hitler to attack the Soviet Union.

Even those who urged a firmer policy in dealings with the U.S.S.R. did not make it clear that Russia was now, not a national state pursuing national interests, but the center of a revolutionary movement dedicated to the creation of a Communist world ruled from Moscow. General John R. Deane believed that for the United States always to be "at the same time the givers and the supplicants" was "neither dignified nor healthy for U.S. prestige." But he also believed "we have few conflicting interests, and there is little reason why we should not be friendly now and in the foreseeable future."[16] Ambassador Harriman shared General Deane's views on the need for tougher bargaining with the U.S.S.R., but he also felt strongly "that the sooner the Soviet Union can develop a decent life for its people the more tolerant they will become. . . . I am satisfied that the great urge of Stalin and his associates is to provide a better physical life for the Russian people, although they will retain a substantial military establishment."[17] Such statements did little to undermine the belief, dominant in Washington, that Russian and American interests were identical, and that the only problem was to bring the Soviet leaders to a recognition of this fact.

But it was not just the Americans who were deceived at Yalta. Churchill also was deceived, and that was indeed a triumph for Soviet duplicity, for Churchill's denunciations of "the foul baboonery of Bolshevism" are among the most magnificent examples of sustained invective in the English language. Here we touch the real root of Soviet success at Yalta: British and American consciousness of the consequences of failure to reach agreement with the Soviet Union. Churchill stated

[13] February 7, 1945, Fourth Plenary Meeting, Bohlen Minutes, printed in Chapter 8.
[14] February 6, 1945, Third Plenary Meeting, Bohlen Minutes, printed in Chapter 8.
[15] February 8, 1945, Tripartite Dinner Meeting, Bohlen Minutes, printed in Chapter 8.

[16] December 2, 1944, Deane to Marshall, printed in Chapter 4.
[17] January 6, 1945, Harriman to Stettinius, printed in Chapter 2, section entitled "Proposed United States Loan to the Soviet Union."

the case with his customary precision when he presented the Yalta agreements to the Commons: "I decline absolutely to embark here on a discussion about Russian good faith. It is quite evident that these matters touch the whole future of the world. Sombre indeed would be the fortunes of mankind if some awful schism arose between the Western democracies and the Russian Soviet Union."

That awful schism did arise. This volume makes abundantly clear that in 1944 and 1945 the American Government made an honest, a desperate, effort to secure Soviet friendship. At Yalta, the professions and promises of Stalin and Molotov convinced the American negotiators that Soviet friendship had been won, that Soviet good faith was assured. Almost immediately after Yalta the conviction was shaken, and slowly, much too slowly, it was destroyed by Soviet aggression. But if that honest and desperate effort had not been made at the outset it is hard to believe that we could now accept unflinchingly the tragically unfolding consequences of the schism between East and West.

The schism is not of our making. So much consolation we can derive from our failure at Yalta. Farther we need not go, and should not go.

18

How the Cold War Began

STAUGHTON LYND

During World War II many people in the United States were convinced that after the war the victorious Allies would continue to work together and to co-ordinate their policies in maintaining the peace. The spirit of cordiality that characterized the wartime conferences at Moscow, Teheran, and Yalta and the agreements reached on many significant matters were harbingers of postwar accord. Stalin's speeches and statements pledging to liberate Nazi-controlled regions and to defend the right of the people to choose their own form of government appeared to give proof that he harbored no aggressive ambitions to dominate these areas. His dissolution in 1943 of the Third International (Comintern), the agency for fomenting revolution throughout the world, seemed to be a clear indication of a renunciation of Communism's historic aim of destroying capitalism in other countries.

To be sure, there were those who did not view the future so optimistically. One American diplomatist suspected that "in spite of all comments and assurances . . . all the Soviets intend to do is to give lip-service and to create certain instances which would give an impression of relaxation without really changing their present practices." And another noted, "Many people here are stating that at the end of the war Russia will do as she pleases, take what she pleases, and confer with nobody." Such opinions, however, were distinctly in the minority. Most people agreed with President Roosevelt, who said in 1944, "I think the Russians are perfectly friendly; they aren't trying to gobble up all the rest of Europe or the world. . . . They haven't got any crazy ideas of conquest. . . . These fears that have been expressed by a lot of people here—with some reason— that the Russians are going to try to dominate Europe, I personally don't think there's anything in it."

Yet, within a short time after the war ended, it began to appear that the President's judgment had been wrong. Soviet armies were setting up Communist-dominated governments in the Balkans and in Poland in disregard of pledges made during the war. On vital questions such as disarmament, peace treaties with the former German allies, boundaries, and the governance of Germany settlement proved impossible. Conflict and hostility replaced wartime cooperation and amicability. What had happened? Why had the prognostications gone awry?

These questions have been answered by some historians in terms of Soviet faithlessness and intransigence. That is to say, Stalin simply did not keep the promises he made during the war to cooperate with the Western powers in

Reprinted from *Commentary*, by permission; copyright © 1960 by the American Jewish Committee.

keeping the peace and to permit the liberated peoples to choose freely their own forms of government. Stalin's "sweet mouthings" and noble utterances during the war concealed his true intentions and were designed only to insure Allied help in the struggle against Germany. Once the foe was destroyed and the assistance no longer necessary, he reverted to his long-standing ambitions of extending Soviet domination.

Staughton Lynd, who teaches history at Yale, does not agree with this explanation of the origins of the Cold War. He lays much of the blame for what happened to the refusal by the United States to appraise the postwar situation realistically. Steeped in a "Wilsonian" and "Utopian" tradition, Roosevelt insisted on self-determination for the liberated areas in Eastern Europe and in the Balkans. He was unable or unwilling to realize that such self-determination might result in the establishment of regimes that would pose a threat to Soviet security. What Russia needed, above all, was a buffer against a future invader; she, therefore, had no choice after victory but to insure that the states surrounding her were friendly.

At the banquet which closed the Yalta Conference, Roosevelt, Churchill, and Stalin all offered toasts. When it came Churchill's turn, he

addressed himself to the years ahead. He felt, he said, that all were standing on the crest of a hill with the glories of great future possibilities stretching before them; that in the modern world the function of leadership was to lead the people out from the forests into the broad sunlit plains of peace and happiness. He felt that this prize was nearer their grasp than at any time in history, and that it would be a great tragedy if they, through inertia or carelessness, let it slip from their grasp. History would never forgive them if they did.[1]

We live today amid the ruins of that hope. Any responsible inquiry into the present controversies between the United States and the Soviet Union must find its way back, from the U-2 to Hungary and Suez, thence to Korea, Czechoslovakia, the Marshall Plan, and the Truman Doctrine, and so, finally, to that time and that failure. In those months of early 1945 which Herbert Feis, in his new book,[2] has called "between war and

peace," the hard core of difference between East and West is to be found.

None of us can presume to dicuss this question without anxiety or passion. One finds it peculiarly difficult to bring to bear on the problem of the cold war the intellectual discipline which, say, the Spanish-American or even the First World War can now readily call forth. The shrill and strained atmosphere, the partisan interpretations of war and quasi-war have been with us for an uninterrupted quarter of a century. We live, move, and have our intellectual being in a habitually clamorous climate of opinion.

Yet how precious would be the gift of seeing the cold war, now, with the kind of perspective which commonly comes only after the passage of much time. There are very few international crises which in the historian's retrospect altogether justify the ideology or behavior of any of the participants. We know today that the War of 1812 began days after, on the other side of the Atlantic, the English Orders in Council which occasioned it had been revoked. Today many of us would be ready to join Henry Thoreau in his Concord jail to protest the war against Mexico. Years after the Spanish-American War, experts exam-

[1] Herbert Feis, *Churchill, Roosevelt, Stalin: The War They Waged and the Peace They Sought* (Princeton, 1957).

[2] *Between War and Peace: The Potsdam Conference* (Princeton, 1960).

ined the torn hull of the battleship *Maine* and concluded that the explosion had taken place not outside the boat but within. The blundering or hypocrisy or chicanery which brought on these wars seems to us today inadmissible. In short, if we could only approximate the historians' collective judgment, a generation hence, concerning the cold war, we might be helped in our understanding of the practical alternatives that are presently before us.

In search of objectivity the American student may attempt to balance the work of Westerners by consulting Soviet accounts. He will be disappointed. It is true that Soviet historians are far more familiar with English, French, and German sources than Westerners are with publications in Russian. For example, V. L. Israelyan's *Diplomatic History of the Great Patriotic War* (Moscow, 1959; in Russian) cites ten American collections of documents and over sixty memoirs and historical works in English. It is also true that the skeleton of events narrated by a work like Israelyan's is full and accurate. But time after time crucial interpretations are woodenly self-justificatory. Human blundering and groping on both sides of the Iron Curtain are underestimated. Thus Stalin's attitude toward the treatment of postwar Germany is made to seem consistent at all times; and he is said to have refused Churchill's famous proposal in October 1944 to divide Eastern Europe into British and Soviet spheres of influence because "the Soviet Union in correspondence with its policy of non-interference in the inner affairs of other nations rejected all plans for the division of Eastern Europe into spheres of influence." Inversely, the Soviets tend to portray American policy as changing from white to black after the death of Roosevelt, whereas among Western scholars even those who are most sympathetic to Soviet behavior in the cold war have stressed the vacillations and

ambiguities in Roosevelt's dealing with the USSR.[3]

One turns back, perforce, to Western scholarship. Here two first-class scholars have been at work: Feis, in the two books already cited, and William McNeill of the University of Chicago, in his brilliant earlier account, *America, Britain and Russia: Their Co-operation and Conflict, 1941–1946* (London, 1953). These works have a quasi-official character. Feis's books were, so he tells the reader, in part inspired by Averill Harriman, America's wartime ambassador to the Soviet Union. They draw both on unpublished papers of Harriman's and on the unpublished papers of the State Department (these have just been closed to scholars). McNeill's volume, similarly, was commissioned by the Royal Institute of International Affairs and scrutinized before publication "by a number of individuals familiar with the events narrated." Thus the works of Feis and McNeill are something more than individual interpretations. To a degree they represent the collective memory of British and American officialdom about their wartime alliance with Soviet Russia and how it broke down.

Perhaps because of their quasi-official character the Feis and McNeill books display the same defect as their Soviet counterparts. They narrate, but they do not really interpret. They do not face squarely the childlike and penetrating question, Why did the cold war start? Some of McNeill's sharpest observations are buried in footnotes. Feis concludes *Between War and Peace* with the moving sentence: "To choose life, the great nations must one and all live and act more maturely and trustfully than they did during the months that followed the end of the war against Germany." Moving, but also

[3] See the final chapters of William Appleton Williams' *American-Russian Relations, 1871–1947* (1952) and *The Tragedy of American Diplomacy* (1959).

banal. Feis does not go beneath the surface of events in search of the specific men and motives that obstructed the choice for life, the inarticulate major premises which led each side to a point from which further retreat seemed inadmissible.

To go beneath the surface means, as I have said, going back. The climactic events of the six months after Yalta—the defeat of Germany, the San Francisco and Potsdam conferences, the testing and use of the atom bomb, all shadowed and confused by the death of Roosevelt and the political defeat of Churchill—brought into the open the conflict in objectives between England and America and the Soviet Union. But this conflict had existed in embryo from the first tentative discussions in 1941 of postwar aims among the three military partners. While the war lasted, each side, intensely needful of the other's military aid, tended to avoid direct confrontation of the latent political tensions. Even at Teheran (1943), perhaps the high point of Big Three harmony, McNeill comments that "Allied co-operation could be and was founded upon agreement on military strategy. Agreement on post-war issues was not genuinely achieved. All important decisions were left for the future after only vague exploration of the issues involved." Victory over Germany, together with the decision of the Truman cabinet that Soviet military assistance was not essential to the defeat of Japan, lifted the lid of a Pandora's box.

The characteristic, continuing objectives of each of the three powers had in fact become quite clear within a year of the German attack on the Soviet Union. When the Red Army, to the surprise of the highest military personnel in both England and America, survived into the winter of 1941–42, serious negotiation as to postwar goals began. Then as later Stalin underscored the fact that twice in thirty years Russia had been invaded

through Poland, and insisted on a more westerly frontier (incorporation of the Baltic nations and the Curzon Line in Poland) and a friendly postwar Polish government. Then as later Churchill, also thinking in terms of his nation's security, showed himself ready to bargain with the Soviet Union on a *quid pro quo* basis but equally ready to invoke the threat of force if negotiation seemed inadequate; it was at this time that Churchill, having just signed the Atlantic Charter with its promise of democracy for "all the men in all the lands," told Parliament that the phrase was not meant to apply to the British Empire. In December 1941, Foreign Secretary Eden went to Moscow to seek an accommodation of Soviet and British diplomatic objectives.

Here American diplomacy intervened in a way which foreshadowed future Soviet-American tension. That December, and again in May 1942 when Molotov visited London and Washington, Secretary of State Hull brought strong pressure on the English government to avoid territorial commitments until a postwar peace conference. On the latter occasion, indeed, he threatened to issue a public statement dissociating the United States from any such agreement reached between Britain and the Soviet Union. The American objective, for Roosevelt and Hull as for Woodrow Wilson years before, was to prevent dictation to small nations so that they might determine their own destinies through democratic processes; and to substitute for the balance-of-power arrangements which seemed inevitable and natural to America's European partners, an international organization to keep the peace. Thus in the Second as in the First World War, American diplomacy sought nothing less than a diplomatic new deal, an altogether new start in the conduct of international relations.

Not only in objectives but in ways and means American diplomatic behavior in this first year of the war was symptomatic of much that was to follow. Avoiding hard bargaining on specific issues, America sought—in the words of a Hopkins memo—to "take the heat off" the Soviet territorial demands by pushing hard for a second front (as well as by talking of a postwar international organization in terms which were, as Feis says, "vaguely magnificent rather than sturdy"). The United States of course had other substantial reasons for desiring a second front. But both Feis and McNeill make it clear that the Americans found it a "happy coincidence" that the military strategy which they favored, a direct assault on Germany through France, was at the same time the form of assistance which the Soviet Union desired above all others. The American hope, Feis writes, was that "the Soviet government was to be lured away from one boon by a choicer one, away from its absorption in frontiers by the attraction of quick military relief."

By championing the second front and postponing to a later day the inherent conflict between the American concern for worldwide democracy and the Soviet preoccupation with the security of its borders, Roosevelt established himself, by the middle of 1942, as a mediator between Churchill and Stalin. As McNeill observes in a remarkable footnote, this relationship was a personal tour de force which rested on a peculiar and indeed artificial basis of fact:

The British public was perceptibly warmer in its feeling toward Russia than was the American public, among whom repugnance to socialism and consciousness of Russia's failure to join in the war against Japan were far greater than in Britain. On the other hand, the American Government in general assumed a more indulgent attitude towards Russia on current questions (for instance Lend-Lease), combined with a more rigid attitude on long-range issues (for instance, the question of the Baltic states) than did the British Government. The secret of this curious contradiction lay mainly in the fact that Churchill and Eden thinking largely in terms of a balance of power, wanted to bargain with Stalin, whereas Roosevelt and Hull thought in terms of abstract principles to which they hoped Stalin could, if treated indulgently enough by his wartime allies, be committed.

When in 1942 and again in 1943 Roosevelt failed to deliver on a second front, a foundation was laid for future ill-will.

Viewed in this way, Roosevelt's approach to the Soviet Union appears fundamentally similar to that of Wilson and to that of Eisenhower: personalities fall away, and the thread of a shared tradition stands forth. All three Presidents attempted to eschew diplomatic settlements based on a balance of power. Like Wilson at Versailles, and indeed in conscious recoil from Wilson's entanglement in secret wartime agreements, Roosevelt and Hull during World War II sought to brush aside concrete, immediate points of difference in order to establish agreement on general principles of world organizations. Feis says of Hull in 1943:

Over each disjointed problem the interested and rival powers were poised—ready to contest, bargain and threaten. This had been the customary way in the past by which questions of frontiers, political affiliations and the like got settled. He wanted to bring it about that all such exercises of national power and diplomacy would in the future be subordinated to rules of principle.

The Americans, McNeill agrees,

tended to think of the establishment of an international organization as a sort of talisman which would possess a powerful virtue to heal disputes among the nations. Instead of regarding international politics as essentially and necessarily an affair of clashing interests and struggle for power, Americans, both officials and the general public, tended to think that international politics were, or at least should be, a matter of legal right and wrong, and that the common interest of all men and nations in the maintenance of peace was so obvious and so compelling that only hardened criminals would think of transgressing against it.

Alike in placing too much reliance on the forms of international organization, Wilson, Roosevelt, and Eisenhower also have shared a tendency to evolve simplistic solutions to the internal problems of foreign nations. For all three men the sovereign nostrum for the domestic ills of other countries has been, "When in doubt, hold a free election." Roosevelt grasped the awakening of the colonial world but conceived it one-sidedly in formal political terms; less than Wendell Wilkie did he perceive the universal challenge to the big house on the hill. Land reform, for example, was as germane to the emergence of democracy in Eastern Europe as were free elections. Indeed land reform was a principal bone of contention between the Soviet-sponsored Lublin government and the Polish government-in-exile. Yet the Big Three paid it scant attention in their interminable discussions of the Polish question.

One cannot avoid the suspicion that Roosevelt's intermittent demand for freedom in Eastern Europe did not altogether escape the tragi-comic quality of Wilson's insistence that the revolutionary Huerta regime in Mexico conduct a plebiscite on its own legitimacy, or—*reductio ad absurdum*—President Eisenhower's recent proposal for a worldwide referendum on communism and democracy. In each of these instances, the American President expressed a sincere and idealistic concern, but a concern which did not really represent a practical alternative in the given situation. McNeill points out that "neither Roosevelt nor Churchill seems frankly to have faced the fact that, in Poland at least, genuinely free democratic elections would return governments unfriendly to Russia." Therefore, he continues,

the democratic process upon which so many eulogies were expended could not produce governments in Eastern Europe (or in many other parts of the world) that would fur-

ther the harmony of the Great Powers and prove acceptable to all of them. Men were not so uniform, so rational, nor possessed of such good will, as the democratic theory presupposed; and in talking of Eastern European governments which would be both democratic and friendly to Russia the Western Powers were in large part deluding themselves.

George Kennan has written in much the same vein of the American Open Door policy in the Far East. "Our constant return to these ideas," Kennan says, "would not serve really to prevent the conflict of interests in China from living themselves out pretty much in accordance with their own strategic, political, and economic necessities." Just so the State Department policy toward Europe during World War II, according to Feis, "tried to arrest the march of armies, the clash of civil wars, the forays of diplomacy by repeated affirmations of the view that principle should govern European postwar settlements."

This syndrome of American attitudes —a syndrome which Walter Lippmann has called "Wilsonian" and E. H. Carr "Utopian," and which has been best characterized by Kennan—threw up significant obstacles to the making of a peace. To say this is not to belittle the American dream of democracy and world organization. It is not so much the American goals in World War II but the lack of realism with which they were elaborated in specific circumstances that is disturbingly prophetic of much which liberals now like to think of as uniquely Eisenhowerian. How similar to latter-day criticisms of American diplomacy's lack of "initiative" are these words of McNeill describing Roosevelt's passivity as the need for postwar decisions bore down on him:

From early in 1942 the American Government had repeatedly proclaimed the principle that no final decisions on matters of post-war frontiers or systems of government should be made until the end of the war.

The theory that a political vacuum could be maintained in Europe was absurd on its face; but this principle helped to hide from American officials the daily necessity of making decisions.

American indecision in the closing years of the war diminished the chances for postwar settlements in both Poland and Germany. Long before Hungary, United States foreign policy was encouraging hopes in Eastern Europe which it had no concrete plans to support. Thus, early in 1944 Roosevelt refused to "back in an unambiguous manner" the proposals for Poland agreed on at Teheran, instead

contenting himself with amiable sentiments about "freely negotiated" and "friendly" settlement of the Soviet-Polish dispute. Clearly Roosevelt did not wish to grasp the nettle, hoping that Stalin and the Poles would come to terms of their own accord. But his attitude only confirmed the Poles in their obstinate disregard of the realities of their situation, and allowed them to cling to the belief that Roosevelt would come to their rescue.

"In this instance," McNeill continues, "and throughout the following year, Roosevelt tried to avoid the responsibilities of the new American power, and by not making himself clear to the Poles he stored up trouble for the future." Thus in October 1944, when Mikolajczyk went to Moscow to consult with Churchill and Stalin about Poland, he was astonished to learn that everyone but himself had thought that Roosevelt at Teheran essentially accepted the Curzon Line. At Yalta, Admiral Leahy warned Roosevelt that the vagueness of the accord reached on reorganizing the Polish government would permit the Russians to make their own interpretation: the President could only wearily reply, "I know, Bill, I know."

Of Germany, McNeil writes that "the American Government, because of its internal disputes and indecision, prevented even the discussion of a common Allied policy for Germany." Alarmed by the furor occasioned by the Morgenthau Plan, Roosevelt put a stop to all American efforts to make postwar plans for Germany from late 1944 until his death. "This ostrich attitude towards the future," says McNeill, "prevented whatever chance there may have been for arriving at Allied agreement upon policy towards Germany through the European Advisory Commission or in any other way, and left the subordinate American officials who were charged with the task completely at sea."

In default of an American initiative, what planning for peace took place in 1943–44 consisted chiefly of British and Soviet attempts to divide Europe between them into spheres of influence. The story of these attempts is an important one, for it suggests that the Soviets, like the West, felt in 1945 that past understandings between the Big Three concerning Eastern Europe were betrayed.

The pattern for postwar spheres of influence in the liberated European countries was established in Italy, however, not in Eastern Europe, and by England and America rather than by Russia. In theory the three military partners were committed to joint decision-making and to democratic self-determination within every European country, regardless of whose armies were occupying it. But in fact, the Big Three tacitly recognized and accepted spheres of influence all over the world. In China, Feis writes, "Stalin and Churchill seemed willing to have the American government take the lead in directing the political evolution of that country; and the American government was assuming it. Similarly, it was understood that Britain could be to the fore in dealing with Southeast Asia." And Churchill said of South America: "We follow the lead of the United States in South America as far as possible, as long it is not a question of our beef and mutton." The habits twined about these long-standing arrangements proved too strong to be offset in meeting the challenge of liberated Europe when it first presented itself in Italy.

England took the lead. Churchill wanted to keep the monarchy in Italy, and deprecated any statement about self-determination. Russia's desire to take an active role through a tripartite military-political commission was deflected by the fact that Western commanders retained power, and when Russia established independent diplomatic relations with the Italian government, its move was strongly resented and protested by the West. The powers which Russia wanted, however, were the very ones which England and America were later to demand in Eastern Europe and which the Soviets denied, pointing persistently to Italian precedents. Some Westerners foresaw the result of the West's behavior in Italy; thus Ambassador Winant wrote in July 1943, that "when the tide turns and the Russian armies are able to advance we might well want to influence their terms of capitulation and occupancy in Allied and enemy territory." But this view did not prevail and the outcome was, in McNeill's words, that "in Italy, Russia had effectually been excluded from participation in Allied decision-making, and the Western Allies could hardly expect to be treated differently by the Russians in Rumania."

As German resistance began to crumple and the Allied armies poured into Festung Europa, the volume and pace of political decision-making in occupied territory necessarily increased. England began to make independent approaches to the Soviet Union looking toward an agreement on spheres of influence which would safeguard the Mediterranean lifeline and put some limit to the Red Army's advance. "Experience," Feis comments,

was showing how hard it was to apply the rule of common consent in each of these unstable situations. And decision could not always wait. In brief, the diplomatic methods in use began to seem defective or unsuitable—awkward for war, ineffective for peace. Hence both diplomats and soldiers began to wonder whether an arrangement which made one or the other Allies the dominant authority in each of these situations was not the sensible way to end the discussion.

Churchill, more tersely, stated that in each of the occupied countries someone had to play the hand, and with this in mind he journeyed to Moscow in October 1944 to make his division of Eastern Europe with Stalin, and thus safeguard British predominance in Greece.

As in 1941–42, so in these negotiations of 1943–44 the United States preferred to remain, in the words of the Monroe Doctrine, an "anxious and interested spectator." Harry Hopkins intervened to change the text of Roosevelt's cable to Churchill referring to the latter's Moscow trip, so that the American President, rather than empowering Churchill to speak for him, insisted on retaining "complete freedom of action." The reserved American veto imparted a provisional character to the Churchill-Stalin agreement. Thus it was that Western policy toward Eastern Europe in 1945 wavered because England and America had not reached full agreement, but the Russians, as in the similar case of the second front, interpreted the wavering as simple bad faith. Stalin protested that he had no idea whether the governments of Belgium and France, created under Western aegis, were democratic; he simply accepted them. Did not the accord of October 1944, although expressly limited to provisional arrangements until German surrender, give him by implication a similar free hand in Eastern Europe?

The first test of the new arrangement came in Greece. In his effort to make the agreement with Churchill stick, Stalin stood aside while British troops crushed Communist-led Greek guerillas: in Churchill's words, Stalin "adhered very strictly to this understanding." At the same time—as Feis, McNeill, and Williams all agree—he attempted to curb the Communist parties in Western Europe, Yugoslavia, and China from bidding for power, lest such an attempt spark off armed conflict between the great powers. It was therefore something of an irony when the Chinese revolution seemed to the West to confirm its image of the insatiable expansionism of Russian Communism.

In the absence of firm tripartite agreements, particularly about Poland, the British government, hitherto the advocate of realistic acceptance of a Soviet sphere of influence in Eastern Europe, at war's end found itself imploring American military assistance to contain the expansion of Soviet power. The upshot was as paradoxical as it was tragic. A sequence of events familiar in Anglo-American diplomatic history then took place. As in the formulation of the Monroe Doctrine, as in the formulation of the Open Door policy, the British government suggested to America a joint declaration of policy for reasons altogether in the realm of *Realpolitik*. As in the two preceding instances, so in 1945–47 the United States government proclaimed the policy as its own and lent it the panoply of a moral crusade. Ten years later, in consequence, England was in the position of trying to restrain the partner which but yesterday it had to prod.

Looking back, it is still difficult to assign responsibility with any sureness for this critical turn of events. America, which realized the importance of creating the United Nations before the bonds of wartime partnership were relaxed, failed to see the comparable importance of more humble agreements about gov-

ernments and frontiers, and this failure complicated the already inherent difficulty where two men so different in their points of view as Churchill and Stalin had to reach firm agreements. A number of prominent Americans, including Roosevelt and Hopkins, were deeply impressed by England's determination to retain its empire: this made them slow to accept Churchill's growing fear of Russian expansion, just as it blinded them to the truth that, in actual hard fact, America had always depended on the English empire to shield it from potential aggressors. Had the Soviet leaders been less suspicious and dogmatic than they were, they might well have been confused in responding to an England which did not have the strength to enforce its realism, and an America which did not seem to realize that idealism must be supported by something more than documents.

For the Soviets, such indecision on the part of the West must have encouraged the hope, championed by Trotsky after World War I, of carrying revolution westward on the bayonets of the Red Army. Advocates of the Russian interpretation of these events have quoted the Forrestal diaries to show that military leaders in the West did not really fear Soviet attack:[4] but these quotations begin no earlier then 1946, when the readiness to mobilize military force to deter such attack had already shown itself. Feis and McNeill reiterate that we possess very little material with which to interpret Soviet intentions in the spring of 1945. But there seems no good reason to doubt that the Russians were ready to carry their influence as far westward as they could safely go without risking the danger of war.

The inertia acquired by supposedly temporary military arrangements, their

[4] See Carl Marzani, *We Can Be Friends: Origins of the Cold War* (1952) as well as the books of W. A. Williams previously cited.

tendency then to turn into a political status quo unless deflected by new agreements for which, after Yalta, the Big Three alliance suddenly seemed no longer capable, posed for the West a genuinely "agonizing reappraisal." It seemed that to keep on a friendly footing with Russia it was necessary to betray (as it appeared to the West) the Polish people on whose behalf England had gone to war. Roosevelt and Truman were not as different in their reactions to this problem as extremists of both the right and the left would have one think: the President who sent the two most pro-Soviet men in American governmental circles (Davies and Hopkins) as his first envoys to Churchill and Stalin cannot have been, initially, bitterly anti-Soviet.

The course ultimately adopted was, of course, containment, and its error lay, surely, in making such a "posture" the *whole* of one's foreign policy. In itself, containment was simply the normal practice of diplomacy which sought to maintain a balance of power, and supported this effort with the threat of force; England has certainly never practiced anything else, and when the United States has tried to follow another course —as between 1801 and 1812 in our dealings with England and France—it has altogether failed. Containment was startling only in contrast with the Wilsonian idealism, today almost hard to remember, which preceded it.

What was novel and alarming was the exaltation of containment from one of many normal means to the entire substance of a policy. There was nothing in the idea of containment itself which would have precluded, for example, long-term credits for postwar reconstruction to the Soviet Union. Even if this had seemed impossible for domestic political reasons, such loans might have been offered to Eastern Europe. When in the Marshall Plan proposals the offer

was finally made, the international atmosphere had become embittered, Communist parties had strengthened their hold throughout Eastern Europe, and it was too late. In a sense, Eastern Europe was the first underdeveloped area where we failed.

In its sudden, totalistic shift from a reliance on ideals alone to a reliance only on the threat of war, American policy after 1945 exhibited a characteristic tendency to go from one one-sided solution to its opposite, equally one-sided. The Darlan and Badoglio deals, the unconditional surrender formula, the dropping of the atom bomb, also suggest an extremism of expediency and violence which all too frequently was the sequel to the benevolent extremism of America's first intentions.

George Kennan has shown how this tendency of American international behavior to oscillate between extremes of idealism and violence is magnified by our habitual self-righteousness.[5] "It does look," Kennan observes,

[5] These quotations are from *American Diplomacy, 1900–1950* (1952). In his writings of that date Kennan altogether failed to apply his general critique of American foreign policy to its dealings with the Soviet Union. Whereas he could say of American conduct toward Imperial Germany in World War I that "you could have refrained from moralistic slogans, refrained from picturing your effort as a crusade, kept open your line of negotiation to the enemy, declined to break up his empire and overthrow his political system . . ." yet these were the very goals Kennan advocated for our policy toward the USSR. Whereas in general he counseled America to "admit the validity and legitimacy of power realities and aspirations, to accept them without feeling the obligation of moral judgment, to take them as existing and inalterable human forces, neither good nor bad, and to seek their point of maximum equilibrium rather than their reform or their repression"—"reform or repression" of the Soviet system were the very goals which Kennan's influential writings of those years urged. Finally, whereas in treating America's relations with Japan before World War II Kennan noted how American policy tended to bring about "the final entrenchment of the power of the military extremists," he notably failed to see that the policy of containment he then advocated would have the identical effect on Moscow.

as though the real source of the emotional fervor which we Americans are able to put into a war lies less in any objective understanding of the wider issues involved than in a profound irritation over the fact that other people have finally provoked us to the point where we had no alternative but to take up arms. This lends to the democratic war effort a basically punitive note, rather than one of expediency.

Again Kennan says, commenting on the intrinsic connection between self-righteousness and total war:

Whoever says there is a law must of course be indignant against the lawbreaker and feel a moral superiority to him. And when such indignation spills over into military contest, it knows no bounds short of the reduction of the lawbreaker to the point of complete submissiveness—namely, unconditional surrender. It is a curious thing, but it is true, that the legalistic approach to world affairs, rooted as it unquestionably is in a desire to do away with war and violence, makes violence more enduring, more terrible, and more destructive to political stability than did the older motives of national self-interest. A war fought in the name of high moral principle finds no early end short of some form of total domination.

Instances of such behavior are legion. One recalls how the "peace without victory" position which Woodrow Wilson proclaimed in January 1917—which meant, if it meant anything, a negotiated peace—gave way in three short months to the complete conviction that autocratic governments could not be dealt with and must therefore be destroyed to "make the world safe for democracy." Again, McNeill has caught this quality in Roosevelt's attitude toward fascist Germany:

The conviction that Germany should be made to suffer for the wrongs done to the world by the Nazis was in a sense the obverse of Roosevelt's belief in the goodness and rationality of mankind at large. If a nation somehow failed to exhibit goodness and rationality, thus challenging Roosevelt's general belief about human nature, it endangered its claim to belong to humanity and deserved, Roosevelt came to feel, the severest sort of punishment.

It is as if, to sum up, the failure of reality to respond to innocent intentions (a lack of forethought as to means being itself considered a kind of innocence) calls forth a thirst for vengeance; then hope may give way to fear of an opaque reality which seems suddenly out of control; and reality be made to suffer for its intransigence.

This transition was the more inevitable after 1945 because English and American policy-makers had persistently underestimated Soviet strength, and the awakening to the real nature of the postwar balance of power came as something of a traumatic shock. One reason for the slow Anglo-American response to Soviet postwar demands in 1941 had been, as Churchill and Hull candidly confess in their memoirs, the conviction that Russia would grow weaker as the war went on. The colossal Red Army rolling east and west from Soviet borders in the spring and summer of 1945 caused latent anti-Communism to come quickly to the surface of opinion and seem sensible policy.

Only then did many sincere and thoughtful persons in the West recall that the Soviet ideology, pressed on to the heroic defensive as it had been since 1941, nonetheless envisaged the transformation of capitalism to socialism throughout the world. Revolution from within was the classical means toward this end; but Marx had never imagined a situation in which socialism and capitalism, represented by different groups of countries, would duel for the allegiance of the rest of the world; and it was a still more basic tenet in the Marxist tradition that means were, in any case, secondary. This underlying tension between opposing social systems facilitated the transformation of cautious cooperation into hostility at a time when public opinion still basked in the glow of victory, and even the leaders of the three victorious powers had far from lost hope in peaceful negotiation. As McNeill puts it: "Each of the Big Three wanted peace and security and recognized that only their continued cooperation could secure these goals. But what seemed an elementary precaution to safeguard the security of the Soviet Union to the one side seemed Communist duplicity and aggression to the other."

If then, we return to the question, Why did the cold war start? the most fundamental answer might be: Because for the first time the challenge of authoritarian socialism to democratic capitalism was backed by sufficient power to be an ever-present political and military threat. It is a far more complicated and potent challenge than that represented by Germany in 1914 or Japan in 1941; it is the kind of challenge associated with the break-up of empires and the transformation of whole societies rather than with the ordinary jostling of diplomatic intercourse. In this sense, those who now speak of negotiation and disarmament as simple nostrums are being superficial, and those who invoke the American way of life are more nearly correct.

Yet containment, while recognizing the seriousness of the problem, would appear to be an inadequate response. Even before the possession of atomic weapons by both sides made reliance on military reprisal archaic, containment was a one-sidedly negative policy which could lead only to slow defeat, and, by way of the frustration and fear thereby engendered, to war. It involved and still involves an identification of the United States with governments whose only qualification for our friendship is their anti-Communism, and which in every other respect go against rather than with the grain of worldwide aspiration. Only a narrow and superficial realism can look to such alliances for strength in the long run.

Is there a moral to be drawn from this alternation between the extremes of Wilsonian idealism and military "realism"? Ten years after he formulated the containment policy, George Kennan saw a moral clearly. "I should like to raise today the question," Kennan stated in 1957,

whether the positive goals of Western policy have really receded so far from the range of practical possibility as to be considered eclipsed by the military danger, whether we would not, in fact, be safer and better off today if we could put our military fixations aside and stake at least a part of our safety on the earnestness of our effort to do the constructive things, the things for which the conditions of our age cry out and for which the stage of our technological progress has fitted us.

"Surely everyone," Kennan continued,

our adversary no less than ourselves, is tired of this blind and sterile competition in the ability to wreak indiscriminate destruction. The danger with which it confronts us is a common danger. The Russians breathe the same atmosphere as we do, they die in the same ways.... Their idea of peace is, of course, not the same as ours.... But I see no reason for believing that there are not, even in Moscow's interpretation of this ambiguous word, elements more helpful to us all than the implications of the weapons race in which we are now caught up. And I refuse to believe that there is no way in which we could combine a search for those elements with the pursuit of a reasonable degree of military security in a world where absolute security has become an outmoded and dangerous dream.[6]

[6] These quotations are from *Russia, the Atom and the West* (1957).

19

The Illusion of American Omnipotence

DENNIS BROGAN

The American people have been singularly blessed throughout most of their history. When they fought Great Britain for their independence in 1776, royalist France rushed to their aid even though the Americans were avowed republicans and hostile to monarchies. Without that help it is extremely unlikely that victory could have been won in so short a time. Then in the treaty ending the war the British agreed to most of the American demands, including boundaries giving the new nation a vast territory stretching from the Atlantic to the Mississippi and from Canada almost to the Gulf of Mexico.

In the first two and a half decades of its independent existence the United States, as the result of a series of astounding concessions by Spain, France, and Great Britain, extended its boundaries to the Gulf of Mexico and to the Rocky Mountains, freed itself from the entangling alliance with France, rid its territory of the last foreign troops, and secured a favorable delimitation and rectification of its northern border. During the next thirty years the boundary was pushed to the Pacific and to the Rio Grande, the consequence of a brief and painless war with Mexico and of a treaty with England. Meanwhile, America was prospering. Industry, agriculture, mining, shipping—all increased, and at the same time the population was growing rapidly. The end of the nineteenth century saw another war, another easy victory, and the acquisition of extensive overseas possessions. In the early years of the new century the United States, by a series of armed interventions, made itself master of the Caribbean and the dominant force in Central America.

Not only in the western hemisphere was American power and influence felt. Twice within twenty-eight years the military forces of the United States journeyed overseas to take part in great wars, and both times they determined the outcome. It was American might that in 1917–1918 and 1941–1945 "redressed the balance of history."

Such was the phenomenal story of American successes. But after the Second World War conditions changed. Reverses replaced victories. The Soviet Union extended its hegemony over vast portions of Europe and strengthened the forces of Communism in the old world. Communists overthrew the Nationalist government of China and took over that immense country in 1949. One year later

"The Illusion of American Omnipotence" from *American Aspects* by D. W. Brogan. Copyright © 1964 by D. W. Brogan. Originally appeared in *Harper's Magazine,* and reprinted by permission of Harper & Row, Publishers. From *American Aspects,* copyright © 1964 by D. W. Brogan, Hamish Hamilton, London, 1964.

South Korea was invaded by Communists from North Korea, and at the end of that year Chinese and North Korean troops inflicted heavy defeats on American forces, who constituted about ninety-eight per cent of the United Nations army defending South Korea.

What had happened to American might, American successes, American invincibility, American omnipotence? Why did the course of world events seem no longer to follow the American wish? Many Americans attributed their country's failure not to any diminution of strength and power but to the existence of knaves, fools, and even traitors in their midst. Dennis Brogan, the eminent political scientist of Cambridge University and a long-time student and observer of the American scene, points to another cause for the American failures and at the same time analyzes the reasoning of those who have attributed them to fools, knaves, and traitors. The problem, as he sees it, is that many Americans refuse to accept the fact that "great as is American power, it is not so great as to quell, by its mere existence, all opposition." Those Americans refuse to admit that there are certain situations over which the United States can have no control, such as, for example, the downfall of Chiang Kai-shek and the Kuomintang. They continue to cherish the "illusion of omnipotence" and in their frustration seek refuge in the plausible but not necessarily valid hypothesis that they have been betrayed by traitors or deceived by fools.

I am writing this on the Pacific Coast, before the election, but in the conviction that the result of the election will very little affect the problem that I want to discuss. Even if the Republicans should make a clean sweep, even if the State Department is cleaned out, from the Secretary to the doorkeepers, even if the Pentagon is purged from the Joint Chiefs of Staff to the leaders of the rescue teams who find lost visitors, one problem of American policy will reman: the problem of the existence, in the American mind, of what I call the illusion of omnipotence. This is the illusion that any situation which distresses or endangers the United States can only exist because some Americans have been fools or knaves.

Such a situation may exist because of conditions about which the United States has, and will have, little to say. For America, powerful though she is, is not omnipotent. A great many things happen in the world regardless of whether the American people wish them to or not. I deeply regret this state of affairs; like

Bertrand Russell, I would gladly settle for an American hegemony; but we are not representative characters, and American hegemony not only does not exist, but is not even universally expected or desired.

I should, perhaps, say that the illusion of omnipotence to which I refer is not shared by all Americans. Nothing could be sillier than to attribute to nearly 160,000,000 people one common attitude, or to assume, as many European intellectuals do, that there is such a thing as "what the American people are thinking." Nevertheless, the idea that I am trying to describe is expressed by Senators and columnists, by candidates, by preachers, by people overheard in taverns and club cars, in drugstores and restaurants—the idea that the whole world, the great globe itself, can be moving in directions annoying or dangerous to the American people only because some elected or non-elected Americans are fools or knaves. When something goes wrong, "I wuz robbed" is the spontaneous comment—the American equivalent of that disastrous French cry, "*Nous sommes trahis.*"

It should also be said that I am not reproaching the American people, or even any important fraction of them, with the sort of mere arrogance that the British displayed in the nineteenth century, the arrogance that made the humiliation of the Boer War so refreshing to the rest of the world. There would be plenty of justification for reproach if the American people were as pleased with themselves today as the English were around the time of Queen Victoria's Diamond Jubilee. But except in the Tribune Tower and a few other strongholds of the spirit of Jefferson Brick, Americans are not overflowing with self-satisfaction.

It would not be surprising if they were self-satisfied. For twice, in a not very long lifetime, America has redressed the balance of history. But for American intervention in the first war, it would have ended in a draw. But for American intervention in the second (which began with Lend-Lease, not with Pearl Harbor), Hitler would have had, with his Axis partners, a free hand. One result of this would, in the long run, have been war with the United States; but that long-run consequence matters little in this context. What does matter is that what stopped the Second and the Third Reich was American power. By 1945—with the greatest fleet, the greatest air force, and one of the two greatest armies in the world—the United States had become a world power such as had never been seen before. Never had plowshares been beaten into swords so fast and on so large a scale.

And never were swords beaten back into plowshares as fast as in 1945. As a demonstration of power, and of pacific intention, the scenario was perfect. The crowd that formed a conga line round the White House on V-J Day represented the American temper of August 1945 to perfection. So did Mr. Leo Crowley cutting off Lend-Lease; so did the immediate pressure to end all the controls and get the boys home. True, there was the atomic bomb—but the thought that there would soon be a world in which the atomic bomb would be a very present hope would have shocked nine Americans out of ten. The war had been won; the fascist menace had been destroyed. True, there was no such mood of high hope as in 1919; but the lesson. of 1919 was not lost. America would not again take mere victory for enough, would not again walk out on the job.

And America has not walked out on the job. American policy since 1945 has, on the whole, been wise, far-seeing, magnanimous. Compare it with the policy of the years after the first war, with the policy of the years of Harding and Coolidge, and the growth in wisdom and responsibility is remarkable. Had there not been such a growth, the Kremlin would have won without firing a shot.

It is partly because the American people feel—rightly—that they have used their great power generously, that in 1952 they are perplexed, distressed, angry, and to some extent deluded. Why is it that, given the power, given the generosity of its use, the United States should be involved in the Korean mess? Why should so great a part of the world have passed into hostile hands? Why should the United States still be in danger, know the irritation of the draft in "peacetime," suffer, in Korea, one of the most humiliating of American military defeats, and nominate, for the Presidency, a soldier not merely or mainly as a reward, but because the times seem to call for a soldier in the White House?

It is my opinion that one reason for American distress is the American belief in American invulnerability and American omnipotence.

II

Belief in American invincibility is, on the whole, a good thing. A corresponding English belief in 1940, without nearly as much material justification for it, probably changed the history of the world. "The English always win, don't they?" asked my intelligent four-year-old son. The English won, but at a cost that has taken away the taste for victory. The Russians won too, but in the recent past they had lost. Probably the only people in the world who now have the historical sense of inevitable victory are the Americans. This belief, in its most extravagant, or McCormick, form, assumes that America doesn't need friends. In the less romantic, or Taft, form, it assumes that America doesn't need friends much. But even in the case of people who laugh at the Colonel and swear at the Senator, there is a lingering suspicion that there must be something grossly wrong when American policy suffers rebuffs; when, in despite of American opinion and interests, things go awry.

That grave mistakes have been made need not be doubted. As Mr. Walter Lippmann keeps on reminding his fellow-countrymen, one of the most obvious was the decision to exploit the victory at Inchon, regardless of the natural interest of the Chinese Communist government, of *any* Chinese government, in the arrival of a victorious American army on the Yalu. For that decision, Mr. Truman, Mr. Acheson, and General MacArthur are responsible, in that order. (For the actual military dispositions, General MacArthur is responsible, unless we are, belatedly, to blame Lincoln for the errors of General John Pope before Second Manassas.) That a naïve view of the world was displayed at Yalta, and long before Yalta, by many powerful Americans, is true. Eyes were kept on the conniving British Empire, as they are still kept by Colonel Mc-

Cormick, Mr. George Sokolsky, and others—eyes which had better have been directed elsewhere. But even had those eyes been more prudently fastened upon Russia, even had American policy been controlled by a Richelieu or a Bismarck, some of the present disillusionment would have occurred all the same. For America, the most powerful nation in the world, was not omnipotent and a great many things in the world were going on and going their own way regardless of the views of the American people.

For, great as is American power, it is not so great as to quell, by its mere existence, all opposition. In the good old days an English fleet could sail into the Bay of Naples and tell that able Bourbon, King Charles III, that he could be neutral or have his capital blown up around his ears. In the good old days before the "good neighbor" policy, the United States (or the United Fruit Company, if they could be distinguished) could lay down the law in the Caribbean. As Cleveland's Secretary of State said, the fiat of the United States was law in America, if the United States chose to insist.

But those days are gone. The United States could insist if she wanted to, but at excessive political cost. Even that American by-blow, the Republic of Panama, can defy Washington, up to the point where the safety of the United States is directly and indisputably involved. These facts are accepted. Yet a great many Americans, when China gets out of hand, or into the wrong hands, think this can only be because of some gross error or even crime on the part of the official rulers of America. Even so simple an explanation as that Chiang made the mistake denounced in all the military textbooks, and exemplified in the careers of Jefferson Davis and of Hitler, of commanding at long range and through favorites, is ignored. People feel that Chiang's defeat (a disaster for America, I freely admit) *must* have been due to American folly or American treason. People refuse to believe that it might have had other, more important causes, above all the one admirably described by Senator Tom Connally: "If he's a generalissimo, why doesn't he generalize?"

The Chinese situation is, at the moment, the most important of these American preoccupations and causes of bewilderment. But the sense of bewilderment is visible in some American attitudes toward Europe too. Why hasn't Marshall aid won over the French Communists—that is, ended a schism in French society going back to the Commune of 1871, if not to the Commune of 1793? Why hasn't it converted "Red Emilia," the Italian district that was in a violent revolutionary uproar in Wilson's first term? Why is it not certain that the inhabitants of the "People's Republic of Germany," after being fought over, and driven here and there, and after having had their social structure destroyed, following the disillusionments caused by the collapse of the Hohenzollerns, the Weimar Republic, and the Thousand-Year-Reich, will welcome slogans admirably designed for Cincinnati or Oakland? In such perplexities there is embedded, at the foundation perhaps, the illusion that the world must go the American way if the Americans want it strongly enough and give firm orders to their agents to see that it is done.

III

This illusion of omnipotence is best illustrated by a very common American attitude toward the Chinese Revolution. In this attitude—apparently the dominant one at the moment—there is a curious absence of historical awe and historical curiosity. The Chinese Revolution, an event of immense importance, is often discussed as if it were simply a problem in American foreign and domestic policy and politics. The Communist triumph in China is discussed as if it were simply the result of American action or inaction, the result of the mistakes, and worse than mistakes, of General Marshall, Secretary Acheson, President Roosevelt, and the Institute of Pacific Relations; and as if the Communists or the Russians would not have "captured" China had American policy been represented and controlled by Representative Judd—or even, perhaps, by Senators Cain and Jenner.

Is this not to display the belief in American omnipotence in very striking form? What is going on in China affects the oldest civilization now in existence. It affects about a fifth of the human race. It must have roots, deep roots, in the Chinese problem as seen by the Chinese. This is no matter of a regime imposed by Russia on a helpless small nation like Romania or Hungary. It is a historical phenomenon that may turn out to be more important than the Russian Revolution. It may well turn out, also, to be disastrous for us and for China. But the first thing to notice is the size of the phenomenon; to notice, for example, that there are five Chinese for every two Americans. What inherent necessity is there that the decision in China is, was, or ever will be in American hands?

It is not only a matter of scale. There is distance. China is six thousand miles from the Pacific Coast of America. How was and is American power to be effectively exercised at that distance? I anticipate one answer—that Russian power *is* being exercised, and that it was Russian power (in the absence of American power because of American folly and treason) that "took over" China. This is not demonstrated and in this crude and popular form is not probable. But even if it were true, Russia is not six thousand miles from China. Russia has had a common frontier with China for three hundred years, and as Russia's center of industrial gravity moves eastward, Russian power gets nearer China and can be more readily exercised there. In a straight contest for control of China between the United States and the U.S.S.R., with the Chinese regarded as vile bodies, the U.S.S.R. would hold the trumps. To ignore that is to show the attitude of mind of those who have complained that, at Yalta, F.D.R. "permitted" Russia to become a Pacific power. Russia was a Pacific power before the United States existed. And she was and is an Asiatic power, which the United States is not. Lake Baikal and Lake Superior are on different continents. Vladivostok and Peiping are not.

But the real lack of historical reverence and realism is in the assumption that Russa "took over" China as she took over Poland. Even if we assume that there is as united an opposition to Communist rule in China as I believe there is in Poland, the scale of the taking-over ought to impose reflection. By what miracle was it done? Could General Hurley or General Chennault have prevented it? Would a sounder understanding of what the Communists were have prevented the Communist triumph? If it would have, then China is a more torpid body, more open to mere manipulation, than it is pleasant to think. If so great an event as the Chinese Communist Revolution could have been prevented by a different American policy, China is "a corpse on the dissecting table," as Charles Gavan Duffy said of Ireland after the Famine. In that case, Mao and Stalin may dissect it and make a monster of it like Dr. Moreau in H. G. Wells' prophetic story. If it was taken over as easily as all that, it will be kept taken over even more easily.

There is some reason to believe and to hope that it is not quite as simple as this. We are in danger of being obsessed with the important and indisputable fact that world Communism is a real and potent force and that it is controlled from Moscow. We tend, therefore, to see the hand of Moscow everywhere and attribute to it an initiating and dominant role that may not always be justified. The Chinese Revolution, we should remember, has been going on longer than the Russian Revolution. Sun Yat-sen was the successful leader of a revolution when Lenin was an obscure and not too hopeful exile in Switzerland. But, I shall be told, that was a *different* Chinese Revolution; that was the *good* Chinese Revolution, the one that deposed the Manchu dynasty and abolished the pigtail and the binding of feet; that was the revolution which was inspired and encouraged by American missionaries and American-trained students. But isn't it a truism of history that when you start a revolution, you can't be sure where it is going and how far?

It wasn't Lenin who overthrew the Tsardom or Robespierre who stormed the Bastille. In a long, bloody, and profound revolution, the extreme party has many advantages. It may not win; it may not stay victorious; the Jacobins learned that. But it may destroy the old order, the old ruling classes, the rival revolutionary parties, Social Revolutionists or Girondins. It doesn't need, in a genuine revolutionary situation, outside aid, outside doctrine, though it may get and benefit by both. The Chinese Communists got aid; they got doctrine. They probably benefited by both (though in 1927 they might have done better without either). But to deny that the Chinese Communists are a large, native Chinese party is to fly in the face of all the evidence. Their leaders may be docile tools of Moscow, but that doesn't alter the fact that the Chinese Communist party which survived the Kuomintang war against it, which survived the "long march," is a formidable indigenous party. On the record, it seems to have been the most formidable indigenous party— the one that, had both the U.S.A. and the U.S.S.R. stayed out, might have won anyway.

Could it have been prevented from defeating the Kuomintang by the provision of "massive and controlled" American aid? I have already suggested that the Russians could play that game too, and their aid could have been both more massive and controlled than the American. But even assuming that they did not so react to open American intervention in a civil war against their political allies, in a neighboring country, how was the aid to be made massive and how was it to be controlled?

Does anyone think that a continuation of what arms aid had been given, or even a stepping-up of such aid, would have done the trick? The Washington wit who said that supplying arms to Chiang was simply a roundabout way of Lend-Lease to the Chinese Communists was a jester, possibly frivolous; but he was not altogether wrong. Lend-Lease to Britain, Lend-Lease to Russia was direct and massive aid to coherent, united, and combative governments. It was not aid to a divided party in a country torn and tired by a generation of foreign and domestic war. More aid to Chiang might have prolonged the war; it might have saved the situation south of the Yangtse; but would it have brought conquest of the Communists by Chiang's forces?

And how was American aid to be controlled—except by exercising a degree of American authority which would not only have inflamed the *amour propre* of the Generalissimo, but would have deprived the Kuomintang of its last political asset, its claim to be "nationalist," to represent the independence of China?

Could the aid have been effective without active American participation—without keeping the Marines in China, without sending in more troops, without, in fact, involving the United States in a greater Korean war? Does anyone who remembers the temper of the American people in 1945, from the White House and Capitol to churches and bars, believe that such a policy was politically practicable?

I have been in America every year since 1944 with the exception of 1949. I have sometimes been twice in America in one year. I have been in all regions. At no time before the Korean war did I find anything like the resolution to make great sacrifices to save China which alone could have saved China.

IV

At first sight, the growing American distress at the continuance of the Korean war seems to show something very different from a sense of omnipotence. It shows, indeed, a sense of frustration, dismay, bewilderment. To find hundreds of thousands of American troops fighting in a remote country, seven years after "the end of the war," is baffling enough. To suffer over 120,000 casualties in such a situation is worse. The Korean war is already, in terms of losses, the third most serious war in American history. An American mother lamenting the fate of her son is a figure to inspire sympathy and understanding. It is natural that the American people should want, not on any terms but on some terms, an end to the Korean war.

But in addition to this common and natural sentiment, there is another American attitude that is less defensible and decidedly dangerous. It might be likened to the attitude of the prosperous and pompous citizen who, in a jam, firmly tells the cops, "You can't do that to me." Many, very many Americans, it seems to me, find it inconceivable that an American policy, announced and carried out by the American government, acting with the support of the American people, does not immediately succeed. If it does not, this, they feel, must be because of stupidity or treason. That the Chinese Communist government should defy—and successfully defy—the policy of the United States, seems to them to fly in the face of a truth which they hold to be self-evident.

Yet such situations exist and may well continue to exist. It is by no means certain that American forces will easily be withdrawn from Korea, or even that they may not have to take part in other wars of that kind. Mrs. Kathleen Norris can no more alter that fact than Senator Taft can really guarantee to keep the military budget to a fixed proportion of the total. In the great power vacuum created by the decline of Europe, the United States is forced, and will be forced, to do a great many disagreeable things—or to surrender. This is a new story for the United States, but it is an old one for Europe. What the American people are enduring now is what the French, the English, the Russian peoples, even the Spanish and Italian peoples, suffered in the process of extending or trying to retain their empires.

But, it will be objected, America is not trying to extend an empire; she is defending public order and morality in Korea. This is very different from the piratical adventures of the old world, from the French in Africa, the English in India, or the Russians in Samarkand or Armenia. Morally, this is true. But, just as the purity of the American cause does not win all American families to an acceptance of the Korean war as necessary and tolerable, so the moral turpitude of European enterprises added very little to the burden of empire. And

that burden was heavy in terms of lives lost.

It has been calculated—and I do not think it is an improbable calculation—that the French conquest of Algeria cost the French 150,000 lives. (What it cost the Arabs, resisting civilization, no one has paused to compute.) I don't know what the British wars in India cost either in great battles, in minor battles, or in disease, but they cost plenty. Even the British peace, imposed on India, cost plenty to the 100,000 white troops permanently garrisoned in that remote, unhealthy land. Do you think it mattered to a French mother that her son, dead in Algeria, was an agent of imperialism? All she knew was that he had paid what Marshal Gouvion Saint-Cyr candidly called a blood tax. And the same story can be told of Indochina seventy years ago—and now. It is one of minor themes of a once-famous novel, Loti's *Pêcheur d'Islande*. "It's a long way to Carcassonne," said the soldier of the Grande Armée, dying in the snow on the retreat from Moscow; and it is a long time since Vergil made the dying Greek remember sweet Argos.

Morally justifiable—indeed, morally splendid—as the American action in Korea on behalf of the United Nations may be, and urgent as the need may be to find an honorable way out of the predicament in which she finds herself, what Americans are paying today is one of the normal prices of being a great power, of bearing the burdens as well as enjoying the advantages of power.

Again, I have no intention of minimizing the horror of the Korean war. I was in New York in December 1950, when it was still not certain that the Marines would get out of the trap sprung on them in North Korea—when, indeed, it was not certain that many of them would ever get home. I felt passionately with the American people. And the situation is not purely American. In a year and a half, my eldest son will be in the army and may be in Malaya or Korea. It is a painful story. But it is an old one.

V

Another aspect of the "you can't do this to me" mentality—which, in turn, is an aspect of the illusion of omnipotence—can best be studied in the writings of Mr. David Lawrence of the *U. S. News & World Report*. To Mr. Lawrence the Korean war, the loss of American lives in it, is not merely painful but unendurable. It must be put an end to, and one of the methods suggested has a real interest—to me a pathological interest. If I understand Mr. Lawrence aright, in order to diminish Communist pressures on the Americans in Korea, Poles and Czechs are to be encouraged to acts of sabotage if not of active revolt, and a "resistance movement" is to be subsidized, with a view to diverting Russian or other Communist resources from Korea—that is, from the Americans in Korea.

This modest proposal deserves examination. Mr. Lawrence apparently does not pretend that the United States proposes to do anything more to liberate Poland and Czechoslovakia than to encourage and equip saboteurs. He does not pretend that such activities, in themselves, will bring down the Stalinist regime. They will, he hopes, cause such inconvenience that the heat will be off the Americans.

It is obvious that Mr. Lawrence does not know very much about resistance movements, or the means open to a totally ruthless government to repress resistance movements. He may have heard of Lidice, of Warsaw, even of Oradour-sur-Glane. But the meaning of those episodes is lost on him (and on many other Americans). To save the lives of Americans, to relieve this new

and heavy but not intolerable pressure on American society, Poles and Czechs are to risk—for themselves and for their families and, if it comes to a pitch, for their countries—total destruction, the execution of hostages, the annihilation of whole villages, possibly the fate of the peoples of the three Baltic states, of whom we do not even know that, as nations, Lithuania, Estonia, and Latvia exist any longer.

These nations, and more especially the Poles, have undergone experiences that not one home-staying American in a hundred thousand, perhaps in a million, can really comprehend. The liberation of Poland, on these terms, might mean the end of Poland. And the Poles are not even promised liberation; merely the satisfaction of annoying the Russians and relieving the Americans. If the United States were in mortal danger, patriotic Poles might be willing to take great risks to aid her, since in American survival "the only hope of freedom lies." But she is not in mortal danger; she is in what a Pole who has known first German, then Russian rule, can hardly regard as more than acute discomfort. To ask the Poles to act, at such risks, to diminish this discomfort is something pardonable only on the grounds of invincible ignorance. And it is something that Americans could hardly seriously recommend unless they saw in the situation a denial of one of "the Laws of Nature and of Nature's God," namely, the immunity of the United States from the common ills of this distressed world.

For is should be evident that only if the United States is willing, in a reasonably short time, to undertake, by general war, the liberation of the captive nations, has any American any business urging kinds of resistance which can pay only in the event of a general—and successful —war. Even were the United States to proclaim such a policy, the problem of encouraging resistance is not a simple one. It can be argued, for instance, that the damage done to France by the resistance movement there—from the torturing and burning of victims to the demoralization that some resistance methods fostered—was far more serious than any damage done to the German occupiers. The only justification for disregarding that calculation was a moral one: that if France took no part in her own liberation, she could not, in fact, be liberated; all that could be done was to expel the Germans, which was not the same thing. But even so, the appeals of General de Gaulle and others, and the organization from London of all sorts of resistance activities, were only just tolerable, because they were not only a means of saving English lives but also of saving French souls.

This is not to say that everything possible should not be done to keep alive hope, the Western tradition, the national tradition in the captive nations. A permanently hostile Poland or Czechoslovakia is a double weakness for the U.S.S.R., a possible future military weakness and a present propaganda weakness. But there is a world between the policy advocated by John Foster Dulles and that advocated by those Americans who say, "This can't go on." It may, and no amount of asserting that it can't will alter the fact.

When policies are advocated on the ground that they will "save the lives of American boys," the implication sometimes seems to be that only the lives of American boys really count. It is often forgotten, in this world of short memories, that one justification of Yalta, of the coaxing and bribing of Stalin to enter the Japanese war, was the saving of the lives of American boys. To save the lives of American boys is a high object of policy indeed. It is one of the marks of a democracy, or of a free gov-

ernment, that the military and political leaders can be held to account on that one point. As the Duke of Wellington pointed out, Napoleon could spend his conscripts as he liked, while Wellington might be summoned to the bar of the House of Commons if he threw away the lives of five hundred British soldiers. But that is a very different matter from giving the impression that American lives, as such, are of any special importance; that, as an American friend of mine put it in some unpublished verses:

Clean-limbed American boys are not like any others.
Only clean-limbed American boys have mothers.

Their lives are of special importance to Americans, but not to the people of other lands. And there would be widespread resentment over the thoughtless implication that it is the first duty of Poles or Czechs to save American lives.

These are hard sayings and they are negative sayings. But they may not be useless all the same. Only by constant vigilance, prudence, willingness to take the long view and to assess the situation, even in its most unpleasant, frustrating, and dangerous aspects, can American policy succeed—succeed in preserving the freedom of the United States and the freedom of other nations as a means to that end. There are no quick, sure recipes for security and power. The Kremlin hasn't got them; the White House will not have them either. This means that the American people will have to learn a great many new attitudes. (They learn fast, as the history of the world since 1939 shows.) They will have to learn that, even in election years, the world cannot be altered overnight by a speech or a platform. Only by accepting this depressing truth can American power, great, flexible, and beneficent as it is, be used to full advantage.

20

On Dealing with the
Communist World

GEORGE F. KENNAN

On March 12, 1947, President Truman appeared before a joint session of Congress to request $400 million for economic and military aid to Greece and to Turkey, whose independence was being threatened by the Soviet Union. Said the President, "I believe that it must be the policy of the United States to support free peoples who are resisting attempted subjugation by armed minorities or by outside pressures. I believe that we must assist free peoples to work out their destinies in their own way." With these words the United States announced its determination to block any further advance by the Soviet Union, and the policy of "containment" came into being.

Four months later an article appeared in Foreign Affairs *entitled "the Sources of Soviet Conduct," explaining the philosophy underlying the containment policy. The author, who was anonymous and was designated only as X, presented an historical analysis of Soviet ideas and attitudes and concluded that the Soviet aim was the eventual destruction of capitalism. The frustration of this ambition was possible, he said, "by the adroit and vigilant application of counterforce at a series of constantly shifting geographical and political points, corresponding to the shifts and maneuvers of Soviet policy...." The United States must not expect "in the forseeable future to enjoy political intimacy with the Soviet regime. It must continue to regard the Soviet Union as a rival, not a partner ... [and] expect that Soviet policies will reflect ... no real faith in the possibility of a permanent happy coexistence of the Socialist and capitalist worlds...."*

Shortly after the article appeared, the author was identified as George F. Kennan, a career Foreign Service officer, at that time a member of the policy planning staff of the Department of State. Kennan was a specialist on Russia, having studied the language in Berlin before the war and having served in Moscow in 1933, 1935–1937, and 1945–1946. In 1952 he was appointed ambassador to the Soviet Union but stayed only one year, retiring in 1953 to devote himself to lecturing and to writing.

After the death of Stalin in 1953 Kennan began a reassessment of Soviet leadership and found some hopes for a relaxation of tensions. At the same time, he saw in the huge military forces, Soviet and American, that faced each other in Europe the possibility of a clash that might lead to a new world war. In a

FROM *On Dealing with the Communist World* (New York: Harper & Row, Publishers, for the Council on Foreign Relations, 1964), 3–20, 37–51. By permission of the Council on Foreign Relations.

series of lectures delivered in England in 1957 and subsequently published in book form, Kennan suggested that a neutral zone be established between the two hostile armies and that this "disengagement" might make easier a political settlement between the two adversaries. It seemed clear that he was prepared to abandon the rigid policy of containment in favor of exploring the prospects for a more flexible position that envisaged coexistence.

The selection that follows is drawn from lectures given in New York in 1963, and may be seen as a further step in the evolution of Kennan's continuous examination of Communism. He asks now that it be viewed not as monolithic and uniform, having the single and unalterable purpose of destroying capitalist societies, but rather as polycentric, willing to pursue a policy of accommodation with the West. He sees the real possibility for a long period of peace and repose if the rigidity that characterized the early postwar years is modified.

THE RATIONALE OF COEXISTENCE

When I first conceived the thought of addressing myself, in these lectures, to the subject matter you see suggested by their titles, I was acting under a sense of irritation over what seemed to me to be the lack of historical depth in much of what was being said publicly in this country about the respective problems concerned. I had only recently returned from a long absence abroad. Much of what was being said here was new to me. When I was told, for example, that a prominent American political figure was advocating the withdrawal of diplomatic representation from—in effect the breaking of relations with—the Soviet Government and other Communist governments, my first reaction was: God help us! Is not this where we came in thirty years ago—thirty years ago this month, in fact—when F.D.R. took the step of recognizing the Soviet Government and when it fell to me, very young and very excited, to accompany our first ambassador to the Soviet Union, Mr. William C. Bullitt, on his first official journey to Moscow? And was this action of F.D.R.'s not actually the culmination of a fifteen-year debate over the whole question of recognition? And did we not all assume that the debate had at least found its final and timely termination with this

act of recognition, whether we liked it or not? Or, to take another example, when I noted that one of our leading conservative columnists was referring to us as being "at war" with the Soviet Union, my heart fell; because I thought of the years of effort, the reams of paper, the entire libraries, in fact, of published materials, which had been devoted to the search for a more meaningful and constructive definition than this of the nature of our relationship to Soviet power, one that did better justice to the complexity of the problem. And I thought: does this, too, all have to be gone over again? Do we have to start once more with all the arguments and counter-arguments of 1918, as though our minds constituted some sort of a *tabula rasa*—as though we had just woken up from some sort of amnesia and were amazed to find an ideologically hostile force glaring at us over the fence?

This, as I say, is the way I began. But I must confess that as I went along I became aware that things more serious than mere shallowness of historical memory were involved in some of these utterances I had stumbled upon. It became evident to me that we had to do here with a great and important body of opinion in this country—and a growing one, I fear—which was fully prepared to reject in its entirety the experience and judgment of all of us who have had to deal responsibly with the problem of Communist power over these past thirty years—a body of opinion which was prepared to throw both hope and patience to the wind, to embrace an outlook which rejected every possibility other than the most relentless and embittered and uncompromising struggle, and to pursue a policy which, in my profound conviction, could lead only, and with inexorable logic, to the final and irreparable disaster which is in all our minds. I became aware, in short, that we had to do here, in the question of our relation to world Communism, with a crisis of opinion of such seriousness as to constitute of itself a great and present danger.

If then, in talking of these things in this first lecture, I speak less from a platform of academic detachment than from that of an engaged and troubled citizen, this is my reason for doing so.

What I should like to talk about today is the familiar subject of coexistence, which lies at the heart of this whole matter. There is a great and real issue here. It is the question whether it should be the goal of our national policy to achieve the early and total destruction, everywhere, of everything that calls itself Communism, even if this goal has to be pursued at the expense of our chances for living with Communist power successfully so long as it is not destroyed. Or whether it should be our goal to find acceptable ways of living with it, and influencing it, even if this has to be done at the expense of our chances for destroying it entirely.

For many years I was under the impression that the first of these views—the one that despairs of living successfully with our adversary and seeks only his destruction—had been debated and tried in earlier times and that there had

crystallized among us an adequate consensus to the effect that this was not the most hopeful way to approach our problem. From 1933 to the late 1940s this was, I think, the case. But during the past ten years we have witnessed the resurgence of a body of opinion which takes the other line, which rejects in effect the whole concept of peaceful coexistence and which would commit us to a policy of "we or they"—a policy which sees no issue to the present contest except in the final and complete destruction of one side or the other.

Both of the views I cited earlier as evidences of historical shallowness fall, as you will note, into this category as well. And they are not isolated examples. Such outlooks are held by a great many people around the country. They have a strong and growing hold on much of our student youth. There are entire geographic regions where they have almost a clean sweep, and where to challenge them at all is to court resentment, misunderstanding, and obloquy. They have rarely affected the attitudes of those who, confronted with over-all responsibility for the conduct of foreign policy, have had to look at these matters long and hard and to take the rap for their decisions. But they have made deep inroads on those aspects of our national behavior which are directly subject to Congressional action or influence—such things as security procedures, visa and passport controls, trade restrictions, export and shipping controls. In this way they have often served to cancel out or to weaken the policy the executive branch was trying, at the moment, to follow. So strong is now their prevalence in Congress and certain other segments of government in Washington that it is not an exaggeration to say that we have today two wholly different and mutually contradictory foreign policies being pursued simultaneously in that city, and you can find whichever of them you want, depending on which door you want to put your head in.

No one will be under any doubt, I am sure, as to my own position with relation to these two alternatives. This is not the first time I have had occasion to raise my voice publicly against these counsels of despair which persist in viewing Communism as the only serious evil in the world, which refuse to recognize in it the elements of either change or differentiation, which insist on treating it as a single conspiratorial force, dedicated only to our destruction and beyond the range of any human appeals, and which, accordingly, would willingly see us sacrifice all the positive values of life to the struggle against it. Naturally, I have to regret that such views still exist and still have the wide currency they do.

But what worries me even more is the combination of amused contempt, or cynicism, or dreamlike complacency, with which I find this outlook treated by most of my friends. I do not think this body of thought can be disposed of by silence or by ridicule.

The question it raises is not a disrespectable one. There *is* this thing called Communist power. There *is* this problem of its hostility toward us. It is a great problem. And if to myself and to many of those who hear or read these lectures, the basic considerations affecting our answer are reasonably obvious, there are plainly a great many people to whom they are not. If these people ever knew the reasons why something called "victory," in the sense of an early and complete elimination of "Communism," is not the answer, they have forgotten them. And I sometimes suspect that many of us who think that we understand these reasons very well might be hard put to it to recall exactly what they were.

Let us therefore take up this question once more. Let us accept the fact that we have this sharp and serious challenge, and let us ask ourselves, as though we had never asked it before: Why, indeed, coexistence? Why not victory?

No objective historian would deny, I think, that the attitude with which the Soviet leaders initially approached the societies and governments of the West was an outrageous one, full of prejudice and intellectual arrogance and intolerable hostility. It was not the same kind of challenge, to be sure, as those common to international life up to that point. It corresponded to none of the established concepts of international hostility. It was aimed, in theory, only against certain classes in the West, not against entire peoples. It did not envisage overt and full-fledged international hostilities. But it did involve attitudes which were insulting and menacing to the Western societies, which had as their aim the violent destruction of the political systems of those societies, and which were clearly unacceptable on any normal standards of international life.

There could be no question in 1918, and there can be none today, of the moral right of a society to defend itself against such designs: to take measures for the disarming and control of subversive elements within its own citizenry, and to take measures of military precaution insofar as these might be responsive to the nature of the challenge.

But it became clear at an early date that if you went beyond this defensive effort, as some of our allies halfheartedly tried to do in the various interventions of 1918 to 1920, and as many people in this country wanted us to do, and made it your objective to overthrow the Soviet Government, you got yourself into a very messy business indeed, even from the standpoint of moral and political responsibility. There were unclarities and ambiguities in the relationship of the Soviet régime to the Russian people which constantly confused the issue. You discovered that the attitudes of people to régime—and particularly the question whether people really wanted to be liberated from it—depended largely on what they thought were, at any given point, the possible alternatives. But these alternatives were often highly obscure. The two greatest non-Communist political parties which had existed in Russia prior to the Communist seizure of power there, hated each other, unfortunately, at least as much as they hated the Communists. It was out of the question that they could ever get together; and neither, as it happened, was capable of governing alone. Those who spoke, therefore, of overthrowing the Soviet Government had no very convincing answers as to what would be put in its place. The problem was not disposed of merely by saying that democratic procedures would be permitted to prevail. This principle had been tried in 1917; but the understanding for democratic procedures among the Russian people had turned out to be not very widespread. A single ruthless minority had easily pushed through the entire parliamentary system. It was not even certain that some of the opponents of Bolshevism had a much greater devotion than did the Bolsheviki to democratic ideals.

Not only that, but you found that a very considerable part of the Russian people preferred to take their chances on adjusting peaceably to Communist rule rather than to have someone try to liberate them by force and in this way compel them to accept all the hardships and dangers and, above all, the excruciating political choices that go with a civil war and particularly one in which foreigners are involved. It was questionable, in fact, how many people in Russia you were going to be benefiting by such an interference into their political life. That some would be pleased to have this effort made was clear; but that many others would not was also clear. On balance, it was a real question

whether such an undertaking, even if successful in the negative sense of bringing about the expulsion of the Communists from the seats of power in Moscow, would have been a blessing for the people as a whole or merely a new source of hardship and horror. One should remember that even the half-hearted and futile little military expeditions which the allies did dispatch to Russian soil in 1918 got vast numbers of people into very serious trouble; the executions that followed them numbered in the tens of thousands.

But aside from all these questions of the political propriety and usefulness of such an endeavor, it was clear that in the sheer physical sense it was an extremely unpromising undertaking. The Russian Communist Party, having had years of experience in the techniques of ousting others from the seats of power, showed from the start an extraordinary mastery of the science of clinging to these seats itself. Once the Communists had established the monopoly of their rule, they had little difficulty in spiking in the bud any really serious attempts at armed opposition. It was plain that they could be removed from the seats of power only by a major insertion of outside force. But any such outside intervention was bound to confuse the very political situation to which it was addressed; for nobody, however opposed to his own government, really feels very comfortable associating himself with foreign military forces coming onto the territory of his country. And the task, in the sheer military sense, was bound to be an enormous one. What was involved, if the intervention was going to do any real good, was not just driving the Communists from power in Moscow. This alone would not have finished them. They were not that breed of cat. They were skilled, as few political movements in history have ever been, in the arts of underground political activity. They knew exactly how to go underground. They would have had to be pursued to the ends of the vast Russian land; and nothing suggests that foreign armies endeavoring to accomplish that pursuit would have ended up in any better position than did, say, the Japanese in the Communist-penetrated areas of northern China during the last war—riveted to the railways, harassed and bled at every turn by guerrillas having closer links with the people and knowing precisely how to exploit those links to the discomfort of an outside force. And this is not to mention the two great subjective questions as to whether, if this were conceived as a joint western undertaking, allied unity would ever have been sufficient to sustain it (it certainly was not in 1918), or if it were to be done by a single Western power, what Western public would ever have consented to bear for long a burden of this nature.

I mention these things simply in order to make the point that even in the early days of Bolshevism, when the Soviet régime was relatively weak and inexperienced, the idea of its overthrow, as a direct goal of Western policy, was never a promising one—either from the standpoint of military feasibility or from that of political effectiveness. Think, then, by comparison, what it would be today, when the Soviet régime has enjoyed a monopoly of power in Russia for nearly half a century; when it has behind it several decades of political and administrative experience; when it disposes over some of the strongest armed forces in the world; and when it has unquestionably achieved a far higher degree of acceptance than was the case in those early years; when large segments of the Soviet population, in fact, have never known any other political system and would be incapable of conceiving of any alternative to this one. The moral is that even if the nature of Russian Communism had undergone no

change—even if it represented exactly the same sort of challenge to us that it did forty years ago (which incidentally is what our ardent liberationists all seem to assume), I should have deepest misgivings about any concept of policy which envisaged, as a sort of an end-product, the overthrow of Soviet power either by the direct use of our forces or by incitement of subject peoples to revolts which we would be vaguely expected to back up if they got into trouble.

I am sorry to have to plunge this way into what seem to be murky and somewhat speculative depths, but these unhappy realities seem to lie at the heart of our problem; for it is hard to conceive of any liberationist policy which would not, sooner or later, run up against them at some point. We are told, for example, by prominent protagonists of the liberationist view, that to achieve the downfall of Communism, we would not have to occupy Russia or China. The vast majority of people in these countries, they assure us, are not Communists. "They will, with proper guidance, take care of their own freedom once they are released from the iron grip of Communist dictatorship." But such a statement raises more questions than it solves. Who, first of all, is to release them from their iron grip? They, themselves? Scarcely. Popular revolt against a ruthless, experienced modern dictatorship, which enjoys a monopoly over weapons and communications, which has its own armed forces under tight control, and which retains its unity and its will to power, is simply not a possibility in the modern age.

And could the peoples of these countries be depended upon to "take care of their own freedom" even if, by some miracle, that grip *was* loosened? This only raises again the tedious question of the possible alternative to Communism. There are no opposition parties in Russia today. There is no fund of political experience outside the Communist Party itself. Russia's previous experience with the concepts of Western democracy was pathetically brief and shallow; and the people who would remember it are mostly gone. The organized political force that could replace the Soviet Communist Party in that vast area today is simply not visible. I would know of no assurance that whatever might conceivably come in place of what is there now would be any closer to liberal ideals. Are we, then, to take moral responsibility for this incalculable change, which may or may not be for the better from the standpoint of the average Russian?

I personally believe that political change will continue to come to Russia; and important change at that. But if it is a question of our own time, I can conceive of its coming, as to some extent it already has, only on the foundation of and within the framework of the present political system, which is now firmly established and which has shaped the political outlooks and assumptions of an entire generation.

But while we are on this subject of political change in Russia, there is one further wrinkle of which I think we should take cognizance. We have here in this country, among the opponents of coexistence, people who argue with great vehemence that there *is* indeed a political alternative to the Soviet régime; that it exists in the form of the non-Russian minorities within the traditional Russian state. These elements, they claim, are thirsting for independence. We could bring about the overthrow of Soviet Communism by supporting them politically—by encouraging them to fight for their independence with the implicit promise of our support—by encouraging them, in other words, not only to destroy Communist rule in Russia but indeed to achieve the permanent break-up of the traditional Russian state.

There can be no denying that the multi-national composition which has characterized both the former Russian Empire and the Soviet Union—particularly the Soviet Union since 1945—is an important political fact. Unquestionably, the unhappiness of non-Russian elements had much to do with the final break-up of Tsardom. It is not at all silly to suggest that this factor may well have an important bearing on the political future of the traditional Russian area. But this is about all one can say with any degree of certainty.

Yet the thesis with which we are now confronted on the part of many of these American "liberationists" goes far beyond this. It asserts with a great show of definiteness that there are known to be a whole series of national groups within the Soviet Union which have long desired independence and which dispose over the necessary prerequisities for an independent existence but which were deprived of that independence by the Soviet régime. They even name a number of entities which allegedly correspond to this description; the list will be found in the so-called Captive Nations Resolution, to which a majority of the members of our Congress—many of them having only the dimmest ideas of the places or peoples involved—were induced to subscribe in 1959.

It is not to deny sympathy for the national feelings of certain of the peoples concerned if I point out that as a question of fact this claim is grossly exaggerated, and in some respects entirely spurious.

There are indeed instances—and I am thinking here particularly of the Baltic states—where a good case could be made for the validity of such claims. But there are other instances in which the whole thesis is fictitious and ludicrous. Certain of the national groups whose names appear in the Captive Nations Resolution as those of nations thirsting for a lost independence never existed at all in this quality; and it is incomprehensible that the Congress of the United States should have been led to commit the policy of this country formally to something called their liberation. Finally, there are still other instances in which we simply do not know the facts. We are often told, for example, that the Ukrainians are all thirsting for complete separation from the traditional Russian state. Perhaps so. But who knows? There has been, and could have been, no proper formal test of opinion on this point over these past forty-five years. The Ukraine never was really independent. History bears no evidence that the majority of the people of the Ukraine have at any time desired a total separation from the main body of the Russian people. And those who assure us that this is the case are for the most part people who have had no personal contact with the central regions of the Ukraine for many years, if ever.

Even should these claims be far better substantiated as assertions of objective fact than they actually are, I can think of nothing more catastrophic than that the policy of our government should be committed to the break-up of the traditional Russian state. Remember that nothing of this sort could be carried forward except at the cost of the violent and total estrangement of the Russian people, at the cost of their embittered armed opposition, at the cost, in fact, of a Russian civil war which would make that of 1918–1920 look like child's play. Nor would the chances of the non-Russian elements be favorable in any such encounter unless they had the foreign assistance on a massive scale. The Great Russians may or may not constitute a majority on the present territory of the Soviet Union, but they constitute by far the strongest national group; they command the traditional seats of political power; they command the centers of transportation and communication. In many of the areas where other nationalities predominate, Russians are heavily intermingled with the non-Russian population. Not only would outside force have to be invoked on a massive scale in order to bring about any such dismemberment of Russia in the first instance, but this outside force would have to remain indefinitely in occupation in order to enforce the maintenance of a *status quo* so violently unacceptable to the strongest national group in the area.

If the dream of popular revolt in the Soviet Union is today unreal in any case, which it is, it becomes doubly unreal if you think of it as hinged to an American commitment to the dismemberment of traditional Russia; for in this case all hope of the achievement of a peaceful consensus among the inhabitants of the region would have been lost; the strongest national element would have been wholly antagonized; and once again, the hatreds engendered over issues not connected with Communism would overshadow any resentment felt towards the Soviet régime.

We have, finally, among the arguments against coexistence, the insistent assertion that the Soviet leaders are largely bluffing and could easily be brought to desist from their undertakings or to yield ill-gotten gains if only we had the gumption to tell them that the alternative is war. This is a thesis which has received a specious appearance of substantiation from the fact that the Soviet government, confronted last year with a choice between withdrawing certain of its installations in Cuba or becoming involved in a war with the United States, preferred to withdraw the installations, and did so at some cost to its prestige.

I can only warn in the strongest way against attempting to draw inferences of this sort from the Cuban crisis. Whatever else may be said of the Russian Communists, history affords no substantiation for the suggestion that they are cowards. If every gesture of prudence or moderation on their part is to be hailed as proof of their faint-heartedness, and cited as an argument for bolder military pressures from our side, I shudder to contemplate the implications for the future course of Soviet-American relations.

The Soviet government is a great power, with a far-flung and complex pattern of international interests, involvements, and commitments. Like any other great power, it can be put on the spot. It can be placed in situations where to yield to bald military threats or ultimata would involve consequences disastrous and unacceptable. Nothing in the long history of its behavior suggests that it would yield, or could afford to yield, to this sort of open intimidation. In general, that school of American political thinking which views the East-West conflict in terms of apocalyptic visions of someone achieving a momentary superiority in weaponry and then saying to others, "Now you do what we say or else..." reflects a very shallow understanding indeed of what makes this world go around. We would not react to this sort of thing, and neither would the others.

The fact is that all these ideas for some sort of violent and short-term disposal of the Soviet problem—disposal of it in ways that would spare us the necessity of talking and dealing and compromising with people whose views we don't like— all these ideas lead sooner or later to war. Let there be no mistake about this. It is going to be hard enough, in the best of circumstances, to preserve the peace. Let no one suppose it will be easier to do so if the very idea of accommodation is ruled out. There is always some point between the undertaking and completion of these militant schemes at which the outbreak of hostilities would become inevitable. And it must be emphasized that the moment we get to this point there become valid and operable, once more, all those ambiguities and uncertainties which were discussed earlier in

connection with the very idea of overthrowing the Soviet government by force. Because war has to have an object. There have to be war aims. If you conduct military operations, you have to be willing to state what you would settle for. And what would our war aims be? Is there any likelihood that, once involved in hostilities, we would be inclined to settle for limited aims—for anything less than the complete destruction of Soviet power? The experience of two world wars would not suggest it. In each of these cases we heeded the demands of the hotheads and the super-patriots, and we insisted in fighting the conflict to its final and ultimate conclusion of the total destruction of the enemy's military strength and his political system: in one case, at the cost of installing the Communists in power in Russia; and in the other case, at the cost of turning over to them half of Europe. And during both of these contests, people in our midst who suggested a compromise peace, as did Lord Lansdowne in 1917, were treated as little short of treasonable.

Now there are two things I have refrained from mentioning up to this point, not because they were not germane to the discussion, but because I wanted, if I could, to make my points without them. The first is the element of change in the Soviet Union. It affects what I have said because it is this that tells us that these desperate and militant policies are not only unpromising but also unnecessary.

This is a great subject in itself. I shall only say here that I find it amazing that men can seriously discuss today these questions of our attitude toward Communist power without taking account of this factor. One can argue about the exact nature and extent of this change; but I do not see how anyone can dispute the difference between the weak and isolated Soviet state of the 1920s and the 1930s and the great power we have before us today, with its far-flung interests and involvements, its embarrassments of empire, its obligations of alliance, its new personalities, and its evolving internal problems. This, surely, is something far more like the traditional, established great power of "Russia" than like the fanatical political personality we faced in the Soviet régime of Lenin's time or the nightmarish totalitarian despotism of Stalin.

We have no need to be thrown off balance by such things as Khrushchev's statement that he would bury us. This does not really mean that he expects to finish us off within his time. He is too much of a realist for this. This, as I see it, was simply a prediction: that his political system would live to assist at the funeral of ours, not vice versa. This is a prediction basic to the Marxist outlook. He cannot do other than to reiterate it. He cannot explain publicly that this is all he means by it; he is a political person and his dogmatist critics would take advantage of it. But there is no reason we should not recognize it for what it is.

I find a great deal that is troublesome in the ideas and behavior of the present Soviet state. There is still a great deal in the way of established procedure and inherited prejudice that Moscow will have to get over before the Soviet Union can coexist tranquilly with other nations. But if I had to choose between dealing with this one or the one we faced thirty years ago, I would take this one any day. While its evolution may not proceed at the pace we would like, it has proceeded at a pace which affords no grounds at all for the total abandonment of all hope that it may some day take an acceptable place in the family of nations. And nothing in the state at which it has arrived justifies us in viewing it as something so far outside the range of ordinary experience that we are entitled to cast aside all the decencies when we deal with it.

The second point I have delayed mentioning or invoking as an argument, is that enormous multiplication of the dangers of war, and of the unsuitability of war as a weapon of policy, which we have before us in the phenomenon of the nuclear weapon of long-range destructive capacity. I have deliberately refrained from introducing this subject; for what I wish to emphasize is that the concept of destroying Soviet power entirely, as a major goal of policy, is and has always been inherently unsound, quite aside from the nuclear factor. It was unsound in 1918 when the allied expeditionary forces went to Russia. It was unsound in 1941 when Hitler's vast conventional armed forces launched themselves upon the Soviet Union. It did not take the atomic weapon to produce this situation. We only confuse ourselves when we ascribe that quality to the weapon.

The presence on this earth today of systems of weaponry suicidal in their implications strikes me as being only a sharp and impatient reminder by the Almighty of a reality which ought to have been visible to us all long ago, which ought, in fact, to have been visible on the example of World War I, but which we stubbornly refused to see: and this is the very narrow and limited degree to which force can ever be the main solution for problems that involve the states of mind —the outlooks and convictions—of great masses of people on this planet. I am startled and disturbed when I hear it said, as I sometimes do, by our military strategists and commentators, that our purpose in war is simply to "kill Germans" or to "kill Russians" or to "kill" whomever else it may be considered to be our enemy. Is this really the purpose of warfare? Are we really served—do American purposes really prosper—just because a life is extinguished, somewhere on this earth, in the agony of battle? And do they prosper in proportion to the number of lives thus extinguished? I cannot believe it. The sources of tragedy in international life lie in the differences of outlook that divide the human race; and it seems to me that our purposes prosper only when something happens in the mind of another person, and perhaps in our mind as well, which makes it easier for all of us to see each other's problems and prejudices with detachment and to live peaceably side by side. The question is not: Why not victory? The question is: What does the word "victory" mean?

I am not preaching a spineless pacifism. Such is the stubbornness and recalcitrance of human nature that the use of force cannot always be foreign to the process of persuasion. Force, too, has its place as an argument, but only a limited place. Force can never be the main argument, or the only one. With it must come, if it is to have any eloquence at all, such things as understanding and patience and the willingness to persuade and, above all, the readiness to restrict force to minimum dimensions and to stop it at the right time.

The trouble with all these proposals for the angry, the militant, the punitive approach is that they ignore the dialectics necessarily involved in every great effort to exert influence on the international scene. They neglect the fact that the hopeful approaches have always to be dialectical ones, embracing contradictory elements, embracing both repulsion and attraction, pressure and conciliation, the readiness to defend where defense is the only answer, but also the readiness to receive, to listen, to concede, to be generous, to take chances, and to give confidence, even while defending.

These suggestions that we should solve our problem by getting angry, by getting tough, by doing something drastic and abrupt, are invidious not just because they involve procedures and concepts which are unpracticable and unfeasible and from which the authors would themselves be obliged to desist, if they ever found themselves in positions of respon-

sibility—they are invidious in an even worse way because they crowd and damage and deflate the hopeful approaches, rob them of their effectiveness and their credibility. The Captive Nations Resolution has freed no captive nations, nor is it likely to do so. But it has irritated and misled and estranged a great many people, including numbers who were by no means Communists. It has given a serious misimpression to our friends as well as our adversaries. It has played into the hands of the hotheads and fanatics on both sides. It has complicated the task of everyone in our government who has been working to avoid the catastrophe of war. And the same could be said for many other of the manifestations of the *simpliste,* die-hard psychology which it reflects. My principal charge against this outlook is not that it is itself without hopeful perspectives, though this too is true. My charge is that, uncorrected, unchallenged, and permitted to have the currency it has in this country today, it cripples the hopefulness of any other approach.

This is why I think it high time that the country clarified its mind on the basic issue of coexistence. If we genuinely wish to avoid the catastrophes of a nuclear war and to find solutions to our differences with world Communism which will render redundant and dispensable the tremendous burden of armaments now resting on mankind, it will not do to let a great part of the vocal segment of our society go on talking as though the search for possibilities of accommodation were unnecessary and undesirable, and anyone who facilitates it were unpatriotic. I submit that a constructive and hopeful policy toward the Soviet Union cannot be conducted against the background of so massive a failure of understanding—against the background of such irresolution and such divided counsel as mark this country today. This is not a question of Russia alone. Behind the Soviet Union there stands as well the great problem of relations with Communist China, to which all the considerations adduced in the lecture will some day be relevant, if they are not now.

If what we require is a new national debate, and something like a public showdown, to clarify these questions and permit this country to speak with a clear and unequivocal voice in world affairs, then let us not postpone this debate any longer. This is a question of fundamentals. Whichever way you cut it, someone—and by that I mean one of two great bodies of thought in our country—is terribly, tragically, and intolerably wrong. If we are to move ahead effectively, the country will have to make up its mind which it is.

POLYCENTRISM AND WESTERN POLICY

Much of the discussion in Western countries today of the problem of relations with world Communism centers around the recent disintegration of that extreme concentration of power in Moscow which characterized the Communist bloc in the immediate aftermath of the Second World War, and the emergence in its place of a plurality of independent or partially independent centers of political authority within the bloc: the growth, in other words, of what has come to be described as "polycentrism." There is widespread recognition that this process represents a fundamental change in the nature of world Communism as a political force on the world scene; and there is an instinctive awareness throughout Western opinion that no change of this order could fail to have important connotations for Western policy. But just what these connotations are is a question on which much uncertainty and confusion still prevail.

The historical development of the process of polycentrism, particularly as it has manifested itself in the growing differences between the Russian and Chinese Communists, is a subject to which a great deal of careful study has recently been devoted and on which there is already an excellent body of analytical literature. There is no need to attempt to recapitulate here the conclusions—remarkably unanimous, in the circumstances—at which leading scholars have arrived concerning the causes and course of this process. Suffice it to recall that it had its origins, generally speaking, in two great events of the year 1948: the forced defection of the Jugoslavs, and the Communist seizure of power in China.

The unity of the bloc never fully recovered from the shock of the Jugoslav defection. Had the Jugoslavs undergone something like a counterrevolution—had they shaken off their own Communist dictatorship, adopted a form of government which permitted democratic freedoms, and relaxed the governmental hold on the economy to a point where the system would have been no longer classifiable as a Leninist-Marxist one—the effect on bloc unity would have been less; for then the defection could have been regarded simply as the loss of a position to the capitalist world: a regrettable setback but not unprecedented, and no fit cause of doubt or questioning for a movement which had always prided itself on its ability to pocket losses and to recover from them. But when the Jugoslavs failed to do any of these things—when the Jugoslav Communist Party remained in power, and Jugoslavia did not go over to the capitalist camp but carried on much as before, claiming to be a Communist state and talking like one but not recognizing the discipline of the bloc or accepting any political obligations toward it—this was really unsettling for those who had remained faithful; for it raised the appalling question whether monolithic unity and discipline were essential at all to the development of Marxian socialism: whether one could not be a perfectly good Communist without taking orders blindly from Moscow and without following slavishly the pattern of institutions and methods established by the Soviet Union.

And since the strains of Stalinist rule were greater in the more Westernized states of the satellite area of Eastern Europe than in Russia itself, this suggestion—that there might be more than one path to socialism—was particularly insidious in its effect on the satellite régimes. Many were the satellite Communists who, in the years following Tito's break with Stalin, groaned under the necessity of pursuing Stalinist policies obviously unfitted to the traditions and psychology of their country and stole envious looks at the Jugoslavs, who could now cut their cloth to suit their own figure and yet maintain the claim to be good Marxian socialists. It is instructive to reflect that precisely that feature of Jugoslav behavior which so many Americans today find it impossible to forgive, namely, that the Jugoslavs did not, so to speak, "go capitalist," but carried on as a Marxian-socialist state, was the factor which more than any other proved disrupting in its effect on bloc unity.

So long as Stalin remained alive, the effects of the Jugoslav defection could be reasonably well contained by the Moscow headquarters. But after his death, this proved no longer possible. The de-Stalinization campaign of the mid-fifties implied at least a partial justification of Tito's earlier defiance of Stalin's authority. It was awkward, in these circumstances, to leave the Jugoslavs wholly outside the camp; and Khrushchev felt it necessary to try to draw them back again—something which could be done only by conciliatory means. But this, implying as it did at least a willingness to forgive the earlier Jugoslav defiance of bloc discipline, proved unsettling in its effect on the other satellites, particularly the Poles

and Hungarians, and had a good deal to do with the events of 1956 in those two countries. For the Polish and Hungarian Communists had to ask themselves: if Tito is to be forgiven and treated with deference, where are the rewards of obedience? Why should not we, too, select our own path?

As for China, rivalry between the Soviet and Chinese Communist régimes was latent from the beginning, but it began to appear on the surface only after Stalin's death; and it was not until 1957 that it began to assume forms which threatened seriously to disturb bloc unity. It is interesting to reflect that it was in part differing reactions to these same events of 1956 that caused the Chinese-Soviet disagreements to become acute. For what the Russians found necessary in absorbing the shock and the lessons of Hungary proved intolerable to the Chinese, whose revolution was in a different stage and who had different political needs. Here is seen how one thing leads to another, how the threads of causality lead on from the original Jugoslav disaffection and the Chinese Communist conquest of China in 1948—the one considered at the time a loss to world Communism, the other a victory—to the polycentrism of today. If there is any lesson in this, it is the demonstration of how poor we all are, even the Communists, at knowing what is a victory and what is a defeat.

We are now confronted with a situation in which what was once a unified and disciplined bloc has disintegrated into something more like an uneasy alliance between two ideologically similar commonwealths: one grouped around the Soviet Union, the other around China. But even that element of order and symmetry which this description would suggest is not complete, because one nominally Communist country, Jugoslavia, is not embraced in either of these alliances, and another, Albania, is nominally and formally embraced in the one (it still belongs to the Warsaw Pact) but is politically closer to the other. And beyond this framework, there are a large number of Communist parties not in power which are greatly torn and bewildered by this division; and some of these parties have an important voice in bloc affairs, even though they lack the prestige that comes of being in power in their respective countries.

Barring unforeseen disturbances in international affairs, I think this state of affairs should be expected to endure, in its essential aspects, for a long time. Efforts will be made, of course, at one point or another, to patch up Soviet-Chinese differences and to restore something like the previous unity. The Poles, who have always had a special hankering for close relations with the Chinese Communists, are apt to be particularly assiduous in trying to assuage the Chinese-Soviet differences. Perhaps at some point changes of personalities in Moscow and Peking will help. But such tendencies can scarcely go beyond a point. An attempt to establish either Moscow or Peking as the unchallenged center of the movement would today involve prohibitive strains. Communism has now come to embrace so wide a spectrum of requirements and compulsions on the part of the respective parties and régimes that any determined attempt to re-impose unity on the movement would merely cause it to break violently apart at one point or another. There can scarcely be any meeting ground today between, say, the Chinese Communist Party and the Communist Party of Italy that would not be disastrous to one or the other.

A complete restoration of unity seems therefore to be out. But a total break, to the point of all-out hostilities and the alliance of one or the other faction with parts of the non-Communist world, seems equally improbable. Excruciating as are the differences which have now de-

veloped within the world Communist camp, all of the disputants are aware that they have nothing to gain, and everything to lose, by tearing themselves to pieces for the benefit of the "imperialists." Chinese and Russians, furthermore, are both highly skilled at the delicate gradating of hostilities of every sort; and while it would not be surprising to see at some point the development of armed conflicts along the Soviet-Chinese frontier comparable in seriousness to those that developed between the Russians and the Japanese along the same frontier in 1938, it would be surprising to see them develop, any more than did those of 1938, into a full-fledged state of war between the disputants.

While this state of affairs, is then, likely to last for some time in its major outlines, it allows of considerable variation and evolution in terms of the relations between various Communist countries and the non-Communist world. This is a point of great flux and uncertainty throughout the bloc. Not only do the Chinese-Soviet differences center around disagreements over this point, and not only are there further differences on this score between the Russians and individual satellite states of Eastern Europe, but almost every Communist party in the world is afflicted by sharp internal differences or gradations of opinion along these lines. It is not too much to say that the entire bloc is caught today in a great crisis of indecision over the basic question of the proper attitude of a Communist country toward non-Communist ones. The question is whether to think of the world in terms of an irreconcilable and deadly struggle between all that calls itself Communist and all that does not, a struggle bound to end in the relatively near future with the total destruction of one or both, or to recognize that the world socialist cause can be advanced by more complicated, more gradual, less dramatic and less immediate forms, not necessitating any effort to destroy all that is not Communist within our time, and even permitting, in the meanwhile, reasonably extensive and profitable and durable relations with individual non-Communist countries.

The lines of division of opinion over this issue are by no means clean; very often both viewpoints struggle against each other in the same troubled Communist breast. But this is in essence the question. It is this which is buried under the long ideological arguments as to whether socialism could conceivably, or could not conceivably, be achieved by means that did not involve violent revolution. It is this that underlies the arguments about the inevitability or non-inevitability of war. This is the explosive substance with which the controversial concept of "peaceful coexistence" is charged. And none of us, I am sure, can fail to note that this is only the mirror-replica of the similar question which divides Western public opinion and tortures the policy-makers of the Western countries.

It is important to recognize that the degree to which polycentrism has already advanced means that individual Communist countries now have a far wider area of choice than was the case some years ago in shaping not only their own relationship to the non-Communist world but also their internal institutions and policies. These two things are, in fact, closely connected; for the more internal institutions and policies come to resemble those that once prevailed in Stalin's Russia and/or prevail today in China, the more one needs a state of apparent tension and danger in external relations, as a means of justifying them. And in both these fields, as I say, the smaller Communist countries, and particularly the Eastern European satellites, now enjoy a far wider range of independent decision than was once the case. At one time there

was only one model; today there are a number of them: the Soviet, the Chinese, the Polish, the Jugoslav, etc. And the fact that Moscow and Peking both need the political support of the satellite parties, and are therefore obligated to compete for their favor, means that neither can afford to discipline them, beyond a point, if the paths they choose are not ones that meet with full approval on either side.

On the other hand, the area within which this freedom of choice exists is not unlimited; it has, in fact, certain very sharp limits, and it is important to bear these in mind.

The satellite régimes of Eastern Europe cannot, first of all, sever the bonds of military alliance which unite them with the Russians. Jugoslavia, it is true, did this in effect; but one must remember that when this occurred, the Warsaw Pact did not yet exist—nor did the Atlantic Alliance. Further, the Jugoslavs had a very special geographic and political position.

Secondly, the satellite régimes cannot abandon the profession of fidelity to Marxist ideals or the monopoly of power which those ideals imply and purport to justify. To do anything like this would be to destroy the very theoretical basis on which their power rests, and to commit, in effect, political suicide.

What the satellite régimes can do, and are doing to some extent, is to shape their own internal economic and social institutions along more liberal lines, or at least individualistic lines. They can, furthermore, ease the restraints—as the Jugoslavs have done—on all forms of contact and dealings between their citizens and people in non-Communist countries. As a part of this process, they can resist—as the Rumanians are doing—efforts to pull them into a tight and exclusive trading association with other Communist countries; and they can insist on the right to expand their trade with non-Communist nations to a point where it constitutes an important element in their economic development.

Finally, while they cannot leave the Communist military alliance, the satellite régimes could, conceivably, if conditions were right, help to deëmphasize the military factor to a point where it would not stand in the way of at least a partial political rapproachement with some of their Western neighbors.

Altogether, then, the choices open to the satellite régimes cover a range which lies somewhere between the extremes of the full independence of the Jugoslavs on the one hand, and a slavish, timid clinging to Soviet patterns and authority on the other. This is a circumscribed range of choice; but what they do within it is by no means unimportant. It could, conceivably, make all the difference between a Communist orbit with which the West could coexist peacefully and without catastrophe over an indefinite time, and one with which it could not.

Now the West has it in its power, ideally speaking, to influence extensively, by its own policies and behavior, the choices that the satellite régimes make in this connection. It can reciprocate or fail to reciprocate moves to relax tensions and to facilitate collaboration in various fields. It can shape its policies in such a way as to create advantages and premiums for efforts on the part of the satellite governments to extend their relations with Western countries; or it can decline to create such advantages. It can exert itself to deëmphasize the military factor in the mutual relationship; or it can take the opposite course. Finally, and of overriding significance, it can show itself reconciled to the existence of these régimes, without accepting responsibility for them; and it can convey to them that they have nothing to fear from it if they will only refrain, themselves, from hostile and subversive policies; or it can hold to the thesis that its object is to overthrow

them, and permit them to conclude that any concessions they may make will only be exploited, ultimately, to their disadvantage.

Obviously, in the totality of these choices, the West is confronted by a pervasive and fundamental problem of policy: whether to promote a trend toward further polycentrism, in the hope that there might prove to be a portion of the Communist world with which one could, in the long run, contrive to live, and that living with it and encouraging it to see advantages in a situation of coexistence might tend at least to narrow the area and power of that other portion with which one could not live, or could not *yet* live; or whether to discourage that trend, on the theory that a differentiation of outlook and authority among Communist powers does not materially affect their status as a threat to the security of the Western peoples, and that the impression of such a differentiation serves merely to disorient and demoralize Western resistance to the phenomenon of world Communism as a whole. This is the question facing Western policy-makers; and there can in my opinion be no doubt that the trend of political decision within the Communist world will be importantly influenced by the answers they find to it. It could well be argued, in fact, that if the major Western powers had full freedom of movement in devising their own policies, it would be within their power to determine whether the Chinese view, or the Soviet view, or perhaps a view more liberal than either, would ultimately prevail within the Communist camp.

Fortunately, or unfortunately, the major Western powers do not enjoy this full freedom of movement. In the case particularly of the United States and Western Germany, but also to some extent of the NATO powers in general, the area in which they could conceivably move to meet the problem of policy posed by the trend toward Communist polycentrism has been severely circumscribed in recent years either by engagements they have undertaken to one another or to parties outside of Europe or by policies to which they have so deeply committed themselves that any early renunciation of them would scarcely be feasible. A glance at their position with relation to the various points of flexibility in the position of the satellite régimes will suffice to demonstrate this.

If it is a question of alteration of the internal institutions and policies of the satellite régimes, it is evident, on the example of Jugoslavia, that neither the United States Congress nor the West German Government is inclined to attach importance to this factor. The Jugoslavs have abolished forced collectivization. They have adopted a system of management in industry fnudamentally different from that prevailing in the Soviet Union. They have practically abandoned the active application of police terror. They have adopted policies on travel, contacts with foreigners and access to foreign informational media which seem closer to those of most Western countries than to those prevalent in the bloc. It is evident that none of this constitutes, in the eyes of our own Congress or of a great part of our public, any reason to treat Jugoslavia very much differently from any other Communist country. A similar disposition seems to prevail in Bonn, if only as a reflection of the Hallstein doctrine, which bars diplomatic relations with any country recognizing the present East German régime. Since all of the satellites do recognize it, they are obliged to see in this doctrine at least a limitation to the possibilities of any future political rapprochement between themselves and the German Federal Republic.

When it comes to economic policy, a similar situation prevails. There are the NATO arrangements for economic controls. There are the various legislative restrictions prevailing in this country.

There is, finally, the Common Market, established and being developed on principles that appear to leave no room for anything like the eventual economic reunification of the European Continent. It will be recalled that in the original Marshall Plan concept, American policymakers were careful to leave open the possibility of the extension of the respective arrangements to the entire Continent, and to phrase the proposals in such a way that if the Eastern European régimes were to be excluded, they would have to exclude themselves, which, in effect, they then did. But the European Common Market has failed to include this feature either in letter or in spirit; and the impression is being given to the Eastern Europeans, including the Jugoslavs, that whatever may be the future of this novel and important entity, they are to have no place in it.

When it comes to the military factor and the question of its emphasis or deëmphasis, the bald fact is that the Western powers, over a period that now runs back for several years, have committed themselves more and more deeply against anything in the nature of a military disengagement in Europe. Not only do they reject the possibility of any extensive withdrawal of foreign troops from the Western part of the Continent, even if this were to be by way of reciprocation for a similar withdrawal of Soviet forces, but they appear to have set their face, in present circumstances, against anything in the nature of a European pact or a nonaggression pact between the NATO and Warsaw Pact members. They are also averse to any sort of arrangement for the de-nuclearization of the European area, even, again, if this were to be on a reciprocal basis. Finally, they have exhibited no very convincing evidence of any disposition to place effective limits on the rearmament of Western Germany, where one restriction after the other, established in earlier years, has quietly gone by the board, and where the Germens are now, in the view of everybody in Eastern Europe, well on the way to becoming in all essential respects a full-fledged nuclear power. Yet at the same time the Western powers, with the exception of the French, have been unwilling to recognize the finality of Germany's eastern frontiers; and the West German Government, with the blessing of the others, still pursues a policy of total irreconcilability toward the East German state.

These aspects of Western policy are not mentioned for the purpose of taking issue with them. Opinions can differ on the degree of their justification, individually or collectively. But even those who are enthusiastic about them should remember that there is a price to be paid for them in terms of their political effect on the Communist bloc. To the East European satellite leaders, faced with these attitudes, and noting the extreme rigidity with which they are adhered to by the Western governments, anything like a de-emphasis of the military factor in East-West relations can only appear today as discouragingly remote. In present circumstances, they can hope neither for the removal of Soviet forces from those Eastern European positions which they now occupy, nor for any further East-West agreements that could take the heat off military tensions. Particularly discouraging and disturbing to them is the progressive rearmament of Western Germany against the background of a West German commitment to the liberation of Eastern Germany, even though that commitment professes to envisage only peaceful means. The effect which the combination of these two things has had on the feelings of people in Eastern Europe cannot be emphasized too strongly. Either one without the other might have been less unacceptable. A strong commitment to the reunification of Germany might have been tolerable

if it had not been supported by a military policy designed to make Western Germany into one of the two strongest states in Western Europe. Or a rearmament of Western Germany, while never fully defensible in East European eyes, might have been more tolerable if it had been coupled with a greater readiness on the part of West German political leaders to *faire bonne mine à mauvais jeu,* to accept the existence of a Communist Germany at least as a regrettable necessity of the present epoch, and to regard the cause of German unification less as a programmatical commitment and more as an historical inevitability, to be left to the healing hand of time. But the spectre of the violent liberation of Eastern Germany, by means not resting on any agreement with the Russians, and coming either against the background of, or by means of, a revived German military ascendancy, unites both governments and peoples in Eastern Europe in a common reaction of horror and apprehension; for the Communist leaders there, however little they may like or respect Ulbricht, know that their own stability would not easily withstand the shock of the sudden and violent overthrow of his régime; and the peoples of Eastern Europe, including the Jugoslavs, see in this eventuality only the beginning of a reëstablishment of the German military ascendancy of unhappy memory throughout Eastern Europe, and 18 years have not been sufficient to allow the horror of this prospect to fade in their minds.

Behind all this, and connected with all of it, is the heavy extent of the Western commitment, and particularly the American and German commitment, to the eventual destruction of Communism generally. We have our Captive Nations Resolution; and the satellite régimes of Eastern Europe and Asia are specifically listed there as ones we have committed ourselves in effect to destroy. In the Far East, there is our similar commitment to the Nationalist Government on Taiwan, with all its far-reaching political ambitions. And Western opinion, not just in the NATO countries but in certain of the neutral European countries as well, is heavily affected by attitudes which are at least skeptical toward, and in some cases strongly averse to, any thought of an accommodation to the permanency of Communist power anywhere.

It is true that the West European NATO governments are in a somewhat better position to face this problem than is the United States. They are not committed to the Captive Nations Resolution. There is no formal reason why they should not, if they wished, shape the policies of the Common Market in such a way as to give to the Eastern European peoples a more reassuring impression of the prospects for their future relation to Western Europe in the economic field. In the case of export controls and other restrictive measures, the degree of their responsibility is obviously smaller than ours; and it would, presumably, be easier for them to take a more conciliatory line. Particularly is all this true of the Italians, whose understanding attitude has already helped to ease Jugoslavia's delicate relations with the West, and who, more than any other Western people, have possibilities for exerting a reassuring and helpful influence on the East European satellites. But further north, the German problem and the aversion to any discussion of disengagement still loom up on the horizon of the Eastern Europeans as impassable barriers to anything like such a lowering of tensions as would make it possible for them to create a basically new political relationship with the West; and for both of these situations, as they well know, Western Europeans are as responsible as ourselves.

It is clear, in these circumstances, that the West has, as of today, only limited possibilities for reciprocating any disposition the satellite countries might evince to reduce the dichotomy of the two worlds and to bridge the gap that divides present attitudes on both sides from the possibility of truly peaceful and mutually profitable coexistence. It is in a sense tragic that this should be the case just at a time when there is so great a longing for a better East-West relationship in the hearts of tens of millions of ordinary people in the East European area, and so important a willingness to move tentatively in this direction even on the part of certain of their Communist leaders. And the fact that things are this way is something which should give pause for thought not just to those who would like to find ways of living peacefully with Communist neighbors but even to those who can contemplate no permanent reconciliation with world Communism; for to deny to the East even the possibility of the development of a better framework for coexistence is to affect the terms of the argument which goes on within the Communist camp and to forego the advantage which a division of opinion there provides. If there is really strength in unity, Communist leaders can only be grateful for a Western policy which slights the values of polycentrism and declines to encourage them; for a rigidly unreceptive Western attitude may eventually enforce upon the bloc a measure of unity which, by their own unaided effort, they could never have achieved.

To say that the West is in a poor position to encourage polycentrism is not, of course, to say that it will not continue to develop. There are instances in which, as in the case of Jugoslavia, the desire for national independence may be so strong that governments will wish for, and seek, relief from the disciplinary strictures of the bloc even if there is no apparent place for them, or even for good relations with them, in the Western scheme of things; and it is not to be assumed that they will find no means of achieving that relief. The West, after all, does not represent the entirety of the non-Communist world. There are other areas where the trauma of the conflict with world Communism have struck less deeply and where both the readiness to forget or ignore ideological differences and the willingness to look at international relations in terms other than those of military conflict will be greater; and people who feel the need of more independence of policy but see no place for themselves in the vision of Western statesmanship can look, as the Jugoslavs are already doing, in other directions for the alternative to isolation.

Polycentrism may thus continue to develop, in spite of, if not because of, the face which the West turns to the troubled and vacillating world of Communism. But there are risks involved here. There is a relatively short-term risk, from the standpoint of the danger of war and of the effect which an absence of polycentrism could have in increasing that danger. But even if military complications do not ensue, there is still the long-term question of the effect on the minds of those tens of millions of people in Communist countries who still look to the West with longing and with hope and who expect from it policies which take account of all the subtlety and contradiction of their position. If such a response on the Western side is not forthcoming,

who can say how this will affect their attitudes in the more distant future? Will they be best influenced by a Western policy which, through its quixotic commitment to a highly unlikely violent liberation, appears to condemn them by implication either to the miseries of a new world war or to an indefinite further period of languishing under oppressive Communist régimes? Or will they be better influenced by a Western policy which accepts as its goal the less ambitious but more promising prospect of a relaxation of the severity of those régimes and, by the same token, of the barriers that separate their peoples from contact with the outside world? This is a question which Western policy-makers will do well to look at all over again, as the Chinese-Soviet conflict proceeds and as its effects continue to make themselves felt.

In the nineteenth century, the colonial mother-countries of the West alienated many millions of people in other parts of the world through lack of imagination and feeling toward those who were in effect within their power. There is, surely, a danger lest history record that Westerners of the twentieth century alienated just as many more through lack of imagination and feeling toward those who were in the power of their ideological adversaries.

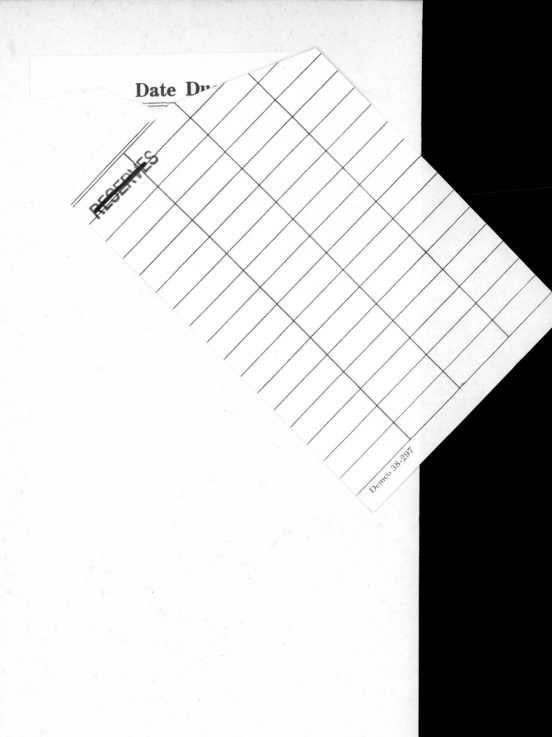

Date Due

RESERVES

Demco 38-297